NEW YORK REVIEW BOOKS
CLASSICS

RINGOLEVIO

EMMETT GROGAN (c. 1943–1978) grew up in New York
City and died there. He was also the author of *Final Score*,
a novel.

PETER COYOTE is an actor who has appeared in more than
ninety films. A founding member of the Diggers, he has
published a memoir of the 1960s, *Sleeping Where I Fall*. He
lives in Marin County, California.

RINGOLEVIO
A Life Played for Keeps

EMMETT GROGAN

Introduction by
PETER COYOTE

NEW YORK REVIEW BOOKS

New York

THIS IS A NEW YORK REVIEW BOOK
PUBLISHED BY THE NEW YORK REVIEW OF BOOKS
435 Hudson Street, New York, NY 10014
www.nyrb.com

Library of Congress Cataloging-in-Publication Data
Grogan, Emmett.
  Ringolevio : a life played for keeps / by Emmett Grogan ; introduction by Peter
Coyote
    p. cm. — (New York Review Books classics)
  Originally published: Boston : Little, Brown, 1972.
  ISBN 978-1-59017-286-5 (alk. paper)
  1. Grogan, Emmett. 2. Radicals—United States—Biography. 3. Authors,
American—20th century—Biography. 4. Counterculture—United States—
History—20th century. I. Title.
  CT275.G7784A3 2008
  973.91092—dc22
  [B]

                         2008018625

ISBN 978-1-59017-286-5

Printed in the United States of America on acid-free paper.
10 9 8 7 6 5 4 3 2

One day in 1965 I was rehearsing a play at the San Francisco Mime Troupe studio in our made-over industrial building on Harison Street. A lithe, freckled man with flinty, Irish features walked in to observe. He had an arresting gait with a leonine head thrust aggressively forward as if it were impatient with the body behind it. His eyes were a cool, unflappable blue, and his face was as still as a mask, suggesting abundant anger and determination. Emmett Grogan had come to audition.

We struck up a conversation that carried us through the afternoon and a long walk to our respective flats, which, it turned out, were on opposite corners of the street. He was a galvanizing story teller and an immediate new friend who subsequently changed my life in more profound ways than anyone I had ever met before, or have allowed to since.

If all of us are "life-actors," more or less consciously creating an identity by our intentions and daily behavior, Emmett was determined to be a "life-star." He carried with him the spot-lit absorption of an actor. Men and women attended when he entered and moved through the room with the detached concentration of a shark, because he had a developed sense of drama in his posture, his cupped cigarette, his smoky, hooded eyes. His being declared him a man on the wrong side of the law; a man with a past; a man who would not be deterred.

This was *Emmett* Grogan, the self created by young Eugene Grogan in a life sentence of hard labor with his soul. Though time and observation have *modified* my early perception, they have never totally obliterated it.

To understand the necessity and purpose of Emmett's alterego, it is necessary to remember the environment in which he became conscious: the mid-Forties and early Fifties in America. Korea had been the first shock to national post-World War II euphoria, interrupting the nation's chow-down of global resources, status and prestige, with the messy business of "making the world safe for democracy." Precipitated under suspicious circumstances, Korea was a bloody hell where troops mutinied and floundered with useless weapons in a struggle between foreign neighbors which they never fully understood.

An overlooked by-product of this war was the growth of the Hell's Angels, formed after World War II. Initially comprised of disillusioned vets, their gang life of blood loyalties, squad- and platoon-sized intimacy and organization was an early intimation of the coming war with the status-quo. The *New York Daily News* featured articles about teen-aged gang-wars, urban snipers, and the spreading blight of heroin in New York's ghettos, and the debacle of Korea was soon successfully covered up by the McCarthy period anti-communist witch-hunts.

The cultural propaganda machinery was in full swing. Rock Hudson and Doris Day were advertising America's consumer heaven to the rest of the world in sexless romps. "Ozzie and Harriet" and "Leave it to Beaver" offered bland television fantasies of family life, intimidating kids from mentioning their personal griefs lest they be considered freaks. In real homes, people drank, fought bitterly, abused their children, had ulcers, and worked themselves into early graves. Young people were pressured to study meaningless subject matter to enter college, to graduate and "make good" like the parents who were dying in front of them.

This divorce between reality and official fiction demanded articulation and voice, and that voice was the unquenchable Youth Underground which leaked its "treacherous" information through street wisdom. It's no accident that Kenny Wisdom is the name Emmett chose for the protagonist of *Ringolevio's* first half, the undirected self which existed before young Eugene willed Emmett into existence.

America's much-touted production of material wealth was not bandaging a lot of people where they were wounded. The forward march of capitalism was killing the nation's gentlest seers and grinding the most tender hopes and aspirations under the heel of economic Darwinism. There were some adult voices calling the shots truthfully, however, but they all seemed to be precisely the people that our parents warned us against*—the

---

*This phrase consciously mimics the title of a book about the Haight-Ashbury, called *We Are the People Our Parents Warned Us Against*, by Nicholas Von Hoffman, a reporter that Emmett distrusted on sight and refused to speak to. He came to the Haight with his teen-aged son as a beard, and in the naivete of the times, counter-culture people, many on the wrong side of the law, gave him free access and spoke frankly with him. Some of his articles for the *Washington Post* were reprinted locally.

voices of rock and roll, jazz, folk music, hot-rods, blues-life and the Beats.

The young's enemy was not Communism but a culture based on the unimpeded demands of capital that rolled over personal eccentricities and predilections, personal power and authority the way Hilter rolled over Poland. We were trying to thrive in a culture whose values and goals were so sublimated to material ends as to be indivisible from them. In such a case, what do you do when the culture itself is the enemy? Eugene created Emmett as his answer to that question.

Emmett quickly became bored with the Mime Troupe and what he considered the "safety" of the stage. With his almost invisible companion, Billy Murcott, the one he called "the genius," Emmett began improvising activities on the streets which laid the groundwork for the Diggers, a group whose action-oriented philosophy and politics were based on autonomy, personal authenticity and freedom. The name itself was an homage to Gerrard Winstanley, the millenarian heretic religious leader of seventeenth-century England who believed in the universal right of man to cultivate wastelands and common lands without paying tariffs to owners of the manors they adjoined. Winstanley's followers were nicknamed the Diggers because they dug and planted on these lands, only to be beaten and dispersed by vigilantes roused by local landowners.

The San Francisco Diggers began producing free food every day in the Golden Gate Park Panhandle. A simple act if you considered it as "charity." But when those who had come to eat were asked to step through a large yellow picture frame called "The Free Frame of Reference" and then given smaller ones to wear around their necks and view the world through, the larger implications of this simple act became apparent. The food was there, the kids were there, why *not* feed them? Without ideology or cant. Just have food there and see what happened. It was a challenging, interesting thing to do, a precedent-setting thing to do. Consider the implications, the organizing, the effort, to make this possible: if you could feed two or three or five hundred people a day, for free, what else could you do? And why not? This

---

In them, Von Hoffman named names, places and dates, which created havoc in the community and caused a number of arrests in its wake, provoking, I'm told, a crisis dialogue about ethics among *Post* staff members.

simple expression of personal power, based on wanting to do something and refusing to be deterred; demonstrating the depth of that desire by performing it not only without recompense but anonymously so that one could not be paid in prestige either, set the stage for the coming years' catalogue of celebratory, culture-shocking, mind-bending events which sprung from the Diggers, many of which are chronicled in the pages that follow.

Emmett's *personal* relationship to these formulations was always ambiguous and complex. His notion of anonymity was to give his name away, so that countless people would claim it for countless purposes. (Eventually, some reporters would assert that there *was* no Emmett Grogan, that the name was a fiction created by the Diggers to confound the straight world.) While it was a way of demonstrating lack of attachment, it also made him ubiquitous, an instant legend.

Life with Grogan was a daily exercise in such contradictions, a daily refinement of one's understanding of "truth." One could never be sure exactly *where* the hair had been split and how. If, for instance, he came into a room late for a meeting, he might apologize with a story about being attacked by street toughs, taking revenge on him for some earlier intervention in their affairs. Usually people listened to these stories, without believing or disbelieving them, enjoying the drama of life with Emmett. If one *were* pushed to incredulity by a particularly outrageous claim and were to challenge him, he might remove his glasses with the air of a smug magician and demonstrate his blackened eye and wounds. The wounds were definitely real, but was the story? If it *was* true, was it completely or partially true? One never knew and never found out.

"Never let them catch you in a lie," he said to me once at the beginning of a three month "run" one summer at New York's infamous Chelsea Hotel. This remark alerted me to Emmett's awareness of his own self-dramatizing, and the extent to which he used his sense of "theater" as an asset in his work. And what was that work?

That summer, we camped illicitly in the Chelsea, pretending to be "managers," in the rooms vacated by Janis Joplin and her band after they had left on tour. We would move from room to room, picking the flimsy locks, confounding the Hotel management who sent the bills on to god-knows-what befuddled band accountant. We spent hours on the phone each day, calling people we had never met, but who might be resources—anyone of whom intimate knowledge could be turned to our advantage—inventing pretexts to bring them into our purview. By the end of the summer we had New York wired: unlimited mobility and access to rooms we wanted to be in; cultural impact; and enhanced prestige. (Of course this last is a contradiction, but we were contradictory people, and, after all, human.)

One high point of the summer's work was brokering a peace-meeting between the New York Police and Puerto Rican gang leaders from the Lower East Side. We'd arranged to have use of the penthouse boardroom of the CBS building after hours. We reveled in the confusion and shock on the faces of the police and the gang-leaders as they were escorted by the doorman, who had unlocked the huge skyscraper, into the executive meeting room. There, at the head of the huge, empty, hardwood table with seating for twenty, were Emmett and I, in blue-jeans, long-hair and earrings, waiting for them like it was our living room. That was a classic Digger ploy—hard politics with style. It was Emmett's art, and he was good at it.

All artists desire an audience, and much as we would criticize and change our culture, we want, at the same time, to be accepted and rewarded by it. Emmett was no different, and it is this contradiction, of simultaneously spurning and yearning an audience, which became the crucifix on which he finally impaled himself. It does not require too much of a stretch of the imagination to see in a crucifix the outline of a syringe, and it is to that ambivalent symbol of healing and death that I must turn for the dark-side of Emmett's "truth."

The Diggers *knew* what was wrong with the culture and believed that if we created enough examples of "free-life" by actually acting them out on the streets, without the safety-net of a stage, then people would have alternatives to society's skimpy menu of life choices. But the strain of inventing a culture is exhausting. Everything comes up for review. No limit or taboo is sacred, especially when the investigation is coupled to belief in a high and noble mission. If our souls know no limits, why should our bodies? Drugs became the fuel for imaginative and physical transcendence.

As edge dwellers, we were proud of being tougher, more experimental, truthful, and less compromised than our peers who seemed more interested in dope-and-long-hair-at-the-office than in real social alternatives. If their Hallmark Card philosophies were fueled by acid, grass, and hashish, we had heroin and amphetamine—champions of the blues life; invincible allies of Charlie Parker, Billie Holliday, foot soldiers in 'Nam, and countless other heroes who had fought the beast up close and turned themselves into the flames they tried to signal through. Hindsight has taught me that there is an invisible ravenous twin haunting each of us. Despite each "good work" and selfless sacrifice in the name of commonly held beliefs, without unremitting vigilance, tiny, daily, indulgences betray these high aims and feed our gluttonous companion.

Emmett stuck me with a needle twice. The first time he pierced my ear. "It'll change you," he said. We were in Sweet William's kitchen, not too long before he became a Hell's Angel. Poet Lenore Kandel, William's olive-skinned lover with a thick shiny braid, smiled contentedly while she sat stringing beads for the glittering curtains that festooned every window in the house. Sweet William was attending the ceremony, his grave, Mayan-Jewish face with high cheekbones and dark eyes bearing solemn witness. Emmett pierced my ear and he was right. It did change me. It drew me a little deeper into our confederation, a little farther outside the pasty grip of convention.

The second time was in the living room of a Hollywood movie star, in a forest of Pop Art paintings. This time the needle was a syringe, loaded with heroin. "It'll change ya," he said, and it changed a lot. The star's wife walked in, took one look at her husband sitting in a circle of freaks shooting up, and left him for good; I began the process of ruining a heretofore healthy body; Sweet William started down a path which took a hard turn at a soured dope deal that left him half paralyzed with a bullet in his head; and Emmett's road petered out "at the end of the line" of the Coney Island subway April Fools Day 1978—some twelve years later, where his body was found, dead of an overdose.

The Sixties turned into the Seventies and the hard-life changed a lot of things. A lot of friends died, all, I believe, mentioned in this book. Tracy, Marcus, Bill Lindyn, Billy Batman, Pete Knell, and wonderful Paula, thrown off a hotel roof in Terra Linda. The list is longer than I have the heart to type. Brooks wound up in a state hospital after blinding himself on an acid trip he never returned from; Moose is lost somewhere in the FBI secret witness program; Freewheelin' Frank did nine years at Folsom; Kathleen had to go underground and disappeared in Europe for 17 years.

Faced with these cautionary episodes, a lot of people got well.

Phyllis went to school and became a nurse and a college professor; Natural Suzanne became a lawyer and will be a judge of international treaties with indigenous people; Nina, Freeman, David and Jane moved upstate to the Mattole River and today look after the wild salmon and fight the excesses of the logging industry. Peter Berg, whom Grogan called the Hun in *Ringolevio*, writes and breaks new ground as a bioregional thinker just as he did as a Mime Troupe director and Digger.

Somewhere in these transformations, Emmett got lost. I went to see him once, shortly after the publication of *Ringolevio* when he was riding high, married to a beautiful French-Canadian actress and living in a luxurious apartment in Brooklyn Heights. He was proud of having returned "so near and yet so far," as he put it.

I admit to envy of him then. I was still without money, living on a commune in Pennsylvania doing no-nonsense farm labor for ourselves and a crippled neighbor, and attending to some details surrounding my father's estate. Most of my energy was going into survival and what was left was dedicated to learning enough about nuclear power to prevent a plant from being erected in our community.

I couldn't help feeling that it was *my* life that had paid for the laundered sheets, elegant rooms, well-stocked refrigerator and bar. Proud as I was of a brother's success, like others in our family, I was sore about the egocentric tone of *Ringolevio* and agreed with one friend's assessment when he said, "Oh yeah, Emmett *sauntered* and we all walked!"

Consequently, when I saw that Emmett's eyes were "pinned" and knew that he'd been using heroin again, I had an excuse to blow up and read him the riot act, while Louise smiled, secretly pleased, I think, that someone was telling him what she could not. I told him that I didn't care if he wanted to die, but why did he want to die such a boring, low-class death? If he wanted to go out, why didn't he take on the nuclear power cartel as his suicide mission and die for *something*? I explained everything that I had learned about it to date, told him he was a boring motherfucker and left so that we could both lick our wounds.

From that time on, our relationship changed, and Emmett began to relate to me as if I were a necessary audience. He was proud to tell me that our bedroom confrontation had produced a new book, called *Final Score*, a nuclear thriller which he felt would outline the perils of the whole system. I declined his invitation to join him at "The Last Waltz," The Band's all-night farewell concert at San Francisco's legendary Winterland Auditorium on Thanksgiving 1976, because I was bored with rock and roll's self-congratulatory flack. Emmett called back two days later to anounce that he gotten Michael McClure, Lawrence Ferlinghetti, Lenore Kandel, and Kirby Doyle—all San Francisco poets and "family"—to come. "Is that good enough, you Jew Bastard?" he laughed, knowing that I would then be there. He had begun writing songs—the Band even recorded two—and was excited that Etta James might record one.

Despite all these activities and interests, by this time nothing much was really sustaining Emmett. The "play" had changed, the perfect role he'd crafted was slightly anachronistic and his inability to make something grand happen was taking toll of his confidence. I felt that he was trapped by the glamor of this persona and needed time to disappear, to take beginner's steps in new directions, beyond the glare of public attention, but he seemed preoccupied with maintaining his identity and status. He developed curious mannerisms, particularly a constant, knowing wink, suggesting that everything had a deeper, hipper side that I would have missed without his warning. It was as if he sensed that his act was getting thin and, instead of nourishing it, resorted to a trick to suggest that it was the *audience's* perceptions which were faulty.

The last time I saw him, I kept a rendezvous at a Malibu beach house and no one answered the door. I prowled around, broke in and found Emmett passed out in bed. I checked his pulse and, satisfied that he was living, shook the place down before I woke him and found enough drugs and traces to open a small pharmacy. We had a knock-down fight and finally, as a strategy for getting me off his back, he confessed to a suicide attempt the previous day. I didn't believe it at all, but I was stunned nonetheless, because, even as a strategy, Emmett was asking me to feel sorry for him. *That* was so uncharacteristic it frightened me.

Because I lived four hundred miles away, I called a trusted friend who lived close enough to monitor him a bit. Duvall Lewis was a brilliant black man who had served as staff on the California State Arts Council while I was Chairman there. A tall and charming hipster and political can-do wizard, Duvall was fearless and never missed the joke. I thought he and Emmett would like each other. They did, and began to hang out together, sharing the same sense of adventure. Duvall called one day, and though his laughter described a hundred-mile-an-hour car race through Topanga Canyon where Emmett chased down a famous cinematographer and forced him to sign a release for his book the man had optioned and ignored for an unconscionable length of time.

When Duvall called with the news of Emmett's death, his call was just one in a long series that crisscrossed the country, stitching friends and the news together. Not so many years after this, Duvall himself was dead by his own hand, in despair at being completely frozen out of the Reagan era's material feeding frenzy. Their two lives, and two deaths, continue to haunt me as unnervingly similar.

There is no way that I can tell you *who* Emmett was; neither will this book. It's like him: part fact, part fiction, a lot of anger and humor, a lot of clear-eyed calls, and some poppycock. Emmett told you what he thought. He was stand-up. He was a man, extreme and contradictory, quarrelsome and kind, charismatic and self-destructive, who *willed* himself to be a hero.

For most people it might have been enough to have been a living legend, an icon to thousands of people that included Puerto Rican gang leaders, presidents of record companies, professional thieves, wealthy restaurateurs, movie stars, socialites, Black Panthers, Hell's Angels, and the Diggers themselves.

So read *Ringolevio* in that light. Don't believe everything you read, but don't be too quick to doubt either. Whether or not he actually did everything he claimed in exactly the way he claimed is immaterial. As Emmett disclaims in his Author's Note, "This book is true." But that doesn't mean it all *happened*. Emmett was a guidon carried into battle, an emblem behind which people rallied their *imaginations*.

Emmett did enough, rest assured. He proved with his existence that each of us could *act out* the life of our highest fantasies. This was his goad and his compassionate legacy. Don't minimize it or let yourself off the hook of his example by quibbling over details. Think about what you read, but more important, as Emmett would have said, "Dig *yourself!*"

Peter Coyote
Mill Valley, California
August, 1989

Peter Coyote came from nowhere and is working his way back.

For

Mr. George J. Hagan

and

my father

RINGOLEVIO

AUTHOR'S NOTE

This book is true. Names, places and some dates in parts one and two have been changed to protect the innocent.

ONE

*For the Greatest Ringolevio Player
to Come Out of the Bronx,
Albie Baker.*

The ultimate game of my childhood was Ringolevio. It was a game of life and death. A game to be fought rather than played. I can think of and still remember the names of several kids from my old neighborhood who either crippled themselves or dashed themselves to death, trying to escape capture or attempting to capture an opponent.

Ringolevio prepared us for life. The violence, the inequities, the poverty, the wars. You learned when to keep your head down and it made you smart and fast, the two principal elements of survival. You may have flunked your mathematics but you made the grade.

I've never met a Phi Beta Kappa, a Magna cum Laude, or a Most Likely to Succeed who really made it in life. Sure they made it in some corporate level or in advertising, but they just bit for the old USA oakey-doke and remained oblivious to the realities of what life is actually about.

The great Ringolevio players of my time all made it in their own *ways — a few went to the electric chair or did terms. Some were great crooks, burglars and stick-up artists but never con men, gangsters or pimps. Others became great athletes, soldiers, radicals, cops, poets and even businessmen. They made it because they learned that you have to move fast in this world. None of them ever got hit by streetcars or automobiles or slipped on banana peels. They were always the ones who caught the ball that was hit into the bleachers and were never the apples who got hit on the head.*

Today I still evaluate the guys I meet as Ringolevio players — were they good ones or bad ones or did they even play. Sometimes I'd say to my good friend Grogan, "Do you think that cat ever played the game?" And Emmett would look across the bar at the guy, study his moves a moment and say, "Never happened." We know. And we may get shot down, Grogan and me, but it won't be with our hands up. It will be in glorious flight soaring across some tenement roof reaching for that elusive cloud of freedom and on our lips the cry "Ringolevio, Ringolevio, one, two, three!"

ALBIE BAKER

It's a game. A game played on the streets of New York, for as long as anyone can remember. It is called Ringolevio, and the rules are simple. There are two sides, each with the same number of players. There are no time limits, no intermissions, no substitutes and no weapons allowed. There are two jails. There is one objective.

Each side tries to capture and jail all the members of the other side, while maintaining the freedom of its own teammates. When everyone on one side is captured, the other team wins.

To jail, or "den" someone, you must catch him and then restrain him, because he is allowed to resist with all the skill and strength of his mind and body. You cannot simply tag him and announce that he's under arrest and expect him to go peacefully. You must get him there. And once he's inside the den, you must keep him there because he can escape (if the jailer gets too close to the prisoners, they may pull him in, and leave), or be broken out (if one of the prisoner's teammates can get to the jail without being caught, he has only to step within its perimeter, shout "FREE ALL," and there's a jailbreak). Bribery is also a possibility, but cheating is not.

Everyone who grew up in the boroughs of New York City and played in the streets knows about this game, which is called Ringolevio.

No one who was there will forget Good Friday in 1956, when the Chaplains and the Aces Wild came to Hester Street — to go against each other in the contest which has gone down in the annals of oral history as one of the great Ringolevio games.

The Chaplains was the largest street gang in the city. It had over three or four thousand members, and they were all black. Nobody knew how it got started, but everybody knew where — Harlem. From there it had spread all over New York City. They had style, these Chaplains, and the thirteen guys who were coming to Hester Street were their Ringolevio team, and they'd never been beaten.

The Aces Wild, on the other hand, didn't belong to anything. They were just thirteen other guys, who happened to be good at what they did. All of them came from Brooklyn, but each of them lived in, more or less, different sections. They had various ethnic backgrounds, but they were all the same color.

These Aces Wild were just a bunch of loners, who came together only when some group claimed it was the best, and challenged anyone to try and beat them at Ringolevio.

Neither team was about to lose, and both of them met with respect for the other. A lot was on the line. It was important. They were twelve years old, and they were going to play for keeps.

It was March 30, forty-three degrees outside, when Willie Pondexteur turned the corner of Seventh, and bounced up 129th Street towards Lenox Avenue. The slush from the Great Snow Storm of '56 had been removed from most of the neighborhoods in the city, but it clung to the uptown curbs, trying to hold its crust for two more days, so that the people of Harlem could have a White Easter. Willie wanted to pour Ronson lighter fluid all over it, strike a lot of matches, and burn the black-frosted sludge into the sewers.

Willie Pondexteur had been born somewhere in Louisiana, by a man no one knew, and to a woman he had only heard about. He lived with his seventeen-year-old sister and her two kids, in a kitchenette apartment with mattresses on the floor and a television set in the corner. Their aunt had brought them North right after he was born, but she died when he was ten. Now there were simply the four of them, and they were on welfare, but mostly on their own.

Willie was a tall, taut-muscled kid with an all-around quickness. He was a Chaplain because he liked the prestige and the power of belonging to the gang, and he dug his role as ringleader of their Levio team.

He passed the Imperial Bar and Grill, and ran up the stoop of the run-down tenement where the Chaplains had a clubhouse. He slammed the door on the cold empty street, and he felt that everyone inside was waiting just for him.

There were thirty-odd people jivin' and carrying on, with the Coasters and the Dell Vikings on the hi-fi, and wine and reefer being passed to make the trip downtown a little easier. Willie embraced his brothers, and goosed a few of the sisters, and talked with Dupree, one of the way-back original founders of the Chaplains, and the man who had arranged the match with the Aces Wild. He was nineteen years old, which meant that everything he said made sense and sounded good.

He told Willie how to get to Hester Street on the subway, and that everything had been set up with the bookmakers and the guys that ran the block. He gave him seventy-five dollars, five for each kid and ten dollars trouble money, and said that he and the other heads of the gang would drive downtown in about an hour with the rootin' section.

"Now goddamn it, we countin' on y'all to show 'em that we the baddest bunch a niggers they ever seen! So, y'all beat dem ofay motherfuckers from Brooklyn, and we'll slide back here wit pockets full a coin, and them knowin' that the Chaplains don't lose nothin' to nobody! Y'hear!" said Dupree — loud enough for everyone to pick up on.

Willie then motioned his team into a group, gave each one five dollars in singles, and said that it was time to split. He kept the extra ten dollars, and nobody questioned his right to hold it. Willie Pondexteur had earned those rights, a long time ago.

Everyone bundled up against the outside, and when they hit the stoop they saw Delmos, sitting in his battered '54 Ford, reading the *Daily News*. Delmos was a plainclothesman who kept an eye on the 129th Street Chaplains' clubhouse. Nobody didn't know that Delmos was a cop. The only reason he was considered a plainclothesman was that he bought all his suits at Robert Hall, and he hadn't bought a new one for years.

Delmos was from the 32nd Precinct. The 32nd Precinct was very afraid of this block, 129th Street, especially where it ran from Seventh Avenue to Lenox. This was because they knew that a lot of Chaplains hung out there. They also knew that this gang did more than play games of Ringolevio.

Delmos had been sitting in that spot for a very long time, and the only answers he ever got were stares. And when he saw the thirteen kids walk down the street toward the subway, he wondered what in Christ's name were they up to now. He radioed in to the station house.

Kenny Wisdom was born on Dean Street in Brooklyn, November 28, 1944, and ever since, he had known that there was more to life than that.

He lived with his mother, father and his six-year-old baby sister in a two-room flat, which also had a kitchen and a bathroom. He'd been there for twelve years, and the only thing that had changed was the place where he slept. When he was two, he made so much noise in his sleep that his parents had bought a folding cot, and set it up in the living room at night, next to the kitchen. His sister now slept where he used to — in a large crib beside his parents' bed.

Kenny made a lot of noise in his sleep because he had asthma, and his wheezing kept his father awake all night and made him think about old men dying in Lyons hotels on the Bowery. So Kenny slept on the cot in the front, and his father got good nights' sleep and was able to get up fresh in the mornings and go to his marginclerk's cage at Delafield and Delafield on Wall Street, and attentively keep track of the stocks and bonds that passed through the brokerage firm, knowing that there was no possibility of a pension — only token bonuses every year at Christmas. The only consolation prizes which his father, Leo, had were that the man who sired Montgomery Clift was in the next cage, and Barry Sullivan, the actor, had once been an office boy at The Firm.

Even then, at the age of twelve, Kenny Wisdom would watch his father arrive home at night, and he'd want to tell him what he could only feel. He loved his father, a kind, generous and gentle man, and Kenny was sad to see him go and come, like all the rest of the mass meat.

The phone rang and his mother went for it, but Kenny grabbed the receiver, and before placing it to his ear, told her that it was for him. She backed off, but listened to whatever she could hear. She heard pig Latin.

"Esyay. Eetmay emay atyay illiamsburgway idgebray and edford-bay venueay in ortyfay inutesmay. Eesay ouyay, othermayuckerfay," he said. And then he hung up, smiled at his mother who wasn't looking at him, and put on his sneakers, grabbed his jacket off the floor, kissed his baby sister, said goodbye, and left.

"Where are you going?" he heard.

"Out to play," he answered, as he closed the door on any further inquiries.

Kenny Wisdom hit the sidewalk with both feet, solid and alone. He headed toward Third Avenue, where the bus would take him to Bedford Avenue, where he could transfer to another bus which would take him to the Williamsburg Bridge. And as he walked up the block, he glanced, as he always glanced, at 340 Dean Street — the building where a certain John Mahoney paid six dollars a week for a room in which he went to bed at ten o'clock every night, and rose at eight thirty every morning, until the coppers found out that Mahoney was really William Francis Sutton.

That was back in February 1952. Kenny was about eight, and was bringing some bottles back to the store for the deposit money, when he saw a squad car stop, and the two cops get out and start talking to this little guy who was taking the battery out of his car, and who nobody in the neighborhood hardly ever noticed.

Kenny sensed something, so he dilly-dallied on the other side of the street, watching, while one of the cops drove away in the patrol

6

car, and the other kept an eye on "John Mahoney," as he carried his battery to Sammy's Servicenter on Third Avenue. Having no idea of what was going on, Kenny followed them to the gas station and hung around, curious to know why this fifty-year-old man seemed about to be getting pinched.

The detective cars screeched the corner of Bergen Street, turning left onto Third Avenue. They slowed down and pulled to the curb in front of Sammy's. Only two men got out of all the cars, a detective and the uniformed cop who had left his partner to watch this guy with the bad battery. That's when Kenny began to realize that there was nothing small-time about this little man, "Mahoney."

The cops questioned him for a few minutes, then they took him by the arm to one of the cars, and they U-turned it back to the Brooklyn police headquarters, which was on Bergen Street, four blocks away.

When they left, Kenny crossed the street with his bag of empties to the Servicenter and approached the attendant, who was dialing the pay phone so fast he kept getting wrong numbers.

"What was that all about?" he asked.

"That was about Slick Willie the Actor Sutton!" came the reply, along with "Beat it, punk!"

Kenny, then, went back across the avenue, into the grocery store, and put the five Pepsi bottles on the counter; got ten cents from Scafidi the grocer; walked outside; stood on the sidewalk; stared at the dime in his hand, and cried for the last time in his entire life.

You see, Willie Sutton had been Kenny Wisdom's Babe Ruth ever since he started understanding the stories which the people told about him, and the newspaper accounts of his life. Sutton had been first arrested in April of '28, they said, after a street corner shooting and gang fight on 7th Avenue and 14th Street in Brooklyn. Willie was badly beaten by the cops before they locked him up. His mother, Mrs. Mary Sutton, who lived at Terrace Place near Prospect Park, fought the case to the Supreme Court, and her son was finally acquitted.

When he was freed, he began to rob banks, and he was so good at it he never had to hurt anyone during a robbery, or at any other time. He became known as "Slick Willie" and "Willie the Actor" after he escaped from an "escape proof" cell at Sing Sing in 1932. He robbed more banks, was arrested, and escaped from prisons in Philadelphia in 1945 and '47. Since then, he had been a fugitive, and the papers and the people said that he engineered the Manufacturers Trust Company robbery in Sunnyside, Queens, on March something 1950. That's about the time he became John Mahoney and took a room in this house on Dean Street, and told anyone who asked him that he worked for Con Edison.

Walking to the bus, Kenny remembered that day in 1952 when Sutton took his last fall, and he also remembered how this Jewish clothing salesman whose name was Arnold Schuster, and who read detective magazines all the time, bragged to the press that he was the one who spotted Willie Sutton on the subway, and followed him, and tipped off the police that he was in the South Brooklyn neighborhood.

A few weeks after the cops captured Sutton, they found Arnold Schuster, dead with several fresh bullet holes in his body. Police headquarters put out an all-points bulletin for the guy they said shot him — John "Chappie" Mazziotta. In later releases they declared that Chappie was seen in the Midwest, Florida, Australia, Japan, and a few other places. These reports made everyone in the neighborhood laugh with their bellies.

Kenny stood at the bus stop, thinking about William Francis Sutton and the seventy-thousand-dollar reward that had been offered for his capture while he was at large for those five years, and the .38 revolver which was stuffed in his belt, but which he didn't attempt to use when he allowed himself to be arrested for the last time in 1952. And afterward, his landlady at 340 Dean Street told everyone that he brought her roses every Christmas and Thanksgiving — after she caught the Puerto Rican woman, who never spoke, in his room one night. She said that all he had of his own in his room were some clothes, a table radio, a chess set, a bottle of whiskey, a few thousand dollars in a shoebox and one book, *U.S.A.* by John Dos Passos.

On that same day in '52, Kenny recalled that he returned from the grocery, and was sitting in the kitchen, when his uncle Tom burst into the apartment with a handful of bills, shouting that he'd just won a bundle on a horse race. "Let's Live triumphed over Hierarchy by two lengths at Hialeah!" his uncle yelled.

The bus came, and Kenny Wisdom got on it — to go and play a game.

The Grand Concourse D Express had stalled so many times, and was barely creeping, that Pondexteur and his brothers finally said "Fuck it!" and got off at 14th Street to walk, or catch a bus, or anything, the rest of the way.

Only a few of them had been downtown before, and when all of them came above ground out of the subway, they walked right into the middle of the Salvation Army Good Friday production in front of SA headquarters. And it tickled the shit out of them.

Some bearded hipster was lugging a two-by-four cross all over the sidewalk, and a foxy chick ran over to him and wiped his face with a scarf, while the blue-red uniformed, capped and bonneted band played a dirge, and the Chaplains tried to give the struggling dude a boost by cheering him on until a Salvation captain, with a tambourine full of money, told them that the point of the whole thing was that "He" wasn't supposed to make it.

Willie Pondexteur asked him what was the quickest way to get to Hester Street. He was told that the least complicated way was by foot, and which route to take. Instead of thanking the captain, he shouted at the guy with the wood, "The meek shall inherit the earth! Six feet of it!" And as the thirteen Chaplains started toward Third Avenue in lower Manhattan, Willie turned back to the crowd, and said goodbye. "Christ was a sucker!" he yelled. Real loud.

The bearded, robed guy with the lightweight cross kept plodding around the pavement without breaking his shuffle, but he threw a quick "you gotta eat" look at this black kid who was doing all the heckling. He missed, the kid was already gone.

At about East Fifth Street in lower Manhattan, Third Avenue becomes the Bowery. And, when you walk down it, like Willie and the others did, on a cold windy day in March, you see lots and lots of white men with hair on their faces and two, three overcoats wrapped around their nearly breathless bodies, with dull-drunk, or sober-frenzied eyes, searching everything for any significance. You hear the coughing everywhere. You look through the windows of the missions, and watch these thirsty souls, as they shake their hands, trying to dance a cup of black coffee or a roll to their mouths. And you notice that there are no women, except for the ones whose tits have fallen into their stomachs, and the scrubbed-faced prims who pimp religion and a moment of steam heat for the price of a prayer.

Every bindle stiff on the street lifted his lids, and eyed this group of black kids coming along the Bowery. They were apprehensive because there were a lot of them. Tradition had taught each person who settled for the Bowery that they were all easy prey for cops, or beefy weekend drunks, or gangs of kids who wanted to spill some blood, break some bones, or burn someone's face off with gasoline. They were very uneasy about this gang of Chaplains.

At East Houston Street, Willie asked a not-so-old black deadbeat how much farther they had to walk to get to Hester. The once-upon-a-time man ran his wet eyes over the faces that were standing in front of him, wiped his snotty nose with his chapped-scabbed hand, and asked them if they was crazy.

"What you mean, crazy?" Willie snapped back.

And the guy told them what he meant. He told them that any colored boys that went to that neighborhood had to be soft-headed fools, because the people down there hated niggers, and they took pleasure in whuppin' the tar out of 'em, and dumpin' them into ambulances like trash into a garbage truck.

"Look who's worryin' 'bout who!" laughed Willie. Then he pushed his face forward and said, "We can take care of our own good goddamn selves, Pops! Now, how far down and where is this Hester Street?"

"Six more blocks and on the right-hand side," came the reply in the simple matter-of-fact tone of someone not caring about anything once again.

It took Kenny Wisdom some thirty-odd minutes and two buses to get from Third Avenue in South Brooklyn to Bedford Avenue and South Eighth Street in Williamsburg. When he got off at the stop, he bumped into Antonucci the Schemer. Antonucci was called the Schemer because his brain maneuvered instead of thought. He wanted to design everything into a plot, and lay a train of money into the right front pocket of his pegged pants. He was never outrageous; just calm, cunning and conniving.

They both walked to and halfway up the concrete ramp on the Brooklyn end of the Williamsburg Bridge, where the rest of the Aces Wild were huddling against the wind — their hands shoved deep into their pockets, their heads crouched into their coats. It was a rough place to stand and wait, but that's the way these kids got together — hard, alone, and fuck the elements.

At about the same time that Kenny and the others were crossing over the East River on the Williamsburg Bridge, Fred Allen was dropping dead someplace in upper Manhattan. And if you'd have asked these kids about what had just happened to Fred Allen, they'd have told you that he had gotten what he deserved — just like Boogie Woogie.

The noise of the BMT trains drowned out anything anybody had to say to one another, so they looked down into the river at the tugs and the barges and thought about things that boys weren't supposed to know. Things that people, low and high money people, use to gap themselves from their childhoods. Things that are supposed to separate them from having been raised some other way, by some other people, in some other place. Things that are personal and essential for anyone who's on the make out of wherever they're from. No, these fellas, watching the river and the cars go by, closing their minds to the sound of the subway trains, weren't supposed to know these things. But they'd grown up quicker than that. They all, already, knew that they wanted out. Each one, simply, wanted to find the stride that would take him there. And it didn't matter to most of them how long it took, as long as they made it. None of them ever considered much of anything else.

When the Aces Wild reached the Manhattan end of the bridge, Delancey Street was Good Friday busy. All kinds of people were bustling every which way to take care of whatever they had to, before the gates went down for the three-day Easter weekend. Pitchmen were all over the street hawking everything from stockings to live, different-colored bunny rabbits. The Manufacturers Trust Company bank looked like it had a run on its hands. And the Jewish merchants on Orchard Street were shouting like crazy about giveaways, fine buys and bargain hunters' joys. The Chinese shopkeepers, quietly, stated that they had the best wares in everything that Christ had to offer and, after all, Formosa was also a town in Arkansas.

The Lower East Side, the beachhead of the Atlantic — where wave after wave of broken immigrants came, still come, to the open-ended ghetto, trying for something which will give them the momentum to a better life, which for most is Long Island. It's a confusing world, the downtown East Side, a mix of Jewish, Old World, Puerto Rican, Bohemian and all those whose lives wouldn't allow them to survive in another neighborhood. It goes back, and stays there, in the early 1900s. It's always been a familiar community to those who've come from foreign shores because these streets always held someone who could speak their tongue.

Where Delancey sort of becomes Kenmare Schiff and heads across Chrystie Street, it cuts into the Bowery — three blocks north of

Hester Street. Kenny Wisdom spotted Willie Pondexteur almost right away. They both eyed each other, and the Aces Wild stayed on the east side; the Chaplains kept on the west side of the avenue until they got to Hester, where everyone turned right, and walked into the Cefalù Social Club on the corner of Hester and Elizabeth streets. One after another.

Jimmy Peerless greeted each of them with a double handshake as they came through the door. And he said, "My pleasure. My pleasure," over and over again. This man, Peerless, owned an import-export company that minored in deportation, but he was lucky and luck pays off. In bags of money, dropped at designated points by invisible men who drove around in '50 Chevies all day, picking up the cash receipts from the many outlets of Mr. Jimmy's varied enterprises, all of which were considered highly illegal by the district attorney's office and the New York State legislature. This bothered Jimmy Peerless about as much as his wife — never.

At the turn of the century, this area of New York became Little Italy because many Italians settled in there. It was also known at that time as Hoodlums' Den because most of the residents were employed in the activity of crime. Hester Street sits in the center of this Italian section, with its four- or six-story tenement walkups, fine Italian restaurants, grocery stores and meat markets which specialize in items imported from the cities from which their owners had migrated, and clotheslines strung from building to building. The label of Hoodlums' Den was lifted during the thirties, as the illegal occupations of the residents became less violent and more organized. Anyway, they usually only killed each other.

Hester Street was picked as the spot for this game because it was neutral territory — nobody on either team lived there. Of course it was a strong Italian environ, and there were a couple of Italians in the Aces Wild club, and, sure, the Chaplains were all black guys — but it was more or less made certain to everyone by Jimmy Peerless, who was the Don, or mayor of the block, that nobody would interfere in the contest, and that the bookmakers would keep everything straight, because there was money to be made, and anyway, everybody in the area really wanted to know, for once and for all, who could play Ringolevio better: them, or us.

Jimmy Peerless introduced his pudgy, twenty-three-year-old law student of a nephew, who showed the teams a piece of paper with lines drawn on it and a different word written along each of the lines. He was explaining the boundaries that had been worked out for the game, but he was making it very complicated by using language that you only hear in a geography class at a private prep school. He had everybody confused, until his uncle reminded him that he was supposed to be talking about three blocks, not the Northwest Passage. His nephew immediately changed his manner of speaking, and pointed out the window to indicate the area that was to be used: the part of Hester Street that starts at Elizabeth, and crosses Mott and Mulberry streets. In other words, he said, the boundary lines were Elizabeth Street on this end, and Mulberry Street on the other, and no one was allowed to run, or hide, or anything on any street but Hester.

Everyone agreed that they understood, so Mr. Peerless smiled and told them that they all looked like good boys, and that he was sure they would put on a good game, and that everyone was excited about who would turn out to be the winners. He also mentioned that his friend was going to start the game in about a half an hour. "With a small-a bang!" he laughed, as he left with his people, so the kids could get a chance to size each other up in the warmth and privacy of the Cefalù Social Club.

The Chaplains and the Aces Wild looked at one another and they knew that it was going to be some goddamn game. They also knew that there were a lot of bets being laid down on the outcome, and that the books had promised a third of the take to whichever side won, and guaranteed fifty dollars to each of the losing thirteen. But there was more at stake than anything anybody could offer. And nobody had to wonder what it was. Everybody, simply, knew that whoever came out on top in this one, would have to deliver more than it was worth.

Kenny Wisdom had met Willie Pondexteur only once before, in Coney Island. So he gave him some skin, and then embraced one Chaplain he really knew, Cool Breeze.

Cool Breeze lived somewhere in Harlem, and had gotten his JD card at about the same time as Kenny. The coppers gave these Juvenile Delinquent cards out in the 1950s to kids who weren't yet teenagers, when they did something of a misdemeanor which they shouldn't have been caught at. And, when you got one of these cards, you had to join some Police Athletic League team, if you wanted to stay out of one of the many state reformatories.

Kenny and Cool Breeze joined the PAL basketball teams in their respective neighborhoods. They were good. So good, that they both made the All City Junior All Star team, and played together against private grammar and junior high school clubs around New York.

Cool Breeze always wore funny clothes. Orange sneakers, no socks, purple pants and a green polo shirt with a neat round hole cut out of the right side, so that everyone could see his nipple. He also had an outrageous way of walking. He sashayed around like he was a girl, or something. Once, when their PAL Junior All Star team was playing this school in Queens, Cool Breeze was sashayin' to the water fountain during the warm-up, and a high school kid called him a sissy.

Cool Breeze hit him four times with two combinations, and before the guy could hit the floor, Breeze grabbed him by the hair and bounced his face against the gymnasium wall. The guy went down like a sack of cement. Cool Breeze looked at him, crumpled on the ground, then he bent at the waist, made his legs stiff and straight, flung his arms out behind his back, and shouted at this guy whose health he'd just impaired, "Now, go home 'n tell yer momma dat a faggot beat y'up!"

Kenny Wisdom liked Cool Breeze very much. The enthusiasm with which they greeted one another loosened up everyone else, and they all started introducing themselves at once.

"I'm Ralphie."

"Name's Basile."

"B.O., here."

"They call me Homeboy."

"Jimmy Taylor."

"Jake."

"Georgie Goodbye."

"Gildersleeve's my tag."

"Joe Stretch is mine."

"Octavius."

"Solly Girsch."

"Lanier."

"Buckeye."

"They hung Ju-Jube on me."

"Benny Levine."

"How's Bull for short."

"Mule will do."

"Antonucci."

"Tommy Lee, Jr."

"BoBo."

"Glen Feet."

"Clearhead O'Keefe."

"Cool Breeze."

"Jesus." And everybody cracked up with laughter.

"No, honest. My name is Jesus Rodriguez. I swear to God!"

Then Willie Pondexteur and Kenny Wisdom, the ringleaders, gave a hello to everyone, and started to discuss the things that had to be talked about, if the equality of humanity wasn't going to be lost in the overzealousness of prejudice, or reality. The discussion didn't last long. They all knew that if things got out of hand, no one would win, and almost everyone would lose. So they agreed on rights and wrongs and shook hands, and when they walked out of the meet, everyone knew that each one was on his own, and that they all had to do everything to win. They just meant every word which no one had to say.

The first car in the caravan of the Chaplains' bleacher section pulled into a parking space at a curb on the Bowery. The other carloads found spots in the same vicinity. It wasn't easy. There were ten cars filled with fifty, sixty young people who'd come from Harlem for the ride downtown to support their team with their spirited, excited presence. Most of them were girls. Little black girls who were charged up, dressed for the occasion, and wanting to see everything they'd heard about midtown and lower Manhattan at Eastertime.

They'd made Dupree and the other drivers crazy, especially when they demanded to see the Easter lilies at Rockefeller Center. They yelled and bitched and rocked the cars, which almost caused some accidents, and caused a lot of disturbance. Dupree finally gave in, and turned his lead car crosstown toward Fifth Avenue, but he wasn't overjoyed about it. Not one bit.

"Lilies!" he said. "It's forty fuckin' degrees out 'n y'all wanna go see some stupid, jive-ass, motherfuckin' lily show! Lilies! You like 'em so goddamn much, whyn't y'all go hang out in a cemetery! Dat's what dey made fo', dead peoples! Sheet! Lilies!"

And when they got to Rockefeller Center there was no place to park. So the girls jumped out and the cars circled the block, which was clogged with traffic and swarming with suspicious cops, who did double-takes at this line of cars being driven by niggers who were, obviously, not chauffeurs.

The security guards at Rockefeller Plaza also were stricken with alarm when they saw the bunch of little black girls heading straight for the lilies. They grouped themselves and lined up around the lily display, determined to protect each and every flower from the clutches of these dirty little nigger girls.

The girls refused to even recognize the arrival of the fat-assed guards. Instead, they just looked at the lilies, walking all around them, making jokes, saying how pretty they were, pointing things out to each other that they'd never seen before, laughing — and when the cars pulled back onto Fifth Avenue the girls bolted through the plaza so suddenly that the captain of the guards almost suffered a cardiac arrest.

That had been over an hour ago. Dupree had simmered down, and as he walked along with everyone gathering around him, and the girls talking, giggling about all they'd seen for the first time, and the other Chaplains, who'd driven the cars, taking swigs of gin to fire away the chill of the air, he pointed up to a street sign that said Hester, and told everybody to shut their mouths and get themselves together.

Hester Street was full of people who came from all over to see this contest. They wrapped their money in paper slips which placed their bets, and they paid to stand inside the heated bar-and-grills, delicatessens, empty storefronts and hallways to watch and see who would win and who would lose. The crowd made the bookmakers, standing around in the Calamari Bar, very happy. And they all bowed to Jimmy Peerless and said all kinds of things which add up to thank you for having permitted this event.

Dupree and his people stopped at the corner of Elizabeth Street, where their Chaplain team was drawing the lines of their jail on the sidewalk with a piece of chalk around a flat metal cellar door. Willie Pondexteur told them it wasn't going to be easy, but they were going to win, and everyone started smiling and trading skin and making statements to the affirmative and grabbing chunks of tits and ass from the girls who were still chattering about the flowers and their ride from uptown.

Then a big hulky man with a wide-brimmed hat came over, and took Dupree and the others who weren't going to play, to a large, heated room with windows fronting the street, a full refrigerator, whiskey, wine, beer, sofas, and a stove with pots and pans and ready to go, compliments of Mister Peerless. The man didn't say goodbye when he left everyone in the room. He said, "No aiding and abetting."

The Aces Wild decided to outline their ten-by-ten-foot den near the intersection of Mulberry and Hester, using a fire hydrant as a centerpiece. A few of the neighborhood girls stood around watching, but nobody looked at them. Everyone was too busy trying to figure out what they were going to do on this block no one knew anything about. They all looked down Hester Street at the Chaplains, and up at the roofs, and at the people fogging up the windows behind the fire escapes, and they talked about how many cars were parked on the block, and which spots looked good.

Guido Spinnelli ran a restaurant in the neighborhood. He was a three-hundred-pound man who stood five feet eight in featherweight shoes, and he was going to start this thing off right. With class.

He came out of his brownstone with a .45 automatic pistol — the kind that they give to officers in the army, that looks like a Hershey bar. It was the starting gun, and he was about to get things going.

As Guido was stepping off his stoop onto the pavement, a little six-year-old named Tony took careful aim and blew the wrapper off his straw. The wadded tip of the paper hit Spinnelli dead in his left eye. He never knew what happened. He just flinched and the .45 went off. The bullet ricocheted off the asphalt, and smashed into Minnetta's Grocery Store window, and blew up a jar of jelly.

That's when the hundred or so people who were still on the sidewalk trying to buy their way into someplace warm, started running. They screamed, and dropped whatever they were holding in their hands, and slipped and slid, trying to get traction out of there. All they knew was that a little guy who was very fat had pulled a trigger that made a lot of noise, and a bullet broke a window and splattered jelly all over a store, and if he did it again someone might get killed, and none of them wanted to be around.

Yes, it was going to be some goddamn game!

Kenny Wisdom had big-boned shoulders, and a lanky-framed welterweight body with no hips, and freckles all over his face. He was pretty to look at, but he was no dummy. Everyone agreed that he had smarts. So when the gun sounded, he didn't care if it was a mistake. It meant only one thing to him and the twenty-five others who'd come face to face to find out who could play Ringolevio better: it was time to get it on.

Nobody goes first in this game, everybody goes at once. The biggest, toughest guys on each side, which were Mule, Cool Breeze and Basile for the Chaplains, and Bull, Solly Girsch and BoBo for the Aces, play cops, and try to find and catch individuals from the other team, and put them and keep them in jail. These cop-guys, or den keepers, seldom try to arrest each other, until there's no alternative, or unless they get a clean shot at each other — otherwise, because of their strength and toughness, the game would become a war. The rest of the players lay-up wherever the cover is good, until it becomes necessary for them to do all they can to free their mates who've been captured — and then, maybe, win.

Out of all the chaotic activity that was unleashed in a frantic burst on Hester Street, the last clear thing that Kenny Wisdom saw before he dove through the front door of a tenement was Solly Girsch running up the back of a Studebaker and leaping onto Chaplain Jake, who collapsed like a paper bag. And as Kenny ran toward the backyards, he knew that Jake was their prisoner. That's all he knew.

Mule was chasing Georgie Goodbye up a fire escape. Cool Breeze collared Joey Stretch by the cast-iron railing outside the tailor shop. BoBo was dragging Octavius out from beneath a truck by his legs. Basile was carrying Buckeye off to jail in a half nelson. Bull was hit flush in the face with a two-foot snowball by Ju-Jube who slid by him into an alley. And Georgie Goodbye ran across some roofs and down a fire escape, leaving Mule wondering where the hell he went.

The score was two up. And it was only the first minute or so of the game. Everyone who could see outside was cheering, and saying things to each other like: "You see dat!" "Dey don' kid around, deese kids!" "I'll be sonna beetch!" "Holy shitta! Gonna be some-a good-a fight to win-a dis!"

Dupree and the rest had their faces pushed tight against their windows as soon as they heard the report of the automatic. And they were even more excited than everyone else, but a little pissed at the stupidity of Mule for hitting the fire escape after Goodbye, instead of trapping Ralphie by the entrance to the luncheonette. And overwhelmed with delight by Ju-Jube's slick getaway which happened ten feet from them. They were laughing themselves into hysteria as they watched Bull pick at the wet filthy crust which covered his eyes and filled his mouth.

Kenny Wisdom looked out into the backyards which formed the alley that stretched all the way from Mulberry to Elizabeth, down to the Chaplains' jail. The wooden fences, sectioning it all into lots, were high enough, and the fire escapes, going up the brick walls of each building, offered a quick way out in a squeeze, but he knew that as soon as someone began moving around out there, it wouldn't be a secret for long. And, if it was one thing that Kenny Wisdom didn't like to do — it was move around in the open. He'd rather sneak all the way. Therefore, he decided to go underground — into the cellars.

When he heard the first footstep on the staircase, Willie Pondexteur jammed himself into the shadows of the hallway, and stopped breathing, until the feet carried whosever step it was down from the second-story landing and out through the front door onto the stoop and into the street. He didn't care who it was, as long as it was gone. He peeked out of the shadow, and looked toward the glass borders of the entrance, and all he saw was rain-gray-cold weather. Only then did he let go of the gulp of air which he'd been holding in his lungs.

He bit on his lower lip, trying to decide. Decide whether to go up or down, above or below — the outside was out. It was too cold to begin with. He knew that he was in a building on the east corner of Mott Street, facing Hester. One block from Mulberry and the Aces Wild jail. He had to find a position where he could see what was going on; who was going into whose jails, and how many the Chaplains were up, or down.

Pondexteur knew that the people in this neighborhood kept pigeons. He glanced at the ceiling and wondered if there was a coop on this roof, or if he'd have to backtrack down the block and find one. No matter, it was better than going into the basement. It cramped his style. Coop or not, roof it was. And he climbed the stairs straight up, using the first three toes of his feet — not making a sound — but the guy in 3-B heard him anyway. He was a professional burglar.

Kenny Wisdom found what he was looking for right away. A cellar that had a window with a clear view of both sides of the street, and a squinty but undoubted view of the corner jail-dens, where the Chaplains and the Aces Wild would try to keep each other prisoner. It was a crooked, close, bowling lane of a place, with garbage cans lined up along the flaking, white-painted right wall. A coal bin was nearly empty, but the boiler was hot and it kept the area warm. There was a storeroom with no door that was full of all kinds of stuff, and there were two real good places where he could stash himself.

The hot and cold water pipes that ran ten inches below the ceiling had rugs hanging over them. He could swing up there and lie on top, if one guy came. Or when he saw that a couple of Chaplains were on their way for a search and seizure, he'd get into the garbage can that he had just emptied out into all the rest. And if they picked up the lid, he'd simply come out swinging and make for the door. Kenny put the garbage can back where it'd been — sixth in a row of nine. Then he went up the short wooden staircase, and released the lock on the outside of the door which led to the hallway, locking himself in, and came back down. The basement window was the size of a cinder block, but it would do just fine. So he took an old battered straw ottoman from the storeroom, and set up shop.

When Pondexteur cracked open the door, the wind cut into him like a knife. He decided to stay on the landing, and just use the roof for quick observations of the scene in the street. It wasn't a bad place to sit it out for a while. The stairwell gave a clear view of all the floors and the stairs that ran between them. There was an inside latch on the door to the roof and a tiny, wired window that looked out over the tops of all the tenements and let Willie premeditate his escape if the Aces Wild happened to come into the building looking for him.

He could see the pigeon coops that he'd figured on, and he could also see that the pigeons were all huddled together on their perches — very still, very quiet, gritting their beaks, waiting out the cold. The ladders of the fire escapes hooked over the edges of each building, and there were enough of them, making it unnecessary to choose which one until the time came to split. He watched the smoke disappearing from the chimneys, and the empty clotheslines beating against each other. He dismissed all the fire doors on the other roofs as possible exits because they were all shut and probably latched from the inside to keep them from flapping and banging around in the wind.

He opened his door again and poked his head out to see if it had an outside catch he could use to hold it closed and stall anyone who was pursuing him, while he jumped down a fire escape. It didn't. "Shit," he muttered, and sat down against the banister, opening the zipper of his jacket to the warm air that was steadily spiraling up the well. He'd wait some time before sneaking a peek down into the street.

Things were settling down outside. Guido Spinnelli had been driven back inside his house by an old woman in a black dress who was determined to beat him to death with a mop handle. She was very upset about the way Guido had tried to give her a heart attack by exploding the noise of a pistol in her ear. She took it very personal.

The people, who had come from everywhere to see this game of Ringolevio, returned and picked up whatever they'd dropped, and bought their way out of the cold — into places that had steam for heat and big plate-glass windows that were constantly being attended to by small kids with rags in their hands, wiping away the beaded fog so that everyone could see what was, or wasn't, happening on the outside.

Every space with a view of the action ground was packed with people, cramming together in a smoke-filled haze, each one trying to find a spot all his own, which naturally caused a bit of commotion. Especially in Anthony's Bar & Grill, when Naked Arthur, who was called Naked Arthur because he had no hair anywhere on his body, got slightly upset with some Irisher whose elbow kept trying to finagle him out of a position which he wanted to maintain. After Naked Arthur thought that he had reasonably put up with enough elbowing, he put his cigar out on the guy's cheek. When the Irishman screamed, everyone in the place held their ears with their hands, Anthony gave him an ice cube to put on the foxhole that'd just been burned into his face, and told him to shut the fuck up.

It was like that in every place, except for the Calamari Bar where no outsiders were allowed in — just regulars, who knew better than to quibble with the status quo of Hester Street.

Kenny Wisdom had been in the cellar for over an hour, when he pulled one of the roaches from his pocket, stuffed it into a Chesterfield regular, and smoked it.

He wanted to relax a little because it was obvious that this contest between the Chaplains and the Aces Wild might last a long time before either side won the decision.

"It may even go a fuckin' week," he thought, "or until each guy starves to death in his hideout or something."

He looked up at the three o'clock sun and at the daylight it made. Some girls started skipping long-rope above and right in front of the cellar window. The grass made Kenny feel good, and he started to get a rise out of watching the girls in their short woolen coats and their little, pleated skirts. The girl turning the nearest end of the rope was standing next to the basement window, with her legs spread apart and her body moving with the rhythm of the rope.

Kenny took his eyes and followed those legs of hers right up to where they ran into her panties, and then he looked between them. He began to want what was there, very much.

He could feel his hands running smoothly up those legs. He dreamed about sliding his fingers under the edge of her loose cotton panties and into the lips of her hairless milky pussy. It was a wonderful idea. The first time he got into a girl's pants something went wrong. Her name was Shirley. They had smoked grass together. Both had their eyes closed when Kenny put his tongue in her mouth as his right hand squirmed gracefully up and between her legs and his finger slowly pushed its way into the slippery flesh of the opening and gradually worked its way inside the dark, tight, dreamy, wet world of her eleven-year-old body.

He moved his finger deliberately and her hand grasped his right wrist and helped his stroke fall into the excitement of the in-and-out-rhythm. Their hearts were thumping. She started to moan with desire and his dick got so big he thought it was going to explode.

He took his left hand and started peeling off her panties without taking his mouth away from her face. He jerked her pants free from her ankles with his foot and lifted her dress with his left hand and moved his head away from hers to have a look at how he was going to stick himself into her.

Kenny got very scared by what he saw. Blood. It was all over everything and he knew that his finger that was jammed up and between her legs had done it. He froze. Shirley opened her eyes, and when she saw the look on Kenny Wisdom's face, she propped herself up to see what was wrong. She screamed. And he didn't blame her at all because he thought he had broken her cunt, and he understood that it was a good reason for yelling.

It was nearly two months after Shirley before he found out that blood don't mean much when you come right down to it. Just something everybody called a cherry and was made to be broken, so they said. After that, Kenny went around cracking cherries like some kids go after baseball cards.

Now, he was simply sitting on an ottoman in this basement as the dusk began to fall. The girls had all gone away. He grasped his knees with the fingers of his hands and pushed himself up to the window to have a look-see.

He saw Bull pacing the chalked square, determined to keep Chaplains Jake and Octavius in jail. Bull was one hundred and eighty pounds of heavy thick bone, and the clouds of mist steaming out of his nose could be boiled down to Ju-Jube.

Mule was guarding Buckeye and Joey Stretch at the other end of the street with similar disdain, while his eyes rolled up toward heaven and his lips prayed for Georgie Goodbye to be delivered.

The only difference between Bull and Mule was their color: one was white, the other black. Everything else was the same, even their noses. They were both broken.

Suddenly there was an explosion of noise coming from the third floor apartment in a building directly across the street. It was really loud. The shades were up and the lights on, and Kenny tried to see if the turmoil had anything to do with the game. It did. Jimmy Taylor, known around Brooklyn as a stiff puncher, had decided to change his place of concealment, simply out of boredom. He was just opening the door of the fourth floor's communal bathroom as Basile was coming up the stairs to check out the roofs. They saw each other immediately.

Jimmy's right hand smashed against Basile's left cheekbone, as he ran down the flight of steps. Before he was halfway to the next floor, he heard Basile coming after him, and he couldn't believe it. He had hit him with his best punch — admittedly, it was thrown a little high, but it should have stopped him for a moment, at least until he shook it off.

"The guy's head must be made of concrete!" he thought, as he felt Basile almost on top of him. His mind didn't even glance at his reputation in the Redhook section of Brooklyn. Fuck history, he would have shouted if he had had the time, as he pulled himself around the railing of the third floor and ran for the door at the end of the hallway.

He kicked it open by raising his stride, his left heel slamming against the frame right below the knob. When the door flung open all he could see were people sitting at a table and jerking their heads up with their mouths open and their eyes wide. Before his foot hit the linoleum, he pegged the fire escape, ran right over the full supper table, flung open the window, and bounded up to the roof.

Basile's attempt to follow Jimmy Taylor was halted by every one of the seven members of this Italian laborer's family, including the grandmother. Basile didn't try to break away. These people weren't attempting to hurt him, they were just gripping him firmly — stunned and awestruck by the interruption. Their questions, shouted all at once, dealt simply with sanity: "Whadda you, crazy?" they all asked.

When they had quieted down a bit, Basile told them to go and ask Mister Peerless about his mental stability, and collect for whatever was broken. Then, as the hands relaxed from his body, he walked around the table, slid out the window onto the fire escape, and climbed quickly to the top of the building.

All of this tickled the shit out of Kenny Wisdom.

Jimmy Taylor slowed down only when he couldn't feel Basile behind him. He was about six or seven roofs away, when he approached the edge and looked back to see if Basile or someone else was coming up the fire escape. It was dark, but he still noticed a small, thin figure huddled against the chimney in the shadows. He made out like he hadn't seen anything, casually faking his attention somewhere else. Then he pounced on top of the form cramped in the corner. Homeboy tried to make a go of it, but his whole body was stiff with cold. Taylor gave him two short ones in the ribs to intimidate any further struggle. He wrapped Homeboy in a headlock and carted him over to the fire door of the next roof, which had no latch, just a folded newspaper for a jamb.

He kept his right arm tightly wrapped around the prisoner's head and face, until he'd reshut the door on the paper. Then he shifted position and slammed Homeboy's left arm up his back to the base of his neck and walked him downstairs, and out the front, and halfway up the block to the Aces Wild jail, as Basile looked down from above.

A few minutes later, Cool Breeze got together with Lanier and Tommy Lee, Jr., to take the two Aces he spotted climbing into the rear of an old bread truck. He stood at the back while Lanier and Tommy Lee, Jr., covered both of the sliding doors in the front. They were very quiet about it. But when Cool Breeze yanked open the rear doors and exclaimed, "Well, if it ain't Jesus!" the silence was broken and Jesus and Ralphie were caught and taken to the Chaplains' chalk-drawn square of detention.

"Kukla, Fran and Ollie" was blaring up from some television set beneath him, but Willie Pondexteur didn't hear it. All he could do was smell the heavy, thick odors of whatever all the people were cooking in all the kitchens of the building, and it panged his stomach. He loved tomato sauce, especially with cheese all over it, on top of anything.

He raised himself up, zippered his jacket, went out onto the roof, shoved an empty cigarette packet between the door and the door-jamb, and cautiously made his way over to the edge near a fire escape, to have a look.

He saw Glen Feet suddenly burst out of hiding with BoBo chasing him. Feet was the fastest, longest-winded runner of whatever length anyone had recently seen in Harlem.

Solly Girsch didn't seem to care. He waited for the right moment and jumped from behind a parked car into the path of Glen's feet, dropping him hard.

When Bobo caught up to where the collision had taken place, Solly hoisted the deflated Glen onto his back, saying, "He sure is fast, ain't he." BoBo couldn't answer — he was out of breath — and he just stood there while Solly Girsch carried Glen Feet back along Hester Street to Mulberry.

Basile was about one sewer away and he started speeding along in a crouch on the street side of the parked cars, and Willie hoped he got there before BoBo could catch back his breath, because it had been obvious on first sight that BoBo outclassed Basile in size and strength. But now, with BoBo out of wind, it might just be possible for Basile to handle him.

Basile crept one car length past BoBo, came up behind him, slammed his right forearm against his throat, and started to choke him. He was succeeding, but BoBo wasn't moving. He was gasping. They both fell to the sidewalk, and Willie started down the fire escape to give a hand, but it was too late. Clearhead O'Keefe came out from hiding and broke Basile's hold on BoBo by poking his finger into his eye, among other things. They all rolled around until BoBo fell on top of this bastard who had tried to strangle him, and explained to Basile that he had a definite choice: he could go along with them to jail, or to the hospital. Basile chose the former.

The Chaplain chicks started yelling their version of Boo! out the windows of the ground-floor flat where they were, and Dupree told them to shut their mouths and cook something to eat. He was depressed by Basile's vain attempt, of course, but he knew that the game wasn't going to be lost because of it. At least, he hoped Basile's capture didn't mean that much. He discussed it with the guys sitting around the room and they unanimously concluded that the turning point of the contest would depend on how successfully each team carried out or defended the inevitable jailbreaks which would occur.

Willie Pondexteur decided it was time he went down on the street where he could group together with his brothers and get some food into the hollow of his stomach. His instincts told him it was either now or stay hungry.

He moved fast, and tiptoed down the stairs. The guy in 3-B flicked back his ears, raised his eyebrows, and silently scoffed at the sound of someone prowling around like an elephant. But no one else heard Willie scamper downstairs and out the side door on Mott Street, or saw him run full-tilt up Hester to Elizabeth where the Chaplains were holding the corner.

He skidded into the Mule, who asked him what was wrong.

"My stomach," said Willie. "It's empty."

So they pooled some money and a delegation went with Cool Breeze across to the restaurant and came back with arms full of hamburgers and Cokes. Ignoring their prisoners, they munched the meat-filled buns, guzzled the sodas, and stacked what was left in a doorway for any of their brothers who might show up hungry.

They talked about losing Basile, but decided that it was too early to make any desperate moves to free him and the others. After all, the Aces Wild were only one up on them, and Mule and Tommy Lee, Jr., could cover the jail while Cool Breeze and Lanier scouted around for someone to nab. Willie, it was agreed, should sink back into the block until it was time for him to pull his specialty on the opposition.

When they finished eating and there was no more to say, Cool Breeze and Tommy Lee, Jr., moved out on the prowl and Willie faded behind the tenements, making his way through the alley, looking for position.

As soon as they left, the Aces in the Chaplain jail began making cash offers for some food. Mule was totally unsympathetic, even at two dollars a burger. But Lanier suggested that eight dollars might get them two buns which they could split. The Aces responded unexpectedly by trying to pull Lanier into the perimeter of chalk to free themselves. They didn't succeed, except in making Lanier very upset.

"Jes' for that, you can try and dance away the cold while you starve, thinkin' bout what you could be eatin', if you didn't try trickin' me!" he told them.

Food was on everybody's mind by now and one by one all the guys who weren't in jail started making their moves for a bite to eat.

Solly Girsch left BoBo and Bull to guard the Aces Wild jail, while he went to buy a bunch of hero sandwiches and sodas. When he got back to the corner, Georgie Goodbye and Benny Levine showed up to share in the groceries. Jimmy Taylor saw Solly come out of the store with the carton, but before he could take two steps toward the food, Lanier and Cool Breeze made him their prisoner.

Gildersleeve, Ju-Jube and B.O. met each other as they walked to the Chaplain home base and the hamburgers. They also met Clearhead O'Keefe, whom they forced to accompany them but didn't feed. All he got was the companionship of his hungry fellow prisoners.

Antonucci was sitting on the third floor of an abandoned building when he started to get hungry. This caused him little concern, because, as usual, he had the situation covered. Wrapped in waxed paper and stuffed inside his jacket were two bologna sandwiches and a half pint of milk. He leisurely satisfied his appetite, pleased with his foresight, while watching the goings-on in the street through a stone-sized hole in one of the soot-covered windows in the empty apartment.

Kenny Wisdom was trying to come up with an idea for a meal when he heard someone at the hallway door. He didn't have time to do anything, but ducked behind the boiler and listened to the footsteps come down the stairs. They were skipping, so he figured it was a girl. He took a peek and saw that she was about to empty some garbage into one of the cans. Suddenly she froze, seeing his shadow cast on the wall in front of her.

Before she could get hysterical, Kenny made himself visible and explained who he was and why he was there and assured her that she had nothing to be frightened about. He helped her dump the garbage and they chatted a bit. She told him that her name was Stephanie and he said that it was a beautiful name. Then he hit on her to get him something to eat and drink.

She said that she would bring him a sandwich and some milk, but she'd have to wait until her father went to work.

"He'll leave in about twenty minutes," Stephanie said, "and I'll be back down in half an hour."

"Good," said Kenny, "and thanks."

Then she left, locking the cellar door from the outside.

On the television in the Calamari Bar, Jerry Lewis was hosting the Academy Awards, and everyone in the place was laying bets on their picks for best actress and actor. Since very few of the patrons in the shellfish bar had any knowledge of the qualities required to win an Oscar, it wasn't odd that they all agreed on two of the nominees as a sure thing — simply, because, after all, they were Italians. It was even less odd that the bookmakers stopped taking wagers as soon as they realized that the money wasn't being evenly spread, because if these two Italian movie stars won, it would bankrupt every bookie in the place.

They were lucky that they closed shop when they did, because a while later Anna Magnani won for *The Rose Tattoo* and Ernest Borgnine for *Marty,* and everyone did a little celebrating for their two paisanos who beat out all those Jewish actors for Hollywood's best prize.

In the locker room of the precinct station house, Patrolman Michael Lowndes was changing into his blue uniform and getting himself ready for inspection.

Michael Lowndes lived in Staten Island with his mother and father. He was twenty-two years old and he'd been on the force a little over a year. He was very proud that he was the first person in his family to become a cop. None of his relatives had ever been able to pass the civil service exam to get into the Police Academy. And tonight he was especially excited, because after one year as a probationary patrolman, Officer Lowndes was getting a new tour of duty and his own beat to pound. Patrolling Hester Street was part of that beat.

An old rusty-gun cop named Malloy had shown him around the area during the preceding week. Malloy had retired to his pension the day before, and now the maintenance of law and order in that section was the sole responsibility of Patrolman Michael Lowndes. He was eager to make good as one of what New York City calls its finest.

Stephanie brought Kenny Wisdom a salami sandwich and a bottle of orangeade. She told him that she couldn't bring any milk, because there was only enough left for her father's coffee, which he always had for breakfast when he returned from work in the morning. Kenny immediately assured her that it didn't matter one bit, and that he was extremely grateful to her for coming through for him.

"I don't know what I woulda done if you didn't help me out like you did."

Then he told her that she had nice hair and began to pump her for some information about Hester Street, hoping to uncover some secret passageway that she might know about.

But he drew a blank. Stephanie didn't know a thing about Hester Street. Her mother was an invalid, and didn't allow her to play outside. So Kenny simply thanked her again and told her that she better get back upstairs before her mother got worried.

She left and he sat and ate the sandwich and drank the orangeade and turned his attention to a loose pile of old newspapers. He picked out a February 1955 edition of the New York *Herald Tribune* which had a banner headline about a two-hour gun battle, and he read the article about August Robles and looked at the pictures.

The news story told about a guy named Joe Aronowitz who had come to New York from Philadelphia to testify against two or more of his former associates who had been indicted for the poor usage of guns, among other things. If they were convicted, it was going to take an adding machine to count up the number of years they would spend in prison. And it was Joe Aronowitz's testimony that would give the district attorney a case, and a guaranteed verdict of guilty.

So these former associates of his allegedly hired someone to do away with him and his blabbermouth. That someone was a five-foot-four, one-hundred-ten-pound, forty-year-old Puerto Rican who wore eyeglasses as thick as ashtrays and who killed people for a two- or three-hundred-dollar fee, and whose name was August Robles.

According to the paper, Robles made Aronowitz drive from midtown Manhattan to Ashland Place in Brooklyn, where he shot him twice in the back of the head and left him slumped behind the wheel of the car, which was parked in front of the National Casket Company. August Robles had a sense of humor.

Two days later, three detectives crashed into an East Harlem apartment only to be disarmed by this tiny little Spanish man. An alarm was put out and the area closed off. Robles, apparently realizing he didn't have a chance to get out of the neighborhood, entered a tenement on East 112th Street, indiscriminately chose an apartment, pointed one of the several guns he was carrying at the occupants, and told them to leave.

They did, and of course notified the police, who rushed to the scene with a swarm of two hundred men. They blocked off the street and a deputy inspector got on a megaphone to ask Robles to surrender because he was completely surrounded and couldn't possibly escape.

August replied that they would have to "wait until I finish a letter."

That's when the gun battle began — it lasted two hours and drew a crowd of nearly ten thousand spectators.

All the neighboring buildings were evacuated and the cops fired thousands of rounds and lobbed tear-gas canisters through the windows of the apartment, from which Robles, apparently not bothered by the gas, was returning the fire.

During the second hour, the cops in charge of the attack discontinued the tear gas which was obviously having little or no effect, and ordered their men to fire live grenades into the top floor flat. They even had an officer from the bomb squad get on the roof directly above Robles and blow a hole in the ceiling with a dynamite charge.

Needless to say, these explosions blew out every window in the neighborhood and set half the block on fire. While three engine companies sprayed water on the flames, one of the detectives who had lost his gun to Robles earlier in the day made his way, along with an army of men and a Catholic priest, up to the top floor landing and the apartment where their man had barricaded himself.

For fifteen minutes they pleaded with Robles to come out with his hands up. After getting no response at all during that quarter hour, the detective who led the way upstairs kicked open the shattered door and pumped twenty rounds of forty-five caliber bullets from a Thompson machine gun into the already pulverized body of the fragile little man who had caused him a great deal of embarrassment by disarming him not five hours before.

The newspaper account quoted the detective, "That guy Robles was too dangerous to take any chances with." The story ended with a description of the priest giving August Robles Extreme Unction posthumously. Two full pages of photos in the *Tribune* testified to that day in February 1955 when two hundred members of the police force declared war on 112th Street and left it looking like a battlefield, simply because a little spic named August Robles made a few of their own lose face by taking their guns away. They were going to get him for that, and while they were at it teach the rest of the spics in the neighborhood a lesson they wouldn't soon forget.

Kenny threw the newspaper back on top of the pile and thought about how chicken-shit cops were, as he finished his sandwich.

Everyone that wasn't in jail had had something to eat by now and some of the fellows on each team thought that it was time for a little action. Gildersleeve, Ju-Jube and B.O. could see that there were only three guys guarding the Aces Wild jail, so Ju-Jube figured that if he and the other two rushed the jail at the same time, one of them was bound to get through and free their imprisoned brothers. They decided to try it. B.O. led the way. They snuck down the street behind the parked cars, but as soon as they crossed Mott, they decided that it would be better to travel the length of the next block across the rooftops. They moved slowly and quietly, until they finally arrived at the building which bordered Mulberry Street, and sat directly across from the Aces Wild jail.

They went downstairs to the foyer and cracked open the front door a tiny bit, so they could get a better idea of how they were going to go about freeing their teammates.

Solly Girsch, Bull, and BoBo were covering the corner, but they were bunched together, rather than spread out in a zone defense. So Gildersleeve said it'd be a cinch, all they had to do was make sure they hit the target from three different angles. This way, he assured Ju-Jube and B.O., the Aces Wild guards wouldn't have time to block all of them. They would only be able to stop two.

They got themselves together for the attempt. B.O. was going to come in from the left flank, Gildersleeve would go down the middle, and Ju-Jube would hit from the right. "Ready," said B.O. "Go!"

They all sprang out the door at once. Ju-Jube ran into a bear-hug by Bull. Gildersleeve faked to the right causing BoBo to slip and fall, but Solly Girsch jammed his hand down on Gildersleeve's collar and stopped him cold. B.O. would have made it if Mister Pulmeri, who was seventy-two years old, hadn't pulled his '49 Buick out of his parking space and if B.O. hadn't run into it and been knocked ten feet into the air. He wasn't hurt — no bones broken — only stunned, and he stayed that way until twenty minutes after they put him in jail.

Mister Pulmeri didn't know anything about B.O. He thought that he'd just hit a bump in the road and he bitched to himself in Italian about this stiff they had for a mayor, Wagner, who couldn't keep the goddamn streets in shape.

Georgie Goodbye and Antonucci got together and cooked up a jailbreak scheme of their own. They were in an abandoned building only half a block away from the Elizabeth Street corner where the Chaplains were keeping six Aces prisoner.

The plan was for Antonucci to crawl down Hester Street on his belly underneath the nine parked cars that lined the curb until he reached the Pontiac on the corner. Then he'd just roll out from under it and into the chalked square and free everybody. Georgie Goodbye meanwhile would create a diversion with his broken field running, which would draw at least two of the Chaplains after him and occupy the attention of the other two.

It almost worked.

Antonucci slipped unnoticed under a car and began crawling on his stomach like a soldier. When he had gone four car lengths, Georgie burst out of the tenement and started making mad dashes to and from and all around the corner with Cool Breeze, Tommy Lee, Jr., and Lanier chasing him all over the place.

He made one mistake. He started running between parked cars. The cars under which Antonucci was making his way to the corner. The inevitable occurred. Between the bumpers of the fourth and fifth cars in the line, Georgie Goodbye stubbed his foot on Antonucci's rib cage and went sprawling to the ground. The three Chaplains jumped on them and they were caught. Antonucci called Georgie a "fucking moron" several times as they were escorted to the den.

Officer Michael Lowndes was standing in formation with his fellow patrolmen in front of the desk sergeant who was taking roll call while the captain walked through the ranks, inspecting each man's equipment and uniform. There followed a brief meeting in which the captain told his men to keep on their toes because a few burglars liked to work this Italian neighborhood on Good Friday night and Easter weekends.

"I know it's cold out there tonight, men," said the captain, "but don't hang out indoors too much. Just keep moving around with your eyes open and you'll stay warm. Only duck inside to shake the chill off once in a while. OK, now go out there and make some arrests."

He didn't mention anything about the Ringolevio game. He forgot.

Dupree and the rooting section were all getting pretty stoned, as were the various spectators who were hanging out in the bars and grills and heated storefronts, but they could still count. They figured that with eight members of each team being held prisoner in jails which were guarded by three guys each — that left only two Chaplains and two Aces Wild who were still moving around. The turning point had arrived and whichever side broke jail first would gain a substantial margin toward victory.

No one knew this better than Kenny Wisdom and Willie Pondexteur, and both understood that it was now time for them to make their moves.

This was the part of the game that Kenny liked best. His part. He looked over the street and immediately noticed that Cool Breeze was not with Lanier, Mule, and Tommy Lee, Jr., defending the Chaplain jail. This meant that Cool Breeze was combing the area, trying to hunt him out. It also meant that Kenny had to wait until he spotted Cool Breeze in order to choose a route that would avoid a confrontation, because Wisdom was physically no match for Breeze.

This was the aspect of Ringolevio which attracted players and made the game a permanent part of the cultural tradition of the streets of New York. Sooner or later during the course of a contest, each participant had to look into himself and face his physical and mental limits. After a kid played the game a few times, he would begin to understand the reality of his makeup by contrasting his abilities with those of the other players. If he was aware of himself, he would soon discover that he had a quality that was unique and peculiar to him, and he would develop it until eventually he became known and respected for it, and would never jeopardize it with whims or fantasy. You just inevitably learned who you really were whether you liked it or not.

Willie Pondexteur also noted that one of the Aces' defensive players was not standing on the corner of Mulberry, protecting the jail with Solly Girsch, Bull and BoBo. And he made the reasonable assumption that Benny Levine was searching for him. This, however, didn't require Willie to keep an eye peeled for Benny because he was already in his position to make his move on the Aces Wild jail.

He was lying on the floor under the steering wheel of a 1954 Chevrolet which he intended to start in a few minutes by wrapping the silver paper from a pack of cigarettes around the ignition wires that were behind the dashboard. Then he was going to slowly drive down the street, pull alongside the jail, leap out of the car and free his brothers.

Now he was simply biding his time with all the doors locked, and enjoying the last of his cigarettes.

Kenny saw Cool Breeze step out of the shadow of a doorway and enter a tenement across the street. He watched him fade into the hallway of the building, and then Wisdom jumped the flight of cellar steps, opened the latch of the door to the hall by slipping a playing card between the tongue and the mouth of the lock, and flew up the stairwell to the roof.

He ran low and fast along the rooftops until he reached the building that sat on the corner of Elizabeth and Hester streets, hovering directly over the Chaplains' jail.

The fire escape which hung down the front of the tenement was twenty-five feet wide of the target, but there was a ledge on the second story that ran the width of the building and Kenny would use it as a path to take him to the spot right above the jail where he would jump straight down into the midst of his teammates and break them out.

He started down the fire escape, stealing his way with the poise and movements of a cat. When he reached the second landing he crouched behind some flowerless boxes which were filled with dirt, and examined the ledge to see if it was strong enough to carry him the necessary twenty-five feet.

There were no breaks in it, which was good, but it sure was narrow and it looked mighty old. But Kenny had no choice, because now it was either win or lose. And the strength of the ledge was a chance he had to take.

He took off his leather Air Force issue jacket which he knew would give him away by scraping against the wall. Also, without it, he would have more room to move between him and the side of the building. Then he eased himself over the cast-iron railing of the fire escape and onto the ledge.

He spread-eagled his arms and pressed them against the bricks, moving slowly sideways, testing every step before putting his weight on each section. He seldom took his eyes off the three Chaplains who were milling about below him.

Then, with only ten feet to go, he met the only obstacle between him and his team's freedom — an empty flower box which was sticking out of a window and blocking his way. He knew that if he stepped in it, it would definitely give way. And he couldn't step over it, because it was too long for his leg span. But he had to get past it. He was still too far away to release the prisoners. So Kenny raised his right arm and grabbed the top of the brownstone window frame which stuck out from the wall above the wooden box. His hand, burned by the ice-cold cement, gripped the abutment like a vise.

Kenny pulled himself up with his right arm, swung completely around, and caught hold of the overhanging frame with his left hand. He was now facing the building with only his hands keeping him from falling backwards — twenty-seven feet to the sidewalk. The wind was cutting into his sweat-soaked body and he began to shiver. But before he inched his way forward, he glanced under his left armpit to the scene below. No one had spotted him.

Suddenly a silhouette passed behind the drawn shade of the window and Kenny flashed on what would happen if the person inside lifted the shade and saw him hanging there. An image popped into his mind of an old lady grabbing her left tit and dropping dead of a heart attack. Kenny had to restrain himself from laughing out loud.

He started to move. He was nearly numb from the cold when he finally lowered himself down to the ledge on the other side of that dumb empty wood box. His hands were black-and-blue frozen. He was still facing the wall. To turn around, he crossed his right foot over his left and moved ever so slowly on the heel of his left foot and the ball of his right until he was facing the street with his back pressed against the wall. He warmed his hands in his crotch and rested a moment.

Patrolman Michael Lowndes was walking down Mott Street toward Hester, swinging his billy club with his gray-gloved hand.

Willie Pondexteur started up the Chevie, waited for the engine to warm a bit, and then put it into gear and rolled away from the curb.

Benny Levine saw him and began to chase after, but Cool Breeze came out of nowhere and hit Benny with a body block that sent him bouncing off the window of a liquor store. The window didn't break, but the jolt set off the burglar alarm. Officer Michael Lowndes heard it. So did everybody else.

The noise distracted the guards of each den. They were all looking the wrong way when Kenny Wisdom dropped twenty-seven feet from the ledge into the chalked perimeter, executing the Aces Wild escape, while Willie Pondexteur pulled up to the Mulberry Street corner, leaped out of the car, and freed the Chaplains by lunging into the Aces Wild jail and shouting, "FREE ALL!"

Benny Levine broke away from Cool Breeze and ran into an alley with Breeze chasing him. Patrolman Michael Lowndes saw them both running from the sound of the burglar alarm. He drew his pistol, gripped his right wrist with his left hand, rested his gun arm on the roof of a car to steady his aim, shouted "Halt!" once, then fired three shots at the two figures who were sprinting down the alley.

The first bullet shattered the base of Benny Levine's spine as he was leaping over a fence. The second one pierced the upper left side of Cool Breeze's back and exploded his heart. The third was a warning shot.

The pandemonium which resulted from the jailbreaks at both ends of Hester Street froze at the sound of the gunfire and at the sight of the cop leaning over the car at the corner of Mott Street with smoke coming out of the barrel of his .38.

As Officer Lowndes began to cross over to the alleyway, the Chaplains and the Aces Wild moved toward the corner of Mott and Hester streets where this cop had fired off his rounds. The people in the bars and storefronts poured out onto the sidewalk as did Dupree with his brothers and sisters. Everyone was speculating on what had gone down.

The burglar alarm was still ringing when the crowd reached the mouth of the alley and saw the cop leaning over the lifeless body of Cool Breeze and the near-dead Benny Levine. Everyone got very quiet.

Patrolman Michael Lowndes holstered his gun and told everyone to stay back and asked someone to call an ambulance. Then he began to notice the several black faces staring out at him from the crowd and he looked back down at Cool Breeze crumpled on the ground, then back at the crowd. Something was wrong.

"They were trying to break into the liquor store!" Lowndes told the crowd.

"You full of shit!" came a reply from someone. "They were playing a game!"

Police Officer Lowndes went for his gun as the Chaplains and the Aces Wild came toward him. He never reached it. Jimmy Taylor cold-cocked him and Mule, Basile, BoBo and Solly Girsch pummeled him to the ground.

Kenny Wisdom took the cop's pistol, wrote Benny Levine's name and address on a slip of paper, and gave both to one of Jimmy Peerless's men and told him to call an ambulance for Benny. Willie Pondexteur wrote down Cool Breeze's home address and name and told the same man that they'd pick up his body at the morgue with his mother. Willie asked Dupree to pull the cars around and get ready to split while they dealt with this fuzz.

Then, as the neighborhood people went back indoors, the Chaplains and the Aces Wild carried this cop across the street to a vacant lot where they stripped him of his uniform and leather belts, shoes and handcuffs, and stuffed them down a sewer. And kicked him half to death. They only stopped when they heard the siren of the ambulance.

The cop's body was left sprawled naked on a mound of garbage as they all crammed into Dupree's caravan of cars which dropped the Aces Wild at Union Square station to catch a train back to Brooklyn while the Chaplains high-tailed it back to Harlem.

The game which is called Ringolevio was over.

Benny Levine was taken to Bellevue and placed in an intensive care unit. The doctors told his family that he'd probably live, but never walk again. Cool Breeze was zipped up in a body bag and a wagon took him to the morgue.

Patrolman Michael Lowndes was carefully wrapped in a blanket by two ambulance attendants, placed on a stretcher and driven to St. Vincent's Hospital, where a medical team tried to set his broken bones back into place with wires and splints.

The area was soon flooded with captains, inspectors, sergeants from headquarters on Broome Street, and regular coppers from the 5th Precinct. The sight of Lowndes's bloody, bruised, nude body made them sick and they asked everyone in the neighborhood what had happened and everyone said that they didn't know anything.

The patrolman's revolver was lying next to him in the vacant lot, right where Jimmy Peerless's man had placed it before the cops came. No one could explain what had happened to his uniform or the rest of his cop's paraphernalia.

An inspector from police headquarters talked to Jimmy Peerless in the Calamari Bar and got absolutely nowhere and was advised to forget about the whole incident.

He did, as did the rest of the police force.

It never even appeared in the newspapers.

Two days later Kenny Wisdom went up to the Salem Methodist Church on 129th Street and Seventh Avenue in Harlem to attend the funeral services for Cool Breeze. He went alone because he was the only one of the Aces Wild who knew him and cared.

The service was brief, but noisy with crying and wailing and repeated demands upon the Lord for a reason why. It ended with the immediate family, mostly women and an uncle who was a bus driver, getting into regular cars for the short ride to the crematorium where the body of Cool Breeze was burned to cinders and poured into a vase.

Willie Pondexteur met Kenny on the sidewalk and invited him over to the Chaplain clubhouse, as plainclothesman Delmos watched from his car and wondered who the white boy was.

Kenny didn't feel nervous when he entered the brownstone which was the clubhouse. He felt mellow — that is, if you can imagine a twelve-year-old pushing thirteen feeling that way. But that's the type of tone that settled into Kenny Wisdom when he was alone with blacks. He mellowed.

Willie offered him some grape and introduced him around. Some of the kids who were on Hester Street a couple of days before asked him how in hell he'd learned to crawl ledges and leap thirty feet to the ground like Superman or something.

"Necessity," Kenny answered. "Necessity."

Everyone was tickled by his response. Especially the foxy little chick whose nipples stood straight up inside nothing but her sweater. Her name was Pearline and she placed a lighted reefer in Wisdom's mouth and had eyes for him. She'd never made it with a white boy before, and this one sure was pretty.

"Where'd you get all them freckles?" she asked.

"They ain't freckles, baby, they're angel kisses," Kenny answered.

And things started to loosen up. It was obvious that this kid Wisdom knew how to party, so they all treated him as if he was simply one of them.

Everyone started dancing and carrying on. Dupree showed up with some cocaine for a chosen few. And after Kenny had some, he took Pearline into a room with a mattress and buried himself in her for close to two hours. They never said a word to each other. They just dug into each other's bodies and made sweat and smells and sounds and sex until they were exhausted, until they dried themselves out.

It was the last time Kenny Wisdom was to enjoy a girl for quite a while, because when he came out of the room, Dupree was standing in the corner with a few bloods who were going to short-circuit his sex life.

"You ever mess with stuff?" asked Dupree.

Kenny didn't understand immediately, but when he did, he said no.

"You wanna try some?" offered one of the guys in the corner.

"Sure," said Wisdom. "Maybe it's time for a little sleep. I ain't learned too much by being awake anyway."

"Well," Dupree said, "lots of things come free, but this one thing you gotta pay for. Just like rent."

Then he asked Kenny if he had any money. He did. And Dupree sold Wisdom a spoon of the best heroin you could buy on the streets of Harlem for ten dollars and threw in a set of works.

"Now you better get goin' back to Brooklyn before it gets dark. And when you get there, you cook a little of that up and remember ole Dupree. But don't you go rememberin' me to no one else, y'hear?"

Kenny said goodbye to everybody, except Pearline, who was surrounded by a bevy of black chicks, asking her all about the white boy's dick.

It took Wisdom almost two hours on the subway to reach South Brooklyn and all he could think about was the needle and the eyedropper and the pacifier and the packet of white powder in the pocket of his jacket. For the first time in his life, he could hardly wait to get home.

When he did, he found his mother in the kitchen making supper. He needed a spoon. He kissed his mother as she mashed the potatoes, told her he had just been out, "that's all," and eased a tablespoon out of the sink and into his back pocket. "Dad going to be late?" he asked as he picked up some matches and made his way to the bathroom.

"No, he'll be home in ten minutes," came the reply.

The door to the bathroom didn't lock or even close properly. He wedged a facecloth between it and the jamb. Then he pulled everything carefully out of his pockets and spread it all out neat on the floor like he'd seen it done a hundred times before. He took a piece of cotton out of a vitamin bottle in the medicine chest, rolled it up into a ball and laid it in the spoon. He turned on the cold water tap and filled a glass of water. He made sure that the collar, a long thin strip of wet paper, fit the needle tight to the end of the eyedropper before he squeezed the nipple of the pacifier and placed the set into the glass to draw-fill with water. When he did, he squirted the water through the needle, cleaning it. He repeated this several times.

Kenny then opened the glassine paper, the same kind of bag that stamp collectors use, very carefully, so he wouldn't spill out any of the contents by cracking the waxed paper with his nervous fingers.

He emptied a very tiny portion of the white powder into the spoon and added a little water from the dropper, spurting the rest of the water through the needle and into the sink. He took one of his mother's stockings off of the shower curtain rod to use for a tie. He held a few matches under the spoon until the heroin dissolved, sucking the heated mixture up through the cotton into the works. He wrapped the stocking tightly around his upper arm and began tapping the dull needle into the vein that was popping out of the pit of his elbow, holding the dropper between the thumb and fingers of his shaking, anxious hand.

He was breathing heavily and hardly felt the needle dig into his vein, until he saw the red blood jet into the dropper. He watched it for a moment, then he loosened the tie, and shot the fluid from the dropper into his arm. The warmth was spreading through his body before he had taken the needle out of his arm. The heroin relaxed his system into a nod, which was broken by a nausea that puked up all he had eaten and drunk that day into the toilet. But it wasn't unpleasant, it was just the routine of a new user and he expected it. Kenny cleaned out the set of works or outfit, rewrapped the paper packet back into its rectangular junkie fold, and covered everything in tissue paper, hiding it all beneath the dirty-clothes hamper. He wiped the blood from his arm with a Kleenex and sat on the edge of the bathtub wondering how long it would take before he'd get over the nauseous stage. He lighted a cigarette which tasted better than any he'd ever smoked before and he knew he was going to join the hyp class and become a full-out junkie now that he had given himself his wings — his first mainline fix.

His body was painlessly pleased with this decision. Kenny began to use stuff several times a day. The first shot in the morning, which is called a wake-up, another in the afternoon, and one late at night. During the course of the two weeks the spoon lasted, his habit began noticeably to take hold. Kenny didn't wash — water is unpleasant to users of heroin; he lost his appetite; his interest in girls and sex was totally unplugged; he stopped wheezing — junk is a sure cure for asthma or the common cold — and his whole life began to narrow down to one junk fix and the looking forward to another. Then the day came when he was out of junk. The bag was empty and when he woke in the morning he could feel himself getting sick. As all addicts do, he had saved the cottons he had used to suck the heroin solution from the spoon into the dropper. He placed them all in a tablespoon, heating the cottons and shooting up what heroin they still held. This took his sick off for the time being, but he knew that he'd have to score before midday.

He had eleven dollars stashed away which was enough for a spoon and carfare up to Harlem, but this time Kenny wanted to score more than a spoon — and he knew where to get the money to cop a fifty-dollar bag. In his building, on the top floor, lived an old maid, a Miss Sadie Grant, who spent every morning cleaning the priest's house of the neighborhood Catholic church. In her small apartment she kept a mission box crammed with bills which she sent every year at Christmas to a missionary society in Africa. It would be months before she'd miss any of it.

Kenny went upstairs and knocked softly on her door to make sure she wasn't home sick or something. There was no answer, and the lock was old and easy to pick with a piece of wire hanger. Once inside, he went straight for the wooden box with an enamel cross on its lid and a piece of velvet covering it. He unhooked the catches on the sides and lifted it open. There was a lot of silver, a neat stack of singles, nine fives and three tens. He took five fives, two tens, and seven singles, folded the fifty-two dollars into his back pocket, and left Sadie Grant's holy-pictured, lace-filled apartment, relocking the door as he did.

All he could do on the subway ride uptown was dream of the pleasure he'd feel at the sight of Dupree. When you use junk, the pusher is your loved one. Your one and only. You can never wait to see him, and after a while your memory can reproduce an exact picture of him, his style, his every mannerism. It's as if no one else existed but you and him. And him first, always — he makes sure of that.

Kenny found Dupree inside the Imperial Bar and Grill next to the Chaplain clubhouse. They went into the men's room and Dupree said that he didn't have a fifty-dollar bag, but he was holding two twenty-five dollar papers which he could let Kenny have. They agreed and Dupree counted out the money while Wisdom checked the papers. Before he left, Dupree gave Kenny two phone numbers and told him to call before he made a move next time. "That way, I'll make sure I got what you lookin' for and we can meet a little downtown — 'cause it looks a little funny for a white boy to be comin' this far up."

When Kenny came up out of the subway in Brooklyn, he met

41

Solly Girsch and Clearhead O'Keefe, who were both on their way to see Benny Levine where he sat paralyzed in a wheelchair inside his family's apartment on Wyckoff Street.

"I've gotta run home for a minute, but I'll meet you there," said Wisdom. Then he went into his family's tenement flat, shut the bathroom door on a towel, and gave himself a fix, the size of which would have killed him two weeks ago — but his tolerance for the narcotic had steadily grown and he saw that the fifty dollars' worth of stuff wasn't going to last him a week.

Kenny Wisdom was becoming what is known as a junk hawk, that is to say, all he ever did from then on pertained to junk, as his tolerance for the stuff grew even beyond his greed for it. He always wanted much more, and not much of anything else.

He hated to leave the bathroom which had become his private chamber of nod, but his mother returned, and he didn't want her to get any more suspicious than she already was. So he went over to Benny's to say hello.

As he walked the block to Levine's building, one could see that Kenny was already developing the gestures of junk movement. Junkies, like faggots, have a distinct way about them and their style is as pronounced as the limp wrist of the fag. A junkie moves with arms dangling and hands swinging with palms up and fingers stiff, as though they were about to pick up a dropper.

Benny Levine was wrapped in a cast and sitting straight up in a wheelchair. He was glad to see Kenny, who sat down on the floor next to Solly and O'Keefe. They talked about all that was going on around the neighborhood, but Wisdom sat strangely silent, thinking how far away the Ringolevio game had become for him. All he could remember were his first two or three fixes. But he did tell them about the services that the Chaplains held for Cool Breeze and about the party they threw in his memory afterwards.

Mrs. Levine, Benny's mother, came home with her older son Max, who was fifteen. She said hello and expressed how glad she was to see them all. Then Max started bitching to her about being hungry.

"There's plenty of sandwich meat in the 'frigerator, so go and fix yourself. Fix yourself!" she yelled back. And Kenny Wisdom knew that he'd just discovered the origin of the word "fix" — it was a Yiddish expression. "Whatta ya know about that!" he thought. "It's a goddamn Jewish term!" He almost laughed, but he had lost his sense of humor back in the bathroom two weeks ago.

They stayed with Benny for another hour, then they all left together, promising to come back and visit soon.

On the sidewalk they stood and talked.

Solly: What you been up to?

Kenny: Nothin' much. You?

Solly: Oh, I did a few numbers.

O'Keefe: Were the Chaplains angry that we didn't all show up for Cool Breeze's funeral?

Kenny: No. Anyways, you don't see none of them comin' down here to visit Benny, do ya?

Solly: What's wrong with your eyes?

Kenny: What eyes? What?

Solly: They're pinned.

O'Keefe: Whadda ya mean, pinned?

Solly: Shuddup!

Kenny (surprised, but not really caring): So?

Solly: How's about a taste?

O'Keefe caught on: You got some stuff?

Kenny: Yea, but I ain't givin' it away.

Solly: What about an outfit?

Kenny: Sure, I got — but you can't shoot up at my house.

Solly: Sell me and Clearhead a dime paper and we can geeze in one of the pads in the abandoned building down the block.

Kenny agreed because he was out to make some money, but was curious about how Solly pinned him: "How'd you pick up on the fact that I was usin'?"

Solly: My brother, Lenny, had a habit ever since I can remember and he's turned me on a few times this past year.

O'Keefe: Lenny gave me my wings, too. Right, Solly?

Kenny: OK, you guys get some water and I'll meet you down the street with the shit.

Solly sent O'Keefe into a grocery store to fill up an empty with some water and told him to make sure that he cleaned the bottle out good, "because if the water's bad, we'll get the chills."

Kenny put together a short-count dime paper and made a slightly smaller one up for himself. He stuffed the outfit under his coat, got some clean cotton out of the cabinet, and met Solly and O'Keefe inside the abandoned building down the street.

They all turned on. Kenny used his own spoon, while Solly and O'Keefe cooked their stuff up in a bottle cap. Then they sat around nodding, oblivious to the cold, and Solly murmured that he wanted to make this scene for a while. O'Keefe went along, agreeing that the time seemed right for him to become a "schmecker," too.

"How much stuff do you have?" asked Solly.

Since greed is the first instinct of a junkie, Kenny answered that he only had a little less than a dime. He really had a twenty-five dollar paper and more than half of another one.

"Well, if we're gonna do this, we gotta cop some more," said O'Keefe.

Solly asked Wisdom if he scored in the neighborhood.

Kenny: No. Harlem.

Solly: Good. The scag is better up there.

Kenny: What about money? Does anybody got any besides the ten you gave me?

"No," Solly answered, "but I know where we can get a bundle. Enough to buy an ounce of horse — some real weight."

Solly Girsch then told Kenny Wisdom and Clearhead O'Keefe about a florist's shop up on Seventh Avenue that was owned by two old brothers who hoarded their money in a box in the back room of the store.

"I used to be their delivery boy," Solly said. "They're little guys. We'd have no trouble with them and they must have over a grand in the place. It's a cinch. Whadda ya say?"

"Sounds good," came the answer from his two listeners.

They decided to use a room on the top floor of the abandoned building that they were in as a shooting gallery; and that each of them would be responsible for his own stuff, and stash it where he thought it would be safe; they wouldn't let on to anybody else what they were up to by nodding out during the course of a conversation or something; Solly would hit on his brother, Lenny, for advice on how to deal with pushers and where to get needles without letting him catch on that he was about to start using; and they'd only pull jobs where the money was enough for them to buy heroin in quantity, or weight, like enough for an ounce or a half ounce at a time. O'Keefe was going to steal thirty goofballs from his mother's sleeping pill collection, and then they all agreed to pull the florist's heist the following night with everyone responsible for bringing their own weapons.

The next morning Solly called for Kenny, and when they met O'Keefe in the luncheonette he spelled out how his brother went about getting needles and where.

"All you gotta do is go into Whelan's Pharmacy and make believe

44

you're a diabetic and ask for, in this order, Protomine Zink U-40, a small bottle of isopropyl alcohol, and a thirty disposable pack of twenty-six-gauge, half inch. And they give you thirty hypodermic needles, syringes and all. You keep the alcohol to keep the spikes clean and sterile. You throw away the insulin. And it only costs five dollars."

"What if they ask you for a diabetic's card?" asked O'Keefe.

"You tell them that you're from upstate or Jersey and that you lost it," replied Solly.

Kenny Wisdom wanted to know how you dealt with a dealer when you were scoring weight. Girsch said that his brother told him to never allow the person making the deal to hold the bread, but only let him inspect the merchandise and case the place for a possible rip-off. When everything seems straight, then the guy with the money should come on the scene and cop the stuff. A third guy should always be outside in case there are dudes waiting to waylay the fellow who just copped. Another thing: always try to be heeled with some sort of weapon. And also, take cabs.

They hung around for the rest of that Saturday afternoon in the top-floor room of the abandoned building — stuffing up drafty holes with rags, dragging a couple of discarded mattresses into this place which was to be their shooting gallery.

Kenny was still heavy-lidded from his morning wake-up. Solly and Clearhead dropped a few goofballs, and after a while began to examine each other's weaponry and to talk about the robbery they were going to pull that night, making sure each of them knew what he had to do.

Clearhead had two snub-nosed, black-metal, fake .38 revolvers which he'd obtained by sending in five dollars and an ad from *Argosy* magazine to someplace in Virginia. O'Keefe was a pistol freak and he got called "Clearhead" because his skull contained no sense of cause and effect, just impulse and illusion. His emotional intensity and the insanity of his fantasies usually enabled him to face down any disturbing reality.

Solly Girsch was the kind that wanted to beat everyone to death during a heist or at any other time for that matter. He had a set of brass knuckles wrapped around the meaty fingers of his left hand. Across his legs was laid a sap made from a wool sock with a quarter of a pound of sand tightly tied into its foot. Solly was a very bad boy.

Kenny Wisdom held a neatly sawed-off, electrician-taped, nine-inch pool cue handle in the belt of his Wrangler dungarees, and also carried a gravity knife which sat flat in his back pocket. But he had no hangups or any peculiarly excessive style of stealing like his two partners — his way was simply to cop and blow. If someone interfered during the course of a job, however, Wisdom would use only whatever violence was necessary to remove that person's presence, as one would remove any obstacle. Sometimes he would get carried away if the guy he was confronting had an attitude or thought he was Sam Spade.

When it got dark and the time came, Kenny, after taking his nightfall fix, went a few blocks away and stole a 1955 two-toned, hard-top Oldsmobile convertible while Clearhead and Girsch kept chickie for him — which was a bit difficult since both of them were goofballed out of their faces and were hardly able to see straight, much less keep lookout.

Anyway, Kenny made sure that they weren't spotted and pulled down the street, picking them up, and drove on to Seventh Avenue and to what became known as the Brooklyn Flower Shop Plunder among the rye-with-beer-chaser-set in the taverns of that area.

After circling the block a few times to see if all was cool, Wisdom double-parked in front of the florist's. Solly Girsch pulled his knitted navy hat down nearly over his eyes; Clearhead O'Keefe covered his head with a stocking which had two holes poked in it so that he could make like he could see. And then they both stumbled onto the sidewalk and into the store.

Kenny sat behind the wheel of the car with the motor running and his eyes peeled. It was suppertime for most people. There were only a few shoppers and strollers and the avenue was relatively quiet — that is, it was quiet, until the florist brothers realized that the two persons who had just entered their shop had not done so to buy any flowers.

This realization caused both brothers to shrill-scream in high-registered harmony, and begin to throw things, like pruning shears, potted plants and anything else they could get their hands on, at the two intruders.

One of the flower pots whizzed by Clearhead and shattered the shop's plate-glass window. This made one of the brothers faint, and cued O'Keefe into pointing his metal-mold pistols at the other owner and making "Pow! Pow! Bang! Bang! You're dead!" noises, as he covered the doorway.

Solly punched an empty vase to bits with his brass knuckles as it

46

flew towards him, stormed through the flak which the stouter of the brothers was still barraging them with, and stiffened him with the sanded-down sock.

Then he went into the back room, kicked in a locked closet door and found the tin money box hidden under a bunch of dried palm leaves.

Kenny Wisdom by this time was very nervous. He saw Solly come out of the back with what they had gone there for in his hands. What he saw next, he couldn't believe.

Solly Girsch, in some brilliant goofball foggy flash of ingenuity, tossed the box to Clearhead who ran outside, threw it into the car, and went back to cover for Solly — who was backing out of the store with the locked cash register hoisted high on his chest.

A crowd was gathering. Kenny wanted to yell and scream and blow the horn NO! NO! but he was dumbfoundly silent.

As Girsch was reaching the front door, he slipped on the pruning shears and began backpedaling, picking up speed until he hit the curb which caused him to fall over backwards and the cash register to fly high into the air — cracking open onto the middle of Seventh Avenue and flinging its contents all over the street.

The bystanders were stilled with amazement. Kenny yelled for Girsch to get up and into the car. He did.

Clearhead O'Keefe, however, was doing his "Bang! Bang! Pow! Pow!" routine, aiming his toy guns at the growing number of very startled pedestrians.

"Goddammit, Clearhead! Come on!" shouted Kenny.

O'Keefe yelled back for Wisdom to shut the car door and start moving. He was coming! "Pow! Pow! Bang! Bang!"

A hard-top convertible gets its name because it has no center post separating the front and back windows. When both windows are rolled down, there is a cinemascopic space from the front to the back windshield — an opening about four feet wide and fifteen inches high.

This is what O'Keefe was aiming for when he dove at the slow-rolling Olds, but his Hollywood fantasy of a getaway didn't quite make it. His make-believe gun-wielding arms made it. His forehead stopped the rest of him. It smacked into the roof of the car, knocking him cold.

And it was only by the grace of Girsch, who caught hold of his arm and ripped him inside, that he didn't fall under the rear wheels when Kenny floored the gas pedal and got them all the hell out of there. Leaving Seventh Avenue bewildered with people snatching up the silver coins which were rolling all over, chasing the dollar bills blowing in the wind, or simply standing in numb-dumb disbelief at what they had, supposedly, just witnessed.

The tin money box was easy to break open and the eight hundred dollars which popped out of it cooled Kenny Wisdom's rage and cut off the stream of "Stupid cocksucker!" obscenities he was directing at his two crime partners.

They ditched the Oldsmobile on Atlantic Avenue and subwayed to Manhattan. At 49th Street and Broadway they came above ground and Kenny called Dupree from a telephone booth on the corner.

Willie Pondexteur answered. He was now working for Dupree, who came to the phone, took Kenny's order, and told him that it would be three or four hours before he could locate and deliver the ounce. The price: six hundred dollars.

Dupree: It's eight o'clock now. I'll meet you at midnight, corner of Eighth Avenue and 49th. 'Cross from the Garden. Willie'll be with me.

Kenny: What'll I do till then?

Dupree: Go to the movies.

Kenny: OK. See you at twelve.

Dupree: Later.

Then he hung up.

Kenny Wisdom came out of the booth and told Solly and O'Keefe what the man had said. They went to the movies.

The first one they saw was playing at the Victoria Theater, *The Man with the Golden Arm.* They didn't see it all. They left during the scene where the writhing, retching Frank Sinatra lets his girl friend lock him in the closet to kick his habit, alone and in the dark.

Solly commented that the first thing that he would have kicked was the fucking door down.

Across the street they bought tickets at the Rivoli and saw a film which Kenny Wisdom never forgot — *Viva Zapata.* He didn't forget the peon who stepped forward and said to El Presidente, "My name is Emiliano. Emiliano Zapata." He didn't forget the revolutionary theoretician who sought Zapata and became his chief adviser. He didn't forget Pancho Villa telling Zapata to be president after the war was seemingly over. He didn't forget that Emiliano Zapata forgot that he was just representing the people when he had become El Presidente. He didn't forget Zapata's realization that he was replaying the dictatorial role of the man whom he and his army had overthrown. He didn't forget Zapata's return to his village, his people, and his confrontation with his generalissimo brother, who was shot after Zapata tells the peons that the fight is theirs and they must deal with matters themselves and not depend on heroes. He didn't forget Zapata's death by a thousand rifle bullets which tore him beyond recognition. He didn't forget the theoretician standing in the shadows, having ordered the execution of this man who wouldn't accept the reins of totalitarian power. He didn't forget how the people surrounded the disfigured, unrecognizable corpse and said that it could be any man. Kenny Wisdom didn't forget any of this and more for as long as he lives.

At midnight the deal went smoothly. Solly Girsch held the bread, while Kenny got into Dupree's car to taste the product and make sure it had the bitterness of heroin, rather than the sweetness of milk sugar. When he was satisfied, Solly gave Dupree the six hundred and Kenny slid the package into the center fold of the New York Sunday *Times* which Clearhead had purchased for this reason. The *Daily News* and *Journal-American* he carried under his arm he had bought for a different reason — the funnies.

After the exchange was made, Dupree and Willie Pondexteur told Wisdom that it had been nice doing business with him and drove over to the West Side Highway and up to Harlem.

Solly hailed a cab and the three of them returned to Brooklyn and their shooting gallery. Once inside, Kenny spread the various sections of the Sunday *Times* on top of the two orange crates which they used for a table, making a three-inch-thick tablecloth out of the newspaper. He then placed the package of heroin in the center of the table and slit it open with his gravity knife, spreading and chopping the white powder evenly until it covered most of the top section of newspaper. He could have thinned it out more, but there was no room.

"Sure is a lotta shit!" said O'Keefe, as he brought over the water and works. "I hope it's as good as it looks."

Clearhead O'Keefe didn't have a regular bottle of water. He had a small Skippy's peanut butter jar filled to its wide-mouthed brim with water. As he went to place it on the corner of the table, he spilled it. He simply spilled it. The water came out of that jar like a tidal wave and within seconds it had submerged the thin-layered ounce of snow into the New York *Times*.

Nobody moved. Nobody said a word. They just stared at this newspaper which they had never read and which had just soaked up their great expectations. Just soaked it right up! The goddamn New York *Times!* You son of a bitch!

As soon as the shock wore off, Solly picked up Clearhead and was going to throw him out the window, but Kenny reluctantly stopped him by saying, "Fuck it! Let's get high and fuck it!"

And Girsch and O'Keefe watched as Kenny cut out a small square from the front page and cooked it up in his spoon.

Girsch: What about the newsprint?

Wisdom: Fuck the newsprint!

Girsch: But you don't know how much you're shooting up. You can't tell. You may kill yourself.

Wisdom: So, I die in my sleep! So what! Everybody dies!

And he sucked up the solution that he had boiled out of the piece of a headline and mained it into his vein. He felt the rush as he took the spike out of his arm and was high. No more, no less, just high.

When the other two had watched Kenny for about five minutes and were relatively convinced that he wasn't going to keel over dead from an overdose or from blood poisoning, they cut themselves smaller squares from the newspaper and did them up. They also got high. And they also figured like Kenny Wisdom: "What the fuck!"

The attitude and that issue of the Sunday *Times* lasted over a month. Long enough to give the three of them oil burner habits. The only break in the sleepy three-or-four-fix daily routine during that period came in the third week when Kenny Wisdom struck it rich. He cut a photo of a pretty, well-bred bride from the society page and geezed her. Unfortunately that patch of paper contained three times the quality of scag his body could tolerate. He OD'd with the dropper still sticking into the pit of his arm.

Solly and O'Keefe were rummaging around in another room when they heard the thud of Kenny's body hit the floor, and the fish-flopping sound of his convulsions. They ran in and saw him bouncing all over the place, his face turning blue. To revive him, they didn't do any of the wrong things which fools say to do, like slapping him in the face or walking him around the room or shooting salt into his veins. They did the right thing: mouth to mouth resuscitation which keeps a person's lungs involuntarily breathing until they catch on to the rhythm, and the brain signals the respiratory system that the game isn't over yet. Only then, when the body begins to respond by breathing on its own, do you lift the person onto his feet and walk him until his eyes roll down from the back of his head and he slurringly regains consciousness. It's one hell of a job to keep the energy of life inside a body that is seizuring to death. But luckily they did it, and it took more than an hour before they did.

"Wha' happened?" were Wisdom's first words as he tried to focus his eyes.

"You were hit by a lady driving a truck," answered Solly, looking at the faded image of the rich broad — stiff and dry in the cooker with a piece of cotton covering her mouth.

"Anything get broke?" asked Kenny.

"Yeah, my high," responded O'Keefe.

When the succour had been burnt out of the *Times*, and the cottons all used and reused until they were drug-empty, the three were sick, shaky, imagination-dulled, and without any information on a big money score they could pull to get enough bread to buy weight. They were just down junkies and they hit the streets, separately, each one in his own way, trying to scrape together the necessary money to keep the sick off.

School was out, where before it had been in and out.

Harlem was too far to travel, and for the immediacy and the sake of a quick nickel or dime bag, they began copping from the Puerto Rican connections in the neighborhood. And soon all the other hyps on the street, and some other people in the area, became aware that the three were addicts.

Solly got his money by prowling Prospect Park and mugging people, or by extorting high school kids out of their lunch money in the Crown Heights section of Brooklyn.

Clearhead O'Keefe stole a real pistol someplace and became a cowboy, sticking up gas stations, delicatessens, candy stores, anything — always firing at least one shot into a ceiling, or a wall, not at anybody. He worked the Bay Ridge territory of Brooklyn and had the cops in the 64th Precinct running crazy trying to catch him.

Kenny Wisdom kept his habit alive as a thief and a burglar, stealing anything from anybody, anywhere. Once, he found a connection who would take meat in lieu of cash. The "connect" would give him half the price marked on the packages of meat in exchange for heroin. When Kenny brought the man eleven porterhouse steaks worth fifty dollars, he would get twenty-five dollars' worth of heroin in return. Before long, Kenny had every A & P, Bohack's, and Grand

51

Union in Brooklyn crying over the disappearance of their meat. To maintain a hundred-dollar-a-day jones, you've got to steal a lot of meat. A whole lot!

It went on that way, getting more involved, more obvious, and more desperate. Kenny Wisdom's family knew something was wrong, of course, but he never let them know that he was a junkie and they didn't have the knowledge, or the experience, or the eyes to see that he was a dope fiend. They just thought that he was crazy. If he didn't want to go to school, and he wanted to stay out all hours of the night and day, and if he wanted to go to jail, ruin his life, and run wild, that was his business. They had a daughter to raise, bills to pay, and no time for any bullshit. His father told him straight: "You want to be on your own two feet and do what you're doing? You go right ahead, but don't come crawling and expect us to help when you get in trouble, and locked up! Understand?"

Kenny said yes.

But one day he came home in the early afternoon to have a bowl of corn flakes or something, and he found his mother sobbing.

"What's wrong?" he asked. "What's the matter?"

"What's wrong? What's the matter?" she yelled back. "My wedding ring's the matter, you son of a bitch!"

"What are you talking about?" Kenny pleaded.

"My wedding ring!" she cried. "It's gone! Where is it?"

And Kenny said, "Where is it? How would I know?"

"You know! You know! Because you took it!" she shouted. "It was right here on top of the dresser where I put it before I scrubbed the bathroom floor. And when I went to put it back on, it was gone!"

"Are you sure you didn't put it someplace else?" he asked.

"Yes, I'm sure!" And she began sobbing again.

Kenny told her that he didn't take her wedding ring, but she wouldn't listen. She just cried. And then he noticed two of his father's suits hanging on the kitchen door, wrapped in the brown paper sack with the De Luxe Dry Cleaners advertisement stamped in large blue letters on the front. He grabbed the bag and brought it to his mother.

"When was this delivered?" he asked.

"What are you talking about?" puzzled his mother, still crying.

"When was this delivered?" he repeated.

"Before. About an hour ago," she answered. "Why?"

"Nothin'," he said, as he threw the suits on the sofa and left the apartment. There was something, however, and Kenny knew it. The guy who drove the delivery truck for the De Luxe Dry Cleaners was a junkie. His name was Eric, and Kenny had bumped into him several times, while he was copping. They both bought from the same connection.

His mother's wedding ring! His mother's three- or four-hundred-dollar diamond wedding ring! And she thought that her own son had stolen it! "That motherfuckin' punk junkie! If he don't have that ring, he's gonna wish he'd never been born!"

He came out of the basement of his tenement building with a sawed-off fungo bat under his jacket and headed for Third Avenue. A fungo bat is a thin baseball bat which is used to hit ground balls during pregame warm-ups. Kenny had a different usage for it in mind.

The dry cleaner's delivery truck was parked on Wyckoff Street, just below the avenue. As Kenny approached it, he heard noise in the back of the van. Eric was getting some suits off the rack for a delivery when Kenny slipped inside the front and slid the door closed. Eric was startled and jumped, holding the paper bag of dry cleaning in front of him like a shield.

Eric: Whadda ya want?

Kenny: The ring!

Eric: What ring?

And Kenny swung the bat hard, catching Eric solid on the left shoulder, and sending him bouncing off the side of the van and onto the floor. Then he moved closer, and stood over him with the bat raised, and asked him again. "The ring!"

Eric: It's gone.

Kenny: Where?

Eric: I sold it to some guy in Collins' Bar. I never saw him before. Honest!

Kenny: Where's the money?

Eric: I gave it to Ramirez. I was into him for over a hundred and he threatened to tell my boss I was usin' stuff. Look, I'll pay ya back . . .

Kenny: No, I'll pay you back.

He slammed the bat down, over and over again. Smashed it against his arms, his back, shoulders, ribs, and his legs, until Eric slumped unconscious. Then Kenny went through his pockets, finding six bags of heroin. Leaving his money, he carefully removed Eric's left arm from the sleeves of his jacket and shirt, so that the tracks on his veins would show. He kept five of the bags and stuffed the sixth into Eric's sock, where it would be found by a nurse or a doctor when they took his clothes off at the hospital before trying to piece him back together.

"You're a known user now, kiddo," Kenny said, and he left the van and walked away. Eric didn't hear him. In fact, Eric didn't hear anything until the next morning, when he woke up to a whole lot of questions in Kings County Hospital. But he didn't say anything, he was too sick.

The beating didn't solve anything for Kenny, it simply vented his anger. To this day, Kenny Wisdom's parents believe that he stole the small diamond-studded silver band which his father had given to his mother on their wedding day. And it's a drag.

The tick-tock of time flew by, or it stood still. There is no difference. The face of the clock and the directions of the big hand and the little hand mean nothing. A second, a minute, an hour, a day, a week, a month, a year — or two — don't matter. There is no calendar. It's all the same. It's junk time. The alarm only goes off when there is a panic, or the connection's nowhere to be found, or anything else happens that stops the supply of the narcotic which the shmecker needs in order not to feel something he doesn't want to feel, which is life. Which is death.

The odds against tomorrow grew, as Kenny, Solly, and O'Keefe injected themselves deeper into their own cabal of heroin with abscesses, hepatitis, and a long list of croakers who wrote scrips for ten, twenty, fifty dollars, depending on what for and how much one wanted. The episodic downhill race continued, with the participants completely unaware that they were in a contest. A contest of survival.

There was this guy in the 'hood. The neighborhood. Albino Sammy. He was a wrong number, an informer. He was also a junk mooch, who maintained his habit by trading information to the cops for heroin which they had confiscated from arrested addicts and pushers. But he would mooch stuff off of anybody who felt threatened by his pigeon tongue, or felt sorry for him.

This skinny, bleached-faced, bald-headed pink-eyed albino got hip to the outrageous activities of Clearhead O'Keefe, and made the mistake of approaching O'Keefe with the proposition that he would keep his yap shut in exchange for a couple of bags of scag every day. He also mentioned that he knew what Solly Girsch was up to, and that Kenny Wisdom was responsible for Eric's injuries.

Naturally, Clearhead wanted to stick his gun into Sammy's mouth, and pull the trigger until it was empty, but at the time they happened to be standing in front of a police station. So O'Keefe asked Sammy to meet him that evening at the shooting gallery.

O'Keefe: Do you know where it is?

Sammy: Of course. And then he split.

Clearhead contacted Wisdom and Girsch, meeting them later that afternoon at the gallery and telling them the bad news. He also told them that as soon as Albino Sammy showed up, he was going to shoot him full of holes. But Solly said no, there was a better way. "We'll let him kill himself."

He then went downstairs, and came back up with an old dead car battery in his hands. Using a matchbook cover, he scraped a bit of the white powdery acid from the battery and carefully shoveled it into one of the many empty glassine bags which were lying all around the place. He filled two more the same way, sealed the three of them, and stacked them on top of the orange crate. He told Clearhead to hide the battery in another room, while he explained to Kenny exactly what was going to happen to Albino Sammy. His demise.

You see, battery acid looks the same as white powdered heroin, and it dissolves in heated water just like heroin, but it doesn't give you a rush, or get you high, or sick, when you shoot it into your vein. You don't feel a thing, because as soon as it enters your bloodstream, you're dead. And it doesn't leave any trace. This is the sophisticated method of disposal, used throughout the junk-cultured streets of the world by men and women, boys and girls, to get rid of other men and women and boys and girls who become a danger to their status in junkdom. When you become dangerous enough to someone, they usually kill you. This is the way addicts with class kill each other. And it is called a hot shot because you get burned for your life, cheated out of existence, while everyone thinks that you're just another straight OD.

So, Solly Girsch was awaiting the arrival of Albino Sammy and anxious to present him with his three neat little gifts. He figured that Sammy would pocket the bags, and return to wherever he returned to, to shoot up. He figured wrong. When the albino finally showed he graciously accepted the offering, but he didn't leave. He had his gimmicks with him, and he began his regular procedure of turning on.

Kenny almost said something to stop him, or get him out of there, but Solly glared at him. He knew that Sammy would get suspicious, if some objection was made. Therefore the three of them just sat and watched, as Albino Sammy unraveled his outfit, opened the papers, poured their contents into his cooker, added some water, heated it into a solution which he sucked up with his dropper, and mainlined into his body. He died on his feet.

As he fell to the floor, the coldness of the spectacle made Kenny's blood run ice. Clearhead sort of grinned, and giggled briefly through his teeth. Solly Girsch didn't give a shit.

After a few moments Kenny asked, "What do we do with him?"

Solly answered, "We cremate the prick."

They started a mattress fire and left the abandoned building for good. When the firemen finally extinguished the top-floor blaze, the cops found the charred corpse of Albino Sammy with the spike still in his arm. They were a bit displeased that such a good source of information would no longer be available, but they weren't suspicious about his death. Just another junkie who suffered the occupational hazard of his addiction, an overdose, and set his bed on fire with his cigarette.

"I guess, he put more in his spoon than he coulda handled," remarked one of the coppers.

"Spoon doon moon coon, Hey spoon! You're a bundle a joy! You an ugly motherfucker, but you still my boy!" is a junkie rhyme of thanksgiving before a fix, which Kenny was soon going to learn from a hard-core oldtimer. In jail. How did he get there? It was easy.

A few days after the albino's accident, Kenny and his two partners were sitting around Girsch's basement, rapping about how they were sick and tired of scuffling in the streets for nickel and dime bags, when there must be big money sitting someplace, just waiting for them to rip it off.

"It sure would be nice to cop some real weight for a change," mused Solly. Then Clearhead had an idea. He told them about this National City Bank on Flatbush Avenue that was ripe and only had women working in it, and the least they could score would be two thousand from one of the teller's cashboxes or, if they got lucky, more.

"Maybe even forty or fifty grand!" he said. Kenny Wisdom and Solly went for it, but on one condition: Clearhead was to drive the getaway car, and remain behind the wheel, while they went into the bank and took whatever money they could. O'Keefe unwillingly agreed, but said that he was going to hold on to his pistol, even though he'd just be sitting in the car and waiting.

Kenny said that was fine, but warned him, "No shooting, understand! No shooting!" O'Keefe shook his head, yes. And then he was asked if he still had those two fake black snub-nosed guns. He did.

"Good," said Solly. "We'll go in with them."

They went to Ramirez, their connection, and got enough dope to keep them straight for twenty-four hours. They got it on credit, and Ramirez was glad to oblige because they were his best customers and he knew they were also stand-up guys and wouldn't beat him for the stuff.

Kenny stole an inconspicuous '51 Ford, while Clearhead got the two toy guns from their hiding place and Solly got a pair of brown paper bags from the grocer and an extra navy blue woolen knit hat for Kenny to wear. They had decided against masks. They were simply going to walk into the bank, make a teller or two fill the paper bags with money, and walk out.

They met on Third Avenue, and Clearhead got behind the wheel and drove over to the National City Bank on Flatbush Avenue. Kenny and Solly got themselves ready. They put the model guns into the paper bags, intending to carry them, like anyone would carry his lunch. Then they got out of the car and walked slowly toward the revolving door of the bank.

Before they got to it, Clearhead began blowing the car horn and hollering like crazy. Something was wrong. Kenny and Solly didn't know what it was, but it was something. They immediately tossed the two paper sacks with the fake guns in them underneath a parked truck, and started back to the Ford to see what was the matter. The car had run out of gas. The fuel gauge read full, but it was obviously broken. They decided to leave it, steal another one, and try later. But before they could move, they were stopped.

"*Freeze!*" came the order. "*One of you moves, and I'll blow your fucking head off!*" shouted the detective who had spotted the car as the one which had been reported stolen, its description and plate numbers having just come over his radio.

He covered them and loudly repeated several specific descriptions of what would happen to any one of them who made a foolish move, while his partner spread-eagled them against the car, and frisked and handcuffed them. Then he made them sit cross-legged on the street, as he searched the car. He found O'Keefe's pistol under the front seat, which made him very happy.

It made him happy because it meant that he and his partner hadn't just arrested three joyriders on a Grand Theft Auto charge, they had nabbed three armed-robbery suspects. But he was very disappointed when, after ripping the car apart, he found nothing else incriminating. He showed the gun to the other detective, who was also delighted and disappointed.

A large crowd had gathered by the time several squad cars arrived to take them separately to the 78th Precinct station house. On the way, each one was asked the same obvious and corny questions by their cop escorts. None of these questions were answered, unless you consider silence a form of response.

When they got to the station, Kenny and Solly were left hand-cuffed and placed in separate cages at different ends of the detective squad's room. Clearhead was taken into another room for interrogation.

The names of the two detectives who busted them were Ray Roppollo and Chuck DeBlaze, and one of them had a hunch about Clearhead O'Keefe. He fit the description of the stickup artist who had been rampaging all over Bay Ridge for more than a year, and the gun was the same caliber as the bullets which had been dug out of the walls and ceilings at the scenes of the robberies.

Roppollo called the 64th Precinct and told the captain in charge that he might be holding the man they were looking for. He asked him to have one of his detectives bring up a witness to one of the robberies, to see if they could make a positive identification of the suspect. The captain said he would have someone over there within two hours.

When they were arrested, none of the three had anything in their pockets but a few dollars — no drugs, or paraphernalia. Girsch and O'Keefe had identification cards in their wallets. Kenny Wisdom didn't even have a wallet.

So the detectives knew that the big guy's name was Girsch and that he was fifteen and that he lived at an address on President Street. They also knew O'Keefe's name, address, and that he was fifteen. But they didn't know anything about Wisdom, and when they asked him, he lied.

He told them that his name was Johnny Mullane and that he had no fixed address and that he was sixteen. The reason he told them that he was sixteen, instead of fourteen, was because he didn't want to go to the hellhole of the juvenile detention hall. He knew his people weren't going to bail him out, therefore he wanted to go to jail — a man's jail, not a kids' insane asylum.

They believed him. You don't have to show them a birth certificate. You just tell them how old you are, and that's what you are. Of course, they informed him, he was in much more serious trouble than the other two because his age made him an adult and the consequences of his present circumstance might land him in a state penitentiary.

His response went something like: "Prison don't have to be a waste of time. A lotta people come out learning a trade."

That's when Dick Tracy DeBlaze started in on his freckles, calling him "flyshit face," and asking, "Who threw the shit at you through the screen?" This needling ended abruptly when Kenny told De-Blaze to go fuck his dead mother.

Wisdom woke up an hour later, alone in a cell in the basement of the 78th Precinct, with a very bad headache and his left eye swollen shut.

Several Bay Ridge merchants and their wives came and positively identified Clearhead as the crazy son of a bitch who had held them up. They also said that they had never seen Solly Girsch or this Johnny Mullane before, and expressed hope that they would never see them again.

Girsch and O'Keefe were remanded over to Juvenile Division for custody. Kenny Wisdom was booked as "John Mullane," and the next morning a paddy wagon took him to Brooklyn Criminal Court where he was arraigned on charges of possessing a dangerous weapon, conspiring to commit armed robbery, assaulting a police officer, and impairing the morals of a minor. Bail was set at ten thousand dollars. He was chained to a string of other prisoners and taken in a Department of Correction bus to the Raymond Street jail, where he was processed, deloused, and locked in a six-by-eight-foot cell on the seventh tier. The seventh tier was what is known as high power section of the jail, where they put men who were considered dangerous or security risks because of their past records, or because of the charges brought against them.

Kenny had been arrested at one o'clock the previous afternoon. It was now five o'clock the following evening, and as he lay down on his bunk he felt the first symptoms of withdrawal. He knew he was going to be very sick. But he was damned if he was going to cop out to anyone that he was a junkie, and try to get some medicine, or something. Nope, it was cold turkey.

His nose began to run, his eyes began to tear and smart, his stomach knotted hollow. Skin fever set in, soaking his body with sweat, chilling his bones with spasms of hot and cold flashes. Too weak to move, but moving and twitching and jerking all the same. Up and down, from side to side. He wasn't nauseous, or vomiting, but suffering what most asthmatics suffer during withdrawal: uncontrollable, brutal fits of wet sneezing, and the raw ache of a steam wheeze respiring through his lungs.

Bolts of electricity raced over him, in and out of him — making his flesh painfully sensitive to the touch of anything, even his own hands. Every cell in his body became startlingly and uncomfortably aware of his condition. His imagination suddenly awoke, screaming at the inescapable horror and anguish of the sickness. His memory cried, begged for a little sleep. His thoughts wondered, asked, demanded, if it wasn't possible for the shin-split aches in his legs to stop. He ached to be free of his flesh which was crawling with terrifying frenzy. His bowels, solidly constipated for months, began to drip, then flow from his rectum and flood the bunk with a lake of stench. Energy surged into his rapid thumping heart, and his lungs heaved with almost suffocating excitation.

He wanted to detach himself from the pain, but he couldn't. It got worse and clung to him, as the actuality of time jarred its way back into his consciousness. He just hung tight and groaned, listening to the old hard-core black junkie in the next cell, every once in a while, repeat his "Spoon doon moon coon, Hey spoon!" ejaculation, and the various blacks from singing groups and street corners harmonizing through the tiers. They helped. They helped a lot. Because they are a people who dig music and music helps, when you lie in your own shit on a straw-mattressed metal bed for days, living through hell — trying to resurrect yourself from the dead.

> *Jes one thing, Baby, Child, before you go.*
> *Jes one thing, Baby, Child, before you go.*
> *There's gonna be judgment in the mornin', Baby.*
> *There's gonna be judgment in the mornin', Baby.*

"Yes, Baby, 'n you gonna reap for what you sow," are the last words Kenny Wisdom remembered hearing, as the aura of a grand mal seizure enveloped him in the blindspot of unconsciousness on the fourth night of his third day at Brooklyn's Raymond Street jail.

The next morning, he came to — strapped to a bed in the jail-house infirmary. But his consciousness was absorbed in a total state of hallucination, and he only glanced at the realities of the leather belts which buckled him down and the thick glass walls of the ward he was in. He was motionless and calm, completely rapt in the scenes of his childhood, as they flowed across the magic screen which filmed his eyes.

Slow-motion scenes of stickball games with Kenny swinging a broom handle with the still, quiet grace of a mime, sending a pink rubber Spalding ball floating high into the air and straight down the center of the block, traveling long and far out of view — for a three-sewer home run.

Pedaling a stolen Schwinn bicycle, his legs moving with the stillness and leisure of a blossoming flower. Running from someone in a game of tag, his feet gently, softly, smoothly bouncing across the peaceful grass of Prospect Park — the trees swaying silently in the wind. Swinging on a set of monkey bars with unhurried elegance. Sublimely dribbling a basketball down court and gently laying it up and into the hoop; the net languidly exploding as the ball gradually fell through for two points.

Pitching pennies which hung in the air before sliding calmly along the sidewalk and skidding indolently to the base of a wall. Leaping dreamingly down and lightly landing on the ground to break his teammates out of the Chaplains' Ringolevio den. His shout of *"Free all!"* echoing off the buildings, overlapping into a multiple mix of sound.

Watching Albino Sammy slowly fall stiff to the floor. Watching Albino Sammy fall, slowly, stiff to the floor. Again and again; again and again; over and over; over and over; always the same; again and again, until the repetition of the sequence became unbearable, and Kenny snapped awake, struggling violently with the bindings which tied his arms and legs — furiously trying to escape from the constantly recycled film clip of Albino Sammy's death.

"All right, take it easy. Take it easy!" said the big black male nurse, finally, slapping Kenny across the face to bring him out of his nightmare.

"What happened? Where am I?" asked Kenny.

The Chinese doctor, who ran the infirmary, came over and told him that he had a seizure the night before. A guard had found him unconscious on the floor of his cell, and they brought him down here on a stretcher, and placed him in bed. The straps, he explained, were for his own good — to protect him from falling out of bed and hurting himself.

The doctor then asked him if he was an epileptic and had suffered seizures before. Kenny wasn't, of course, but he said yes anyway, rather than be labeled a junkie on his record.

"Do you have these seizures often?" questioned the doctor.

"No, only once before," replied Kenny.

"When was that?" continued the doctor.

Kenny told the doctor that when he was about eight years old a teacher had beat him at school, and "later that evening, I suffered my one and only convulsive fit prior to this one."

The doctor asked him if he had any idea what might have caused this recurrence. Kenny offered that it may have occurred because of the knockout blow he had received from the detective at the 78th Precinct a few days ago.

There was no mention, or question about the use of drugs, or the possibility of addiction, or the symptoms of withdrawal. Kenny was surprised, but he shouldn't have been. The apathy of the people who staff the infirmaries of the detention centers and correctional facilities in the city of New York makes them glad when a "patient" doesn't ask, plead, cry, or beg for help and relief from whatever agony he is in. The doctor seemed satisfied with Kenny's explanation and told him that they were going to keep him in the infirmary for a few days. Also, they were going to give him a pill, called Dilantin, three times a day. This medicine, he said, would calm his system down from the shock it had just gone through and, hopefully, prevent any further fits of epilepsy.

Kenny thanked him, and they left him alone. He stayed alone, strapped in the bed, unable to eat, or sleep, taking the pills which did absolutely nothing to relieve him of the hallucinatory movie of his life that kept dancing in front of his eyes and waltzing through his mind. Only time was to relieve him of that. Standard Time.

Kenny Wisdom's single consolation was his ability to maintain control over his mind and body during the question and answer period with the doctor. It had taken every ounce of his strength not to crack, and he was proud of himself.

After nearly a week in the infirmary, Kenny had kicked his habit enough to begin to eat. He nibbled at a cereal-filled hamburger patty, but devoured a small glob of Jell-O. This excessive desire for sweets is the beginning of what is known as the chucks, an enormous hunger which addicts experience in the last stages of withdrawal, enabling them to eat everything they can get their hands on.

Apparently, this first taste of food was also a sign to the infirmary staff that Kenny was well enough, and no longer needed to occupy bed space in the ward. So, he was returned to tier seven, assigned to a cell, and informed by the guard in charge that, due to his illness and his stay in the infirmary, he had missed his preliminary hearing, which was postponed indefinitely.

Kenny didn't know quite what that meant, but he also didn't care very much about it at that particular moment. This was the first time he'd been on his feet for practically two weeks, and he was feeling pretty shaky. He didn't give a fuck about much of anything except getting into his cell and flopping on his bunk. Anyway, he didn't ask, or answer no questions to no cops no how.

"Okay, Mullane," said the guard, when he was satisfied that he wasn't going to be asked a question, "Go and stand in front of your new home, Number Eight. And holler when you get there."

The guard then pulled the lever which automatically slid open the door of bars to the inner chamber, and Kenny waited while they closed behind him and the guard pulled another lever which slid open the door of bars to the tier's walkway.

They had given Kenny a new set of blues at the infirmary, and, as he walked to the door of Number Eight, he noticed that the shirt fit all right, but the pants were too big and baggy, slapping against his legs as he stepped.

He stood before his cell door and yelled back to the screw that he was doing so. The bars slid open and he went in, and loudly informed the screw of that fact also. "Okay, watch your hands!" shouted the guard, as the door clanged shut.

Kenny lay back on his bunk, propping his pillow under his head, and stared at the cloudy rays of spring sunlight which somehow penetrated the thick bricks of frosted glass that were stacked in the shape of a window on the unreachable outside wall of the jail. He was weak from the brief and sudden physical activity he had exerted in his transfer from the infirmary and his return to the seventh tier. It was only a matter of getting out of bed, putting on some clothes, walking to an elevator which took him back to High Power, and taking a few steps to his new cell, but it had completely tired him out. It didn't make him sleepy, however. His nerves still jumped and jerked and shook to awaken him from his two-year nod and lack of feeling.

He was moderately hollow sick at his stomach but felt a real hunger and desire for food. His bones continued to ache and groan in their marrow. His awareness was heightened, and the seizure and hallucinations had just become something to worry about. He was feeling better, but couldn't wait to feel fine.

This is the uniquely brutal point of junk sickness and withdrawal — the waiting. Most junkies would stop using if it wasn't practically impossible to endure the agonizing length of time it takes for the cure. The length varies from eight days to weeks to months, depending on the individual's physical and mental makeup. That's why no one takes the cold turkey route voluntarily — only involuntarily, when they're arrested and locked up. For Kenny, it was a long haul because his brain waves had been smacked, his asthma was acute, and he was undernourished and thin. So everything became waiting and hanging on, with no escape from time. He could only wait, and while he did, Kenny Wisdom developed a healthy respect for eternity.

When he returned from the maximum-security tier-seven mess, after gobbling up his four-thirty "supper," Kenny looked into the stainless steel mirror embedded in the wall of his cell above a porcelain sink. He could hardly believe what he saw. His face was ashen and shallow; his eyes were clear, but the pupils were enlarged and wildly spinning — like two blue saucers in a white enameled sky. He took off his shirt and examined the sticks that were once his arms, and the knobby bones that were once his shoulders, and his sunken chest and flabby belly. He was repulsed by what he'd done to himself, and determined to whip his body back into the strong, agile, alert shape it had once been.

His sexual desire returned and for the next five months he used it to motivate himself in a steady schedule of physical exercise. He played basketball and chinned himself on the workout bar when his cellblock was allowed onto the caged-in rooftop court three times a week. He did situps and pushups in his cell until he reached the point where he was doing a thousand of each every day. He ate everything on his tray at mealtime, no matter what it tasted like. He smoked very little because he had no money to buy tobacco, only butts that he found, or shorts — the few last puffs of someone else's cigarette.

He became friendly with a lot of guys on the tier, and they lent him books, and taught him a lot of things he had never known, but always wanted to learn. The books were generally anthologies of poetry, which are highly prized by long-termers because you can read them over and over without getting bored; the abstract phrasing of the words stimulates your imagination, and gives your mind opportunity to think for itself. Kenny also got himself tattooed while there; a sparkling pair of dice, showing up a winning roll of seven, was pinned into his left forearm; a clawing black panther was drawn, clinging to his right bicep.

The tracks in the pits of his arms faded into scars, along with the memory of how they'd gotten there. One day, however, a new prisoner was admitted into the cellblock, who brought Kenny's heroin experience back into focus: Willie Pondexteur. Willie and his Chaplains had been in a rumble with another gang in the Bedford-Stuyvesant section of Brooklyn. It had been a front-page battle. Two guys were killed, and several eyewitnesses told the police, who broke up the fight, that the two were shot dead by bullets from a pistol fired by Willie Pondexteur. He was charged with Murder One, and they had him cold.

Kenny hadn't seen Willie for about two years, and after he exchanged "fancy meeting you here" greetings with him, he explained his situation, and listened to the impossibilities of Pondexteur's. They hung out together when they were out of their cells, Kenny showing him the routine and who was who and what the advantages and disadvantages of High Power were: "The screws treat you with respect, because they know you got nothin' to lose, or you wouldn't be in this section. But if you get out of line, or show any riotous tendencies, they throw you into the hole immediately. And it's dumb to go to solitary, when they'll give you 'most anything you want here, to keep you quiet. If you gotta be in this jail, this is the best room in the house. These old cons will let you in on a lot of things you oughta know before you go to the penitentiary. And, Willie, if it's like you say it is — that's where you goin'."

During the months Kenny spent in the Raymond Street jail, he was taken several times to both the Brooklyn and Manhattan police headquarters, and made to stand in lineups. The various coppers in charge of the Lines would read off his John Mullane name, and the immediate charges and circumstances of his case. They obviously wanted to get something concrete-heavy on him, but nobody ever identified him, positively or tentatively, for anything.

Finally, he was notified that his preliminary hearing had been reset. And on a Monday morning in the last week of July 1958, he was taken to the Brooklyn Criminal Court building, and placed in a holding tank to await his turn to appear before the judge.

A young, lean, ambitious, horn-rimmed-glassed lawyer from the Legal Aid Society, named Richard Langly, called "Mullane" over to the bars of the tank, and told him that the court had appointed him as his attorney.

Then Langly asked, "Are you crazy?"

Kenny looked around to make sure he was the one being addressed.

"I don't understand," he replied, after he was certain that the question was directed at him.

Attorney Richard Langly explained. He told "Mullane" that his name was really Kenneth Wisdom, and that he wasn't even fifteen, much less sixteen years old, and that he had no right to be in this place. He said that Patrick O'Keefe had revealed Kenny's real name and age to an assistant district attorney the previous week. He also told the assistant D.A. that it was Kenny who stole the Ford. O'Keefe did this, Langly said, because he was charged with umpteen counts of armed robbery, and was trying to make a deal with the D.A.'s office.

"Did he say anything else?" asked Kenny, as visions of Albino Sammy, the flower shop, and other episodes of his junk experience flooded his mind.

"No," replied Langly, "and if there is anything else, you're lucky he didn't talk about it, because the D.A. wants to get something on you very bad. As it stands now he has no case, because the only evidence against you is the testimony of an accomplice, which is not permissible evidence, much less grounds for conviction. So I talked it over with him, and he has agreed to dismiss the charges against you if you agree not to bring any civil action against his office for having allowed you, as a juvenile, to be incarcerated in the Men's House of Detention."

"Agreed," responded Kenny, and then asked the lawyer if he knew what had happened to Solly Girsch.

He was told that Girsch had been positively identified by several persons as the individual who mugged them in Prospect Park, and that he had been tried and convicted, and was now awaiting sentencing at Juvenile Hall.

The attorney continued, finally delivering the punch line which

66

Kenny had been waiting for: "Your parents are in the courtroom and I talked with them. They thought you had run away. They only found out that you spent the past five and a half months in jail on Friday afternoon. The D.A.'s office notified them.

"There's a priest from your parish out there, too, and he told me that you were now expelled from your parochial school.

"Also, there's a Jesuit who I think they said is the nephew of your mother's cousin.

"Now apparently from what I could gather, you've given your parents a very hard time, and they don't know if they want to, or are capable of resuming the responsibility of your custody. If they decide not to accept custody of you, the court will make the decision of either sending you to the Warwick State Reformatory, where you will remain until you are sixteen, or to Riker's Island, until you are twenty-one.

"Would you like to talk with your mother and father about it?"

"Yes," Kenny quickly replied.

"All right," said Attorney Richard Langly, "I'll arrange it immediately." Then he left. A few moments later, a bailiff took Kenny from the tank and walked him down the hall to an empty courtroom, entered with him, and took a position by the door, blocking his prisoner's only possible route of escape.

Kenny didn't even notice him, as he approached the circle of people who were talking to his Legal Aid Society lawyer.

When his mother turned and saw him, she burst into tears, and his father said, "Do you see what you've done to your mother?"

The parish priest said that Kenny should be ashamed of himself, for having been expelled from school, for having caused pain and humiliation to his parents by running around, stealing cars, and "the Good Lord knows what else," like a common street urchin, when his family had provided him with a good home, and sacrificed themselves to give him the opportunity of a fine Catholic education, only to get a slap in the face by a cowardly and ungrateful son for "the suffering and hardships they both had endured in order to raise their boy to be a good, upstanding Catholic gentleman. "Well what do you have to say for yourself?" he concluded.

Kenny didn't want to say anything. He wanted to punch this roly-poly Irish priest in his fucking bullshit mealy mouth, but he didn't.

Instead, he turned toward his father and mother, and performed for his freedom.

He told them that he loved them very much, and that he was

sorry that he had disgraced and hurt them so. But that he had tried not to, he pitched, by giving a false name and standing on his own two feet, accepting the responsibility for his actions without getting them involved.

"I knew that I had done wrong, and took the punishment that my childish mistakes had warranted. I committed the wrong alone, and accepted the consequences alone. I love you and understand all that you have given up for me. That is why I lied about my age, and was incarcerated for five months in an adult prison for my juvenile foolishness. I could have made it easier on myself by telling the authorities my true name, age, and address, but that would have made it harder on you. I love you too much to have done that. I was solely to blame. And I didn't want the slightest speck of my faults to be borne by you.

"And, please, believe me when I say that I tried my best to protect you from any of the consequences of my foolhardy prank, and that, for as long as I live, I will never be able to forgive myself for the pain which I have caused you, and that I will try to make retribution to you and to God for that pain and sorrow, by devoting myself to the education of my mind, and, someday, hopefully graduate from Notre Dame University, as a successful man and a good Christian.

"Please, forgive me."

And they did.

Attorney Richard Langly couldn't believe that the plea, which he was hearing, was actually and mellifluously coming out of the mouth of the kid whom he had just talked to in the tank.

The parish priest believed what he was hearing. He believed it was a bunch of crap, and that Kenny was an incorrigible delinquent who should be sent to the Catholic reform school in upstate New York. He had mentioned that previously to Wisdom's parents, and felt that now it was "in the hands of the Lord." Or some such copout like that.

The Jesuit was intrigued and impressed by the boy's quick-witted intelligence, and elocution.

The bailiff thought the punk should become a lawyer, and remarked the same, as he returned Kenny Wisdom to the courtroom where his case would be dismissed, and the matter of his custody would be adjudicated by the judge, Samuel Liebowitz.

Now, there are a lot of people who know about this man, and there are a lot of people who don't and will never have an opportunity to get any firsthand knowledge of him, because he retired from the bench. He didn't want to, but somehow the powers that be got this aged old man to give up his dealership of justice.

During the twenties and thirties, Samuel Simon Liebowitz was the most brilliant and successful criminal lawyer in the state of New York. His clients were also very successful. Most of them were gangsters. He defended all of the big racketeers of the city and seldom got less than an acquittal. He always got enormous fees. He defeated seventy-eight prosecutors in seventy-eight murder cases, in which most of the defendants were "Legs" Diamond types. After each case, he'd make statements to the press that he opposed the death penalty, but favored the whipping post.

He was a contradictory as well as a controversial figure. He said that the most significant case of his life occurred in 1933, when the United States Supreme Court ordered a new trial for nine black men who were convicted in 1931 of raping two white women, and sentenced to death by an Alabama superior court.

Samuel Liebowitz was appointed chief counsel for the defense in what was and is still known as the Scottsboro Case. His legal strategy and skillful tactics during the trial incensed the prosecutor to the point where he began shouting things like, "The State of Alabama is being violated by Jew money and a Jew lawyer from the State of New York!" He was right. Due to Liebowitz's successful arguments for the defense, the state of Alabama, and other states in the South, were forced to allow blacks to sit on juries for the first time. In 1940, after twenty-one years as a lawyer, he was elected to a judgeship in Kings County, which is Brooklyn. His postelection statement was, simply, that he intended to "temper justice with mercy." The severe toughness of his courtroom style, however, negated those words, and forced the New York Police Department to assign round-the-clock guards to protect him from the numerous threats made on his life.

Especially in 1951, when eighteen cops were indicted for taking bribes and protecting a bookmaking ring, which was allegedly headed by one Harry Gross. Harry was on the stand, and refusing to answer any and all questions. This enraged Judge Liebowitz and he informed Mr. Gross that he'd give him a "thousand years, if you don't talk! I'll bury you in prison!" Gross still refused to respond to the questioning, so the judge ticked off one six-month contempt citation every minute for an hour, and also imposed a fifteen-thousand-dollar fine on Harry the Bookmaker. And that was that.

Now, Kenny Wisdom was sitting at the defense table with his

attorney, awaiting his turn to stand before Judge Samuel Simon Liebowitz and receive justice tempered with mercy. There were two convicted defendants ahead of him; each one about to be sentenced. The first guy went before the bench, and the judge read from the record that he had been found guilty on two counts of armed robbery, and asked him if he had anything to say before sentence was passed. The nineteen-year-old said that he didn't. Then Liebowitz asked him to look at the clock which was on the wall over the door leading to the judge's chambers, and, please, to tell him what time it was.

"It's five to ten, Your Honor," replied the youth.

"Well, that's what you get," the judge told him, "Five to ten years at the state penitentiary of Ossining, New York."

He slammed his gavel to finalize the judgment, and called for the next one to be brought before him.

Kenny Wisdom was incredulous.

The second convicted felon was a swaggering seventeen-year-old mugger, who thought that he was a tough guy. The judge went through the same presentencing routine, with the exception of the clock, and gave the kid two years at Riker's Island. But before he made the length of the term decisive with the slamming of his gavel, the kid made a wise remark.

"I'll do that standin' on my head!" he cracked.

"In that case," the judge replied, "you can have another two years to do on your feet, which will give your blood enough time to recirculate properly. Four years." Slam! went the gavel.

Kenny Wisdom was becoming ill.

When the judge called for the next case, an assistant district attorney stood and said that his office wanted a dismissal because there was no case. He informed the court that it was now simply a question of who should take custody of the boy, his parents or an institution.

Then, he began reading from affidavits by the arresting officers and the parish priest which testified to the incorrigibility of Kenny Wisdom. Defense Attorney Langly rose the moment the prosecutor had said his mouthful and came to the defense of his client, directing his comments at the prosecution rather than the judge.

"The boy's parents want him returned to where they think he rightfully belongs, their home. They know that Kenneth is a promising young student and they want to give him the opportunity to get a good education and a college degree. He has . . ."

"The young should be sued for breach of promise," muttered the judge.

Kenny's stomach turned over.

His lawyer had an angle of legality up his sleeve however, which was going to save the court some time and also save Kenny from going to a reformatory. Langly crossed over to the prosecutor and conferred briefly with him, advising him that Kenneth Wisdom's parents were prepared to file a publicly scandalous suit against the City of New York for the Police Department's oversight which had allowed their son to be incarcerated in the Men's House of Detention for over five months, subjecting him to the terrifying environs and corrosive atmosphere of hardened criminals. He ended by saying, "The boy shouldn't even be in this court!"

The assistant district attorney acquiesced to the defense counsel's logic and motioned that the boy be released into the custody of his parents, if they'd waive any and all action against the city.

The agreement was made and Kenny was released into his parents' custody without having to face the "justice tempered with mercy" of Judge Samuel Simon Liebowitz.

After the decision, the parish priest huff-puffed back to his rectory, and Kenny Wisdom and his parents were driven to their home by the Jesuit, who wasn't ordained as yet. He was a scholastic, teaching at a high school, studying to take his final vows. He was introduced as Father Francis Kelly.

When they got to their two-room apartment, Kenny played with his sister, and the Jesuit and his parents drank coffee in the kitchen. The Jesuit told them they had made a wise and courageous choice in allowing their son to return to their home, because he was an extremely bright boy with great potential. The Jesuit also had an idea about a way in which that potential could be developed, but he didn't mention that until a while later. Because Kenny's father had some bad news to tell his son, and he called him into the kitchen.

He told Kenny that while he had been away Grandpa had died.

"And he left you this," he said, handing him a small package. Inside the envelope were all of his grandfather's union cards. Kenny took them with him into his parents' bedroom and closed the door.

He wasn't surprised at the sorrow which he felt for the loss of his grandfather. He didn't cry. He just sat on the floor and looked at all the union cards with his grandpa's photo on each of them, and remembered.

His grandfather had been orphaned by a fire when he was seven years old, in some coal town outside Pittsburgh. Some neighbors took him into their family, and when he was nine, he was sent to work in the Mellon Corporation's mines, giving most of his wages to the people who had taken him in.

But, by his sixteenth birthday, he had saved enough money to come to the city of New York. He worked there, as an ironworker, a bridgeman and a riveter. He was proud of the things he had helped to build — the Brooklyn Bridge, the Brussels World's Fair, and many more structures.

He had been married to a fine woman who was still alive, and he had been a stern but sagacious father, raising a family of four girls and a boy.

His age forced him into retirement long before Kenny was born. His chest was still big-boned enormous, but his legs and arms sagged with the passing of time. He had never set foot inside of a classroom, but he was a wise man. He would take Kenny for walks, using a cane for support — a cigar always between his teeth.

A doctor once told him that smoking was going to take two or three years off his life. And Grandpa replied, "What difference does it make. They'll be the last ones, anyway."

He'd been Kenny Wisdom's guru, if you will, and taught him how to meditate simply by staring at a tree until it became everything. He never said much, just watched and absorbed. Now life had absorbed him.

He was a good and honest man, and the honesty of his toil was recorded on the union cards which Kenny held in his hand. He was dead, but he'd been one of the few who lived.

Kenny went back into the kitchen, and the Jesuit told him he taught at a boys' preparatory school on Park Avenue in Manhattan. This school was attended by the sons of diplomats and wealthy people of the various professions. He said that the school had decided to give scholarships to a few bright underprivileged boys. The entrance exam and the scholarship tests were being given on the following Saturday.

If Kenny wanted, the Father said, he could arrange for him to take those examinations. If Kenny scored high and was scholarship material, he would be placed in the junior high school, rather than have to go back to the sixth or seventh grade in some public grammar school.

Kenny looked at his mother and father, squeezed the union cards which were still in his hands, and said, "Sure."

Mr. George J. Hagan

Pop

It took Kenny more than an hour on the subway that Saturday morning to get to the preparatory school, which was near 86th Street and Park Avenue.

The series of tests and examinations lasted from nine to about four in the afternoon. At one point he had to write an essay on why he wanted a private school education. Kenny never realized how much he learned about words from all those anthologies of poetry he read in the Raymond Street jail.

When he was finished he took the subway back to South Brooklyn, thinking he didn't even have a chance of passing the entrance exam, much less the scholarship tests. As he entered the apartment, and before his parents could ask him how it went, the phone rang. His mother answered, and it was the headmaster of the Jesuit Preparatory School for Boys. He told her that Kenny showed outstanding ability and awareness with his answers to the questions and had won a scholarship. The headmaster personally called to inform her because he wanted to relieve Kenny and his parents of the unnecessary anxiety of awaiting a written announcement. He closed by asking her to tell her son to come over to the prep school on Monday morning, because he wanted to talk things over with him.

Kenny had never seen his parents glow with such happiness. They were elated and very proud of their son. It obviously meant a lot to them.

Kenny didn't know what it meant to him.

On Monday morning, one week after he had been released from jail, Kenny entered the Preparatory School for Boys, and was met by a Jesuit priest named Father Berrigan. They talked while he showed Kenny around the school's luxurious facilities. The talk amounted to the uniqueness of Kenny's position as a member of a student body of swells, with the advice that he should keep his past experiences to himself.

When they got to the newly built gymnasium, they were joined by Father Daley, the headmaster of the school and a Marine Corps chaplain. Kenny was introduced to him by Father Berrigan, who left them alone.

Kenny watched as Berrigan walked away and then turned his attention to the lacquered-wooden-slat floor of the gym.

The headmaster said, "I understand that you play ball."

A grin began to swell inside of him, and a smile turned up the corners of his mouth, as Kenny Wisdom replied, "Yes. Yes, I play."

TWO

*For Graziano Mesini
and Dario Sambuco*

I'm no hoodlum! And I don't like to be called a hood. I'm a thief.

A thief is anybody who gets out and works for his living, like robbing a bank, or breaking into a place and stealing stuff, or kidnapping somebody. He really gives some effort to it. A hoodlum is a pretty lousy kind of scum. He works for gangsters and bumps off guys after they've been put on the spot. Why, after I'd made my rep, some of the Chicago syndicate wanted me to go to work for them as a hood — you know, handling a machine gun. They offered me two hundred and fifty dollars a week and all the protection I needed. I was on the lam at the time and not able to work at my regular line. But I wouldn't consider it. "I'm a thief!" I said. "I'm no goddamn lousy hoodlum."

Alvin Karpis, *The Alvin Karpis Story*

It was September 15, 1958, and Kenny Wisdom was climbing the stairs of the IRT subway station to begin his walk along 86th Street and his first semester at the private preparatory school for boys. He knew that he was far from home, but he had no idea nor did he even consider the social and academic situations he was about to encounter as a classmate to the sons of the rich and powerful. He was only preoccupied with the cleanliness of the streets, the tall stately buildings with penthouses on top of them, the limousines taking the residents of those apartments to wherever they made their money, the doormen, the imported food shops, the dignified gait of the women and the funny hairdos of the poodles. It was all very impressive and it sure wasn't Dean Street.

But Kenny didn't look out of place. He was wearing one of the two conservative Brooks Brothers' suits which he had purchased from a booster in his neighborhood who assured him that this was the style of clothing that high-class people preferred to wear and look at. "Sharkskin suits from Phil's Style Center on Broadway don't go over too big on Park Avenue and they tend to make the people of that area a little nervous and sometimes quite suspicious of the person who is garbed in one. Especially if he's carrying books and going to school with their children. Believe me, take 'tweeds' and forget the 'threads,' " he said, and he was right.

It didn't matter, however, because Kenny's first course on that first morning of his arrival at the knocked-up-with-opportunity preparatory was physical education. When he went to the locker that was assigned him and stripped off his conservative cover and bared his jailhouse tattoos, the loud "How have you beens?" of the returning students became gapes and hushed whispers about the new boy with pictures drawn on his muscles. Kenny immediately knew what every kid in the place would be telling anyone with ears that day, and their parents over dinner that night. Without Brooks Brothers' help, Wisdom was just "rough trade" to the Fauntleroys who suppressed their giggles and were afraid to ask him anything because his cartooned arms weren't exactly the size of comic strips and there was also nothing particularly funny about the look on Kenny's face.

The only person who said something was the phys. ed. teacher, a layman named Ralph Farina who was also the basketball coach. He said, "Kenneth, please come into my office a minute." There he told Kenny that he had been previously informed of the scars which testified to Wisdom's unfortunate past and he gave him a jar of Rose Dark Waterproof Covermark and explained that in order for Kenny to avoid any further embarrassment for himself or the school, he should apply the makeup to the blemishes on his skin every morning before class and to do so in the upstairs lavatory out of the other students' sight.

Kenny complied, but not because he was embarrassed. He simply knew full well what would happen if he didn't. The only complication with this cosmetic routine resulted when Kenny joined the basketball team. He was always scrambling under the boards for rebounds, and the body contact with the other players rubbed off the greasepaint. So he was forced to wrap an Ace bandage around his upper right arm and cover his small pair of lucky seven dice with a piece of adhesive tape.

Father Berrigan was transferred to another Jesuit prep school in Brooklyn, but Kenny remembered the advice that the priest had given him about not discussing the particulars of his street background with any of the well-bred members of the student body. Kenny never said a word, and he put on such a strong silent act that most of the students didn't dare pry into the privacy of his upbringing, or even talk with him about matters which weren't directly concerned with the academic or extracurricular activities of the school. They preferred to conjecture about his past among themselves, rather than face the reality of an unanswered question.

Eventually, however, one of the forwards on the basketball team, who had become more or less familiar with Kenny, struck up a conversation which he began by commenting on some strategic game plan and ended with an inquiry about Kenny's tattoos. Wisdom dead-eyed him and coolly replied, "What tattoos?" And that was that.

Kenny was just barely six feet tall, but he could spring from a standstill and touch the rim with both hands. He was a good playmaker and could shoot equally well with either hand. His all-round ability and scrappiness allowed him to control the key and score against opponents who were much bigger. His eighteen-point average per game didn't interfere with his flashy around-the-back ball handling, which always delighted whoever was watching, particularly the girls from the private schools in the area who in turn delighted Kenny with their approval. He played center. And he played that position so well that it minimized the need to fence with questions which he didn't want to answer about himself. He just remained intriguing, which was exactly the way he wanted it.

The subjects he was required to take didn't differ that much from those of any other junior high school. There was math, English, religion, an elementary course in logic which Kenny enjoyed, and Latin which was a bitch, and a combination political science–civics course which was taught by a priest who demanded that each student read the New York *Times* every day and prove it by answering questions on a quiz which he'd chisel from the *Times* in the afternoon. In fact, the whole course was nothing but the New York *Times*. It was the only book one had to read and every time he did, Kenny got a yen.

Now at first this yen was just a cellular yearning for some dope — which had been Wisdom's way to escape from his parochial family dormitory in Brooklyn — but after a while the yen became a simple urge to steal. To steal all the things you can find out in the New York *Times*. Where else?

You see, Kenny didn't want to get up at six in the morning five days a week to beat the rush-hour crowds that pack the subways he rode to his school. He didn't like to stay at the school until seven each evening to miss that same bunch of white-collar stiffs on his way home. He didn't even want to go to school — much less come home. He wanted more than that. Kenny Wisdom wanted to be a thief and steal Park Avenue. This dawned on him early one morning as he was leafing through the *Times* on the train. He came to a full page of pictures in the society section which were photos of some of the swells who had been to a fund-raising benefit for somebody's leper colony the night before. He looked at the faces and he read their names and some were familiar. In fact, he had met a few of them. They were the parents of the boys and girls who came to watch him play basketball. They were the fathers and mothers of his classmates. "I'll be a son of a bitch!" he thought, before he started to dream. A dream that was not going to come true all by itself. He had to do it and it wasn't easy. But the motive was there and it was strong. It wasn't something that you can buy or have given to you. It was something that you have to take: freedom. Kenny wanted to do it all by his lonesome, because it was a personal thing, this freedom of his. It had nothing to do with this or that, it just had to do with Kenny Wisdom, and some new tailor-made suits maybe and some soft alligator shoes instead of the dumb clod-hopping cordovans he had on! And no more goddamn subway trains, just taxis! Here, there, everywhere! And ringside seats for the fights at Madison Square Garden! And nightclubs! And first-class hotels with room service! And trips to Vegas sitting with the boys at a blackjack table with a chorus girl keeping your shoulder warm with her hand! And above all else, a suntan! Not one of them Coney Island, Far Rockaway, Breezy Point, dry, red-skinned, phony tans, but a real smooth bronze job that you get on the Riviera where the soft Mediterranean sun melts over you like butter, blending your freckles into a solid golden brown! Yes, a fucking suntan! That's what Kenny Wisdom's freedom was all about, a fucking suntan! "Fifteen years old, my ass!" Kenny shouted to himself. "I'm as old as I'm ever gonna be! It's now or never!"

"What the fuck are you lookin' at?" he yelled at an old startled watchman who was returning from a long night's work of boredom. *"Ain't you ever seen somebody with angel kisses on his face before?"*

But he wasn't angry. Kenny was just excited over the possibilities of his discovery. When he got off at his station he was bubbling with so much enthusiasm that he laughed all the way to what had just become his very own Private Preparatory School. It was going to teach him how to get into these Park Avenue luxury apartments for a look around, and the New York *Times* was going to tell him when the owners of those apartments were going to be out of town on a vacation in Jamaica or at a funeral or a wedding or making a film in Los Angeles or something.

Yes sir, the good old New York *Times* with "All the news that's fit to print." God bless 'em! Kenny didn't just restrict himself to that paper's society section. Nope, as soon as he caught on to the angle, Wisdom read every entertainment section, obituary, society page, and gossip columnist in every daily newspaper in New York. He felt special gratitude for Earl Wilson, Leonard Lyons, Walter Winchell and those wonderful ladies Louella Parsons, Hedda Hopper, Sheila Graham. They were great, the best! "Thank you! Thank you! Thank you!" Kenny would say and kiss the mug shots which accompanied their bylines whenever one of their columns contained an item of interest to his trade. Which was burglary.

Instead of studying Latin in the kitchen every night, Wisdom would spend three hours going through all the day's papers, combing them for clues and copying any relevant information into a tablet notebook. While he was doing this, his parents would be watching television in the living room and were especially careful not to disturb their son's studies which were going to make him a professional. They were right about the professional part, but wrong about the doctor, lawyer, or architect type.

At school, Kenny continued playing basketball to meet new faces, and he maintained a B grade in all his subjects. He did this by cheating, which wasn't very hard to do because the quizzes and tests were given under the honor system. He had everything covered except his "Toity-toid 'n Toid" manner of speech, which he had to do something about before he began dating any of the thoroughbred adolescent chicks from the private sister school on Madison Avenue, or getting palsy-walsy with his fellow students to be invited to dinner and parties. He needed to do both of these things in order to enter and case the homes of the Park Avenue Kingdom. But he had to learn how to talk without sounding like Rocky Graziano. He did.

There was another kid in his class who had been awarded a scholarship because of his brains and his family's low economic status. His name was Louis, and he had been raised and educated in London where his Greek parents had owned a small restaurant which went broke, and they had all come to America because his father had been given a job as a waiter by one of his cousins in another small Greek restaurant. Kenny liked Louis. He was a square shooter and there was no bullshit about him. He was very bright and all he did was study very hard and read a lot and all he wanted to be someday was a professor of English literature. He was already somewhat of a scholar and he had a beautifully accented voice — one of those British public school tongues which never slurs any words and always crisply enunciates the *th*'s and everything.

Kenny talked with Louis a few times about English poetry, which Kenny had read in one of the anthologies in the Raymond Street jail. He had even memorized one, a poem by Chidiock Tichborne who'd written it as a letter to his wife only a few hours before he was hanged for having conspired to assassinate some queen of England about two hundred years ago. Louis was impressed because he had heard neither of the poet nor the poem before and they were both good, and Louis liked to learn about things he didn't know before. He even wrote it down.

So Kenny approached Louis with his problem which was quite obvious and asked him what he could do about it. Louis told him that it was simply a matter of strengthening the muscles of his tongue, which were lazy and had to be exercised by reading English poetry aloud with marbles in his mouth. Kenny trusted Louis and he did what he had told him to do. He did it every night for a month wherever he could.

One evening he went up on the roof of the Dean Street tenement where he lived and he took the marbles out of his mouth because he felt that he'd put in enough time with them and he wanted to hear what he sounded like without them. Besides, his tongue was getting muscle-bound. He read a speech from a Shakespeare play and he read it very loudly and deliberately. Because he wanted the sky to hear and understand him. "This is the excellent foppery of the world, that, when we are sick in fortune, often the surfeits of our own behaviour, we make guilty of our disasters the sun, the moon, and stars; as if we were villains by necessity; fools by heavenly compulsion; knaves, thieves, and treachers, by spherical predominance; drunkards, liars, and adulterers, by an enforced obedience of planetary influence, and all that we are evil in, by a divine thrusting on — an admirable evasion of whoremaster man, to lay his goatish disposition to the charge of a star! My father compounded with my mother under the Dragon's tail, and my nativity was under Ursa Major, so that it follows I am rough and lecherous. 'Sfoot! I should have been that I am, had the maidenliest star in the firmament twinkled on my bastardizing!"

Kenny didn't sound like a mug anymore. He sounded like John

Garfield, and he was satisfied. The neighbors all had their heads stuck outside their windows looking up, trying to see "What the hell goin' on up there?" Wisdom leaned over the edge and panned all their inquiring faces and told them that nothing was wrong. '*I just lost my marbles!* That's all!"

From then on Kenny was in the stretch, but he had to work fast because it was mid-November and he had to infiltrate the fat cat duplexes on Park Avenue by going to all the parties and dating all the chicks he could before they all went away to the Bahamas or someplace for their Christmas vacations with their families.

He must have gone to ten parties in those few weekends. And each time he'd take a different girl. He did this because he not only wanted to have a look-see at the homes where the parties were being held, but also case as many other flats before his time ran out. He would always arrive ten minutes early to pick up his date and chat with her parents about the Yuletide Season and how nice it was in New York City at that time of year, which usually prompted the mother to agree but explain that they were going to miss the holiday glories of the city this year because they were going to spend time with their relatives in California or Europe or with the beachboys in the Caribbean. Then he'd ask where the bathroom was and on his way there he'd make mental notes of everything within the periphery of his vision. When he'd return, the girl would waltz out of her room with a "sorry to keep you waiting" and she'd be all coiffeured and chemised and they'd go to whatever party with a "not too late" goodbye from her father.

Now these weren't spin-the-bottle-post-office parties, and if you've ever buried your dick in the mouth of a chiffon-dressed adolescent chick with a beehive for a hairdo, you know what I mean. They were come-quick-through-the-fly-of-your-herringbone-suit parties and no chaperones, only West Indian maids who saw everything but didn't so much as do a Tsk! Tsk! And mirrors everywhere.

The first time Kenny went to one of these things, he was directed to a private wallpapered elevator by a doorman in a building on East 74th Street. His date was a cocky jane with a petulant mouth and he liked her because she was feisty and not a creampuff like the others, and also because her parents were very big movie stars and had lots of money and all the material things that affluence provides. The elevator stopped at the top floor and its door opened into the apartment. To the right was the master bedroom with a huge four-poster canopied bed, surrounded by an array of ornate furniture.

To the left was the living room or rather the salon, completely paneled with mirrors. All four of the long walls, the high ceiling, every inch of space was a mirror. There were no windows and the floor was a very thick white rug. The few couples who'd been invited were sitting around this visually dimensionless room listening to cha-cha-cha and drinking. The bar was just to the left of the kitchen which was between the salon and the master bedroom. Several doors leading to a study, the kids' rooms, guest rooms and maids' quarters lined the wall from the kitchen to the master bedroom.

Kenny and the chick said hello to everybody and went over to the bar. She asked the maid-bartender for something and Wisdom said, "Me too, please." What he got he didn't expect, a glass of yellow cloudy water which tasted like licorice. He looked at the green bottle that it had come out of and the label spelled Pernod. After three or four glasses of the stuff he began to get a headache and the girl he was with started coming on randy.

She tugged at his hand lightly and motioned towards the bedroom. They got up and Kenny followed her, rubbing the nape of her neck with his thumbs, his fingers massaging her collarbones. He laid her down on the cloudlike mattress of the four-poster and told her to wait there and that he'd be right back. His head was splitting with ache and he went to the bathroom to see if the medicine chest held anything in the way of relief. He found a bottle of 222's, which is the Canadian equivalent of aspirin, but instead of containing some ingredient known as a buffer, each pill has about one eighth of a grain of codeine in it. Kenny swallowed eight of them and in less than a minute the full grain of narcotic killed his pain with a dull, numbing warmth that spread throughout his body with a buzz.

He dangled while he took a piss and the buzz turned into a mellow sort of high and when he came out of the john his eye caught something that he had never seen before. In a quietly decorated studio adjacent to the bathroom was a piano. Not an ordinary upright piano, but a big black Steinway grand piano, squatting proudly on three thick delicately carved wooden legs, its gleam filling the room. Kenny walked over to it and slid his fingers over the polished finish and stared at the glistening ivory keyboard. They were like a full set of magical teeth and he was afraid to touch them. He just stood and looked at them and was sad that he couldn't run his hands over them and make them do what they were made to do — create music. For an Irish kid who was raised during the fifties in Brooklyn by parents whose cultural tradition went back to people who came over on a boat from Ireland in the late 1880s and settled on Fifth Avenue between 116th and 117th streets six blocks north of what is now New York's Central Park and which was then Shantytown, music was to be listened to and sports were to be played and money was to be made and pianos were something you heard when you put a nickel in a jukebox. If you went to the Catholic church of your parish you could hear a nun pedal an organ and listen to a choir sing "Tantum Ergo Sacramentum."

Kenny wondered where guys like Fats Domino, Jerry Lee Lewis and Little Richard learned to dance those keys into sound, a sound that could make you feel the way they wanted you to feel. He could understand the power of that sound with his body, but his mind couldn't comprehend the mechanics of how it was made. That grand shining piano and the variety of instruments that accompany it were things that Wisdom had never learned to use. Christ, it was even too big to steal!

He slid back into the bedroom and relaxed on the silk-cased pillows next to the sweetheart, who unzipped him and gobbled up his joint giving him head. He let his flesh ride the rhythms of her waving wandering tongue, but he kept his eyes open and his brain alert and detached from the hot juices of her mouth. He was thinking. He was trying to figure out a way to get into an apartment that has a private elevator for a door. He could see that the fire exit, which was in the kitchen and led to a staircase in the rear of the building, was a triple-locked slab of metal with a burglar alarm attached to the top of its frame. That was no way.

The chick had turned the lights out in the bedroom and it was dark. Kenny could see everything in the front of the apartment reflected in the mirrors of the salon at the end of the hall. He watched the bartending maid as she went into the kitchen to fill the ice bucket. She went to the refrigerator, took out a brown insulated bag of ice cubes, removed a towel from a rack to dry her hands, and revealed the vehicle that Wisdom was going to use to enter this apartment: the dumbwaiter.

If the ropes were good, he'd just pull himself up to the appropriate floor and kick open the unwired door, which wasn't locked or bolted but simply sealed shut with dried paint. It would be a cinch. Still, it was a dangerous route to take when you consider that once you're inside there is no other out but the way in, and if they discovered that a burglary was in progress and the coppers blocked the dumbwaiter exit in the basement, you were trapped. But the

Moroccan leather jewelry box that Kenny could barely see on top of the dressing table in the darkened room was all the encouragement he needed to risk that possibility.

The jane lifted her face from his crotch and rested her chin on his stomach and asked him if something was the matter.

Kenny said, "What, sweetheart?"

She flicked his limp dick with her finger and asked if anything was wrong.

"Oh, no, no. I just have a bad headache and it won't let me get into it, that's all," he softly lied.

The codeine made it impossible to get an erection and the chick was getting lockjaw trying to give him a hardon and make him come in her mouth. He pulled her up onto his chest and kissed her a few times to show his appreciation for her labor and she said, "Oh, Kenny, I . . ." And he said, "Let's go."

Before they left, Wisdom memorized the three different numbers for the various phones in the flat. He also wanted to take a peek inside that jewelry box, but he didn't because he was afraid that he might blow his cool and cop a ring or something, which might give him away or at least alert the owners of the place and spoil the surprise that he had in store for them.

By the time school closed for Xmas vacation, Kenny Wisdom had cased the insides of thirty luxurious apartments by going to parties of this kind or simple suppers with classmates, or by taking dates to Saturday afternoon movies before the basketball games that he played in the evening, or walking with chicks for a Sunday stroll and make-out in the park. He knew who was who and where they were going and when and for how long. His notebook was filled with the layouts and phone numbers of the places he was going to hit. He was ready.

Five days before Xmas, he went on his first score. He had no money, but he had devised a plan: he was going to play it like a kid. He wore an old pair of corduroy pants, a black turtleneck sweater with a sweatshirt underneath, a navy blue wool cap and sneakers. He carried a satchel which the athletic department of the school had given him for his game gear. Inside of it were the tools he thought he might need, an old football which he was going to use as a prop, and a pair of unlined leather gloves he had stolen from a kid at school.

One of the cardinal rules of burglary is that when you go on a job you should never take anything with you that might identify you if you have to split in a hurry and drop everything. Or even if all goes well, you might absentmindedly forget something that can be recognized as yours. A good thief should go in clean, with a new set of clothes with the labels torn out and nothing whatsoever in his pockets, not even a handkerchief, which might have a laundry mark on it. Only a pair of gloves and a screwdriver. Everything else you need in the way of tools or a Gladstone bag to haul away the goods, you can usually find at the scene. But Kenny had no money for a new suit or for a hotel room to make the change or any time to get any. So he knew that he was doing wrong by costuming as a kid and using his own stuff on his first run; however, he didn't have much of a choice. He was desperate and his tight-timetabled schedule demanded that he move right away and in the only style that he could afford. He was totally aware of the risks of his situation and he was counting on this awareness to get him through the number without leaving any identifiable traces.

Wisdom left his house with his parents thinking that he was going to play ball at the Knights of Columbus gym near Prospect Park. He took the subway to the Union Square station, but before changing to the Lexington Avenue train which would take him uptown, he went into a phone booth and called the three numbers which he had written down on a piece of paper along with several other particulars of the residence he intended to knock over. The first two numbers he dialed were answered by a service and he hung up after asking for a nonexistent party. The third was the one he wanted. It was the direct private line into the apartment. He let it ring about fifteen times and no one answered. He took the Lexington Avenue local to 77th Street, got off and dialed the number again with the same result. He took the football out of the bag while he was in the phone booth and tossed it around in his right hand as he walked the short distance to his destination. To make sure that someone wasn't taking a long bubble bath or something, he called the apartment again from a telephone booth on the corner of Madison Avenue. He even asked the operator to try it, making certain that he wasn't dialing wrong or that it wasn't out of service or disconnected. It was early afternoon and there were only a few people on the street and snow flurries began to fall. He had cased the building the previous week and he knew that the janitor-custodian would be burning trash in the incinerator at that hour. The incinerator was at the opposite end of the basement and around a corner, hiding it from the dumbwaiter shaft which was right inside the service entrance. Someone working back there had no view of the entrance or of anyone near the dumbwaiter, and the noise of the furnace obliterated any other sounds.

Kenny made his move. He tucked the football under his arm and opened the door of the service entrance. No one saw him go in and if anybody had noticed, all they could see was a boy with a football returning home and going in the back way so as not to track any mud into the carpeted foyer of the apartment house. How considerate. Inside, Wisdom bolted the door shut and waited until he was sure that his calculations about the janitor were right. They were. He could hear him moving cans around and the flames from the furnace silhouetted his movements on the wall. Kenny kept his eyes on those shadows as he dropped the football into his bag and took out a claw hammer to pry loose the several hastily driven nails that sealed the door of the dumbwaiter shaft. He did it quickly and quietly, putting each nail he took out into the back pocket of his pants. The door was old and cranky, but without the nails it swung open freely. Kenny tugged on the rope and the cart rose a few feet. It worked, but he couldn't tell how much noise it made because of the sound of the furnace. He could only hope for the best and fuck it!

Watching the shadows at the end of the basement, he took the nails from his pocket and threw them into his satchel which he placed inside the cart. He kept the hammer in his left hand as he crawled into the dumbwaiter and closed the door with his right. It was a tight squeeze and he was propped inside the box in a fetus position and it was pitch-black dark and so dusty-dirty that he could hardly keep from sneezing. He laid the hammer in his lap and held the rope firmly with both hands.

Before pulling on the rope, he thought about it all for a moment. About how the dumbwaiter cart might make too much noise and he'd get caught. About how the rope might be frayed and snap while he was hauling himself up the eight stories to the top floor. About how the pulley might get jammed up and he'd be trapped in the shaft alone and suffocating in the musty dark. About how the cops and firemen would be called to rescue him and how no amount of explaining would explain away the burglary tools and he'd land in jail for a long term. About how he was already locked into a jailhouse routine of playing it straight for the squares who had awarded him the privilege of a fine education in the Grade-A-Prime social circle of rich people who had two last names and how the long-time-coming-future held degrees from Ivy League universities which would make him a professional man who could marry into money and find his stature and fortune and fame in his in-laws' corporation or law firm or on his own if he preferred, like a real Horatio Alger.

"No," he thought, "that future's a long time gone!" The rest he just chalked up as possible occupational hazards.

But he was nervous about the dumbness of the dumbwaiter route, and he sighed as his hands followed each other along the rope, steadily raising him from the basement. He was soaking-sweat-wet and the cart cramped his body and forced him to rely solely on the strength in his arms to carry the weight upward. He moved slowly on purpose to minimize the muffled rumble of the cart. His fingers became his eyes and carefully examined the rope as it passed through his hands for weak spots. His right elbow grazed up the side of the shaft wall, counting the large spaces which occurred at each landing and signified what floor he was passing. Two, three, four. His right leg was ready to wedge itself against the shaft to prevent a freefall crash to the bottom in the event that the towline gave way or broke loose from the roof of the cart.

Suddenly his ears gave the alarm to stop, to freeze! Someone was yelling, screaming! Kenny was scared. He held his breath and listened. The shouts came from above, from the next floor — five. It was a woman. Two women. Were they shrieking because of him or what? He couldn't make it out. He lifted the dumbwaiter toward the sounds. He had to get closer to hear why they were upset. As he moved, it got louder and louder until he was directly behind the wall of the kitchen it was coming from and it couldn't get any louder. He stopped and held his breath and listened again. They were arguing. It was a lady and her maid. They both had accents and the dispute was about more nights off and the arrogance and inefficiency of servants these days and Wisdom was glad that it had nothing to do with him and he relaxed back into the tension of doing what he'd come there to do. He moved on, drifting up through the darkness and away from the resounding racket of the fifth floor.

He could still hear them going at each other when he pulled next to the dumbwaiter door of the eighth floor apartment. He wrapped the rope around his right leg and jammed his foot into the corner of the landing space to steady the cart and hold it in position. He wiped the sweat off the palms of his hands on his pants and put on his gloves. He listened at the door for a few moments, then knocked on it softly but repeatedly a few times. He didn't hear anything from inside and there was no response. He tried to make the door give way by pushing on it with his arms, but they were still weak from having hauled him up from the cellar. He unraveled the rope from his leg and wound it around his hands and wrists. He raised his sneakered right foot, placed it on the middle of the side of the door where he knew the latch was, and began to shove it open a little bit at a time to avoid the unnecessary noise of splintering it open with one solid kick. It took about thirty seconds to bust in and the only sounds were the paint cracking, the latch jumping off the wall and clinking on the tiled kitchen floor and the hammer slipping from his lap to the back of the cart.

Kenny pushed the door full open. The dim daylight of the room made his eyes blink and he took a deep breath of the relatively clean, fresh, cool air. He looked around before easing himself out of the dumbwaiter. His legs were stiff and he flexed them as he tied the slack from the rope once around the door. He removed the satchel and the hammer from the cart and wedged the door shut on the ropes. He took some kitchen towels and stuffed the cracks around the door to prevent any light from entering the dumbwaiter shaft so that if anyone did notice that someone had finagled with the basement door and they discovered that the cart was up somewhere instead of down there, they wouldn't be able to tell right away which floor it was on, and they would have to tug on the rope, warning Kenny who would split out the fire exit, alarm or no alarm, and maybe get away. At least, he'd have a chance.

He stretched his cramped muscles for a minute in the kitchen and looked at how filthy his clothes were. "You sure can get dirty playing football," he smiled to himself as he quickly checked out all the rooms in the apartment. Most of the doors were open except the ones for the study which had a desk in it, and the master bedroom, which contained what he had come there for, jewelry.

Kenny found the leather case in the top drawer of the dresser. It wasn't even locked. When he opened it, he was disappointed. There was only one small diamond brooch, a pair of emerald earrings, a ruby ring in a gold setting, some strings of pearls, and lots of silver, platinum, gold bracelets studded with turquoise and other equally inexpensive stones. Not one diamond necklace! The stuff in the case was nothing but small change. Kenny couldn't understand it. The woman whose bedroom he was in was noted for her extravagant jewelry. She couldn't have taken it with her. You don't wear diamonds when you take your kids to a small country chalet in Vermont on a skiing vacation. He started rummaging through all the drawers and closets of the bedroom. He had been in the apartment for five minutes when he discovered the safe embedded in the back wall of a walk-in closet. He looked it over. It was a Diebold box and it was really flush into that wall. He wondered how deep it went and how thick was the plaster-coated cement that held it in place.

It's no big thing to rip a box out of a wall when you're in a house, but in an apartment you've got to be very careful because when you start chipping at the cement, the noise travels down through the wall to the apartment below. In either case, whether it's in a house or an apartment, you never try to pop the door of the safe itself by peeling it or punching it till the pin hits the back of the safe. That takes too much time. The object is to get the box out and take it with you someplace where you can open it at your leisure. You learn things like this when you talk to an experienced burglar for twenty minutes in places like the Raymond Street jail.

Kenny was reluctant to crack the box loose from the wall, but he knew that the big stuff was in there. He could smell the smoke. The trinkets in the leather case were only worth a few hundred at best. Then he remembered the desk. Sometimes people write the combination in a memo pad or something because they have bad memories. They only do this, however, when the numbers of the combination aren't the same as a significant date in their lives such as their birth date or the day they were married. In most instances, this is the case, but Kenny decided to look the desk over anyway.

He picked up his satchel and walked into the study. Only one of the drawers in the desk was locked. The rest were full of paper and pencil insignificance. He pried open the locked drawer which contained a bunch of receipts and bills and a half-filled-in, unsigned application for a new life insurance policy. On it were the dates of birth of the father, mother, and their two children and the day, month, year of the parents' marriage. Kenny put the crowbar which he used to open the drawer back into the satchel and returned to the closet with the paper in his hand.

Most combinations dial to the right for the first number, one full turn to the left for the second number, and to the right for the third number. Kenny tried this sequence of dialing and the vice versa of it, twice for each of the dates listed. None of the codes worked. So he decided that the guy must have a good memory and it had cost

Wisdom six minutes to find it out. He had been inside the apartment for twelve or thirteen minutes.

He threw the paper on the floor and left the bedroom to check what was behind the back wall of the closet. He was in luck. The wall was just a partition for another closet in one of the kids' rooms. He had to work fast. He took some clothes from their hangers and spread them at the base of the wall of the kids' closet to make sure that any chunks of debris would fall soundlessly onto the wooded floor. He didn't have to repeat that when he returned to the safe. The floor of the master bedroom closet was shielded by carpeting.

He dug into his satchel and came up with a long, thick screwdriver and a ballpeen hammer with a hard-rubber head. He began to chip away at the plastered cement around the edges of the box. After a couple of minutes a crack formed near the top right corner. He worked on it and it split the cement along the top and down the right side of the box into more cracks. He angled the driver until it was nearly parallel with the wall and hammered at the loosened cement. In no time he was picking large chunks from around the twelve-inch-square border with his hands and laying them on the rug. He could see that the box was less than six inches deep, and when he had cleared about two to three inches of cement from the top and right side, he laid down his tools and grabbed the top and side with his hands and started tugging at the box with his arms to see if it had a bolted retaining bar in the rear. It didn't and moved easily, crumbling the wall all around it. Soon it was completely free and just sitting on the jagged ridges of the plaster and concrete which had kept it sealed inside that wall for God knows how long.

Kenny removed the football from the satchel to make room for the box. He eased it off its perch and lowered it into the satchel which he had to squeeze tight to close the zipper. The box was about sixty pounds heavy and Wisdom hoped that the bag was able to take the weight without busting at the seams. He was just able to fit the screwdriver in by sliding it underneath the zipper. The football he was going to have to tuck under his arm. The hammer he wanted to keep beneath his sweater in case he ran into any opposition.

He took the diamond, the emerald, and the ruby pieces from the case and wrapped them in a sock and shoved them into his left front pocket. He looked out of the bedroom window and saw that it was still snowing lightly. He had been in the apartment for thirty-one minutes. It was time to leave.

He made sure that he didn't forget anything, took a piss into the soil of a potted plant because he didn't want to flush the toilet or leave any urine floating around in the bowl, and went into the kitchen. He removed the towels, opened the dumbwaiter door, unwound the rope and raised the cart to look down the shaft to see if everything was cool. It seemed to be. He lowered the cart and lifted the load satchel onto it, placed the football on top of the bag, and holding the rope tight with both hands, he finessed himself into the dumbwaiter and resealed the shaft door to the kitchen by using a towel as a wedge.

He lowered himself and his goods quietly but quickly down the dark inner sanctum of the dumbwaiter shaft, letting the towline slip through his gloved hands and keeping track with his right elbow of the number of floors he passed. Four, three, two, one. He stopped. Listened for a moment and when he heard nothing, he slowly continued to the bottom, zero.

Again he listened for some sound of activity. There was none. Even so, he took the hammer from under his sweater and held it in his right hand as he carefully opened the cellar door to the shaft and slid out of the dumbwaiter. He stood still and looked around the basement. The furnace had quieted down and there was no sign of the janitor. He waited for a moment, then he shoved the handle of the hammer into the belt of his pants, took the satchel and football from the cart and placed them on the ground, and closed the door of the dumbwaiter, shutting it tight by pressing against it with his body.

He grabbed the handles of the satchel with his left hand, tucked the football under his left arm, cracked open the service entrance door to the basement, slipped out onto the sidewalk and walked up the block, fondling the football which was now in his right hand.

After a few feet, Kenny realized that he had made a mistake. He should have stolen an overcoat, too. His body was still soaking wet and it was so cold outside that he began to shiver and his nerves caught on and he started trembling. He Saint Vitus danced to the subway as fast as he could, painfully lugging the load and contemptuously clutching the stupid football close to his side. He thought that he was going to rattle to pieces.

He bought a token, went through a turnstile and walked to the end of the station platform. His teeth stopped chattering and his body was able to shake off the chill in stuffy, windless underground and return to its state of perspiration, the beads of sweat rolling down his face, chest, back and underarms. His left arm was stretched with exhaustion and the fingers of his left hand were stiff and numb from hanging on to the sixty-some-pound satchel. He wanted to get rid of the fucking crappy football. He set the bag down and looked around to see if anyone was watching. There weren't many people this two-thirty-early in the afternoon and most of them had their heads buried in newspapers and none of them were near his end of the platform. He threw the ball underhanded far into the unlighted tunnel and onto the tracks. He clocked the crowd again, making sure that no one had spotted him.

The train came and he got on it and returned to South Brooklyn.

It was Friday, December 19, and Kenny Wisdom had just pulled off the first of many successful burglaries. He was delighted with himself but anxious to crack open the box and take out what was in it. He had put a lot of work into the notebook organization of his scheduled plans and he needed to know how worthwhile his beginning effort had been.

The school had recessed for the holidays at midmorning of the previous day after the celebration of a High Mass for the students and a benediction and blessing for their safe return. Kenny's timetable planning called for a theft every day and sometimes two in the same day, up until the last opportunity on Saturday, January 3, 1959. By then everyone would have returned to the city or be on their way back into town and Kenny would have to begin attending classes again, early Monday morning on the fifth. There was no getting around that. He had to show up and continue at the school, no matter how much loot he scored, or someone might get suspicious.

"It's going to be a lotta rough work to keep all the appointments on my tight calendar. Everything has to be precise because I'm cutting it pretty close. And I also have to figure a way to beat that fucking dumbwaiter routine. It's too risky," he thought.

Less than an hour after he had come out of the subway, Kenny had busted open the box at the seams with a five-pound sledge and a chisel on the asphalt ground floor of an abandoned warehouse in his neighborhood. It was dusk and the light wasn't too good, but he could see what he was taking out of the busted box, and what he saw made all the hassling that he went through that day a pleasure. There were two large and exquisite diamond necklaces in separate satin-lined cases. Another velvet-covered case containing diamond bracelets, brooches, earrings, and wedding rings which looked like heirlooms. Some legal papers, wills, policies, passports, an old gold railroad man's watch and chain, books of blank personal checks and $1,700 in cash. "Hot damn!"

Kenny counted the money twice to make sure that the stack of twenties, fifties and hundreds really did add up to $1,700. When he was satisfied that there was no mistake, he folded the money into his back pocket, tore up and burned the pile of papers, and put the three cases of jewelry into his satchel, dumping the contents of the sock into the larger, flat, velvet one. He put a match to the sock and let it flame beside the paper ashes. He hid the broken-up safe in the corner of the building, intending to dispose of it later that night. Then he went home to Dean Street, dropping the gold watch and chain down a sewer. "It isn't worth nothing besides sentiment and it's too dangerous to keep around!" He also stuffed the pair of gloves down into the sewerage.

There was no one home when he got there. His father was still on his way from work and his mother had taken his sister to a pediatrician. He put the tools back into their chest in the hallway closet, stashed the three cases of jewels and all but sixty dollars of the money deep into the center of his mattress, remaking the bed and refolding it to its upright position and wheeling it back to its place against the wall of his parents' bedroom. He tossed the nails which he had pried loose from the basement dumbwaiter shaft door out of the window into a garbage-strewn courtyard, scrubbed the dirt off the cloth satchel in the kitchen with soap, hot water, and a sponge, and put it out on the fire escape to dry.

Then he got a clean set of underwear, a fresh pair of pants, some socks and his wing-tipped shoes, and went into the bathroom, stripped, threw his filthy clothes into the hamper after transferring the sixty dollars to the pocket of the other pants, and took a long, hot shower, washing his sneakers as well as himself.

The rhythm of the hot water beating down against his back and shoulders and his head and neck calmed him down and loosened him up. He relaxed and he felt great. He only had one nagging thought, *"Fuck dumbwaiters!"* Other than that, the sole thing on his mind was the fact that his dream was coming true. Along with the cheerful knowledge of all the homecoming surprises which he was going to engineer for about twenty vacationing Park Avenue swells. He was gassed.

At 8:30, he went out. He glanced up at the kitchen window where his parents were finishing off their mackerel supper with

95

coffee, and up at the fire escape where his sneakers were drying next to his satchel. He was wearing a short black raincoat over a dark brown turtleneck and he nodded with respect as he passed the boardinghouse at 340 Dean Street. He got a large brown paper bag from Scafidi the grocer and hustled over to the empty warehouse. Inside, he checked around for anything that he might have forgotten or which hadn't been completely burned to ashes. When he was satisfied, he put the twisted safe into the bag, walked up to Third Avenue and hailed a cab.

Kenny had asked his father for two dollars to go to a movie and that's what he gave to the cabbie for driving him to the corner of 39th Street and Third Avenue in Brooklyn. He had hit on his father for the deuce because the sixty dollars in his pocket was a secret and he wanted to keep it that way. His family was very suspicious and he'd have to cover that by asking for fifty cents here and a dollar or two there.

He walked down to one of the piers near the Bush Terminal and dropped the bagged box into the water of the Narrows. It was quiet on the waterfront at that time of night. The only noise came from the stamping machines at the American Can Company and the water slapping against the piles. The ferries crossing over to Staten Island from Brooklyn and Manhattan and returning were all that was moving in the harbor. It was peaceful, but the dock he was standing on had been and was the setting for several memorable events and plenty of simple, physical, grunting, routine longshore activity in the daytime.

Kenny Wisdom recalled a notable scene which he had witnessed and which had occurred in this same place when he was eleven years old. The longshoremen who worked this pier had gone on a wildcat strike for something or other, and since the Brooklyn waterfront was controlled by the Anastasia brothers, along with an additional branch of the reputable family of organized crime, Tough Tony Anastasia came down to the dock to enforce a settlement to the dispute. He pushed and shoved and bellowed at the stevedores and told them that he was going to break all their fucking legs if they didn't start unloading the ship. He wasn't successful. Nobody moved. Now don't get me wrong, he wasn't called Tough Tony for nothing. He was a mean, cruel, brutal heavyweight of a goomba who would just as soon have strangled you as look at you, and was reported to have done so to lots of people, even during the course of a meal. But on that day and in those circumstances his approach was all wrong, because longshoremen aren't exactly altar boys themselves, and they knew that as tough as he was, Tony couldn't break all their legs, and even if he did, the ship would still remain unloaded on account of them being in the hospital having their bones set and wrapped in casts so that they'd heal properly.

Therefore, Tough Tony continued shouting his threats and getting nowhere for half an hour. He finally stopped when a black Cadillac Coupe de Ville pulled onto the pier and a bodyguard-chauffeur opened the rear door for his passenger, Albert Anastasia. All the dockworkers immediately turned their backs, faced the opposite direction and stood motionless, staring across the harbor to avoid looking at the man who had just arrived.

Albert Anastasia wasn't outwardly emotional or as rough-and-tumble looking as his brother Tony. He was a cold-blooded, ruthless, logical man whose black-clad presence was terrifying. He waved his brother aside and walked alone toward the semicircle of backs. He stopped a few feet from the middle and stood in the center of the about-faced-longshoremen, and he waited with his gray-gloved hands folded at ease behind his back. There wasn't a sound and nothing moved. There was just a still, dead silence as Albert Anastasia waited. Waited for one of the stevedores to sneak a peek at this man they had all heard and read about, this terrible man who had incorporated murder, this powerful man whose turf they all lived, worked, loved and died on, this intriguing man that they had only seen photos of, and who was flesh and blood standing behind them, granting to any of them a look at the hidden and physical mystery of the man himself, which would put an end to the fables and might offer some clue as to how one little man could control so many.

Albert Anastasia had been patiently waiting for a mere three minutes when the inevitable happened: a young longshoreman glimpsed from beneath the peak of his cap at the infamous figure, and Albert caught his eye and beckoned him with a gesture to "come over here." The young guy was scared, but Albert was smiling and gestured again for him to "come on." None of the other workers turned around for even a look. In fact, most of them shut their eyes.

The stocky youngster walked hesitantly and awkwardly over to Albert Anastasia who linked his arm with the guy's and strolled around the pier and talked with him, making sure that the semicircle of men heard every word that was said. He looked at the stevedore's I.L.W.U. nametag which was pinned on the outside of his peacoat and told him that Michael Sheehan was a nice name and asked him, "Are you a Catholic?"

"Yes, sir."

"No 'sir.' This ain't the army here. It's a brotherhood. We all brothers in the same union, no?"

"Yes."

"You gotta wife? Kids?"

"Yes, two girls."

"The goils, they go to school?"

"No, they're too young. Only two and three."

"Ha, ha. Wha' happened to one?"

"My wife's pregnant. One's on the way."

"Ha, ha, I like you. I like people that have a sense of humor."

"Thank you."

"For what? You live in the neighborhood here?"

"Yes, up on Fourth Avenue."

"You like it there? It's a nice place?"

"It's not bad, but the boiler's on the blink and the owner don't show no interest. And we complained, but . . ."

"What's the address? Maybe I make the owner show interest. I like to help my union brothers."

"Thank you. Thanks a lot. It's 4325 Fourth Avenue."

"Good. Good. I'll see what I can do."

Albert Anastasia shook the guy's hand and told him that he wished his wife had a baby boy this time because there'd always be a place in the union for him when he grew up to be a man like his father.

"See ya 'round, kid," he said after accepting the youngster's many thanks, and then he walked back to his Cadillac and his chauffeur drove it off.

The crowd of longshoremen turned to watch his car move away and Tough Tony waded among them, shouting, "Now back ter woik 'n no more nonsense!" And they did. They went back to work because they knew that if they didn't, Michael Sheehan, his wife, their two girls and their unborn baby would be dead by the morning. The boiler would blow their building at 4325 Fourth Avenue to smithereens or something else would happen. It didn't matter how, they simply would be dead. Albert Anastasia had just told them.

Kenny Wisdom thought about the fried ice which was Albert Anastasia's style and he was contemptuous of the respect that he had for the man without really knowing why. He quit thinking about it, as he walked along the railroad tracks on Second Avenue towards the corner of 42nd Street where he was going to spend some of his money in a bar called Mom's.

It was called Mom's Bar because the men who ran it were the sons of the woman who owned it and they were naturally known as the Mom brothers. There were five brothers, but Jimmy and Joey Mom were the two who really managed the place and maintained it as a going concern. They tended the bar as gentlemen and kept things under control like professionals. They didn't take any shit from anybody. Most of their customers were neighborhood people who worked hard on the waterfront and had been nasty a long time and liked it that way. The other regular patrons came from nearby sections of Brooklyn and did other things for a living. They all had one thing in common, however. They disliked strangers. This dislike gave the store a bucket-of-blood reputation which warned anyone who wasn't already known by, or friendly with, someone in the establishment, to stay away unless his head was made of concrete. Kenny was on a first name basis with the Mom brothers and most of the regulars. He was quiet, polite, and respectful with everyone, but duked when a situation demanded that he handle himself. Nobody cared about his age because he looked old enough, and he never went there without money to spend on more than bottles of beer. He always came alone, relaxed on a stool, drank Cutty Sark until he was mildly juiced, and was glad that he had a place to go where no one knew anyone he didn't want them to know, like his family, and where he could ease the tension of his Park Avenue masquerade among people who would appreciate what he was doing and who unknowingly hardened his motives to keep doing it. The closest most of them ever got to Kenny Wisdom's idea of a suntan was Atlantic City or the Jersey shore or up at Greenwood Lake.

Most of all, Kenny liked to drink at Mom's because they were people just like him. They were happy and joked about their hard knocks. The only trouble was that the world they lived in made it necessary for them to laugh a lot. He knew this and wanted to live in a world where you didn't have to laugh anymore if you didn't want to. Not a cry-in-your-beer world either, a world all your own with no time clocks to punch and no one to answer to but yourself.

The bar itself was the only non-Spanish joint in the area. It was an oasis on Second Avenue. Besides the quality of the people, there was nothing special about it. Just a regular bar with a back room full of formica tables, and a jukebox which had everything from Buddy Holly and the Crickets to Ezio Pinza's recording of "La donna è mobile." There was no telephone. Detectives had come in one afternoon and ripped the pay phone out of the booth because, they said, some schmuck had left a few betting slips lying around on the floor of the bathroom, and if it ever happened again they were going to close the place down. It didn't, and neither did the guy who dropped the slips of paper. He was told to go play someplace else. The Mom brothers ran a hard-drinking bar for family and not a playground for morons.

Kenny walked inside, exchanged "How ya doin's?" with Jimmy Mom, ordered a double Cutty over ice and said hello to a few of the guys he knew. It was still early but it was Friday night and everyone was already into the partying mood. Pineapple, a dock worker from Hawaii, was lushed and nursing a beer at a table. Matty was sitting alone next to his German shepherd, rolling cellophane from a cigarette pack in his fingers and drinking shots of rye. Matty had been a professional lightweight fighter until he was blinded in the ring when he was in his early twenties. And now he was in his fifties and the only blind shylock in the world. He didn't depend on anybody. He was his own muscle. When someone would get fresh with him or tease his dog or something, Matty would tell the guy that he was a nice fella and pat him on the shoulder a few times to figure out the location of his jaw and coldcock him with a short right hand. Nobody fucked with him.

Mikey Mom was telling his brother Joey about some basketball player who lost a game for the New York Knicks the night before, and Doc Brown, who told everybody that he was going to medical school to become a doctor, was trying to butt into the conversation and kept asking them who they were talking about until Mikey finally turned to him and shouted, "Who? Who? Who? What are you, a fuckin' owl? Who! Who!" The Doc turned red and everyone laughed and continued juicing and was happy that it was the weekend.

Kenny was enjoying himself, shooting the shit with the guys who only had nicknames, and they all bought each other rounds, and by eleven thirty he had half a bag on and decided that it was time to leave because he had a lot of work to do tomorrow. But just as he was about to go, they came in. Seven or eight college weight lifters who wanted to test the water at Mom's. They were all big, bulky, two-hundred-pounders who hung out in some academic tavern in the Bay Ridge section of Brooklyn. They stomped into the back room, took off their jackets to show everyone the muscles that were clearly visible in their skin-tight T-shirts, and asked for trouble by demanding waiter service.

No one was impressed or amused, just annoyed. Annoyed that after having hassled all week to scrape together a little extra dough — by working overtime or through some larcenous activity — to have a brief good time on Friday night, Saturday and Sunday, they were going to have to hassle with some allowanced punks to spend it. The women were more annoyed, because they only got a few hours a week away from their stoves and kids to go out with their old men like before they were married, and as usual someone was trying to spoil those few moments. These someones weren't even a part of their own crowd and this was their bar. It was for them, for people who knew each other and worked and gambled and lived and did numbers together. It was their neighborhood bar! The only bar that remained neighborhood after the spics flooded in and took over everything else. It was the only place they had left to themselves. It was Second Avenue and they were Second Avenue and everybody from somewhere else should stay somewhere else. Stay where they belonged and not come to bother, because they've got enough bother among themselves and with the spic dynasty, who wanted to take over but could only take it over their dead bodies. Now some Bay Ridge bunch was trying to move in and disturb their privacy. They had gotten the Moms' off-limits message like everyone else had in Brooklyn. They still didn't stay away, so now they were going to get got.

The women moved into the luncheonette — which was connected to the barroom but only open during the day for ham 'n egg breakfasts and meatball sandwich lunches for the men who worked in the factories and warehouses and piers on this stretch of the waterfront. The women did this after Jimmy Mom loudly notified the collegiate slobs in the back that if they wanted a waiter they could go to the Waldorf Astoria. Nobody had to get ready when one of the muscled shirts bounded up to the front. Everybody was always ready.

Muscle Boy leaned over the bar, stuck his face out and ordered two pitchers of beer. Jimmy replied that they only sold bottled beer and the punk said, "Okay, give us eight bottles of your fucking beer!" Jimmy asked to see his draft card and Mr. America flexed his twenty-inch bicep of baby fat, pointed to it and said that was his draft card. Jimmy Mom showed him his reserve-the-right-to-refuse-service-to-anyone sign. But he only showed it to him for a moment because it was his fist. A fist that was as thick and as wide and as hard and as flat as a brick, which Jimmy flashed for a split second before he crashed it against the wise ass's mouth, knocking him over to the far wall, where he slumped to the floor and began unconsciously choking on his caved-in teeth.

The other muscles came running up to the front of the bar and were hit with everything but full bottles of whiskey. Feet, fists, bar stools, softball bats, clubs, ashtrays. Kenny sidestepped one guy who was trying to run out the front door and split his forehead open with a capped bottle of beer. "You forgot your jacket! You can't leave without your jacket!" he yelled at the guy while he used his head for a soccer ball.

The melee that those muscle-bound punks started, and which they were never going to be able to forget because of the existence of mirrors, ended in less than three minutes. The denouement occurred immediately afterwards, when they were dragged outside and dumped in the street like so many limp pillows of lard, and left to crawl back to the singles bar of their Bay Ridge campus.

Kenny returned with everyone else to continue the pleasure at Mom's. It had been a long hard day for him and the scuffle had blown his high and made him weary. He needed another couple of drinks to cool him out before he went home.

A young, curly-yellow-haired longshoreman whose name was Johnny Be Good made a pile out of the dumbbell boys' jackets and threw them out the back door and into the gutter. The women appeared from the sanctuary of the luncheonette and were still pissed off at having their night out so rudely interrupted, however briefly. The men turned their mood from anger into laughter and were telling each other, "Did you see the look on that one prick's face when I . . ." anecdotes about the scene that had just gone down. And the party went on happily after.

Kenny said so long to everybody and left about one o'clock, walked up to Third Avenue and caught a cab back to Dean Street. Once upstairs, he stripped off his clothes and flopped down on the cot which his mother had unfolded for him in the living room, as she did every night. He could feel the goods that he had stashed in the center of the mattress, and their presence lulled him into the deep sleep of a tired but satisfied man who had a schedule to complete and a dream to fulfill in the days ahead.

He awoke at nine o'clock, fully rested and anxious to get going, but he stayed in bed until his father went out for his Saturday morning stroll and his mother took his sister with her to shop for groceries. He put on a turtleneck under one of his going-to-school suits and stepped into his pair of cordovans. He filled his satchel with the jewelry and the tools that he had used the day before, put the money in his pocket, grabbed his overcoat, and cabbed it to 59th Street and Fifth Avenue in Manhattan.

There he checked into the Ritz Hotel. He told the desk clerk that his name was Edward Walsh and that he wanted a room with a private bath and that he'd be staying for about two weeks. He paid for a week in advance when he noticed the clerk eyeing the satchel as his only piece of luggage. A bellboy showed him to his room, and after he left with a dollar tip Kenny double-locked the door from the inside and went to work stashing his goods. He took a razor blade from the satchel, flipped over the mattress of the three-quarter bed and sliced a small slit in the center of it and pulled out some of the kapok stuffing. He carefully fitted the three cases of jewelry into the space and replaced the stuffing to cover them up and mask the open slit. He pulled the mattress back onto the springs and remade the bed.

In the bathroom he cut a full-length, foot-wide strip from the end of the plastic shower curtain, wrapped his tools in it and placed them inside the water tank of the toilet bowl. He flushed the razor blade down the toilet and waited to see if the tank would refill itself properly and without any interference from his improvised tool kit. When it did, he tossed the empty satchel into a closet, unlocked the door and left the hotel without leaving the key at the desk.

As he walked up Fifth Avenue, he rechecked the details of the day's score, which he had copied onto a piece of paper from his notebook. It was a nighttime job because the custodian-janitor of the Park Avenue building was a juicehead and was usually stone drunk by 9 P.M. or out drinking in a Lexington Avenue saloon on a Saturday night. There was a private elevator leading to the apartment and Kenny had no intention of using a dumbwaiter for this one. He figured on getting the key that unlocked that elevator and made it move from the service area of the basement and up into the apartment. That key and others like it were somewhere inside the janitor's digs in the cellar. Kenny was going to find it.

He put the piece of paper into the pocket of his overcoat and entered Browning King's Fifth Avenue men's clothing and apparel store. He bought a blue blazer and gray flannel slacks, a green woolen sports jacket, a dark brown leather three-quarter-length car coat, several pairs of black pigskin gloves, four camel's-hair turtlenecks, some underwear and socks, two pairs of charcoal-brown widewale corduroy trousers, one pair of desert boots with crepe soles, and a black leather Gladstone bag.

No alterations were necessary for any of the clothing he had purchased. The sales slip was made out in the name of Stephen Rogers and he paid for everything in cash. He returned to his room at the Ritz and ripped the labels out of all the stuff and burned them in an ashtray along with the sales slip. The cardboard boxes he tore into little pieces and flushed them down the toilet in small portions. He disposed of the ashes from the tags in the same manner.

He put everything in the closet, picked up the telephone, and asked the bellboy to bring him all the day's newspapers and some shaving gear and after-lotion. When the bellboy arrived with the things, Kenny realized that he forgot to buy a watch. The guy told him it was 12:30 and left after he was paid for the items and tipped for his service.

Kenny took a long hot bath and scanned the papers to see if anyone had changed their plans due to a death in the family or some other account. Apparently no one had, but there was a news story that set Wisdom to thinking about things which he seldom remembered. It appeared under a MURDERER GETS LIFE headline on the fourth page of the New York *Daily Mirror*. The murderer was Willie Pondexteur and he had been sentenced to life imprisonment for the double slaying of two rival gang members during the rumble in Bedford-Stuyvesant six months before. He was going to do that life term in the penitentiary at Dannemora and Kenny made a mental note to write him a short letter and mail him some money. "The diddy-boppin' fool!" he thought, and shook his head sad.

Bathed, shaved, and dressed in his new shoes, trousers, sweater, and coat, Kenny walked over to 42nd Street and bought a cheap watch. He boarded the Lexington Avenue subway at Grand Central Station for his ride uptown. There were lots of empty seats on the train but he had to stand because he was carrying a long screwdriver, a hammer, and a crowbar in the waistband of his corduroys, which prevented his bending to sit. The gloves were skin-tight and he flexed his fingers to loosen them up a bit.

It was five o'clock and he had about eleven hundred left in his pocket when he got to the building on 88th Street and Park Avenue. He was in luck. The janitor was just coming out of the back entrance to the place. He was wearing a clean set of khaki work clothes and walking towards Lexington Avenue. Kenny followed him on the other side of the street and watched him enter the working-class gin mill where he did his social drinking. Kenny accurately concluded that the guy was calling it a day and was going to hang around the saloon for a few hours and jawbone with his cronies. He wanted to blow the janitor a kiss but decided that it was no time for any Damon Runyon sentiment. He did appeal to Saint Patrick, however, and asked him to ensure that the fellow had a long and pleasant evening and enough money to drink himself into a proper stupor.

He quickly returned to the rear of the building and entered through the service entrance. He checked out the basement area to make sure no one else was there. There was no sign or sound of anyone. The only thing that he'd have to watch out for were kids making deliveries from the neighborhood liquor stores and food markets. He wanted to leave the service door unlocked, so that nobody would go around to the front and bother the doorman and possibly make him suspicious. Kenny knocked on the door of the janitor's basement flat and when there was no answer he tried the door. It was locked, but he opened it easily with a plastic-coated holy picture of the Sacred Heart, the kind that is given to the mourners at a Catholic wake by a priest or a friend of the family. Kenny found a couple of them outside a funeral home in Brooklyn and always carried them with him for use in such situations. He slipped inside and flicked on the overhead light in the small foyer of the two-room flat. The keys that he was looking for were hanging neatly on a rack of hooks inside a closet door in the living room next to the television, and he found them right away. He removed the one he wanted, closed the closet door, turned off the light and left.

He had already telephoned the apartment from the subway station and no one answered, so he didn't hesitate in pushing the button for the penthouse elevator and unlocking the door when it arrived. There were only three buttons in the elevator: up, down and emergency. He pressed "up" and relished the convenience in comparison to the crudeness of the dumbwaiter as he rode in style to the penthouse. Once upstairs, he fine-tooth-combed each of the rooms, turning the lights on and off as he went in and out of each one. There were no valuables lying loosely around anyplace in the apartment, but he located the safe where you usually locate safes, on the back wall of a bedroom closet. It was a small box and with only the light on in the closet and the door closed, he worked on getting it out with the screwdriver. He didn't need to use the hammer because the plaster and cement cracked and crumbled easily. In little more than twenty minutes it was free and he took it out, placed it in a Bloomingdale's shopping bag that was on the closet floor, covered it with an old raincoat from one of the hangers, and left the same way he had come, returning the key to the rack in the janitor's flat on his way out. On Fifth Avenue he hailed a taxi and went to Brooklyn. He arrived at the empty warehouse before seven o'clock and sledgehammered the box open. It contained the customary assortment of legal papers, $600 in fifties, an opal bracelet, two pairs of good-sized diamond earrings, a small emerald brooch, an old-fashioned gold locket adorned with diamonds, and a small silver Spanish comb studded with diamonds and rubies which were set into a mother-of-pearl inlay. Kenny examined it for a moment with the flashlight that he had hidden in a hole in the floor beside the sledgehammer and chisel. It looked very expensive, but it sure was ugly. Then he put the money and the jewelry into his pockets, the tools back where they were stored, the stashed box into the shopping bag and, in order to avoid the possibility of attracting any attention with the flames of a small fire, he tore the stack of papers into little bits and tossed them into the shopping bag, placing the raincoat on top. He checked out the immediate area to see if he had taken care of everything, and when he was satisfied he picked up the bag and walked to the west end of Dean Street, crossed Boerum Place onto Amity Street, continued through Van Voorhees Park under the Brooklyn-Queens Expressway and back onto Amity Street until he arrived at its dead end between piers seven and eight. There he dropped the weighted sack into the East River, trusting that the undercurrent would scatter the sunken evidence around the Buttermilk Channel and perhaps someday float the raincoat over to the shores of Governors Island, hopefully causing consternation among the dim-witted United States Coast Guard stationed at Fort Jay.

Kenny went back to Manhattan, phoned his parents, and told them that he was going to an all-night party with some friends and he wouldn't be home until late Sunday afternoon. "What friends?" asked his mother. "My friends," answered her son before he hung up. He bought a bottle of Cutty Sark and returned to the Ritz and stashed the jewelry with the rest of his goods in the mattress and replaced the tools in the toilet's water tank.

He went over to Downey's Steak House on Eighth Avenue and had a few drinks and a big meal. There was nothing exceptional playing at any of the first-run Broadway movie theaters, so he settled for a film at a dollar house on 42nd Street. It was *Detective Story* with Kirk Douglas, William Bendix, and the actor who had portrayed the revolutionary theorist in *Viva Zapata*, Joseph Wiseman, playing a four-time-loser dope fiend. He carried the film, outclassing the other actors. Kenny liked to watch professionals who were good at what they did and Joseph Wiseman never let him down as an actor.

On Sunday morning, Kenny broke into a janitor's basement flat while the guy was at mass and entered and cleaned out another luxurious apartment. He followed the same warehouse-East River routine of the day before, a routine he was going to repeat a dozen times in less than two weeks. He returned to his hotel room, stashed everything in its proper place, changed back into his school clothes and shoes, and hung a Do Not Disturb sign on the doorknob before he left. He walked over to Times Square with more than two thousand dollars in his pocket, carrying his now-empty satchel, and bought all the New York Sunday newspapers. Then he took a train back to Brooklyn because he wanted to read through the thirty pounds of newsprint before he got home, but by the time he arrived at his stop on Pacific Street, he hadn't even unfolded the Sunday *Times*. He dropped it into his satchel, left the others on the seat, and went to have a normal late-Sunday dinner with his family, wondering what he should buy them for Christmas.

Early the following morning, Kenny returned to the Ritz Hotel, changed his clothes, removed the jewelry from the mattress, and took it to a branch of the Chemical Bank on the corner of 42nd Street and Fifth Avenue, where he rented a safe-deposit box under the alias of Edward Armstrong O'Neill. In answering one of the questions of the application form, he named Thomas E. Henneberry, who was the head of the New York province of the Society of Jesus, as his beneficiary in case of death. He deposited all the jewelry and most of the money in the box, keeping five hundred dollars in his pocket. During the entire operation Kenny never once removed his gloves because he wanted all the fingerprints on the box to be someone else's. He thought he was being shrewd but actually he was only being melodramatic. The handwriting on the application form was clearer evidence of his presence than any finger dabs.

By January 1, 1959, the day that Fidel Castro's forces overthrew the Fulgencio Battista regime and the Cuban people were sacking the casinos of Havana, Kenny Wisdom had successfully burglarized thirteen locations, and unsuccessfully attempted four more with only one insignificant close call. He had about nine grand and five cases fat with jewelry in his safe-deposit box at the Chemical Bank. The bottom of the East River was cluttered with the leftover debris from his two-week assault on Park Avenue and he had bought his father a tie, his mother some flowers, and his sister a Mickey Mouse watch for Christmas because he didn't want to cause any suspicion. He did what he set out to do and he adhered strictly to his schedule of plans.

Now he was lying on his bed in his room at the Ritz and he was satisfied and tired. "Enough was enough," he said to himself, and he got drunk and fell asleep on Cutty Sark.

In the morning he awoke with a hangover, and went out for something to eat. It was a Friday, but hardly anyone was on the street and almost everything was closed. He walked up to Broadway, bought the newspapers, and had breakfast in Toffenetti's. The Russians had stolen the headlines from the Cubans by putting the first manmade planet into the solar system and they called it "Lunik." Kenny was exhausted and it was cold but his headache was gone and the noon sun was blinking through the clouds and he wanted to walk. To walk to nowhere in particular and for no special reason other than to take the air. He was coming down from the high he had maintained for over a month. His nerves were frayed by the tension, the anticipation, the apprehension, the anxiety, the overall excitement of his dangerous two-week burglary run. He had carried out most of the possibilities on his notebook list and it had worn him out. His vacation had been a vocation and he had worked hard at it and he had learned a lot. The most important thing he learned was to recognize when to quit for a while, to give it a rest, to take a breather. That time came when he ceased to be desperate and began to get greedy: when the jobs started to become routine and his alertness to detail careless and he had to remind himself that he wasn't exactly taking candy from a baby but doing things they called felonies and put you in prison for.

As he walked along Broadway towards Central Park, he thought about those people whose apartments he had entered and whose stuff he had taken, and he gleefully imagined the expressions on their faces when they returned from their holidays and found that the security of their sheltered dominions had actually been violated by someone who wanted what they had and took it! Kenny got a kick out of that and he hoped it blew their minds and made them crazy. He didn't like those people because . . . Just because, that's all! Especially the ones with two last names, whose people had come over on the *Mayflower* or something and whose English Protestant ethic and ancestral background gave them inherited money and a patronizing attitude toward people like him. They got a real good education where they learned how to steal legitimately from everybody, more and better than any of the great hard-earning crooks in the country, who at least worked for a living and simply accepted the possibility of punishment as a hazard of their occupation. The highfaluters robbed people blind and never got caught because they and their kind made the rules — and if you make the rules you don't have to break any, you just change them when they interfere with your larceny.

"Fuck them!" Kenny muttered, and wished they would get heart attacks when they saw the gaping holes in the walls of their closets.

All of a sudden Kenny stopped walking and his body surged with energy, as he realized what was going to happen when those people did get back from wherever they had gone. Yes, they were going to be flabbergasted and raise hell, but they were also going to dial their telephones and tell the operator to connect them with the police department. After the detectives from the local precinct had received enough one-after-another calls and surveyed the damage that had been inflicted to the property of their protectorate, they'd contact police headquarters and ask for the assistance of none other than Inspector Raymond Maguire and his legendary Safe and Loft Squad which was probably the best team of professional investigators in America and definitely the only uncorruptible segment of New York City's police force. The inspector and his men were relentless; they captured the top burglars in the business and they couldn't be bought off. Kenny knew he had a few loose ends to take care of before the heat was turned on by all those phone calls.

He went back to the Ritz, changed back into his Brooks Brothers' outfit, packed the tools and the clothes that he bought at Browning King's into the Gladstone bag, made sure that he hadn't missed something in the room, checked out of the hotel, deposited the Gladstone in the baggage room of Grand Central Station, and returned to Dean Street in a taxi, where he burned the only physical evidence that could link him to the scenes of the burglaries — the itemized notebook. The baggage claim check and the safe-deposit box key, he stashed in the mattress of his folding bed along with five hundred dollars in cash.

He spent the weekend at home with his parents, playing with the Smith-Corona portable typewriter they gave him for Christmas, and on Monday morning he rode the train to school with two dollars in his pocket, just as usual.

Kenny Wisdom's uncle was a detective in the homicide bureau of Brooklyn police headquarters and had pulled Kenny's rap sheet from the local, state and federal files as soon as he matriculated at the Private Preparatory School for Boys in September. His mug shots, arrest record and fingerprints destroyed, Kenny was therefore never considered a suspect in any of the cases by the Manhattan detectives. Since he was so meticulous in his modus operandi on each of the jobs, the Safe and Loft Squad was sure that they were looking for an experienced professional and definitely not some kid with a knack for burglary.

Several old-timers were picked up during the first weeks of the investigation and the tabloids were full of the matter. They speculated that another Matinee Mob had been organized in the city and suggested the possibility of a connection between the recent series of burglaries and the quarter-million-dollar Arthur Godfrey caper. At least one columnist wanted to know if Raffles was really only a character in a play.

Within a month all the hoopla died down and Kenny continued to attend school regularly, maintain a B average and keep up his straight front. But by spring, he felt that it was cool enough for him to modestly spend some of the money he had acquired. Every weekend he'd get the Gladstone bag out of Grand Central Station, rent a room in a different midtown hotel, and go to the Garden for the Friday night fights. He liked boxing and the skill it required of the two men who were together inside a ring to prove to each other that one of them was better. It was a business like any other business, the only difference was that the blood showed. Kenny would always sit at ringside and he would usually bring a chick with him, because for a regular Friday night main event, a woman escorted by a man didn't have to purchase a ticket, just pay the tax on it. So Kenny would get two ringside seats for the price of one. Of course he never told the chicks that he only paid twenty-eight cents tax for their ticket, and since none of them had ever been to the fights before, they all thought Kenny was a very generous guy and they would show their appreciation for the thrilling ringside experience in whichever hotel his bed was in that night.

From the get-go, Birdland became one of his favorite haunts. He always went to the 52nd Street club alone. He'd pay two dollars to the cashier at the bottom of the stairs after hassling with a midget-spade about his proof of age, and stand at the bar or sit in the gallery and drink Cutty Sark while watching and listening to musicians like Bobby Timmons, Cannonball and Nat Adderly, Charles Mingus, Stan Getz, Jackie McClean, Miles Davis, Dizzy Gillespie, James Moody, Herbie Mann, Philly Jo Jones, Leroy Vinnegar, and Horace Silver, whose piece "Senor Blues" was a melody which Kenny considered as a theme along with "Filthy McNasty."

Between sets, Kenny would hang around the bar and get acquainted with some of the folks, telling them his name was Eddie. He got friendly with a few people and with one dude in particular, a middle-aged jazz aficionado from Holland who owned a jewelry store in Brooklyn and had a display case in the Diamond Exchange in Manhattan. Kenny told the guy that his grandmother had died and left him her wedding ring, which he wanted to get appraised, and if it was worth anything, possibly sell to cover the cost of his education. The jeweler gave him his card and invited him to drop into his Brooklyn shop anytime.

Kenny knew he was taking a risk, but he had no idea how much the jewels in his safe-deposit box were worth and he didn't want to sell the whole haul to a fence for a fraction of its value, even though that was less dangerous. He wanted to eliminate the fence as middleman and deal directly with the bent jewelers themselves, intending to get rid of the stuff piece by piece, rather than in one lump. He figured this would get him a better price for the goods. He figured right but he also figured wrong.

Instead of going to school one day, Kenny went to the Chemical Bank and took somebody's grandmother's wedding ring (at least it looked like somebody's grandmother's wedding ring) out of one of the cases in his safe-deposit box and brought it to the Dutchman in his jewelry shop in Brooklyn. The guy put a jeweler's glass to his eye and examined the band of diamonds for about thirty seconds.

When he was finished he said, "I'll give you seven hundred dollars for it." Kenny ask him if it wasn't worth more and the jeweler replied, "Sure it's worth more but I'll give you seven hundred for

the stones. The setting I can't use, you understand." Kenny understood and took the money. As he was leaving, the Dutchman told
him that he would buy anything else that his grandmother might
have left him. It was the beginning of a mutually profitable relationship which lasted until Kenny had exchanged all of his merchandise for nearly forty thousand dollars.

During these business transactions, Kenny would talk to the
Dutchman about Europe and the man gave him some addresses of
people in Rotterdam and Paris who, he said, would be most oblig-
ing "to you, Eddie, if you mention my name when you have something which you inherited and wish to sell."

Kenny didn't know it at the time, but those addresses were going
to come in handy sooner than he expected because he was in trouble, real trouble, and not with the law, but with men who were
beyond the law.

You see, the gentleman who ran the fencing operation in that
section of Brooklyn where the Dutchman had his store, had picked
up on the fact that somebody was bypassing him and his family and
was dealing directly with one of his customers. His name was Syracuse Frankie on account of his being born in Syracuse, Sicily, and he
was a very mean and impatient man who had no respect for free
enterprise, especially when some cocksucker was freely enterprising
in his territory. He was a bad motherfucker and it didn't take him
long to find out that the person who the Dutchman said he knew
only as Eddie, was really a fifteen-year-old "son-uva-beetch" named
Kenny Wisdom. The word went out right away to find him.

Fortunately, Kenny got a phone call from a friend on that Saturday morning when Syracuse and his people discovered that he was
"Eddie," and he was told that he should go and bury himself someplace because Frankie Syracuse planned to use him for sauce on his
spaghetti.

There was nobody home but even if there had been he wouldn't
have hesitated. He snatched the baggage check, the safe-deposit box
key, a few hundred dollars, and the passport he had acquired during
the previous month from their stash in his mattress, and ran out of
the house and smack into Joey Antonucci, who had come over to
show Kenny his new car.

"Show me!" said Kenny. "Show me how fast it can drive to Manhattan!" Kenny stayed in a hotel in the city that weekend. On Monday he collected his money from the safe-deposit box and booked
passage on the S.S. *Nieuw Amsterdam* for Holland. As they had

arranged, his good friend Joey Antonucci picked him up and drove him over to the pier in Hoboken in his brand-new car for which he had bought a license to drive.

Kenny didn't have time to buy any new clothes, so he played it like a student and boarded the ship in a schoolboy crewneck sweater, carrying the last New York daily newspapers he was going to see for a long time. Joey followed him up the gangplank with the Gladstone bag full of rumpled clothes which were stuffed with money. Kenny had thrown away the set of tools weeks before.

When it came time for all visitors to disembark, Joey and Kenny embraced and said goodbye. Joey had never asked Kenny what his reasons were for leaving in such a hurry. Joey didn't talk to friends that way, he just did what he could do for them. Joey Antonucci was lovely.

It was the first time Kenny had ever been out of the city of New York, and as the tugboats guided the ship through the Narrows and into the Atlantic Ocean, he watched Brooklyn fade into the blanket of Manhattan's smog and was glad to be leaving. He had sent his parents a telegram from a Western Union office that morning, informing them that he had run away with a rich young girl to Phoenix, Arizona, where they planned to get married because they loved each other very much. "Love and please don't worry. Your son, Kenneth."

He decided against taking a plane to Europe because he didn't like the idea of arriving in an unknown place that quickly. The cruise would give him time to adjust himself and find out something about all those countries that he had neither heard nor read much about. It would also give him time to figure out a way to get all his cash through customs.

When the coastline of America became a thin bump on the horizon, Kenny, using information he had acquired from a ship's third engineer who used to drink at Mom's, approached the purser and told him he was dissatisfied with his tourist class accommodations and, flashing a fifty-dollar bill, inquired about any possible vacancies in first class. The purser took the fifty and assigned him to an unbooked cabin on the main deck and had a steward smoothly affect the transfer.

Kenny rang for the steward and gave him his wrinkled sports jackets, slacks, sweaters and blue silk suit, and told him to have them cleaned and pressed as soon as possible. He also ordered a bucket of ice, a bottle of Cutty Sark, a carton of Chesterfield regular, and something to eat. He put five grand in his trouser pockets and distributed the five hundred fifty- and hundred-dollar bills inside the lining of his bag, as evenly as he could. He phoned the shopping center on the promenade deck and asked them to send six white shirts and some underwear and socks to his stateroom, giving them the proper sizes.

Then he relaxed on a chaise longue and read the newspapers. They were full of headline stories about some kid called the Cape Man and another called the Umbrella Man, who allegedly had killed a pair of rival gang members in a rumble in a Hell's Kitchen playground during the night. Kenny remembered with anger at himself that he had forgotten to send Willie Pondexteur some dough up at Dannemora penitentiary.

The S.S. *Nieuw Amsterdam* was a well-run ship and the voyage was comfortable and enjoyable. Kenny spent several hours reading tourist information books about the countries of Europe, concentrating on France and Italy, the Riviera and Sicily. The rest of the time he passed with a gorgeous young model who was nineteen and whose name was Bunny Ranier. She was going to spend the summer in London with her father, who managed the American Express office in that city. When asked, Kenny told her he was twenty-two, a graduate of Stanford's School of Dramatic Arts and that he planned to travel throughout Europe studying the various techniques of the New Wave cinematographers with the hope of being able to work with one of them on a film project. (He had known a girl in New York whose brother went to Stanford, so he knew that it was in a place called Palo Alto, California, and he had read an article in some magazine like *Esquire* about these New Wave film directors and he remembered enough facts and names to be able to cover his story.)

Bunny was a gift. Kenny dined with her, drank with her, swam with her, Ping-Ponged with her, laughed with her, slept with her, and everything else that two people on a boat can do together, he did with her. When her beautifully erect, blond-haired body disembarked at Southampton, Kenny Wisdom meant every word he said in his goodbye to Bunny Ranier.

Immigration and baggage inspection took place between Southampton and Rotterdam, the authorities having boarded the ship at Southampton. Everything went smoothly because Kenny fashioned a money belt out of a sleeve of one of his white shirts and it fit comfortably tight around his waist. He also bought an air ticket to

Paris at the purser's office. He only intended to stay a few hours in Rotterdam, just long enough to get briefly acquainted with the town. He bought a street map before leaving the pier and took a taxi to the street of the only address in Rotterdam that the Dutchman in Brooklyn had given him. Looking out the window of the taxi, he expected to see everyone wearing wooden shoes and full colorful skirts with white bonnets on their heads. They weren't, and he felt strange. He was a foreigner and he didn't like it. He couldn't even speak with the cab driver, the way he spoke to cab drivers in New York. The guy only knew a few words in English like where to, please, thank you, and some numbers. He gave the driver a dollar when they arrived and he wouldn't accept any change.

He walked along the street to the shop listening to the alien guttural sounds of people talking to each another. It was scary, this being a foreigner business. It made you feel more alone than you really were. He went into the small jewelry store and responded to the English-speaking owner's "Can I help you?" inquiry with a pleasant "No" and a short statement to the effect that he simply wanted to browse around. He wanted to check the place out without letting the guy know who he was. He just wanted to satisfy himself that the shop was there and would be whenever he needed it. Only one person from his neighborhood knew he had gone to Europe and he wanted to keep it that way. After a few minutes he spoke with the jeweler and asked him if he was indeed the owner, and when the man replied that he was, Kenny looked carefully at his face so that he would be able to recognize him again when the time came. Then he said that the man was fortunate to have such a nice shop, goodbye, and he left.

Kenny had a sandwich and a few beers in a café, but he was still unnerved by the feeling that he was different from everyone except the dumb tourists with their fingers pointing at everything. He stood out too much. The town was too small to blend into. He was getting paranoid and sensed that everybody was looking at him. He didn't like it. He didn't like it double because of the money he had wrapped around his waist. He went to the airport and got on the first plane he had ever been on in his life and flew to Paris. At least it was a big city and maybe it would be easier to go unnoticed there until he could get his bearings and the language down.

It was midafternoon of the second Tuesday in May 1959 when Kenny landed at the airport of the city he had heard so many songs about and seen so many movies of, but none of those films prepared him for the scene which confronted him as he walked through Orly airport. He couldn't believe it. Everywhere he looked there were a pair of gendarmes standing by entrances and exits and around ticket counters. One of each pair had a submachine gun, a Sten gun, or a burp gun slung loosely over his shoulder, ready for some kind of action. People were hovering over transistor radios in little groups all around the place. Kenny was very nervous and wondered, "What the fuck is going on here?"

He went into a bar to get a drink and it was packed solid with people who were all staring at the television set in the upper corner of a far wall. Everyone was silent as they watched and listened to the face on the tube. When the face on the screen finished moving his mouth, Kenny asked the English-speaking barman who it was and what it was all about. The guy told him it was Michel Debré, the French premier, making a nationwide address to mark the first anniversary of the May 13, 1958, French putdown of the uprising in Algeria and that he had made clear his intention to maintain and affirm French permanence in Algeria.

"What about the cops? The police? Lee gentarms?" Kenny asked.

"Oh, les gendarmes, les flics. They are for Kennedy," replied the barman.

"Kennedy who?"

"Your Kennedy."

Needless to say, Wisdom was very confused and he had a straight double shot of Black and White to calm his anxiety and to keep him from screaming something like, *"Let me the fuck outta here!"*

Shortly afterwards, he took the wildest cab ride ever to a small hotel on the Boulevard Raspail. Once inside and behind the closed door of his room, he began to relax until he saw the small porcelain bowl with a waterspout in the middle which he thought was the Parisian version of a bathtub, and he became convinced that everybody in Paris was out of their fucking minds. Just as Kenny plopped down on the bed to consider his situation, there was a loud explosion outside. He jumped up and ran over to the window which he almost fell through because the sill was only ankle high. People were running every which way in the streets below him. Bunches of cops were rushing in the opposite direction of most of the people, and every other one of them was holding an unslung submachine gun with both hands tightly at hip level. There were some rat-tat-tat, rat-tat-tat bursts farther down the street and he opened the window to have a look. Some of the cops were firing into the air to scatter the crowd that was forming near a small smoking clump of rubble where the explosion had obviously occurred.

They were successful in dispersing the growing mob, but rather unsuccessful in firing their automatic weapons harmlessly into the thin air. Several rounds of their deadly ammunition fell terrifyingly short of the sky and were actually ricocheting off the outer walls of the upper floors of the taller buildings in the vicinity and going god knows where. When Kenny realized that the *ZING! ZING!!* sounds he was periodically hearing, and the intermittent appearance of little puffs on concrete dust he was seeing on the buildings across the boulevard were the effects of low-flying-at-random bullets, he concluded that sticking one's head out of a window for an insight into insanity was a very dumb move and he hit the floor and crawled away from the giant window to the bathroom where he sat on the rim of the tiny tub between the sink and the toilet and waited for it to quiet down outside. He tried to remember whether Algeria was a country in Africa, the Mideast, or an island off the coast of France. And Kennedy? "What was he doing over here? I thought he was trying to get to be President. I don't know. I don't know. What the fuck's goin' on around here, anyway?"

Kenny didn't leave the hotel that night because he was afraid the cops might stop and frisk him and find the money. He couldn't stash the money anywhere in his room because the door was about as secure as a candy bar wrapper, and he had worked too hard for the forty grand to leave it lying around in a mattress for some penny-ante thief to find. So he lay on his bed thinking that he had to settle in one of the countries bordering the Mediterranean and learn the language and the mores of the people there before he'd be relaxed and unafraid enough to sit still for a suntan. But where? He kept searching for an idea until he eventually fell asleep.

The next day he walked up to the Boulevard St-Germain and had five cups of coffee and a dozen croissants with butter at a café called the Navy Bar. He went for a stroll along the Quai D'Orsay and marveled at the beauty of the river Seine and the grandness of Notre Dame. He could see the Eiffel Tower stretching above the city in back of him. The bookstalls and the out-front activity of the merchants selling their wares in the streets were just like he'd seen in the movies. He was amazed by the splendor of it all and he wanted to get into it, but the money belt made him anxious and the pairs of submachine gun-carrying gendarmes who were walking all over the area kept his anxiety at a high level. He bought the international editions of the New York *Times* and *Herald Tribune* and returned to the Navy Bar which had become at least slightly familiar to him in this place where everything seemed strange and possibly dangerous.

The café was packed, and before he could say anything a waiter plunked him down in a chair at a table with two men he didn't know but didn't mind the looks of. Kenny was nervous and tried to bury his face in the newspaper. One of the guys asked him if he was an American, and when Kenny replied that he was, they introduced themselves as Dominic Lorenzo and Jean Massot of Quebec, Canada, both professors at the University of Montreal. They were about thirty years old and quite sympathetic to Wisdom's plight which he skillfully explained to them after introducing himself. He told them he was twenty-two and that he had worked on the Brooklyn waterfront ever since he graduated from high school and that he had saved his money for nearly five years to get enough for an inexpensive year in Europe where he hoped to learn a language or two and perhaps further his education. "But what the hell's going on here? A war?"

"Yes, sort of," said Jean, and explained about Algeria and how it was a French colony and how the Algerian people were sick of being French possessions and wanted to be independent and have their own country and form their own government. To accomplish this end they were having a revolution in Algeria, and since there were so many Algerian laborers living in France, they also were taking part in the revolution by attacking the various citadels of French imperialism in the capital city of Paris. Their activity was basically terrorism, and they bombed government buildings with *plastique* explosives, and yesterday they blew up one of the offices in the Ministry of War only a few blocks away. The gendarmes carried automatic weapons because they frequently engaged in gun battles with groups of Algerian rebels in the streets of Paris as well as in other cities of France.

"Why doesn't France let them have their independence?" Kenny was told that it all came down to oil. Algeria provided most of the fuel that kept the machinery of France running and France was not about to give up that oil-producing territory without a fight, because then they would have to pay for the oil which they now simply took out of the ground for free. And, yes, the Algerians were going to win their battle for freedom because they had not given themselves any alternative to victory.

Then Jean helped Kenny order something to eat and Dominic explained that they were going to an Alpine village in northern Italy to stay with his brother and spend the summer climbing mountains in the Alps. They were driving there through Switzerland on the following day and would be glad to take Kenny with them as far as he wanted to go. They were very sympathetic guys and easy to be with and since Paris wasn't exactly fun city, Kenny accepted the offer.

That night the three of them went to a bar on some rue off of the Boulevard St.-Germain. The place was called Storyville and the walls were lined solid with thousands of jazz records. These were selected individually by the house disc jockey and played on the turntable of an elaborate stereo system which filled the narrow room with the beautiful music Kenny thought he had left behind. He got turned on by the sounds, had a few drinks and decided to let the money belt think for itself for awhile. He didn't intend to get careless or sloppy drunk, it was just that he wasn't as alone as before and the tension of the last couple of days demanded that he relax a bit. He didn't come on like a big spender either, he played it small. After all, the only things he knew about Dominic and Jean were what they had told him and what he was able to learn with his instincts. They seemed straight, but if he could tell a good lie, probably so could they. Kenny remained on his toes; only his paranoia was gone, not his wits.

Storyville was a hangout for expatriates, beatniks, artists and jazz buffs. Between records, some lame who called himself a poet recited something entitled "No More" which he dedicated to James Dean. It went more or less like this: "No More Drive-ins or Floridian Senior Citizens, Little Leagues or Baton Twirling, Park Avenue Buildings or Bomb Shelters, Eisenhower or Douglas MacArthur, Charles Van Doren or Adlai E. Stevenson, 3-D Movies or Hula Hoops, Chlorophyll Gums or Color-Code Paint Kits, Army McCarthy Hearings or Crime Kefauver Hearings, Teresa Brewer or Pat Boone, American Bandstand or Lip-Synch, My Fair Lady or West Side Story, Betty Furness and Refrigerators or Dinah Shore and Chevrolets, Ozzie and Harriet or Burns and Allen, Mama or Dragnet, See It Now! or What's My Line, Jack Paar or Mrs. Calabash-Wherever-you-are — NO MORE!!!" Someone suggested that he keep his ignorance a secret by shutting his mouth. Another yelled that "James Dean was a pussy-whipped-crybaby!" thereby starting a fight with the rhyming, expatriate soapboxer. Both clutzes were pushed into the street where they began to have it out. They weren't even into their first round when the two flics came jogging down the cobblestones and settled the altercation by swinging their capes at the combatants, knocking both of them cold. Kenny didn't understand what he had seen at first, but soon correctly concluded that the hems of the capes were weighted with lead, a very neat trick, not unlike a similar method used by some patrolmen in New York to clear kids off street corners without provoking cries of police brutality from the neighborhood women. There, they would roll their billyclubs in the folds of a *Daily News* and smack the kids on the shoulders to get them to move on, while the women of the area would watch and comment on the gentle firmness of the officers.

Kenny was impressed with the sophistication of the cape routine and looked on as the pair of gendarmes gave the two fallen scufflers a beating for their disorderly conduct. When they had finished, they stopped a passerby and frisked him. He showed them some kind of identification as they searched a small brown paper bag of pastries. They took out each of the half dozen tarts and crumpled them one by one, dumping the crushed remains back into the paper bag. "Why are they doing that?" asked Kenny. "Plastique," said Jean. 'They're looking for plastique, the explosive I told you about this afternoon." Wisdom fingered his homemade belt which was strapped around his waist and began not to feel too good again.

Early the next morning, Dominic and Jean picked Kenny up at his hotel in their secondhand Volkswagen bus and drove over five hundred kilometers through Troyes and Dijon to Geneva where they spent the night. The following morning Kenny got rid of the cumbersome belt by opening an account and depositing the money in a Swiss bank while his companions were having breakfast. He also bought a thousand dollars' worth of American Express travelers checks and exchanged $200 for its Italian equivalent of 120,000 lire. It was quite a relief.

They moved on to Turin where Dominic was to meet his brother. The drive through France to Switzerland had been the first trip Kenny Wisdom had ever made out of any city. He had never seen forests or fields or lakes or farms or their animals before, and they all seemed very beautiful and were brand new to him. The road from Geneva to Turin was spectacular with its passes through the colossal

Alps, beneath the snow-capped peaks, through the luscious green depths of the valleys and the centuries-old villages. It was all so overwhelmingly real, authentic, energetic and powerful. He was awestruck by the permanence of the mountains, yet none of it made him afraid and he wanted to stay in these mountains for a while. He felt that he could learn what he needed to know in them.

He asked Jean and Dominic if he could go with them up to the small village they had mentioned and maybe climb some mountains too, but mostly study the language of the people and get acquainted with their ways so that he wouldn't feel like that much of a stranger any longer. They said, "Sure, you can come with us, as long as you pull your own weight and do your share of whatever has to be done."

"Agreed," he said.

In the very clean, quiet and linearly designed capital city of Piedmont — Turin — they pulled into the courtyard of the Liceo di Don Bosco school where Dominic's brother was the headmaster and a priest. Kenny was naturally surprised, but Don Lorenzo was a warm, rugged man who obviously worked hard and wasn't anything like most of the priests Kenny had known in New York who were all pasty-faced lames and corpulent leeches. He liked Don Lorenzo because he looked and acted like and was a man, which is difficult, especially when you're wearing skirts. He had a shovel in his hands when they drove in, and his thick wrists, forearms, and sweat-beaded neck testified to the fact that he probably used the shovel more often than he did a pencil.

They spent the night in an empty dormitory at the school, and the following day the four of them traveled up the Valle d'Aosta, passed the headquarters of the Fiat industrial empire in the town of Ivrea and finally arrived at the village of St. Jacques where Kenny was going to learn all he wanted to and more in the next four months.

St. Jacques was approximately 1700 meters above sea level and the weather was brisk in the middle of May. It was a small Alpine village surrounded by mountains and capped to the north by the glistening snow-covered peaks of the 4600-meter Monte Rosa. There was one general store, several little dairy farms which produced milk and excellent cheeses, a tiny hostel maintained for mountain climbers by the Alpine Club, a few thatch-roofed-stone-walled cottages which were the homes of the villagers, some mule and horse-drawn carts and wagons, a couple of cars and trucks, no tourists' shops because they seldom came this far up, and a two-room, single-floor cement building which was the village center and police station, manned by green-uniformed Alpine soldiers who had eagle feathers in their pointed hats and who were posted there to rescue stranded climbers and to catch smugglers, packing cartons of American cigarettes over the Alps from Switzerland.

There was also a café-bar which sold espresso coffee, vino bianco e roso, snacks, Italian cigarettes over the counter and most brands of American and other foreign cigarettes under the counter, bottled beer, and two types of liqueurs: a white lightning called Grappa and a green lightning called Lampi Verdi Alpini. They parked outside and went into the bar. It was late afternoon and there were many men of the village inside, standing around in their wooden shoes and talking, or sitting at tables playing a bridgelike card game known as Scoppa. When they saw Don Lorenzo, Dominic, Jean and Kenny, they all sat down and had some wine while one man went and rounded up the rest of the villagers.

Most of the people who gathered in the bar were red-cheeked, fair-skinned and blond-haired and spoke Italian with a clipped, sing-song accent, but there was a group of about eight men who were dark, more subdued, and spoke the language in a heavy, deep tone and looked like Italians look in New York. It was at this point that Kenny discovered why Don Lorenzo was so loved by the people of this particular village and what they were going to be doing in St. Jacques besides eating and sleeping and climbing mountains. The priest had been raising money for and gradually constructing a church in St. Jacques over the past two years. The eight darker men were from Southern Italy and had been convicted of minor offenses and sent to prison in Turin, where they had been paroled into the custody of Don Lorenzo to complete their sentences working on the church, which was to be completed during that summer.

Before it got dark, everyone walked down the road to the site of the half-constructed church. Don Lorenzo talked over his plans with the group of workers, gesticulating here and there to clarify what he said. Kenny didn't understand much, but he understood the gist of what he was hearing. Unfortunately, the altitude and the thinness of the air had activated Kenny's asthma and he was wheezing audibly.

Later that evening, when they were moving their gear into the cabin where they were going to stay, Jean and Dominic noticed Kenny's irregular breathing and suggested that he take it a little easy until he got used to the climate, but Kenny reminded them of their bargain and struggled to keep up with them. It was a week before he found his pace and was able to handle whatever it was without overexerting himself.

Dominic drove him to the town of Champoluc to buy some proper clothing at the weekly open-air market which was set up every Saturday. Kenny got himself a set of work clothes and purchased a complete outfit of climbing clothes, boots and equipment, including a pick, a pair of metal spikes that strapped onto your boots for crossing ice, thick-lensed, dark glasses with blinders on them, a knapsack with an aluminum frame and a Carta Sciistica Della Zona Del Monte Rosa, which was a detailed map of all the trails on all the mountains of the area. Jean and Dominic had the remainder of the necessary gear, such as nylon ropes, buckles and pitons.

In two weeks, Kenny was used to his wooden work shoes which were handmade to order for fifty cents American and kept his feet warm and dry — and which he had expected to see on the feet of the people of Holland and never on his in the Alps of northern Italy. He was getting into the language, but his accent varied according to whom he was speaking to — a Piedmontese or a Neapolitan. His asthma quieted down to a point where he seldom noticed it and the work on the church was exhilarating because it put him on a common basis with the people of the community and dislodged his feeling of being a foreigner in a strange land. He took on the attitude of the other Italian workers and considered himself simply one of them.

At night they would have plates of pasta and lots of Barbera red wine, which was necessary for the proper digestion of food at that altitude. All the workmen ate in the same room and at the same long table with Don Lorenzo at the head. After dinner some of the villagers would come by, and the men would tell each other stories of the days when they were partisans with their fathers and fought against *I Fascisti*, and nineteenth-century tales of the conquests of Garibaldi who, they said, liberated Sicily and Naples and united Italy in 1860 — and of course they spoke of contemporary politics. Kenny was told that about 25 percent of the Italian population were Communists and that they formed the strongest Communist political party in the Western world, but he couldn't believe it when a few of the men he worked with actually told him they were Communists. Real Communist party members! It was the first time that he had ever seen a flesh-and-blood Communist, never mind met one! But he got over it.

Kenny also began to read the Italian newspapers every evening to advance his knowledge of the language. *Il Messaggero* and *Il Correre della Sera* were the two papers that used to arrive by mail days after the news had become old. There was always lots of coverage of American affairs, but from a viewpoint with which Kenny was unaccustomed. Like when John Foster Dulles died that May, Wisdom discovered that a whole lot of people didn't like him very much and were not particularly unhappy at his passing. There were nearly daily reports about Negro sit-in demonstrations at lunch counters all over the South, which prompted Kenny to wonder if there were any Negro-Italians, and when he asked one of the workers he was told no, but there were Sicilians. He also read the words in all the balloons of the comic strips.

Kenny amused himself by thinking about what his family and friends in Brooklyn and the people he knew in New York would say if they could see him walking around the Italian Alps in his wooden shoes building a church. They probably wouldn't say anything because they would be speechless. He did hope his mother and father would get over his sudden disappearance without too much heartbreak and worry. He knew that it must have hurt them a great deal to see all their aspirations for their son's future destroyed, but it was better this way than being sooner or later caught in one of his acts and sent to an upstate prison, or taken for a ride to the Island and his body dumped into Gravesend Bay. Wasn't it? That question didn't really matter, it already was. He promised himself he would write his parents a letter as soon as he was about to leave this place for another.

Dominic, Jean and Kenny were shortly taking twelve- and fourteen-hour-long walks up to the 3300-meter Testa Grigia, carrying fully loaded packs to strengthen their legs and whip their bodies into the rhythmic shape required for mountain climbing. Kenny's asthma completely receded and he enjoyed the quickening pace of the walks. He knew he was preparing himself for the scaling of some great peaks with his two companions, but he had no idea that one of the mountains he was going to attempt would be Il Cervino, the Matterhorn. They never mentioned it to him and he didn't consider asking them about the which's or where's.

These walks up huge hills soon became climbs up small mountains, when they took a week off from their construction job and crossed along the 2700-meter ridge of the Bettaforca to the 3500-meter Q Sella refuge cabin where they ate only bread and drank only wine and slept. It was July, but the snow was deep and it was as cold as a bitch when the sun went down and the clouds moved over your ankles. Kenny felt nothing short of pure astonishment as he watched the billowy clouds roll beneath him. It was all too incredible for somone whose previous vision of wilderness was Central Park.

Around four or five each morning, they would leave the refuge and attempt different climbs. There was the 3700-meter peak of Perazzi which they practiced on from all angles. They crossed the Castore Glacier (yes, a real fucking-honest-to-god glacier!) to the base of the 4200-meter Castore mountain peak where a blizzard forced them to go back to the refuge on their first try. They later scaled it twice from opposite directions on two different days.

A week after they had been back in the village of St. Jacques, they left again. This time they climbed to the Alpine Club's refuge cabin of Mezzalama, and from this 3000-meter perch they twice made the very difficult and dangerous climb up the flat, black surface to the 4100-meter top of La Roccia Nera. It was something else with Jean leading on the first successful attempt, Dominic on the second and Kenny always in the middle. What with hammering the pitons and pulling up the slack on the nylon cord and loosening it again and nothing to stand on but little slits of cracks in the back-breaking rock and the wind whistling and pushing against you and the cold freezing, and finding that it's harder to get down than it is to get up, and looking below at the Verra Glacier and across to the gigantic Breithorn Plateau and now you're in Switzerland and now back again over (a border?) to Italy, and the early afternoon sun melting the ice, and the water dripping and the stone softening as it gets warmer and you have to go back before it becomes hot, and there is very little support and the oxygen is so pure that you have difficulty believing that everything is real — it's glorious!

At the end of July before the sun became August, the three of them set out on their last series of climbs. From St. Jacques they crossed over the 3100-meter Piccolo Tournalin to the village of Cheneil and through the town of Valtournanche to the ski resort of Breuil which sits at the foot of the Matterhorn. From there early the following morning, they climbed to the 3700-meter Lion's Head of the mountain and on to the 3800-meter Luigi Amedeo di Savoia refuge hut where they wrote their names in the book like they had done in the other books in the other refuges, and went to sleep. Before three in the morning they raced the sun in their climb to the 4270-meter Pic Tyndall, but couldn't make it to the top of the 4478-meter majestic Matterhorn because of a flash storm. They were successfully back down to the refuge hut by midmorning, and to Breuil the next day where they celebrated.

They took their time in returning. A cable car carried them up from Breuil to the 2500-meter Plan Maison where everyone was skiing in the August sun. They walked across the snow to the ice and camped for the night in the pass of the Piano Rosa. At sunup, they climbed over the 3000-meter Cime Bianche and down along the blue lakes to the hamlet of Fiery and on to the village of St. Jacques with a greeting of Welcomes! and Bravos! and their fill of eat and drink and many ears to listen to the tales they told of their eleven-day adventure with the earth.

The erection of the church was finished during the first week in September when the last piece of slate shingle was slid into its place on the roof. Along with all the other men who had worked on the structure, Kenny scratched his name in the wet cement on the top of the small but sturdy bell tower. It was dedicated on the following Sunday to the memory of Dominic Savio and the first mass was celebrated in it by Don Lorenzo. The people of St. Jacques were very happy that they finally had a church and they held a feast which got everybody bloated with food and drunk with wine. By the end of the evening all agreed it was the most splendid church they had ever seen, with the exception of course of Il Duomo in Milan.

On Monday, Kenny Wisdom said goodbye to St. Jacques and its people and to Don Lorenzo to whom he gave all his climbing equipment with the request that he make sure it got to someone who would put it to good use, and he drove away in the Volkswagen bus with Jean and Dominic. Along the road to Torino, Kenny looked back at the Alpine mountains and realized that the last few months in that little village had been one of the best times he had or would have in his life and he had only spent $140. He also noted that he hadn't been laid during that whole period, but had also never missed it. Yes, the Valle d'Aosta had been good to him.

Kenny shook hands and embraced Jean Massot and Dominic Lorenzo outside of the railway station in Turin. He was taking a train to Milan, and they were driving on to Genoa where they were going to board a ship back to Canada and Quebec. He couldn't thank them enough for being what they were and for having allowed him to share their experience.

On the train, Kenny wrote his parents a long letter in which he described the wonderful time he had in the place he had been in. The motive for going there, he wrote, had been his growing involvement with a group of people in Brooklyn who were a very bad influence on him. In order to continue his education he had been forced to escape from their grip before it was too late by hopping a freighter to Europe. He had been studying Latin in the Alps all summer and had received a scholarship to a boarding school in Northern Italy where he was going to prepare for his matriculation at the Sorbonne University of Paris, intending to graduate with a degree in international corporate law and join a large firm and become their international lawyer. "So, please don't tell anyone that I'm in Europe because I want to remain undisturbed in my quest for a professional career. Thank you for understanding. I love you all very much and I'll give you my address in my next letter after I get firmly rooted in my classwork. Please don't worry about me because I'm only doing what I have to do to make you proud of me. Your loving son, Kenneth." He enclosed some edelweiss in the envelope and mailed the letter from the post office in the railway terminal of Milan.

He stayed for about a week in that city, having several suits made and buying new shoes and other stylish Italian apparel to go with them. He was amazed at how well he spoke the language and he enjoyed going around and rapping with anybody about whatever happened to be in the papers that day, or arguing over the price of something, or anything which he could use as a subject of conversation to demonstrate his fluency and to let whoever he was talking to know that he wasn't the new kid on the block anymore, *vedi*.

When his suits were ready, he put one of them on, a splendid Principe di Callas wool which fit him like a glove, and packed the rest of his new things into a Gucci leather suitcase, and rode a first class compartment on the express train to Geneva to get some more of his money out of the bank. While in Geneva he met a pretty Belgian girl named Michele who was attending a German language and culture *collegium*, a finishing school, in Heidelberg. She had come to Switzerland with some friends for a skiing holiday and they were just stopping in Geneva for a couple of days before returning to school. She spoke English as did the rest of her party whom

Kenny got to know. There were about twelve girls from various countries and a few men. Two of the men were very interesting and persuaded Kenny to travel back to Germany with the group, which wasn't that difficult, considering his involuntary period of celibacy and the lovely expensive smell of the well-born bodies of noble, young ladies.

Kenny ended up spending over eight months in Heidelberg and nearly twenty thousand dollars on an apartment that caught fire, a car that got totaled, hashish, cocaine, weekend trips to the gambling casinos of Baden-Baden, the ski resorts of Innsbruck and Bavaria, parties in Berlin, Paris and Brussels, and on an investment in the prosperous Egyptian-styled Semiramis Club which amounted to less than his bar tab in whiskey alone, forget the champagne. It was a bat, a lengthy run of pure debauchment, and by the end of April 1960, Kenny was bored with the country, the town, and the circle of dissipating people he gathered with in Heidelberg, especially since the only serious criminal activity they were capable of committing successfully was suicide. He split.

The one reasonable routine which Kenny enjoyed during his stay was eating two and three meals a week at the Sole D'Oro Italian restaurant on the Hauptstrasse of Heidelberg. It was there that he met Alfredo Rizzo, who was a native of San Remo, and who was part owner of the Ristorante Italia in Baumholder/Idar-Oberstein, Germany. The two men became good friends over the months, and Alfredo promised to take Kenny with him when he returned to his hometown after Easter and show him around the Riviera as only one who had grown up there could.

Alfredo was a big, stout, good-natured man and he called Kenny the night before to tell him he was planning to leave for Italy in the next couple of days and if he still wanted to come, he'd better tell him now and catch the next train to Baumholder. His family was going to have a festa for his thirtieth birthday and he didn't want to disappoint them or himself by arriving late, so, *"Vieni subito! Hai compito?"* Kenny said, *"Si,"* and was in Baumholder early the following afternoon.

Now Baumholder is supposed to be a town in Germany, at least that's what the map says. But what it doesn't tell you is that it is also the site of the largest concentration of Allied troops in Europe, allies meaning whoever on America's side at the time. These soldiers don't sit around all day either, no, they play endless war games in the eleven-kilometer-square wasteland between Baumholder and its twin town of Idar-Oberstein. They go out on maneuvers for a month at a time, these freedom-fighting forces and they take with them every conceivable type of weapon, explosive and armored vehicle used in conventional warfare. Paratroopers even fall from the sky on cue to overrun a barren mole of a hill being held by the enemy who are easily identifiable in their red-colored vests. It's not make-believe, because the ammunition is live and the combatants gung-ho, and some of them die real dead practicing their roles as pawns in these games called war. Kenny didn't know this when he stepped off the train in Baumholder. Oh, he knew that the U.S. Army was there, but they were everywhere in Germany. Christ, the U.S. Army headquarters was in Heidelberg. There was a difference, however. In Heidelberg all the soldiers were clerk-typists. Here they were all members of combat-ready-dog-faced-crazy battle units.

The town was a block long, a low-class ghetto sitting at the edge of one of several rolling hills. Next to it was the base, where the various armies maintained their enlisted men's barracks, officers' quarters, homes for their dependents, a bowling alley and other similar facilities giving the air of a small American town divided into neighborhoods in accord with the economic brackets of its residents. The street and the alleys of Baumholder, however, were unpaved and muddy. The buildings were all saloons and above them were rooms where the hostesses lived and catered to the sexual fancies of soldiers on pass. Each of these girls had been bonused by a baby during the intercourse of their employment. The only men in the town who were not in the military were the owners and managers of these Gasthauses where the women plied their trade.

There was a bunch of kids whose colors ranged from white to cocoa playing in the mud of a single street, as Kenny walked under a sign proclaiming the Velvet Kitten and into the bar. He ordered a bottle of beer, noticing that the barmaid was reluctant to give it to him. There were no other customers, only some girls who obviously worked there, sitting in a booth behind him, and they also seemed not too happy with him. He thought that they were uptight because his well-tailored clothes, expensive suitcases, and nonmilitary hair length made them suspicious. He asked the barmaid how far it was to Idar-Oberstein and where was the pay phone. She said eleven kilometers and over there on the wall by the W.C.

He called Alfredo who told him that he was glad that he'd made it and that he would pick him up in fifteen minutes. Kenny sat down on the stool to wait and drink his beer. The silence was cold. They were just staring at his back. He could see their looks in the mirror behind the bar and he understood that they didn't want him in there, but he didn't really give a shit. He put some coins in the jukebox and played some loud rhythm and blues. It was a good box with a lot of heavy music selections, but the sounds didn't thaw the ice. He was halfway through his beer, when the eyes turned from him to the front entrance. Two MPs had just come in and were standing there, giving their undivided attention to the back of Kenny's neck. They walked over, one on each side of him. They were both big white guys and the one with the mustache asked Kenny if he was an American. Kenny watched them in the mirror and nodded yes.

Moustache: Let's see your passport.

Kenny: This ain't no military installation and I don't have to show you nothin'.

The other MP unholstered his .45, leaned against the bar, pointed it at Wisdom's face and ordered, "Boy, you do what the man said." Kenny didn't move, he sat there expressionless and didn't do anything. The MP with the gun cocked it, and a bullet jumped into the chamber. Kenny lifted his head and stared blankly at the nervous bully eyes behind the automatic piece of chocolate, while he moved his hand into his jacket pocket and removed his passport. He threw it on the bar in front of Moustache.

Moustache: You kinda young, ain't ya? Says here, you're a student. Where you study?

Kenny didn't say anything, he just kept his gaze fixed on the eyes of the punk who was insulting his humanity with a pistol.

.45: Answer the man, boy.

Kenny: Heidelberg.

Moustache: What are you doing here?

Kenny: Drinking a beer.

Moustache: Listen, schoolboy, don't go wise-assin' with us, you hear? Now, what you doin' in Baumholder?

Kenny: I'm waiting for a friend to come 'n pick me up. We're going on vacation.

Moustache: Well, you finished waitin' here, boy. You go do yer waitin' in a bar 'cross the street. This bar's fer niggers only, understand? Now git across to a place on the other side 'n wait there for yer buddy.

Kenny put his passport back into his jacket pocket, picked up his two suitcases, and walked toward the door without looking at anyone.

"Hey, fella! You didn't pay for the beer!" yelled the barmaid after him.

"I didn't have any beer," replied Kenny as he went outside. At that moment Alfredo pulled up and Kenny piled in and they drove to Idar-Oberstein. After greeting each other, Kenny told Alfredo about the scene that just went down in the Velvet Kitten and asked him if that was the way things normally were around that town, or had he simply run into two bastards who didn't like his looks — not an infrequent occurrence in Kenny Wisdom's case. Alfredo was genuinely surprised and slightly confused by the question. He suggested that maybe Kenny had been away from his country too long and had forgotten what it was like in America. *"E lo stesso, no?"*

Kenny remembered all the newspaper articles that he had read during the last year about the Negro civil rights demonstrations in the States and the nonviolent-civil-disobedient activities for the total integration of schools, neighborhoods and transportation, for better job opportunities, for dignity, and for a bigger piece of the American pie. Alfredo told him about the numerous bloody racial conflicts between the white and black soldiers whenever they returned from field maneuvers and went on weekend passes to Baumholder, where with the exception of disinterested MPs, there were no cops to prevent them from engaging in race wars involving hundreds of fever-pitched men. Some of them were left dead and a lot of them wounded, and they didn't just go at each other with bats and balls either, Alfredo said. They used bayonets, guns and anything else that they could steal from ordnance. Once, somebody had even tossed a grenade into a black or a white hangout — Alfredo couldn't remember which color the men had been who were killed and maimed by the fragmenting explosion. He twirled his forefinger in a circular motion near his temple to indicate that he thought all those GIs were fucking crazy.

Before dawn the next morning, Kenny was scared out of his sleep by a thunderous rumble that shook the building and didn't stop. He looked out of the window, and along the cobblestoned street below were passing miles of tanks and other heavy equipment with columns of foot soldiers marching on both sides of the vehicles. He ran downstairs where he met Alfredo, who said that he had no idea what was going on. Kenny opened the door and stood in the entrance and asked a passing soldier what it was all about.

"The Russians!" came the answer.

"The Russians what?" Kenny demanded.

Another replied that the Russians had shot down an American plane and the troops were leaving Baumholder and marching to Berlin because it looked like war.

"War? War?" Kenny shouted to no one in particular. "That's fuckin' ridiculous! War." Then he went back inside and told Alfredo what the story was and suggested that they get the fuck out of there before whatever shit there was hit the fan. Alfredo thought that was good advice and within an hour they were packed and driving south on the Autobahn to San Remo, Italy. The car radio informed them that an alleged U.S. spy plane was shot down by the Soviet Union when it transgressed that nation's borders, and the pilot was captured. The Russians called it a deliberate act of provocation and demanded an apology. The Americans denied that anything at all had happened and claimed that the Soviet Union was seeking a confrontation on totally false pretenses.

By the time Kenny had withdrawn the rest of his money from the Swiss bank in Geneva and he and Alfredo were blissfully in San Remo, the United States admitted that there had been a plane downed by the Soviets and that a pilot had indeed been captured. The plane was the U-2 and the pilot was Francis Gary Powers and on that first day of May when that inanimate object and its driver were dropped from their spying mission in the sky by Russian anti-aircraft, everyone in Europe had shit bricks for a week over the possibility of a world war with a difference, a nuclear difference. Kenny didn't shit no brick, but it was then that he finally understood that politics wasn't just a word you read in newspapers. It was a category of life or death, depending on which way the wind blew, which facts were ignored, which truths were lies, which policies and their makers were wise or expedient, crafty or cautious. He concluded that politics were men, and that some men were political animals and aware of the actuality of politics, while most others were simply duped into the fold of one politic or another because of any number of self-interested reasons. Level-headed, independent individuals avoided the plague of the political arena and went about their business, regardless of who was running the show. This was Kenny's position and he intended to maintain it.

There was also another front page story in the European press that week about another American who had gone down which filled Kenny with a mild sense of disbelief at its absurdity, and if he had known anything about pataphysics, he would have become a pataphysician on the spot. This other American was Caryl Chessman who had been convicted in 1948 on seventeen counts of robbery, sexual abuses, and attempted rape, and had been sentenced to mandatory execution in the gas chamber of San Quentin for "kidnapping with bodily harm." During his twelve years as a resident of Death Row, Chessman had become a public symbol for people all over the world who opposed capital punishment, had written some books, and had been granted eight stays of execution. Caryl Chessman's eighth and last stay was the kicker which convinced Wisdom that a senseless irrational cabal existed in the hierarchy of U.S. democracy. Chessman had been given his last stay a year previously, only ten hours before his scheduled execution, because some presidential advisers had suggested that the man's death at that particular moment might mar the "We Like Ike!" goodwill tour of South and Latin America. Chessman's departure had been postponed rather than Ike and Mamie's. "Would wonders never cease?" deliberated Kenny, with an afterthought of "Probably not."

San Remo was everything and even more than Kenny had known it would be. He was living with Alfredo and his family in a swell house in the back neighborhood set into the hill overlooking the hotels and the central part of town. All of Alfredo's friends and neighbors worked either in San Remo or at the casino in Monte Carlo. (Residents of San Remo are not permitted to work or play in that town's casino, but are employed by the casino of Monte Carlo whose residents are also bound by a similar off-limits rule and are only allowed to frequent, or work in, the San Remo casino. The reason for these nonresidency requirements is perfectly obvious when you consider that both towns are small and anyone who lives in one of them knows everybody in it and if you grew up there, half of the population are probably your relatives.)

Kenny didn't have any time to lie on the beach in the sun during his week's visit there, because he was too busy getting to know the people and the setup of San Remo. Alfredo had him running around all over the place, introducing him to so-and-so at the early morning flower market, or showing him the operation of this and that in some part of the town. Alfredo helped Kenny to everything and everyone he needed to know in that short time before he had to return to his restaurant business in Germany. Kenny was very grateful because he planned to settle in San Remo and his role was made easier as a friend of the family.

A day or two after Alfredo left, Kenny decided to go to Rome for the 1960 Olympic Games. He bought tickets to all the events he wanted to see, and he only intended to spend a few weeks there. He packed all his belongings, told Mama Rizzo that he'd be back soon, "as sure as ten dimes'll buy a dollar," or so he thought, and he caught the train to be shortchanged in Rome.

He had been in Rome's railway terminal for not even five minutes when some joker tried to cop and blow with his luggage. He caught the guy immediately and punched the lame son of a bitch out. A couple of regular city cops came running over, and a few carabinieri, and they pushed their way through the small crowd that had gathered and demanded an explanation from Kenny. He told them the punk had tried to lift his luggage and he had stopped him. Then they asked the cheesy little bastard who was sniveling on the corrugated rubber floor of the terminal what had happened, and when the rotten prick told them that all he had tried to do was aid a foreign traveler with his suitcases and that he had received a beating in exchange for his courteous offer of a Roman citizen's hospitality, Kenny blew his cool and tried to kick him in his lying-mealy mouth. The cops grabbed him and placed him under arrest for assaulting a man who was simply living up to his responsibility as a Roman to make the visit of foreigners to the Olympiad a pleasant one.

Kenny thought they were kidding, but they weren't. He was driven to a police station across from the Piazza Esedra where the gentle Roman who had tried to steal his suitcases put on an act of indignation and proceeded to file a denouncement against him. A police lieutenant was admonishing Kenny for his violence. "You can't go around Rome beating people up, Signore! This is not New York or Brookolino! We have laws against such things!" Kenny wasn't interested, he was talking with his hands to the guy who was denouncing him as an unprovoked assailant. He told him to tear up the affidavit and he would pay him twenty thousand lire. The guy signaled that he would but for thirty thousand lire. Kenny nodded his head "Yes," which sent the hustler into a forgive-and-forget act with the police officials, pointing out to them that Rome's reputation for hospitality would be tarnished if its citizens couldn't overlook an unfortunate accident caused by the misinterpretation of a Roman's customary politeness toward all strangers to their great city.

The cops were reluctant, but finally agreed, and they let Kenny go after a ten minute harangue in which they assured him that if he ever assaulted another person in their jurisdiction, he would be sent to prison for a very long time.

When Kenny left the police station, he saw the cop-and-blow artist waiting for him on the other side of the piazza. He wanted to push him in front of a bus because if the coppers had ever opened his Gladstone bag and seen all the money in there, he would never have been able to explain its presence. He approached the character, gave him his fifty dollars and also a detailed description of how he was going to break his fingers and tear his tongue out, if he ever saw him again. The guy could see that Kenny was aggravated and he understood that he was very serious and by the way he spoke Italian that he wasn't much of a stranger to the streets of Italy, so when Kenny said, *"Vatene!"* he split in a hurry.

Kenny checked into the Hotel Excelsior on the Via Veneto soon after that. The Excelsior was one of the two hotels which Kenny had considered, the Grand Hotel being the other. He'd decided on the Excelsior because of its subtle flamboyance, its access to the Via Veneto, its guests, who were for the most part movie stars and wealthy vacationers from the U.S.A., and its security — distinctly below the standards of the Grand Hotel, which was so good you never saw any of the hotel detectives. Besides all that, the people who stayed at the Grand Hotel, as well as the employees, were highly sophisticated in the mores and styles of the very rich and/or aristocratic, and Kenny Wisdom was still too rough around the edges to blend properly into that type of refined, polished background. He hoped his stay at the Excelsior would smooth his appearance and sharpen his form, until it all became comfortably second nature to him.

After checking in and depositing seventeen thousand dollars with the unimpressed assistant manager for safekeeping in the hotel vault, Kenny went to the American Consulate to get the official U.S.I.S. booklet for American visitors to the Olympics, and the detailed list of events and a street index from one of the clerks.

As he was leaving the consulate, Kenny bumped smack into a familiar face which returned his stare with equal curiosity. His mind backpedaled all the way to Brooklyn for a name that went with the face, which was still searching to recognize his. He tilted his head slightly and inquired of the face, "Charlie? Charlie?"

"Yes," replied Charlie. "Where do I know you from, the neighborhood?"

"Yes, my name's Kenny. Kenny Wisdom. I used to see you around the 'hood with Joe Denave and Johnny Conte, those guys."

Charlie and his friends in Brooklyn were all about twenty years old now to Kenny's sixteen. They never hung around together, but just said hello when they'd see each other on the streets. They were the older crowd and because Kenny hadn't been in Brooklyn too much after he began going to that Park Avenue Private Prep School, he actually hadn't seen Charlie since he was about fourteen. And he didn't know, yet, if he was glad to see him now or not.

Charlie had some passport business to take care of and while it was being handled, he told Kenny that he had been in Rome for a few months with his wife and that John Conte had also come over but had returned to New York the week before. It was originally just a straight honeymoon-in-Rome trip, but Charlie had turned the temporary vacation into a more permanent one by becoming partners with an Italian in an auto and scooter rental agency. He had gone into the place to rent a car and started talking to the guy about his business, and one thing led to another, and now he was making the money for his extended vacation *from* his extended vacation with the business venture — and enjoying it more.

All Kenny knew about Charlie's Brooklyn days was that he had hung around up on the Parkway and had been on the television program *Strike It Rich* where he was permitted to win some money on account of some grave injustice which the City of New York had done to him. What it was exactly Kenny couldn't remember, and he didn't ask because it was none of his business.

Now, standing with him in Rome, Kenny could see that he was good people and a likable dude and he was smart and had a quick-witted way which made you laugh. Physically he was of average height, stocky frame, and his round-light-skinned-cheerful-Italian face was dotted with sparkling eyes. Kenny listened and looked and became glad he had met him.

They left the consulate and had a few drinks at the Café de Paris across the street, where they promised each other that they would get together for dinner sometime soon. Charlie gave him his business card and suggested that Kenny drop around during the daytime to check out the hustle he was running on the square tourists. He commented that the operation was totally unbelievable, before he said goodbye.

After two weeks of watching Ralph Boston broad jump, John Thomas balk, Oscar Robertson, Jerry West, Walt Bellamy and

Company basketball, and Cassius Clay T.K.O. for a gold medal which he wore as a medallion on his chest in the walking tours he would take up and down the Via Veneto for all to see the body psychology of The Greatest! — after having balled a lot of ingenues who were always in and out and around the Hotel Excelsior, Kenny Wisdom walked over to the Via Torino and Charlie's place of business. It was only about an eight-block beeline from his hotel, but it took him more than two hours to get there on that afternoon because the Communists were rioting bloody all over that part of Rome in an attempt to topple the Christian Democrat and neo-Fascist coalition government which they eventually succeeded in doing later in that month of July. It was quite a sight with buses burning, tear-gas canisters being thrown back and forth, heads being cracked, cops dividing the huge mob into small groups and pummeling them to the ground and retreating when the mob came back together and charged. It was one hell of a street fight and it was going to continue sporadically for several weeks. But it wasn't like Paris, there were no submachine guns and no one was firing weapons. They were just intent on destroying property, which made the merchants sick as they pulled the corrugated steel shutters down over their storefronts.

Kenny was very careful as he slipped through the raging chaos. He wasn't afraid, he just figured that whatever it was all about was their blues and had nothing to do with him, so he avoided confronting any side of the action by circling around it, but he watched the goings-on like a critic watches a play. He thought that whatever they were up to, they were all very sloppy at it. He finally made it to the Viminal Agency which had a "Special Rates By Week or Month — All Services Included No Extras — Agency Under American Direction" sign alongside the entrance.

Kenny walked in, and up the ten-yard driveway to where Charlie was reading a newspaper behind a counter with "The Right Kind Of Car And Scooter For You At The Right Kind Of Price" slogan painted on it. Charlie was in the middle of a giggle when Kenny announced in Italian, "This is a stickup!"

Charlie glanced up from the newspaper and said, "Oh, how are you doin'? You startled me for a minute there. I thought you were a disgruntled customer coming back to make a little crazy."

Kenny: You get many of them?

Charlie: Well, if they ain't pissed off at something when they get back here, we make sure they are by the time they leave.

Then he pointed to the English language daily American newspaper of Rome and said, "Listen to this. 'Brotherly Lover. A 22-year-old Sicilian has complained to the Roman police today that his bride ran off with his brother while he was changing clothes to leave on his honeymoon a few hours after their wedding!' How's that for a fuckin' burn, ha?"

A priest came running up the driveway screaming, *"Accidente! Accidente! Un altro incidente!"* Apparently, a sailor from the Seventh Fleet had rented a scooter not ten minutes before and had driven it straight down the street and up the steps and into the door of the church at the end of the block. Kenny thought it was very funny and Charlie in an aside said it happened all the time and that was why the priest was so upset. The door of his church was turning into splinters. Charlie asked the priest if the sailor was dead or something. He wasn't although he had been taken away in an ambulance, but the priest wasn't concerned about that, he just kept yelling about his door. Charlie suggested that he might try leaving it open from now on and then nobody would crash into it anymore. The priest left the same way he'd come in, but this time he was tugging at his hair.

Kenny and Charlie were making their faces red by laughing so hard. Charlie rang a buzzer and a small, black-haired mechanic named Cosimino came bouncing up from the basement garage with a red jump suit on, and Charlie told him what had happened and to go collect the smashed scooter from the church steps. Cosimino was also delighted by the incident but seemed a little disappointed that the guy was still alive. Before he left, he drew a line with a pencil on the wall next to fourteen other lines and Kenny understood what it meant.

By that evening, the rioting had moved to another part of town and Kenny went to dinner with Charlie and his wife, Anna Marie. He recognized her as someone he had seen around Brooklyn and discovered that he knew her younger brother, but not too well. She was very attractive, slender with a fragile type of beauty, nice tits, limbs and ass, and a good sense of humor which gave her a full, honest laugh, rather than some nervous, twatty titter. Kenny thought that Charlie was a lucky man to have such a fine woman and he also thought a little about adultery, but he made that consideration a memory after a while, because his friendship with them blossomed and he came to love them both as people very dear to him. It was mainly their presence in that city which made Kenny decide not to return to San Remo right away, but to remain longer in Rome. They and the city of Rome itself helped temper Kenny's on-again-off-again nostalgia for New York. There was a warm "You can go and fuck your dead ancestors!" attitude about Charlie, and Anna Marie and the people they knew in the city that made Kenny feel at home there, or at least not that far away from home. They seldom took themselves seriously but they rarely were ever kidding.

Like one day, Anna Marie was driving Kenny around the old section of the city, Trastevere, where he was looking to rent a flat and this soldier was waiting for them to pass so that he could cross the street and Anna Marie accidentally ran over one of the guy's feet and he started hopping around, holding his toes and yelping about *"My foot! My foot!"* She stuck her head out of the car window and demanded to know *"What foot?"* before she drove away, looking back at the soldier jumping up and down in the rear-view mirror and commenting about what a "Silly, crazy son of a bitch!" he was to dance around the street like that. Now if that's not New York, you've never been there!

Kenny got himself a place on the Via del Mattonato, which means "the street of the crazy-born," in Trastevere, which means across the Tiber River. It was an unfurnished duplex apartment over the only other thing in the building, the landlord's grocery store. The bottom floor had the bedroom, living room, dining room, kitchen and bath. Upstairs was a large, airy, multi-windowed studio surrounded by a wide balcony, and on top of that was a terrace that doubled as a roof. It cost ninety dollars a month and Kenny signed a one-year lease, bought himself lots of good furniture at the Porta Portese Flea Market, checked out of the Excelsior Hotel, banked his money and moved in, and was happy that he had a place of his own.

Kenny Wisdom stayed in Rome, coasting on his money, palling around with a lot of movie people, making it with chicks from all over, getting to know the ins and outs of all the important streets of the fancy Appia Antica villas and luxury hotels, meeting many underworld characters of the city who hipped him to the various ways that they handled anything from American cigarettes to furs, educating himself by touring the museums and churches with their fine paintings, sculpture and architecture, reading books the way they were written in Italian by everyone from Machiavelli to Moravia, seeing films almost every other day, visiting the opera at La Scala once and again at Parma, eating meals in restaurants carved into Etruscan caves and learning many of the Italian ropes by simply hanging out with Charlie and his friends at the Viminal Agency, which was always good for a guaranteed laugh anyway.

Othello was Charlie's partner and a heavyweight put-on artist. In the early fifties, his car had stalled in front of a trolley and the conductor went bananas and had threatened him with a metal pipe if he didn't immediately push the car off of the tracks. Othello had laughed and the conductor had swung with the pipe and missed, and Othello had taken it away from him, parted his hair with it, and killed him. When Othello was released from the penitentiary, he opened the scooter/car rental agency. There was only one other place in Rome where you could rent scooters and it mysteriously burned down some weeks prior to the Olympic games, leaving all the tourist action to Viminal.

At least once a week Othello would scream his fucking head off about nothing in particular at the guys who worked at the agency. He just did it to keep them all in shape. His favorite trick was to pull out from behind a corner at oncoming traffic in his Alfa Romeo, sending the first line of speeding cars up onto the sidewalks in their attempt to avoid the horror which they envisioned as imminent when they saw Othello's car make its leaping appearance out of nowhere. He would also drive around sometimes in a big, bulky, bashed-up Fiat 1200 which he used to play bumper-cars with, slamming it into the cars nearest him when the traffic was particularly annoying or if he just didn't like the look on the driver's face next to him.

Then there was Sergio, whose nickname was The Fish because he used to be a ballroom dancer and worked as an extra in the movies and he looked like a fish. He was less than five feet tall and the best at what was known as the Viminal Eyeball, which was the look that everyone got when someone returned a rented car or scooter. The vehicle was moved to a position under a spotlight about seven feet from the counter, and the mechanics and Sergio and anyone else who was involved in the comic opera at the time would walk around and around the car or scooter, checking it out and moaning about all the damage that had been done to their poor baby. Of course the customer was usually astonished by the sincerity of the act. One mechanic named Franco would even break down and cry about all the work that he'd have to do to get the vehicle back in shape, if some customer wasn't responding in the expected manner. And true to the philosophy of W. C. Fields, they never gave any of the suckers an even break. Kenny never saw anybody leave the place without at least forfeiting his fifteen-dollar deposit because of some damage to a car or scooter which had been damaged long before the tourist had ever thought of coming to Rome. There was also quite a profit to be made on the gasoline. Sergio was always charging some foreign clutz 10,000 lire ($16) for two liters of gas.

The Fish was stone-cold-blooded about collecting for damages after a real accident occurred. He didn't putz around. One time he went to the hospital where a guy was lying in traction with two broken arms and legs from a car wreck and Sergio tortured the son of a bitch until the guy confessed that his travelers checks were in the pocket of his pants, but explained that he couldn't possibly sign them because of his broken arms. Sergio proved that he was wrong about this by removing one of his arms from its sling and forcibly helping the guy to sign his name on ten fifty-dollar checks.

Most customers who returned with their rentals would pay what was asked just to escape the incessant moaning and groaning routine, and would stomp out of the agency with their faces flushed from the familiar slow burn caused by the Viminal Treatment that they had just received. Some of the clientele, however, wouldn't go for any of it and would threaten Sergio with bodily harm if they didn't get their deposits back. That's where Dog came in. Dog was a big, vicious husky that Sergio would use to chase away angry marines or college football players. He never had to let him loose because even a moron could take one look at Dog and realize that fifteen dollars wasn't worth a gamble with probable death.

Charlie had a friend named Burt who was a medical student, actor and cocksman. He was also a six foot eight, three-hundred-pound giant who wore twenty-three-inch-long shoes, played the role of Hercules in those chintzy Italian colossal flicks and had a pleasant mean streak running all through his huge-brick-shithouse of a body. One day Burt decided that he wanted to fight the dog. So they did, and right on the floor in front of the counter at Viminal. Burt slipped on some grease and went down and Dog was all over him. They beat the piss out of each other in a furious, growling, tearing battle. Burt was punching, kicking and wrestling with the animal. Dog was ripping at Burt's massive chest with his teeth, trying to get a clean shot at his throat. He never did because Burt was hitting him in the head with his boulder fists and kicking him in the underbelly with those mammoth feet of his. After ten minutes both of them were beaten and exhausted. Dog's head was swollen from all the shots he had taken and a couple of his ribs were broken. Burt's chest and arms were torn and bleeding like a faucet runs water. Each of them would have been dead if either of them had been someone else. It was a draw.

Kenny had more belly laughs hanging out with the people at the Viminal Agency than he'd ever had anywhere else. Charlie hadn't exaggerated when he said that the scene there was totally unbelievable. He'd just neglected to mention that it was also hilarious.

In January '61 Anna Marie gave birth to a dynamite baby girl and they named her Roma. And Kenny became an uncle by proxy. The Congo was big in the news and Patrice Lumumba was murdered. Yuri Gagarin from the Soviet Union became the first man in space and in the same week the U.S. sponsored a fiasco called the Bay of Pigs Invasion. Kennedy established the Peace Corps to aid impoverished peoples of foreign nations, while CORE sponsored freedom rides which led to violence all over the South. The large community of wealthy Latin and South Americans in Rome didn't interrupt their routine gaiety when Trujillo was assassinated in the Dominican Republic. Even his grandchildren kept right on partying with the money their fathers had taken with them when they'd fled their homeland. Algeria was still on Kenny's mind and he followed the on-and-off French-Algerian talks closely because he wanted to spend some time in places like Marseilles and Nice, but the activity of the terrorists kept disrupting the plans of most tourists. Slick Jack and elegant Jackie visited Vienna, London and Paris, assuring everybody that everything was all right, and Dr. Robert Soblen was convicted of being a spy and sentenced to life imprisonment on the testimony of Jack Soblen, his brother. The Goya art theft from the National Gallery in London touched off a wave of burglaries in France and the U.S. in which seventy-some-odd paintings were stolen. Apparently, the Goya job had sharpened the appetites of several art collectors who'd had their eyes on various works which were either priceless or not for sale, so they simply commissioned thieves to get whatever their little hearts desired for them.

Kenny met one of these collectors, who wanted to pay him five American grand to lift an Etruscan vase from the small museum near the town of Sacrofano on the outskirts of Rome. Since Kenny was running a little low on funds, he decided to do the job to beef up his bank account. It was easy. There was only one sleepy old wino of a watchman, and the museum building was so ancient it was on the verge of crumbling. He jimmied open a window which almost fell apart and climbed inside. There was no alarm system and the only way you could have waked up the watchman was with a bomb. He took the tiny vase from its case and put it into a thick canvas sack filled with popcorn, left through the window, drove back to Rome in a car which didn't belong to him, abandoned the car, stashed the objet d'art in his pad where it was going to stay until the collector gave him the five thousand in cash on the following afternoon, and without changing from his black sweater and pants, Kenny went to have a late dinner with the former heavyweight champion of the world, Ingemar Johansson.

After eating, they both left the Da Meo Patacca restaurant and picked up Charlie and Anna Marie at their apartment and drove out to a party in a villa on the beach of Fregene. It was a crumby affair. All the broads were old or ugly and there was this well-known cowboy actor who had made it big in an American television series. He was lushed and kept coming on to Johansson about how he didn't think he was so tough and he was going to prove it just like Floyd Patterson had. Needless to say, Ingemar wanted to bash this guy in his pasty face, but his fists were lethal weapons not to be used outside of a Marquis of Queensberry ring under penalty of the law. Kenny put his arms around the cowboy and led him into a clump of trees, whispering in his ear that he had a secret he wanted to show him. The secret was that the porcelain caps that made a person's teeth look like Chiclets have a tendency to snap loose when the person is hit in the mouth with a stiff right hand. Kenny gave the guy a private demonstration of this phenomenon and then he left the dreary foolishness of the party with the three people he had come there with.

Othello and Charlie used to race an Alfa Romeo Zagato sports car in places like St. Vincent and in September Kenny went with them to watch the racing of the Grand Prix at Monza. Kenny had never seen a Grand Prix so Charlie and Othello explained a little about it and both of them said that they thought a driver named Von Tripps was going to win. But it didn't turn out that way because Count Wolfgang Von Tripp's low-slung car went out of control, jumped an embankment, and killed him and eleven other people who were in the crowd of spectators.

It happened so fast that it seemed like a hallucination. The car careened through the mob and exploded with the slow-motion fury of a napalm bomb. People were running all around in shock, terrified and overwhelmed by the split-second-horror-striking disaster. Men and women were kneeling, praying gratefully to some deity for having spared them or sobbing with grief for the ones who hadn't been spared. The screams of pain from those who had been twisted and burned but were still alive after that moment of dread, were only dulled periodically by the roar of the remaining cars speeding past in the race which Kenny often wondered whether anyone won.

A week or so later, Kenny was talking with some black students from Africa about another crash, the one that killed Dag Hammarskjöld as he was on his way to mediate a solution to the strife-torn Congo which Belgium insisted was their property. The black students were unanimous in their belief that it hadn't been an accident. They emphatically contended that Hammarskjöld was murdered to prevent him from reporting to the United Nations and the world the slaughter and atrocities that the Australian mercenaries were carrying out on the Congolese people. Kenny thought that their theory was a bit far-fetched and anyway he said, "What difference would it have made if Dag Hammarskjöld had revealed what was going on there? Everyone already knows about it and nobody seems to give a shit except in cocktail conversation." They replied that his stature would have taken the quality of rumor out of the stories and that was plenty of difference. Kenny agreed they had a point, but he still didn't think the Belgians would be concerned enough by the possibility of U.N. pressure to rub Hammarskjöld out. The logic of the Africans couldn't convince him that Belgium or any other country for that matter would be afraid of the kind of public opinion that a bunch of lame U.N. delegates could arouse in the world. The discussion ended in a stalemate.

At Christmas, Kenny telephoned his parents for the first time since he had been in Europe. He told them that everything was fine, that he was studying, and that they could write him care of American Express in Rome. They were happy to hear from him and he was glad that they were all okay and everything. When asked how long it would be before he was coming home, Kenny said he really didn't know but as soon as he was finished with school he'd try to come back for a visit. "Give my love to everyone and best wishes for a Merry Christmas and a Happy New Year and please, don't worry about me because I'm working really hard to make you all proud of me. Goodbye. I'll call again."

In the last week of January '62, Kenny went to Naples with a fiery, nineteen-year-old, German redhead who was raised by her mother to be a "gentleman's mistress," and that she was, right down to the smallest, sophisticated bone in her gorgeously firm body. The gentleman in question was a big wheel art director from Hollywood who was living and working on American film productions in Rome. The only trouble with this was that he was over fifty and a young lady needs a little respite now and then from the fatiguing ordeal of flabby sex and hardened arteries. *So*, when what's-his-face went to Yugoslavia to choose some locations for a film that he was working on, Neillie ("Not Nellie, stupid! *Neeeillie!*") drove to Naples with Kenny for a remembrance of things past: things which occur when two young people with tight, hard bodies entangle themselves for an hour or two, making sweet-sour love.

They didn't intend to stay in a Neapolitan hotel but drive on to the town of Posillipo and spend their few days together there. Kenny, however, had made an appointment to buy some grass, which was very hard to come by in those days in Italy. There were some Chicanos stationed at the naval base in Naples and they had a little operation going, having their friends and relatives mail them kilo bricks of grass from Texas. So Neillie and Kenny were going to have lunch in Naples and afterwards he was going to make the pickup.

When they arrived at the central part of the city near the waterfront they ran into a roadblock, and a cop informed them that there was a funeral procession in progress and they would have to turn back or park their car and wait until the ceremony was completed. Kenny didn't know whose funeral it was, so after he curbed the car they walked over and into the huge crowd. It had to be somebody very important and dear to the Neapolitans because all the women were crying and the old men were beating on their chests and pleading with the heavens to have mercy on his soul.

Kenny politely asked a young man who had died. The young man seemed a little disturbed by Kenny's ignorance but answered, "Il Cavaliere Salvatore Luciana, Signore." Kenny thanked him but he had to ponder the name for a few moments before he realized that Salvatore Luciana was none other than "Lucky" Luciano. "I'll be a son of a bitch. It's Lucky Luciano," he said to Neillie who didn't know who he was by either name. Kenny told her that he was one of the guys who ran the gambling rackets in New York City and that he had been deported back to his Neapolitan birthplace.

Kenny had heard about a lot of funerals for gangland bad guys in

America, but even though he had never seen one, he was sure that Lucky Luciano's funeral was going to be hard to beat, even for the Queen of England. The hearse was a nineteenth-century, hand-carved, black wooden coach drawn by a dozen black stallions with violet plumes attached to the crowns of their heads. The last time the coach had been used was when the last king of Naples died long ago. Every Neapolitan who had a brace of horses and a wagon had draped the horses in black, filled the wagon with flowers, and was following Lucky Luciano's body.

Behind them were more Cadillacs than Kenny had thought existed in all of Europe. Half of the population of Naples were thronging the procession and wailing *"Gesu! Gesu!"* and throwing flowers under the hooves of the horses and the wheels of the passing hearse. Someone in the crowd got a little overenthusiastic in expressing his grief and hit the coach driver in the head with a bunch of lilacs, almost knocking off his stovepipe top hat. If there was a system of grading funeral processions and the sincerity of the carryings-on of mourners, the final departure of Lucky Luciano would have won hands down. It was a two-hour orgy of totally convincing baroque despair that day when the people of Naples said goodbye to their favorite son, whose last words to the American public before he had been deported were, "If you want a license to steal, become a politician."

Kenny Wisdom copped the kilo of grass, wrapped the brick in brown paper, went to the post office and mailed it to his address in Rome. He didn't keep the weed with him because in Naples the dealers have a tendency to turn their customers in to the police for a reward which is five times the price of the kilo itself. He returned to the restaurant where he had left Neillie and they drove to a small, rustic hotel, near the hulking volcano of Vesuvius, located by the edge of the sea with a panoramic view of the sparkling waterfront and the magnificent Bay of Naples.

After four delicious, juicy days together, Neillie had to get back to her job in Rome. She returned by train because Kenny was going to take the boat to Messina and drive around Sicily for a couple of weeks. Later that evening, after she had been gone for several hours, someone knocked on the door of Kenny's hotel room as he was packing his things for his trip the following morning. Kenny thought it was an employee of the hotel, but it wasn't.

It was the guy who had introduced Wisdom to the art collector who wanted the Etruscan vase. The theft of the vase had caused a minor stir in the newspapers because all Etruscan art objects were national property and forbidden to be bought or sold, much less stolen and smuggled out of the country by a Scandinavian connoisseur for his own personal enjoyment.

The connect's name was Squint Laszlo, a twenty-six-year-old American, born and raised in Florida by Italian parents who had returned to their native Napoli on the husband's pension. Their son had come with them. Kenny didn't particularly like Squint because there was something about him that smelled wrong, but his reputation was on the up-and-up and you don't necessarily have to like people you do business with, so he said hello and let him in.

Kenny: How'd you find me here?

Squint: I live up on the hill and I saw your car in front of the hotel, so I just asked the manager and he told me your room. It's nice here.

Kenny: Yeah, it's beautiful. What's up?

Squint: You have anything to drink?

Kenny pointed to a bottle of Scotch on a small table and watched him pour some into a glass and sit down in an armchair. He waited for Squint to say why he had come around, because he knew that Squint didn't like him very much either and he wasn't just dropping by for a friendly visit.

Squint: You been doing anything lately?

Kenny: Yeah, I've been minding my own business.

Squint: Easy. Easy. I was just tryin' to be sociable.

Kenny: Well, I don't need no sociable.

Squint: Where's your girl friend?

Kenny: Look, what did you come here for — to talk about my social life, or what?

Squint: Okay. Okay. 'Member the Scandinavian dude you worked for?

Kenny: Yeah. What about him?

Squint: He never paid me nothin' for gettin' him together with you.

Kenny: So?

Squint: Well, I figure I got somethin' comin', seein' that you both got what you wanted. And now he's gone back to wherever he come from 'n I got no way of makin' him come through with some coin, so I figure that you may be able to help me out some. See what I mean?

Kenny: Yea, I got good eyesight. How much did you expect to get from the cat?

Squint: 'Bout ten percent of what you got, five hundred dollars.

Kenny: How come you let the dude go by without payin' you?

Squint: I just wasn't thinkin', that's all. You know how it is sometimes. You . . .

Kenny: Uh-huh, here's two hundred. Next time you're in Rome, you call me up and I'll let you have the rest.

Squint: Thanks man, I really appreciate this. I didn't mean it to be this way, puttin' the bite on you 'n all but I'm in a bad way . . .

Kenny: Forget it. Now, look, I got things to do, so if you don't mind . . .

Squint finished off his drink, pocketed the dough, and lingered by the door. "Sure, I just want to make it clear that I know that you don't have to give me nothin' and I want you to understand that I know that, and . . ."

Kenny: What's the matter, don't you know how to open the door?

Squint: I'm leavin'. I'm leavin'. And thanks, Kenny, I really mean it. And I'll definitely call you when I'm in Rome, definitely. See ya, 'n thanks again.

Kenny didn't believe that Squint hadn't been paid by the Scandinavian but it was worth the two hundred to string him out on a line waiting for the rest of the promised five. Kenny figured that this way Laszlo wouldn't go wrong on him for some loose change. "The cut-rate parasitical prick!"

Kenny traveled around Sicily for a month and while he was there, he found out that his beef with Syracuse Frankie in New York had been forgotten through the intercession of somebody's father whom he had met in Rome. It was very good news and it made Kenny's trip extra worthwhile.

Charlie, his wife Anna Marie, and their child Roma returned to the States late that spring. Kenny was sorry to see them go because of all the good times they had had together, but Charlie wanted to attend school in New York and study architectural design. He wanted to build and rebuild everything from stores to houses to country cottages and within a few years he was successfully doing just that, without ever having gotten a high school diploma. He didn't need one. He already knew how smart he was and he learned how to do what he wanted to do and he did it. It was as simple as that. *"Arrivadella!"* Kenny assured them that he would be seeing them, as they boarded their Alitalia flight for New York.

Ever since Kenny had returned to Rome, Squint Laszlo had persistently telephoned him collect from Naples at least once a week. Kenny finally refused to accept the calls and early one afternoon, guess who showed up at Kenny's place. When he opened the downstairs door, Kenny blew it. "What the fuck are you doin' here? Huh? How'd you find where I lived? You miserable cocksucker! Get in here!" and Kenny grabbed Squint by his shirt and pulled him inside, off the street, pushed him upstairs, and made him sit in the kitchen.

Squint: Listen Kenny, I . . .

Kenny: No, *you* listen! I told you I didn't have no fuckin' money for you! And what do you do, you come here to bust my balls! You fuckin' punk! How many times I tell you that I'm broke and can't give you nothin' until I find some work, huh?! *How many times!* And you come here! What is it, you don't believe me, huh? *Huh?*

Squint: No, you're wrong, man. I didn't come here to hit on you for any bread. In fact, I forgot all about that. I just need some help, that's all. It's nothin' to do with money, honest, Kenny, nothin'.

Kenny: What kind of help?

And Squint produced a kilo brick of grass from under his shirt. Kenny didn't say anything. He went into the adjacent room and returned with a Lupara shotgun which he had bought in Sicily. He had two shells in his hand and he cracked open the weapon and said to the now terrified Squint, "If you're not outta here by the time I load and cock this, I'm going to blow both your arms off."

Squint Laszlo split so fast, he fell all the way down the stairs with the shout of "And I never want to see you again, *you cheese-eatin' motherfucker!*" in his ears as he opened the door and ran away.

Kenny Wisdom paced around his apartment. He was furious because he had been right about Squint Laszlo being a wrong number. *"The cocksucker!"* And it was no good staying around Rome while the Squint tried to figure out a way of setting him up for a fall. No, it was time for a suntan!

Kenny hurriedly packed some gear together, called the phone company and told them to temporarily disconnect his service, locked up the apartment, advised the landlord in the grocery store that he was going on a vacation to get some sun and to please keep an eye on his place. Across the street he told his good friend Maurizio Grana, who ran the rackets and most of the underworld activity in that section of Trastevere, to spread the word about this Squint Laszlo and to please make sure that no punks broke into his place while he was away. Then he got into his car, went to the bank where he withdrew about five hundred thousand lire and got a letter of credit for the rest, and drove straight up the Via Aurelia to San Remo, stopping only for food and gas.

Alfredo was still busy with his restaurant in Germany and hadn't been back since his thirtieth birthday but Mama Rizzo was alive and well and very happy to see Kenny. She fed him an enormous meal and told him to go sleep in Alfredo's bed.

The next morning, he explained that he wanted to find a place of his own in San Remo, because he wanted to stay for a while and the hotels were too expensive. In two days, Mama Rizzo introduced him to one Giuseppe Tiberi who had a small place he wished to sublet for a few months while he and his wife went to visit his son, the doctor, in America. Kenny went to look at it and it was exactly what he'd wanted. A two-room stucco house with a kitchen, bath, and a corner terrace with a view of the sea. It was set into the side of a hill overlooking San Remo and Kenny gave the man three months' rent in advance, plus a little extra for security, a total of less than three hundred dollars. That's not counting the number of kisses Kenny bestowed on Mama Rizzo for having come through like the champ she was.

Kenny Wisdom did nothing but work on his suntan religiously for the next two months. He must have used three gallons of suntan oil in coaxing his skin into a bronze blend, puttng it on before, during and after he sunbathed to avoid any burning or peeling. At first, he only took the sun on his terrace because the paleness of his body embarrassed him too much to expose himself on the pleasantly crowded Riviera beach. But when he arrived at the point where he couldn't see his freckles for his tan, he began swimming in the Mediterranean surf. Besides sunning and swimming, Kenny would eat dinner once or twice a week with Mama Rizzo and her family; go drinking with Alfredo's younger brothers and friends; pick up foreign girls and offer them the hospitality of his humble abode; read newspapers to learn how the games played by the men of the world were turning out — and read books. Not books about other books, or books that teach things they pay you for, just books of prose, poetry and both.

The Russian spy, Colonel Rudolf Abel, was released from prison and exchanged for the American spy, Francis Gary Powers. John Glenn became the first American in orbit and was a national hero. And Kenny was damned if those Algerians didn't pull it off, when he read the news of the cease-fire in Algeria, and the subsequent declaration of independence and the proclamation of one of the leaders of the revolution as the independent Algeria's premier, Ben Bella. But a short time later Kenny was astonished to discover that the fighting over Algeria hadn't ceased on the home front of France. The Algerian immigrants were peaceful enough, but the rebellious right-wing faction of the French army, the OAS, wasn't very happy about the way things turned out in the granting of independence to the people of a colony whom they'd been fighting against for so long to prevent just such an independence. It made them look like losers in the eyes of the world, while the truth of the matter, they said, was that they had been sold out and dishonored by bureaucrats and the government of France itself. So, to revenge their loss of face, they started their own little wave of terrorism throughout France and even attempted to assassinate Charles de Gaulle a few times. The turmoil of the Algerian crisis wasn't over yet, goddamit!

One news item, however, pleased Kenny Wisdom no end: The $1,500,000 Mail Truck Robbery in New England. The heist was perfectly carried out by five or six men and a woman who didn't leave a trace of a clue as to who they were or where they went, and they didn't have to use violence to accomplish their goal, either. It was a slick number, planned to precision, an admirable event. "Bravo!" In October, Kenny went to lie on the beach at Nice for a while and he met a beautiful girl on the sand. They were getting along fine, with Louise running her fingers and eyes all over his body and noticing his now-faint freckles and saying, "*Regardez les taches de rousseur!*" and him saying, "*Ce ne sont pas des taches de rousseur, ce sont des baisers des anges!*" and they laughed and kissed and his hands massaged her strong, soft back and made it feel good, and they rolled around in the surf and ran along the beach and played and were very happy with each other and glad that their lives had brought them together. They made elaborate, detailed plans of how they were going to enjoy each other that evening — and all of a sudden a fat man with a straw hat jumped up in the shade of an umbrella and screamed, "*Mon Dieu! Mon Dieu!*" over and over and attracted a group of people which soon became a crowd around his deluxe portable transistor radio. They too began to exclaim things like "*Mon Dieu!*" and "*Merde!*" and Kenny and Louise thought that it was a very funny spectacle until the crowd kept growing and the faces of all the people looked somber and most of them were picking up their towels and hurrying back to their hotels. Kenny stood up and asked someone what was going on and the man rapidly replied as he gathered up his air mattress and stuff that World War Three was about to erupt and Kenny collapsed on the sand pebbles and kicked his feet and slammed his fists in a *"No! No!"* tantrum. Louise took him by the hand and they went to her hotel and made love in bed thinking that it was the last day in the rest of their lives because John Fitzgerald Kennedy had given Nikita Sergeevich Khrushchev an "or else" ultimatum about something which was the Cuban Missile Crisis and everyone thought that it was all over now baby blue.

It wasn't of course. Just a game in a war as cold as a dead celibate's balls and it pissed Kenny off at the puppeteers who ran those scams in the name of the puppetry of peace. However, he wasn't as angry as he became when he returned to San Remo and one of Alfredo's brothers told him that the cops were looking for him, why, he didn't know.

Kenny had an idea and no intention of sticking around to confirm it. He packed his stuff into his car and drove the hell out of there and back down to the Via Aurelia to Rapallo where he turned off onto highway 227, passed through Santa Margherita and checked into a small, elegant hotel in Portofino. It was a stupid thing to do. He should have left the country.

He realized this at five o'clock one morning a week later, when the door to his room was turned into firewood by the banzai charge of a half dozen cops who ran in and all over his bed, waving their Berrettas all at once and shouting that he was under arrest and to get up and get dressed but not to make a move or they would shoot him. Kenny lay naked on top of the bed waiting for the coppers to get over their Keystone jitters. He didn't dare respond to any of their demands to move for fear of being shot by one of them who didn't want him to move. They were really freaky and he didn't want to do anything to spook them so he just froze and made like he didn't understand what they were all yelling about.

A lieutenant finally came into the room and the raiding party got off of Kenny's bed and simply stood around it, covering him with their guns. No one had even turned the lights on. The only illumination came from a lamp in the hallway and the officer told one of his men to switch on the light, unless they wanted to wait for the dawn. He ordered another two to search Kenny's clothes before allowing him to get dressed and the rest to give the room a thorough going-over, before stuffing the suspect's belongings into his bag.

Every one of the hotel staff was waiting for them, when they went downstairs. The manager expressed his sympathy for Kenny's unavoidable inconvenience and presented him with the bill, which he accepted but didn't pay. This caused the manager to have a change of heart and he adopted a very hostile attitude that soon turned into self-pity when the lieutenant informed him that whatever money the suspect had was now state evidence and couldn't be used to pay any hotel bill. The manager began to weep at his misfortune and Kenny left with the police.

Two cops followed the siren-wailing-flashing-light caravan in Kenny's car, as they all drove to police headquarters in Rapallo. The lieutenant asked Kenny all kinds of questions which he didn't answer and probably couldn't have even if he had wanted to because the cop who was driving the car they were in was trying to maintain control of it without reducing his speed of a hundred and sixty kilometers an hour and he wasn't having too much success. Maybe he was trying to break some kind of record by driving the eleven kilometers to the station in eight minutes but he certainly almost broke all their necks at least a dozen times during the ride. It was quite a wake-up, especially when they slid sideways through a turn and almost flipped over and into the waters of the Rapallo Gulf.

Kenny sighed with relief when they screeched to a halt in front of the headquarters and he was glad that his arms were handcuffed behind his back because he wanted to pound the driver's nose into the back of his head. Inside, they ushered him into a captain's office which had a desk full of American detective magazines. The captain was sitting behind that desk. He was given Kenny's passport which he scrutinized while Kenny stood in front of him surrounded by a battery of cops. The captain looked at the photo in the passport carefully, then examined Kenny's face, then back to the photo, then the face, photo, face, face and photo. He put a cigarette into his holder, lit it, took a few drags, blew the smoke towards Kenny, and asked his first question, "What's your name?" The guards around Kenny all elbowed each other, commenting on how clever their captain was to ask the suspect his name even though he had his passport in front of him. One of them called it, "Not missing a trick."

Kenny was inclined to call it something else but instead he just answered, "Kenneth Wisdom."

The second question by Captain Clever was "How do you spell it?"

And the peanut gallery elbowed each other again and Kenny knew that it was going to be a long day. "K, E, N, N, E, T, H, W, I, S, D, O, M."

The third question was "How old are you?" To which Kenny answered, "Eighteen."

Captain Clever went, *"Ha-haaa!* You lie, Signore! According to your passport you are still seventeen for two more weeks! Now, we continue and no more lies, only the truth! The truth, understand!" He slapped the desk for emphasis and the gallery started murmuring things about his being a genius at interrogation, and the questioning went on and on with Kenny playing D & D to Captain Clever's I.Q. for hours.

Kenny was driven to Rome the next day for arraignment on charges of addiction and possession of narcotics for sale. They had apparently found an ounce of marijuana and what they claimed were five bags of heroin in his Rome apartment. Kenny knew that he had smoked up all the grass in his pad months ago and he hadn't even seen heroin, much less used it, since the spring of 1958. Therefore, he came to the obvious conclusion: Squint Laszlo, "That *motherfuckin' cheese eater!"*

Captain Clever had boasted of his fine detective work in locating Kenny at the hotel in Portofino. When a foreigner checks into a hotel, he must register with his passport, and a name, address, and date-of-birth report is sent to some bureaucrat in the local government who routinely telephones the captain of the local police department when he notices that a man they are looking for is staying in such and such a hotel. Yes, you couldn't outsmart the likes of old Captain Clever. No, he was some Sherlock all right. *The pudgy little runt!*

Kenny was questioned again in Rome and again with the same inane line of interrogation. Afterwards, he was booked into the Regina Coeli jail. The name means the Queen of the Heavens jail. It was built at the orders of the king of Italy back in the nineteenth century and when he saw what a magnificent jail his royal architect had constructed, he was so pleased that he told the man he could have anything that he desired, within reason of course. The architect replied that his only request was for the king to spend the first night there before it was opened to the public, and then the architect hanged himself from the Garibaldi Bridge which is less than a hundred yards from the prison's entrance.

Kenny Wisdom spent seven months without bail in that cramped-

moss - ridden - rat - infested - syphilitic - conjunctivitic - tuberculous-
marasmic - anemic - choreal - cancerous - scabied - ringwormed - rotten-
crippling-languishing-ulcerated-septic dungeon of bronchopneumo-
nia and there was only one thing on his mind, the bitter thought of
Squint Laszlo. When he came to trial, the prosecutor waived the
charge of addiction for lack of evidence and dismissed the case. The
five bags of alleged heroin turned out to be five unmarked packets
of soap powder and the ounce of marijuana hadn't been on the
kitchen table when Kenny had left for his vacation because the
landlord had checked the apartment out several times after Kenny
had been gone and the informer who had telephoned the tip into
the police was nowhere to be found, so they let Kenny Wisdom go
free after having taken away the only suntan he had ever had in his
life.

His young defense attorney made an ardent, grandstand speech
about the injustice of it all, and pointed out the obvious failure of
the intelligence of the police to the three judges, and demanded to
know how his client was ever possibly going to achieve redress for
the torturous time he had spent in the Regina Coeli and for his
Alfa Romeo Giulietta which had been sold at the police department auction in Genoa. The defense attorney was advised by the
chief of the three judges that redress was available through the
courts and his client only had to file a civil suit against the state for
compensation for his grievances. The lawyer suggested to Kenny
that he would be more than happy to handle a suit against the state,
if Kenny would retain him with a slight fee. He was told to forget
it.

Kenny Wisdom was interested in justice but he just wasn't in the
habit of expecting it for himself. As far as he was concerned, justice
always ran a poor second to injustice which was almost perfect. The
wrong people went hungry. The wrong people were being loved.
The wrong people were dying. He wasn't angry, he just wanted to
get even, and he had no intention of going about it through the
folly of the judicial system.

Later that afternoon of June 2, 1963, Kenny was processed out of
the Regina Coeli and his belongings were returned to him. He took
a taxi to his flat on Via del Mattonato. Thanks to the strong-arm of
Maurizio Grana, the landlord-grocer had been persuaded not to
lease the apartment to someone else and he was delighted to see
Kenny step out of the cab in front of his store. He beamed with
affection for his lessee because the rent was long overdue, in fact, he

hadn't received any money for nearly nine months. Kenny thanked him for his kind trust and assured him that he would pay a full year's rent in the next day or so, to show his appreciation for the landlord's benevolent and sympathetic consideration of his unfortunate plight.

The cops had ransacked the apartment and it was in a shambles but Kenny didn't care. He only cared about one thing, the shotgun, and it was still under the floorboard in the bedroom where he had left it. He looked it over to see if it had gotten rusty or anything, and when he was satisfied that it was still in good shape, he put it back under the board. He took a shower, scrubbing away the clammy stench of the Regina Coeli until the hot water ran out. He dressed and went downstairs and across the street to speak with Maurizio Grana but he wasn't there. When asked, one of his strong-arms said that he was in Saint Peter's Square at the Vatican, because "Johnny Walker is dying."

Johnny Walker was the name given to Pope John XXIII by the people who make their living in the streets of Rome because he was always sneaking out of the Vatican palace in the normal, black cassock of a simple priest and walking around the slums of the city, rapping with the class of people that he belonged to and had never turned his back on. He was seldom recognized, but on one occasion he was talking to a guy selling fruit from a pushcart and he was talking straight, not riffing any Hail Marys. He wanted to know what kind of economic shape the guy and his family were in; he wasn't concerned if the guy was in a state of grace or not. He asked the vendor whether he and his family got enough to eat, was their home adequately comfortable, were they catching any breaks, and so on. Now, you would have to go to the People's Republic of China to outdo the anticlericalism of the poor Italian working man, so it wasn't unusual for the vendor to become annoyed with the prying of the priest who was distracting him from his work. When the priest said that the fruit was certainly ripe and fresh and wondered if the vendor would be so kind as to give him a peach which he couldn't pay for because he hadn't any money, the guy turned red and looked up from his cart for the first time at the priest's face, and the name of the place where he was going to tell the priest to go clotted below the adam's apple of his throat, the moment he recognized the face above the starchy collar. When he'd recovered from his near-stroke, he tried to kneel down on the sidewalk to ask forgiveness, but Johnny Walker stopped him and told him to cool it because all he wanted was a peach and he'd pay him the four cents for it, if the vendor would accompany him back to his rectory which was the Vatican.

The whole police force of Rome had been alerted to the pope's disappearance and there were rumors that he had been kidnapped and was being held for an enormous ransom. There were cops all over the place when the little priest showed up at the rear gate of the Vatican garden and asked the gardener if he could borrow twenty-five lire from him to purchase a peach from the dumbfounded vendor. The gardener had to postpone his epileptic fit in order to loan him the change to pay for the peach. Within hours the push-cart vendor's photo was on the front pages of every Italian newspaper and he was interviewed on nationwide radio and television and from then on, mobs of people were fighting to buy the fruit from the man and his pushcart because both were obviously Papal Blessed.

Kenny bought a pack of Chesterfields from the strong-arm and went over to Saint Peter's Square to find Maurizio Grana and pay his final respects to the dying Johnny Walker.

The sun had gone down and it was early evening and the square was filled with people who were standing vigil for a good man who had refused to be corrupted by power. A good man who had a lot of heart and the class to go with it. The crowd of people who were waiting there, quietly saying goodbye to a man they knew was good, were not a bunch of sob-sisters, breast-beaters or hand-wringers. They were low and high money people, pimps and hookers, movie stars and producers, waiters and beggars, boosters and killers, gamblers and fugitives, drunkards and dopers, gangsters and thieves, aristocrats and riffraffs, peddlers and vendors, farmers and landscapers, bartenders and mechanics, prizefighters and soccer players, owners and renters, bastards and mothers, pickpockets and fat-wallets, swindlers and graft-takers, tough and tender, heavyweight and lightweight, legit and illegit, educated and illiterate, creative and mercenary, all with one thing in common among them, their badness. And that night, the baddest of Rome interrupted whatever villainy they were into and came together to show their class to the world by standing up for the goodness of one of their own. The politicians of the Catholic Church stated that John XXIII was an interim pope, but they were wrong. He was the last pope.

Johnny Walker died the next evening and it was business as usual again. Kenny had a few drinks with Maurizio Grana and he learned that Squint Laszlo had indeed set him up and snitched to the coppers and that shortly before Kenny had come up for trial, Squint had split back to America and was living alone in Norfolk, the seaport city of Virginia. There he was involved in a small operation, distributing hash and heroin that was smuggled into the States by sailors and other seamen, to fourth-rate pushers from Philadelphia. It was strictly a penny-ante operation, said Grana, and the Outfit let it exist because it took some heat off of their own dope syndicate.

Maurizio offered to have someone in America take care of Squint Laszlo for a nominal fee but Kenny said no. "Just try and make the proper arrangements for me to go there myself without having to use my own passport. Can you do that?" Maurizio said sure but it would take a little time. And that it did. Kenny didn't arrive in the United States until late October. He only took one bag with some changes of clothes, his shotgun and shells.

Squint Laszlo had gotten married when he returned to America and he kept his wife clear of his business by renting a house in a small town outside of Raleigh, North Carolina. She was nearly six months pregnant according to the information Maurizio had gathered and Squint visited her at regular intervals of once or twice each week. That's where Kenny decided to hit him, as he was coming home.

Kenny rented a motel room in a neighboring town under an assumed name. He had cased the house where Squint's wife lived and he had watched Laszlo come and go a few times, in order to pick a good spot to waylay him when the time came. During the month Kenny spent checking and rechecking the area, running and re-running the roads, and acquainting himself with whatever activities occurred at certain hours of the day in that locality, he also learned about the town where he was staying and its people. His motive was simple curiosity. He hadn't been to the United States for over four years and he had never been to the South.

His motel was on the outskirts of the town and the first day Kenny went out for a beer, he had to walk half a mile before he saw a bar sign. He walked into the Petite Birdland Club and ordered a rye with beer chaser, feeling a little strange in the place because everyone else was black. He used the name Eddie Walsh again when the bartender started a conversation and he told him he was from nowhere in particular. There was a rag-tag pool table in one corner, booths along one wall and tables in the center of the room, and the jukebox music was good and loud.

He hadn't been in there for more than five minutes, when a young blood walked over to him and asked him if he was "Lookin' for some black cock?" Kenny thought he was being called a faggot and was about to split the guy's face with his bottle of beer but an older dude stepped in and explained to Kenny that the guy hadn't been putting him down but just asking him if he was looking for some black pussy, that's all. "Cock mean pussy down here, boy. So, don't you go takin' no offense, y'hear." Everybody had a giggle and Kenny went there often to get drunk and eat hot chili, ham hocks, black-eyed peas and have a piece of black cock now and then.

When he wasn't keeping Squint Laszlo's house under surveillance or hanging out at the Petite Birdland Club, he would watch all the civil rights marching that was going on downtown and the sit-ins and demonstrations. He saw crackers use the nonviolent, passive demonstrators as punching bags. One time, he clocked a group of customers in a diner gang up on a half dozen girls who were sitting in the doorway and break all their ankles and pour Clorox down their throats, smashing their teeth with the mouth of the bottle. The woman who owned the diner squatted down over the girl who had led the sit-in and pissed on her face, calling her *"A pig!" A pig!"* over and over while her yellow urine sprayed down from beneath her hoisted dress to the hysterical glee of her applauding customers. When the cops came, they arrested the demonstrators and carted them off to jail not to the hospital.

Kenny thought a lot about that nonviolence and concluded that it was an ideological crock of shit. "It's got nothing to do with human nature or being a human being. Turn the other cheek, bullshit! You kiss my ass!" He couldn't understand the logic of not defending your right to eat, sleep, sit, work, shit and go to school where you wanted to and make love and marry whom you wanted to. "These people are doing nothing but asking for their civil rights, when they should just take them and let anybody try to stop them. They claim that passive resistance is the only way to avoid bloodshed. Whose blood? Certainly not theirs. They say that they are fighting a struggle, but as soon as the battle starts they lie down and cover their heads and get whupped. They were going to overcome? What? When? Did they figure that the crackers would get tired of stompin' and shootin' them? Or maybe they were playing for the sympathy of the closet-queen-liberals with that line about four hundred years of enforced Negro servitude to the white man. Well, how can any man, be he good or bad, have any respect, never mind sympathy, for a people who have allowed themselves to be oppressed for so long, by so many, by even their own, and have done nothing about it, except ask, 'Please may we integrate and vote now?' Yea, sure you can come in now, James Moody, and play if you want to, we're through. 'Free at last! Free at last! Great Gugamonga, we are free at last!' Who the fuck was he kidding. They sure are a strange bunch of niggers, these civil righters."

The only hitch in the plans that Kenny Wisdom had laid for Squint Laszlo was that the Squint always arrived from and returned to Norfolk in the daylight when there were people on the roads, making it difficult for Kenny to carry out his premeditation without risking being spotted by someone. So, he altered his plan and went to a sporting goods store in Raleigh where he bought a shotgun-cleaning kit as a prop in the implementation of a new scheme.

The civil righters were at it again, marching, demonstrating, picketing, sitting-in, and going limp when the state troopers arrested them. Kenny was passing an alley about two or three blocks from the center of the action when he heard them. Two burly, drunk crackers working over five civil rights kids who were rolled up in the nonviolent defensive position, protecting their skulls and their vital organs from damage. Kenny shoved the cleaning kit into the waistband of his corduroys and snuck up behind the guy with the axe handle in the rear of the alley. The other guy was busy trying to kick in some kid's ribs and he didn't notice Kenny take the headache-stick away from his partner, but he heard the sound it made when Kenny crushed in the side of his friend's face with it, and he turned just in time to catch a glimpse of the club as it linedrived his jaw into right field. Both of them were on the ground, creamed unconscious. Kenny tossed the axe handle down and told the civil rights activists that it was all right to get up now and that they'd better split before the coppers noticed what had happened. The two white girls, the two white boys and the black girl looked up at Kenny and back down at the K.O.'d bullies, and one of the white girls, a black-haired Jewish bohemian from New York or New Jersey, stood up and demanded an explanation from Kenny of why he had done what he did.

Kenny was slightly astonished but he answered, "Well, you see, last night I had a dream and I was trying to think of it when I passed this alley here and those two guys interrupted my train of thought with all the noise they were making, beating on you like that, so I made them be quiet."

Only Kenny and the sixteen- or seventeen-year-old black girl thought he was funny. The other four to his disbelief started shouting things like, "Who do you think you are, anyway?" "Why don't you mind your own business, this is our thing and we want to do it our way!" and "You shouldn't hit people like that! You should pity them because they don't know what they're doing!"

Kenny raised his hands and yelled, "*All right! All right! Enough!* I see. I see. Forgive them for they know not what they do. Okay, I'll mind my own business and you do it your way. I learned my lesson and I promise that I won't stick my neck out for nobody, no more. Nice meetin' you!" And as he turned to storm out of the alley, the black girl caught him by the arm and said, "Thank you, brother."

"Forget it ever happened, sweetheart. You better get yourself and your friends outta here before they come and lock you up and throw the key away."

The last thing to reach his ears when he walked away was a muffled cry from one of the white kids. "We're not afraid!" he said. And Kenny was very happy for him.

Kenny spent most of the weekdays in the motel looking at television. Besides watching Lassie put her life in danger to rescue a pair of small boys from the raging rapids of one river or another, he watched a quiz show entitled, *The Senate Permanent Investigations Subcommittee Hearing* which starred John L. McClellan and Joseph M. Valachi. It got great reviews. The New York *Times* which Kenny had bought at the bus station in Raleigh said, "Not since Frank Costello's fingers drummed the table during the Kefauver hearings, has there been so fascinating a show."

Valachi was a great performer and should have been awarded an Emmy. He talked about "La Cosa Nostra," which means our business, our matter, or our thing, and he told how he went about doing his thing as a soldier for the Vito Genovese family in and around the New York City area. He helped to identify 317 members of the Mafia, most of whom were dead and buried or had been reported missing in action.

One of the great segments of this situation comedy series occurred when Joe Valachi recounted how he and a kid named Tommy fulfilled a murder contract one night. He said that they had brought the marked man out to a restaurant in the Bronx for dinner. Then he started talking about his accomplice whom he obviously liked very much. He said things like, "He was a nice kid. You could talk to him. A real collegiate type. He even dressed Ivy League 'n everything. I mean, you could have a conversation with him. He was real intelligent. A collegiate type. A gentleman. He could put words together right, so you could talk easier to him. He wasn't a stupid. He was educated. He read lots of books. A real collegiate type. He even wore a vest once. He knew about all sortsa interestin' things. We used to converse good together. He was a real likable kid," until he had the senate subcommittee crazy and Senator McClellan interrupted him and told him that he could appreciate Mr. Valachi's admiration for the young man but would he please get to the point of the story and explain if and how they killed their dinner guest.

Joe Valachi replied, "Yea, sure. During the course of the meal, we strangled him," and then, "He was a real nice kid. You know, a collegiate type . . ." Kenny convulsed with laughter, as did most of the reporters and spectators at the hearing, and he thought that Joe Valachi should be given his own prime time TV program and be allowed to make the people laugh who were missing his comic routine because they had to work during the day.

This first figure in the history of the crime syndicate to break the "Omertá" blood code of silence was the best comedy actor in the most entertaining show that was ever produced on television, with the exception of Peter Falk in his short-lived series, *The Trials of O'Brien*, God bless him!

Kenny paid for his room at the motel every three or four days in advance to keep the manager from fearing that he was going to skip out without settling his bill. He also talked with the guy about how difficult it was to get a job, to hold him over until he found the right farm to buy because that was what he said he intended to do. "I like to be independent and I figure if I find a place for the right price, I can work it and me and my girl can get married and raise a family in this lovely part of the country . . ." was the type of line he used to satisfy the man's curiosity.

On Monday afternoon of November 18, 1963, Kenny Wisdom got even with Squint Laszlo. He had watched him arrive home earlier that day from behind the tree line that bordered his property and he had waited for his wife to drive into town for some groceries. When she left, he checked to see if anyone was around and walked over to the house with the cleaning kit under his belt and the loaded shotgun beneath his raincoat. He opened the unlocked back door, went inside, and surprised the shit out of Squint Laszlo, who was watching a soap opera on TV. He leveled the shotgun, which he had wiped clean of all fingerprints, at Laszlo, and motioned for him to get up and go sit at the kitchen table.

Squint: Kenny! What are you doin' here? My God, what's wrong?

Kenny: Shaddup! Do exactly what I say and don't try anything.

He put the gun-cleaning kit — also wiped free of his prints — on the kitchen table and told Squint to open it and take everything out and unscrew the tops on the bottles of cleaning fluid. Squint did, putting his prints all over everything. He was shaking so much he even spilled some of the fluid on the table.

Kenny noticed that Squint was right-handed, like he had hoped he was. He crouched down beside the table, next to Squint's right knee and held the double barrels of the shotgun six inches from the point where Laszlo's throat curved into his chin.

Squint Laszlo whimpered, "I didn't mean nothin! I'll make it up to you. Please don't! Why?"

Kenny Wisdom said the word "Suntan," a moment before he squeezed one of the triggers and shredded Squint Laszlo's head from his body.

The noise was very loud and half of the kitchen was splattered with blood, bone and brains. Kenny was careful not to get any of it on him as he opened and closed Laszlo's hands around the barrel, trigger and butt of the shotgun. He took the box of shells out of his coat pocket, placed them on the table, and put one of the shells into the second barrel which he had left empty because he had been afraid that it might have gone off with the first round. He wanted a live round to be in the barrel next to the spent cartridge of the other. He laid the shotgun down across Laszlo's right ankle, made sure everything was properly arranged and went over to the curtained window, took a hard look around, and when he was satisfied that no one was out on the road or peeking out of the windows of any of the three houses which were fifty yards away, he turned off the TV and beat it back to his motel, leaving Squint Laszlo for his wife to find.

The news on the local radio and TV stations and in the local papers the following day reported that one of the town's residents, a Mr. Squint Laszlo, had been cleaning his Italian-made shotgun the previous afternoon and his head had gotten in the way and it had been blown off. His wife had discovered her husband's body and was now under sedation. The sheriff's department and the coroner's office ruled that it had been an accidental death and also that it was the fourth such case in the area that year and warned the community to check and make absolutely sure that their weapons were unloaded before proceeding to clean them. And the funeral services were going to be held at . . . Et cetera.

Kenny burned the gloves, shoes and clothes that he had worn when he paid Squint Laszlo his last visit. The only emotion he felt was satisfaction. The bitter thought of Squint Laszlo had been on his mind for over a year and now it was just a memory which he found easy to forget. He was even Steven, that's all. In fact, he even believed he had let the Squint off lightly by simply killing him because when you sit in a damp, diseased prison, hating someone so much that your hate becomes dispassionate, you calculate ways to make him live horribly for what he has done, rather than just die for it. The suffering of being blown away by a shotgun blast is slight, compared to the suffering that a person would have to endure, if he was forced to continue living after his tongue had been cut out or his hands or feet cut off or after his liver had been infected with cirrhosis by the injection of a particular poison into his bloodstream. No, a quick death is easy going in contrast to a dwindling life of anguish. The only reason Kenny had quick-killed Squint Laszlo, instead of making him live a life of torture, was that it had been more convenient.

Kenny decided to spend the rest of the week in the town where he had been staying for nearly a month because his passage back to Italy from a Canadian port wasn't for another twelve days and he liked the Southern town and the people he had met there. He was drinking beer and shooting pool at La Petite Birdland, early one Friday afternoon, when a hefty woman ran into the place and shouted for Choice Horse, the bartender, to turn on the TV, "Cause someone just shot de President!"

At one thirty in the afternoon, Walter Cronkite with his voice wavering and his eyes watering, announced that the President of the United States was dead, was dead, was dead. And for the next seventy-two hours, Kenny and the black men and women who crowded into the club because they had no television sets in their homes drank a lot of liquor and ate some food and watched and listened to the news coverage surrounding the assassination of the thirty-fifth President of the United States.

They saw stiff-upper-lipped Jacqueline remain tearless because as one reporter put it, "She seemed to know that there is a way to act when the President of the United States has been assassinated."

They saw the Texas Book Depository and the six'
from where, the authorities said, a man whom they
movie theater after he had shot a patrolman nar
aimed his mail-order rifle at the back of the Pre
fired the shots which killed him and wounded
Texas, as they drove down Elm Street in a moto
city of Dallas. The man's name was Lee Harvey Oswald anu —
supposed to have done it all alone — they said.

They saw a still of Lyndon Johnson standing next to Jacqueline Kennedy, being inaugurated as the next President on board the
plane that was to carry the body of the former President in a bronze
coffin back to Washington, D.C. There it was draped with an American flag and placed in the center of the rotunda of the Capitol
building and surrounded by an honor guard of six men from the
armed forces who stood at parade rest while two long lines of people
passed by the coffin in silence. The commentaries and the statistics
and the analogies and the editorials which blamed John Kennedy's
death on every American because we all hated each other too much
became boring and redundant and had everybody turning away
from the television set by Sunday morning, only to have their interest aroused again with the promise that in a few moments the assas-
sin was going to walk out of a basement elevator and the TV cameras were going to show you what a man who has murdered a President looks like when he moves.

The crowd at La Petite Birdland got more than they were promised because a bit player named Jack Ruby pulled out a gun and
performed the first actual murder recorded on a live national tele-
cast when he put a bullet into Oswald's stomach because he had
taken little Caroline's father away from her. Everybody in the club
went "Oooooeeeeee!" and their enthusiasm returned and they
began drinking and laughing again, until the video tape replays of
Jack Ruby's big scene also got monotonous.

On Monday, the funeral procession was a spectacle of important,
powerful, famous faces marching behind the flag-covered coffin that
sat on top of a black caisson and it reminded Kenny of Lucky Luciano's funeral in Naples. All the men and women in the club were
pointing out people they recognized to each other as close-ups of
their faces appeared on the screen, and then there was Johnson
standing by the grave at Arlington Cemetery and the coffin was
lowered into the ground and the American flag was properly folded
and presented to the widow and it was over.

ite was summarizing the various reactions of important
can figures to the death of John Kennedy and he said that
e had only been one sour comment received and that it hadn't
een completely unexpected, considering the man who'd made the
statement was Malcolm X, who, when asked how he felt about the
assassination, had replied that "the chickens had come home to
roost." Everyone in La Petite Birdland laughed and raised their
glasses to Malcolm X because as someone there said, "He was one
bad nigger!"

Kenny was glad that there was a man out there like Malcolm X to
tell society it was full of shit. Personally, Kenny had no hankering to
fight society or reform it; he just wanted to rob it. But he knew that
Malcolm X had been Detroit Red and had gotten religion while he
was doing a term in the penitentiary and that when he was released,
he began saying all those things that nobody wanted to hear and the
way he said them, made all the squares piss in their pants. Kenny
liked him very much and wished him everything good you can hope
for a man.

Kenny stopped for a day in New York on his way back to Italy but
he didn't contact anyone he knew, especially his parents whom he
had corresponded with from Rome from time to time. He didn't go
uptown either, he stayed downtown and walked around Greenwich
Village because it was the section of Manhattan which had no
facsimile in Europe and he wanted to take a piece of it back with
him. He saw six films in succession that afternoon and early evening,
six films that he had never seen the likes of before. They were *Guns
of the Trees*, *Shadows*, *The Connection*, *On the Bowery*, *The
Flower Thief*, and *Cool World*.

He went into a bookstore on Eighth Street and bought a shopping
bag full of prose poetry which wasn't available in the English lan-
guage bookstore of Rome. Books by Gary Snyder, Michael McClure,
Philip Lamantia, Lawrence Ferlinghetti, John Weiners, Allen
Ginsberg, Samuel Beckett, Philip Whalen, Jack Spicer, Kenneth
Rexroth, Eugene Ionesco, Jack Kerouac, William Burroughs, Rob-
ert Creely, Charles Olson, Leroi Jones, Henry Miller, Gregory
Corso, whose poetry he liked the best, and Norman Mailer, whose
Presidential Papers explained to Kenny what he had missed while
he was away from America.

He read all of these on his return trip and in his apartment in
Rome. He liked the way these people used words to report the news.
It was all news to him, information about an impending indictment

against the U.S. of A. announced by broadcasters who gave detailed dissections of life in these United States by sitting down wherever they were with pencil and paper and writing about things that Americans had on their minds. They gave Kenny an itch, an itch to say something to a whole lot of people, an audience. But he didn't know what it was that he wanted to say or even if he had anything to say or how to go about saying it if he did or to whom.

There was a young girl living on his street who was the slum goddess of the neighborhood and a student actress at the Center of Experimental Cinematography at Rome's Cinecitta. Virna told him about a film exposition, a two-week series of daily double features being presented by someone who thought that the films he had selected were relevant to the life and times of 1964. She asked Kenny if he wanted to go with her and he did. Every evening for two weeks, he went to the Salone Margherita, a nineteenth-century music hall and the most beautiful movie theater in the fucking world, and saw *Breathless* and *Contempt; Shoot the Piano Player* and *Sundays and Cybele; Last Year at Marienbad* and *L'Avventura; Saturday Night and Sunday Morning* and *Taste of Honey; Virgin Spring* and *Term of Trial; One-Eyed Jacks* and *Young Lions; Salvatore Giuliano* and *The Bandits of Orgosolo; Ashes and Diamonds* and *The Pickpocket; The Manchurian Candidate* and *The St. Louis Bank Robbery* (the first film Steve McQueen ever spoke in and the best movie ever made about a funky gang of armed robbers and a bank holdup); *Rocco and His Brothers* and *Accattone.*

It was this last film, *Accattone*, made by Pier Paolo Pasolini, that opened Kenny's eyes, because it was about a gang of real-life guys in the cruel and violent squalor of the backstreet Roman slum, Trastevere, which was where Kenny lived. The movie was about the people of his neighborhood and it showed the way they really were and what some of them wanted to be. It hipped Kenny to the idea of using film as the medium to express what he knew about.

Virna got him an application for the Center of Experimental Cinematography and he filed it along with a certificate of Good Conduct from his uncle at the New York City Police Department which advised the authorities in Italy that the police files failed to show any record under Wisdom's name, or any fingerprints. He also submitted a twelve-page critical essay entitled, "Reflections on the State of the Short Film as Social Document and Art" in which he stated that documentaries and their makers were irresponsible in their attitudes toward their subjects, operated with old kinds of imagination in a new kind of society, and were basically just propaganda tools for the exposition of a world which they refused to show clearly. This essay was accompanied by another which dealt with the importance of poetic logic and catharsis in making the realism contained in art a purer reality and concluded that "an artist through the use of his imagination can articulate his sensitivity toward reality and thereby create an actuality more actual than actual actuality."

Kenny also adapted T. S. Eliot's poem *The Waste Land* into a screenplay. The prologue went like this:

FADE IN

A windowed elevator on the ground floor of a luxury, baroque apartment building. The camera is directed through the rear window and focuses on a ragged, gypsy fortune teller as she enters the lift, closing the cage and glass doors behind her.

With her back to the camera, she stares, transfixed by her image reflected in the glass of the door. A group of children are seen through the mirrored reflection of her face, as they come running down the corridor towards the lift.

They brake themselves at the sight of the wretched woman and cringe in fright. Everyone remains still for several moments. Finally, a boy speaks hesitantly, hiding himself in the fold.

BOY

What do you want?

GYPSY

I want to die.

The fortune teller presses a button and, as the elevator slowly rises above the group of children, the camera follows it and focuses on the vibrating cables while the credits appear on the screen.

MUSIC

A BASS SOLO by CHARLES MINGUS.

CREDITS

It took Kenny nearly two months to research and write the essays and to adapt *The Waste Land* into a shooting script. Virna helped him translate all of it into Italian, when he had completed the drafts in English. The competition for acceptance into the Center was strong. There were two hundred applicants seeking admission to the two-year course of film direction and there were only four openings in the class, which was restricted to nine students composed of six Italian nationals and three foreign auditors.

Ten days after Kenny had delivered his application and the required essays and script, he was called to the Centro on the Via Tuscolana for an interview with the institute's board of directors. It lasted for more than an hour and when it was over, Kenny had demonstrated his fluency in the language and had engaged the board with his discourse on why he had adapted T. S. Eliot's poem to manifest the apathy of society and his intention to use it as a cinematic vehicle to express the need for a relevant change in a decaying system. Three days later, Kenny received a letter from Dr. Leonardo Fioravanti, the director of the Centro, advising him that he had been accepted at the institute for the two-year course on the direction and editing of film.

He was surprised and happy with himself and amused by the thought that his people back home might end up being proud of him after all. He wrote them a letter and enclosed a Xeroxed copy of the Centro's announcement of his acceptance, telling his parents to go and have Tony Caccetta, the butcher, translate it for them, if they didn't believe him.

For the next six months, Kenny Wisdom saw forty hours of film a week; dismantled and re-edited a movie called *The Four Days of Naples*; attended lectures by famous film directors; visited the sets of films being produced at the Cinecitta Studios; learned how to work with the 35mm. Mitchell camera and the lightweight portable Arriflex camera; rehearsed acting students for roles in closed circuit television plays; directed cameramen in those same TV productions; and made and acted in two films of his own.

The Italian National Film Library was at the Centro and it enabled the curator to screen all of a particular director's films for the students in a chronological order, thereby allowing the members of the class to watch the development of the film maker's ability and to witness the emergence of a skill which might distinguish him from other directors.

For instance, Elia Kazan's films were viewed, starting with *A Tree Grows in Brooklyn* and continuing with *Boomerang, Gentleman's Agreement, Pinky, Panic in the Streets, Sea of Grass, Streetcar*

*Named Desire, Viva Zapata, On the Waterfront, East of Eden, Baby
Doll, A Face in the Crowd, Wild River, Splendor in the Grass* and
ending with *The Anatolian Smile (America, America)*. It took four
eight-hour days to see those films and on the fifth day there was a
discussion about what was so special about Kazan compared to other
film directors. Everyone agreed there were better film makers
around and also that no one was better with actors than Kazan. It
was further decided that he was one of very few directors to consist-
ently bring good writers to work on a film and to have them write
directly for the screen.

The investigation of Elia Kazan as a film director was a normal
academic one, until one young student pointed out that for an artist
whose films were heavily concerned with certain sociological problems in the United States, Kazan had found it relatively easy to rat
on all his friends during the McCarthy years in order to avoid being
placed on the blacklist. Yes, it indeed seemed strange to Kenny and
the rest that the man who'd organized the Actors Studio with Cheryl
Crawford and Lee Strasberg, would have done a cheese-eating thing
like that. "Would the world never starve for want of wonders!"
someone said.

Of the two films Kenny made and played the lead in, one wasn't
very good because the cameraman kept going in and out of focus
and he wasn't much better at reading a light meter either. The
second one, however, was very good both technically and artistically.
The films were shot on various locations around the city and the
only facilities of the Centro that Kenny used to make them was an
Arriflex camera and some of the acting students, as well as the
cameraman. No one was paid for working on it and the film stock
itself was obtained for free as raw stock which hadn't been used
during some productions at the studios of Cinecitta. The only cost
was for the laboratory fees and they totaled three hundred dollars
for the processing of the film. The first one was called *Now I Live
and Now My Life Is Done* after the poem of the same name by
Chidiock Tichborne. It was the story of a man who was respected
and envied because of his wealth, education, success and physical
attractiveness. The camera followed him through a calm summer
day, examining his impeccability of grace, manner and design.
Everywhere he went people sighed and dreamed of being in his
shoes. Road workers reluctantly carried on when he passed by and
social climbers took notes of his attire, commenting to one another
about him. In all, he was everything that most people want to be —

an Apollo of a man, unafraid and seemingly capable of anything. As dusk fell over the city, our man returned to his villa and, in the solitude of his bedroom, calmly put a bullet through his head. *Fine*.

The second film had no technical flaws and Kenny had much better control over its direction and himself. The title of it was *Billy Brown, Sunday Afternoon*. *"Let Them Look Me Up and Take Their Own Sweet Time!"* and it ran thirty-seven minutes with a magnetic musical sound track of jazz and it was chosen as an entry for the Student Film Festival of Salerno. It told this story: A young man wakes up one morning, slips into a sweater and jeans and confronts himself in the mirror on the wall of his dumpy slum dwelling. He plays to his reflection, constantly switching characters and moods. Fed up with himself as an audience, he runs out to the morning and strolls the exclusive streets of the better part of the city. As he walks, he imitates famous actors in their portrayal of violent roles. Lost in one of these roles, he comes upon a man walking along the bank of a park lake. Believing that the whole scene is part of his fiction, he attacks the man and viciously beats him to the ground and rolls him into the lake. He stands there, reacting to the floating body with caricature poses of Marlon Brando, James Dean, Richard Widmark and Montgomery Clift. He walks away and over to a café where he throws over one of the sidewalk tables and points and yells at the startled old man who is having his morning coffee, imitating Brando's scene in *One-Eyed Jacks*. Across the street, he enters a snack bar and becomes Cagney when he sees a woman eating a grapefruit and he takes it and pushes it into her face. Police cars are swarming into the area and he sees them. There is a sports car double-parked with the motor running, the driver having jumped out to buy some newspapers. The youngster gets in the car, closes the door, looks directly into the camera and says (subtitles), "I am only twenty-one years old," copying Anthony Perkins's portrayal of Alexis in the film *Phaedra* which leaves the audience with little doubt as to the final outcome when he speeds away. *Fine*.

As Kenny Wisdom watched himself move around for the first time on a larger-than-life big screen at the festival theater in Salerno, he became very confused. "Who is that guy up there? Is it me? Do I walk like that? Move my hands that way? No! That's not me, it's him! Who? Who is he? He's not me! He's just making believe he's me. It's a movie, that's all. He's a character in a movie. Who? Not me! Him! Who's he? An actor. But what's he doing? He's making believe he's me making believe I'm someone else. *No!* I'm making believe I'm him making believe he's someone else. That's it! I'm him being someone else. Who? Him. But who's he? Me. No, I'm him. Yes! I'm him making believe he's me making believe I'm someone else. No, that's not right! I'm him making believe he's me making believe he's someone else! Who?"

Kenny got up and rushed into the men's room. He sat on a toilet bowl and held his face in his hands and tried to keep from blowing his mind. He'd been there for about twenty minutes, when one of his fellow students came in and knocked on the stall where he was sitting. "Kenny, are you in there?"

"Yes, what is it?"

"They want you outside. They're going to give you a prize!"

"Okay, I'll be right there."

They gave Kenny the best actor award at the Salerno Film Festival for his performance in his own film. Two days later the director of the Centro called him into his office and expelled him because one of the student's fathers who had been a spectator at the festival was also one of the three judges who had presided over Kenny's trial in Rome in 1963. He had recognized him on the screen and had demanded his immediate dismissal from the institution because persons with criminal records are not allowed to attend the Center for Experimental Cinematography, and Kenny had lied on his application and had been mistakenly permitted to matriculate and, "Now, if you don't mind, please leave these premises immediately or I'll have to call the authorities and have you removed. Goodbye!"

Kenny didn't really give a shit because his mind was still fogged out by whoever or whatever it was he had seen in his film at the Salerno Festival. He took a bus back to his apartment in Trastevere and plopped into the big, brown, tattered, leather armchair and was tired. There was a book lying on the floor beside him which he hadn't read but intended to, *A Portrait of the Artist as a Young Man* by James Joyce. He picked it up and absentmindedly flicked the pages, until something caught his eye in the front part of the book. "— What is your name? Stephen had answered: Stephen Dedalus. Then Nasty Roche had said: — What kind of a name is that? And when Stephen had not been able to answer Nasty Roche had asked: — What is your father?" And Kenny Wisdom said, "Irish. An Irishman. I'm Irish! What the fuck am I doing in Italy, anyway!"

He withdrew his last five hundred dollars from the bank, packed one bag full of clothes and another full of books, threw both his films and the paper award certificate from the festival into the Tiber River without saying anything to anyone, took a taxi through the Anti-Tsiombe demonstrations in central Rome to the airport at Fiumicino where he bought a ticket and boarded a plane for Dublin, Ireland, to see if he could get himself straight in the Ould Sod of his forefathers.

From the Dublin airport in Collinstown, Kenny rode an airport coach the six miles south to the city. It was a cold, damp, drizzling December Friday and when he arrived at the Busaras depot on Store Street, he felt a touch of the flu coming on. He asked a cab driver whether he knew of an inexpensive hotel and the fellow said that he certainly did and, "Climb in, lad, and I'll take you there meself." The first thing Kenny noticed, when the cabbie said, "Here we are now," was the doorman standing under the canopy of the Gresham Hotel, so as not to get his uniform wet or his brass buttons tarnished.

Kenny asked the driver if he understood what the word inexpensive meant and told him to take him to another hotel. The taxi continued on and pulled into the curb across from Saint Stephen's Green in front of the Hotel Shelbourne. Kenny didn't see a doorman this time because the fellow had run down the block to fetch the Rolls-Royce which belonged to the couple who were standing in the entrance and Kenny recognized the man as Rod Steiger and the woman as Claire Bloom and he told the cabbie that he had a strange habit of getting angry when he was being hustled and to forget the word "hotel" and "Let's see if we can get anywhere by concentrating on 'Boardinghouse.'"

The cabbie drove around to Harcourt Street and stopped in front of an elegant Georgian house in a row of handsome Georgian houses. The subdued sign above the wooden door read "The Abbotsford Hotel" and the cabbie told him that they were giving low–season room tariffs this time of the year and for a single with breakfast in the morning, the rate came to twenty-two and six, "or 'bout tree dollars a day, meboy." Kenny said okay and the cabbie insisted on helping him inside with his luggage. He understood why, when the manageress of the hotel and the cabbie greeted each other by name. In the off season in a small city like Dublin, cab drivers get paid commissions by hotel owners for bringing travelers and tourists to fill their vacant rooms.

Kenny didn't like the place because it looked and smelled like a bishop's rectory. It was too clean and prim and polite and had the

air of a British townhouse. He had come to Dublin to be "Ginger Man" Irish and he wondered if a man like Behan would have stayed in such a morgue as the Abbotsford Hotel. But he felt too ill to lug his bags around in the rain looking for a better place, so he paid the cabbie and advised the manageress that he was a student and intended to remain for a few days and no longer than a week. She showed him to his room and he went to sleep for a couple of hours.

It was early evening when he woke up, and his chill was gone only his stomach wasn't doing too well. He thought that some soup might help. He dressed warmly and walked down Harcourt Street past Saint Stephen's Green to Grafton and went into Neary's pub on the corner of Chatham Street. It was packed crowded with neatly dressed, middle-class people talking about the theater, and it was stuffy and hot. The lights were globes with brass fixings, the walls were mahogany and mirror, and the bar was made of pink marble. Pink marble! Kenny didn't really want to stay there because it was too stuffy, he was sweating, and he didn't like the self-righteous looks on the faces of the two chubby men or the sound of their hollow laughter, but he really needed something in his belly so he squeezed in beside them and told the waiter to get him a bowl of bouillon or something. When asked what he wanted to drink, he pointed to a mug of black beer on the chubby guys' table. They were talking very loudly now about radio.

Kenny peeled off his coat and scarf and for want of any other place put them, he dropped them on the floor beneath his table. This caused a few of the patrons who noticed, to adopt an attitude toward Kenny, who couldn't have cared less. The soup came with a "Here's your pint a stout, sir." Kenny thanked the waiter, remembering that, "Yes, that's what it's called. Stout."

The clear soup tasted good and went down easy but the stout was another story. Kenny had never had any before and since his stomach was a little topsy-turvy anyhow, the first couple of swallows of the black porter brought on a definite sensation of nausea and there was no doubt about it, he was going to puke. He called the waiter and asked how much and was told it was five and six and Kenny had all his money in his hands which he had gotten from the Ulster Bank at the airport in exchange for Italian lire and his head was spinning and his face flushed and whatever had been in his stomach was floating around in his clamped shut mouth and if he opened it again to ask what the hell was five and six, the waiter was going to be splashed with vomit and have to take a bath to remove the stink, so Kenny motioned for the waiter to take whatever was five and six from the pile of coins in his hand and grabbed his coat and scarf off the floor and ran to the back exit, holding his hand over his mouth now to signal everyone out of the way and when he hit the outside air, he released his hold and the barf blew from his mouth like a gale and splattered Chatham Street and two actors who were coming out of the stage door of the Gaiety Theatre.

The force of the vomiting practically broke the capillaries in Kenny's face. It finally ended after several minutes of dry-pukes, when nothing was left to come up. He stood leaning against a wall, exhausted and deflated. He put on his coat and wiped the cold sweat from his face with his scarf. He took a few deep breaths to revive himself and walked down Chatham Lane to Harry Street where he saw a sign for another pub, McDaid's. He felt better now that his stomach had done what it had to do and he went in to see if he could get a sandwich and acquire a taste for Guinness's stout which the fat-bellied Irishmen of New York City called "the wine of Ireland," but only sipped at between glasses of whiskey from Scotland on Saint Patrick's Day.

He liked the saloon with its high-ceiling, scattered tables and solid wooden bar. It was a big, funky room and the only decor was the people in it. They were hearty and whether they were laughing or arguing, discussing or pontificating, they were enjoying themselves and each other. They weren't dressed up to impress anybody. The noise they were making was a racket of music, and within seconds Kenny had picked up on the accented sounds of the flavored phrases of language. When the barman asked what he would have, Kenny replied, "Givus a pint a stoot 'n one a dem ham sandwitches." And when the barman did, "Tanks."

Standing alongside Kenny at the corner of the bar was a not-too-tall, chunky, dark-haired man in his twenties, wearing a dull-gray suit jacket over a black sweatshirt and baggy-brown pants, and a pair of black work boots laced with yellow twine. He was a manual laborer and those were the clothes that he worked in and did his weekend drinking in and lived in and went to sleep in, when he was too drunk to take them off. They were his clothes.

He told Kenny his name was Eamonn and asked if he was an American. Kenny said yes and introduced himself and they shook hands like they really meant they were glad to meet each other.

Eamonn's eyes had a sparkle but there was also a deep sense of anger about them. He hated something very much and had for a very long time. The scars that showed through his three-day beard and lined his thick eyebrows, and his busted nose testified, by the way they were situated in the features of his face, that he hadn't gotten them from slipping on a wet pavement or in an accident. No, they were carved by lefts and rights and kicks and other things that men use to keep a short, stocky bull like Eamonn from running them over like a locomotive. Kenny asked him about the big guy with the cap and eye glasses who was presiding over a group in the back corner of the room and delivering verse after verse of resounding poetry. Eamonn said that he was Paddy Cavanaugh and had taken over the poet's residency chair at McDaid's after the untimely death of Brendan Behan, himself. Then Eamonn told Kenny the story of Himself's last night at McDaid's. He came into the place besotted and slammed the door with loud shouts of *"Bejasus!"* and *"Bullocks!"* There were two women and five men sitting at the back end of the bar and Paddy the barman told Himself to shut his yap and show some respect for the ladies who were present or he'd serve him nothing to drink. Himself belched and nodded his head, agreeing to the demand. After he was served his pint of porter and double glass of Powers' Irish whiskey, Himself stood in front of the empty stool next to one of the women whose back, like the other's, was turned on him. While he downed his whiskey and gulped his pint, Himself quietly unzipped his fly and took out his bologna of a penis and laid it out flat on the seat of the empty stool without anyone noticing. When he finished his whiskey and had only a little porter left to his pint, he tapped the woman on her shoulder and she turned her head towards him, and Himself took his right hand and without saying a word he pointed down at the stool, and when the woman craned her neck and saw what he was pointing at, she screamed so loud that even Himself had to cup his hands over his ears to keep them from being split. Then she fell off her bar stool and onto the floor in a dead faint, revealing the sight which had startled her to the other lady, who also shrilled and took a dead fall, leaving the long, fat, round, uncircumcised muscle resting on the stool for her gentlemen companions to stare at with eyes bulging and mouths gaping. They didn't faint, and Himself thought they had a poor sense of humor indeed when they dragged him outside and gave him a thumping which left him in the gutter with a cracked skull. He was taken to the hospital and there his liver failed due to the lack of proper alcoholic sustenance which it regularly required. " 'N tat was t' last time Himself had been to tis store, 'n that's t' trut!"

Kenny Wisdom told Eamonn that he was a longshoreman from Brooklyn, New York, and that he had just come to Dublin on an impulse because his grandfather had been born in Munster Province, County Tipperary, outside the town of Tipperary, and from there he'd come with his father to Dublin and they'd emigrated to America. Kenny said he was also a writer and wanted to write about what the city of Dublin and Ireland were really like, "because the only information you ever get about this place is how green it is, or some such nonsense!" He also said he didn't have much money and was renting a room in a Georgian hotel because he didn't know his way around enough as yet to locate a less expensive place where the absurd pomposity of the Irish middle class wasn't residing.

They talked for over two hours and bought each other four or five pints and two rounds of Powers, and Eamonn said he was staying at an inn which was very reasonable and if Kenny wanted, he would take him there and introduce him to the proprietors and he could ask them if they had any vacancies available. Kenny was very glad to hear Eamonn say that, because he was searching for such an invitation — or at least a lead — with the line he had spun to him.

They walked down Grafton Street feeling no pain, and as they were approaching Westmoreland Street, Eamonn laid his thick right hand on Kenny's left shoulder blade and squeezed twice to feel if the body under the coat was as solid as it appeared, and when he was satisfied, he stopped him and said, " 'Tis nice, t'meet a man 'n perhaps make a friend, t'ain't it." Kenny could see his eyes in the light from the window of a café and the look he saw meant what his mouth had said. Kenny answered, "Yes."

They went into the café, bought some fish and chips, and ate them on the bus which they rode up the quays along the River Liffey to a stop in front of the Four Courts, where they got off and walked across the river on Bridge Street until they came to Lower Bridge Street and Number 20, the Brazen Head. They stepped into the stone-paved courtyard and Kenny thought he was really drunk because the windows and the whole frame of the building itself seemed cockeyed. He wasn't, it was.

The Brazen Head is a small, antiquated residential inn built in the early seventeenth century. The pub is a thick-beamed, low-ceilinged room, dimly lit by funky brass-banded lanterns, and its lead-gridded windows face into the courtyard. It received its liquor license in 1666 during the reign of Charles II and is not only the oldest drinking place in Ireland but is also the only legal after-hours' pub in the country because the license permits the bar to remain open until 2 A.M. for the residents of the inn. These residents live in rooms upstairs and they're all men.

Eamonn took Kenny inside to the bar and introduced him to Mr. and Mrs. Cooney, the owners of the place, and told them that Kenny was looking to rent a room. Mr. Cooney just grumped and ignored the statement about renting a room. Mrs. Cooney said, "Oh, have y' had any luck?"

A little spic-and-span old man asked Kenny what he was doing in Dublin trying to find a room. Wisdom looked around and saw portraits of the individual heroes of the many movements of Irish resistance to British domination and at the penned sketches of the Troubles and the Easter Rising in 1916. He could see they were all authentic originals just by their warped frames and yellowed glass and browned paper and he answered, "I came to see what my great-great-grandfather and his brothers died for in the Great Rebellion of 1798."

"What was his name 'n where was he from?"

"His name was Sean Ó' Gruágain, 'n he came from Tipperary."

"What's your name 'n where are you from?"

"Wisdom. Kenny Wisdom, 'n I come from New York. Brooklyn."

A tall, big-boned, lanky man of sixty turned and announced, "Fifty-seventh Street, Times Square, Thirty-fourth Street, Union Square, Canal Street, DeKalb Avenue, Pacific Street, Thirty-sixth Street, Fifty-ninth Street, Eighth Avenue, Fort Hamilton Parkway, New Utrecht Avenue, Eighteenth Avenue, Twentieth Avenue, Bay Parkway, Kings Highway, Avenue U, Eighty-sixth Street, Stillwell Avenue 'n Coney Island!" and asked Kenny, "Well, wat do they mean to ya?"

"They're the subway stops the Sea Beach Express makes from Manhattan to Brooklyn."

"Right y'are! Right y'are!"

"What d'you do in New York or is it Brooklyn?" asked a man with a hook for a hand and a face as cold as his eyes were dead.

"Brooklyn. I work on the waterfront, unloading ships 'n stuff."

"Why're you here this time o' year?" asked little spic-and-span.

"I wanted to beat the tourists and the prices they cause."

"When did y'arrive?"

"This afternoon."

"Do y'have a bed to sleep in tonight?"

"Yes. A cab driver took me to a place on Harcourt Street, the Abbotsford, 'n I rented a room for the night 'cause I had no idea where to look for what I wanted."

"And what is it you want, then? The Abbotsford's a fine, clean, comfortable place."

"Bed 'n breakfast in a place where I can find out why and what people died for in Ireland. A place that don't cost much and the people have something to say besides 'Isn't Siobhan McKenna a marvelous actress.' A place with a room where I can sleep and drink and write about what happened after men, women and children died for the Republic of Ireland and the papers and treaties that were signed compromising their deaths and the economic incompetence of the government which demands an emigration unequaled since the famine, 'n a place where I can discover the reason why Eamonn and I are the only two young men in a bar that is dedicated to the past and the freedom fighters who fought for the present — and if you can't tell what a man is by lookin' at him, all the answers to all the questions you can ask won't help you none!"

Kenny took his bottle of stout with him over to the wall where he read Robert Emmet's speech from the dock. It was framed in glass and had been hanging on that wall since the week they executed Robert Emmet in 1803. While Eamonn, the proprietor, and the other residents of the inn conferred among themselves, Kenny could see that the judge who had been presiding over the trial kept interrupting Robert Emmet in an attempt to break the course of his thoughts and confuse him to prevent him from making a proper speech before he was sentenced to death. The boorish interruptions from the bench, however, had an altogether different effect from the one expected, and the young man fended off the spurious remarks by the judge with an eloquence that was as cool as it was brilliant:

"Does the sentence of death, which your unhallowed policy inflicts on my body, condemn my tongue to silence and my reputation to reproach? Your executioner may abridge the period of my existence; but while I exist I shall not forebear to vindicate my character and motives from your aspersion; and as a man to whom fame is dearer than life, I will make the last use of that life in doing justice to the cause and that reputation which is to live after me, and which is the only legacy I can leave to those I honour and love and for whom I am proud to perish."

Eamonn called Kenny over and Mr. Cooney told him that they had decided he could board at the Brazen Head and he should go back to the Abbotsford now for a good sleep and return with his belongings in the morning when Mrs. Cooney would have a room ready for him. And the rest was "Two pound a week for bed 'n breakfast."

Kenny had known by the way Eamonn had spoken about it, that the Brazen Head was more than just another residential hotel and that the men who lived there were not simply ordinary boarders. That's why he answered their questions and made that kind of a pitch for himself. He hadn't been lying about his grandfather's grandfather and the tone of the barroom gave him the proper frame of reference for his closing remarks. As he lay in his bed at the Abbotsford he was excited that he had come to Dublin and felt fortunate that he'd met Eamonn and delighted that he was going to be living in a place in the bowels of Dublin where he could learn just how deep his Irishness ran. As far as Rome and his traumatic film experience, he concluded that what he had seen on the screen that day in Salerno was just two sides of the same man acting like a third.

He only had two hundred and fifty dollars left and he opened a thrift account at the Munster & Leinster Bank on Grafton Street where he deposited the two hundred and changed the fifty into about eighteen Irish pound notes and some coins. Then he carted his bags of books and clothes onto a bus which took him near Lower Bridge Street and he walked into the Brazen Head Inn.

There was no one around but Mrs. Cooney, who gave him a cup of tea and showed him something which he hadn't noticed in the bar the night before, a small, very old desk made of black wood that she said had belonged to Robert Emmet himself. She remarked that Kenny had a lot of luggage and he explained that it was mostly books. "Oh, so you are serious 'bout writin', then. Well, good. We haven't had a writer take bed 'n board here for quite a while, and seein' what you said last night about your intentions and all, the other residents decided that you should have a good room and one that would inspire the truth from yer pen t' paper. Now, come upstairs and I'll show you your room."

Mrs. Cooney was a hard-working woman in her early thirties and there was a sturdy pale beauty in her face. She had a warmth about her which made you feel at ease and pleased by her company. Kenny carried his bags up the flights of wooden stairs and stopped behind

Mrs. Cooney in front of the door which she said was now his room. It was a thick, black-stained, wooden door and Kenny noticed that there were several impressions dented deep into the front of it. He asked Mrs. Cooney about them, as she opened the door and showed him into the room. She told him they were made by gun butts, when the soldiers had come for the man who had been living there at the time and taken him off to the Kilmainham Jail. His name was Robert Emmet and this had been his room, "And breakfast is at six and eight each morning and the bedding you change yourself once a week on Tuesday when the laundry comes, and the washroom's down the hall and it's got a tub in it which I hope you have no aversion to usin' now and then like some o' the gentlemen who reside here. Now make yourself at home and if you got any questions 'bout anything, you kin always find me in the kitchen." She closed the door behind her and went back downstairs.

There was a hard-mattress bed with a cast-iron headboard placed flush against the wall to the right of the door as you came in; an old dresser of drawers and a large portable closet, both with a peeling varnish; a bent-wood chair in front of a small, rectangular wooden table, both of which were stained dark; a single light-bulb hanging bare from the ceiling over the table and chair desk-set; the walls were tanned with age and even though it was cold and there was no heat, Kenny cracked open the window to relieve the mustiness of the air in the room.

"Robert Emmet's room, mmm. Well, it doesn't make it any warmer," Kenny thought, as he kept his coat on and removed his books from the bag and piled them on top of the dresser and spread his clothes in the drawers and closet. He was surprised at how much stuff he had left back in Rome for anyone to have or the landlord to sell. He hadn't even brought a suit, just warm clothes, a pair of shoes, leather gloves and his heavy, charcoal-brown, three-quarter-length leather coat.

For the next month, Kenny Wisdom ate only fish and chips at a café down the quays and drank and talked and listened to the men in the bar of the Brazen Head. They told him about Brian Boru and Phelim the Burner; Edmund Burke, Wolfe Tone and Daniel O'Connell who all had resided at the Brazen Head Inn; the age of the secret societies — the Steel Boys, the Oak Boys, the Catholic White Boys, the Protestant Peep O'Day Boys; Charles Stewart Parnell and how he invented the use of social ostracism as a political weapon, known by the world today as "boycott," and how a bitch named Kitty O'Shea caused his political suicide by citing him in her divorce — "The banner of Kitty O'Shea"; King Carson, the Protestant voice of Ulster and his arms; Roger Casement's attempt to obtain arms from a German submarine which was intercepted by the British and him subsequently hanged in London for treason; the Sinn Fein, meaning "Ourselves Alone," and Padhraic Pearse who led them in the six-day battle which began on Easter Monday of 1916 and took place at the General Post Office in the center of O'Connell Street, and the terrible sense of one's enemies being of one's own house; the Black and Tans coming to restore order in the autumn of 1919; 1920, eighteen-year-old Kevin Barry, the first Irish patriot to be hanged since Robert Emmet; the Freestaters versus the Republicans, antitreaty versus treaty; the thousand-pound reward for and the great influence of Michael Collins and his organization of a highly efficient counterespionage network for the IRA during the guerrilla warfare against the British; Collins' ambush by members of the IRA dressed in British uniforms and sent by de Valera whom he was on his way to see for a consultation about The Treaty (or Articles of Agreement); de Valera, with Collins out of the way, issuing a cease-fire proclamation and becoming Prime Minister and Ireland remaining partitioned.

These men who lived and drank at the Brazen Head were members of a section of the 1923 IRA who had not accepted the cease-fire order, had refused to lay down their arms, referred to de Valera and his Government Assembly as Murder, Incorporated, and sang this song together:

Take it down from the mast, Irish traitors,
Tis the flag we Republicans claim
It can never be owned by Free Staters
Who shed nothing on it but shame.
Then leave it to those who are willing,
To uphold it in war or in peace,
Those men who intend to do killing
Until England's tyranny cease.

The big man who had named the various stations where the Sea Beach Express train made its stops was Mick Quirk. After he had shot several British intelligence agents to death in their homes in 1920 when he was seventeen years old, he'd been sent to New York, where he was given thirty-five dollars a week and slept on the subways, until he was allowed to return to Ireland in the winter of '23 after the cease-fire and that's how he knew all the names of the subway stations in their proper order. When he did return, he was given a job as a doorman in one of de Valera's government buildings with a promise of a twenty-pound-a-month pension when he retired. He was only one among many who killed men and women in their beds and ended up as lackeys for de Valera and his incorporated gang.

Besides all the talking and drinking and singing, these old-timers gave Kenny copies of periodicals which explained convincingly what they had killed people for. One pamphlet written by a Sinn Feiner read: "Nationality is our great object, a nationality which may embrace Protestant, Catholic and Dissenter . . . the Irishman of a hundred generations and the stranger who is within our gates; not a nationality which would preclude civil war, but which would establish internal independence — a nationality which would be recognized by the world as a comparative economic State, rather than a competitive capitalist society . . ."

Other articles confirmed that the Sinn Fein was the oldest progressive movement in Ireland, a socialist republican organization which fought on the platform of building a workers' republic. Its armed wing, the Irish Republican Army, was a revolutionary army. Those men back in the first quarter of the twentieth century and the century before fought not only for their freedom from the British but also for their freedom from exploitation at home. They fought for the freedom to be equal men in their own country in a classless society. They were shortchanged by de Valera and his pack of cronies, these Sinn Feiners and old IRA boys, and condemned to bitterness, a meager pension, and a glass of booze or two at places like the Brazen Head.

Kenny's money ran out but he didn't need much because it didn't cost a lot to live in the Northside of the city of Dublin. Eamonn took him to the National Insurance office where he got his blue registration card and insurance number by saying that he had been born in Tipperary, had gone to America as a child for an education and returned to his native land for a visit. Now he had decided to stay a while and he had been offered a job at the Guinness Brewery and needed the card, please. He got it.

Every weekday morning at 6 A.M., Kenny and Eamonn would shape up with a lot of mostly older men outside the St. James Street

gate of the largest brewery in Europe with four thousand steady
employees known as Guinness Men, and wait to be picked by the
hiring boss to work as casual laborers until 5 P.M. Even when the
work load was light, Kenny and Eamonn were always picked because they were young and strong. Kenny's first job at the plant was
to stand atop a pyramid of empty aluminum kegs which had a base
fifteen barrels wide and was fifteen deep and fifteen layers high,
about twelve hundred and fifty barrels all told, and toss them down,
carefully aiming each one to bounce on thick woven-cord pillows
rather than on the cement. He became so adept at hitting the pillows in such a way as to make the kegs slide off them and softly roll
along the concrete floor, and he did it so quickly without ever missing, that after a while the foreman permitted him to go home with a
full day's wages when he had dismantled seven or eight of these
pyramids in three or four hours rather than the normal nine. The
rest of the casual labor gang stacked the loose kegs onto the carts
which carried them inside the plant where Eamonn worked, filling
them with the porter and sealing them with a bung.

Kenny liked working outside in the yard and when he finished
around ten or eleven, he would go into the employees' taproom and
drink as much free porter for lunch as he could con out of the
counterman and return to his room at the Brazen Head to sleep,
until four or four-thirty in the afternoon, when he had to get back
to the plant to punch out on the timeclock. Then he would have
some fish and chips with Eamonn for supper at a little Italian café
on Usher's Quay and walk back with him to the Brazen Head to buy
a half-dozen bottles of stout in the bar and take them up with him to
his room, where he would remain alone, writing about people and
things he knew about.

The first piece he did was about a jolly, middle-aged man who
used to frequent the bar at the Brazen Head early every evening,
and who had lived in a room across the street. It was published in
one of Dublin's newspapers, as a letter.

It was 10:30 and Swillbelly Logan tucked his bike under his arm and
went into a Southside pub for a pint. He was a big fat man with a cherry
face and a punchy voice and every working day for the past thirty years,
he downed a stout as soon as the gates were opened. Then he'd wheel his
bike into the street and make his late morning rounds.

Swillbelly Logan was a messenger and he'd never been anything else.
He'd worked for the same firm all of his life and he knew the city like

187

few other men. Every street, road and line was fitted into his memory and he knew the quickest way to get to each of them. He didn't even know what a map of Dublin looked like but he knew where everything was.

Except for his eight on-the-job-pints, Swillbelly loved to ride his bicycle more than anything else. And he was the best, especially during rush hour traffic. He'd slip into his saddle and race down Grafton Street with intent. He seldom used his brake. Instead, he'd look at the women and drive them back onto the pavement with a swerve. Sometimes he'd manage to knock a few parcels into the gutter or give someone a splash and when he did he'd giggle and celebrate with an Irish. He'd fly into Suffolk Street and ride the kerb with buses leaning on top of him, cars cutting in front of him and old ladies calling him dirty names.

Swillbelly Logan had heart.

When he came into Church Lane, he always met the jam by walking along the pavement until he reached the Bank of Ireland where he'd pedal like hell right down the center of Westmoreland Street and nobody would pass him.

Swillbelly never had an accident and was never made to pay a fine but a lot of people hated him.

One time a schoolteacher chased him down the quays until he finally caught him at a crossing. Logan was ignorant of the intended assault, so he relaxed while the pedestrians passed in front of him and mused about his next pint. The driver got out of his car and began beating him on the shoulders with an umbrella.

"I've been after you for ten years!" he screamed, and continued to rain blows on our man, until Swillbelly arrested the weapon and held the fellow at bay and listened to him yell about "recklessness!" and "I've had two — *Two!* — accidents because of *You! You . . .*"

Logan didn't like to be abused, so he knocked the teacher's hat off with a swipe, tossed his umbrella into the Liffey and raced to the Brazen Head.

He was pleased with his fame and proud of the havoc he'd been causing for the past three decades and he wanted to give himself a reward.

You'd meet him in the bar and he'd talk about Dublin and the people he'd seen and the changes that came and the things that were gone. He'd describe the old Davy Byrnes and tell you the way O'Connell Street used to look and about the tourists who asked him directions in the summer and about the kids who threw snowballs at him in the winter. He'd talk about the city's arms and legs, about her eyes and ears, about what she felt like today, yesterday, any day.

It was "his" city and he never left her. He hadn't been outside of Dublin for forty years and he wasn't planning any trips, he would say. He was in love with the town and each morning he kissed her and toured every line in her body on his bike.

Swillbelly Logan liked his job very much but yesterday somebody put him out of work. He was coasting down Bridge Street when that somebody knocked him down with his car and ran over his chest and left him there to die. To die with the buildings that he loved so much and that were condemned and being ripped down because an authority on renewal said they were a hazard and ugly. This big fat man with a cherry face and a heart as big as a lion. A man who'd fought to free his country so Irishmen could have cars just like the one which killed him. A man who saw his sister splashed all over the pavement during the Civil War by somebody who'd thought that she was someone else. A man who took everything in his stride from dowagers asking him questions to kids trying to hit him in the face with empty bottles. A simple, quiet man who wanted to be comfortably poor and ride around "his" city on his bicycle and have a few pints and a whiskey now and then and go to church and read an evening paper is dead.

And the messengers of this city can be proud that he had never been anything else.

Kenny Wisdom was still reading all the newspapers he could get his hands on but he concentrated less on the stories of international politics and more on news items dealing with the local issues of Dublin because that's where he was living. One announcement by the government made him crazy: they passed a bill allowing persons who'd been declared incompetent and insane and who were locked up in asylums to vote, and at the same time they stated that they were seriously considering the revival of the cat-o'-nine-tails to punish juveniles who were delinquent.

He wrote an article which was rejected by every newspaper, even as a letter to the editor. It wound up being published in a student radical bimonthly periodical.

It was Sunday afternoon and he was standing in front of one of those cafes on O'Connell Street. A sixteen-year-old middleweight, five foot eight, whose name was Filthy McNasty. He stood there with his left hand jammed into the pocket of his tapered pants and he flipped a cigarette into the gutter. He looked through his hair at the passing girls and whistled when he liked what he saw. He was an imitation of all that is new in the world. But he felt good with himself and that was all that mattered. He had an identity and so he slouched against the window and let everybody look at him.

You talked with him and he told you he was a delivery boy. It wasn't a bad job, he said, but he was looking for something better. You had coffee with him and you sat at one of those plastic tables and listened to him tell you that he was waiting for his friend, Puppet Magurk, and they were going to the movies. *The Hustler* was playing and they'd seen it but wanted to see it again. They liked to watch Fast Eddie shake his fist at the world and beat it at one of its games.

Filthy McNasty was a kid who'd been in three or four gang fights. A kid who had smashed a guy in the face with a sugar-shaker because he'd tried to dance with his girl. A kid who'd beat up an old lady in the street for laughs and had stabbed an old man in the head because there was nothing better to do. And you sat there and looked at him and wondered why.

"What you think 'bout them loonies votin' in the election?"

I told him that I didn't think it was very funny but he did. He said it was a gas. He said that the lunatics probably knew more about what they were doing than most of the other voters. He didn't see why anyone should vote anyway and he grinned at the thought of the politicians standing there, ready to tell you lies — lies about the past, lies about the future, lies about the present — and nobody would be there to listen.

"Tey wouldn't know what t' do with all their spewf!" he said.

You told him that politics is based on unkept promises but that in their hearts, each politician wanted to do his best to further the progress of his country. And the kid who's called a "Ted" looked at you with disbelief and laughed at your naïveté. He said that he wanted to tell you something and leaned forward on the table, spreading his elbows for leverage. And he told you that half the people who run the government also run businesses and that most of them have outside financial interests to protect. He told you that anyone who wanted to start an industry in this country had to be certain that he wouldn't be in competition with any of those interests. They're always talking about progress, he said, but let some guy come into this city and try to build a match factory and they wouldn't even let him lay a brick.

"That's politics, pal. Be seein' ya," he finished, and left with his friend.

Filthy McNasty was a kid with a lot of heart and everyone was trying to take the mickey out of him. They wanted to bring back the "cat" and cut off his hair and change his clothes. They wanted him to dance reels and speak Gaelic because that, they said, is what they freed this country for.

That's why they walked down the streets with their caps on crooked and faced the Black and Tans like heroes. That's why they fought their hearts out and killed their brothers, they said. And they wanted it that way.

But Filthy McNasty and Puppet Magurk and all the rest who are like them don't want it that way. They have their own ideas about Ireland and you can threaten them with the cat, the rack, or the garrote but you won't frighten them. They're tough, these kids, and they're not afraid to fight and die just like their fathers weren't afraid when they fought for the basic human right of freedom.

Well, these kids want to be free too. Free to be different from their fathers. Free to think their own thoughts and find their own place in this country. Free from the social intolerance which drives them to senseless crime. And free to be decently poor if they want to and keep out of the rat race.

A lot of people think that these kids are "non-Irish" or "anti-Irish" but they're mistaken. They're some of the best-spirited Irish around and they know what it means to have a flag of your own. Their gangs uphold the tradition of the White Boys and the Steel Boys and they cover their own territories just like them. And they're bomb throwers, these kids, just like their fathers. They bomb the mediocrity of the radio and television services. They bomb styles in clothes, speech and haircuts. They bomb education right out of their lives and they talk of James Bond and go out in the streets to beat up old ladies and smash windows because they're angry.

Angry at grown-ups. Angry at the woman in charge of the Society for the Prevention of Cruelty to Animals who said in The Irish *Times* the other day that she mourns the poisoning of the rats that live along the banks of the Liffey but that she realizes it has to be done because the tourists are coming! While these kids and their little brothers and sisters are walking around with scars on their faces from rat bites. They're angry because this city is out for them — seeking revenge. The city which lets them live in slums like the Northside, the finest breeding grounds for crime, and places where kids like Filthy get their names. They're angry at intolerance and at the adults' fear of understanding.

Fear of understanding that people should look to themselves for the causes of the kids' anger. That people should look forward to future generations and not back at past generations. That the city should have sports facilities not only for clubs but for individuals as well. That the courts should lean on the side of compassion rather than severity. And above all, the people should understand that by trying to squash the McNastys and the Magurks and by seeking to conform their tastes and attitudes to middle-class customs, they will only succeed in taking the mickey out of the men who are going to be the backbone of this country.

Men who will have realized the absurdity of partition and will do something about it. Men who will keep this nation alive by building and working together. Men who will lead, who will follow, who will produce another generation. Men who will care about life and who won't have an unhealthy attitude towards death. Men who will remain Irish citizens and not become Irish emigrants only if the people look to themselves and make relevant changes in a political and economic system which, as it now stands, is totally irrelevant to the futures of these kids as Irish men and women.

Kenny kept working at the brewery and taking home his twelve pounds ten shillings' pay a week and drinking and rapping and writing and reading. He'd been at the Guinness plant for two months and had hardly said more than a passing word to anyone, when a guy named McShane asked him if he'd like to have a drop of whiskey with him and his pals after the whistle blew.

They went to a booth in the smallish back section of a pub on a lane off the quays. Over double glasses of Jameson, Kenny was told by McShane and the others that they'd been watching him and had heard him talking in places like McDaid's and the Brazen Head and they'd read some of the things that he'd written and they were surprised but glad that an American Irishman had the wits to understand properly the situation of the Republic and express a righteous attitude about its partition. They asked him how deep his concern was and when he told them that his outrage over the misrepresentation of the Irish people by de Valera and his mob and his anger at their acquiescence to partition was imbedded in the marrow of his bones, they invited him to be a man of action as well as letters and to go north with them that weekend and he accepted and he went.

They blew the wall out of a tiny post on the border of Armagh near a place called Forkill late that Saturday night, and they were back in Dublin when the pubs opened for the Sunday afternoon session. They had drunk quite a few bottles of an illegal white lightning made from heather by the country folk of Ireland in hidden stills and called poteen. McShane said, "It's a shame that people drink it, 'cause it's so fine, they should baptize babies with it instead!"

McShane and his pals had a few years on Kenny but they were younger, just the same. The news of the previous night's bombing had been on Radio Eirean in Dublin and rather than separating and cooling it, the group insisted that Kenny come along with them to Neary's pub and upset the chatter of the patrons with songs of bravado. As soon as they entered the door, Kenny could see that everyone in the place knew who they were and what they had just returned from doing, and the ones who didn't were finding out by whispers.

They staggered and shoved their way through the parting crowd to the bar, and McShane took the pipe from his mouth and ordered *"Some jars for me 'n me boys, barman! 'N hurry up about it, o there's goin' t'be a few strange faces in heaven t'night!"* And the pints of stout were lined up on the bar before them and they sang about downin' this and upin' that and the pints kept coming and someone in the crowd was paying for them and even provided a round of Irish, and the singing got louder and the boasts got bigger and everybody was slapping them on their backs when Kenny got into the act of damning things and shouted, *"Fuck the Pope!"* which he thought was a reasonable thing to demand — but the gathering froze with a sudden heavy silence and McShane said that Kenny had had too much to drink and it was beginning to affect his brain, and when Kenny replied with a *"Bullocks!"* McShane and the others ushered him out and over to McDaid's where Kenny shouted it again and McShane told him, "You're walkin' on the fightin' side of us, now!" and Kenny insisted that they *"Fuck the Pope in his Pauline bunghole!"* and they thumped him and drove him back to the Brazen Head and dumped him in his bed. The next morning he went to the brewery as usual but with a hell of a headache. He couldn't remember what had happened but he knew that something had occurred because his lip was swollen and his left eye was black. After work, he asked McShane how his face got knocked about and he was told he'd been drunk out of his head and had collapsed against the bar at McDaid's and to "Forget about it 'cause it was nothin', just too much drink."

A short time later, Kenny went with them on another run to the North where they got juiced on poteen and used so much gelignite on a stone footbridge which only had a twenty-five foot span across a shallow tributary of a river near Cullaville in County Armagh, that it turned into dust and they almost blew themselves up. They couldn't hear what any of them was saying on the drive back to Dublin because they were all deafened by the *Boom!* of the explosion.

At one o'clock in the morning of the first day in the second week of March, Kenny was posted on the corner of North Earl and Marlborough streets where he stopped pedestrians and traffic from entering O'Connell Street, while McShane and the other members of his band along with several additional groups of men were doing the same on Bachelors Walk, Cole's Lane, Parnell Street and on all the rest of the avenues which led into O'Connell. They turned away men and women and cars and cabs and told them to go somewheres else and stay away, while a man who was very good with explosives was inside the Lord Nelson Tower, stringing plastique like a garland around the underside of the statue's shoulders in such a professional manner that when the explosion occurred, it severed the Lord's head clean from its body and dropped it neatly below to O'Connell Street in one piece. Even though the police arrived in quick-time, Nelson's head, which was as big and as heavy as the largest fermenting vessel at the Guinness Brewery, was gone. It had been taken away and transported to the backyard of a well-known saloonkeeper where it remained on private display for Dubliners who had an appreciation for bronze sculptures with dented noses.

After that, Kenny decided that he had enough goofs and that he was sick of eating fish and chips all the time and taking wages for a living. Besides, he hadn't been laid since he'd been in Dublin, because women weren't allowed in the rooms at the Brazen Head and he didn't like to pay hookers for the clap. The few girls he met weren't much to look at and had only allowed him to do a bit of pantsing, so he figured it was time to pull a score and pull out.

He let his feeling slip one Saturday when he was talking alone with McShane at McDaid's pub.

McShane: I know it's difficult. Freedom always is. It's slavery that's easy!

Kenny: Look, I know that one family has ruled Ireland for eight hundred years and that the Irish government pays ground rent to the Penbrooke estates, but you gotta handle it yourselves. I got somethin' else I gotta do.

McShane: You got somethin' else you gotta do! It exists and it'll go on existin' because good men like you do nothin' about it!

Kenny: Do what? D'you think blowin' up footbridges and border posts is goin' to make the border disappear?

McShane: It's somethin' . . .

Kenny: It's nothin'! And never will be 'cause it's a bark that doesn't bite! You're all so involved in gettin' your message across that nobody knows what you're sayin' but they laugh anyway because it's funny.

McShane: Well, what about your pals? Do you want to see them go to gaol . . .

Kenny: Of course not! But that's where they're goin' just the same 'cause they're dumb, so dumb that they could even get arrested in Times Square on New Year's Eve for loitering!

McShane: But Kenny, they wouldn't go to gaol, if you would help us in our . . .

Kenny: Fuck that *Odd Man Out* shit!

McShane: You're drunk!

Kenny: Yea, I'm drunk! *As usual,* and you're crazy and I'll be sober in the morning but you'll be fuckin' crazy forever! And I don't intend to end up as a down payment for the future, like all those guys at the Brazen Head. So, leave me be!

He did, and for the next few days Kenny didn't go to work but read all the newspapers like he used to read them in New York, until he saw the type of item he was looking for. There was an American film production in town and they were shooting scenes every morning at the studios in Bray, outside of Dublin. One of the actors in the film was a big star and when Kenny was in Rome he'd heard that the guy always traveled with lots of cash.

Kenny cleaned himself up the next morning, dressed, and carried some books like he was a student, and took a bus to the Gresham Hotel on O'Connell Street. He walked in and up the stairs to the movie star's sixth floor suite which had been mentioned in a gossip column in one of the papers. The door was easy to open with a piece of celluloid. When he was inside the salon of the suite, he heard someone snoring in the bedroom. He knew that the actor had to be on the set by six or seven and it was eight o'clock now. He peeked through the crack in the door and saw a woman sprawled naked on top of the bed wacked out in a Seconal sleep. He looked at her for a moment because it'd been a long time since he'd seen a naked lady, too long. He even felt like fucking her, but an attaché case caught his eye and he took it from the chair next to the bed and snapped it open in the salon. There was money in it all right and plenty of it. He counted out forty-three hundred dollars in hundred- and fifty-dollar bills and put back twelve hundred dollars to cause a little confusion when the movie prince returned and tried to figure out whether or not he had been robbed. He left the same way he came in.

He changed three of the fifties at the American Express office into Irish notes. He wasn't afraid about any inquiry because the American Express office would be closed by the time the star got back to the hotel and did or didn't discover Kenny's gain, and it'd be closed the following day also because it was Saint Patrick's Day, and by the time it opened again Kenny would be gone to wherever he had decided to go in the world which he once again thought of as a candy store because he now had the money to pay the checks for sodas.

Kenny bought himself a new pair of shoes, an expensive dark blue turtleneck of Irish wool, and a ready-to-wear pair of tan corduroy trousers. He changed into them back at the Brazen Head, where he also packed his bags but left them in his room. Downstairs in the bar, he bought several rounds of doubles for everyone and went with Eamonn for a night on the town. Eamonn didn't ask how Kenny came by his new prosperity, but he did say he was sad that he was leaving. They were good friends, and on the raids up to the North and at the decapitation of Lord Nelson, they had stuck close to each other with an instinctive trust. They drank a lot together and had quite a few brawls in the pubs along the quays and they had talked. It was in those conversations that Kenny learned what it was like to be a young Irishman and poor and lonely. Eamonn was twenty-five years old and had never had a woman lie next to him in bed. It was sad, and Kenny refrained from telling him tales about his experiences with women. It just wouldn't have been right to make a man, a friend, feel less than the man he was. They were the best of pals, but earlier that afternoon Kenny had decided not to have a dumb, drunken goodbye with Eamonn, and he made arrangements with a lovely little harlot from O'Connell Street to meet them at McDaid's, where for ten pounds she was to tear Eamonn away from Kenny — and without letting him know either that she was a hooker or was paid — take him back with her to her room and make love to him for the entire night, even if she had to rip his clothes off to get him in bed.

Her name was Kate and she was waiting at the bar when they walked into McDaid's. Kenny said hello to her and introduced Eamonn, who became dazed and perplexed because, after Kenny had slipped Kate the ten and given her the nod, she was all over him, grabbing and pinching and coming on and tugging at him to go away with her. Eamonn was turning a little red and getting angry, but Kenny pulled his head close and whispered in his ear, "What are you, a stupid man or something? Can't y'see promiscuity when it's starin' you in the face? She wants you to go home with her 'n poke her, you dummy! Now, go along before she changes her mind or I'll take her meself. What're you, afraid? Go ahead then an' I'll see you in the morning."

Kenny said goodbye to Eamonn as Kate was pulling him out the door by his arm. "Before the night is over she will probably be thinking that ten pounds is a small price to pay a girl for being devoured by the likes of a bull such as Eamonn," Kenny thought, as he watched them pass by the window and on down Chatham Lane.

"What kind of a trick was that to do?" questioned a strong-throated voice with no Irish inflection in it. Kenny turned to see that it belonged to a full-bodied brunette in her mid-twenties with a hard, beautiful face. "What did you say?" he asked and she answered, "I was just wondering if you always dogged birds for your friends that way."

Kenny: What do you mean?

She: Nothing. Forget it. I'll buy you a drink — and she did and told him her name was Peggy McCoy. She was an actress and she had just completed a role in a film in London and returned home to spend the Saint Patrick's holiday with her father in Dublin — but she should have known it'd be a waste of time, she said, because her father was already passed out in bed from too much drink, and he didn't like her much anyway on account of her profession, and she had just stopped in to McDaid's to say hello to a friend who was an actress with the Abbey Theatre Company only to be informed by the barman that her friend was working in a film being shot on location in the west of Ireland. Rather than return to her room at the Shelbourne Hotel to wait for the next flight back to London in the morning, she'd decided to "get a little pissed myself, and you're an American, aren't you?"

Kenny said that he was and that he had come from Rome where he also worked in films, to vacation for a while in Dublin because he'd never been here before — and he was also planning to fly to London, "sometime tomorrow and I intend to get a little pissed myself tonight, so why don't we do it together." They did, returning to her room at the Shelbourne afterwards where they made love to each other, until both their bodies were raw, neither of them caring whether the other one was telling the truth or not.

They were, however, and the next morning Kenny awoke with a hangover so bad his eyes hurt as he returned to the Brazen Head to collect his belongings. The place was empty, everyone downtown watching the Saint Patrick's Day parade, so he wrote a short good-bye-and-thank-you note to the Cooneys and enclosed ten pounds in an envelope which he set on the table in the kitchen. He left his bag full of books outside Eamonn's door and carried his bag of clothing back with him to the Shelbourne where he told the desk clerk to mind it for him. Then he went upstairs and woke Peggy who wasn't

feeling too chipper herself. They had a pot of hot coffee for breakfast. After she'd showered and dressed and was recognizable, they
went to the lobby and she checked out and paid her bill and Kenny
retrieved his bag.

They walked across to Saint Stephen's Green and down Merrion
Row to O'Donoghue's pub which was supposed to be closed for the
holiday but wasn't, and they had a couple of pints of stout to get
themselves back together and telephoned Aer Lingus for two reser-
vations on the midafternoon flight to London.

The flight wasn't crowded but it was a bit surreal. Most of the
passengers were men handcuffed to other men. Ever since Ireland
won its independence and became a republic it had been a haven
for British crooks on the lam, because it had never signed an extradition treaty with England. After the $7,200,000 Great British
Mail Train Robbery in August 1963, however, the British government offered the Irish government an incredible deal involving
trade agreements and sizable loans which didn't have to be paid
back, if they would only sign an extradition treaty, because some of
the Great Train Robbers were in the Republic of Ireland and were
being watched by detectives from Scotland Yard whose mouths were
watering. England wanted them arrested and returned to be tried
for a crime which caused the Empire a great deal of embarrassment
and a hell of a lot of money. So, de Valera and his Incorporated Mob
did sign the extradition treaty and before the ink was dry on the
secret document, the Scotland Yard boys nabbed the robbers who
were all asleep in their beds and hauled them back to London jails.
There was no way for them to fight being extradited in the courts
because there was no such clause or provision in the treaty for doing
so.

The men who were being returned by the law to London on the
same plane with Kenny Wisdom and Peggy McCoy were not any of
the Great Train Robbers but merely British crooks who were
caught in the sweep over Ireland by Scotland Yard after the treaty
had been put into effect. Some of them had been living as respecta-
ble citizens, operating small shops in Dublin and smaller towns in
the various counties for years. The government of Ireland had all
but put a stop to immigration with the signing of that bloody treaty
and the Republic was worse off for it.

Peggy McCoy was not only vigorously attractive, she was also
smart, tough, feisty and knew her way around without being foul-
mouthed and cunty. Kenny liked her, and lived with her in her flat

on Hollywood Road in Kensington, S.W., for a month, until she was called to go to Spain for six months' work on two pictures being filmed back to back. While she was with him for that month, however, she took him around London where he met several people over pints of bitter in pubs and glasses of gin in clubs. They became his mates and worked with him after she was gone.

One of these was a big-bearded, boisterous man named Jess whom he met in Finch's pub on the Fulham Road. Jess was in his forties and knew everything there is to know about drinking in London. He took Kenny for pints of hard cider drafted from wooden kegs in a house on the Edgeware Road, the only local in the city where all they served was hard cider. The men who were regulars there were old-timers, as addicted to the cider as absinthe drinkers are to absinthe but twice as crazy. Then there was Henecky's near Fleet Street which served glasses of its own distilled whiskey from spouts which were tapped into the bungholes of huge wooden vats. There was a tier above and surrounding the barroom where, in the eighteenth century, the aristocrats would look down on the lower classes, watching them drink and fight and make fools of themselves. And the French Pub on Greek Street where everything was bottled and nothing on tap except people. It was here that Kenny met the bloke whose sparsely furnished flat on Old Compton Street he sublet, after Peggy McCoy went away. He didn't want to remain in southwest Kensington and had given up Peg's flat to move to Soho where the action and money were to be had.

It was also at the French Pub that Jess introduced Kenny to Matt, an East Ender who earned a handsome bit of money each week producing hard-core pornographic literature which he wholesaled to the porn shop proprietors in Soho for a quid or two apiece. They in turn retailed them to their customers for a fiver per book. Matt was temporarily out of business when they met, because the woman who had been authoring the books he was manufacturing with stencils, bonded paper and a mimeograph machine, was arrested and sent down for stabbing her old man in the chest while he was asleep in bed because, she told the magistrate, his snoring had driven her temporarily insane and she had just tried to wake him up, " 'at's all!"

It was an opportune meeting for Kenny because he was practically skint after he paid six months' rent in advance for his digs. He was therefore very interested in Matt's operation, and when he told Matt he was a writer of sorts and could put together words in a book which would give the reader wet dreams while he was still awake, they left the crowded French Pub and walked down Old Compton Street to the empty bar in the Swiss Hotel — where over several pints of Charington's bitter they talked money. They finally agreed on a fifty-fifty proposition which called for Kenny not only to write the fiction but to help in the production and distribution of it as well.

Matt was a short Black-Irishman who was born in the East End of London around 1940 after his parents emigrated from Dublin to open a fish and chips café with his uncle. He was a warm, friendly, muscular guy but a little tense, and that tension would sometimes turn into paranoia when he got drunk as an elephant's trunk. His tightness would become a taut apprehension and he would explode and strike out at anything or anyone near him, giving or getting a kicking. When it was over and he was sober, he wouldn't remember anything. It didn't happen often. He was a stand-up character and a decent partner, and Kenny liked him. They became good mates.

Three days after Kenny and Matt bought a gross of Gestetner stencils and a stolen portable typewriter, Kenny had written his first of many porn books. The typing was difficult and the stencils made it twice as hard because he couldn't see what he typed. The fiction, however, was easy and he wrote in longhand before he typed it onto the stencils. It was a one-hundred-page story, two hundred words a page, about a middle-aged man who was the physical education teacher at a private boardingschool for little girls and how he would massage the insides of their soft, fuzzy, pale thighs after he told them they showed signs of an ailment which was peculiar to girls their age. It was only his wisdom and attentiveness to such ailments, he said, which prevented the eventual and painful cramps and spasms they caused. "So you just be a good girl and lie here and relax and close your eyes and concentrate on feeling good while I just slip off your tiny panties for a moment to see if there are any symptoms on your little tummy and use my finger to check the inside of your lower abdominal wall for any of those nasty little bumps . . . and I know the Vaseline is chilly but doesn't it feel good and warm inside . . . if you lift your legs up a bit, that's it, and spread them, like a good girl, fine, now that's better isn't it . . ." And how he would take them over his knee and spank their little bare bottoms when they were naughty and after he had trained a pair of them enough, he would get them to take off their clothes and direct them on how to play with one another's little creamy bodies. When he had tutored them to the promiscuous point where anything was allowed, he would strip and they would all play together with him masturbating and, placing their faces cheek to cheek so that their mouths were side by side, he would shoot half his load in one, hold it for a second, and shoot the rest in the other. The end of the story came when he widened one of the little girls' peepee enough to poke his large prick inside. He lay down on his back and got her to sit on his Vaselined tool and told her to ride on it like she was on a horsey, "Up 'n down, up 'n down. That's a good little girl, up 'n down." Although she was just wide enough, she wasn't deep enough and he pierced her insides causing her to hemorrhage all over him and die. But he continued, having gone from sodomy to necrophilia.

It was called *Teacher's Pets* and after the first mimeographed two hundred copies sold out in the shops for five pounds apiece in three days, Kenny had to retype six sets of stencils to keep the machine running constantly to supply the demand for the book. It ended up selling over fifteen hundred copies in less than three weeks, making Kenny and Matt each a bit over a thousand quid richer after expenses. It also made the organized porn mob in Soho very angry that a pair of independent operators' gear was outselling theirs and they did something about it.

They didn't have a line on Kenny but they knew Matt, so they settled for him. It happened in the same week Ronald Biggs and his gang of Great Train Robbers were sentenced to thirty years because one of them coshed the train's engineer on the head with an axe-handle, making it a crime with violence. The magistrate said he was giving them the maximum penalty with no chance for parole to make sure that they'd all be old men before they'd have a chance to spend any of the unrecovered £2,600,000.

A couple of members of a small firm that specialized in hurting people they were paid to hurt, nailed Matt to the floor of his flat by driving a railroad spike through the back of his left knee into the wood. He would have bled to death, if his kid brother hadn't come by to pay a visit and bum some money. As it was, he remained in shock until the following day and a cripple for the rest of his life.

Kenny was sitting in the Kismet Club off Leicester Square at three o'clock that afternoon talking with Jess about how amusing it seemed to him to have been writing articles demanding relevant reform in Dublin just two months ago, which only a few people wanted to read, and now every queer loaf of bread on Brighton Pier was spending five quid to read some rubbish he scribbled off in a few days. They were both laughing about the absurdity of taking the politics of the world and society seriously when *Wham!* Rudolf the Yid did a front-wheel skid down the steps of the club and over to their cain and abel where he nearly blew his tin-lid screaming, "God forbid what just happened to Matt wouldn't also happen to Kenny," who couldn't make out exactly what he was saying because he was rhyming his slang so fast and the Yid got more upset and shouted, "Don't no one rahn' 'ere unnerstan plain English!" Jess understood though and spelled out every word to Kenny as they MacNabbed a cab to the hospital on Roehampton Lane where Matt had been taken by ambulance from his flat near Putney Heath.

Matt's wife Katheleen and his younger brother Chas were sitting on a wooden bench in the vistors' waiting room with Matt's year-old son, Jim, when Kenny and Jess came rushing through the door. It had been five hours and Katheleen was now dry-eyed but tear-stained. She said she went out with the baby at about nine o'clock that morning to buy some milk and stuff at the deli and had stopped off at her mother's for a chat, and when she'd returned there were coppers all over and Matt had been put in an ambulance and was about to be taken away when Chas spotted her and told the attendants to hold it a minute so she could ride to the hospital with her husband.

Chas said that Matt must have been taking a bath when whoever did it came in because he was all wet and naked and the tub was full of water. It must have happened right after Katheleen stepped out because he found his brother nailed to the floor at nine thirty according to what the clock read that was lying next to the door when he opened it. He described how the whole flat had been turned upside down and it wasn't on account of a struggle either, he said. The bastards had been after Matt's money as well and they had gotten it too.

Katheleen nodded her head yes it was true and they took all of it because Matt hadn't hidden it very good, just underneath the mattress the night before, and he planned to bank it in a mate's safe before noon that morning. The coppers asked her questions for two hours straight and told her it was a professional job by a gang that was hired to do these things to people and did she know what kind of business her husband was in and she replied, "Of course not!"

Jess said they knew by now because they probably pulled his file at Scotland Yard and he had only just finished doing a prison term last year.

Kenny told Katheleen not to worry about money because he would take care of it and asked her when they could see Matt. She answered that the doctors were operating on his leg at that very moment and had said that no one could visit him until tomorrow or the day after.

He gave her a hundred quid and said he would go and bank another five hundred with the same bloke that Matt had intended to see that morning and "Use it 'cause it's yours 'n there's plenty more where it came from, unnerstand?"

After Chas assured them that he would stay with Katheleen until Matt was out of hospital and help her put the flat back in order, Kenny and Jess said goodbye and went to bank the five hundred quid in the iron tank in Frank Henry's betting parlor, where Kenny and Matt and a few of their mates for a slight fee used to keep large amounts of cash that they didn't want to walk around with or stash in their digs, for fear that the coppers would tumble to it and confiscate it as taxes which all loyal subjects owed to Her Royal Majesty Queen Elizabeth.

Every geezer in Soho knew what went down with Matt, and Kenny walked all over that racketland looking for a gun he could buy to shoot the elbows and kneecaps off of the berk who paid to have Matt done. He knew who it was, and that Saturday night he also got to know what happened to people in those days who went around London looking for a gun to use on somebody. Word got to him that if he was at the intersection of Clapham Park and Bedford roads at 8 P.M., he would meet a man who had a pistol to sell him. Kenny met him all right and he did have a .38 Webley revolver, but he didn't give it to him, he arrested him with it and took him to a police station and charged him with assaulting a police officer, attempted murder and possession of a loaded revolver. He had been set up, by one of any number of persons, and the man who arrested him wasn't any ordinary copper, he was Inspector Blandler who considered himself the scourge of Soho. The inspector felt it was his spiritual duty to clean up the area with his own private methods in what he maintained was his own private war against crime.

The inspector filed a report stating that he had heard it about that Kenny was planning to waylay a certain so-and-so at such-and-such a place and it was only by the justice of the Lord that he got there first and singlehandedly disarmed him and placed him under arrest. Of course Kenny kept screaming *Frame!* but he was told he would have his day in court and that he didn't have to have his fingerprints taken but they were taken anyway and he was asked some questions, only one of which he answered.

"How did a young lad like you get started in all this?" asked a Metropolitan Police sergeant.

"*I went down 'n applied!*" answered Kenny, and he was given a sound thumping by the spinning-top cop and thrown into a station house cell. There he lay on a plank with some thoroughly disinfected blankets for a pillow until Monday morning when he was driven in a Black Maria to magistrates' court where he was remanded to Her Majesty's Prison of Brixton.

Being remanded to prison for custody to await your trial differs very little from being sentenced to one after you've been convicted. In fact, there are only two dissimilarities: you can buy certain food from the canteen and you can have a visitor each day instead of the regular half-hour-a-month visit permitted guys doing terms.

Katheleen and Chas were the only people who visited Kenny; everyone else he knew had records and weren't allowed. Matt was out of the hospital after a while and very upset by what happened and they were all doing the best they could, but it really just came down to Kenny's word against the inspector's. On the first Tuesday in June, 1965, Inspector Blandler was believed and Kenny was sentenced a while after to not less than ten years and no more than life at Parkhurst maximum security prison. Kenny's mind boggled at it all and there was no place he could turn because all he had to say was what everybody had to say and just as loud: "*He planted it on me! I'm being framed!*"

Before he was transported and sent down to Parkhurst, "the Bastille of the Isle of Wight," to begin his sentence, however, Inspector Blandler, thank fuckin' god, blew it, and Kenny remained in Brixton to hang tough while Scotland Yard investigated an accusation that was made against the inspector.

Apparently a group of students were demonstrating against Queen Frederica of Greece in front of Buckingham Palace where she was having tea with Queen Elizabeth and Inspector Blandler arrested a young medical student, claiming that he had taken a brick from his coat pocket and was just about to throw it at the Greek queen when the startlingly observant inspector pried it from his hand. The young medical student, however, was having none of that and he demanded to speak to one of the higher-grade detectives who worked out of Scotland Yard. When he did, he told him the inspector was full of shit and to prove it he gave the detective his raincoat to bring back with him to the Yard to have the lab boys there check it for any traces of brick dust. They did and after they found not a speck of brick dust on the raincoat or on any other article of the student's clothing, they confronted Inspector Blandler. The inspector did a stone portrayal of Captain Queeg, saying that he had been appointed by God Himself to abolish scurvy in this district and by God he was doing just that and any way he could too by God, and not only on his shift either and his wife could testify to that (and she did) but twenty-four hours a day, as God was his judge, and sometimes right in the middle of a sound sleep there would be a flash and it would become clear how to deal with one particular individual or another by God. When they examined the raincoat that the inspector wore that day, guess what they found. Kenny and some twenty-odd persons who claimed at their trials that Blandler had planted evidence and framed them were freed. Some of them after having served three or four years for things that the sick Inspector Swine couldn't catch them at.

Kenny never saw a newspaper photo of that young student and he wasn't even able to pronounce his name but by Jesus he loved him for having the tenacity and the smarts to get himself cut loose from that phony beef. Thanks to him for having saved his life and the same goes for a lot of other dudes who owe their liberty to that quick-witted young man. "Thanks and have a nice life, fella!"

Soho wasn't particularly hospitable any longer because the coppers now had his number, and the berks who had Matt done didn't fancy the idea of Kenny Wisdom's presence, so he moved out to a house in East Dulwich with a safe blower he met in the Brixton nick. He only went into town once during that month of June after he had been released, and that was to the Royal Albert Hall for The International Poetry Congress of the poets of the world and of our time, which was a pompous way of saying a poetry reading.

Many of the poets whose books had given him that itch back in '63 and '64 were there: Allen Ginsberg, Lawrence Ferlinghetti, Anselm Hollo, Alex Trocchi, Simon Vinkenoog, Andrei Voznesensky, Ernst Jandl, Pablo Neruda, Gregory Corso — and they did it to him again. This time, however, what they did was give him the simple desire to go back to America because that's what he was, an American, they told him in their poems, and that's where it was happening and if he wanted to do anything that's where he would have to begin, in his own backyard. He decided that as soon as he blew this warehouse safe which he and his mate in East Dulwich were planning, he would return to the States. Yes, it was time to go home!

The job wasn't set until early November and there was a lot of planning and worrying and hard work to get through before he could pack up and leave, but East Dulwich wasn't a bad place. Kenny had himself a good girl friend and a stand-up mate and a lot of dart games and laughs at a pub called the Cherry Tree. There were the fathers, brothers and uncles of several of the Great Train Robbers who used to hang out and drink at the Cherry Tree. One of them was the father of Charles Wilson, who had been broken out of the Birmingham jail in August of '64 by two guys who just walked inside, unlocked the door to his solitary cell, and went away with him. Wilson's father wasn't losing any sleep waiting for his son to turn up though,

There was one big celebration at the Cherry Tree that lasted joyously into the night of July 8, when the news was full of Ronald Biggs, the man who planned and carried out that greatest robbery in modern history, and the details of his escape from Wandsworth maximum security prison at three o'clock that afternoon. The radio and television were on full blast and everybody was hoisting their glasses as the commentators described the clockwork precision of the elaborate operation which had been handled with a skill akin only to the Mail Train Robbery itself.

At three o'clock that afternoon, a dilapidated red moving van scraped alongside the twenty-foot gray wall of Wandsworth prison while Ronald Biggs and other top security prisoners were exercising in the yard, and a "cherry-picker," an elevator platform of the kind used to repair streetlights, pushed up through a hole in the van's roof with two men in it. They covered the four unarmed guards with shotguns, lowered two rope ladders and yelled, "Okay, lads!" to Biggs and three other cons who climbed up the ladders and jumped down from the wall through the roof of the van onto an improvised trampoline which was set up inside to break their fall. They all swiftly changed from their prison garb to ordinary clothes and hopped from the van into three waiting cars which sped away with the van following. The whole operation took thirty seconds and made Parliament so crazy they wanted to call out the British army to recapture Ronald Biggs. Biggs had truly inspired Kenny Wisdom and his mate who were finally able to pull their score on the third weekend of November with Joan Baez and Donovan leading a peace march right past the warehouse where they had just tied up the watchman and were working on the very large but old Hobbs safe.

Kenny unscrewed the keyhole covers and Truman, the professional safe blower, rammed the correct amount of gelignite into the keyholes with a dowel, connected the copper detonator to pieces of wire which he stuck on top of the gelignite with plasticine, and wrapped around the door handles so that they would stay firmly in place while he pulled the bare ends of the wires outside the office into another room. After Kenny covered the safe with a rug, Truman connected the wires to a three-volt doorbell battery which triggered off the explosion. It wasn't very loud but it was successful. The locks were broken, and the handles turned, and the box was so old that the antiblowing device which should have pushed bars across the inside of the doors to jam them, didn't work. They discovered why the warehouse had such an old and easy safe when they opened it and found less than three hundred pounds — which made them both mad because of all the work and planning they had put into the job. Truman asked the watchman why there was so little when there should have been so much and the old codger said that the warehouse owner had been held up a week ago by some black fellas and that it hadn't been reported to the police or the papers because the money that was stolen was cash acquired by not paying his proper income tax!

Truman and Kenny were disgusted. They knew that the guy who owned the warehouse had been beating Her Royal Majesty out of tax revenue, but because they were living way out in East Dulwich, they weren't too up to date on the goings-on about town and were especially ignorant of any activity in the black underworld.

They returned to their digs and Truman simmered down and started talking about another score, but Kenny said he'd had it and was going to go away for a while.

He didn't have many belongings left, only a few clothes which he stuffed into a bag. He did have 142 quid, though, and that was enough for a plane ticket back to New York. But he almost didn't get a chance to buy one because, as he was saying his farewells to Truman, two police patrol cars came hot-lotting it up to the front of the house. Kenny leaped out the back window and scarpered over some fences, leaving his bag on the kitchen floor.

When he felt he had run far enough, he hid in some bushes and looked to see if the coppers were coming after him. They hadn't even seen him and he watched them take Truman away and post a guard by the door. The old watchman must have gotten loose when they left and fingered Truman's photo which was one of a dozen photos detectives carried in their pockets to show anyone who saw a safe blower cracking a box.

Kenny waited a while before taking a bus to the underground and the underground to the airport bus terminal and another bus to Heathrow Airport. All he had in his pockets was the money and fortunately his passport. His coat had even gotten torn when he scarpered over the backyard fences. "Some way to return home after being away for six and a half years. Fuck it!" He bought a ticket on a BOAC flight to New York and considered himself lucky to be alive.

THREE

For Matthew "Peanut" Johnson

For when you're alone
When you're alone like he was alone
You're either or neither
I tell you again it dont apply
Death or life or life or death
Death is life and life is death
I gotta use words when I talk to you
But if you understand or if you dont
That's nothing to me and nothing to you
We all gotta do what we gotta do

T. S. Eliot, *Sweeney Agonistes*

It was the last Sunday in November of 1965 and his twenty-first birthday when Kenny Wisdom landed at Idlewild airport, which had been renamed John Fitzgerald Kennedy.

A lot of things had changed. Kenny's parents had moved to a different section of Brooklyn a few years back. He took the crumpled letter they had written him about their change of address from his pocket and dialed their new phone number from a booth at the airport. He didn't yell "Surprise!" when his mother answered, he just asked her what was for dinner because he said he would be home in half an hour. He hung up before she could express her astonishment.

He caught a cab for Brooklyn which took him on the Belt Parkway past the fishing boats returning to Canarsie from their early morning trawl, the red-tiled roof of the Lundy Brothers' huge seafood restaurant in Sheepshead Bay, and the parachute jump in Coney Island and . . . "What's that?"

"Whadda ya mean, 'Wat's dat?' " said the cabby. "Dat's de bridge. De longest suspended bridge in de woild, de Verrazano, dat's all! Where you been?"

When they arrived Kenny paid the fare and stood for a moment looking at the six-story, gray, sixty-unit building with the name "The Royal Poinciana" cut into the cement above the front entrance when the building was constructed prior to World War One.

He went inside and checked out the mailboxes for the right apartment number, took the elevator up to the proper floor and rang the doorbell. He heard the joyful commotion even before it exploded-open the door, and pulled him in and spilled all over him. His mother was hugging and kissing his head, his sister wrapped her arms around his waist, and his father was shaking his left hand with both of his.

His mother began crying with happiness. Her hair had turned gray with streaks of white and she had gained a little weight since she had the operation she wrote him about. His sister was also laughing-crying. She was a teen-ager — tall, blond, shy and pale from anemia. His father was smiling broadly with honest embarrassment. He had suffered a cardiac thrombosis a while ago but he was over it now, and his hair was still thick and jet-black, and his shoulders and back were as straight and erect as they always had been.

Kenny sort of felt like a stranger but he knew he was home with his family and it was good. Good to be back where they could see each other in the flesh instead of through letters and photographs. His sister hardly knew her brother any other way, and his parents remembered their son as a boy they watched grow up in words on pieces of paper. Now they saw that their boy-son-brother was indeed a man. He looked at them and saw the adolescence he had spent as a twenty-two-year-old in Europe on their faces, which had grown older in the way that people age in Brooklyn.

After Kenny phoned them from the airport that Sunday afternoon, his mother and sister had dressed back into the clothes they had worn to church that morning and his father had put on a clean sports shirt to greet their world-traveling son, the film director — who arrived with unshined, scuffed shoes, dirty, wrinkled trousers and sweater, torn coat, and a two-day beard. "Don't you have any luggage?" was the first question he was asked after the Happy Birthdays and Welcome Homes.

"There was a baggage mix-up, it seems, at the London airport and half the passengers on my flight lost their bags in the shuffle, including me. But the BOAC people said they'd notify us on Monday or Tuesday when they found out where our stuff ended up. It's probably all in Tunisia by now or some other remote godforsaken place."

While Kenny took the first real shower he had since he left his pad in Rome and changed into different clothes, which still fit and had been mothball-stored in a dresser by his parents in a bedroom which they said was his "own room," his mother was on the phone notifying all the relatives and friends of the family that the prodigal had returned and they should all come over. And come over they did. As soon as Kenny finished eating a pot-roast dinner with his father the doorbell started ringing, and aunts and uncles, first cousins and second, by blood and by proxy, all sorts of people he hadn't seen in six, seven years, and some little children he'd never seen before, crowded into the kitchen and living room of the five-room, eighty-five-dollar-a-month apartment, and Kenny was as glad to see them as they said they were to see him.

When the initial greetings were finished, the booze was broken out and someone asked Kenny if he wanted ice and he said yes because he hadn't had any for a very long time, and everyone relaxed into a party mood. He told them pleasant stories about Italy and the Center of Experimental Cinematography in Rome and the films he made, and how he went to Dublin and grass-rooted it with the people there to find out what it meant to be Irish and whether he had any distant relatives still around. He gave up trying to locate them after a while and accepted an offer from the Granada television network in London to assistant-direct some documentary shorts, which he did for half a year until they discovered he wasn't an Irish citizen but an American and took his work permit away. So he decided it was time to come back home anyway and he did.

An aunt mentioned something about his being a citizen of the world, which prompted Kenny to tell them about a small town in Italy called Rocca Sinibalda which had a big castle constructed in the shape of an eagle with its wings spread in flight. The castle was purchased by a woman from Washington, D.C., whose family had made millions selling brassieres. She turned the spacious castle into a series of studios where artists could live and work for free. The woman also became the town's benefactress and she changed the jail into a hospital and bought farm machinery for the people and made sure that everyone was well fed and housed. One day she had someone hoist a flag with a blue circle on a white background up the pole on the castle's tower and she proclaimed that the people of Rocca Sinibalda were now citizens of the world and the town itself was going to secede from the nation of Italy. The people of the town were confused at first, but when they were informed that secession from Italy meant they wouldn't be bothered by paying taxes any longer, and also that they would no longer be subject to Italian law or authority, they immediately became citizens of the world and enthusiastic advocates of secession.

It went on like that until Kenny had polished off a fifth of Seagram's Canadian whiskey and was smashed, and everyone else had to go because tomorrow was Monday which meant getting up early for work or school. They all said "Goodnight" and "Nice to have you back" and "See you again soon, maybe next weekend" and "Take care of yourself" and left without asking him about what he intended to do now that he was home. Even his parents didn't question him that way, and he could see they were proud of him simply for his presence and for having returned home. They were happy to have their son, and his sister her older brother, and he was too.

When he regained consciousness late the following morning, he had a difficult time remembering where he was, because he feared that if he opened his eyes to the daylight he might be permanently blinded or suffer a brain hemorrhage in his splitting head, which was already reeling from an alcoholic concussion. He deliberated for a time and finally figured out he was home. He cupped his hands over his eyes and made his way to the bathroom where he delicately sprinkled water on his fractured face and washed the ashtray from his mouth with toothpaste and some Listerine which he almost swallowed because the rye whiskey shakes had taken over his spastic reflexes.

He was still dressed in the clothes he wore the night before, except for his shoes which someone had thoughtfully removed. He shuffled slowly to the kitchen in a trance, aware only of the painful effort it took to move. He made some instant coffee and sat down at the table, trying to focus his bloodshot eyes on a note braced between the salt and pepper shakers which was signed, "Mom." It wasn't until he was drinking his second cup of coffee that he could read it. His mother wrote that she had gotten a job in the personnel department of some company because, with his sister grown up, there was really nothing to keep her occupied around the house. And there was plenty of food in the fridge and his sister would be home from school around four thirty and she and his father would get back at about six that evening, "Love, Mom."

Kenny had three more cups of coffee and walked around the apartment. It was a comfortable place with green wallpaper in the carpeted foyer, which doubled as a dining room, and reupholstered furniture in the yellow and brown living room, with thick green drapes over the windows. His parents' bedroom was all white with a crucifix tacked to the wall, overlooking a woven, white, woolen bedspread. The French doors that had separated it from the living room had been removed, his mother told him, because they were warped and wouldn't close properly, and anyway, without them the living room had a more open feeling. His sister's room was also painted white and the three-quarter bed, like the rest of the furniture in her room, was new and made of light-colored wood. The furniture in his "own room" was also new and manufactured with the same wood by the same company in the same style. There was a desk, a dresser, a single bed and a row of waist-high bookcases along one of the blue walls. There was a red nagahide armchair below a reading lamp which gave the room the finishing touch of a study. The room had been designed for a young boy to do his high school homework in, or write his university term papers. Besides his sister's furniture, "his" was the only new furniture in the apartment, and it was obvious his parents bought it with the hope that their son would have returned a long time ago to continue his education — a fantasy the study-styled room encouraged, even though the blue linoleum floor had only been worn by his mother's entering the empty room over the years to hang her wash on the clotheslines outside the windows.

Inside the closet, hanging on a wooden rack in long, zippered plastic bags, were the suits and clothes he had worn when he was a student at the private preparatory school on Park Avenue. Even the cordovan shoes were there, on the floor with trees in them. Rummaging around in the closet, he noticed something that was ironically funny. On the left, behind an old Eisenhower jacket, was an ancient wall safe that was built into the closet when the building was constructed as a fashionable residence at the turn of the century. Kenny couldn't help but laugh, and he was curious to see if anyone had left anything in it. He got a small crowbar from the tool chest in the kitchen and easily pried open the door of the antique box. There was only a letter inside which was written in German, and as far as Kenny could make out, it was about love. There was also a small photo of a very distinguished gray-bearded man with a high collar in the envelope with the letter. Kenny was disappointed because he expected something more extravagant. He put them back into the box and banged-jammed the door shut on someone's fading lonely-heart memory.

He was still hangover-tired and he sat down in the armchair and thought about it for a moment: about how his family had more money since he left them with one less mouth to feed and his mother had gone to work; about how they spent their money to make a nice home for themselves and give him and his sister their own rooms; about the disappointment they must have felt all the years his room remained empty, except for an occasional guest staying the night or his cousin Paul, whose family's nearby apartment was too small for him to have any privacy and whose books were on top of the desk. Paul at least used the room as it was intended to be used. He also thought about what he was going to tell his parents when they eventually asked him what were his plans for the future. He would really have to think about the answer to that one.

For the next couple of days Kenny stayed around the house reintroducing himself to New York's television, daily newspapers, and AM and FM radio stations. He was impressed more by the quantity of the media barrage being pumped into the homes throughout the city for the entertainment of its residents and by the incredible amount of things advertised for sale, than he was by the quality.

Everything from the six o'clock newscasts to the FM midnight-to-dawn, musical-interlude interviews, to the search-for-tomorrow soap operas at noon, was nothing short of hypnotic. He concluded that if you had enough beer and pretzels and a radio and TV you could barricade yourself inside a room for a week and just sit and listen and watch and switch stations. Whether you wanted to or not, you would learn what they wished you to know about so-and-so and such-and-such in a way that left little for you to decide except what station and from whom you wanted to hear it. The content was always inoffensively the same — only the styles of delivery and the images of the performers varied slightly.

By that Wednesday, Kenny had enough of home entertainment and he took the subway over to Manhattan to see for himself what the voices on the airwaves were trying to tell him about the city streets. He got off at a stop in Greenwich Village and stood on the corner of Eighth Street and Broadway for a moment to get his bearings.

"Kenny! How you been, man?" wanted to know a very long-curly-haired guy wearing a floppy brown car coat which hung below his knees and made him look shorter than he was. He was standing in front of him with his hand outstretched waiting to shake Kenny's. Kenny didn't recognize him for the hair but shook his hand anyway and said he was fine and "Okay, I give up. Who are you?"

"Billy. Billy Landout from Brooklyn. Remember?"

"Billy! I'll be a son of a bitch! My mother wrote 'n told me that you were away at some college studying to be an engineer. What happened?"

"Nothing happened. I graduated last summer with a degree in engineering and just decided I didn't want to be an engineer for a while, that's all."

"Well, are you in a play or something?"

"What do you mean, in a play?"

"I mean your hair and everything."

"No, man. I just felt like a change, and besides the chicks like to run their fingers through my curly locks and make believe I'm Donovan or somebody but I'm just me, man. Just me."

"Are you still living in Brooklyn?"

"No, I got a pad in the East Village."

"The East Village? Where's that?"

"Oh, that's just a name some real-estate dudes gave to the Lower East Side to promote it as sort of a new bohemia, an extension of

Greenwich Village. Come on, walk over with me and I'll show you around, and you can buy me a beer and tell me what you've been doing with yourself."

"Listen, tell me something."

"What?"

"How'd you recognize me after all these years?"

"Your freckles, how else?"

"Fuck you, too!"

The sky darkened with gray clouds hovering as they walked across Third Avenue into the wind. Billy mentioned that the Lower East Side had originally been marshland, which is what the word Bowery meant if you spelled it *bouwerie*. A group of panhandlers were huddled against the cold on the corner outside the Gem Spa candy store, and Kenny was confused for a moment by their juvenile, well-fed, cherubic faces, until Billy explained that it was just a new game the kids from the other boroughs played in Manhattan. On Saint Mark's Place just before First Avenue they passed a building where, according to Billy, Trotsky, and two of his comrades had edited a political journal during the months prior to the Russian workers' struggle for power in 1917. They crossed one of the city's largest and least-known parks at Tompkins Square, continuing along Avenue B to Tenth Street and the Annex.

The bar had a late afternoon crowd of mostly Jewish chicks, and black guys dressed like aesthetes and coming on like noble savages. Kenny bought a pair of Ballantine ales and carried them over to a table where Billy had piled a couple handfuls of peanuts. They drank ale and shelled peanuts for a few hours and talked about themselves and the news. Kenny ran down a précis of his more than five years in Europe. Billy talked about what was happening on the Lower East Side of Manhattan. About how it had evolved from the violent battleground for opposing ideas of immigrant peoples to the frontier of adventure for the East Coast of America's aggressively searching youth who kept time to Kerouac's *On the Road* beat, but settled for a more stationary scene here, and let their hair grow long. About how people who wrote in newspapers for a living had categorized the place as a "new Bohemia" and the young who came there "Hippies." About the low rents; the Kerista free love cultists who set up a floating sexual kibbutz which daily congregated in various pads; the cafés, bars, clubs, theaters, galleries, magazines, papers, films that were springing out from underground throughout

218

the area; the young people who were dropping out of their generation like flies and pushing further toward a vision which was out of sight. About acid and how it just might be one of the keys to the locks on the door of that empty room filled with nothing, nowhere.

After nursing beers at the Five Spot while listening to Charles Mingus and crashing the rest of the night on a floor-mattress in Billy's walk-up apartment on Avenue C, the next morning Kenny dropped two 300-microgram capsules of this LSD drug he had only heard about. Billy had taken it several times and was by far the best person for Kenny to trip with, since he never took himself too seriously and knew how to calmly chart a course during a psychedelic experience. He suggested that Kenny take 600 mics rather than the usual 300 because it would insure a total high. A lesser dosage would probably allow Kenny to resist the possibilities of the drug and chalk the trip up as simply another kick, thereby negating or blocking the chance for him to glimpse into the blindspot of his consciousness. Billy took just one 300 cap because he had been there before and it didn't take him much to get there again.

Within an hour Kenny was zonked. Inanimate objects and irrelevancies melt-twisted free of importance and drip-faded into the waterfall of pretension. Remembered images invoked from the past exploded into a kaleidoscopic burst of day-glo spirochetes wistfully dancing in a chaotic, nostalgic, timeless cascade of moment, like a drowning man's thoughts. Everything moved at the speed of light, with yesterday's light gleaming in one direction and tomorrow's in another. He saw that what was and will be — only is. There was a glimmer inside the privacy of his being, and he immediately understood that if he became anxious or panicky, he'd miss the clear light of his own death which is part of life. Then everything that was supposed to happen happened, until he was flashed-out-spaced. It seemed like he was going to stay that way forever and just when he started to feel that enough's enough, it was over and he began to come down. His kidneys ached.

Now that the psychedelic storm was over, Kenny's thoughts settled into a calm. He knew that most people were simply in trouble with themselves because they feared who they were. He dug that no matter how much he begged to know whether he might be the hero of his own life or its victim, he would be unable to discover his destiny. He understood that everything always happens and that his

219

needs were just his needs and didn't reflect some universal principle. That there were some things even more important than being alive and one of them was being alive the way you want to be alive.

He walked over to the sink, picked up a nearly empty bottle of Cott orange soda and finished it. He studied the empty for a moment and ran his thumb across the "Deposit" impressed in raised glass. He slammed the bottle against the porcelain, and the glass shattered into the sink. The noise startled Billy and he came into the small kitchen to see what it was. He saw Kenny standing over by the sink. There was a funny, intense look on his face which made Billy a bit apprehensive.

Kenny: Why was that bottle worth five cents?

Billy: Because it was a re-usable commodity.

Kenny: Why wasn't it worth a dollar?

Billy: It didn't have enough value . . .

Kenny: Magic.

Billy: Magic?

Kenny: The magic of property. Inanimate objects have no intrinsic value except what they can do for you, but in our culture they're invested with all sorts of magical properties, and cops protect that magic by making sure property has to be paid for — the unimaginative flunkies. Everything revolves around profit and private property. Those are the premises. I just questioned the logic by destroying the magic.

The seriousness in Kenny's face broke and he began to laugh. Billy relaxed and smiled too, wondering what brought on that dissertation. They went outside and over to Tompkins Square Park with Kenny concluding that it was good to be wacked out on acid because it made it difficult to be reasonable, and that way you could see right through things while looking incomprehensible and mad and you could make statements that were frightening and true.

It was cold and there were very few people in the park. They each bought a pint of warming red wine and walked the streets looking at the faces of the people and the curious activities in which they were involved. After a while the wine was finished, and Kenny decided to return to Brooklyn before it all got boring. He told Billy he would see him in a day or two and went over to the Eighth Street subway station.

There was a girl standing on the platform who looked vaguely familiar. They stared at each other for a moment, and when the train pulled in they entered the same car and sat down together.

Her name was Lucille Collins, and he had gone to grammar school with her and hung around with her brother. "Don't you remember?" she asked Kenny. He remembered and he also recalled he hadn't liked her very much or her brother either but he forgot why. The acid was still making it difficult to consider anything other than absurdity, and he answered her questions with a slight flipness he felt they required — especially when she said her brother was in Vietnam and asked Kenny what he was going to do about the army now that he was back in the country.

He replied that he wasn't going to do anything about the army and added that the next time she wrote to her brother she should advise him to "watch his ass because no matter how good his wages are, those little yellow people have been in the business of war for a long time and they don't consider it employment but rather a co-op in which they all own shares." She got a little snotty after that and countered with a remark about how the draft was going to get him, like it or not. Kenny laughed and blurted out that they didn't even know he existed because he had never registered.

Lucille Collins said something like, "Don't bet on it!" before getting off the train at her stop. The following afternoon Kenny Wisdom remembered why he had never liked her when they were kids: she was a snitch. He remembered this as soon as he answered the bell and the two men at the door, who identified themselves as FBI agents, presented him with two possible choices: he could go into the U.S. Army or to a federal penitentiary. Needless to say, this blew Kenny's mind and he kept protesting the fact.

"This can't be happening! Man, I just got here!"

But the agents simply suggested that the brevity of his return home was his own blues and three days later, on Monday, December 6th, Wisdom was inducted into the army and bussed to CoB, 6th Tng Bn, 2nd Tng Bde, USATC, Fort Gordon, Georgia.

It was only in boot camp that Kenny finally knew, through the haze of his amazement, that he was actually in the service. He also knew he had no intention of remaining. He wasn't about to try some dumb faggot routine, however, or pull a cornball lunacy stunt to get an immediate discharge. No, there was a war on and they would lock you in the stockade before they would let you out if you tried something stupid to fake a Section Eight. He remembered all the stories he heard when he was a kid about all the guys who ended up in Leavenworth after trying to cop out on the so-called police action in Korea. Now, with Vietnam on the stove, they were nabbing the same stiffs who were giving the same scams a whirl, making vain attempts to receive a medical discharge. Kenny was going to play it smart and smooth his way into a reverse, arriving at the psychological point where they would pay him to leave. There was no other way except walking AWOL, and so he decided to be stone-cold-blooded about it until he regained his freedom.

Kenny kept himself cooled out by smoking reefer in the barrack's boiler room with a few black dudes from Philadelphia whenever he got a chance, which was frequently. In fact, he spent so many of his off-duty hours hanging out with his black buddies that the group of pink-faced appleknockers from upstate New York who talked about becoming suburban Kiwanians formed the opinion that Kenny was probably a "moulonjam" himself. They even suggested that his freckles were proof of his being a mulatto. Of course no one ever expressed these insights to Kenny himself, but he picked up on the vibes and would joke while high with the brothers about all the suckers in their squads who were terrified that someday they would find their women fucking a nigger in the backseat of the family Ford.

Kenny coasted through the eight weeks of training at Fort Gordon, and angered the chumps who wanted to make good in the army and bewildered his goof-off, hipster friends by being classified a high achiever. He scored a top rating on the written I.Q. tests, placed second in the physical fitness trials, and won a trophy as the best rifleman in the company. With these laurels in his file, he applied for officer candidate school and signed up for the Airborne before returning to New York for his two weeks' leave, glad that everything had worked out as straight as he planned.

Billy laughed himself silly when he saw Kenny in uniform, saying he was sorry about his predicament but it was hilarious just the same. They spent some time together in that city and Kenny explained his good soldier scheme to him and confided that it was really easy because most of the schmucks who got duped into the service were losers from the get go, anyway. "The way I got it figured, the army will cut me loose with an honorable discharge before Easter."

Kenny had only been home a few days when his orders arrived. He was to report to Fort Ord, California, within a week, to begin advanced infantry training, a prelude to OCS. He liked the idea of going to California and he remembered a girl who lived in San Francisco, a model he met in Rome. She had written him a letter which had been forwarded halfway around the world before finally arriving in Georgia, enclosed in an envelope from his mother. He had copied her phone number from the letter into his little book, and now he called and told her to change the sheets because he would be there early the following evening.

The next day on the plane, he felt good about his move to the West Coast and more than confident that his time in the service was nearly over. The flight took about five hours, and he phoned Rhea from the airport. She was waiting for him when the coach pulled into the air terminal in downtown San Francisco.

Kenny hadn't seen Rhea for two years, and then he had only known her for a couple of months. But when he saw her standing on the sidewalk — all slender, firm, tall and beautiful with her chestnut hair full like a mane — he gave her a long-lost-lover embrace and the kind of kiss he felt the woman who was going to remove the celibate state which he had endured since returning to America, deserved. She was glad to see him, too. He left his duffel bag in the trunk of her car, and they had something to eat in a Chinese restaurant before retiring to her North Beach apartment. There they made love in a hard, solid, tender, active expression of life, until they felt it beautiful to stop and sleep in each other's arms — no longer anxious about being alone.

They spent the week together and it went by much too fast. Kenny liked the North Beach section of the city and he only left it to watch the sun set from the beach over the Pacific Ocean. He'd heard a lot about the area from the poets who had been turning him on with their books for years now. The Co-Existence Bagel Shop was gone, but the bars were still there, as was the only tangible evidence of the San Francisco Beat Renaissance during the late fifties — the City Lights bookstore. It remained open till two every morning with Ferlinghetti and his partner Shig competing against the topless clip joints along Broadway for a piece of the street action, and simply by its presence, giving notice to whomever it may concern in the tourist crowd that there were other poets in America besides Robert Frost who had miles to go before they slept.

City Lights published a series of paperbacks called Pocket Poetry and Kenny bought one entitled *Gasoline* by Gregory Corso, and several others which he took with him on the two-hour bus ride to Fort Ord. His processing began when he arrived that Wednesday and was completed by midafternoon Friday. The unit he was assigned to wouldn't be made up till the following Monday, so he was given a weekend pass. He phoned Rhea and she suggested they spend the two days with friends of hers who had a house in Carmel. They did, and it was West-Coast-wonderful with horseback riding along the beach and into the surf at dawn each morning, and Bordeaux-and-steak suppers outdoors each evening. It was March but the sun was warm and boot camp had put Kenny into such great, high-keyed, physical shape that his vigor matched that of the sea. The beauty of nature in that area reminded him of the wilderness he had enjoyed in the Italian Alps. He hadn't felt so good in years, and now more than ever he knew he wanted to live for a while in northern California. "But first things first," he said to himself, thinking about the army.

When he returned to his barracks, he saw a notice on the bulletin board saying that the company had been formed and training was to begin in the morning. Bright and early it did, with a march out to a firing range where they sighted their rifles. Kenny liked to march. The cadence relaxed him and allowed him to think. He decided that the best time to pull anything was right away, in these first few days before they got to know him. He had brought half a dozen Dexamyls with him from New York and carried them in his pocket, intending to use them whenever the moment came to heighten whatever contradiction he would cause.

The right moment came two days later on another firing range. Kenny realized this while sitting in the bleachers and listening to an instructor rap about what not to do when firing a bazooka. The sergeant explained that the most important thing to worry about was not the shell itself, but the exhaust of the explosion caused by firing it. The concussion that burst from the rear of the bazooka was known as the back-blast, and he demonstrated its action on an empty orange crate. He knelt and another sergeant loaded the bazooka with a blank shell, telling the training class to keep their eyes on the crate, which he lined up with the tail end of the weapon. Then he tapped the instructor on the head and there was a loud, rumbled crack-sound, and the wooden crate disappeared into a puff of dust as the blank shell leaped across the field and curved down into the open turret of a tank target, eighty yards away.

It was very impressive and Kenny dropped the six Dexamyls with a gulp from his canteen in preparation for what he knew was going to happen. The instructor again cautioned the class to be aware of the back-blast and told them they would be firing two rounds from the weapon, using that same tank as their target. The first round would be a dud, but the second contained a phosphorous explosive. Kenny decided to wait until his platoon was on the line to fire their live round, before making his move.

By the time he finished firing the blank round, the amphetamine was coming on, and he began to have an overwhelming sense of well-being. He already knew what he was going to do and waited for his platoon to be called forward, while his mind raced time and went nowhere. He sneaked a cigarette and sat in the bleachers, watching the blue-white phosphorous explode in bursts around the tank. It was like a fireworks display, and he wondered what it would be like at nighttime in battle. He remembered all the films he had seen about war. How the realism was always muffled to keep it from becoming unpleasant for the audience, and how they would leave the theaters going, "Tsk! Tsk! War is hell," but remark also that some men were able to measure their manhood by the sword, like Audie Murphy. Like George Armstrong Custer.

His platoon moved to the firing line and he knelt next to the weapon. Everything was going *Ziiinnggg! Ziiinnggg!* as the instructor ordered the gunners over the loudspeaker to raise the weapons into position and the loaders to ready the shells. The weapons were loaded, and as soon as this was acknowledged with a tap on his head, and while everyone else was sighting their aim on the target, Kenny stood up with the loaded bazooka resting on his shoulder. He just stood straight up while his firing partner made like an ostrich and covered his head with his arms. A closet-queen corporal standing nearby alerted everybody by screaming with terror and running away. The loudspeaker began shouting, *"Hold your fire! Hold your fire! No one move! No one move!"* But when the other trainees turned and saw Kenny standing and pointing his bazooka all around, they panicked. Some of them laid down their weapons and split, while others carried them and ran.

The confusion was frightening. With noncoms diving for cover and trainees running all over the place with primed bazookas in their hands and the loudspeaker pleading with everyone to *"Stop! Stop!"* and calling for the *"Captain! Captain!"* If someone had fired his weapon it would have caused a chain reaction, and they all would have gone off. It was scary but Kenny wasn't particularly concerned. He even considered walking back to the barracks but the bazooka was too heavy. *Ziiinnggg! Ziiinnggg!*

The loudspeaker yelled and finally wheedled him to, *"Please, Wisdom, lay the weapon on the ground, that's an order!"* while a second lieutenant crawled on his belly over to Kenny's blind side. There was no way the lieutenant could secure the bazooka in a struggle without causing danger to himself and the others, so he thought he would use some lame, junior-college logic to beg Kenny to be reasonable. Kenny didn't see the lieutenant sneaking up alongside him, and when he begged his first "Please!" into his left ear, Kenny jumped in surprise. The lieutenant froze, wetting his pants while everyone else cringed and hid their eyes. Even the captain began to weep and mumble something about his seventeen years in the service.

After a moment Kenny resumed his calm and looked all around surveying the scene. Two sergeants ran up to the lieutenant and one of them tore the officer's .45 out of its holster, cocked a round into the chamber, placed the barrel next to Wisdom's temple, and was about to blow it open when Kenny abruptly sat down, cradling the weapon in his lap. He studied it briefly, then looked up at the startled sergeant clutching the pistol and asked, "How do you unload a bazooka?"

The sergeant handed the lieutenant back his .45 and squatted down beside Wisdom. "Here, I'll show you," he said and took the bazooka. He walked about ten yards away, and the loudspeaker sighed, *"All clear! All clear! Return to your firing positions! Return to your firing positions!* and cajoled the trainees carefully back to their posts on the line, where they discharged their weapons at the target downfield and then returned to their seats in the bleachers.

The lieutenant pointed his pistol at Wisdom while both sergeants held him firmly between them. The black sergeant kept asking him why he wanted to go and do such a goddamn fool thing, but Kenny wasn't listening. He was looking at the chubby figure running awkwardly toward him from the far side of the training area. The rest of the trainees were watching, too, as their company commander huffed and puffed his fat-assed way past them with his belly bouncing in front of him like Jell-O. He was going full-tilt, and Kenny could see that his face was flushed red. As he came nearer, he cocked his right hand, and about two feet away he threw the punch at Kenny, leaping into the air like a baby elephant. The two noncoms eased themselves to one side, and the captain, widely missing Kenny's head, slammed into the lieutenant. The collision sent both of them to the ground with a groan and caused the .45 to fire a round into the sand, sending everyone ducking for cover again.

The captain struggled to get up, his face changing through the colors of the American flag. The lieutenant leaned over to help him and invoked, *"Put that fucking pistol away!"* Pointing toward Wisdom the captain screamed, *"Take that son of a bitch back to company headquarters! And if he gives you any trouble, ram your feet up his ass!"* As the captain was trying to overcome the difficulty that a bloated panda faces in regaining his footing, Kenny was tied to a fixture inside an armored personnel carrier and driven back to his company area.

After the first sergeant was briefed, Kenny was led into his office at headquarters. The topkick was an old soldier right out of the movies. The veins in his face were broken from whiskey, and his neck was thick-red with wrinkles. His enlistment had begun in Asia back in '44 when he served in Burma against the Japanese, and now it was ending while an undeclared war was being waged in that same part of the world. He didn't want to hear any bullshit, he just wanted to know whether the private standing in front of him was trying to punk out of that war, or was truly bat-shit.

Kenny's brain was completely jangled with tension, and when the first sergeant asked him for his full name and service number, he flipped out and started to scream hysterically. The shrillness of his tantrum forced everyone to cover their ears and the first sergeant yelled for his men to *"Get him outta here! Now!"* Kenny screamed all the way to the hospital. He only stopped after a doctor ordered him strapped in a bed and locked in a private room.

The doctor reviewed Wisdom's file and later reported to the captain that the young man's previous high performance record as a soldier convinced him that he went bananas at the bazooka training area because of some severe strain and he recommended his immediate transfer. The next morning Kenny was wrapped in a straitjacket, strapped into an ambulance, and driven north to the Letterman General Hospital at the Presidio military base in San Francisco.

The neuropsychiatric building was a separate annex of the hospital. It had been constructed at the turn of the century by the government to house inmates who became criminally insane while imprisoned at the federal penitentiary on Alcatraz. When the foot-thick, steel-plated, front door opened, and Kenny saw the three-hundred-pound black orderly standing inside, grinning — the name WASHINGTON on a plate pinned to his uniform — he moaned. They sat him on a bench in the receiving room, and he wondered what sort of fun and games were in store for him and how long it would take before he would be disqualified as a pawn and get released from the war team. He had been wide awake for the last thirty hours, but now the speed was wearing itself out of his system and he felt tired and shaky. They removed the straitjacket and he stretched out and relaxed. He longed for a bed and some sleep, but he had to wait while his papers were sorted by the staff sergeant in charge and his transfer orders processed.

When that was over, Washington, the buffalo nurse, brought him upstairs to be interviewed by a psychiatrist named Kruze, who questioned Kenny briefly and studied him for a moment until he felt satisfied that he was fairly sober and safely subdued. He told Washington he could leave them alone.

They talked for about forty minutes and it was a congenial conversation. At one point Kenny even admitted that, yes, he wanted out of the army as soon as possible. Dr. Kruze was sympathetic and offered to arrange for his honorable discharge from the service, but said it would take a few weeks to be effected and asked, "Do you think you'll need any medication?"

"I don't know, doctor. Why?"

"Well, you're going to be here for a while and there's very little to do. Most of the patients are pretty sick and a tranquilizer will help relieve any anxiety which may occur during your stay."

"Sure. Whatever you say, Doctor."

"All right, I'll prescribe a fifty-milligram Thorazine in the morning, one in the evening, and a chloral hydrate for sleep."

"Fine."

"What about work? It says here in your file that you have cinematographic experience. They have a fair-sized film unit and photo lab on this base. I think one of the patients works over there now. Should I see if they can use you? It'd be good to have something to do for a few hours a day, to break up the monotony of just sitting around here and waiting."

"Okay, Doctor."

"Good, I'll talk to them about it. Now, there's no bed available downstairs in the sign-out-patient ward, and there won't be until after the weekend. So you'll have to stay locked up in the control ward here on the second floor till Monday, when they'll move you below, where you can go and come as you please. I'll call Washington to get you set. Is there anything you want to know?"

"Yes, Doctor. What about visitors?"

"Do you have family in San Francisco?"

"No, just a friend."

"Oh. Well, until Monday you'll only be able to visit in the reception room during the day. However, when you're moved downstairs there'll be no restrictions other than the usual requirements that you remain on the base and return to the ward before lights out."

"Thank you, Doctor."

"Be seeing you."

The control ward had eighty beds in four rows — two rows along the walls and two down the middle of the floor. It was a cramped, barren, austere place with everything colored white or drab green. The patients all wore dark blue pajamas and shuffled around instead of walking. They were either temporarily lobotomized from electric shock treatments or too phenothiazined to lift their feet. There was no conversation. Just what was left of people sitting on beds in dumbfounded silence or talking to themselves with vacant stares. There was also a lot of openmouthed dribbling.

The patients in the control unit ate in a mess hall which could have been designed by the Marquis de Sade. It was the basement of the building: a dark, high-ceilinged, concrete dungeon with a stainless-steel steam table and long metal benches attached to several long metal dining tables bolted to the cement floor. There were no windows, and the lighting was purposely bad so no one could see anyone else's eyes without it being obvious.

There were a dozen girls and a handful of women. The girls were young dependents of career soldiers, and pretty in that raw, simple way girls are when they're vulnerable and fragile. The women, on the other hand, were old and tired. They were either in the army or the wives of men who were, and they had reached their own rock bottoms without any intention of bouncing back. The girls and boys and men and women sat together at the tables during mealtime but there was seldom any contact made. Nothing was said to anyone, and even the food was left practically untouched. Sometimes, someone would laugh or cry but only to themselves.

Kenny was nearly overwhelmed by the sadness of it all. The sadness of seeing so many young people with their minds broken — knowing that none of them were faking. He wondered whether they could tell that he was . . . and how long it would be before he wasn't. He had been locked inside the ward for three days and had conformed his appearance to its style of madness, remaining silent and shoveling himself around. How long would it take before the role he was playing ate its way into his being and enveloped him — before he actually became what he only appeared to be?

He was glad, very glad, when they moved him downstairs to the other unit. There, he was allowed to sign himself out and roam around the Presidio base and eat his meals at the mess hall in the main building of the hospital. Rhea visited often, bringing him civilian clothes and books from City Lights. Kenny used these books to defend himself against the self-recrimination and guilt which some of the patients in his unit continually displayed, convincing themselves that they were to blame for their illness. Visions of God were also big, and the group therapy sessions struck Kenny as merely self-indulgent self-pity. These guys weren't very sick, they were just flake-outs who liked to think they were ill because it satisfied their masochism. When their wailings became persistent and loud enough to upset him, Kenny would retaliate by reading aloud poetry from the *Antonin Artaud Anthology.*

God does not exist, he withdraws, gets the fuck on out and leaves the cops to keep an eye on things. He separates from himself 3 cops divided into 3. Okay, but why not 4 or 2 or 1 or zero or nothing at all? And from where did these 3 incorrigibly filthy accomplices of the father, the son, the holy ghost (the father, mother, son), come to equal 1 and not 3 ?

HANGING FROM THE
    INNER CADAVER

and 2) *palelark puuuling*
        larglark cawwling

    3) *tuban tit tarting*
            with the head of
            the head ogling you
    4) *homonculus frontal*
        punch
        from the pinch whoring you
rocking to the stinking boss
this arrogant capitalist
from limbo
swimming toward the stickisome trinity
of fathermother with kiddy sex
to empty the body whole,

wholly of its vitality
and put in its place . . . who?

230

he who was made by Being and Nothing-
                                                            ness,
the way one puts a baby to make peepee.

    AND THEN THEY ALL GOT
        THE FUCK OUT OF THERE

I tell myself that there's scum and crud abroad and god's sucked Lenin's
ass: and that's the way it's always been,
and it isn't worth talking about anymore,
it doesn't matter, it's just another fucking bill to pay.

Kenny didn't read out loud any of Artaud's words on electric
shock in deference to the truly sick patients in the ward who belonged upstairs. There was no room for them up there because the
unit was already overcrowded with casualties from Vietnam —
young guys who were plucked from their farms and small towns and
big city tenements all over the country and shipped to the other side
of the planet, to a foreign culture where the people only thought of
them with hate or in terms of money. Men high on drugs for the
first time and memories of fat-backed America, torn by helicopters
from some behind-the-lines recreation, and thrown into the mouth
of fury, maybe to be hit in the back by a bullet that comes from
nowhere, surely to become paranoid and inhuman. Men who shot
down women and babies because they were terrified, and who later
collapsed with overwhelming guilt — their minds blown by the horror of what they'd done.

Some of these men ended up in neuropsychiatric wards, some
more in VA hospitals with their limbs lost and their minds teetering
on the brink, others in prisons for fragging officers who ordered
them about, and still others, paradoxically, didn't live to regret it.
Only the glory boys escaped, but home wasn't the same for them
either.

Kenny was quickly sick of looking at the splintered results of his
country's insidious scheming in Indo-China. Boredom set in and he
was fired from his work therapy at the photo lab for using the
equipment and chemicals to process almost 5000 eight-by-ten prints
of a snapshot of his own face taken by one of the other patients. He
went AWOL frequently and spent those nights with Rhea. Dope
was all over the base and he mixed it with booze. His response to the
junior officers who wanted to punish him with Article 15 fines, was
always the same — he said he was crazy.

231

He was anxious to be discharged and live in the city. He wanted to get involved with theater. He read about the San Francisco Mime Troupe in the newspaper and thought about working with them. They were a radical company who had developed their theater arts into a medium for revealing the lies on which the U.S. Government based most of its foreign and domestic policies. Since Kenny's political awareness had grown into a need for action, he wanted to become a part of that. He knew, however, that most radical groups had a built-in, self-destructive energy that was dangerous not only to their ability to perform, but to the individual as well. They were always too quick to identify themselves with progressive such-and-such and insurgent so-and-so, and always signing their names to whatever was resisting, defiant of, or agin the government. Kenny didn't think that was too smart. Set yourself up in clear view, and someone is bound to set you down. The one thing he learned, especially during the time he spent in prisons, was how not to satisfy anyone's curiosity. Jails are built to feed the curiosity of the guards and the voyeurism of other inmates. There are few solid doors, and the lights are always on. A prisoner quickly teaches himself to hide his feelings and whatever he's into from everyone, mostly because he knows it's dangerous to reveal anything, but sometimes for no other reason than to spite a prying system and its lackies.

This had become second nature to Wisdom, and because it had, he decided to change his identity before hitting the streets of the counterculture. He thought about it for a while. The longhairs were all changing their names to more romantic-sounding, rough 'n ready, American tags — like William Bonney, Mitzi Gaynor and John Wesley Harding. He wanted to reflect his Irishness and rebellious ancestry. He hit on the name of Robert Emmet but felt it was too corny. However, he liked the sound of Emmet. He played around with it for a time, linking it to various others, until he finally chose to translate his grandfather's name from the Gaelic Ó Gruágain to Grogan. He added another *t* to Emmet and he had it. Emmett Grogan — double sixes, boxcars and a good, solid, Irish name for someone classified a schizophrenic by the Defense Department.

He had been at the neuropsychiatric ward nearly four weeks when his papers were finally processed and he was mustered out of the service. He was happy it was over and even happier when the army made a considerable mistake in the amount of back pay and travel allowances owed to him by giving him seven hundred dollars, three times his due. He celebrated with Rhea that night in North Beach and lived with her while trying to find a place of his own. She was a little confused at first by his new name but began calling him Emmett after a while, like everyone else he got to know.

A cultural alternative was being tried out in America by some young people who adopted their cause with evangelical fervor in the face of the secular establishment. They were a generation utterly separated from their parents by the unbreachable gap of acid. San Francisco's Haight-Ashbury district was the focal point for most of them. Unlike New York's East Village, it was empty when the long-hairs began arriving in search of a community. The predominately black neighborhood was sparsely peopled with Filipinos, Japanese, Russians, Czechs, Scandinavians, Armenians, Greeks, Germans and Irish before it became the city's "West Beach," or new bohemian quarter. Old-timers and newcomers were attracted by the low rents of the houses, but that soon changed. The old, wooden, Victorian homes were quickly divided into flats by brokers looking for fast money, and who preferred renting to faggots because they were thought to always improve the places they lived in. The shopkeepers were purported to be the pulse of the neighborhood's development. They left their shopwindow lights on all night to brighten up the area, and the straights simply considered them brave eccentrics on the side of virtue.

Emmett rented an unfurnished studio apartment in a huge, wooden building owned and divided by an art dealer. The rent was only fifty dollars a month and the place was in the Fillmore district on Fell Street, below the borderline separating that black ghetto from the Haight-Ashbury love ghetto. He painted the room a soft, mustard yellow and built a bed and a long, thin worktable out of lumber he copped from a construction site. He only used the communal kitchen down the hall for coffee or to store beer in the fridge. He ate regularly at a barbecue-and-booze parlor on the corner.

He signed up for unemployment as soon as he was discharged, and when he went down to pick up his first thirty-five-dollar check, he walked over a few blocks to the Mime Troupe. His hair had filled out from the boot-camp crew cut but it was by no means long, and he was wearing a green sports jacket, slacks and a turtleneck. He seemed to attract a bit of attention and even disturb a few people when he entered the office. One of those he put on edge was the company's founder-director, R. G. Davis, who asked him what he wanted, and also, "Are you a police officer?" After Emmett smiled

No, he wasn't, and carefully introduced himself by his new name and recent medical discharge, he was given a form to fill out and told to arrange for an audition with a middle-aged insurance salesman, one of the most talented comedians on anyone's stage, Joe Bellan.

Emmett rehearsed a monologue from an eighteenth-century Goldoni play for two days and returned to audition at the troupe. His performance was strong but his style was too tight for the broad, open manner of acting demanded by commedia dell'arte. He was told he needed to work hard if he wanted to develop his skills, and was invited to learn what he could in a mime class conducted for members of the troupe early every afternoon by Davis.

Now, mime isn't the pantomime of Marcel Marceau. Although it incorporates the same physical movements as pantomime, it is neither silent nor restricted from using props to dramatize a dialogue. On the contrary, it uses everything from loud buffoonery to slapstick travesty to perform dramas in which scenes imitated from life are exaggerated and broadened to make obvious what is usually subtle. Ronnie Davis had studied with Etienne Decroux in Paris during his early twenties and Emmett could only compare his mimic action to that of Jean-Louis Barrault whom he saw perform the role of Battiste in the film version of the nineteenth-century play, *Children of Paradise*. He was good, very good.

The season began and Emmett played small, baker-candlestickmaker roles on the weekends, while continuing to develop as a mime in workouts during the week. The plays were performed outdoors on a portable stage the troupe would set up on the grass of the parks around the city. The performances were free with only a hat being passed around afterward. There were no government subsidies or foundation grants but every moment — from the preshow, warm-up songs like "Avanti Popolo" to the tits-'n-ass-costumed deliveries of the actresses — was professional. The performers were paid five dollars for each show when the money was available, which was seldom, after the resignation of the troupe's business manager. His name was Bill Graham and he left the company to follow up an idea he got at a benefit party thrown for the Mime Troupe. He leased a hall for dancing, hired the same groups who had played at the party, and charged people admission to get in. It was simple and an immediate hit. Within weeks the Jewish war hero had a booming successful operation going at the Fillmore auditorium and the purists all over the Bay Area felt they were being burned by his shorthaired attitude towards business. They began calling him the antichrist of the underground and a cultural rip-off artist. Graham reacted in turn by raising his middle finger and inviting them all to "sit on this and rotate!" He was one of few public figures on the scene not to give credence to the bullshitters.

Rhea was working full time at her career, traveling to Los Angeles for modeling gigs, and Emmett saw her less and less. Instead, he hung out in the Haight, where he maintained a diet of hallucinogens and developed a heavy crush for teenyboppettes, falling in love with every young, runaway girl he met. All these relationships were always beautiful. He would get high with a soft teen miss turned flower-lovely, and they would ball with their knuckles and knees, the ends of their hair, the tips of their fingers, and insides of their eyes. There was very little talk involved in these wonderful dialogues. The young always feel more poignantly without words.

Billy Landout traveled into town from New York during that first week in August when the former Eagle Scout, Charles Whitman, demonstrated his easy familiarity with guns by climbing to the top of the University of Texas' observation tower in Austin and opening fire on campus strollers for ninety minutes, killing sixteen, wounding thirty-one, and being shot to death himself by a cop to become the U.S. title holder for a single-handed, mass-murder rampage. Two days later, a flash-talking Brooklyn-Broadway hipster was killed by an overdose in his Hollywood Hills house overlooking the Sunset Strip. Lenny Bruce was suicided by society. His death-blow had actually been dealt years before he was found stretched out naked on his bathroom floor with that curious, serene expression on his face. New York City District Attorney Frank Hogan, fulfilling his role as one of society's most insipid henchmen, ordered his office staff to turn the spiv-dressed comedian into a fat, mad, abject figure. Vincent Cuccia, one of his assistant district attorneys who tried the case, repented to Bruce's lawyer, Martin Garbus, in Garbus's book *Ready For The Defense*: "I feel terrible about Bruce. . . . I watched him gradually fall apart. It's the only thing I did in Hogan's office that I'm really ashamed of. We all knew what we were doing. We used the law to kill him." To no one's great surprise.

Billy arrived shortly after the comic was put into the ground by stand-up, old-timer Milton Berle. He moved in with a girl friend who was a student at the Experimental College of San Francisco State. He also joined the Mime Troupe, working as a technician on the weekly outdoor productions and studying mime with Ronnie Davis. Billy and Emmett would get together and talk about the evolving phenomenon in the Haight-Ashbury, until the wee hours of nearly every morning. Other members of the troupe would sometimes take part in these discussions, particularly Coyote and the Hun. Coyote described himself in a book as having grown up with very smart, wealthy parents in Englewood, New Jersey. He was a very imaginative but fat child who only learned to like his body after having graduated from Grinnell College and then dropping out of graduate school and beginning to work at the Mime Troupe, studying with Davis. At twenty-five, he was no longer fat, but was tall and handsome. He had an affinity toward Zen discipline and a scholarly, intelligent mind, due in part to the emphasis his family put on education. He was performing the lead role of Pantalone, an eighteenth-century Jewish-Italian shylock in the current commedia dell'arte production. He played the part well.

The Hun got his name because some believed he was his own horde, while others felt he looked like a Mongolian Iago. He also profiled himself in that same book. Born in New York City in 1937, he spent his adolescence as a car-hiker in the potpourri city of Miami which, he would point out, was only built in 1927 and represented the Pow! Pow! naked power of the South. He was a child genius with an I.Q. of 160 and a Quiz Kid, but in high school he hung around with "fourteen-fifteen-year-old hillbilly boys that used to stand in Levi's and boots, with thunderbird belts and kind of like denim or, y'know, a shirt with whaddaya-call-it, a Western shirt, pearl buttons on the things, drunk, drunk, and going like this and looking like Montgomery Clift in that flick he made with Arthur Miller's script and lookin' like that, y'know, with brass knuckles." He picked up a political orientation from his father, an H. G. Wells *Outline of History* libertarian, who thought the Russians were good people. He went to the University of Florida on a work scholarship, got a degree, concentrating in literature, and after getting over the New York blues-life mystique, drifted to San Francisco to meet the older members of the beat generation. He joined the Mime Troupe as a writer-director and was in the process of directing a one-act play about police harassment and brutality called *Search and Seizure*, which he wrote from the actors' improvisations.

These discussions that Billy, Emmett, and the others had, dealt with the freedom being assumed by young people in Haight-Ashbury and throughout the world. They agreed that the ultimate goal of the Haight community seemed to be freedom and a chance to do your thing, but they felt one could only be free by drawing the line and living outside the profit, private property, and power premises of Western culture because, as Coyote remarked, "The idea of changing anything from within has been exploded long ago."

"Hope was the shot" for the Hun, and he believed along with everyone else that the foundation of a civilization was growing, being built, on young people who were really very wishful: forms of a civilization coming after the deal went down. The deal being roughly the same as in the Soviet Union in 1917, with the young going for hard kicks as a way out, and paying heavy dues because "you can't have the beauty of being a hard liver without payin' those dues. You're not gonna do it. You try it, you're not gonna do it."

Emmett wondered whether anything viable was going to come out of all of it: whether the powerless might for once obtain enough power to make some sort of relevant change in society. He immediately dismissed as ridiculous the notion that everything would be all right when everyone turned on to acid. It was noted that LSD was used during World War Two to solve naval tactical maneuvers, and they concluded that although the drug might facilitate understanding, or the process of doing something, it offered no moral direction or imperatives.

In quick time, Emmett and Billy decided to get things real by challenging the street people with the conclusions they arrived at during these sessions. They mimeographed their thoughts, using a different color paper for each set of leaflets, which soon became known as the "Digger Papers." The name "Diggers" had been tossed forward by another member of the troupe who read about the seventeenth-century group in a British history book and felt that Emmett, Billy and their ideas about freedom resembled those of Gerrard Winstanley, William Everard and their one hundred supporters. These men began to cultivate the common parkland they appropriated in 1649 around Saint George's Hill in Surrey, to feed themselves as a protest against the astonishingly high food prices and to give the surplus to other poor. Cromwell and his Roundheads answered the cries of the food merchants and local farmers, who wanted the land themselves, by using the army to suppress that small, hardy, radical band of agrarian reformers who intended "No other matter herein, but to observe the Law of righteous action, endeavoring to shut out of the Creation, the cursed thing, called

Particular propriety, which is the cause of all wars, blood-shed, crime, and enslaving Laws, that hold the people under miserie."

It was stone idealism — something neither Billy nor Emmett had tried before but felt was needed to shake up the street's rite of purification: a purification of the young people which began with their depurification on the streets. Every few days, after dark, Emmett would sneak into the SDS office next to the Mime Troupe's studio with Billy, and they would mimeograph their handbills on the students' Gestetner without anyone knowing. Late afternoon of the following day, Emmett would walk on one side of Haight Street, and Billy down the other, giving them out.

The Digger Papers were also a reaction against the pansyness of the S.F. *Oracle* underground newspaper, and the way it catered to the new, hip, moneyed class by refusing to reveal the overall grime of Haight-Ashbury reality. Essentially, however, the Papers were an attempt to antagonize the street people into an awareness of the absolute bullshit implicit in the psychedelic transcendentalism promoted by the self-proclaimed, media-fabricated shamans who espoused the tune-in, turn-on, drop-out, jerk-off ideology of Leary and Alpert. The first paper successfully antagonized the acid community with its mocking refrain: "Time to forget because flowers are beautiful and the sun's not yellow, it's chicken!"

Another and probably the most famous Digger Paper was a response to statements by self-appointed spokesmen, and to notices placed in shopwindows by the Haight Independent Proprietor (HIP) merchants association, which advised the people to invite policemen to share a meal with them — to build up better community relations with the force. It said:

Take a Cop to Dinner Cop a Dinner to Take a Cop Dinner Cop a Take

Mr. Answer Man		
what is		
a *weapon*	*Why a cunt*	
worse	*which is*	
ten times	*ten times*	
worse,	*larger*	
than the	*than the largest*	*Degoutante,*
Hydrogen	*cock*	*said Mickey*
Bomb?	*extant,*	*kissing cops.*
	Mickey.	*to hedge the bet.*

238

Take a cop to dinner.

Racketeers take cops to dinner with payoffs.

Pimps take cops to dinner with free tricks.

Dealers take cops to dinner with free highs.

Business takes cops to dinner with graft.

Unions and Corporations take cops to dinner with post-retirement jobs.

Schools and Professional Clubs take cops to dinner with free tickets to athletic events and social affairs.

The Catholic Church takes cops to dinner by exempting them from religious duties.

The Justice Department takes cops to dinner with laws giving them the right to do almost anything.

The Defense Department takes cops to dinner by releasing them from all military obligations.

Establishment newspapers take cops to dinner by propagating the image of the friendly, uncorrupt, neighborhood policeman.

Places of entertainment take cops to dinner with free booze and admission to shows.

Merchants take cops to dinner with discounts and gifts.

Neighborhood Committees and Social Organizations take cops to dinner with free discussions offering discriminating insights into hipsterism, black militancy and the drug culture.

Cops take cops to dinner by granting each other immunity to prosecution for misdemeanors and anything else they can get away with.

Cops take themselves to dinner by inciting riots.

And so, if you own anything or you don't, take a cop to dinner this week and feed his power to judge, prosecute and brutalize the streets of your city.

n.b. Gourmet George Metesky would remind everyone not to make the same mistake as Arnold Schuster who served the right course at the wrong time.

the diggers.

These Papers, which only cost $1.50 per thousand, more than aroused the so-called leadership class of the Haight-Ashbury, and they tried to find out who the Diggers were. They were answered with telegrams: REGARDING INQUIRIES CONCERNED WITH THE IDENTITY AND WHEREABOUTS OF THE DIGGERS; HAPPY TO REPORT THE DIGGERS ARE NOT THAT. Emmett and Billy wanted to maintain their anonymity in the hope of achieving the kind of autonomy Gregory Corso talks about in his poem, "Power." They sought to dramatize that power of autonomy by performing Corso's only play, *Standing on a Street Corner*, before the morning, lunch, and evening rush-hour crowd of Montgomery Street office workers, without letting on that the performance was a staged event — the point being to lead the white-collars into believing they were witnessing an actuality which thrice repeated itself. However, something happened that made the one-act play seem relatively unimportant, and it never got beyond rehearsal.

Mid-Tuesday afternoon in that last week of September, a sixteen-year-old kid named Johnson was shot three times dead in the back by a fifty-one-year-old, pot-bellied cop named Johnson, who was only a few feet away from him on "the Hill" overlooking Palau Street in Hunter's Point. The boy was black, the cop was white and said, "I did everything I could to avoid doing what I did. I'm sure sorry."

His apology didn't satisfy the black community, which had emerged during World War Two when the white trickle to the outer cities became a tide and the myth of suburbia was built. The black population of San Francisco swelled from four thousand to eighty thousand. They came to work in the war industries, and after the war was over they were deposited in an outer-city slum instead of an inner-city ghetto. Hunter's Point was their outer city. It's a peninsula, and when the insurrection erupted a few hours after the boy had been killed running away from a car, which wasn't reported stolen until the next day, the cops effectively cut off the peninsula from the mainland by blocking off the linking span at Third Street for ten blocks. .

As soon as black tempers began to flare, and the young ones started to run through the streets, looting and setting fires, Mayor John Shelly declared that a state of emergency existed in the Bay-view-Hunter's Point Area and proclaimed a curfew from 8 P.M. to 6 A.M. He also announced that he wasn't going to permit a repetition of what had occurred "in that other city south of here," and he telephoned Governor Edmund Brown, who was on tour campaigning against Ronald Reagan for reelection in Imperial County, and asked him to order out the national guard.

Many of the two thousand troops were veterans of Watts, and most of them were stashed in a makeshift outpost at Kezar Stadium when they arrived in the city. Police Chief Thomas Cahill ordered the entire S.F. police force, on duty together for the first time since

V.J. Day in 1945, to try and restore some semblance of imposed order. They wore helmets and carried shotguns against the rock-and-bottle-throwing blacks who were massed around the E.O.C.'s Bayview Community Center, which had been the S.F. Opera House before the earthquake.

It was Indian summer weather and the mass media gave hourly reports of the temperature readings; City Supervisor Terry Francois begged his "black brothers" to cool it; Assemblyman Willie Brown demanded the dismissal of the cop and more jobs for black men; at the request of both Governor Brown and Mayor Shelly, the S.F. Giants–Atlanta Braves baseball game was televised to the home audience with a special tape-recorded feature of Willie Mays appealing to his people to remain inside and "root for your team."

The heatwave continued with record breaking ninety-five-to-one-hundred-degree temperatures, and the violent outbreak spread to the Western Addition, inner-city areas of Fillmore and Haight-Ashbury. Several unfounded reports of sniper attacks were radioed to the authorities, and the national guard was ordered into the streets with M-1's and rapid-firing Browning automatic rifles. The cops began shooting at the kids and laid down a thunderous barrage of fire into the Bayview Community Center, riddling the place with bullets. There was a photo in the next morning's *Chronicle* of a black man cakewalking in front of the police line cordoning off Third Street, shouting, *"Shoot me! I'm not armed! Shoot me!"* They did.

SNCC, SDS, and the Progressive Labor Party organized a demonstration of less than forty University of California students against the presence of the national guard. They marched with picket signs outside the Mission Street Armory, demanding that the troops "Get Out of Vietnam and San Francisco!" and "Go Home!" A few of them surrounded three military trucks in the street behind the armory and shouted, "No soldiers are going to leave this place tonight!" before they were rousted by the cops.

Emmett was up in the Haight-Ashbury when middle-aged, self-asserting radical Paul Jacobs and his attorney-wife, Ruth, led seventy-odd SDS and Community for New Politics members in a demonstration up Haight Street, with signs proclaiming their solidarity with the "Psychedelic Community." The white, radical-liberals of the Bay Area had quickly turned to the equally white people of the Haight-Ashbury after they had been told to go fuck themselves by the blacks with whom they sympathized. But the longhairs weren't having any either, and there were shouts of *"Go back to school where you belong!"* and lots of outside-agitator jokes hurled at the condescending Berkeley crowd as they submitted to peaceful arrest.

Billy showed up, just as a car full of Students for a Democratic Society pulled down the street with a bullhorn blaring out instructions to "Stay on the Avenue of Psychedelics after the curfew hour and confront the fascist police!" The HIP merchants countered with signs in their fog-lighted shop windows advising, "For your own safety and for your own good, stay home and off the streets!" Emmett and Billy disagreed with the SDS and HIP, because both used the curfew for their own petty interests. They decided simply to ignore the curfew and do or not do whatever they wanted. They put up a few scribbled posters to notify the street of their alternative to foolhardy confrontation and cowardly acquiescence.

A short time later, Emmett spotted a number of the Leary-oriented leaders from the psychedelic *Oracle* staff, standing under the marquee of the Straight Theater near the top of Haight Street. One of them was a chubby thirty-year-old named Michael with a penchant for white cotton clothes that invited comparison with yesteryear prophets. He was also the Mickey put down in Norman Mailer's poem that was liberated into the "Take a Cop to Dinner" leaflet, and he was actually tearing down a poster — a poster Emmett had just fastened to the lamppost in front of the theater.

"What the fuck do you think you're doing! Huh!" Emmett yelled, as he came up from behind and spun him around. He was about to paste him one in the face, but Billy caught him because the area was full of heat whose attention he was already attracting by shouting, *"Well, what the fuck do you think you're doing with our sign?!"*

"Take it easy, Emmett. We didn't mean anything. We just have a different way of dealing with the police, that's all. Why don't you come over to the office with us and we'll talk about it, okay?"

"No, there's nothing 'okay' about it! We already know your ingenious plan! You're gonna love 'em to death with fancy suppers 'n suffocate 'em with smoke from burning incense! Well, we got our own way, see! Like standin' on a street corner waiting for no one, if you want, 'n defendin' your right to do it or anything else! That curfew's for you! So, you better hurry home before the nasty policemens give you all a spankin'! 'N leave our signs alone!"

"Emmett, why do you have to be so hostile? We're —"

"Oh, get outta my face, willya! *Just Get Outta My Face!*"

Afterwards, Emmett and Billy went down to Fillmore Street for some barbecue. While they were ordering, the twenty-block area of Fillmore was sealed off from Fulton to Geary streets. They took their paper plates of food with them and stood outside the eatery, watching the surreality of the paramilitary operation unfold on the sidewalks where children had been playing only moments before. They got caught up in a crowd of black people who were trying to get back to their homes, and it felt strange being white but nobody said anything.

Some kids started throwing bricks from the vacant lot at an official car that was passing, and suddenly someone hollered, *"Lock 'n load!"* Fifty cops immediately dropped to their knees and jacked shells containing pea-sized charges of buckshot into the chambers of their riot guns. Everyone scattered in hysteria, as a sergeant called, "Bag that kid in the red sweater!" The kid was pinched and thrown into a squad car.

The crowd re-formed with everyone muttering about the insanity of fifty loaded shotguns on a city street. Their faces were all flushed with anger and the heat — the heat that made the tar on the streets soft and sticky and the apartments too hot to stay in. It took most of those people over two frustrating hours to get back to their own places, only to spill back out onto the street again until 3 or 4 A.M.

Billy returned with Emmett to his room and they were hassled by cops and soldiers all the way. By the time they arrived, they were pissed off and bent on vengeance. They made a brace of Molotov cocktails with a couple of half-filled bottles of turpentine and went up to the building's roof. Down below passed personnel carriers with armed national guardsmen patrolling Fell Street. Both of them knew that if they dropped the fire bombs onto a truck, they wouldn't be immediately suspect, because they were white. They also realized that it would touch off a murderous, repressive on-slaught by the soldiers, in which black people would suffer a far more devastating and wholesale oppression than they did already. They looked at each other and quietly decided it wasn't their play to make. They hid the rag-wicked bottles in a corner of the roof, and drank up the rest of the beer in the icebox downstairs.

The insurrection simmered down and the newspapers claimed that it was caused by the "cancer of discrimination," and they gave notice that President Johnson had ordered an investigation into the severe unemployment of black San Franciscans. The president of the Chamber of Commerce, Cyril Magnin, immediately announced an urgent crash plan to provide some two thousand quick jobs for the minority-race unemployed, and Congressman Phillip Burton claimed that one thousand jobs would be made available in the city's post office during the Christmas rush. Judges Elton Lawless and Joseph G. Kennedy declared a "San Francisco riots amnesty" and freed three hundred adult prisoners, ninety of whom were white and had been arrested in the national guard curfew protests and were bruised and shaken when released because they'd been knocked about by the black inmates of the jail. The House Un-American Activities Committee launched an inquiry to probe the "riots" for subversive elements, and sought the support of moderate civil rights groups like the NAACP and the Urban League "to purge black action groups of subversion." The Artists' Political Action Committee of the Artists' Liberation Front paraded in front of city hall with a black coffin labeled "Another 16 Year Old." Connie's Haight Street restaurant, along with the Socialist Workers Party–Young Socialist Alliance, laid two large, bright, yellow wreaths on the dirt of the rubbish-strewn hillside where Matthew "Peanut" Johnson had been shot dead, as a poignant memorial — "In Brutal Memory of Black Justice."

Then it was all over and the riot headlines were pushed off the front pages by a sensational exposé of a former Kentucky governor's grandson named Augustus Owsley Stanley III, as the "LSD Millionaire," and by the "LSD Fugitive's Strange Story" concerning Ken Kesey's totally unstrange return trip to San Francisco while everyone had been preoccupied during the insurrection. After having fled the city ten months before to escape a pot bust, he came back from Mexico, he said, "as a fugitive, and as salt in J. Edgar Hoover's wounds," and also to help with a "graduation ceremony." He confused everyone with his change of heart about LSD and angered some former friends by wanting to convene seventy-five hundred people for an "acid test commencement" on Halloween, to show the way to a new style of communal interchange. At the same time, he wanted to deemphasize chemical turn-ons by graduating acidheads out of LSD. All it finally amounted to, after the hoopla died down, was a by-invitation-only, private party held in a warehouse with a lot of booze and plenty of group analysis. For weeks the press had everyone hyped about what a Slam! Bang! party-bash it was going to be, but it turned out to be something less than a whimper. *"Spargere voces in vulgum ambiguas,"* someone said a long time ago in the prologue of the past.

As the weather and black people continued to cool out, the press kept up its graphic coverage of the hippies. In fact, the word hippie was itself a fabrication of the mass media, and in order to do it justice, there was a flood of newsprint devoted to the subject of hipsterism, ranging from stories about the "Beatnik-Anarchist Provos" in Holland, to profiles of various Haight Street characters like Super-Spade, a twenty-five-year-old, leather-clad, black grass dealer, who wore a button proclaiming himself "Faster than a speeding mind." The media launched such a concentrated, focused assault on the Haight-Ashbury that it soon became the most over-exposed neighborhood in the country. Only Washington, D.C., and other seats of government have been more closely covered by journalists.

The Mime Troupe's outdoor season in the parks ended, and the company accepted a few indoor bookings around the Bay Area. Emmett and Billy performed together nightly in a comedy-farce called *In-Put, Out-Put,* a one-act written and directed by the Hun about the basic absurdity of computer programming. The performances ran for a week at a Berkeley coffeehouse and died the way live theater always dies when it upsets or embarrasses audiences. Emmett's unemployment checks stopped shortly afterwards and he was broke, which was no big thing because everybody was. Neither he nor Billy could see what was so hip about it, however, or what was soulful about panhandling. Since being fleeced was the daily condition of most Haight people, the two of them resolved not only to relieve their individual strapped conditions, but to try also to aid some part of the larger down-and-out community. After all, that's what they were talking about and demanding in the Digger Papers: collective social consciousness and community action.

Billy and Emmett wanted to pull some sort of score which would benefit others besides themselves — some job that would provide a take big enough to share. Plain money wasn't the answer because greed would probably never permit a sizable cash haul to be properly divided among the people and besides, no one would learn anything about collective interaction from it. What was needed that they could buy with a sackful of stolen money?

"Bread!" exclaimed Emmett. He got Billy to drive his '55 Ford station wagon to the San Francisco Produce Market on the outskirts of the city. The sun had only been up for half an hour when they pulled through the chain-link front gate and drove into the lot, past the loading platforms stacked high with crates of fresh fruit and vegetables. One of Emmett's uncles used to truck wholesale produce from the West Side marketplace in Greenwich Village to some small supermarkets around Brooklyn, and at age ten or eleven Emmett had helped him quite a few times when his uncle's regular helper was sick. He learned his way around produce during those brief assists and stole meat from the same markets to pay for his junk habit. Now he attracted a lot of attention because of his very long hair, but Emmett's fluent Italian compensated for that. He spoke with the immigrants who ran the wholesale stalls lining both sides of the market. At first most of them were suspicious, but they became friendly after he handed them a line, and within an hour the Ford wagon was packed tight with crates of food. There were tomatoes, turnips, green beans, cauliflower, Brussels sprouts, onions, eggplant, squash, potatoes, lettuce, yams, apples and oranges. From a particularly generous Italian named Paddy, who managed the only poultry plant in the market, they got fifty pounds of chicken and turkey parts. That was all there was to it.

Driving back to town, they discussed different ways of distributing the food. The problem was that the street people, who really needed it, had no place or means to cook it.

"We can get it cooked. We'll make a stew."

"What do we use to cook with? What'll be big enough?"

"Cans."

"Cans? Garbage Cans?"

"No, milk cans. They're sterilized 'n durable 'n you can handle 'em easy."

So they snatched a pair of twenty-gallon milk cans from a dairy plant in the Mission district and transported everything back to Emmett's place. It was around 8 A.M., when they began boiling down the fowl to make a stock for the stew. They worked hard for hours preparing the vegetables, Emmett working as hard that first morning as he was going to daily for over a year. He worked harder than most blue-collar folks work for a living — something Emmett had done only occasionally to the probable chagrin of the ghost of his late grandfather whose union cards he still carried in his pocket. They talked while they worked and decided to give away the stew in the Fell Street Panhandle of Golden Gate Park at 4 P.M. that afternoon. While Emmett ladled the inches of grease away from the surface of the stock and continued to ready the greens, Billy went downtown to mimeograph and hand out several hundred leaflets notifying the Haight community about

246

```
         FREE FOOD        GOOD HOT STEW
        RIPE TOMATOES        FRESH FRUIT
         BRING A BOWL AND SPOON TO
        THE PANHANDLE AT ASHBURY STREET
         4 PM   4 PM   4 PM   4 PM   4 PM
         FREE FOOD EVERYDAY FREE FOOD
            IT'S FREE BECAUSE IT'S YOURS!
                              the diggers.
```

They added the greens and potatoes to the stock only minutes prior to leaving, otherwise they would have lost their solidity in the boiling hot soup and melted into a mush, instead of becoming a stew. It was just before 4 P.M. when the two of them drove over to the Panhandle and set the hot milk cans on the grass with the boxes of tomatoes and cartons of fruit. There were already fifty people waiting and another fifty-odd showed up immediately, some of them carrying their bowls tied to their belts. The number of people increased to a stationary two hundred, as the Free Food continued through the week in the Panhandle, every afternoon at four. The bowls dangling from the waistbands took on an immediately recognizable significance.

The word quickly spread and soon such underground papers as the Berkeley *Barb* were nibbling around, trying to scoop a story on who was behind the Free Food event. They only ended up running into an anonymous wall, and finally were discouraged enough to simply chalk it all up to that "mystery-shrouded Haight-Ashbury group, the Diggers." The hipsters who knew Emmett and Billy searched them out in the cold fog and found them sitting on the grass among the young newcomers to the Haight and the old-timers from skid row, gobbling up the soup du jour. The Hun remarked that it was a great idea. "Try to keep it going for another week, if you can, and you'll really get your point across. Just another week. Terrific!" The straight New Lefties came around and turned a little green with envy that they hadn't thought of the food angle as an organizing principle themselves. If they had, they would have done it only as a one-shot for the publicity. The liberals, hip and square, would watch the hungry crowd being fed and grope around, looking for someone to offer a donation to. Conservatives would ask why everyone didn't get a job.

Emmett and Billy knew that Free Food everyday in the park was a popular act, but they didn't intend it solely as a symbol. No, they were hungry and so were a lot of others, and they were going to keep the Free Food going every day, in spite of everything and for nothing. When donors would offer notes of vicarious approval, they'd take the bills, strike a match, and burn them to the amusement of those eating. The young kids squatting in the Panhandle were hungry and afraid all right, but they were on their own for the first time for no matter how long, and they wanted no material support from members of their parents' world. The burning of the ten- and twenty-dollar bills typified, more than anything else, what they felt and what the Diggers believed.

A half-dozen young women, a few of whom were dropouts from Antioch College, shared a large pad together on Clayton Street and volunteered to take over the cooking indefinitely. Two other members of the Mime Troupe, Butcher Brooks and Slim Minnaux, undertook the everyday delivery of the prepared food to the 4 P.M. Panhandle feed. This left Emmett to make the early morning round of pickups at the Produce Market, the Farmers Market and the Ukranian Bakery. On his way back to Clayton Street every A.M., he would try to steal some beef for the stew. They didn't have access to any freezer storage space, so he could snatch only a side of beef at most from a meat packing plant, or from one of the trucks making deliveries, and take it back for the group to butcher themselves. He tried hustling a head butcher at the Allen Meat Company for a daily box of scraps and bones for soup stock, but he only got himself whacked on the head with the flat side of a cleaver — and no meat. Of course, he could have hijacked a whole trailer full of meat and fenced the goods, but that would have only been a one-shot deal, and the importance of Free Food was its steady continuance everyday at the same time for as long as it was needed.

Billy hustled some dough and Emmett rented a six-car garage on Page Street that was filled with empty window frames. He was joined by some young dudes from the 4 P.M. feed, who helped him nail the window frames all over the wooden front of the garage and clean up the inside. Simolean Gary had come down from Redwood looking for parts for his motorcycle; John-John had roamed out from Brooklyn, riding the rails, sleeping in freight cars; Motorcycle Richie had also wandered from Manhattan, driving out on a hot Harley-Davidson. John-John was Leo Gorcey personified, and if he had been born during the thirties, he would have undoubtedly been one of the Dead End Kids in the movies and he knew that. The combination of the three of them was enough to keep life from ever getting boring. They stenciled a sign below the roofline and opened the doors to the street within a few days. The place was called the Free Frame of Reference and it was the first free store.

Emmett didn't bother to make clear to the community something which was very important. He didn't bother because he didn't want to at the time. That something was that the Free Food was not begun to prolong the economic usefulness of day-old bread or vegetables or bad cuts of meat, and the free stores were not set up to prolong the economic usefulness of secondhand clothes and other items. Only a fraction of the goods used or accepted were secondhand and they were made available and displayed to effect a Salvation-Goodwill-salvage cover to conceal the fact that the rest of the stuff was new and fresh and had been stolen. People who tried to deposit their refuse at the Free Frame of Reference were told to go and recycle their garbage someplace else. And when the stiffs wanted to speak with whoever was in charge of the operation they were told, "You're in charge! You wanna see someone in charge? You be in charge!" This was done not only to dramatize the concept of assuming freedom, but also to prevent the cops from vamping and busting someone for being in possession or receipt of stolen property. For the same reason, the leases for these places were always signed by some drifter passing through town and not by Emmett or Billy or anyone else. No one ever accepted responsibility for anything.

Butcher Brooks was a photographer and he had a battered VW bus painted a bright yellow, with a slogan written on the outside panel in orange Day-Glo, "The Road of Excess Leads to the Palace of Wisdom!" He had been working as a Digger for about a month, and his bus became known around the streets as the yellow submarine, often carrying the Digger women — Natural Suzanne, Fyllis, Cindy Small, Bobsie, NanaNina — in the back with the prepared food. The crowd would see the yellow submarine coming down Ashbury Street and they would mill around near the curb in the park. Brooks sometimes felt the people were taking the Free Food too much for granted so, instead of parking and unloading, he often teased them by continually passing, until he sparked them into some sort of action, like waylaying the bus when it became delayed in traffic, removing the ignition keys, and seizing the cooked food. He also made them work for it by sealing the milk cans tight, banging the lids firmly shut with a hammer. It would take some time for several guys in the park to tug the jammed cover free of the blister-hot can and ladle out the stew. This Free Food theater evolved to a point where Billy constructed a giant, thirteen-foot square Frame of

Reference from four two-by-fours bolted together, and Emmett painted it a golden orange. The frame would be set up between two large oak trees in the Panhandle every day before 4 P.M. When the Free Food arrived, it would be placed on one side of the frame and the hungry would be made to walk through it to get at the stew and whatever else was being shared on the other side, changing their frame of reference as they did.

The Hun was anxious to get involved in the theater aspect of the Diggers' activity and he proposed an event for Halloween. The hero of Kerouac's *On the Road*, Neil Cassady, was driving the Kesey-Prankster bus around the Panhandle that afternoon, holding a lively conversation with the traffic. The bus was a regular school bus that had been Rorschached with almost every color of paint, and had a sign above the windshield spelling "Further," instead of "Bread" or "Meat." Emmett wondered briefly if there was an analogy to the Russian Black Marias that were painted various happy colors and labeled "Bread" or "Meat" to camouflage them from their citizens. That evening, while Ken Kesey furthered his prank-sterism with a diploma from his own graduation, Emmett and Billy carried the two-by-four Frame of Reference up to the corners of Haight and Ashbury, where they stood it against a lamppost. Sculptor La Mortadella showed up with a pair of his nine-foot puppets, which he'd made for a Mime Troupe presentation, and the Hun, Slim Minnaux, and Butcher Brooks. Dozens of three-inch-square yellow wooden frames made by the Digger women were given out to the gathered curious, who hung them around their necks like medallions. A puppet show was improvised on the corner about the in's and out's of being on either side of the Frame of Reference. Billy and Brooks held the frame steady, as the other four paired off to handle the gangly puppets — one maneuvering the hands, the other holding the stilt and performing the voice. Each puppet remained on the opposite side of the frame from the other, but both changed sides frequently, commenting on the differences between them.

A crowd of five hundred formed, blocking the sidewalk and traffic, and were quickly followed by the cops, who ordered everyone to "break it up! And move along!" No one moved, so for some reason the cops turned and addressed the puppets instead of the puppeteers, and warned them they were violating the law by causing a public nuisance and obstructing traffic and further informed them they would be arrested if they didn't cease and desist. This dialogue between the coppers and the puppets tickled the people silly, and continued until reinforcements arrived and the puppets were busted along with their maker and the puppeteers. The cops had a difficult time placing the dolls in custody because of their size. In fact, they were almost too large to fit into the paddy wagon, but were somehow squeezed inside after much effort.

Brooks got enthusiastically fanciful and tried to incite the crowd to *"free the prisoners!"* They began to rock the patrol wagon, and for a moment it seemed about to go over, but the people retreated when Brooks was popped and thrown in with his comrades. The cops drove the wagon away to the park police station, leaving Billy to dismantle the frame and carry it back to the Free Frame of Reference on Page Street with John-John, Gary and Richie. The rest of the Diggers, mostly women, scattered to raise bail money from the community.

At the station house, Captain Keily tongue-lashed Butcher but didn't charge him for attempting to incite a riot. Both puppets stood against a side wall, and cops entering and leaving the station would make startled comments like, "Will ya look how fuckin' big they are! Jesus, if one of 'em fell on somebody, it'd probably kill the son of a bitch! Why the hell does somebody make something so fuckin' big in the first place? They gotta want to hurt people! Look at how big those fuckers are!"

All five puppet showmen were charged with violating penal code 370, creating a public nuisance and were booked and locked up together in the same back cell. Emmett, like the rest, felt it was a "fun bust," the only time being arrested has ever been a fun thing in his life. It was fun when you consider that arrest was the moment he feared most during his career as a thief. This bust was just a goof — a misdemeanor punishable by a small fine, a reprimand and/ or a couple of days in the city jail, not by a term behind bars in some penitentiary.

None of the Haight Independent Proprietors, or HIP merchants, as they were called, came across with even a portion of the $625 needed to bail them out. But, after being transferred downtown to the city prison's misdemeanor tank in the Hall of Justice building, they were able to sweet-talk the head of VISTA's O.R. Project and get themselves released without bail on their own recognizance. They did this by proving to him through a series of telephone calls to the Mime Troupe and a signed affidavit from Ronnie Davis that they all lived in and had roots in San Francisco.

The case went before Municipal Court Judge Elton C. Lawless within forty-eight hours — on Emmett's 22nd birthday. His honor reluctantly dismissed the case before anything got started, at the urging of Deputy District Attorney Arthur Schaffer, who said, "Further investigation indicates that the charges of creating a public nuisance should be dismissed in the interests of justice." The further investigation he mentioned was some cocktail conversation he had with the defendants before eating lunch with them. This penal code 370, which they were charged with violating, had been chosen by the park station cops as the main weapon in their declared war of harassment against the Haight Street people, and the puppet quintet was happy to be cut loose. They were in a good mood when they walked out of Lawless's courtroom, and their loudness attracted Bob Cambell, a newspaper photographer who was assigned to cover the municipal court building, which was quiet with the inactivity of a dull afternoon. He got the story from the deputy D.A. and asked the five defendants if they would stand on the outside steps for a photo. They did without thinking anything of it.

The next morning, Emmett walked down his block for a newspaper and a cup of coffee. On the corner there was a sealed container that unlatched a *Chronicle* when it was fed a dime. He dropped his ten cents into the slot, opened the lid, and what he saw made him lift out two copies instead of one. On the front page was a five-by-seven picture of him and the others, outside the court building after their release the day before. The photo was headlined, "In the Clear" and captioned with their names and a brief synopsis of who they were and what had gone down. He was referred to as an actor, but thankfully there was no mention of the Diggers or even the Mime Troupe. The photo captured each of them striking a pose: La Mortadella was shown with his pinky and forefinger raised in the sign of the cornuto or the cuckold; Slim Minnaux was leaping with arms-stretched, fists-clenched ecstasy; the Hun had his thumb jammed up into an imaginary asshole, and his face was pinched like someone who just smelled a load of shit; Butcher Brooks was dressed in someone else's style and leaning forward in a stiff, fraternity stance, Emmett, still wearing his army boots, with a scarf knotted around his neck, an IRA cap flopping on his head, and a cigarette loosely hanging from the corner of his smile, was one step upstage from his pals, staring out at the reader from above the middle finger and index finger of his right hand, raised in the sign of a backwards

253

BOB CAMPBELL

V which to the English and Irish means "Up Your Ass!" and is the equivalent of the American, lone, uplifted, middle finger.

The photo seemed as big as life to Emmett, and he wondered if it meant any trouble. He didn't like too many people knowing about him, and now half the city was probably going to know all their names before the day was out. He finished his coffee and then thumbed a ride up Haight Street to Clayton. As he was walking up the hill to the house where the stew was being fixed and the station wagon was parked, several people called out to him by name and flashed him a V-sign. He stopped a few of them and explained that they had it all wrong. "You've got to turn your hand around 'n flash it backwards. Like giving someone the finger. See . . ." and he showed them. But there were too many to bother about and by the time he went over to the Panhandle at 4 P.M. for something to eat, everyone was waving the V-sign to him and to one another, saying things like, "Peace, brother." "When are you going to run for mayor, Emmett?" It was depressing. There he was, on the front page of the town's only morning newspaper, telling everyone to shove it all up their ass, and they thought he was just imitating Winston Churchill or something. "Fuck it!" He decided there was no way to make the hippies hip to it, and besides he had better things to do.

The *Chronicle* photo also had another effect: it clued in photographers who covered the Haight-Ashbury that the Diggers were newsworthy, and fed the Hun's enthusiasm toward media takeover and newsmaking. Emmett asked several hip, freelance photographers — and warned some straight, establishment cameramen — to refrain from taking his picture because it would interfere with his work and ultimately impair their health. The Hun was charged up and laid plans for the disruption and possible takeover of a radio station in San Jose and another in Berkeley, both of which had invited the Diggers to appear for an interview and telephone discussion with the listening audience. Meanwhile, the pick-up, preparation and distribution of Free Food was left to Emmett, Billy and the women, with everyone else opting out for the more exciting and adventurous game of guerrilla theater.

Emmett hustled some twenty turkeys from Paddy at the Produce Market, got them cooked in ovens all over the Haight community in the morning, and shared them with the people who gathered at the Free Frame of Reference on Page Street at 4 P.M. that Thanksgiving afternoon, 1966. He also went on radio with the Hun, Coyote and the others, but was careful not to say anything. He just remained closemouthed and listened to the rap they laid down about what was happening in the Haight-Ashbury, and how the material affluence of America was permitting many of the young people to live off of society's surplus and enabling them to use wampum items that were already made, or that they created themselves instead of money. These points were further discussed in a meeting a few nights later at the Page Street Free Frame and developed into a theatrical event to "celebrate the death and rebirth of the Haight-Ashbury and the death of money."

To the stone disapproval of R. G. Davis, who felt his company was being co-opted by the Diggers and their street activities, most members of the Mime Troupe organized the celebration for that Saturday afternoon and Emmett invited the Frisco Hell's Angels to take part. Two hundred car mirrors were removed from wrecks in the junkyard and a thousand penny whistles, candles, incense sticks and several hundred lilies were collected, and two reams of two-foot wide posters were printed with the word NOW! blocked in six-inch-high, red letters on a white background.

The event began with the NOW! posters being silently handed to everyone on Haight Street, while members of the Mime Troupe, having split into Group 1 and Group 2, walked parallel up and down on both sides of the street, chanting. First, Group 1 would go, "*Ooooo!*" Then Group 2, "*Aaahhh!*" Group 1, "*Ssshhh!*" Group 2, "*Be cool!*" Back and forth like that, over and over, louder and louder. At the same time, the penny whistles were distributed through the swelling crowd, and they used them to join in, blowing up an eerie, high-register shrill. Young girls dressed in white-sheet togas gave everyone a flower, and the car mirrors were passed around to reflect the light from the sunny side to the shaded side of the block. The smell of burning incense was everywhere, as the people surged onto the blacktop, blocking traffic. A muni-bus driver got out of his coach and danced in the street with a girl, and his passengers disembarked to mix in the fun. The Frisco Angels rode their chopped 74s along the white line between the stalled, bumper-to-bumper cars. They rumble-roared past the crowd in a procession with NOW! banners flapping from their sissy-bars. Hairy Henry was up front with Fyllis standing on his buddy seat, wailing, "*Frrreeeee!*"

Soon there were three or four thousand assembled, and the noise of celebration rose to a jubilant crescendo, as the sound of a mantra began: "The streets belong to the people! The streets belong to the people!" The beat went on as the tactical police force bunched up on a side street toward the top of the Haight. They were summoned by Captain Kiely because the people had neither applied for nor been given a permit for their gathering, therefore it was unlawful and had to be stopped. But how do you try to stop four thousand people from partying? They didn't, and the beat set in, "The streets belong to the people!" "The streets belong to the people!"

Their parade completed, the Frisco Angels parked their bikes up at the end of the block. As Hairy Henry was helping Fyllis from his scooter, a pair of TPF cops came over and told him he had committed a violation by allowing her to stand up on the seat while his machine was in motion. They asked to see his license, and then ran a radio check at headquarters to see whether he had any outstanding warrants. There were no traffic warrants out on him, but they learned that Henry had just been paroled from San Quentin, having finished an eight-year bit. They told him to come with them over to the station house and they would return his license to him there. Hairy Henry told them to keep it. More cops came over, and he was arrested for resisting arrest. "What resist? You never told me nothin' 'bout no arrest! What arrest? What for?" They dragged him into the paddy wagon, but his tight friend and Hells Angel brother, Chocolate George, started pulling him back out again. He was bystanding during the incident and felt that the coppers were doing Henry wrong. The cops piled all over the two, and after a struggle, shoved them both inside the wagon, locking the wire-mesh door.

The rest of the Frisco club had walked back to the party long before the cops had made their move against Henry, but several persons witnessed what went down and one of them ran over and told Emmett about the bust. He decided to lay it on the people and see if there was enough solidarity on the street to warrant the continued talk of community. Slim Minnaux, who was tall enough to be seen and heard far back in the crowd, bellowed out the news and told everyone to march on the park station for their release. There was a loud shout of unanimity as the people turned as one and started towards the station house. The party mood continued with poet Michael McClure strumming his autoharp and Hells Angel Freewheelin' Frank shaking his tambourine, both walking in front with everyone singing, *"We want Hairy Henry! We want Chocolate George!"*

Reinforcements were called in by Captain Kiely when he heard what was happening, and the cops surrounded the station. The crowd turned along Stanyon Street, went through Golden Gate Park and across to the parking lot in front of the station house. The line of cops fell back in face of the two to three thousand marchers who were lighting the candles now and still maintaining the song, *"We want Hairy Henry! We want Chocolate George!"* Some of the people even pushed their way past the surprised coppers and inside the station and almost succeeded in releasing both prisoners, but were driven back outside at gunpoint. A coffin, used to symbolize the death of money, was held up and quickly filled with the $380 bail required for the two. This was handed over to the Frisco club's president, Angel Pete, who remarked that he had never seen anything like it. The people had never stood up for the Hells Angels before, and the speed with which the money was collected really surprised him and he yelled, "Thanks!" to the crowd as he left with his brothers for the bondsman.

Chocolate George was bailed out later that night, but Hairy Henry was kept locked in the felony tank at the city prison on a parole hold with no possibility of bail until the case against him was tried. That's what you call being burned, and Emmett was pissed off. He got Henry an attorney who said he would defend him gratis. He even got to see Henry at the city prison — but not as a visitor.

Emmett was spotted lifting a one-hundred-pound box of prime round steaks from the rear of a truck being loaded at the Armour meat company. A truck driver, who was goofing off in the cab of a trailer parked nearby, clocked him as he slid the meat into the back of the Ford wagon and drove away. The fink also wrote down the plate number before calling the cops. Emmett had just dropped the haul at Clayton Street and was driving back to his pad with a steak he intended to fry for himself before collapsing asleep. He heard the sirens and the order to pull over at the same time. There was a .38 staring at the left side of his face and he didn't argue. They found the piece of meat on the floor underneath the dashboard wrapped in a sheet of paper. He had carefully pulled the car into a parking space along the curb, so it wouldn't be towed away, and he was then handcuffed and taken downtown to the Hall of Justice in a squad-rol. There he was booked for possession of stolen goods and suspicion of grand theft. He said hello to Henry when they locked him inside the same felony tank, and was asked what he'd been popped for.

"Possession."

"Possession of what? Grass? Coke? What?"

"Meat. Possession of a fucking piece of meat!" And everyone laughed.

But this one wasn't a fun bust. The Armour meat company, as well as a couple of others, had been reporting frequent thefts to the police, and he was going to be in real trouble if someone could place him at the scene of any other grabs. He sweated a little, but he could hardly keep his eyes open or his mind on the problem. This was his first day off in nearly three months and he just crashed on one of the bunks until his bond was posted the next day.

There didn't seem to be any witnesses to any of the other heists, or at least they weren't coming forward, but the company still wanted to prosecute him to the full extent of the law and set an example of him in the newspapers. Fortunately, his attorney, a strong man named Richard Wertheimer, who studied law after becoming crippled as a longshoreman, was able to talk with a few of the company's directors and make a deal. Emmett was to make restitution for the one hundred pounds of round steak and they would ask the court to reduce the complaint to simple petty theft and to grant clemency. At the preliminary hearing, Dick Wertheimer spoke with the judge in chambers, and when the court was in session continued his plea from the floor, asking that his honor understand that "the boy wasn't stealing the meat for himself or to sell for cash but he did it to divide among the poor and hungry, disenfranchised, young people who've been crowding into the Haight-Ashbury . . ."

Judge Joseph G. Kennedy was presiding and his response to that argument was, "Well, son, even Robin Hood had to pay his dues. Six months . . ." — and he hesitated long enough for Emmett to mutter, "Shit!" for having copped a plea — ". . . suspended. And six months probation." With the stipulation that he reimburse the Armour people before the completion of that probation.

A week later, Hairy Henry and Chocolate George were in the same courtroom with Brian Rohan, the attorney Emmett had asked to defend the two. As soon as the court was called into session, the prosecution dismissed the charges for lack of evidence, and Rohan flipped out because Henry had already spent weeks in jail, and Rohan had put in long hours preparing for the defense. Why had the D.A.'s office waited until now to drop the charges? Why hadn't they notified him and his clients sooner? But there was nothing to be done. When he stormed out of the courtroom into the hallway, he ran smack into one of the arresting officers, a punk-faced bastard named Kerrens, standing next to a crowd of newsmen. Kerrens had made a quick reputation on the streets in the Haight as a brutal, lying prick, and Rohan knew this. He really let it fly in a good, solid, five-minute tirade, which he closed by promising the cop he was going to build a harassment-brutality case against him that wasn't only going to get him kicked off the force, but also give his wife grounds for divorce. Emmett enjoyed the at-the-drop-of-a-hat performance and so did Rohan. The cameras had recorded every moment of his displayed outrage and the cop's embarrassment for the six o'clock newscasts. It was plenty slick.

The Frisco Angels wanted to repay the people of the Haight for having come through with their brothers' bail. The club wanted to throw a party and Angel Pete talked about it with Emmett. They decided to have one in the Panhandle on New Year's Day and they did. It was called the New Year's Day Wail! and the Angels bought beer, which they gave away to everyone, and paid for the PA system. Emmett arranged for an eighteen-foot, flatbed truck to be used as a stage. Since it was early Sunday afternoon, Emmett had to go wake up Big Brother and the Holding Company, as well as the Grateful Dead. Pearl cursed his being to infinite damnation, and Jerry Garcia suggested he go play Russian roulette with a loaded automatic, but they came and he played his beautiful guitar licks and she sang her trashy soul out for the people.

It was a great day and a hell of a party — the first free rock-concert-party in any city park put on solely by the people for themselves. By late afternoon everybody was high and happy. The cops came, saw the way everyone looked wasted, and split, muttering something about the absence of a park permit. The crowd shouted a goodbye after them: *"The parks belong to the people! The parks belong to the people!"* Even so, Emmett believed the cops would have vamped, if the music had continued past dark. But the bands had to gig at the Fillmore and Avalon ballrooms that night, so there was no music. None that was played over the loudspeaker system, anyway. The "Wail!" ended with the falling sun and the Angels rode off on their scooters and everyone else drifted away, smiling with the feeling of having had a good time.

Emmett got loaded after he returned the truck, and bedded down with Natural Suzanne — a high-hipped, eighteen-year-old Michigan girl with sharply etched cheekbones, who dropped out of Antioch to live in the Haight-Ashbury. She had been staying with Emmett for a few weeks and they both liked it. The past three months, since the

Free Food began, had been ball-breaking lonely for Emmett. No one was really into the food but him and the women. In fact, if it hadn't been for those women there wouldn't have been 4 P.M. Free Food in the park everyday or any day. They were the real strength in the Haight-Ashbury community, the real Diggers. Cooking two or three twenty-gallon milk cans full of stew for two hundred people can be a goof, if you do it once a year, but try doing it for two or three days in a row, for two or three weeks, for two or three months. And not get paid — not make any money from it at all. It's a bitch!

The news media began referring to the Diggers as "a sort of hippie philanthropic, do-gooder organization based in the Haight-Ashbury"; as "Mod Monks," and as "a new breed of hip Salvation Army social workers without portfolio." No matter how deep into the streets they delved, they couldn't come up with anyone who would claim responsibility for any of the Digger above-ground activities. Emmett was enormously popular on the streets and because of this, and because he continued to shun publicity, giving the press the go-by, the HIP class regarded him with a certain apprehension and dislike. He didn't care. He knew what he was doing and he just didn't care. However, the growing spotlight scene annoyed Billy Landout who split for the East Coast to see if he could rustle up anything in New York. Everyone, including Coyote and the Hun, thought Bill was an innocent, holy, little guy, but Emmett knew better. He knew him when he was a tough kid on the streets of Brooklyn, and he hadn't changed. The toughness was still there, he was just very quiet about it. William Everard seemed to have been the same way. He also pulled the same kind of a fade back in the seventeenth century, leaving the historians puzzled as to what kind of a man he had been and what type of a role he played within *that* Digger movement. It's doubtful Billy Landout had the same sense of history, he simply wanted to have a chocolate egg-cream at the Gem Spa candy store on the Lower East Side, that's all. After he had gone, the Hun started a rumor that Billy had left because the city of San Francisco wasn't big enough for both Emmett and him. Emmett only heard that dumb gossip weeks later, after he had just spoken with Billy long distance, and it was too late to do anything about it. It was a pretty cheap shot to take at someone, Emmett thought. "But what the fuck! Some people are just small that way," and he forgot about it.

A public health eviction notice was slapped on the Page Street Free Frame because several people were crashing there. But an employee of the Quakers, called Fish, found a new and much better location right away and they moved. It was a storefront on Frederick Street with a kitchen, bathroom, a spacious interior and a large empty basement. Motorcycle Richie, Gary, and John-John transferred what stuff was needed from Page Street, and Emmett stenciled the name of the new place over the front window: The Free Frame of Reference. He thought about putting up Number Two but decided it would have been too corny. Quaker Fish got his wife to sign the lease before she divorced him and returned to her parents in New England. There was a room in the back, to the right of the kitchen, which John-John, Gary, and Richie made into a bunkhouse, building beds and stealing some furniture. It was too small to sleep more than six or seven, so everyone else who wanted to crash used the basement floor which was covered wall to wall with mattresses. The women continued to cook the 4 P.M. Free Food at their house on Clayton Street, leaving the kitchen to be used only for coffee and whatever snacks had been lifted from somewhere.

The Ford wagon finally up and died one day, and it looked like the yellow submarine wasn't going to last much longer either, being driven sixteen to twenty hours a day. Emmett and a crew of Diggers were discussing the need for another vehicle, when in the front door walked Richard Brautigan, a tall, carrot-haired, thirty-five-year-old poet wearing grandpa glasses, a peacoat and a floppy, wide-brimmed, felt hat. He also sported a golden bristled moustache, which drooped over his upper lip like a nodding eyelash. Richard called his poems "Tidbits" and he wrote quite a few for the free handbills which were mimeographed and distributed by the Communication Company, a small organization set up by two office-staffers of *Ramparts* magazine. Their names were Claude and Chester and, turned on by the style of the Digger Papers, they effectively replaced the need for them by printing single-sheet newspapers which were handed out along Haight Street several times a day. The Communication Company was one of the best newspapers any community ever had.

Brautigan had some news himself that day — an item about a wealthy, young woman named Flame who wanted to buy the Diggers something they could use, and needed.

"Would she go for a pickup truck?" someone asked.

"Sure," came the reply, and Butcher Brooks jumped to his feet, asking Richard to take him to her and telling everyone else that he would be back that evening with a pickup he had his eye on. And that evening he did return, driving a '58 Chevy pickup in great condition with a brand new set of tires. Next to him on the front seat sat a stunning redhead with long, full hair and skin the color of ivory. She was Flame all right and she soon became Brooks's old lady, living with him in another storefront on Webster Street in the Fillmore.

The pickup truck almost became a serious problem. Since it was registered to a nonexistent person, everyone wanted to drive it and make believe it was theirs. Emmett put an end to all that by taking the keys and either driving it himself or only allowing someone like Butcher Brooks to use it to take care of Digger business. The need was too great and it was too valuable in those terms to be squandered on tripsters who wanted to drive around Haight Street pretending they were hot-shot characters in a B movie. The truck was used as a free bus, however, picking up passengers along the streets who didn't have the fare for a regular one. This was done whenever it wasn't being used for something more important to the community as a whole. In fact every time the Diggers moved the vehicle, it was filled either with people, or stuff to be given away — it was never empty.

In the rear of the Frederick Street Free Frame of Reference was the free store, brimming over with liberated goods to be shared with whoever needed them. In the front of the place was a large space kept clear of furniture and made available as a lounge or hangout for the casualties of the so-called Love Generation. Kids who were beaten down by the mean streets or the cold, wet, foggy, San Francisco climate. Doctors would come by almost every evening to examine lines of them for things like hepatitis and bronchial disorders, sending them to the S.F. General Hospital when they showed symptoms of a serious illness. The Free Food continued to keep everybody from malnutrition except for the heavy dopers who stone-refused to get next to anything nutritional — so they died. Emmett had to be cautious about stealing meat because of his probation, and therefore the stew was usually made from a poultry stock. He met some right guys in a halfway house, however, who had just been released from Folsom and San Quentin, and they fingered some easy food scores for him. For a while things picked up, but only for a while.

It was at this same halfway house that the Quakers offered Emmett a ten-thousand-dollar-a-year job to do the same work he was doing, but as a member of their organization. They balked, however, when he asked them to give him the year's salary in advance, in one lump sum. Other churches and social organizations became interested in the Diggers and the work they were doing, but they were usually put off by Emmett's purposely hostile attitude, especially when he told them to go and take care of their own backyards, starting with the redistribution of their sect's wealth to the poor. The HIP merchants and others like them seldom approached Emmett, and when they did they treated him as if he were a combination of John Garfield, Timothy Carey and Pat O'Brien. That is to say, they showed him a condescendingly fearful respect.

The dope dealers usually stayed away, too, but one day the biggest dealer of top quality LSD, who was known as Bear, sent someone around with ten thousand tabs of white-lightning acid that had just been produced in the lab and was not as yet marketed. After the delivery was made to Frederick Street, the dealers sat back and waited to see whether the Diggers and their free giveaway were for real. You see, the ten thousand tabs were all the same color white and none of them had appeared in public. Therefore, they were identifiable. It didn't take long for the word to get around about what was being done with them. When it was certain they had been freely distributed among the Haight community, Bear came around himself to meet this Emmett Grogan and give him some more, along with seventy-five twenty-pound turkeys, in anticipation of the Human Be-In.

The Human Be-In was the brainstorm of the Haight Independent Proprietors and their market researchers and consumer consultants — who'd pointed out the need for national publicity, if the HIP associates hoped to merchandise their hippie paraphernalia to the international department store chains and to the smaller shops throughout the country. The HIP merchants were naturally afraid that Emmett and the Diggers might seize upon the moment to disturb their sweet, lovey-dovey courtship of the media by revealing the unstrained, unclean truth about the Love Ghetto. That's what the gifts of acid and turkey seemed to Emmett to be about — sort of a HIP version of a Jaycee basket of cheer. The Diggers had been working in the community for over four months, and even though the HIP merchants claimed in interviews to have helped, they never gave them a hand with anything. The acid was to have been their insurance against any outbursts to the press, but it didn't work out that way because it wasn't sold by the Diggers, so there was no debt owed. The only reason Emmett accepted the fowl and dope donations in the first place was that it wasn't entirely up to him. The others, like John-John and Gary, all dug the idea of themselves in the benevolent roles, giving away free acid to the people they knew on the street. All the street people were handed five hits of LSD apiece, and were asked to share them with others. But if they dealt the five to someone, for some needed cash, or swallowed all of them, or flushed them down the toilet or whatever, that was okay, too. It was free, it was theirs, they could do what they wanted with it.

The ironic part of the bribe was its total unnecessity. The HIP merchants didn't have to worry about Emmett's talking to the press and exposing the dreg of casualties in the Love Ghetto because he was cultivating his anonymity as a line of defense; a first line of defense against being devoured by a glut of cheap, fashionable notoriety; self-protection from arrest, prosecution and anything else that might impair his ability to perform. He wasn't denying his leadership by doing this, he was just seeking to maintain a distinctly low profile of himself as a leader. The Haight-Ashbury was jampacked with reporters from every medium, and Emmett never said a word to any of them about the "Love Generation." The only scribe he did speak with was Poet Allen Ginsberg, who came to the city to counsel the HIP merchants on the structure he felt the Human Be-In should take. He invited Ginsberg over to the Frederick Street Free Frame one evening to hang out with the people there. He came, bringing Timothy Leary and Richard Alpert along with him. Many things can be said about Allen Ginsberg but only one really matters and is completely deserving: he's a good person and there aren't many around. The same didn't seem to be true of Leary or Alpert; and the young street people sitting close together around the floor in the Free Frame of Reference seemed to understand that. Especially one very young girl whose eyes were flirting with vacancy. As the two LSD shamans pitched their psychedelic banter, riffing about the transcendental importance of an inner life, this little girl stood up and announced, "You don't turn me on!" She held her ground and kept repeating the same accusation: "You don't turn me on!" And the others agreed with her and also began to chant, until everyone was shouting — *"You don't turn us on! You don't turn us on!"* — forcing the two of them to leave with a good man who should have known better than to squander himself on a pair of charlatan fools.

That's what the young street people were bitching about. They weren't worried about what either of them were saying or particularly concerned about the truth or falsity of it. Their beef was with the way they were saying it, and neither Leary nor Alpert could carry the tune. But there they were every time you turned around — on the covers of magazines, on the radio and TV, all over the fucking place — representing them, the young people, the alternative culture. Two creepy, whiskey-drinking schoolteachers! It was sad and the young people in the Free Frame that night rejected out of hand the lie they were fed by the media and felt disappointed in themselves for having ever believed in the psychedelic duet.

Adjacent to the Free Frame of Reference was another storefront which had been leased by a Krishna consciousness group and fixed up for the arrival of His Divine Grace, the Swami. The dozen or so members of the Krishna commune were vegetarians and they used to eat an afternoon and evening meal while sitting around on pillows in a circle on the straw-matted floor. The only other activities these disciples seemed to engage in at their storefront, which they called a temple, were chanting mantras and listening to lectures by their Swami-Guru after he arrived from the East — the East Coast, that is. The disciples' heads were all shaven and they served their Swami twenty-four hours a day, believing that "if the spiritual master is pleased, then one can make great advances in the spiritual life." Nothing displeased the Swami more than "the disorderly bunch" that gathered inside the Free Frame of Reference next door to him, "clattering about like rowdies" and "creating a deafening din" which made it nearly impossible for his disciples to meditate. It didn't disturb his meditation, of course, he was a pro. His major ire, however, stemmed from the fact that the Diggers grabbed up most of the surplus from the Produce and Farmers markets, making it difficult for his disciples to elicit any religious offerings from the men who worked in the two wholesale outlets.

One night when Emmett was showing some movies in the Free Frame and the audience's laughter was particularly loud, the Swami became exasperated. He halted his talk and one of his disciples went to the pay phone on the corner and telephoned a complaint in to the park police station. The cops were evidently pleased by the call because they came immediately. The station was only around the block from the Free Frame and it was easy for them to mass together for a crackdown. A sixty-year-old lieutenant led two dozen cops and two paddy wagons the short distance. W. C. Fields' film *The Bank Dick* was being screened on a sheet draped across the front window and Emmett was standing by the door. He saw the cops begin to arrive. Little Robert, a tough, young Indian with some Chicano blood, long black hair and nobody, also saw them, and he locked the door after Emmett went outside to speak with the officer in charge about whatever it was all about.

There were cops all over the street now, and all of them were staring at the images moving around on the sheet-covered front window. There are several scenes in *The Bank Dick* where Keystone Cops chase equally bizarre robbers, and one of them was being projected at that moment. While Emmett was talking over the fire laws and the alleged overcrowding of the premises with the lieutenant, the Cops were running all over the screen after a pair of bank robbers, one of whom's name was Repulsive Grogan. It was a very funny scene with a hilarious chase sequence and plenty of slapstick laughs, but none of the cops, who were standing in full view of the images being projected on the sheet in the window, seemed amused. Not one of them even cracked a smile or made a joke, in fact, they even appeared to be embarrassed. Watching the flick over the lieutenant's shoulder, Emmett could also see that the coppers were eyeing him with obvious annoyance, apparently feeling he had planned everything that way to make them look stupid. Their looks were getting Emmett a bit edgy because he knew what they meant. He was glad the cops felt like assholes, just the same.

The lieutenant wasn't a prick but he was an old man who should have been retired. He informed Emmett that the gathering inside the Free Frame was in violation of all sorts of fire codes and health regulations, but he agreed that his patrolmen didn't have to enter the premises and that there was no need for any arrests. The crowd could exit in single file, he said, without any fear. Emmett nodded for Little Robert to open up and he went back inside to inform everybody about what was happening. He did it quickly and all of them got to their feet and began filing out onto the sidewalk.

The lieutenant was standing by the front door, with his men positioned in back of him making nasty cracks to the dispersing crowd. Just about everyone had left when there was a loud noise from inside and to the rear of the building. Emmett turned in time to see Patrolman Kerrens, the rat himself, come crashing through the kitchen window, knocking over all the food being warmed on the stove and the piles of plates used to share it. He was running up toward the front with his right arm raised and waving, shouting that he found an outfit, a set of gimmicks. He was lying, of course, having brought the works with him when he jumped through the window.

Little Robert caught Emmett's eye, and he slipped downstairs to the basement. It was a smart move. There were a few needle freaks crashing in the cellar and they had probably left behind their spikes when the lieutenant had ordered the place vacated. If the cops found their paraphernalia, Emmett would be rousted and probably convicted on a narcotics charge, but Little Robert's snap thinking insured that nothing was found in the basement.

Kerrens's shouting triggered the other coppers standing out front and they surged inside, actually, bowling over their rusty-gun lieutenant, as they moved. Seeing Kerrens running toward him, Emmett blew it and caught him full flush in his guileful mouth with a roundhouse right which he hooked practically from the floor. Kerrens galloped *Smack!* into it, his legs kicking out from under him as he smashed *Bam!* onto the floor, stretched flat. He went down so fast and stiff, it was just like the rapid-speed antics of the Keystone Cops in the *Bank Dick* movie, which no one bothered to shut off. The coppers almost stomped on the cold-cocked Kerrens as they all piled over one another for a clear shot at Grogan — imitating the Keystone Cops on the film-screen, who were also colliding into each other while attempting to apprehend the other Grogan. It was a comedy, all right, with cops mimicking cops, and Emmett thought he was dreaming. The last thing he saw before a blackjack put out his lights, was Repulsive Grogan firing at the Keystones from the back of a vintage convertible roadster driven by W. C. Fields who was mouthing some astute observation about the poor quality of modern firearms compared to the sound reliability of the flintlocks of yore.

The cops tore the Free Frame of Reference apart and destroyed all they could. They poured the foodstuff on the kitchen floor and added water until it became slop. They ripped up the clothes hanging on the free store racks and threw paint over them. When everything was smashed and broken, they brought Emmett around and dragged him into a squadrol. They drove him away, and the crowd, which had grown to about five hundred, remained quiet. No one else was arrested. Little Robert snuck out of the Free Frame while the two sets of cops were trying to pounce on the two different Grogans.

At the park police station, Kerrens was still shaken, with a split, fat lip and a swollen mouth, and Emmett thought he was going to catch one hell of a fucking beating — the kind of beating that doesn't give you time to worry about disfigurement, just allows enough thought to hope you'll continue breathing after you pass out. His partner drove Kerrens to the hospital for treatment, and Emmett wondered whether they were going to bring him there, too, because of the way his forehead had been cut by the sap. The lieutenant was still peeved at having been disobeyed, disregarded and kicked aside by his men, and he ordered a plainclothesman to drive Emmett to the city prison. He wanted the prisoner to be booked and locked up downtown because he felt there would be more trouble for him if he put Grogan into one of the back cells where the rank and file could get at him and probably beat him to death. Needless to say, Emmett felt that the lieutenant had made a wise decision.

The next morning he woke up in the felony tank, all bruised and very sore. After a lump of oatmeal for breakfast, he was taken downstairs for arraignment. The courtroom was filled with spectators and a murmur rose as he entered. Both his eyes were puffed, but he could see the familiar faces of people he knew, sitting on the rows of seats in the gallery. He returned their signs of encouragement with a smile before turning to face the bench. He felt good that they were there, good that the people were behind him, good that he wasn't alone.

Butch Hallinan, the eldest son of the famed attorney, Vincent Hallinan, was his lawyer. He had tried to get Emmett out on bond earlier that morning but no bail had been set. He was being held on a probation hold because he violated his probation by getting himself arrested, and bail could not be posted or set without the approval of his probation officer. The P.O. was in the courtroom, seated alone near the empty jury box.

The prosecutor began to read off the charges that were filed against him and — as they always do — he simply read aloud the number of the penal code that was alleged to have been violated and not the name of the crime it represented. As the prosecutor was mouthing off a whole string of these numbers, he came to one which no one seemed able to identify — not him, or the defense counsel, or even the judge, who finally asked his court clerk to look the number up in the California book of penal codes. When the clerk located its meaning, he brought the lexicon over to the bench and his honor announced that it meant maintaining and operating an opium den. The courtroom burst into laughter, and the judge had to gavel for order before continuing. "It says here that there has to have been an Oriental present at the time of the offense in order for this to be a valid charge. Was there an Oriental present when this defendant was arrested, Mister Prosecutor?" The courtroom began to convulse, and even the judge seemed to think that it was mildly amusing for he pointed out that "no one has been arrested or charged with this crime, since the year 1891."

When order was restored to the court, Butch Hallinan began the defense argument by shouting that the cops and the D.A.'s office were harassing Grogan and conspiring to violate his rights guaranteed under the Constitution. He was getting a bit carried away but the judge calmed the proceedings by asking him to approach the bench with the prosecutor. Emmett's P.O. joined the huddle and his honor accepted the prosecution's advice and dismissed all the charges against the defendant. The tremendous deluge of unfavorable publicity that was bound to stem from the opium den charge, the prosecutor felt, would surely lead to other charges that the police had infringed upon the rights of the defendant and so forth. These claims would probably be accompanied by an outcry of "frame" and it all wasn't worth it, as far as the assistant district attorney could see.

Emmett was impressed because they even dropped the charge of assaulting a police officer, and after a brief chat with his P.O. he was cut loose. Several reporters from both the establishment and underground media tried to interview him when he was released from the city prison. Their persistence finally forced him to break the story in the press so they would all quit trying to scoop an exclusive out of him. He did it by contacting a radical weekly that had just begun publishing and wasn't going to last very long — *The Sunday Ramparts*. The newspapers were apparently hot about his story because of the mutiny angle and he was careful to emphasize that part in the short interview he telephoned into *Ramparts*. He said the lieutenant "seemed to be getting on in years and his men showed him nothing but an incredible disrespect. He lost charge when his subordinates pushed him to the ground out of their way and actually ran over him in their absurd, uncontrollable and childish anger with me for having accidentally knocked off one of the patrolmen's hats. It was sad and certainly disgraceful for the bystanders to witness how a bunch of grown police officers disregarded their lieutenant and commander in charge, tossing him aside as if he was a piece of trash or something." The story broke under headlines on the front page of the citywide weekly and it caused a mild controversy at city hall. There was serious embarrassment for the park station's commanding officers. They were quizzed by other reporters who investigated what became "their discipline problem" with probing questions that disturbed the status quo of the station house for a while. It wasn't much of a revenge, of course, but it did offer a bit of satisfaction. And a week or so later someone fired a few rounds through the front window of Kerrens's house as he sat down for supper. Apparently the bullets weren't aimed at him, just a few warning shots, splintering a glass and the salt and pepper shakers. Emmett wondered who'd done it, and also what sort of a cordial prank he could pull on the swami in his Krishna reservoir of pleasure. But he forgot about all of it when he cooled and resigned himself to the fact that there were more important things to do than begin a religious war.

The Human Be-In was publicized as a "Gathering of the Tribes," but it was actually more a gathering of the suburbs with only a sprinkling of nonwhites in the crowd of three hundred thousand. It was a showcase for beaded hipsterism with only one stage for the assembly to face. On it sat the HIP merchants, their consultants, and several psychedelic superstars, while the Quicksilver Messenger Service, the Airplane and The Grateful Dead played their sets over a PA system guarded by Hells Angels who were asked to do so after several incidents had occurred. The turkeys had been made into thousands of sandwiches under John-John's supervision, and the bread was salted down with crushed acid. Gary organized the free distribution of the sandwiches to those who looked like they needed something to eat, physically or spiritually. Afterwards, Emmett walked to one side of the stage and stood below it, watching the so-called luminaries of the alternative culture. He felt a sense of anger and despair over the way the Be-In had been set up and presented. Their advertising had assembled three hundred thousand people, and all they gave them was a single stage with a series of schmucks schlepping all over it, making speeches and reciting poetry nobody could hear, with interludes of music. It was even more incredible to Emmett that the crowd crushed forward for a better spot where they could stargaze at the feeble spectacle. The HIP merchants had invited the Berkeley radicals to participate in the Be-In, as a placating gesture to the left-wing, liberal media. They were more than happy to come, of course, and were represented on the stage by the baby-fat runt himself, Jerome Rubin. All made up in the image of a true

Russian theorist complete with a Trotsky-Stalinesque moustache, he called for a marriage between the Haight-Ashbury and Berkeley tribes, proclaiming that "our smiles are our political banners and our nakedness is our picket sign!" He was awed and shaken by the enormity of the crowd and several times he seemed about to wet his pants, ecstatic over his getting to speak to so many at once. But he was afraid to begin sounding like the cornball square he is, so he gave up the microphone after a few minutes and sat down to ask his gooseberry, Stew Alpert, whether he had come on like a hippie or an old straight. Stew Alpert is to Jerome Rubin what Clyde Tolson is to John Edgar Hoover and he was quick to assure him that he flashed everyone with his ability to make hip-sounding remarks and even shocked some with his new image. Timothy Leary followed and he seemed to be a bit juiced, only able to mumble, "Tune-in, turn-on, drop-out," once or twice to the crowd before he sat back down with that same old shit-eating grin all over his face.

Allen Ginsberg, like everyone on the stage, was pleased with the giant, press publicity–engineered turn-out of people. He even appeared to believe that the mere assembling of such a crowd was a superworthy achievement in itself, negating any need for further action. In a way it did. Since the body count of three hundred thousand assured the HIP and their friends of worldwide media coverage, why give the press anything to photograph or write about other than the people who gathered? That way it was one great big fashion show, that's all.

More ham chewers trouped up to the mike and kept saying how wonderful it was with all that energy in one place at the same time. Just being. Being together — touching, looking, loving, embracing each other — that's what it was all about, they said: "The New Consciousness!" Then, the mantra began: *"We are one!" "We are one!"* Three hundred thousand people shouted repeatedly that they were one, and Emmett just sat on the grass and watched them pretend, wondering how long it was going to take before people stopped kidding themselves.

Someone parachuted out of a single-engine plane into the middle of the meadow and several thousand people began swearing that they just saw a vision of God. Poet Gary Snyder ended it all by blowing on a conch shell and everyone turned toward the falling sun and walked toward the Pacific Ocean to watch the dusk from the beach.

Later that evening and throughout the following week, the mass media kept applauding and broadcasting the news about what they called the dawning of a new era for the country and for the world. They pointed out that everything had been peaceful with no fights among the *gigantic crowd* of three hundred thousand. Well, no large, serious slugfests, at least. Just a few dozen minor stompings. The love shuck was given momentum by all the coverage, and the press even began calling the Love Ghetto of Haight-Ashbury things like "Psychedelphia" and "Hashbury." The HIP merchants were astounded by their own triumph in promoting such a large market for their wares. They became the Western world's taste makers overnight and built a power base upon their notoriety and their direct line into the mass media. The city's officialdom began to take the HIP leadership class a little more seriously. They held public conferences with them about token problems, like the rerouting of the municipal buses to avoid clogging up the Haight Street traffic, which was already overburdened with squares, shopping for a far-out purchase to bring back to suburbia.

Emmett was angry. He didn't give a fuck about how much bread the HIP merchants were making, or particularly care that only a chosen few in the community were actually benefiting from these profits. He was simply angered by the outrageous publicity that the Haight Independent Proprietors had created to develop new markets for the merchandising of their crap — angry about how their newsmongery was drawing a disproportionate number of young kids to the district that was already overcrowded — thousands of young, foolish kids who fell for the Love Hoax and expected to live comfortably poor and take their place in the district's kingdom of love. Angry with most of the heads in the community who were earning a dollar doing something, like the rock musicians, and kidding themselves by feeling that all the notoriety was good and would bring more money into the underground and expand the HIP shops, providing more jobs for those who wanted them. The truth was that the disastrous arrival of thousands too many only meant more money for the operators of fly-by-night underground-culture outfits, the dope dealers, and the worst of the lot, the shopkeepers who hired desperate runaways to do piecework for them at sweatshop wages. It was a catastrophe and there was nothing to be done except leave, or try to deal with it as best one could. Whenever someone sought to reveal the truth of the situation, they were put down, ignored or dismissed as being unhip by the longhaired, false-bottomed hipsters who had money in the bank. Emmett understood that he might be making a mistake by judging his anonymity more important than exposing the hype that was going down, but he felt it would be dumb to open his mouth to the media. He would only end up as down payment for the future of a mob of middle-class kids who were just experimenting with hunger — youngsters who were playing hooky from suburbia to have an adventure of poverty. He felt that most of them would return to the level of society which bred them but he also knew that some of them would never, ever get back home to compare their stories of wantage with their parents' "You'll-never-know-what-it-was-like" tales of the Depression.

"Emmett Grogan" had become an anonym to the public and he understood that. It would have been relatively easy for him to have captured the media spotlight, gain recognition, and finesse his own acclamation as a leader by broadcasting to the youth of the nation, telling them to stay where they were because they had been deceived. But it already seemed too late to stop them. They were thoroughly duped into coming to the Haight-Ashbury and they were eagerly on their way and there was nothing to be done. He decided to continue in his attempt to effect something substantial and relevant to cope with the oncoming invasion, instead of exchanging his anonymity for the notoriety which would have accompanied his denunciation of the HIPs as pigs to the press.

He had been dealing in Free Food for over four months now, and things like Free Food do something to a person when he keeps them going for a long time. They tend to give him a healthy respect for reality and a deep disdain for the fake political ploys of the fraudulent Left. And so, he went on as a Digger, doing things that were, at least, pertinent and to the point of some community need, and he left the performance of trivial, unavailing antics to the fatuous publicity seekers who were most of the self-proclaimed radical spokesmen of his generation.

His seemingly resolute adherence to anonymity confused the political careerists, and he enjoyed watching them try to figure out whether he was just a sucker or someone with an angle up his sleeve. But he never thought about the semantics or tactics of politics long enough for him to become bitter. His work kept him too tired and busy to want to hassle himself about mere words and people who did nothing but use them. There was, however, a large group of men in the city who functioned only with words, but whose use of them was very important to Emmett. They were the poets who first broadcast the news to him — the news that he now needed to know. They had all come to San Francisco for a sort of reunion, using the activity surrounding the Human Be-In as their point of convergence. Emmett wanted to meet and speak with all of them and was knocked out when Richard Brautigan told him that the poets felt the same way about the Diggers and wanted to have a poetry reading for them.

The arrangements were quickly made for a reading to be held in Gino and Carlo's bar in the beat section of North Beach. It was advertised by word of mouth, and by a newspaper columnist as a "benefit for the Diggers." So many poets showed up to read that night, and so many people came to listen, that the gathering had to be divided in half between Gino's and another bar, forcing the poets to walk back and forth to each place if they wanted their poetry to be heard by everyone.

The people who made up the audience that night had been reading news stories and had been hearing about the Diggers and "their philanthropic social work" for months, but never anything about where the Diggers got the money to do all those things. So when the word went out that the reading was to be a benefit for the Diggers, they naturally assumed that meant a donation. But it didn't. There was no admission or cover charge or money collected in either bar — it was all free. Allen Ginsberg and Gary Snyder accidentally passed a hat around Gino's for a collection, however, while the Diggers were arranging things at the other location. When Emmett and Coyote arrived, the money had already been collected and the hat was given to them. But, instead of accepting it, the two immediately asked for everyone's attention and announced that there was a mistake. "The only type of benefit that could be thrown for the Diggers is one where everything is free!" Then, they gave the hat to the bartender and told him to count the money out on the bar in front of everybody, and to continue buying rounds for the crowd for as long as the bread held out.

"That's a Digger benefit!" laughed Coyote, and everyone applauded.

And Gary Snyder remarked to Allen Ginsberg, "Did you see that? They gave it all away — back to the people!" The money lasted a long time because there was a lot of it in that hat. "An awful lot of it," Emmett had thought when it was handed to him. It was far into the morning before the sound of poetry turned into conversation, and everyone agreed that a good time was had by all. The only other poets the people would like to have seen there that night were Charles Olson and Gregory Corso, but they were well represented, even though they hadn't been able to make it to San Francisco.

Emmett admired all the poets but valued one in particular because, unlike most members of the Beat Generation, he spoke about the discipline of Eastern philosophies with more than abstract knowledge. Gary Snyder went to Japan and became a Zen Master. On returning to the United States, he wrote a poem which the editors of the S.F. *Oracle* wanted to publish in their psychedelic paper as an example of his new work. He gave it to them but they only ran it in the first couple of copies of an early edition, pulling it out of print because, they claimed, it was "too hostile" to be compatible with their mild approach toward "consciousness raising." The poem simply seemed to indicate the need to relate man back to nature by calling for the correction of man's overall white, Anglo-Saxon way of thinking with American Indian, Japanese and Hindu thought. At least it seemed that way to Emmett, and he asked Gary Snyder if it was all right for him to have it printed up by the Communication Company and given away free. It was and he did.

A CURSE
ON THE MEN IN WASHINGTON, PENTAGON

om a ka ca ta ta pa ya sa svaha
As you shoot down the Vietnamese girls and men
                    in their fields
          Burning and chopping,
          Poisoning and blighting,
So surely I hunt the white man down
          in my heart.
The crew-cutted Seattle boy
The Portland boy who worked for U.P.
                    that was me.
I won't let him live. The "American"
          I'll destroy. The "Christian"
                    has long been dead.
They won't pass on to my children.
I'll give them Chief Joseph, the Bison herds,
Ishi, sparrowhawk, the Fir trees,
The Buddha, their own naked bodies,
Swimming and dancing and singing
                    instead.

279

As I kill the white man,
            the "American"

                        in me
And dance out the Ghost Dance;
To bring back America, the grass and the streams.
To trample your throat in your dreams.
This magic I work, this loving I give
            That my children may flourish
            And yours won't live.

                hi 'niswa ' vita 'ki 'ni

A short time after that poetry reading, there occurred an event
which was a turning point in the lives of many people. Several
Diggers were still members of the S.F. Mime Troupe and they also
belonged to the radical Artists Liberation Front, an organization
comprised of Bay Area artists who sought to make visible the
latent and often evil stupidity inherent in the American government's handling of our city, state and country's affairs. They would
attempt to accomplish this through the sponsorship of art exhibi-
tions, films, plays, concerts, or any event which had an educational
theme geared toward heightening people's awareness of what was
being done by politicians in their name.

Emmett, Coyote and the Hun frequently talked about the wealth
of talent represented in ALF and discussed various ideas for getting
them all to work together as artists on one giant project, on one
colossal "liberating" event. The only real difficulty in organizing
such a collaboration was finding a suitable location where the entire
ALF membership could freely convene to perform en masse. They
mentioned this one afternoon during a conference with two Methodist ministers who were also officers of the Glide Methodist
Church. The parish of Glide Church is the Tenderloin or the
Times Square district of San Francisco, making it one of a few
churches in the world with a congregation composed largely of pros-
titutes and homosexuals of either sex. Because of this, Glide Church
naturally placed much importance and effort on working to relieve
social problems and to insure the welfare of its parishioners, as well
as on maintaining a foundation which studied their sexual habits
and did statistical research in conjunction with the Kinsey Institute.

When the two ministers pressed the topic further, they were told
that the Artists Liberation Front simply needed a place to hold "a
carnival of the performing arts" or a "happening." The ministers

conferred for a moment, then gladly donated the use of any space or facility in their building, including the church itself with its cathedral-like interior. They did this without actually knowing what they were committing themselves and their church to, and Emmett and the ohers made a point of not telling them more of their plans than they thought was wise.

Later in the day, they telephoned around and arranged for the people they felt could organize a meaningful ALF event, to meet that night in the basement of Glide Church. By 9 P.M. everyone who had been asked to come had arrived and the planning session got started. There were poets Richard Brautigan and Lenore Kandel; Quaker Fish who acted as brilliant soft-pedaling liason with the Glide officialdom; Claude and Chester and the Communication Company; Coyote and his full-out blond Louisiana old lady, Sam, who had a distinct and widely known penchant for undressing any time socially; the Hun and his woman, Judith, a fine dancer and body psychologist extraordinaire; Butcher Brooks and Flame; Emmett and Natural Suzanne; Slim Minnaux and NanaNina, and soft, warm, beautiful, lonely Fyllis, who was jinxed with always being in love with someone else's man, more Diggers, more ALF members and a dark-haired, powerful-looking man of medium height who arrived with his wife, Lenore, and stood by himself during the entire meeting, periodically staring at Emmett with his intense, black eyes. The man's name was Tumble and he was thirty-three years old. At first, Emmett became confused by the attention Tumble was giving him, but quickly dismissed the looks to concentrate on the discussion at hand.

The talk began with everyone asking each other what sort of improbabilities they would like to see happen in the different rooms, and it didn't take long for the suggestions to become bizarre. After a while, the separate offices and rooms of the Glide Church building, the interior of the house of worship itself, and the outside area and adjacent parking lot were marked off and designated to different groups of persons at the meeting. These individuals were to use the space or spaces they were assigned, and their various talents to design and create an assortment of permissive settings or scenes in which they themselves and others would be able to act out their own fantasies. They named the event "The Invisible Circus" and decided that in order for it to be effective it had to run for an entire weekend or a full three-day period. They also resolved to limit publicity to word of mouth with the exception of one thousand tricolor poster-handbills of a sketched circus-wagon announcing The Invisible Circus as a seventy-two hour environmental community happening sponsored by the Diggers, the Artists Liberation Front, and Glide Church, with the time, place and date. Emmett was enthusiastic and he worked hard on the event, whenever he could get away from the Free Frame of Reference and the Free Food for a while. Like the others involved, he wanted to show up the feebleness of most public gatherings, like the Human Be-In, by providing an ample opportunity for everyone who came to enjoy themselves as active participants in the happening, not passive stargazers.

He also became tight with Tumble during the time they spent realizing all the elaborate possibilities of the circus. Tumble lived in an apartment in North Beach, and often after they finished at the church late at night, Emmett would go back there with him and sit at a large, round table in his kitchen, talking about the Diggers and what they were into. Natural Suzanne would come along with him, sometimes, to watch Lenore sit at a little table over to one side of the kitchen, moving her intelligent, graceful hands quietly making the strong, exotic jewelry she sold to the large San Francisco Import Mart in North Beach. Tumble was turned on by the things Emmett spoke about and he began working with him, driving the Digger truck around on food runs and making pick-ups for the Free Frame of Reference. Emmett was very glad that Tumble wanted to lend himself to work because most of the Diggers, especially the former and/or continuing members of the S.F. Mime Troupe, had switched their attention and energies to the Invisible Circus and other guerrilla theater activities, leaving only a few who were willing to stand up under the pressure of the other work.

It didn't take long for some, like John-John, Gary, and Richie, to become bored with the monotonous heavy chores required at the Free Frame, and they would disappear during the day, returning there only to sleep at night. That left only the women, who came through like champs as usual, Little Robert, and a handful of others whenever they weren't in jail, and Emmett, who was getting irritable and very touchy under the strain, snapping at people and yelling all the time instead of talking. Now Tumble came, who was strong enough and had more than his share of the street-wisdom acquired by most men who had done terms, to lighten the load for everyone and allow them to relax a notch.

The night of the Invisible Circus, the officials and ministers of Glide Church began to get rather nervous, wondering what they had gotten themselves into. They had accepted all the lies and half-truths liaisoned to them by Quaker Fish, but it was difficult to be deceived about what they saw with their own eyes. There was an elevator that ran from the street level entrance of the church to a large hall in the basement below, and Emmett had filled that hall with literally tons of shredded plastic he had spent days trucking over from a plastics factory. When people descended to the hall in the elevator, they stepped out into three feet of plastic strips and it was quite a struggle for them to move around, falling all over themselves as their feet got tied up in the strewn cord. Once they made it through the plastic jungle, they were confronted with a crush of people feeling each other up inside a low-ceilinged, cramped rec room that was sweltering hot because of its proximity to the boiler, and blustering with outrageous noise from a rock band whose amplified sound was so loud in that tiny space that it brought many to tears. The barren Formica church cafeteria took up the rest of the basement, and it had been turned into an R and R center, with a huge punch bowl on one of the tables filled with Tang spiked with salutary doses of acid. Upstairs, a row of a dozen separate offices had been redecorated as "love-making salons" with candles, incense, floor-mattresses covered with colorful spreads made in India, bottles of oils, perfumes and lubricants, doors with locks on their insides and all the light bulbs removed. Down the corridor from "love alley," Richard Brautigan, working with Claude and Chester, had set up "The John Dillinger Computer Service." Using the machinery from the Communication Company, they printed Flash! bulletins and news items, notifying everyone about what was going on where and how to get there and also telling them the news right after it happened. This was done by dispatching reporters all over the church to cover various events and report back to "Dillinger" headquarters to type their stories on stencils. With these stencils several hundred releases were immediately mimeographed and rapidly distributed to the crowd. One reporter even went across the street to a "Tenderloin" bar, bought a beer, and eavesdropped on a heated argument between the bartender and some of his patrons, while also jotting notes. Then he went back to the church, typed it all up, had it run off on the Gestetner, and returned to the bar with copies of the word-for-word report of the argument, which correctly named everybody in the bar who had been involved. It nearly blew the juiceheads' fucking minds to see themselves and what they were doing only a few minutes before, described in print.

The Hun was holding a conference "On the meaning of Obscenity" with a lawyer, a minister, a police-community relations cop, and himself seated at a large table with hundreds of spectators standing around watching. Behind them was a glass display case which was built into the wall with a door on the back of it that opened into another room. In that room was Slim Minnaux who opened the rear door of the case a crack and stuck his cock through, laying it on the only shelf. While the Hun was conducting the three knowledgeables in their serious discussion of obscenity, Slim was wagging his cock around on the shelf behind them, displaying it to the audience and none of the panel could figure out what was so goddamn funny.

The obscenity conference ended with a naked couple being carried into the room on a canopied mattress by four bearers, as if they were transporting an Egyptian pharaoh. They lowered the carriage onto the conference table, and the young man and woman began making love, as an enormous sheet of paper that was taped across and between the sidewalls to hide one third of the room burst open, and a dozen belly dancers leaped through. Sam led with her milk-white skin moist and glistening, her nipples puckered taut and blushing pink, and a black silk scarf floating against her white hair and across her sloping back which was covered with prickly heat. Judith following with the others, dancing around the lovemakers to the beat of six or seven drums, and enticing the gathered to join in their erotic warmth.

The cathedral-like interior of the church itself was alive with hundreds of people actualizing their fantasies, while someone played Chopin's "Death March" on an electric organ. Several couples were draped over the main altar, fucking, as a giant, naked weight lifter towered above them, standing on top of some sort of tabernacle in a beam of light, masturbating and panting himself into a trance. Other persons were screaming their testimony, or giving witness over the loudspeakers from the microphones in the pulpit and the missal stand and beside the altar lectern. A dozen conga drums beat their rhythms against the walls, echoing high up in the archway. A man sat cross-legged on the carpet and traced the altar-facing with a set of multicolored, magic-markers. A pair of excited doves flew round and round, while people stripped off each other's clothing in the candlelight, and clouds of smoke from a thousand burning incense sticks swirled aloft to the center of the cupola. A group of drag queens stood in the vestibule giving each other head in an orgy of mmm's and ahhh's and being looked at by a small band of teenyboppers who were turning red in a flurry of giggles. Some Frisco Hells Angels were in the back pews being entertained by a beautiful woman dressed in a Carmelite nun's habit who kept shouting for "More! More!" and they were giving it to her. A black transvestite was on his knees screaming in contrition for his sins, as he was lashed with a whip by a grinning toothless albino. An old, white-haired, bearded man announced he was god and loudly accused the overflow congregation of having taken his name in vain. "You did!" "You did!" he said, again and again. Some youngsters felt one another's recent pubescence, pantsying in the balcony, while a few naked bodies raced up and down the aisles, pedaling bicycles. Two hookers walked in off the street with a horny john and gave him some behind a statue of Christ with blood all over the front of it from a dude who had just got his head cracked during a scuffle.

It was like the set of an incredible Fellini wet-dream, and it went on and on with the sights and sounds interlacing into surreal harmony, and everyone moving, watching, seeing it all, and no one afraid, but laughing joyfully, happy, and now and then a scream followed by a hushed silence with everything still for a moment until the person who screamed would laugh and give away the joke, and it would all get back to normal again with the music wailing, moaning for a lost soul, loud like tears, as the faces bobbed up and down in a sensual parade of assumed freedom taken, making it all one big happy prickly pussy crab-lice moment of eternity.

The press got wind of the goings-on at the Invisible Circus, of course, and showed up with photographers and television news cameramen, but no one would talk with them and they just hung around bug-eyed, ogling the activity with their mouths gaping. The cops also came with several fire marshals who brought court orders that ordered the building vacated immediately because of an assortment of violated regulations which presented fire dangers, such as the mountain of plastic in the basement. Needless to say, the officials of Glide Church, who had been hovering on the brink of cardiac arrest all night, were relieved by the court orders which were announced throughout the building over the PA system and in bulletins handed out by the John Dillinger Computer Service around 4 or 5 A.M. that Saturday morning.

During the eight or nine hours since it began, over twenty thousand people had passed through the Invisible Circus and there's no telling how many would have finally showed, if it had been permitted to continue. When it was forced to end, the few thousand who remained went out to the Pacific Ocean to herald the dawning of the sun, and to roast pork sausages over a bonfire for breakfast, listening to Michael McClure play his autoharp and sing his song, "Oh, Lord, Won't You Buy Me a Mercedes Benz" with Freewheelin' Frank singing, too, and beating on his tambourine. Even though a dozen reporters spent nearly two hours at the church, not one line was written nor one word spoken about the Invisible Circus in the news media. It had been too incredible to explain, and so it and the fantasies that were realized during its brief existence became personal memories cherished by the people who were there and were part of an event, the likes of which has never been seen again in the city of San Francisco.

The Invisible Circus proved to be a much-needed respite for Emmett who got himself blind-wasted, but was back on the street the next afternoon with Tumble, delivering the Free Food to the throng in the Panhandle. A few Diggers, like one talkative twenty-five-year-old named Tobacco, got it together during the week and hustled rent money for several crash pads. There were three on one block alone and they slept over 120 people a night with only two rules enforced: no needles or sets of works and no weapons allowed. Besides the four or five people who lived at and operated each of these crash pads, there were few others older than eighteen. They were runaways.

The runaway situation had become critical since the Human Be-In, with the kids not only running away from something but running to something. The myth of the Haight-Ashbury had been manufactured to appeal to the young and they were running as fast as they could to it. White middle America was outraged that their children were leaving, and since a runaway has no constitutional rights, and is merely the property of his parents, they demanded their return. The liberal Democratic senator from Connecticut, Abraham Ribicoff, proposed a bill which would have brought the FBI into the search for runaways and further called for a computerized system of federal investigation on behalf of "American motherhood" and its preservation. San Francisco Juvenile Court Judge Ray J. O'Conner became publicly irate and said that all the Digger leaders should be jailed for contributing to the delinquency of minors by harboring runaways.

There was a montage of runaway photos tacked to the "Wanted" bulletin board at the park police station and Police Chief Cahill ordered his men to begin "daylight raids" along Haight Street. These raids were quickly renamed "haul-ins" by the kids because the coppers would sweep everyone up off the street, not just the very young suspected runaways. Within a short time the S.F. police department formed a special team to conduct these haul-ins which also rousted kids sleeping at night in Golden Gate Park. This tough special cruising force was named the S-Squad or the SS, and each member of this team had a particular fondness for cracking their billy clubs upside the kids' heads.

The SS didn't discriminate either, they arrested everyone, even a couple of HIP shopkeepers and a couple of their straight customers. It was getting to be bad for business and the HIP merchants formed another ad hoc committee for police-community relations. They were aware of the power base the Be-In gathering had afforded them and they spoke with Chief Cahill about the overzealousness of some of his men in enforcing Penal Code 370 or public nuisance, on persons who had money in their pockets to spend in their stores. Afterwards, they held a press conference stating that they were all going to work together to solve the problems that were occurring in the Haight-Ashbury and the chief publicly agreed to see them whenever a discussion would be helpful. The newspapers quoted the merchants as saying it had been a "cordial, meaningful meeting" and carried a story listing all the HIP merchants' names, the names and addresses of their shops and what was sold in each of them. The papers also mentioned a statement by one of the owners of the Psychedelic Shop who proposed to arrange for some sort of a finger signal and mantra chant with Allen Ginsberg to clear the streets, so that whenever P.C. 370 was being violated, the crowd would disperse as soon as the signal was heard, and no one would have to be arrested.

Well, that never happened but the HIP merchants did sponsor a Council for the Summer of Love, which was supposed to have been a service to aid the thousands of kids who were coming to the Haight when school let out. It just turned out to be a clearinghouse, however, for a bunch of bad artists and their equally bad art. The only thing the council tried to do on behalf of the expected hordes was ask the city to purchase an outlandish tent larger than two football fields where a hostel could be set up for the kids to crash. Since the size of the tent seemed so preposterous, they didn't get it, and of course they naturally never thought of hustling the bread for it themselves. The Haight Independent Proprietors also created the HIP Job Co-op to locate employment for those who wanted it. The trouble was that most of the jobs available were for unskilled labor or office workers, and since the kids had a better educational background and were white, they took the openings away from the unemployed minorities. Even the post office jobs promised to San Francisco's blacks during the "riot" were given to the newly arrived hippies because of their higher scores on the department's examinations. This aroused the black and Chicano communities, causing friction and animosity between them and the longhairs who began arrogantly to consider themselves the "new niggers."

The apprehension generated by the approaching so-called Summer of Love also led to the creation of three other organizations which were regularly funded by proceeds from benefits, as were all of the community's organizations, except the Diggers. The first of these organizations was Happening House founded by Leonard Wolf, a professor at S.F. State, who once pleaded to be arrested during a naked dance recital by Jane Lapiner at the Straight Theater on Haight Street, to publicize his solidarity with the community. And he was. In fact, he was the only person arrested, the coppers finding it difficult to refuse him, since he kept insisting. Afterwards, he opened Happening House with a few of his fellow academicians and they called it a "community center," but it was really only a teaching venture where faculty members from S.F. State taught classes, and their college students planned artistic diversions for the amusement of the kids who were flocking to the district.

Huckleberry House, the second organization, was as lame as its name. It was started with money from the Glide Foundation which also salaried the staff of ministers who operated it. It was basically a referral center where some runaway kids would come when they became disillusioned with the Haight-Ashbury. Their parents would be notified, and the kids would be given room and board for a couple of days, until their family made the necessary arrangements for their return home. It was a nice, mild, safe, responsible way for the church to become involved in "hippiedom" and the hierarchy was probably glad that the turnover at Huckleberry was as slight as it was. But, no matter how minimally, it did relieve a desperate situation.

The last of these enterprises was the Switchboard. It was also a referral center, but really worked as an answering service for messages from parents to their runaway kids. Each week, they published a long list of names in the Bay Area underground papers like the Berkeley *Barb*, notifying persons that they had received messages for them. The more relevant side of the Switchboard functioned by locating bed space for travelers in volunteer crash pads, and advising people in trouble about "free" lawyers, and providing a "free" bail service in collaboration with the Vista O.R. Project. The Switchboard was the only one of these operations that did any amount of substantial work for the welfare of the Haight community.

The Diggers had developed their medical services and health examinations at the Free Frame of Reference to a point where some of the doctors were even making house calls to treat people who were too sick to move, or had too many sick children at home to leave their house. These services were not restricted to the hip alone. The word about them spread among the other poor people, the blacks and Chicanos, and they, too, took advantage of the free health care. The doctors were mostly young and worked as residents in various hospitals around the city. To protect themselves from any sort of possible malpractice suit, they had a form mimeographed which each of their prospective patients had to fill out, giving the doctor involved permission to treat him. None of the patients ever complained about any treatment they'd received, and in fact they had nothing but praise for the doctors. A large part of the antibiotics and other medicines used in the treatment of the patients was hustled by a few nurses and the doctors themselves from the pharmaceutical houses in the area.

One of the heads of San Francisco's health department, Doctor Joel Fort, approved of these types of medical services, even though the Diggers had no facilities to speak of, but he was soon removed from his position on account of his "liberalism" and replaced by Dr. Ellis Sox who became quickly known as L.S.D. Sox because of his campaign against the Haight-Ashbury. He would make outlandish statements to the press about the health conditions in the Haight, claiming the possibility of dangerous outbreaks of every disease carried by rats from the bubonic plague to leptospirosis and sending teams of inspectors into the district to examine the private sanitation of private house interiors, while never enforcing any of the regulations against the filthy neighborhood businesses and restaurants. Since the landlords wanted to break the leases with the hippies, who had been the first tenants in years in most of the buildings, and rent to secretaries and junior executives who would pay higher rents, the health inspections served as justification for the eviction notices that usually followed.

During this same time, a doctor named David E. Smith became friendly with Professor Wolf and set up an infirmary at Happening House which he modeled after the Digger operation. At first, everyone was glad about this new medical service and was happy that there was another benefit for the people, but those feelings soon changed. Everybody became disheartened when Smith, M.D., began his own self-aggrandizement with even more sensational press releases than L.S.D. Sox. He talked about an epidemic of "marijuana cough" and about drugs only he seemed to know anything about. One of these he called Love Juice, which he said was made by mixing DET with DMT — a concoction invented by syndicate mobsters in the East who brought it West to peddle in the Haight-Ashbury.

Smith, M.D., seemed to be more concerned with the pharmacology of the situation than with treating the ailing people who came to him for help. He seldom prescribed anything more beneficial than aspirin or thorazine, while keeping a log of his activities and compiling a mound of statistics about drugs and their abuse, which he used in his pitch for the funding of his own medical clinic, separate from any other facility. He had only been at Happening House for six weeks when he had raised enough money to open that kind of operation and cover the cost of paying himself a salary. It was an apartment on the second floor of a building on the corner of Haight and Clayton streets and he converted it into an office complex which he called the Haight-Ashbury "Free" Medical Clinic. But it was far from being free. Just because no one was made to pay a fee when they went there, didn't make it a "Free Clinic." On the contrary, the patients were treated as "research subjects" and the facility itself was used to support whatever medical innovations were new and appropriate to the agency. And at least once a week there'd be an interview with David Smith, M.D., in the newspapers, or on the television, or in the folds of some national magazine, like *Life*, in which he'd expound on his feelings toward such dangerous drugs as STP, or B-2, a combat weapon and incapacitating agent created by the U.S. Army which was somehow being sold in hip communities across the country.

Everyone was sad that the doctor contented himself with making speeches about drugs like "68" which nobody had ever heard anything about, instead of seriously devoting himself to the care of the community's health. It was also a waste, as well as a shame.

Besides the H. A. Medical Clinic, the district sprouted a group of short-order lunch counters which sold "Loveburgers" and "Love Dogs" and gave away a "Love Guide" to the HIP shops. Film producers, like Sam Katzman, used the community as a location for cheap, Hollywood quickie-films like *The Trip* and a young entrepreneur started a firm that rented one or more hippies for parties called Hire a Hippie Unlimited. Storefronts in the area were being leased for forty thousand dollars and Grayline ran a bus tour through the district for tourists. Droves of evangelists descended on Haight Street to bring the young people closer to Jesus, and the S.F. police department jumped on the publicity bandwagon by organizing a series of ridiculous narcotics raids for reporters, which only netted an ounce or two of grass. An example was the "Super Jean" fiasco where the cops claimed to have broken up one of the Bay Area's biggest dope rings but really only arrested a harmless pothead.

The street people of the Haight reacted to the police harassment with Sleep-Ins at night in Golden Gate Park to protest the city's ordinance against such activities, and with Mill-Ins at the main intersections of the district to demonstrate for the repeal of Penal Code 370 and express their belief that "the streets belong to the people!" Realizing that the overly centralized Haight-Ashbury was only necessary for the shop owners, the older residents of the area — folks who had been there a while and had their own pads — started to move away to Marin County and Berkeley, trying to get out before the "Summer of Love" arrived. The underground press continued to ignore things like this migration of the old-timers from the Haight and remained concerned with other, more frivolous matters. For example, the straight merchants in the district tried to con everyone into believing they'd get high from smoking dried banana peels and the underground papers got wind of the story. The Berkeley *Barb* even devoted its entire center fold as a pullout, which explained various recipes for browning and baking the banana skins and described several methods of smoking them, once they'd been dried.

A thing like that would have been funny but it happened all the time, causing the Diggers to blast the underground press for printing nonsense rather than publishing the news the people had to know, and serving the people they claimed to represent. The Diggers also called for a conference among themselves, the HIP merchants, and anyone who was actively involved in the Haight-Ashbury, to discuss what could be done for and about the waves of young immigrants heading for the district. Because it was neutral territory, the basement of Glide Church was used for the meeting, which was more than well attended. The main figures or speakers at the conference sat on a dozen or more chairs that were arranged in a circle in the middle of the one hundred fifty to two hundred spectators. Emmett sat next to Tumble, Coyote and the Hun, facing the editorial staff of the S.F. *Oracle* and the members of the Haight Independent Proprietors association.

The meeting began with Coyote asking the shopkeepers what they planned to do about the continuing constant assault on the community by the cops. He was answered by one of them who read a proposal that had been adopted by the HIP merchants' recently formed organization, The New Community, and drafted by its Ad Hoc Committee for Better Police-Community Relations. "We invite all law enforcement officers, news personnel, firemen, health inspectors, judges, barristers, detectives, narcos, military personnel, and state and local government representatives and their families to join us for a meal — a dinner — to advance our understanding of each other and promote community goodwill and service."

Emmett couldn't believe he heard that and said so. "Are you serious! Haven't we been through that 'Take a Cop to Dinner' rubbish before? You gotta be kidding! When are you guys gonna take your fingers out of your assholes and —"

Another HIP merchant interrupted by commenting, "We used 'Love' successfully in dealing with the media during the Human Be-In, and Tim Leary said that if we continued to share our love with the other establishment agencies, and with the persons who run them, we'll eventually win our right to —"

Emmett jumped up, cutting him off. "Lookit, nobody wants to hear that dribble, understand! The only relevant thing to our situation Leary ever said was that 'Tune-In, Drop-Out' metaphor of his, and the only right anybody'll get by following his advice is the right to go mad — to become a gibbering idiot! What do you think we are, chumps? We don't wanna hear that shit! You're the only ones doing

292

well by 'Love,' and all we wanna know from you people, you who're using the Haight-Ashbury as a marketplace to sell your cheap artifacts of the so-called New Consciousness, is what and how do you intend to affirm your responsibility to the community? Huh? How?"

A bearded shopkeeper muttered something about the HIP Job Co-op being affirmation enough of their responsibility to the community.

Emmett remained standing and shot back, "Yes, the HIP Job Co-op! That's a fine example of what's going on here. Sure, it manages to get some helpless runaway girl a job. A job in an attic-sweatshop making dresses for a dollar an hour! Say it takes her two hours to make a dress. That's two dollars, right? Well, then the people who employ her — the incense-burning hippies — take that dress 'n sell it for twenty-five or thirty dollars. After a while she gets disillusioned about this kind of short action and she drops further into the street. Then, we end up with her. An' that's where your HIP Job Co-op's at, motherfucker!

"You HIP merchants and some of you other people around here have done the most to build the myth of the Hippie-Longhair, the incense-burning, bead-stringing freedom, and now you ain't doin' a goddamn thing to cope with this immigration crisis you ticked off. You ain't concerned about it, are you? What are these kids goin' to do, when they get here 'n find out that the myth is just that — a myth? There are already enough hungry confused people on the street and now there's going to be a lot more. An' you cloud-dwellers better come up with some alternatives about what to do about 'em 'n cut out all this metaphysics shit you're all so fuckin' fond of 'n quit playin' Monopoly or someone's going to take it personal 'n stuff an I Ching up yer ass like a suppository!"

As soon as Emmett sat down, the two brothers who owned the largest and most successful of the HIP shops agreed that the hippie world was being marketed without conscience, and promised they were going to limit their commercial operation and turn the back half of their Psychedelic Shop into a "calm center," so that the kids could wander inside off the street and meditate in pleasant surroundings. The proposal made Emmett bow his head in disgust and hold it with both his hands, wondering what preposterous, lunar logic could inspire anyone to think that a "calm center" would even slightly alleviate any of the problems which had to be faced in the district. He looked up after a moment at Tumble, who was flexing his mouth and jaw muscles with contempt for the silly proposition, and they both shook their heads at one another as the Hun mimicked applause, offering a heavily sarcastic, "Terrific! Terrific!" He went on to explain some of the Diggers' plans for dealing with the summer months, concluding by asking the Haight Independent Proprietors to aid in any way they felt they could.

The merchants reacted with approval for the ideas he spelled out, but announced that the association had previously decided, as a group, to concentrate all their financial assistance on helping Doctor Smith's H.A. Medical Center, the HIP Job Co-op, Happening House, and the Council For The Summer of Love projects, which they thought would be able to handle satisfactorily the influx of young people arriving during the next few months. They did remark that if the Diggers could continue their "exemplary, charitable work," all the better! But, of course, their HIP association wouldn't be able to afford much in the way of aid to the Diggers because of its already overburdening economic involvement with the aforementioned social-activist organizations.

Emmett felt that did it. There was no reason to continue the meeting. It was over and he ended it. "Uh-huh! You're all going to financially ensure the existence of a pharmacist's center for the research of drug abuse and abet his persistence in building a career for himself, an employment agency which either places runaways in lowly sweatshops owned by the same employers who supervise the agency itself, or gives out-of-town college kids the jobs that are needed by San Francisco's poor, an uninspired experiment in education conducted by the academic community of multi-million-dollar universities, and a platform for the city's unimaginative artists to display their utterly bad art! You're going to allow these pitiful scams to remain throughout the summer to hopefully provide you all with a façade which'll represent your deep, heartfelt concern and empathy for the community. A community which ain't gonna keep letting you guys off forever because you play stupid. No, someday it's gonna find out that all of you have been aware, conscious of what you were doin' 'n not doin' all the time. That you knew what you were makin' all along! An' when they do find that out, they're gonna bomb everyone of you 'n your shops, 'n the banks where you been depositing the money you been makin' out of existence! Blow every fuckin' thing away! Everything! Ha! Ha! Come on, let's get outta here!"

The Diggers got up together and headed for the staircase, glaring back at all the eyes who followed them out the door. Someone in the crowd wished aloud, "Peace, brother. Peace." Emmett stopped, turned a quarter of the way around toward the direction from where the voice had come, and answered the farewell: "Peace? Listen fella, there's very few people that have peace on this planet, why should we?"

Then the Diggers left, and Tumble remarked as they walked up the stairs, "That's one room we forgot to include in the Invisible Circus. They're talkin' up more fantasies in there right now, than a lot of the people carried out that night in the church next door!"

Unknown to Emmett and the others, there were several reporters in the crowd during the rap session, and that weekend the underground weeklies hit the streets with news of the Glide Church meeting spread all over them. One was headlined CLASS WAR IN THE HAIGHT, and detailed a story about a battle that was being waged between the street people led by the Diggers, and the monied, hippie class headed by the Haight Independent Proprietors. In several different newspaper accounts of the Glide meet, the name Emmett Grogan was connected with a description of a "demanding spokesman who had the aquiline nose of a leader" and he was spot-quoted and misquoted.

In one version which appeared in the Los Angeles *Free Press,* and was written for that paper's three hundred thousand readers by Jerry Hopkins, Emmett was said to have actually threatened the HIP merchants with the bombing of their stores, unless they gave over a percentage of their profits to the community. It even further alleged that he inferred a bombing had already occurred, and would be followed by another, if the shopkeepers didn't comply with his demands for the distribution of a part of their wealth to the people.

Needless to say, Emmett was flipped out by the generally false coverage, and in the case of the "bombing threat" story, at least one instance of vicious, deceitful reporting. He wanted to choke every one of those lying, yellow-journalist throats, bend all their fingers back until the bones of their knuckles snapped, rip their snide tongues out of their smug faces. That's what really got him crazy about these small-time reporters who took cheap shots at people — their petty self-regard for their own minor self-importance. "Who the fuck do they think they are? Making up all that shit that never happened, putting words in my mouth that no one ever said? Everybody who reads those fuckin' lies is gonna believe we're all just another bunch of punk anarchists who want a piece of the pie, a bunch of lames who're just jealous of the bread the HIP merchants are makin' n are tryin' to extort some of it for ourselves. Those cocksuckers!"

Tumble pointed out that the HIP merchants had spread the word about the Glide meeting, and that was the reason there were so many people there, making it impossible to screen out the press. "Yea, 'n they probably called the papers themselves, too. Why else would reporters from L.A. be there?" They continued talking about it for a while, but there was nothing they could do to prevent what was already taking place because of the rotten newspaper stories.

The pay phone in the Free Frame of Reference kept ringing with reporters who hadn't been at the Glide meet and wanted an interview from "Emmett Grogan" or another "qualified Digger spokesman" for a follow-up story on the "Class Warfare in the Haight-Ashbury." Emmett didn't speak with any of them. He wanted to keep his low profile as a leader as low as possible. He also felt that if any more publicity was created about himself, it would just serve to cause friction between him and the rest of the Diggers who would feel he was copping the spotlight all for his own. No, the Diggers didn't need any more notoriety and everyone seemed to be in agreement about it.

However, when KQED, the city's National Educational Television station, called asking whether Emmett Grogan was available to be a guest on a talk show, Coyote answered, telling them that Emmett wasn't, but that he was and they invited him. He rationalized his appearance on the show by saying that he had accepted as a member of the Mime Troupe and not as a spokesman for the Diggers. Emmett watched and listened to him say, "Hippies are the fruit of the middle class and they're telling the middle class that they don't like what has been given them by the American Empire's materialistic-oriented society. And what had begun as a cultural revolution is now shaping up and heading toward a revolution of violence."

Coyote delivered his statements in a suave, earnest style, and Emmett enjoyed his charming performance because he knew that all the Bay Area New Left men and women who were watching the show were comparing Coyote's quick, intelligent rap and hip-radical appearance on the tube with the dry-crusted, moth-eaten riffs and stale, banal manners of the corny, run-of-the-mill, radical spokesmen who were regularly on the tube. He was colorfully different from these stiffs, all right, and a dynamically-hip spokesmen, but as a leader he was in trouble. His problem was that he couldn't say

"No!" — didn't know how to say "No!" — and it was something he had to learn.

Emmett was also a bit confused by the very fact of Coyote's appearance on the tube. The two of them had often talked about the necessity of remaining anonymous, as had the Hun and the others, and about the need to safeguard against revealing any secrets with slips of the tongue. But, while Emmett had protected his anonymity, Coyote, the Hun and some other Diggers had repeatedly gone on radio, given interviews, and now appeared on television. The academician-director of Happening House, Leonard Wolf, had even gotten Coyote and the Hun to tape separate biographical interviews with him for his book of hip profiles, *Voices from the Love Generation*. Emmett wondered if they just meant it was dangerous for *him* to make appearances in the mass media. He didn't know, but guessed it was all right for them to deal with the matter in any way they wanted, as long as they didn't cause too much attention to be focused on the Diggers. And they didn't, and he forgot about it.

During the week, the brother-owners of the Psychedelic Shop limited their operation and redecorated the back of the store as a "calm center" where the kids quickly began congregating to sit around on the floor cushions all day long, trading dope with each other. Emmett was arrested twice on traffic warrants, which had been issued because several tickets for parking and moving violations had been ignored. Rather than waste the money paying fines, he paid the penalties by spending a few days in the city prison. When he got out, he found that the Frederick Street Free Frame of Reference had been closed by order of the fire and health departments. In addition to the cop standing outside the vacated premises, the landlord had placed a wire gate over the rear windows and had padlocked the front door. He had received a score of complaints from his other tenants about the Diggers and he was obviously relieved about the city's order calling for their eviction.

Slim Minnaux, Coyote, Tumble, the Hun and other Diggers had already located another place, however, and it was only a few blocks away on the corner of 901 Cole Street. It was a much bigger and better location with a second floor balcony-promenade surrounding the entire inside, and front walls made of banks of connecting plate-glass windows, leaving the whole interior visible from the streets outside. The free store was soon stacked with goods and crowded with customers, two of whom were hefty, black welfare mothers who hung around day in and day out, waiting for prize merchandise that they could take and sell to one of the secondhand stores in the Fillmore for some extra cash. Whenever anyone said anything about this practice to either woman or one of their many friends, the reply was always a sharp, *"Well, it free, ain't it? What you talkin' 'bout, then!"* These two women did offer a service of their own to the many girls who needed it: they generously advised their hip sisters about the machinations of the California welfare system and held a daily class in how to overcome the bureaucracy's basic stinginess and comfortably provide for themselves and their children.

The free store took up two thirds of the main floor, which had a wall dividing the other third of it into a separate annex or room where Judith organized a free sewing shop and tie-dye center. In there, women were taught how to tie the knots and use the dyes, and people would come in off the street all day long to have the clothes they were wearing mended, or made more interesting with colorful tie-dye patterns and sewn-on patches. Because the free center was the only place in the city actually producing tie-dyed garments at the time, several persons approached Judith and the others with business offers, asking them, for example, to tie-dye a few dozen white T-shirts for a percentage of the profits of their sale at one of the HIP clothing shops. But none of the women would go for it, noting that if they were in it for the money, they would open their own shop and make a mint from their unique designs, especially since they were the first fullscale tie-dye operation in the Haight. Soon, their tie-dyed clothing was seen everywhere in the district, and a handful of girls who learned the basics from Judith and the others, went to work for the HIP shops, mass-producing tie-dyed items into a fashion that eventually spread throughout the country.

Every evening, the doctors who were working with the Diggers would provide their free health service which was named "Home Free." Besides the medical examinations and free treatment, a legal aid service was also set up, which made a group of lawyers available who were willing to defend community residents free of charge. These lawyers did much to make the city aware of the rampant police brutality and harassment tactics being carried out against the longhaired residents of the Haight, and also gave the kids a feeling of security that someone would be in court to defend their rights whenever they were swept off the street by the cops.

The Hun hustled the rent for the storefront and even signed the lease for it himself, which surprised Emmett and some of the others at first. But it soon became obvious that the Hun considered it his free store, and sort of took charge of the place. Before, he only visited the two previous free store operations and occasionally dropped by the Panhandle Free Food at 4 P.M., keeping himself from getting too involved while maintaining his position at the S.F. Mime Troupe. But, when it became apparent to him that the Diggers weren't just a short-term thing, he embraced the Cole Street free store as theater and approached the project with a different attitude. The place was named "The Trip Without a Ticket," referring to a comment made by an anonymous Digger regarding his unwillingness to pay for someone else's trip — to end up as the price of someone else's ticket. The Hun used the store as a base for implementing his ideas and thoughts on guerrilla theater. He resigned from the Mime Troupe, and with his old lady, Judith, tie-dying in the next room, he spent all his time at the Trip Without a Ticket, observing everything that took place in and around the free store as theater, and the people involved in the activity as protagonists, actors consciously and unconsciously improvising their roles in life.

Most of the life-roles people were cast in had been given to them — handed to or forced on them by one hierarchy or another, or by circumstance which seldom made them interesting, simply "types." But the people who hadn't acquiesced, the ones who hadn't accepted the worn-out, hackneyed caricatures as substitutes for their lives, for their being themselves, were interesting and exciting. These people were conscious of their existence and aware of the roles they were playing. They were "life-actors." And Emmett, the Hun, Tumble, Coyote, and several others would get into long discussions about life-actors and about why the things they did were to be considered "life acts." All the conclusions they made during these sessions were utilized in the Cole Street free store operation, and everyone connected with the Trip Without a Ticket worked hard at creating theater all the time.

Emmett and Tumble continued with the Free Food, driving the produce around in the pickup, along with the goods for the free store. Tumble wanted to organize a fleet of trucks, so that the entire city could be covered in the same day and so that Haight-Ashbury, which seemed to be ignored by the privately owned municipal sanitation company, could be cleared of the mounting piles of garbage. Slim Minnaux and Coyote went on tour with the S.F. Mime Troupe, performing in the brilliant and skillful production of *The Minstrel Show*, an old-time, darky, vaudeville-musical of poignant, biting social criticism, with all the performers in blackface, so that the audience remained unable to tell whether they were black or white until the actors removed their gloves at the end. The Hun developed his concepts about theater in "his" free store, and from mental notes he had taken during discussions with Emmett, Tumble and many others, he wrote an intelligent, perspicacious manifesto, which was published as an eight-page pamphlet by the Communication Company and distributed freely throughout the city. It was also mailed to different parts of the country, giving the Hun a reputation among the Tulane Drama Review Set, as one of the brighter, more ingenious, radical minds involved with "liberating theater" in America. The perceptive article was also an attempt at correcting the underground's concept of the Diggers, as a "hip Salvation Army." It was an effective piece to a degree, and naturally, entitled "Trip Without a Ticket:

Our authorized sanities are so many Nembutals. "Normal" citizens with store-dummy smiles stand apart from each other like cotton-packed capsules in a bottle. Perpetual mental outpatients. Maddening sterile jobs for straitjackets, love scrubbed into an insipid "functional personal relationship" and Art as a fantasy pacifier. Everyone is kept inside while the outside is shown through windows: advertising and manicured news. And we all know this.

How many TV specials would it take to establish one Guatemalan revolution? How many weeks would an ad agency require to face-lift the image of the Viet Cong? Slowly, very slowly we are led nowhere. Consumer circuses are held in the ward daily. Critics are tolerated like exploding novelties. We will be told which burning Asians to take seriously. Slowly. Later.

But there is a real danger in suddenly waking a somnambulistic patient. And we all know this.

What if he is startled right out the window?

No one can control the single circuit-breaking moment that charges games with critical reality. If the glass is cut, if the cushioned distance of media is removed, the patients may never respond as normals again. They will become life-actors.

Theater is territory. A space for existing outside padded walls. Setting down a stage declares a universal pardon for imagination. But what happens next must mean more than sanctuary or preserve. How would real wardens react to life-actors on liberated ground? How can the intrinsic freedom of theater illuminate walls and show the weakspots where a breakout could occur?

Guerrilla theater intends to bring audiences to liberated territory to create life-actors. It remains light and exploitative of forms for the same reasons that it intends to remain free. It seeks audiences that are created by issues. It creates a cast of freed beings. It will become an issue itself.

This is theater of an underground that wants out. Its aim is to liberate ground held by consumer wardens and establish territory without walls. Its plays are glass cutters for empire windows.

Free store/property of the possessed

The Diggers are hip to property. Everything is free, do your own thing. Human beings are the means of exchange. Food, machines, clothing, materials, shelter and props are simply there. Stuff. A perfect dispenser would be an open Automat on the street. Locks are time-consuming. Combinations are locks.

So a store of goods or clinic or restaurant that is free becomes a social art form. Ticketless theater. Out of money and control.

"First you gotta pin down what's wrong with the West.

Distrust of human nature, which means distrust of Nature.

Distrust of wildness in oneself literally means distrust of Wilderness."
— Gary Snyder

Diggers assume free stores to liberate human nature. First free the space, goods and services. Let theories of economics follow social facts. Once a free store is assumed, human wanting and giving, needing and taking, become wide open to improvisation.

A sign: *If Someone Asks to See the Manager*
        Tell Him He's the Manager.

Someone asked how much a book cost. How much did he think it was worth? 75 cents. The money was taken and held out for anyone. "Who wants 75 cents?" A girl who had just walked in came over and took it.

A basket is labeled *Free Money.*

No owner, no Manager, no employees and no cash register. A salesman in a free store is a life-actor. Anyone who will assume an answer to a question or accept a problem as a turn-on.

Question (*whispered*): "Who pays the rent?"

Answer (*loudly*): "May I help you?"

Who's ready for the implications of a free store? Welfare mothers pile bags of clothes for a few days and come back to hang up dresses. Kids case the joint wondering how to boost.

Fire helmets, riding pants, shower curtains, surgical gowns and World War I army boots are parts for costumes. Nightsticks, sample cases, water pipes, toy guns and weather balloons are taken for props. When materials are free, imagination becomes currency for spirit.

Where does the stuff come from? People, persons, beings. Isn't it obvious that objects are only transitory subjects of human value? An object released from one person's value may be destroyed, abandoned or made available to other people. The choice is anyone's.

The question of a free store is simple: What would you have?

Street events

Pop Art mirrored the social skin. Happenings X-rayed the bones. Street events are social acid heightening consciousness of what is real on the street. To expand eyeball implications until the facts are established through action.

The Mexican Day of the Dead is celebrated in cemeteries. Yellow flowers falling petal by petal on graves. In moonlight. Favorite songs of the deceased and everybody gets loaded. Children suck deaths-head candy engraved with their names in icing.

Street events are rituals of release. Reclaiming of territory (sundown, traffic, public joy) through spirit. Possession. Public NewSense.

Not street-theater, the street *is* theater. Parades, bankrobberies, fires and sonic explosions focus street attention. A crowd is an audience for an event. Release of crowd spirit can accomplish social facts. Riots are a reaction to police theater. Thrown bottles and overturned cars are responses to a dull, heavy-fisted, mechanical and deathly show. People fill the street to express special public feelings and hold human communion. To ask "What's Happening?"

The alternative to death is a joyous funeral in company with the living.

Who paid for your trip?

Industrialization was a battle with 19th-century ecology to win breakfast at the cost of smog and insanity. Wars against ecology are suicidal. The U.S. standard of living is a bourgeois baby blanket for executives who scream in their sleep. No Pleistocene swamp could match the pestilential horror of modern urban sewage. No children of White Western Progress will escape the dues of peoples forced to haul their raw materials.

But the tools (that's all factories are) remain innocent and the ethics of greed aren't necessary. Computers render the principles of wage-labor obsolete by incorporating them. We are being freed from machinistic consciousness. We could evacuate the factories, turn them over to androids, clean up our pollution. North Americans could give up self-righteousness to expand their being.

Our conflict is with job-wardens and consumer-keepers of a permissive looney-bin. Property, credit, interest, insurance, installments, profit are stupid concepts. Millions of have-nots and drop-outs in the U.S. are living on an overflow of technologically produced fat. They aren't fighting ecology, they're responding to it. Middle-class living rooms are funeral parlors and only undertakers will stay in them. Our fight is with those who would kill us through dumb work, insane wars, dull money morality.

Give up jobs, so computers can do them! Any important human occupation can be done free. Can it be given away?

Revolutions in Asia, Africa, South America are for humanistic industrialization. The technological resources of North America can be used throughout the world. Gratis. Not a patronizing gift, shared.

Our conflict begins with salaries and prices. The trip has been paid for at an incredible price in death, slavery, psychosis.

An event for the main business district of any U.S. city. Infiltrate the largest corporation office building with life-actors as nymphomaniacal secretaries, clumsy repairmen, berserk executives, sloppy security guards, clerks with animals in their clothes. Low key until the first coffee-break and then pour it on.

Secretaries unbutton their blouses and press shy clerks against the wall. Repairmen drop typewriters and knock over water coolers. Executives charge into private offices claiming their seniority. Guards produce booze bottles and playfully jam elevator doors. Clerks pull out goldfish, rabbits, pigeons, cats on leashes, loose dogs.

At noon 1000 freed beings singing and dancing appear outside to persuade employees to take off for the day. Banners roll down from office windows announcing liberation. Shills in business suits run out of the building, strip and dive in the fountain. Elevators are loaded with incense and a pie fight breaks out in the cafeteria.

Theater is fact/action

Give up jobs. Be with people. Defend against property.

Emmett appreciated the Hun's brainy semantics and his sapient analysis of the Diggers as life-actors, and their activities as theater, because it provided a very good cover and satisfied the curiosity of the authorities and general public, as well as exciting the hipper members of the New Left. Of course, it was just a superficial description of what was really going on — the same thing as classifying the Saint Valentine's Day Massacre as "Theater of Cruelty." It was simply an account of the casual, outward, conscious style of the Diggers and some of the things they did, and not an examination of the heightened awareness of the intrinsic essence of the Digger operation or its motives. The elements of guerrilla theater and street events were merely accessories contingent upon the fundamental reality of Free Food, the free stores, the free goods, and the free services made available to the people. The San Francisco Diggers attempted to organize a solid, collective, comparative apparatus to provide resources sufficient for the people to set up an alternative power base, which wouldn't have to depend on either the state or the system for its sustenance.

When the people — meaning the various ethnic, lower economic, oppressed minorities of the United States of America — were able to drop out of the system and become independent within their own power structure, rather than dependent on the state's, then they would have the chance to eliminate their considerable racial prejudices toward one another, and unite themselves as a single popular class to fight for equality, forming a united front to abolish all classes through a prolonged series of uprisings embodying a socialist revolution.

That's what the mass media called the philanthropy of "a Haight-Ashbury band of hip social workers without portfolio" and the Hun "Guerrilla Theater" and Emmett "Free Food."

"Some Salvation Army!" Emmett often thought to himself. But he was glad that the mass media joked about the Diggers as mod monks and that the so-called heavies of the New Left slighted the Diggers as lightweights and claimed that they were politically naïve and irrelevant. He was glad because it was going to be a long haul of determined action and not just one "revolutionary" outbreak by a bunch of leftist rhetoricians, before the stage would be set for the total reconstruction of society into a popular social democracy. And Emmett knew that if he revealed the innermost truth of the Diggers and their work, it would have only provoked their annihilation by the government. So, even though it was frequently hard to do in the face of the smug logorrhea chattered by punk radicals, he just kept his mouth shut and tried to take care of business.

It was after the Hun's piece had been printed, and while Emmett was up at the Communication Company's office-pad that he discovered *Ramparts* magazine was preparing a story about the Haight-Ashbury, concentrating on the district's leading figures, their political attitudes, or lack of them, and focusing special attention on the Diggers, particularly Emmett Grogan. Fully aware of *Ramparts'* facile dependency on muckraking and frequent reliance on falsifying "for the good of the cause," Emmett figured he had to try and do something about the article or at least the parts about him and the Diggers. He thought about it for a moment and decided to appeal to the editors on the grounds that, if they publicized him and the Diggers as radicals in their national magazine, it would seriously interfere with their work and definitely hamper them in their attempts to serve the people — the same people whom the magazine purported to wholeheartedly support.

Tumble drove Emmett over to North Beach and dropped him off a few blocks away from the magazine's offices before continuing on home. As he walked over to *Ramparts*, Emmett wondered whether the editors would sacrifice the kind of colorful copy that satisfied the voyeurism of their readers, "For the good of the cause." But he never got to ask them that question because, when he turned the corner onto Broadway, he saw a scene going down which made talking to ink-slinging calumniators seem less important that day than usual. At first glance, it looked like a stick-up was being pulled with a short, black kid holding an M-1 across his chest and standing on the bottom steps of the front entrance to the *Ramparts* offices.

A squad car had just driven up and Emmett planted himself against a parked truck for a better view, as one of the cops got out and walked over to the young, armed black, leaving his partner to burn up the police radio frantically reporting into headquarters with his eyes bulging and his face all twisted, flapping words at the microphone. An older black man, about thirty, with a moustache and a .38, came out of the front door and stood on the landing at the top of the steps, watching the cop talk to the younger guy below him. In addition to both having guns, the two blacks were dressed the same way, in car-length black leather coats and black berets. Emmett looked closely at the older one and remembered seeing his picture somewhere wearing similar clothes. It only took him a moment to match the face with the name of "Bobby Seale" and quickly figure out that whatever was happening had to do with the "Black Panthers."

The little dude with the M-1 snarled something about the Fifth Amendment to the cop, who took a couple of steps around him and up toward the landing, until he was right next to Bobby Seale. Seale stared at the copper real hard, which made the cop visibly nervous causing him to talk louder, shrilly like he had a red-hot poker up his ass. "Who's the leader?" he asked and Seale answered by gesturing toward himself. The copper said something else which angered Seale, and he stuck his face into the cop's, yelling, *"Goddamit! I don't want to talk to you! So, you can go away from here! Go on, git!"* And the copper apologetically muttered, "Oh!" turned around and walked back down the steps, as more cops drove up.

These were plainclothesmen, and as soon as they got out of their cars, they began talking heatedly among themselves. One of them pointed towards the little dude who looked very young, but they didn't do anything, just kept on talking back and forth to each other. More of them drove up and Bobby Seale opened the front door at the top of the stairs and shouted inside. Two more black men came outside carrying M-1's and stood with him on the landing.

Warren Hinckle III, the bilious editor of *Ramparts* at that time, appeared behind the glass front doors, wearing a moth-eaten patch over one of his eyes. A police lieutenant clocked him standing inside the entrance and called out to him. When he stuck his head out between the doors, the copper asked him what the trouble was all about, indicating the gun-toting blacks. Hinckle III replied that there was no trouble and assured the lieutenant that everything was under control. This got the coppers mad because it meant they couldn't make any moves on their own, since the person who owned the place had no objection to the guns, making it perfectly legal for the blacks to be carrying them, unconcealed.

Television news cameramen and reporters began showing up to take part in the drama, and one of them, of course, immediately attempted to provoke a bit of action by trying to barge up the stairs and inside *Ramparts*. But an M-1 blocked him and he was shoved back down the steps. The newsmen didn't seem to understand that if their self-righteous arrogance provoked any shooting, they'd end up shot like everyone else — the only difference would be that the bullets that hit them would've been fired by both sides. Apparently, they were either unconcerned about this fact or simply too fucking dumb to realize that nobody was kidding except them, because when three or four more bereted black men came outside of the offices, and they all started to leave, surrounding a striking black woman like guards, an ABC newscaster and camera crewman almost incited their own demise.

Bobby Seale was coming down the front steps alongside a bulky, muscular, strong-looking black man of medium height who was carrying a shotgun. Emmett recognized him from a newspaper photo as Huey P. Newton. The two of them were walking one on each side of the black woman, holding up magazines in front of the cameras and blocking any attempts to photograph her, when one of the TV crewmen grabbed at the periodical Bobby Seale was using for cover. Seale grabbed it back from the asshole and Huey P. put his magazine over the lens of the camera trying to focus in on the woman who obviously didn't want herself filmed. Suddenly, the six o'clock newscaster, who was standing by the camera with his microphone ready, caught hold of the magazine and pushed it into Huey P., striking him in the stomach. At this point, two other blacks, who were trailing behind, scooped up the woman and hustled her across the street into a waiting car.

The newscaster's blow was slight but it was plain to see that the blatant audacity of it outraged Huey P. and he dropped the magazine and belted the newscaster square in his mealy face, knocking him flat up against the wall which rebounded him into his cameraman. All the cops tensed up and their hands began fidgeting around the butts of their holstered pistols, and Bobby Seale motioned to his brothers that the time seemed appropriate to split. But Huey P. didn't think so and he stood out in front of the others, pointing at the dazed newscaster and shouting for the cops to *"Arrest that man! He assaulted me 'n I want you to arrest him! Go on, arrest him GODDAMMIT!"* The cops all began flipping the straps off the hammers of their .38's, and Huey P. jacked a shell into the chamber of his shotgun and ordered his brothers to *"Spread out!"* behind him, and they did, facing the cops with their M-1's gripped tight in both hands and angled toward the sky.

It looked like it was all going to blow any second, and Emmett moved off the sidewalk into the street, positioning himself for cover out of the line of fire a hundred feet away on the other side of the row of parked cars. Just then, a fat, chunky cop started coming forward yelling, *"Don't point that shotgun at me! Stop pointing it at me, I tell ya!"* The traffic coming from and going to the Bay bridge was bottled up at the freeway ramp behind Emmett, and the copper's screaming had all the people in the cars staring with their mouths open wide in utter disbelief at the showdown occurring only a short distance away from them.

There were about thirty cops all crowded together on the sidewalk now, and the chunky one kept hollering and making threatening motions towards his pistol, and Huey P. held his ground in front of him with his shotgun tilted, ready for action. He wasn't going to let that fat cop bully his way any closer and he started challenging him to remove his gun from his holster. *"Go on, you big fat racist pig, draw your gun! You goddamn coward! Go on, I'm waitin'!"* The fat cop froze, startled at being called. The other cops began moving away from him out of the line of fire, and when he saw that, he sort of sighed, hung his head low and gave up. Huey P. Newton laughed in his face.

All of a sudden, one of the black guys who walked over to the car with the woman and the other two, came running across the street screaming, *"Please! Please! Don't shoot! The cops are goin' to kill all of us! They're going to kill all of us! Please! Please!"* Huey P. shouted for him to shut up his sissy-ass mouth, but it was too late. His cry-baby bleating had startled the cops back into their bully-boy attitude, and they began to come on cocky once again, trying to take command of the situation by ordering the Black Panthers not to move or wave their weapons. But Huey P. didn't go for any of their shit and he replied back to them with a bit of his own advice, "Don't any of *you* go for *your* guns!"

Everything became shattery at his response and seemed about to burst into a shoot-out, but the Panthers began backing off, having successfully made their point several times over: that cops aren't so quick to push people around when they aren't the only ones armed. The Panthers stepped carefully backwards, easing their way through the traffic and moving across the street where they quickly got into their cars and split, to the amazement of all onlookers. When they had driven away, the cops broke into a flurry, scurrying all over the place to their squad cars. The sirens all began blaring, as they tried to bull through the jammed traffic — all the while radioing into headquarters about the two "carloads of niggers driving around the fucking city with loaded guns!" It really got them crazy.

Emmett had also been sincerely impressed and he walked over to one of the staff writers who was now standing on the front steps of the *Ramparts* building with a group of his coworkers and asked him what it was all about. He was told that the Black Panthers were accompanying the widow of Malcolm X, Betty Shabazz, as her bodyguards, while she was in the city for a speaking engagement and an interview with the magazine. Emmett also discovered that Warren Hinckle III and the other editors were all too busy enjoying their vicarious experience to want to diminish "their" few precious moments by talking about the particulars of the "Hippie" cover story. Through the office's plate-glass window, Emmett could see them swilling from paper cups, laughing and slapping one another on the back at having been participants in the memorable put-down of the cops, and he decided to let it go for a while and split back to the Haight for something to eat.

Emmett first heard about the Black Panther organization back in October '66 around the same time Free Food started. Bobby Seale had been a stand-up comedian and Huey P. Newton a tough, street blood, when the two of them met as students at Merritt College, where they both became student leaders. It was after they dropped out of the school, to work as community organizers for the North Oakland Poverty Program, that they created the Party by writing out its ten-point platform and program. The "points" were divided into "What We Want" and "What We Believe" categories of practical, specific demands for things they felt were needed, and should be — things that were guaranteed by the U.S. Constitution and had been demanded by black people for a hundred years, things that were directly related to what they had before they were forced to leave Africa. The language used to express the ten points was concrete, easily understandable, and seemed to cover all the ground concerning a man's right to existence on the planet, be he black or brown or whatever.

Emmett felt that the articulation of the Party's platform and program was far more inspired than the choice of "Black Panther" as a name. It was too narrow a title for a group which stressed "intercommunalism" and besides, one of the Ku Klux Klan's first dens or local chapters in nineteenth-century South Carolina had also been named after the same predator — one of the only animals to kill for sport, not just food. Emmett assumed that the name had been chosen as a follow-up to the SNCC group, which had been formed to protect black people and civil rights workers in Lowndes County, Mississippi, during the early sixties, and not in emulation of the "Black Panther squads" of the U.S. Army's special forces division. He also wondered how all the low-money people in America, not just blacks, were reacting to the Party's alien titles of "Chairman" and "Minister of Defense" assumed by Bobby Seale and Huey P. Newton.

These were only minor details when one considered that the Black Panther Party was not fundamentally a black racist organization, not racist at all. They worked hard in the Bay Area black community to teach the people their rights, especially their right and duty to defend themselves against brutalization by the "racist power structure." They did this by patrolling the black neighborhoods on weekend nights with loaded weapons to make sure the people weren't terrorized or murdered by some "racist pigs" or local "coon-hunters," the way they usually were in Oakland on Friday and Saturday nights. Their concern for self-defense, with arming the people, and with guns branded them undesirable to the moderate and cultural nationalist black organizations, but that was okay with them because as far as they were concerned all them "Negroes" and "jive-ass esoteric motherfuckers" weren't taking care of the needs of the people, and were just out for whatever they could get their hands on for themselves. This attitude gave the government and the spot-quoting press the opportunity to paint the Black Panthers as a ruthless gang of vicious, black-racist, terrorist, back-shooting cop-killers, rapidly making them targets for every trigger-happy lawman and every political candidate who was riding on the back of the "law 'n order" frenzy which was spreading throughout the country.

At that same time, the cultural revolution was in full swing in the People's Republic of China, and the news media in San Francisco was always full of stories about the Chinese waving their little Red Books. Since there was so much free advertising going on, Bobby Seale and Huey P. Newton, like two free-enterprising young men, took advantage of the situation by standing on street corners, selling the *Quotations from Chairman Mao Tse Tung,* using the scratch they made to buy shotguns and pay the rent on their storefront-office, where they recruited their cadre, many of whom were still in their teens, like little Bobby Hutton, the first rank-and-file member of the Black Panther Party.

They were an energetic and ambitious black revolutionary organization, and it was soon after they put the cops down in front of *Ramparts* that the magazine's only black staff writer, who interviewed Betty Shabazz that day, joined the Party. He had just been paroled from San Quentin where he had done an eight-year-bit at the bottom of the prison's pecking order as a rapist, which afforded him plenty of quiet time to write a book. His name was Eldridge Cleaver, and he was given the title of Minister of Information after he helped Chairman Bobby and Minister Huey P. begin publication of the Black Panther Party newspaper which transformed the organization into an armed propaganda unit no one could ignore. No matter how outlandishly and crazily Cleaver jerked off his rhetoric, there was always something in the paper which made its existence worthwhile to the black community and to the country's other low-money people as well.

Emmett understood what the Panthers were doing and respected them as brothers in the same struggle.

David Smith, M.D., still managed to maintain his quest for public recognition, striving toward "success" at his Haight-Ashbury Medical Clinic, which he continued to insist was "Free" simply because no one was made to pay him a fee for being a research patient. One of the clinic's statistics briefly interrupted the "experimental" operation, until he was apprehended and singled out for the press by the doctor, as an example of the type of psychosis which he claimed was rampant in the Haight-Ashbury. The statistic called himself Joe SuperSex and he gained his notoriety by stealing a box of urine testing tablets from the H.A. Medical Clinic and giving them away as dope, poisoning several young people. But he wasn't the only one to nearly tarnish the clinic's "wholesome record of unselfish humanitarian service" — there were many others. A few of the more cunning were imposters, posing as doctors working on the staff of the H.A. Medical Clinic and going around making house calls. It was a pretty funny scene, at least if you weren't one of the young females who'd had the canals leading from their uterus to the external orifice of their cloacae probed in examination. It was shortly after the series of imposters that the clinic discontinued making any house calls. The Diggers wanted this Mickey Mouse operation replaced with really "free" competent medical clinics in the Fillmore, Potrero, Mission, Hunter's Point-Bayview, and Haight-Ashbury districts.

One afternoon, Emmett left the truck with Tumble and took some time off from the Free Food to see whether anything could still be done to effect some sort of control over the *Ramparts'* Hippie article which had him deeply worried. He went over to the Communication Company to see what Claude and Chester knew about it, and found them mimeographing a letter from Neil Cassady in Mexico to Allen Ginsberg, who was preparing to leave San Francisco to return to New York by way of the college lecture circuit.

Neil Cassady was an intense, strong forty-year-old with rippling muscles, an unequaled tolerance for alcohol and drugs and a voracious desire to communicate everything he knew, or whatever he was thinking about, to everyone all the time. He was a gypsy-traveler with no money in any bank, and the hero of at least one book, who lived his life with a velocity that seemed to preserve his prime, but would have killed most men twenty years younger. The style of the letter offers a brief but accurate glimpse at Cassady's makeup and a quick poetic insight into one of the things which concerned him besides pleasure, which was always on his mind until he died from it a short time later.

San Miguel'Allende, GTO — MEX 3-31-7 6p.
i know it looks like my mind's gone — but No — still, i'll recapitulate. But first — Bro. against Bro., almost, in USA. (Bloodless for most part)

Civil was as Rite Rite cleans up for year or more — i.e. R. Reagon now as governor has already appointed Big Business/man as Labor Commisioner, Welfare Chief is a Lawyer who opposed welfare, State Conservator (redwoods) is a big lumberman; real estate czar is supposed to be fare housing crusader, as Clemency Sect., and ex-D.A. who favored capital punishment — get the idea? — then, late '68 — not slow, but fast adjustment as new awakening spreads throughout our culture — meantime, watch out, fishes coming to the surface are to be caught — hooked if your beard's long or hair more than 3 inches. all emotion, no reason, etc. etc.

Many hip folk thought that same way at the time, which was why the Communication Company was printing up the note. After they completed running it off, Emmett got Claude and Chester to take him over to see Warren Hinckle III at his house, so he could find out whether the editors of *Ramparts* were writing a serious, investigative report on "hippiedom" or just using the fashionable popularity of anything "hip" to boost their circulation and pocket more subscriptions.

Claude and Chester were an odd couple but appeared made for each other, working well together. Claude was a Topanga Canyon beat from Los Angeles who seemed to be trying to wear out his black Mennonite clothing and extra-wide-brimmed, flat, high-crowned, western-style hat — the kind worn by morticians in the Old West. To add to his graveyard look, he sported thick, black-lensed glasses to partially correct his near blindness, and at the same time, prevent anyone from seeing his eyes. He was only a little over twenty but was married to a pleasant woman nearly twice his age, and even though he seldom talked, he made most people laugh just by being around. He was also a slick hustler and a talented mechanic, skillfully maintaining the mimeograph machines that had been bought on time from the Gestetner Corporation but never paid for, leaving their repair entirely up to him.

Chester, on the other hand, didn't have any mechanical ability and was too obvious to be a good hustler. He was in his early forties, but the speed with which he carried out most of his activities gave him a much older look. His frequently haggard appearance blended in with the prevailing taste of the youthful "hippies" and none of them ever called him "Pops." Being a veteran of the "underground culture movement," though, he might have enjoyed and probably would have nurtured such a fatherly tag. He also considered himself an unofficial historian, having authored a sensational catalogue of footnotes on the Beat Generation as well as several other cheap paper pulps about the drug-oriented, bohemian way of life to appeal to the insatiably prurient appetites of middle-class suburbia. While Claude operated the Gestefax stencil maker and printed up handouts on the machines, Chester would scour the Haight-Ashbury district, looking for "hot" news items which he jotted down in one of the many composition books he carried around in a weathered canvas bag that hung from his shoulder by an adjustable strap which had been in the same position for about fifteen years.

The Communication Company had been modeled after the Digger Papers' operation, and the service it provided the people of the Haight was exceedingly valuable because the news it disseminated was for the most part, essential and needed. The only trouble was that both Claude and Chester also worked on the staff of *Ramparts'* advertising department where they spread all the newsworthy information about the Haight-Ashbury to the magazine's editors, as a matter of conversation. Since Chester had a well-marked and unrelenting ambition to become a famous underground journalist, Emmett suspected him of feeding those editors too much "news" about the Diggers that was nobody's business. So, he remained wary, and considered himself alone, when he entered Warren Hinckle III's house with the two of them. His sole mistake was in going there at all.

Hinckle III glad-handed him at the door and invited them all inside an expensively furnished, tastelessly comfortable salon where Emmett planted the grimy seat of his dungarees on a large, clean, white-tufted sofa. After he was asked his preference, he was handed a giant tumbler filled with practically half a pint of Southern Comfort and several square chunks of ice, which clinked around in the thick, heavy glass, making that rich, solid sound you hear in Hollywood movies. It was all right and Emmett enjoyed the juice, even though he had to use both hands to drink it.

Warren Hinckle III was pouring himself a fist of whiskey from a bottle on a portable liquor cart. He appeared to be one of those middle-aged, heavy-drinking, college fraternity types who operate as journalists in the radical-liberal political arena for their own personal prestige and self-importance, as well as for the money they make from their usually short-lived publications and the exaggerated influence they feel they assert on minor public officeholders. Their motives are seldom, if ever, based on any progressive, humanitarian or beneficent interests. Hinckle III began by informing Emmett that the article in question had already been written and was presently at the printers where the plates were being offset for the presses. He also noted that there was only a passing mention of Emmett and the Diggers in the story, and that there was nothing to worry about. The conversation continued with Emmett having downed his first glass of booze and working on an equally large second, while chatting about his career in the army and telling a few humorous stories about the work he was doing as a Digger in the Haight-Ashbury.

He only stayed for about twenty, twenty-five minutes, and two weeks later, *Ramparts* magazine was on almost every newsstand in America with a picture of poster-artist Stanley Mouse on the cover and "A Social History of the Hippies" written by Warren Hinckle III inside. The article amounted to nothing short of stone fabrication — a farfetched piece of snide bunko about a fictive "summit meeting of the leaders of the new hippie subculture," which the Diggers had supposedly "convened in the lowlands of California's High Sierras during an early spring weekend" to discuss "the state of the nation of the hippies." As a preface to the plated concoction, there was a full-page photo montage of the alleged "Dramatis Personae" of whom "Emmett Grogan" was one, representing the Diggers. The picture they used was a snapshot taken by a girl one day, when he delivered some Free Food from the produce market to her commune. It was a black-and-white shadowy print, while all the others were bright, clear technicolor shots, and its murkiness was a consolation, because few people who didn't already know him could recognize him from it. But it did capture his image all right, showing him in his fatigue jacket wearing his IRA cap at an angle.

As soon as Emmett saw that March issue of *Ramparts,* he knew it meant trouble. And he became more certain of the ticklish situation it was to cause, after he read the two pages of copy which described him in unreal, outlandishly romantic terms, as the Frodo Baggins of the Haight-Ashbury and "roguish hero and kingpin of the Diggers." The profile of him also outlined several of the anecdotes which he told to Hinckle III during their brief drinking session, and concluded with a lambent flame of intellect by advising the hippies that if they didn't start actively protesting with marches and rallies, instead of just living their protest, more and more youngsters would begin "to drop out of the arduous task of attempting to steer a difficult, unrewarding society" and the driving would be left to the

Hells Angels. Whatever that meant, besides being an obvious attempt to strike terror into the hearts of lily-white liberals with a vision of descending anarchist hordes of outlaw bikers stuffing their wives' vaginas with Nazi swastikas and jamming motorcycle chains into their rectums with mental institutional force.

But Emmett wasn't concerned with the basic absurdity of the article's premise. He was preoccupied with the problem that was certain to stem from the publication of the crap in the first place. The kind of trouble he was anxious about wasn't anything the authorities or their law-enforcement flunkies might do, but rather, the brand he felt sure was going to be put on him as a result of the magazine's cheap glorification of him as a mock-hero. It was bound to cause friction with his brothers and sisters, and sure enough, when he walked into The Trip Without a Ticket, everyone acted like he had betrayed all of them by revealing himself as "their leader." Persons on the street greeted and waved to him with false respect but his own people felt cheated, and cold-shouldered him.

He tried telling them what happened, that he had nothing consciously to do with the setup, but they kept coming on like he intentionally hurt them in order to accept the plaudits of strangers. The HIP merchants were also undoubtedly convinced that he was behind the *Ramparts* story from its inception because the magazine spot-quoted him putting them down heavily.

The situation was bad and bound to get worse. All the people whom Emmett worked with and had turned on, even Tumble and especially the Hun, felt they had been used for his aggrandizement and fame. He decided to split, to hang it on the limb, until things cooled and the impact of the *Ramparts* story faded. He talked it over with the women who assured him the Free Food would continue, as long as somebody trucked the produce to them to be cooked. Tumble said he would see to it. Then, Emmett walked over to where Super-Spade, the black grass dealer, was standing in the cold, predusk fog outside the Mnasdika clothing shop on Haight Street and borrowed three hundred dollars from him, as a long-term loan.

Back at his pad on Fell Street, Emmett laid out his plans to Natural Suzanne, removed five hundred tabs of LSD from the one thousand he'd stashed before the Human Be-In, as a source of emergency funds, and flew to New York for half fare, using a youth card someone had given him for Christmas.

No sooner had he gone, than the San Francisco press and other newsmen from the national mass media swooped down on the Trip Without a Ticket looking for a story. They all wanted to interview the "longhaired hippie" who scoffed at his generation's talk of "love" as being merely a bullshit shuck, and who claimed that the Haight-Ashbury was nothing but a "Love Ghetto" populated by middle-class kids who were having "an adventure of poverty" and whom he fed from his Digger free soup kitchen. He was handsome with "the aquilined nose of a leader" and he had a good, jaunty, rebellious image about him, with that bold cap of his, and most of all, he wasn't Jewish! Yes, he had definite qualities and was good "star" material, but "where'd he go?"

When anyone inquired about him at the Trip Without A Ticket or any place in the Haight-Ashbury for that matter, they were laughed at and told "Emmett Grogan" was just a myth and didn't exist. The FBI eventually came around and took the Hun back to their offices for "routine questioning" about the Diggers, their Free Food and free store operations, and about the whereabouts of "Emmett Grogan." The Hun was careful to maintain the Salvation Army–Goodwill cover line, while expounding on his ideas for new wave theater, and claiming that the Diggers had simply made up "Emmett Grogan" as a mythical, nonexistent, heroic figure to fool the press. As for the photo in *Ramparts,* the Hun offered that it was a picture of an actor who had been a member of the Mime Troupe a while back, and had played a small part in an adaptation of Brendan Behan's *Borstal Boy.* The eight-by-ten glossy, he said, had been given to the radical magazine as a lark to perpetuate the legend of the nonexistent "Emmett Grogan." The FBI regarded the long-haired, shaggy Hun with such contempt and ridicule that they unquestionably fell for his "myth-making" line, and they dropped the "Emmett Grogan issue," filing it away as a prank.

Emmett returned to New York City on a Sunday. He always seemed to travel from place to place on Sundays because there were fewer people around, and it had become a habit when he was in Europe. He seldom if ever made any moves on a Saturday, which he considered a wrong time of the week for him, a jinxed day, for no other reason than that he was born on a Saturday, whatever the fuck that had to do with anything. But it did.

On the plane, he sat across the aisle from a young college student type dressed in a conservative suit and vest which he tried to academically liberalize with a wide-knot, cotton tie that had Day-Glo flower patterns all over it. His hair was also a little long in the back, but just a little, and he was intently reading Warren Hinckle III's fake "Social History of the Hippies" in *Ramparts.*

Emmett looked at this kid who would graduate to a mild, pageboy haircut and tie-dyed clothes within the next year or so, and he watched closely as the student read the last two pages of the article which were about him. It certainly seemed strange to Emmett to be sitting next to somebody who was reading about him and smiling and chuckling aloud over a few of the things he'd done as a character in some clown's idea of a short story. Very strange! For a moment Emmett wanted to take his IRA cap from his back pocket, put it on, tap the kid on the shoulder, point to the name "Grogan" in the article, then point back to himself and laughingly say, "That's me!" But only for a moment, because that wasn't what it was all about. "Nobody's on the make in this game. At least, I ain't," he thought to himself, and if he had been, he wouldn't have to tap no college kid on the back to be recognized, that was for sure. Every student in the country would know what he looked like, if he wanted them to. "Every motherfuckin' one of 'em!" he assured himself before falling asleep in a seat designed by a moron.

When he got to New York City, Emmett called up Candy Sand, a young, bouncy-cute woman who was secretary to an American literary figure and a sympathetic twenty-four-year-old with whom he had only recently become friendly over the long-distance telephone. She had gone to the same midwestern school with one of the women who now worked with Digger Free Food on the West Coast, and she told Emmett, "Of course, you can come over!" And further invited him to stay in her place for as long as he needed to, because she had lots of room, she said. "And lots of warm, bubbling hospitality, too," Emmett thought.

Her pad was on the Lower East Side at the corner of Second Street and Avenue A on the third floor of a turn-of-the-century tenement walk-up above a Spanish grocery store. It was rent-controlled at sixty-five dollars a month and the roomy interior had been inexpensively, but wisely renovated with natural colored, rough pine covering all the walls and cabinets, hiding the cracked plaster and peeled paint underneath, and giving the whole place an expensive, West Village modern look. It was also very comfortable and intelligently furnished with lots of cushions and soft places to sit or lie, and a red checkered cloth over one table to tell you it was part of the kitchen, which wasn't closed off, but open-walled toward the large front room. The light that came through the many clean windows on every side, filled the space with an airy, Scandinavian feeling.

It was hard to believe that it was just another walk-up pad in a Lower East Side tenement, and Emmett was very glad he was offered such pleasant digs where he could lie back and relax, refreshing himself with a few days' vacation for the first time in six months of Digger-free activities.

Candy was as sweet and cheering as her apartment, and she was graciously considerate of her guest, staying out of his way and giving him plenty of quiet time to rest and think about what he was into. Emmett thought quite a bit about that during those few days, comparing the Diggers with the other politico-social activist groups and their ideologies. He even came up with a name for the integrated assertions and aims of the Diggers' visionary theorizing. He called it the ideology of failure — "You got nothin', you got nothin' to lose." That's why everything the Diggers had done and did was "free."

Emmett also thought about all the radicals who were always so quick to call him and the Diggers anarchists, simply because they didn't openly espouse one revolutionary program or another. In their narrow, bigoted view, one had to be either a Marxist, Leninist, Trotskyite, Maoist, or hold to some combination of these ideologies, or else be politically categorized an anarchist. All those radical labelers ever did was read, write about or discuss the different revolutionary theories, dealing with semantics, while Emmett and the Diggers refused to discuss publicly or define the political dialectics of the work they never ceased to continue to do. Work which was alien neither to Marxism or Maoism, but at the same time needed neither to endure.

The Diggers didn't particularly care which ism they were putting into practice with their work and were also, in fact, mildly amused at the word-slinging radicals, who were as full of puritanical shit as the country's right wing was cowardly absurd.

Emmett lay lazily around the pad for three solid, quiet, fat days before he finally got an urge to go out and gander around the neighborhood. He decided not to look in on his family this time for many different reasons, but mainly because he didn't feel like making apologies for his new life-style. He tried to locate Billy Landout, who was off somewhere apparently traveling around the country. So, he was more or less alone, with everyone he now met in New York being a fresh face with no reference to his past.

The streets were windy with smoke from the boilers, and cloudy with flakes of soot from the Con Edison plant on Fourteenth Street, which blackens the sky and pollutes the air of the Lower East Side. He walked north on Avenue A towards Tompkins Square Park, past bundled-up longhairs and thin-clad Puerto Ricans bopping along with their fists clenched inside their pockets against the cold, on their way to cop. He bought a *World Journal Tribune* and an East Village *Other* and entered an old-time ice-cream parlor and lunch counter called the Sweet Shoppe, where he sat in a booth and had a cup of coffee and a toasted English muffin.

It was two o'clock in the afternoon, and he felt good and rested from the long hours of sleep and doing nothing but eating Candy Sand's cooking and thinking about the past six months, which now seemed so long ago to him. But a short article in the East Village *Other* newspaper snapped it all back home. On the top of one of the inside pages was a story about the Glide Church meeting between the San Francisco Diggers and the HIP merchants that had been held several weeks before. The story was the same one which had been printed in the L.A. *Free Press* under Jerry Hopkins' byline, and it told about Emmett Grogan threatening to bomb the HIP merchants' shops if they refused to kick back some of their profits to the community.

Emmett got real fucking sore about the article all over again. He paid his check and steamed out of the Sweet Shoppe along Avenue A towards Ninth Street, and the address he read on the underground newspaper's masthead. The East Village *Other*'s office was a storefront across the street from Tompkins Square Park and Emmett had no trouble finding it. There was a girl sitting at a desk which guarded the entrance to a back room where the next edition of the newspaper was being composed. Emmett told her he wanted to speak with the editor. She asked his name and "what about," and he said it was none of her business, and she replied that if he didn't answer her questions, he wouldn't get to see the editor. But he insisted, saying it was an "urgent personal matter," which seemed to make some sort of sense to her because she got up and went into the back room, giving him the cool eye as she turned.

The whole front portion of the outer office was crowded with back issues of the paper piled all over the floor, and the walls were entirely covered with the different poster-size front pages representing each and every edition of the newspaper that had been published since its birth. Emmett scanned the series of headline graphics papering the walls and noted that most of them dealt either with the bestiality or brutality of the police. He wondered whether the publisher and the editorial staff of the newspaper really hated cops that much, or were just catering to their readers, most of whom were students.

The girl returned and pointed him out to a paunchy, pale, bald-headed man in his early thirties wearing a baggy buttoned-down shirt turned brown at the collar by the stuffy steam-sweat-heat of three days' wear.

"Yes, can I help you?"

"Are you the editor?"

"I'm one of them."

"I want to speak with the person who's the head of this operation."

"You do, huh? Well, what's your name, and what's it you want to talk about?"

"The name is Grogan. Emmett Grogan, 'n what I want to talk about I'll tell the person in charge."

"I'll be right back," he said, and turned into the rear room.

The girl at the desk overheard the dialogue and was giving Emmett a different kind of once-over stare, now that she figured he was "somebody," but when skinhead returned with another dude, he told her to go for some coffee, and waited until she split before introducing the founder-publisher-executive editor of the East Village *Other*. Emmett immediately recognized him and his showy, auburn, handlebar moustache, as the guy had been bartender in Stanley's saloon on Avenue B, where Billy and he often went drinking during his leave from the army a year ago. But he didn't mention this to either of them, just shook their hands and stated his beef, pointing out that the article was stone bullshit and asking them if they understood the position it had placed him in, now that he was in New York.

"You see, when the mugs who own the territory around here find out that I'm in the neighborhood, they're going to think from reading this crap about me threatening to bomb the HIP shops out in San Francisco that I'm going to try the same thing here, try to strong-arm the hippie merchants who lease store space from them, the same way 'n they're going to get mad when they think that I'm muscling in on their thing, because that's what it comes down to in their eyes. There's nothin' political or social about it to them — just some guy tryin' to get a piece of the action 'n they're gonna take that personally — very personally, 'n fuck knows what'll happen! Now I gotta go see that they get set straight about what I'm into before they get the wrong idea about why I'm here, 'n do something I'll be sorry for — so, if anybody asks you about this article about me, you just tell 'em it was a mistake, 'n it's bullshit, because that's all that it is — bullshit! An' don't print anything else about me, either, understand. I don't need, want, or care for my name being in newspapers. So do me, and in the long run yourselves, a favor 'n don't write anything about me because you'll only interfere with what we're trying to do for the hip community, 'n I'm sure you wouldn't want to do that. Good! So we understand one another. Be seein' you." And he shook their hands again and left before they could reply or even say anything.

Later that night Paul Krassner, the lampoon editor of the satirical, leftist periodical newsprint magazine catcalled *The Realist,* which government authorities continually contended was blatantly pornographic, told Candy Sand about a community meeting being held that night in a Lower East Side loft to discuss the problems facing the "hip community of the East Village." Emmett had met Krassner in San Francisco when he was taking a VIP tour of the Haight-Ashbury with some of the HIP hierarchy, and he was impressed at how a man of such tiny physical stature could be such a gross smart-alec. He burned some of Krassner's money in response to a series of journalistic inquiries and also gave him some free acid, the mere giving of which had, for some cryptic reason blown Krassner's mind. So Emmett went to the community meeting with Candy Sand and Paul Krassner, where he was introduced to the East Coast's version of HIP. They weren't united under the same or any other name but were certainly uniform in their "hippie" manner and style, affecting a similar and possibly weightier identification with the psychedelic experience.

Most of the thirty-some-odd persons present at the meet were in their twenties, had been raised in upper-middle-class environments, had finished college and had dropped out of their establishment futures because they were bored and wanted a chance to put creativity back into their lives, to make an art out of living. They were more wordy and less spaced out than their San Francisco peers, and since the Lower East Side didn't exactly border any spectacular woodland or rolling green hills, they were more concerned with community politics than with the ecology of their environment. Even though they tried to dress up their surroundings by constantly

referring to them as the "East Village," the neighborhood still refused to allow them room enough to escape or transcend the reality
of its mean streets. The Haight-Ashbury, its population being
largely hippie flower children, encouraged the myriad activity of the
esoteric sciences, but the Lower East Side, peopled predominantly
by blacks and Puerto Ricans and some Eastern European immigrant
families, most of whom were either Ukrainian or Jewish, was a low-
money environment where people thought flowers were a luxury
because they died too easy, even when they had thorns, and transcendentalism an annuity a person got from the government when
he reached age sixty-five.

No there was scarcely enough room to breathe, much less make
believe on the Lower East Side, and Emmett listened as the talk
centered on the ill treatment the arriving hippies were receiving
from their black and Puerto Rican neighbors. He kept quiet until
he felt that those assembled were wrongly, but eagerly convincing
themselves that the Puerto Ricans and blacks were prejudiced
against them solely because of their long hair and life-style, making
them the country's "new niggers." This conclusion, that the hippies
were the new niggers of America, seemed to delight the group, and
they quickly began exchanging different tales of outright bigotry
they had experienced.

Their histrionics in describing their scenes of personal discrimination sounded like the blackface hokum of the San Francisco Mime
Troupe's minstrel show with lines like, "You know what really gets
'em crazy? Bare feet! When they see a longhair walkin' down the
sidewalk in midwinter just after a snowfall with no shoes on, it
blows their minds! 'N they don't know how to deal with it, so they
get angry!" "Yea, 'n when they always see longhaired dudes with
their arms around hippie chicks, it gets 'em wild because they know
the hippies are makin' it together 'n they're not gettin' any!"

Emmett interrupted and ultimately curtained the show by simply
pointing out that the Lower East Side of Manhattan had always
been a tough neighborhood and in tough neighborhoods the new
kid on the block always got beat up and ". . . in this case, the hippies
who're moving into the tenements now are the new kids on the
block, that's all, 'n they're being put down just like every other new
group that moved there before 'em, 'n that may not be the way you
want it in the East Village, but as long as the East Village is part of
the Lower East Side, that's the way it's gonna be. But there's more
to this trouble than the traditional old-slappin'-down-the-new rou-

tine or the longhairs freakin' out the shorthairs crap you've been shootin'." And he continued his rap by laying down a few of the other beefs that the longer residents of the neighborhood had against the hippies.

They were especially upset, he said, because of the hippies' readied willingness to pay the higher rents and whatever-the-market-will-bear prices fixed by the slumlords. This overcharging, coupled with the fact that the poor residents of the area knew damn well that most hippies came from the wealthy white suburbs of their American dream and therefore didn't really have to live in their low-class poverty neighborhood, aggravated their already deep dislike for the outgoing, jubilant hippie style, and ticked off a series of violent outbreaks to "wipe the smiles off their faces," because what the fuck were they so happy about anyway!

This spawned an attitude that the hippies could afford to be happy, paying the increased rents and inflated prices with "money from home," while the people who were really poor and not just "tripping," suffered the ironical burden of their presence. Thus they became the fair-game targets of people who needed some quick money fast, which was nearly everyone. The sight of a pair of well-fed hippies walking through the neighborhood, panhandling change against a backdrop of desperate bleakness may have appeared farcical to strangers, but to the people who lived their entire lives in the area, grew up there, it was a mockery, a derisive imitation of their existence and it got them angry. Plenty angry.

Besides this basic false role-playing of theirs and the increase in prices and rents they caused by moving in, Emmett went on to tell them that the hippies were also being blamed for the spreading of infectious hepatitis and venereal disease among the families in the area, as well as for the intensified police campaign of inundating the area with beefed-up squads whose patrols were spreading heat all over the place and putting an impossible strain on all illegal operations. This seriously hurt the community, because those "outside the law" activities were its financial backbone and constituted between 35 to 40 percent of the economy of the Lower East Side.

"So, as usual, it comes down to money again, but that's the way it's always been when a new bunch comes into a territory where another group has previously taken up residence, settled in, and has come to consider it their turf. The hippies present an economic danger to those people who've never been anything else but poor, and they've already proved to be a threat to the community in more ways than one. A threat not only to the neighborhood's flimsy economy, but also to the neighborhood people's values, hopes and dreams. You see, most of these people *want, more than any of you could ever not want,* things like a pre-fab house out in the suburbs or a pre-fab apartment or bungalow back in Puerto Rico. They're just like all the other lower classes that came before them, dreaming of becoming middle class with all the trimmings that go with it. The difference between the Puerto Ricans and the others before them is that the Puerto Ricans aren't white, so they've become static in the low-money bracket, but they don't smell as bad, therefore they're not going nowhere as fast as the black people and are being permitted token breakthroughs here and there.

"What I'm getting at is that their dreams of someday makin' it out of what they regard as a sewer are very important to them, 'n when hippies come along riffin' about how unhip it is to make it into middle-class society 'n how easy it would've been for them to make it, but they didn't because it was insignificant, these low-money people get confused and upset because here are these creepy longhaired punks who grew up with meat at every meal and backyards to play in and the kind of education which is prayed to God for, and they threw it all away for what? To become junkies like at least one member of every family on the Lower East Side? To live with garbage and violence and rats and violence and no heat or hot water and violence and disease and violence? Is that what hippies thought was the hip thing to do with their lives? Well, to these people and their sons and daughters who've had no alternative but to live their lives in the disaster of the Lower East Side, there ain't nothin' hip about junk or poverty or violence, and they have nothing but contempt for young, educated fools who think it's exciting to live in a world they really know nothing about, the kind of world these kids' middle-class parents built the suburbs to protect them from.

"However, these parents never figured their children would attempt suicide by scaling the fortress walls of suburbia and running to the ghettos which had become part of their generation's fantasies — fantasy ghettos like the Haight-Ashbury and the Lower East Side where sidewalks were more real than the lawns of Westchester and where people were red-blooded human beings, instead of blanched, bloodless, cardboard automatons. The poor have no sympathy for these young whites who're searching out what was kept hidden from them. They have none at all because of the hippies' arrogance, an arrogance they wear on their sleeves, an arrogance which mocks the poor for wanting what they've rejected, and insolently pities them for not comprehending or understanding the reasons why they left the 'American Dream' behind.

"So, you better face the straight goods, brothers an' sisters. You ain't the new niggers or spics, 'n you're never gonna be. You have too much to fall back on whenever you want to or have to — good education, a home, family, the color of your skin — 'n the people in the neighborhood know that, an' also that you're still the children of the ruling classes, whether you like it or not. As far as they're concerned, you're just having an adventure — an adventure in poverty which, if you aren't careful, may prove more real than you're ready to deal with."

The crowd in the loft didn't seem to like a thing Emmett said, primarily because he burst the underdog image they were casting for themselves. Nobody said anything after he stopped talking because, like it or not, everything he said seemed to be true. There was a silent pause for a moment, then a tough-looking Jewish bohemian woman in her late twenties asked Emmett what he thought could be done to relieve the troubled situation the hippies were facing in the Lower East Side and how they could hip the poor to the inherent lie of the American Dream and its middle-class accoutrements.

First of all, he said, they had to jettison the self-satisfying impression that they were the "new niggers" — which was going to be difficult. It was very comfortable on the bottom of the social heap where you could lie back, stay doped up and not accept any individual or community responsibilities, feeling perfectly hip about having been classed the new losers and doing everything by doing nothing to justify the classification. If they could get past that, Emmett continued, then they could apply their "fortunate" backgrounds in serving the needs of the neighborhood, not as "hip social workers," but as members of the community who wanted to develop it for themselves as a place where they could enjoy life and where their children could grow without being forced to attend the stifling institutions run by the city government.

They could start on their own by opening free day-care centers for the children, and later, free schools and free stores where they could hip the community to the truth about the American Dream and show them that the hippies weren't just passing through the neighborhood on a trip, but settling down and trying to build a life there for themselves. Afterwards, they could organize free block parties and free rock concerts and Latin festivals in Tompkins Square Park, and clean the streets and vacant lots of their garbage and abandoned cars, so they could be used by the people and their children without the danger of being bitten by rats. Then they could set about fixing up the tenements where they lived.

Someone who said he was a member of the Progressive Labor Party remarked: "That's all well and good, but don't you think that the people who will ultimately benefit from all this proposed cleaning up of the neighborhood and the renovation, say of the tenement dwellings, will be the persons who own all the buildings — the slumlords, and that if the area is made more pleasant, the people themselves will become more or less content with their situation and try to keep what they have, rather than revolt against the forces which keep them in oppression?"

"No!" Emmett fired back. "That's a trap: keep everything bad, in fact, make it worse to heighten the contradictions and educate the people, making them aware 'n letting them see the oppressor. Everyone vote for Ronald Reagan, so when he's governor of California repression will become real to the people and they'll rise up in revolution. Bullshit! They'll just turn in whoever's threatening them financially or personally, like the Jews on Long Island during the McCarthy fifties, and vote for Reagan again.

"People dig dictators and being told what to do, as long as they're benefiting from it, getting paid. As far as the Lower East Side slumlords go, if the streets of the neighborhood and the buildings get fixed up so they're pleasant and livable 'n the landlords try to evict the tenants who made the repairs so they can rent to faggots and secretaries who want a hip address, we'll defend ourselves and we'll kill them! It's as simple as that. An' don't anyone say that we won't be able to get at them because we won't be able to find out who they are or where they are. That's a myth! Because it's already been done before and will be again. We'll find out and don't nobody worry about that. We'll find out, even if they live in Dayton, Ohio, and we'll kill them. Once the people get it together and have a chance to live with a degree of comfort and in surroundings that aren't rat and disease infested and without having to scuffle all the time or hassle against impossible odds, nothing will be able to stop 'em until they get just as much as everybody else. Nothing! Until everybody's equal in a classless society and all have enough of what they need 'n nobody has to go hungry, so some fat man can eat baked Alaska at the Four Seasons, or his fat wife imported smoked salmon from Nova Scotia at Grossinger's.

"No, when the people get that inch they're going to want more than the proverbial mile. They're going to want all of it 'n the ones who own it are going to have to give it up or have it taken from 'em! 'N it's up to guys like me, up to us 'n others like us to get that inch for the people, so they can taste what it'll be like when those few who own everything are knocked out of the box, and the many can finally live like human beings, instead of like serfs in a kingdom run by a handful of aristocratic, robber-baron families. Up to ones like us, because we know about what low-money people can only dream about. We've experienced what they still hope for 'n we know what has to be done 'n how to do it.

"Most important, we don't have to do it. We don't have to do anything. We can survive comfortably without hardly hassling at all because we know how the monster works 'n thinks 'n we can manipulate it for our own ends. That's easy. But suppose we took it a step further 'n didn't fuck with it specifically for ourselves. Suppose we did what we know how to do for nothin', for no other reason than we know how to do it. Suppose we did it for free! Did what was necessary, so the people would have the inch they needed to get that first mile on the road to a social democracy, 'n did it all for free! We couldn't lose, 'cause when you start by doing it for free, for nothin', you got nothin' to lose and you're beyond the possibility of defeat! That's what's called the ideology of failure, and if you brothers and sisters would apply that to your lives and roles in the community instead of just playin' out your adventure of poverty, dead hands of fantasy, we'd be able to get it on in the Lower East Side, and rip-off that inch before anyone knew we weren't kidding! And the hippies would soon become an integral part of the community, rather than just depending on the passage of time to earn them acceptance."

Then Emmett spent an hour laying out what the San Francisco Diggers did in the Haight-Ashbury, explaining the overall difficulty of their work, and how they actually went about getting it all done. He was careful, however, not to give away any secrets or discuss how they obtained free goods by theft, because he didn't feel it was appropriate for a room full of people he didn't know, and in the end, would probably prove dangerous to him and his West Coast comrades. He did make a point though of showing the absurdity of the news media's description of the Diggers as "philanthropic do-gooders" and went on to explain the importance of anonymity in any attempt to achieve individual or collective autonomy.

All the thinking Emmett had done during his lay-up at Candy Sand's pad had charged him with a new surge of energy, and he rapped for over two hours. When he finished, there was nothing really left to say or ask, except the obvious question which each of the New York City hip people assembled in the loft that night to discuss their "community problems" had to ask himself: was he or she really serious and together enough to begin the difficult work of serving the needs of the unrewarding Lower East Side and its people for nothing, for free, totally and uncompromisingly free. It was a question no one asked out loud, for each person had to deal with the answer to that one himself, later, and alone. "For the time being, anyway," Emmett thought, and everyone adjourned downstairs to a bar for a couple of beers before going their separate ways.

The group crowded around Emmett because he impressed them with his rap, and they pressed him for more answers to questions no one should have had to ask. It was funny how people at first always thought of him as just another "handsome lug" and a gang leader because of his reticence and rough exterior, until he began to talk, revealing that he knew fucking well what he was doing and exactly how to take command when he had to. It always seemed to amaze them that he wasn't an illiterate imbecile or a dumb dead-end kid or something. He often wondered why they had that image of him, and concluded that it was part of a "noble savage" hangup which made them imagine him as some sort of existential primitive hero who depended on his primate instincts and not much else to fulfill his assigned duties given to him by some mysterious cabal of revolutionary intellectuals who sought a merger of hippie radicalism and New Left politics.

It was a joke, all right, and Emmett often used it on people who insisted he was a "truly great leader," by replying that he just took orders over a pay telephone in a prearranged public booth in whatever city he was in. "They just call me up 'n I go 'n do what they tell me."

Less than a week after the "community meeting" in the Lower East Side loft, Emmett stopped into the East Village *Other* office to look over the latest issues of the few West Coast underground weeklies which were available there. He had been on the phone with his brothers and sisters in San Francisco several times during the previous two weeks he had spent in New York, and they'd told him everything was going all right with the Diggers and the Haight-Ashbury, but he still wanted to see what else had been occurring in the West. The skimpy and often fallacious news about those other activists and happenings was to be found only in the self-indulgent folds of California's underground press which, much to his regret, Emmett was forced to skim for some slightly relevant information.

He never got around to looking at those California weekly undergrounds, however, because his eyes caught a glimpse of something tacked to the side wall as he was walking into the back room: the galley proofs of the copy for the next edition of the East Village *Other*, and one article's headline caught hold of Emmett and stopped him. He read the bold letters, DIGGER LOGORRHEA, and pulled the copy off the wall, reading it fast and wincing every time his eyes ran over the name Emmett Grogan. The girl who was sitting at her desk post got up and went into the back room when she saw from the look on Emmett's face what might happen.

He was furious! Not only had they not respected his appeal to them not to print anything about him in their paper, but either through incredible stupidity or malicious intent, they falsely reported the rap he gave a week before at the loft, attributing things to him which neither he nor anyone else had ever said that night. The article quoted him as having declared that an outbreak of terrorism was necessary to educate the people and force the exploiters of the counterculture to their knees to make them give away all their goods to the community for free! It was outrageous! Stone fucking lies, all of it! He could hardly believe it, and when he looked up and saw the skinhead editor standing there alongside the handlebar-moustached founder, publisher, executive editor, he blew it!

"What the fuck do you call this shit, huh? Well, what is it, motherfucker!"

"Hey, listen, this is a newspaper and we print . . ."

"You're fulla shit, it's a newspaper! It's a bloody, fuckin' rag!"

"We print stories our readers expect us to."

"Stories?! Fuckin', bold-faced, bullshit lies, you mean!"

"Look, we were there, both of us, 'n we heard . . ."

"You heard shit! There's not one thing in here that's even half true. It's all lies and you know it. Both of you motherfuckers know it! Nothing but fuckin' lies!"

"Look, that's debatable. You may think . . ."

"Debatable, my motherfuckin' ass! It's all a lie, 'n a stupid, dumb corny pack of lies, too! You're not even slick enough or smart enough for anyone but a cretin to believe that I said any of this bullshit, that anyone even talks this way! You two-bit mother-fuckers!"

"Well, why don't you write your own version of what happened and we'll print both of them to let . . ."

"You'll print shit! Nothin'! you hear! Not one fuckin' word about me, ever!"

The two of them looked at one another, and realizing that Emmett wasn't going to give them back the galley proof of the article, the handlebar moustached publisher grabbed for it and Emmett shoved him away, sending him crashing into a pair of file cabinets. Skinhead only moved his hands to adjust his glasses, apparently trying to call Emmett's attention to the fact that he was wearing them, and the look on his face seemed to say, "New York State gives persons twenty years in prison for hitting a man with glasses." The founder-publisher stood his distance well behind the desk and nervously threatened, "Listen, if you don't give us back that article and leave this office without any more trouble, I'm going to call the police!"

Emmett had to laugh. Here he was, standing in the middle of a room whose wallpaper pictured cops as vicious storm-trooping Nazi animals, and the publisher of the East Village *Other* was going to call them to arrest him! Incredible! Emmett continued to laugh as he tore the galley proof into tiny pieces and threw them into the air. Walking toward the front door and the street, he kept laughing, and the founder-publisher twitched his handlebar moustache and trembled furiously as he tried to make like he was really dialing for the cops. Emmett tried to encourage just that by prompting him to "go 'n fuck your dead mother!" as he walked out the door into the brisk, early spring afternoon, wondering whether he had provoked the punk-faced dude into actually completing his call to the police.

Emmett didn't intend to lose any sleep over it, and for the next couple of days, he roamed around the Lower East Side looking up the people he met at the loft meeting and checking out their various activities. He spoke about guerrilla theater with the Angry Arts, a group of politically conscious artists, and described the Communication Company operation to the Black Mask, a band of radical pamphleteers who were printing leaflets. He talked about how to finance economic collectives and business cooperatives to achieve financial independence and token autonomy from the state with

Chino Garcia, a mammoth twenty-two-year-old Puerto Rican and affable ex-gang leader who was in charge of the Real Great Society. This was a Puerto Rican cooperative business venture and community action group which also ran a free school, appropriately called the University of the Streets. He discussed hip political issues over a telephone hook-up with the audience on Bob Fass's midnight WBAI listener-sponsored radio show called *Unnameable*. He got to know the black leaders of the neighborhood by drinking a couple of beers every day in PWee's bar on Avenue A and spoke the language with the Italians while shooting pocket billiards with them in their pool hall across the street from PWee's.

When several members of the San Francisco Mime Troupe were performing their controversial minstrel show at the University of Calgary in Alberta, and got jailed by the Royal Canadian Mounted Police for having a marijuana seed lodged in one of the wardrobe trunks, Emmett, with the help of the friends he made since he arrived in the city, organized a series of demonstrations in front of the Canadian Consulate in New York. He also spoke to the consul in charge, with poets Allen Ginsberg and Gregory Corso, whom he had finally met at the Chelsea Hotel and with whom he'd shared several hustler-gourmet meals at Grant's restaurant on 42nd Street. The consul took quite a battering during their conference, with Gregory slamming his fist on his desk and loudly demanding the actors' release, and Emmett firing unanswerable, hard, quick questions at him, and Allen calmly implying it all seemed to be highly repressive, while also remarking that the facts lent themselves to a possible charge of collusion on the part of the Royal Canadian Mounted Police to interfere with the rights of American citizens.

The protests and news coverage of the demonstrations helped, but it was Emmett's phone call to the Canadian theater critic Nathan Cohen, and Cohen's subsequent column in the Toronto *Star* that freed R. G. Davis and the others from the inevitable long prison term which would have followed their trial on trumped-up charges. The charges were dismissed because of the adverse publicity in Canada stirred up by Cohen's dynamite column, and R. G. Davis and the Mime Troupe are forever grateful to Mr. Cohen for his righteous defense of socially relevant theater.

It was only after Emmett had acquainted himself with the various action projects on the Lower East Side that he realized there was really no feeling of community among the hip artists, and no real sense of belonging to the neighborhood. They were more involved in protesting national issues like the war in Vietnam, than in getting their own streets cleaned of filth and made livable. In fact, they seemed to dig living in a slum and like the smelly garbage strewn all over the place. It gave it a romantic look, one of the members of the Angry Arts commented.

One thing was for sure. If any of the things he talked about at the loft meet were ever going to get done, it was certain that he would have to take a large hand in the work, and he wasn't sure he wanted to spend that kind of time in the East. His brothers and sisters in San Francisco had told him the West Coast was clear for him to return, and he was anxious to get back there and continue the work he started. But Natural Suzanne, Fyllis, the Hun and a new poetic plum of a woman named Lacey Pines, who joined in the Free Food activity of the San Francisco Diggers a month before, were all on their way to New York, and so Emmett decided to wait for them before going back. Until then he continued to immerse himself in the neighborhood, working with the action groups and offering the advice of his experience.

The one thing Emmett really wanted to accomplish on the streets of the Lower East Side was their cleaning. He felt that if all the garbage and abandoned cars could be removed from the alleys and vacant lots of the neighborhood by late spring, the community would have a better chance of making it happen during the summer. The East Village artists could construct playgrounds for the kids in the empty lots and the hippies could organize block parties and street fairs on the weekends. After their streets had been cleaned, the black and Puerto Rican residents would be put in the position of keeping them that way and defending against persons from other blocks dumping their refuse there. When the whole area was completely cleaned up, Emmett felt it would breed a community spirit and lay the foundation for the solidarity needed for more community action.

Everyone with whom he talked about it agreed that the removal of garbage from the area and a general cleaning of the neighborhood was the first major service that had to be completed before the people would respect or see any value in forming a coalition among all the community groups. It was the kind of action that would make the advantages of joining forces obvious and would be accepted as totally neutral since it benefited everyone equally. But how do you get rid of years of waste, tons of heavy-duty debris from the nearly one hundred separate streets which make up the neighborhood, and get it all done before summertime? It was no small feat and Emmett went around discussing it with the different community groups, trying to come up with an angle, a way to get it taken care of. At the same time, Bob Fass began talking about the problem on his radio program, and after a few nights of discussing it with his audience and his guests he came up with the lame idea of having a series of "Clean-In's" to be held every weekend until the Lower East Side was cleaned up. He invited all the members of the listening audience to come to a specific street in the neighborhood that Saturday to participate in the first Clean-In.

They came, all right! About two hundred of them from all the different boroughs and suburbs of New York City, carrying protest signs about the various social evils which were bred by filthy streets and sporting the buckets and mops and the wire brushes and cleansers with which they intended to realize the first of the Clean-Ins. They were all in a jocular brotherly mood as they grouped in the middle of the street for what they considered to be a social event, something like a hayride. The people who lived on the block hung out of their windows looking down on the milling, mostly white kids, who were discussing how they should go about attacking the problem of "helping the poor help themselves."

They were quite a sight, these boys and girls — who grew up in places where there were lawns to play on and trees to climb — as they separated into pairs and walked to different spots along the block, wearing their casual "Saturday work clothes" which they always wore whenever there was a car to be washed or leaves to be raked at home. They kept to themselves and the people who lived there left them alone, just watching as they swept up paper with their brooms or actually got down on their hands and knees to scrub a patch of sidewalk spic and span.

That's what was really so pathetic and absurdly futile about the Clean-In. In the center of a neighborhood which averaged six to eight abandoned cars per square block, you had a group of weekend hippies on their hands and knees frantically washing away some stain of middle-class guilt from the pavement, while tons of real garbage remained untouched, clogging all the lots and alleys. The arrogance of it was so outrageous and obvious to almost everyone, that Bob Fass announced on his radio show that there would be no more Clean-Ins because most people from the Lower East Side neighborhood felt that they were a bummer, and he had to go along with their feelings because, after all, they did live there!

Emmett pondered the depths of vanity and self-indulgence required to organize such jive-ass events as the Clean-Ins, before directing his attention to the serious matter of relieving the neighborhood of its abundant and weighty loads of trash and scrap metal. He was convinced it was going to require a fleet of trucks to make the number of hauls needed to clear the area, and that fleet would have to meet some sort of schedule if there was to be any hope of getting the job done before summer. But how was anyone ever going to arrange for the trucks to appear in the first place? "Where are they all supposed to come from?" Emmett was thinking to himself over a cup of coffee one morning. He hadn't made very much progress in locating the trucks when he noticed what turned out to be the solution to the problem on the front page of the morning paper — the good old New York *Times!*

In the lower right-hand corner of page one, almost lost — like only a front page story can be lost by the *Times* — was a brief headline announcing a developing scandal within the city's private sanitation companies. This one-liner was followed by an article reporting the progress of some committee that was investigating several reports of kickbacks and payoffs to various city officials for their help in assigning city contracts to the area's private sanitation companies which were alleged to be controlled by organized crime. The story went on to detail a specific instance of alleged corruption on the part of one city agency official in collusion with the head of a reputed crime syndicate family "with its headquarters on Elizabeth Street in Lower Manhattan's Little Italy." The reputed head of the Elizabeth Street crime family was none other than Don Signore Jimmy Peerless himself, and Emmett, immediately understanding the kind of trouble the private sanitation companies found themselves in, flashed on the idea that they could use a sizable dose of good publicity in the New York press. He wondered how receptive they would be to a little public relations advice from him. Well, he would know soon enough because he was going to speak with the men in charge in the same place he spoke with them almost exactly ten years ago to the day, as one of the Aces Wild who came to their section of Little Italy to go against the Chaplains in a game called Ringolevio.

There was also a good precedent for the offer he was about to extend the "family" men who used the Elizabeth Street Cefalù Social Club as the headquarters for the overseeing of their private sanitation companies, as well as their other varied business interests. The precedent showed that active concern for the welfare of the poorer elements in a "family's" territory was always good for business, as well as being beneficial to the family's public image.

The precedent which Emmett recalled later that afternoon in Italian to the gentlemen of respect at their Cefalù Social Club on Elizabeth Street, took place in South Brooklyn during the summer of '66, less than a year before. The possibility of a dangerous and potentially disastrous giant rumble occurred over the integration of a predominantly white high school in the East New York-Flatbush section of Brooklyn, and hundreds of cops were sent to patrol the area between the last days of July and the first week in August while thousands of kids roamed the streets fighting, looting, and burning down whatever stores they considered part of enemy turf. In a desperate final effort to end the madness and avert the colossal rumble which was set to be staged at any moment, the Lindsay administration got Relocation Commissioner Frank Arricole to contact the Gallo brothers, Larry and Al, through their lawyer, and arranged for them to get past police lines hopefully to persuade the Italo-American kids, who ganged together to stomp the niggers from integrating, to go home and stop making trouble.

At that time, the Gallo brothers were still involved in a much publicized gangland war with the Profaci-Colombo family that began back in '60 and escalated in the summer of '61, after the oldest of the three brothers, Larry Gallo, was lured one Sunday afternoon to the Sahara cocktail lounge in Brooklyn, where two men came out of the back of the darkened saloon while Larry was standing alone at the bar and tossed a piano wire around his throat and started to strangle him. A police sergeant happened by, intervened, and got a bullet in his face. The two shadowy hit-men got away and Larry Gallo lived to step up the war along with his two brothers, Crazy Joe who was eight years younger and kept a full-grown lion in his office on President Street for protection during the gangland warfare, and Albert "Kid Blast" the youngest of the three, who turned out to be an ineffectual leader which got him renicknamed "Kid Blister."

The Gallo Gang's continuing warfare in Brooklyn earned them a lot of very bad press because of the twelve dead bodies that were found and the twelve more missing and wounded. So, Larry Gallo naturally jumped at the chance to muster a little public goodwill for himself and his gang by doing the community a service it had asked of him. He arrived in a black Riviera at the intersection which served as a meeting place for the Italo-American gang kids and was greeted with a VIP celebrity welcome by the kids and cops alike. With his kid brother Crazy Joe in prison, and his youngest brother, Kid Blister Al, having proved a washout, it was left up to Larry Gallo himself to get the leaders of the Italo-American kids to tell their gang to break it up and go home. He approached those kids who he knew had influence and control over the gang, and simply told them all to go home. One white kid began with a "But the niggers — " and Larry Gallo smacked him in the mouth, dropping him cold to the ground. By nightfall, there were no kids on the streets and there was no more trouble, big or little, after that.

For his service to the community, Larry Gallo got his picture taken with his arm around Mayor Lindsay and another city hall guy, and the next day the photo was on the front page of every newspaper in the city with Larry Gallo's broad smile grinning from ear to ear right above the ligature scar on his throat where the piano wire had left its mark. All the captions in the metropolitan newspapers had remarked something to the effect that Larry Gallo was probably a good guy at heart.

The gentlemen of respect listened as Emmett went on to detail the proposal he felt would aid them in their present unfortunate situation and afford them a public platform to prove their goodwill by cleaning up their neighboring Lower East Side community — from which they could exact a series of tributes in the form of press conferences and releases implying the moral and social responsibility of their private sanitation companies.

Then he laid out a plan whereby the eighty-five separate blocks making up the Lower East Side could be cleared of all debris within the following two and a half months. By dividing the area into ten distinct sections, he figured that a fleet of ten or more of the private sanitation companies' giant green garbage trucks could haul away enough of the rubbish to clean all of the lots and alleys of the community in eight consecutive Saturdays' work, leaving the city glaringly responsible for the removal of the abandoned cars.

Emmett spent over an hour rapping about his idea and making his proposal clear to the gentlemen of respect, assuring them that he would guarantee total press coverage of any community service they chose to perform on the Lower East Side. Now it was up to them, and he sipped at his very hot cafe espresso and Grappa Liquore, as the gentlemen of respect discussed his proposition among themselves in a Sicilian dialect only they could understand.

336

Finally they turned their attention back to Emmett and informed him that they would agree to try it out to see how it worked on the following Saturday morning, which was only three days away. " 'N you better make sure you got everything covered, kid, 'cause we gotta pay our men overtime from the time they show up at eight o'clock on Saturday morning to the time they finish up. So don' you go fuckin' up, 'cause there's lots a money we puttin' out to see this thing gets done right. So you better do your best like us, see, or you're gonna have a lot to answer to us for, if you fuck things up somehow. So, don't! It's a good idea, but we don' wanna throw no money away for nothin' you understand?! So, you make-a damn sure it counts front page! Okay, you a good kid. Now, what you gettin' outta all this?"

Emmett told them a line about how he wanted to give everyone on the Lower East Side a chance to live together in peace and harmony without the filth of garbage that had accumulated because of the city sanitation department's criminal neglect of the neighborhood. It was exactly their criminal neglect which he hoped to expose with the generous cooperation of the private sanitation companies who were being wrongly slandered by those same city hall officials.

Emmett shook all their hands before walking out into the crisp evening air of Hester Street for his long but enthusiastic walk back to the pad on Avenue A, thinking for a moment about the last time he was on Hester Street and what he came there for then, and also briefly wondering whether Willie Pondexteur was still in the penitentiary at Dannemora, or paroled by now, or dead. It seemed such a long time ago that Emmett hurried to push the thoughts of that day out of his mind, thinking instead about how he had to keep the upcoming Saturday cleanup very quiet, and at the same time organize slick press coverage of the event.

But even though Emmett maintained tight security about the project for Saturday, word of the cleanup by the private sanitation companies got to the wrong people in the East Village and they leaked it to the city government administration, who flooded the Lower East Side neighborhood with their own department of sanitation trucks on Friday, and copped all the publicity for the city of New York. Several Puerto Rican gangs — with whom Emmett had discussed the proposal he made to the Elizabeth Street "good people" — were outraged by the city's publicity stunt cleanup, after having always avoided their community in the past. They printed

337

up reams of paper on the Black Mask's mimeograph machines and went up to the rooftops bordering the streets and tossed them into the air to float down to where the department of sanitation men were working. The leaflets all said the same thing in big black block letters: PICK ME UP, MOTHERFUCKER! And the sanitation men did, just as they picked up the other symbol of the modern slum, the mounds of broken glass which were everywhere. In the contemporary nonreturnable world of the Lower East Side, bottles were only good for throwing and not for the regular two cents or nickel deposit they had been worth a few short years before.

The fire department was there too, giving out stuffed fluffy animals to the children as an expression of their goodwill to the inner-city ghetto community. There were two types of small stuffed animals packed by the gross in boxes. One set was small black kittens with white faces and the other was a thousand or more tiny gray mice with black button eyes. As if the children of the Lower East Side didn't have enough real mice to play with in their own kitchens! Was it just that the firemen were all so blind dumb from their weekly whiskey-beer bashes in Staten Island and strangers to the reality of the neighborhood they were paid to protect, or was the giving away of the stuffed mice to the children a conscious insult meant to demean the residents of the community? The children didn't really care to figure it out, assuming instead that the firemen knew what they were doing. When the fire department officers sitting on top of their bright red hook-and-ladders cheerfully handed the tiny gray cotton-stuffed playthings to the children lining the sidewalk, the kids didn't return the smiles, but simply stared blankly back at the men who were supposed to be "public servants," and dropped the little toy mice into the gutter where the water being used to wash down the back alleys ran off the sidewalks and carried the hundreds of make-believe rodents to the whirlpool over the sewer at the end of the block. The last thing that could be seen of the sinking toy mice was the glimmer of their shiny black button eyes, as they congested at the mouth of the corner sewer, like a rush hour crowd pushing and shoving and cramming together into subway trains to get somewhere ahead of god-knows-who.

At first, Emmett had no idea who informed the mayor's office of the planned Lower East Side cleanup on Saturday by the private sanitation companies. But it didn't take him long to figure out that it was one of the self-proclaimed leaders of the East Village hippies who did it just to make Emmett look bad in the eyes of the gentlemen of respect, and also to prevent him from accomplishing the kind of community service which would make him a more powerful neighborhood figure. And he didn't believe it was done to him out of pure jealousy either, by some political careerist dude who was on the make for a piece of the area's leadership pie. No, it was the work of a person or persons who didn't want him taking care of business in their territory and thereby disrupting the status of their already established hierarchy of East Village hipsters. However, Emmett had no time to waste at that moment playing "Who done it?" He had to contact the "good people" and let them know what went down and that he hadn't been directly responsible, and "maybe next time."

He thought it was wiser for him to talk with the gentlemen of respect over the telephone just in case they felt it was all his fault for some off-the-wall reason of their own. Early that evening he called the Cefalú Social Club, but nobody wanted to talk over the phone, and before he could make up some excuse about not being able to go over there, they sent a car to pick him up and bring him back to Elizabeth Street. The gentlemen of respect were a bit cold toward him, but their stone-faced looks seemed to understand that Emmett wasn't entirely to blame for whatever had gone wrong, and there was no reason for them to believe that Emmett had anything to do with leaking the information of their planned operation to the mayor, so they shrugged it off as a try, as a "You win some, you lose some." They told Emmett it was a good idea. "You have any more, you come tell us, understand? Maybe it works out better next time, okay? Good. But you gotta learn the people you dealin' with over there on the East Side, a little bit about *Silencio*, before you come back with any more ideas, right? Or it just end up to be a waste of time. So long now. See you sometime. An' remember, tell everybody to keep their goddamn mouths shut from now on, 'n you, too. This should be a lesson to you that you need to have some respect for *omertá* if you ever want to get things done, right? *Allora, arrivedella. E stai attento, capisci?*"

"*Si, d'accordo, Don Signore. Arrivederci, Signori.*"

"*Addio.*"

Emmett forgot about most of that business shortly thereafter, only thinking once in a while about how long the city's department of sanitation was going to keep up their goodwill cleanup of the Lower East Side, and about exactly who tipped them off in the first place. But after a while he even forgot about that, since once they started removing the tons of garbage from the area, public pressure insisted that the department of sanitation continue until the job was done, and slowly but surely they were doing just that. As far as figuring out who the informer was, Emmett narrowed it down to someone connected with the East Village *Other,* and there was no great need for him to peg whoever it was any further, because it really didn't matter who the individual had been, as long as he knew which cabal the dirty rat motherfucker belonged to.

One evening Emmett was walking crosstown to the East Side from the lower West Side where he had just cased that district's wholesale produce market and meat-packing houses. He was thinking about hustling some vegetables and ripping off a truckload of meat to give each block on the Lower East Side two sides of beef or a full steer to butcher and distribute among themselves. It was a good idea, and he was assured by at least one Puerto Rican street gang and by a few blacks at PWee's saloon that they would help get the meat shared through the neighborhood as quickly as humanly possible before it went bad, or before the cops, who were known to be stealing meat themselves, got pissed at someone else taking what they considered to be their private loot and caught on to who did it and where the haul had been taken.

It was only when Emmett remembered that the neighborhood was comprised of approximately eighty-five separate streets without counting any of the avenues, that he was able to realize the enormity of the job. It added up to a whole lot of fucking meat! About 170 sides of beef or eighty-five whole cows would have to be liberated and distributed among the people, if everyone was going to get an equal taste and the community was to be treated as a whole with no one section being left out to later claim unfair treatment.

"*Ooooeee!* Is it ever gonna be one motherfucker of a score!" Emmett smiled to himself, while also vowing that if he ever did pull it, Robin Hood would have to be goddamn extra careful this time or he would end up paying more dues for this caper than he thought possible. For no matter how popular the heist would be in the eyes of the people, Inspector Raymond Maguire, the crackerjack head of New York City's Safe and Loft squad, had just been recently placed in charge of a special truck unit because of some big midtown hijacking, and he would bury Emmett in some upstate penitentiary, the same way he would have if he had nabbed him back in the Christmas season of 1958, when he successfully worked Park Avenue to pay for the kind of freedom which could no longer satisfy him. It would certainly be ironic, to say the least, for him to be popped by Inspector Maguire after all those years. Busted for stealing some fucking meat! "Hot damn, Vietnam!" as the man said.

Emmett snatched a giant orange from a fruit stand outside an Italian grocery store and continued along Bleecker Street, deftly turning the fruit over and over with the tips of his fingers, peeling it in such a way that the rind remained intact — a two-foot-long streamer of bright orange skin which would have made Ilse Koch proud. He tossed it into someone's garbage can and bit into the pulp, noisily sucking the juice from the fruit and letting it drip down his chin and squirt up his nose. When he finished off the orange, he licked his lips to savor the last of it, and dangled his forearms away from his body, flapping his wrist-limp hands in the crisp cool air to shake them dry. A little further along the 300 block of Bleecker Street, he scooped up a ball of shaved ice from a fish stand in a market and washed away the stickiness.

Emmett enjoyed the afternoon alone among the trucks and stalls in the lower west side of Greenwich Village marketplace which was about to be relocated to the Hunt's Point district of the Bronx. He had been surrounded and hounded by people whom he didn't know ever since he came out of his seclusion at Candy's place a few weeks ago, and today was the first time he really had all to himself. He liked being alone, and he guessed it was because he didn't feel as lonely when he was all by himself which was sort of selfish, but fuck it! It was better than being encircled by lots of people who were all looking at him, hanging on his every word without really caring or understanding what it was he was actually saying. That's when he really felt the almost overwhelming loneliness, which often filled him with despair and a desperate longing for a good woman, a home and some kids to love and be loved by — his own family in a small house in the South of France or in the Southwest of the United States. But it always seemed too much for him to ask, when so much that should have been done in the Book of Revelations wasn't done and now had to be done, so there would finally be something new under the sun. Anyway, he would probably just get bored with a family of his own and blow it. He was still too young, after all, to feel as old as he felt.

His thoughts were suddenly interrupted by someone shouting his name from across Bleecker Street, and he turned to see a young couple crossing over to him from Liberty House, a storefront enterprise that had been organized by the remarkable black woman Fannie Lou Haimer, to retail goods which were handmade by poor blacks in Mississippi to finance various civil rights activities in the South and to provide some small money for their own meager existence.

Emmett watched the pair as they came toward him through the traffic. The guy appeared to be in his early thirties, had a big nose, a stumpy body, and a large head which was made to seem bigger by a mop of curly, black hair. The girl whose hand he was holding was in her middle twenties, had a short-cropped pageboy haircut, buck teeth, and was pertly pretty the way young stenographers in a steno pool look pretty compared to the sagging hags who've been sitting in front of the same typewriters for forty years.

They were both broadly smiling when they bounced over to his side of Bleecker Street, and they seemed delighted to have bumped into Emmett whom they said they had briefly met at the now famous loft meeting weeks before. The guy introduced himself as Abbie Hoffman and the woman as his old lady Anita, and went on to ask Emmett if he was walking over to the East Side, and if so "do you mind if we walk along with you 'cause we live in a pad on Saint Mark's Place, 'n we're on our way there now." Emmett said, "Sure!" he didn't mind, and the three of them began moving east with this guy, whom Emmett insisted on calling Abbot, bending Emmett's ear all the way.

First he remarked how impressed he had been by Emmett's rap at the loft that night and how hip it was. Then he commented about how the *Ramparts* article had been a heavy turn-on for a lot of radicals like himself, showing them all how the hippie movement held a wealth of political potential and should be approached in the same manner and style that Emmett used to establish the socio-political Diggers in the Haight-Ashbury. After that, Hoffman talked mostly about himself, running down his own biography and describing the many roles he had played as a member of the radical movement.

Abbot's old lady Anita didn't say anything, content just to give her old man a glowing look of approval once in a while, as Emmett listened to him tell his life stories: how he'd been a pool shark as a youngster in Gloucester, Massachusetts, and a helluva shoplifter and a slick hustler of all sorts. He also kept pointing out that he'd been a heavy activist in the radical movement for over a decade, "before anyone had ever heard of Emmett Grogan, ha! ha! ha!" And he went on to tell about how he worked for SNCC in the South where he was sort of press agent — public relations liaison man for them and the other civil rights groups, as well as being the man behind Stokely Carmichael, writing his speeches among other things, and on and on.

Emmett could clearly hear the guy's hunger pangs in the anxious sound of his voice. Abbot had been working in the "movement" for over ten years, always in the background, while others reaped the glorious laurels of fame, and now he was approaching his fortieth birthday — within a few years he was actually going to be forty fucking years old! — and nobody would ever have heard of him!

"The guy must fall asleep with fantastic dreams of grandeur every night," Emmett thought, but he didn't think it mattered to him one way or another, and so he accepted when Hoffman invited him inside his pad for a beer. Once they were there, Abbot continued to profile himself as a heavyweight who also knew his way around the East Village, all the while hinting that he would be a good man for Emmett to work with. But even though it was true that Emmett didn't have a tight working partner in New York City, he had no intention of getting next to Hoffman, at least not that way, anyhow. The guy did seem more than enthusiastic and energetic enough, however, so Emmett agreed to work with him now and then whenever something relevant came along to benefit the Lower East Side community. And that was Emmett's mistake. He didn't know it at the time. He might have had a slight inkling, but he really didn't know that he was making a serious mistake in getting involved with Hoffman, in allowing Hoffman to get involved with him. A blunder that he was only to discover he had made after it was far too late to rectify.

They were into their third or fourth can of beer when Emmett became buzzed by the juice and got trapped by his own ego and began riffing about what he was into on the West Coast and hoped to get into on the Lower East Side. He also rapped heavily about the importance of anonymity in getting things done, and Hoffman loudly agreed before he started to quiz Emmett, picking his brains for the secrets to the Diggers' style and their keys to being "political hipsters." Abbot carried on his interrogation like a cop, intently searching out clues, trying desperately to understand what he'll never understand.

The next day, Emmett compounded his initial mistake by stopping by the Hoffmans' ground floor pad at 30 Saint Mark's Place and dropping off a load of San Francisco Digger leaflets and Communication Company news handouts which Abbot had said he would have reprinted and distributed throughout the Lower East Side in the hope of organizing the same type of news service for that lower Manhattan area. But in reality Hoffman had some different plans of his own, which didn't particularly concern the establishment of a Lower East Side Communication Company. He wanted to employ whatever information he could garnish from the set of papers for his own benefit, to study and learn the new words he would need to use if he ever hoped to mask himself successfully as a radical, hip politico, and street theater director. In that pile of papers which Emmett had unthinkingly left with Hoffman, was all the education Hoffman needed to pass himself off as a political hipster. The assortment even included the Hun's bright and original "Trip Without a Ticket" essay on guerrilla theater, as well as all the other significant Digger writings that were printed during the past year in San Francisco and were destined to soon become the private textbook pages of a street theater manual and hip lexicon for Abbot Hoffman and his East Village cronies in their quest for personal recognition as national figures in a mock-revolutionary movement of masquerade, just "for the hell of it!"

Emmett didn't see what was happening and didn't even notice the carnival that was going on around him because he was blinded by his own ego, bathing in the respect that the East Village underground was showing him. A respect he was being granted by the counterculture hippies because he refused to become a public figure to the squares, never giving any interviews to the press or accepting any of the many offers he received to appear on various radio and television talk shows. His strict adherence to his own code of anonymity quickly made him a unique and legendary figure in the underground, and he knew that. So he nurtured that image by being more secretive and making his simple anonymity seem unnecessarily mysterious.

One night a beat political group who called themselves the Anarchists were going to throw a party in an Avenue B loft which belonged to the founder-publisher of the East Village *Other,* and they invited Emmett as well as all the people he could get to come. "Are you guys *sure* you want me to invite *all* the people I can get in touch with to come to your party?" "Yes! Invite as many people as you can. Invite the whole fucking city if you want! Everyone!"

So he did. The party was called the Anarchists' Ball and Emmett demonstrated his own anarchistic touch by telephoning Bob Fass at WBAI and a few other radio personalities who had their own shows on different stations, informing them of the Anarchists' Ball and asking them to make spot when-and-where announcements about the party to their listeners who were all to be told they were invited. " 'N tell 'em to bring their own refreshments!"

So many people showed up at the Avenue B loft that night that the Anarchists' Ball had to be relocated across the street to Tompkin's Square Park with everyone telling everyone else they had been invited by "Emmett Grogan" whom nobody could find because he wasn't there. He went to the movies to see *The Thief,* a modern quasi-silent film starring Ray Milland, which has only a bit of dialogue and is seldom revived in theaters since it was made over twenty years ago. The estimated crowd of three to four thousand at the Anarchists' Ball had the cops freaked and thinking that there was about to be a riot or that some sort of gang war was going to happen. The Anarchists were delighted that their Anarchists' Ball had really turned into something chaotic and a true expression of their love for Kropotkin, Proudhon, and nihilist Dadaism, and they all agreed that Emmett Grogan was an anarchist extraordinaire. Since so many people who didn't know what he looked like were looking for him, one of the head Anarchists, Paulsky, assumed the name "Grogan" and went around through the gathering, passing as Emmett and shaking hands and making cracks about how the cops, who encircled the streets bordering the park with lines of blue-coated reinforcements from neighboring precincts, were all scared shitless by the mob.

There was certainly no doubt that the cops were definitely confused and perplexed by the large gathering of people, who were in a cheerful party mood, chugging wine from half-gallon jugs, toking on reefers and dancing to music being blared from several portable radios. Perplexed because at least half of the crowd were not from the immediate area, having traveled there from sections of Brooklyn, Queens and even Staten Island. Throngs of neighborhood young people whose cheap transistors were tuned in to either Latin or rhythm-and-blues stations dead-eyed the middle-class hippies who swarmed into their turf for a night of dancing to the songs of the Loving Spoonful and the Mamas and the Papas resounding from the FM bands of their more expensive wireless receivers.

The black and Puerto Rican kids kept their distance from the clean-faced strangers, but they didn't just stand around staring at them. They jumped and shouted, danced and laughed to prove to themselves and to everyone else that they could out-party any bunch of white kids. Some of the hippies who lived on the Lower East Side moved around, coming on to the bunches of cute chicks who had driven in from the suburbs, while others panhandled change or tried to deal drugs to the visitors. Most of the East Village longhairs were partying hard themselves alongside their neighbors, however, trying to make some sort of contact with their black and Puerto Rican brothers and sisters.

The cops were bewildered all right, and when they asked some kid what was going on and were told it was the Anarchists' Ball, it all still didn't make much sense to them. Yes, they were confounded about not exactly knowing what was happening and bothered that they had no advance warning or information that such a gathering was going to occur that night. But they were by no means "scared shitless" by the mob and far from afraid that things might get out of hand or beyond their control.

You see, Tompkins Square Park had been the setting for many riots earlier in the century, and after they took place, several city departments and agencies got together and redesigned the park, stringing it with so much cast-iron fencing that it gave the place the look of a labyrinth and made it virtually impossible for any crowd to move anywhere en masse. The four-foot-high iron railings were placed randomly throughout the park, successfully dividing it up into small sections, and at the same time, separating into easy-to-handle groups any large mob that might gather. Also, in case of trouble, there were handball and basketball courts in the northeast section of the park enclosed and encircled by thirty-foot-high chain-link fences — that could quickly be converted into a makeshift jail or temporary holding facility for prisoners apprehended during a mass arrest.

Since the long hot summers of the mid-sixties spawned so many insurrections throughout the country, the cops held monthly pre-dawn maneuvers on the Lower East Side, which they considered a "trouble area," and the sealing off of Tompkins Square Park was the main concern of those riot control exercises. Emmett had seen the cops do their thing very early one morning when he was returning to Candy's from the East River, and it only took them about three and a half to four minutes to secure the park — which was quite impressive, even if there really was no traffic at that hour for them to contend with.

Therefore, the cops were hardly shitting in their pants in the face of that crowd that night. In fact, they were probably hoping something would explode so they could do it for real and set in motion the master game plan they had been rehearsing for so long.

The Anarchists' Ball ended at 11:30 P.M., the bewitching hour that puts the "disturbing the peace" ordinance into effect for the general public. It was agreed that a good time was had by all, even the few from the suburbs who got beat for some of their money in dope transactions which turned out to be nothing but burns. The crowd dispersed peacefully, and even though it was a relatively simple thing to arrange, nothing like the Anarchists' Ball in Tompkins Square Park has ever been seen again on the Lower East Side.

Emmett got back to Candy's pad about midnight, and no sooner took off his jacket and poured himself a short glass of wine, when the phone rang. The caller identified himself, but immediately swore Emmett to secrecy before he would say what it was he phoned about. Emmett promised he would never reveal the person's name to anyone ever, and then listened as the dude excitedly related what he had heard with his own two ears and had been privy to less than an hour before.

"Emmett, they're gonna get you killed! They were all there tonight, in the park at the Anarchists' thing, all of the East Village heavies, the hippie leaders, 'n what you did by inviting all those people to the ball freaked them out. There were thousands of people there from all over, 'n all night long, everywhere you went in the park, all you heard was Emmett Grogan, Emmett Grogan. Your name was all over the place! Everyone was talking about you 'n asking questions 'n looking all around for you! Well, it really got the head hippies who've been running things around here since before you came East crazy, 'n they talked for a long time about how something had to be done about you before you copped all the power from them 'n took over things in the East Village by yourself! They're scared, real scared, because you're always putting them down 'n pushin' them around, 'n they're really afraid that you'll put them all out of business if you're allowed to go on like you have been. So they're going to pay somebody to kill you before you get control of everything 'n force all of them to knuckle under or get out of the picture! 'N they mean it, too! What's-his-name already has someone lined up for the job, 'n they're all gonna put up the bread together tomorrow to pay the guy's price, so you'll be hit before the week's out. I don't know what you're gonna do! You know who they are. I don't know what else to tell you. I can let you have some money if you need to split. Anyways, I just thought you oughtta know what they're up to. If I can help in any way, call me, okay? 'N don't worry. I'll let you know right away when there's anything new or I hear about any other developments. Wish I could do more. Talk to you later, man, hear?"

"Yeah. Thanks. Be seeing you."

Candy was already asleep because she had to get up early for work the next morning, and she'd been out very late the night before at a party at Casey's Restaurant, where many people who're involved in the publication of words for a living hang out and hold casual but classy get-togethers. Casey is, of course, the name of the owner, an affable Chinese man with waist-length black hair whom Emmett had met at the same party with Candy. It had been sort of a lark for him to rub and bend elbows with so many literary notables, as well as making him just as tired as gracious Candy Sand. But the phone call sparked his adrenalin and gave him the type of second-wind surge which always renewed him. He was glad Candy was already in bed, leaving him completely alone with the incredible thought that his death was being purchased the same way housewives pay exterminators to get rid of insects, or farmers put up bounty for hunters to go after varmints.

It was unbelievable, all right, and there was very little if any reason at all for Emmett to disbelieve the person who phoned him with the news. He was in his mid-thirties and was a responsible figure in the New York radical-hip political circle, a respected member of the East Village leadership set and a person who also happened to secretly feel a personal friendship for Emmett and who just didn't cotton to killing or any use of violence, that's all. He was definitely not some scatterbrained kid looking to create a little excitement by making up a nifty story or by crying wolf to scare up some action. No, what his man had told him was for real. Emmett was certain of that.

His problem now was to figure out how to prevent it from becoming "for keeps." It was no good for him to waste time trying to pin down how the contract man would go about hitting him without making it look like what it was — a hired killing. But he did squander some time on the various ways he might be killed. He would either simply disappear which was already part of his myth anyway, known as "doing a Grogan," or get his skull caved in and his pockets rifled, to be found dead in the streets and be labeled just another robbery victim by the cops. But that might cause too much of a storm in the ever-tenuous relations between the hippies and the Puerto Ricans and blacks, and therefore might prove too risky a method in the long run.

When he'd given enough thought to how he might be done, he turned his attention to various methods by which he could avoid it. Every once in a while, as he thought, Emmett's belief would be staggered for a moment by the simple preposterousness of it all — by the undeniable probability that he would be dead within the next couple of days.

When he flashed on that, on the downright outrageousness of that pack of scumbags paying somebody to snuff him, of even insinuating they'd do such a thing, Emmett began to shake with rage. Once he actually put on his jacket, laced up his boots, took the Walther PPK automatic which a brother laid on him back in Frisco out of his bag along with several extra clips of 9 mm. ammunition, and started to go out and get a few of the punk motherfuckers before they could pay somebody else to do him. But he stopped short of the door, holding the Walther loosely in the sweaty palm of his hand, considering it a foolish move, the kind of ploy that should only be left to Mike Hammer's fantasies, and certainly not something for a man alone in the concrete reality of a city like New York to do against impossible odds and with nobody to back him. But he came close, awfully close, and that group of psychedelic asshole suckers who decided to pay to have him taken care of would never know how close they came to having a burp gun jammed up their noses and the trigger pulled until it didn't work anymore.

Emmett finally went to bed around three or four o'clock with his Walther under the pillow and the extra clips in one of his boots. He didn't particularly like automatic pistols, preferring the sturdy reliability of a .38 revolver to the fickleness of an automatic, but even though he would trade it in a minute for a good snubnose Smith & Wesson, he was glad it had been given to him, and he always kept it close and clean to reduce the likelihood of it ever jamming up on him in a spot. He tried to remember the last time he took the Walther apart and gave it a thorough cleaning, but he fell asleep before he could recall.

Candy Sand had just split to her literary secretarial job when Emmett awoke at 10:30 A.M. with a poisoned headache from an unrestful night of bad dreams. He was sipping a cup of light coffee and smoking his first cigarette of what was apparently going to be a very long day when there was a knock on the door, and every thought he had the night before suddenly added up and told him that this was probably it. He tiptoed quickly, barefooting it into the bedroom where he snatched up his piece and two extra clips and slowly came back out, positioning himself flat against the wall on the right side of the door, out of the way of any possible line of fire.

There was a second volley of knocks which was more aggressive and louder. A quick chill ran up Emmett's naked back, and he flushed, with beads of sweat breaking out all over him, making his dungarees cling uncomfortably tight at his crotch and the balls of his feet moisten the wooden floor. No one had ever before knocked on the door of the pad during the morning, at least not since Emmett had been there. There was no buzzer downstairs, so maybe it was just a Con Edison man wanting to read the meters. "No, if it was somebody like that, he'd of announced himself. They always announce who they are. Everyone knows that. An' I don't give a fuck what he says he is if he does say so either. Even if he's Western Union, I don't want any! And I'm gonna tell him I don't want none, too, to let him know I'm here, because that way, if he's the one who's supposed to do me, he won't know I've got a piece, 'n he'll brazen it, maybe even come bargin' in, 'n I'll blow his fuckin' head off. That way it'll all be over 'n done with right away instead of getting dragged out 'n makin' me crazy."

The knocking started again, but this time it was more like someone pounding on the door with their fist. Then came the giveaway, and at first Emmett didn't believe it, but it sounded again loud and clear. A girl's voice calling out his name, "Emmett! Emmett!" shortly followed by, "It's me, Natural Suzanne!" All the taut tension seemed to slip out of his body. He sighed and took a deep breath, letting his arms relax to his side and his gun dangle limp in his hand. For a moment he was disappointed that it hadn't been what he thought, because then it would at least have been over. But only for a moment. It was actually better it turned out this way. He remained cautious, however, asking Natural Suzanne casual questions through the still-locked door about things only she knew about, while making believe he just got up from bed and was still drowsy stupid with sleep.

But it was her all right, and she was alone, with a suitcase, jumping excitedly across the threshold after he opened the door, and going into an immediate impassioned description of her trip from San Francisco to see her mother and sisters in Michigan before coming to New York and Emmett. Her overwhelming joy at being in the Big Apple city for the first time, and the sprightly, cheerful depiction she gave of her journey as an adventurous voyage made Emmett feel very old, hardened by the reality of the weapon stuffed in his waistband and the unhesitating intention he had only moments before about using it. She was very young.

Her arrival, however, had changed the spot he was put on by the East Village hippie leaders, and when she further told Emmett that Fyllis, Lacey Pines and the Hun were also on their way to the city and should arrive within the next twenty-four hours, it made his situation drastically different from what it formerly had been. He was no longer alone. He immediately called the person who phoned him the night before with the news that he was deemed too dangerous to live, and told his friendly contact about the arrival of his sisters and brother from San Francisco and asked him to spread the news among the East Village leadership who wanted him out of the way. He told him to inform them that he would be returning to the West Coast with Natural Suzanne and the others as soon as possible, within a week or two, hoping that the news of his imminent departure would give the hippie punks enough reason to cancel their plans for his dispatch.

Emmett was satisfied that it would work, and by the time the others arrived from San Francisco later that same day, it had. The East Village hippie hierarchy conferred about the new development and they unanimously resolved to drop their plans since he was leaving anyway, which was all they wanted in the first place. Emmett's friend phoned him with the news of their decision, but also warned him that the postponement was based on the grounds he would split the city within the next two weeks, and further advised him to plan accordingly. "Okay, thanks a lot. You really saved me this time around 'n I won't forget it. Be seeing you!"

Emmett continued meeting with the East Side community's activist and social-political groups, such as the Angry Arts, the Black Mask, the Anarchists, the Real Great Society and the Group Image, and talked over the possibility of their forming a coalition to organize a New York Communication Company of their own and establish other services for the people in the neighborhood by cooperating, instead of competing among themselves and bad-mouthing each other.

He knew he had very little time left to get anything relevant started, but he tried just the same to turn some sort of trick before he would have to leave and return to the West Coast with the women and the Hun — who were also meeting with the different Lower East Side factions, trying to turn them on to consolidating their energies for the solution to some of the more important community problems.

Emmett didn't tell anyone about the plot the handful of East Village hipster marketeers had made against him. He only implied to his San Francisco comrades that his presence in the neighborhood wasn't particularly welcomed by those who used the area as a marketplace for their own benefit. He could have revealed the story of the plot to the mass media and thereby the people, but he felt that they probably wouldn't have believed it unless his contact also came forward to corroborate his testimony, and that was more than unlikely. He also couldn't figure what real good it would serve to bring it out into the open. For a man who was alone like Emmett to give something of himself away to the press, he had to be damned sure he was going to get something for it. So he decided to keep it quietly private between him and the hip marketeers, only letting them know that he knew about their pipe laying against him.

The East Village market operators, however, didn't react to his knowledge of their plotting as quietly as he had, and they set a campaign in motion to discredit his work in the community, knowing full well that any statements he might make about their conspiring against him would quickly sound like the paranoid ranting of a man looking desperately for a way to save face. This public campaign to discredit Emmett and his work was made necessary because of an article by Richard Goldstein that had just appeared in the *Village Voice*, the Greenwich Village radical-liberal weekly founded in the fifties by Norman Mailer, among others. This article successfully made Emmett seem the center of a personality cult by labeling the Diggers "Grogan's people."

Emmett had bumped into Goldstein over a month before in the Clayton Street house where the Free Food was prepared for the Panhandle, and he thought he was just another young kid who'd run away from home, because he was only a little more than five feet tall and had a neat, blond, childlike appearance. When Goldstein identified himself as a reporter for the *Voice*, Emmett at first figured he was jiving, but told him that if he was a reporter, he was wasting his time around the Clayton Street place, because there wasn't anyone there who was going to talk to him. Then he left to go make his daily rounds with the truck. Goldstein stayed, however, and somehow got Fyllis to open up for an interview, calling her "Miss Metesky" in the article.

The story was entitled "In Search of George Metesky," Metesky being the man who exemplified for Billy Landout and Emmett the absurdity of protest, with his twenty-five-year career as the Mad Bomber of New York which began when he was denied disability payments after being blasted in the face with steam while working for Con Edison. Goldstein based his report on the same sort of hippie leadership meeting in the Haight-Ashbury that Warren Hinckle III and Jerry Hopkins used as the premises for their unfactual articles. Goldstein didn't rely as heavily on fabrication, contenting himself with a snotty description of the meeting as "Emmett Grogan's debut, because the Diggers are his thing," and prophesying that "it will be interesting to watch the crucifixion when the Diggers drive the money changers from the temple, and Grogan may attempt just that."

The story went on to make Emmett and "his people" into an image of "hip resistance" and called them "the new realists, committed to an existential ethic of direct responsibility," as well as the "social workers of the Haight," who "give food, shelter and, ultimately, protection from what Grogan views as a hostile, murderous establishment."

It was just the kind of personal publicity that Emmett always avoided and tried to thwart, because he knew it would only lead to further friction between him and his brother Diggers, and it did. Even though he himself didn't speak with Goldstein, the reporter wrote about him in personal terms, using the *Ramparts* piece and "Miss Metesky" for the basic information he needed to give rise to a hero whose fall he seemed to await with relish. Emmett blew it and tongue-lashed Fyllis for having talked to Goldstein about their work together, because ". . . now all the dude's waiting for is to write a follow-up story about our crucifixion — about how we got wiped out because we proved to be too much of a serious threat to the establishment hippies! Sure, it'll make good copy for the papers, won't it Miss Metesky? And you can give them another interview when you're in jail!" But he didn't stay angry long, because, after all, Fyllis was only seventeen, and fidelity was her name.

Since the *Voice* story publicized Emmett to New Yorkers as a popular hip leader of the West Coast underground, his East Village enemies felt compelled to publicly denounce the role he was playing in the East. They gave Candy Sand's unlisted phone number to their friends in the media, and calls began coming in, asking for interviews with Emmett or inviting him to be a guest on radio and TV talk shows. One prime time television show was particularly persistent in their efforts to get Emmett to appear, phoning three and four times a day. He finally accepted their offer after he dreamed up a scheme for dealing with them.

The program was the Metromedia talk show moderated by Alan Burke, a backbiting, venom-tongued carper who was the New York version of L.A.'s TV personality and evil-speaking knocker, Joe Pyne. Both of these stupid sarcastic interviewers relied heavily on insulting their usually dumb or eccentric guests to amuse their studio audiences and to get home viewers to watch their programs. Emmett's plan was to dress Natural Suzanne up in his recognizable clothes and IRA cap and have her appear on the show as the mythical and legendary "Emma Grogan." The Hun was more than willing to accompany "Emma" on the program and act as a Digger spokesman, while Fyllis and Lacey Pines were to perform their walk-on roles in the "guerrilla theater" piece, as members of the studio audience, using lime and cherry pies as their props.

The show was being taped, of course, but everyone had been assured that no matter what happened it would be televised, because the point of the whole program was to make people look ridiculous, even Alan Burke himself. The taping was to begin at 6 P.M. that Sunday evening, and an hour before, the three giggly, nervous women and the Hun, who was musing over the possibilities of his television appearance, entered the Channel 5 studio with a suitcase filled with melting custard pies and phoned Emmett, who remained back at the pad, to tell him everything was going as planned.

When it was showtime, Alan Burke smugly introduced "Emma Grogan" and "her shaggy Digger sidekick," the Hun, as his guests for the evening, not knowing that it was going to be the last time he would have the upper hand or, for that matter, any control for the rest of the program. The Hun immediately stole the show away from the not-too-bright Burke, after he made some rather stupid and derisive remarks regarding the questionability of "Emma's" sex. The interviewer was upset by the Hun's quick-witted comebacks and sharp counterattacks which ultimately destroyed him by capturing the attention and applause of the audience and even the admiration of the technical staff. The Hun was coming up seven and eleven every time, and Alan Burke finally tried making friends with him, which Fyllis and Lacey Pines took as a personal affront to their integrity. So one of them ran up and pelted him swoosh! in the face with a cherry pie, while the other bombarded the audience, flinging pies every which way from the stockpile in the now open valise.

The scene was chaotic with a fat lady running around screaming, *"My dress! You've ruined my dress!"* and Alan Burke slumped stunned in his chair trying hard not to choke on the cream filling his mouth — unable to talk or see because of it — and children picking up lumps of cream from the floor or the backs of the seats and eating it or throwing it around the room, and the Hun rising from his chair and masterfully commanding the cameramen to follow him as he walked toward the exit, delivering a monologue and directing the camera work: "I am in a box looking at you through a box. And you are in a box, watching me through a box. I am leaving my box and the things which make up my box. I've made my decision. What are you going to do about the box you are in?" And he walked toward the door marked Exit, directing the attention of the different cameras to the rafters of lights and to the various other things which were part of the studio, — and then centering them on a close-up of himself as he opened the door and walked out in silence, leaving the sound of chaos behind him and the camera focused on the slowly closing door. The picture on the home screens faded to a commercial station break.

Afterwards, the "motley group of Diggers" trouped over to a Broadway cafeteria to get something to eat, and Natural Suzanne phoned Emmett to give him a brief account of what happened, saving the blow-by-blow description for later. While he was waiting for them to return to the pad, Emmett got another call. This one was from John Gruen, a reporter at that time for the *World Journal Tribune* and a devotee of East Village bohemia, who wanted an interview. Emmett told him no, but made the mistake of not hanging up immediately, giving Gruen enough time to ask him what he was doing interfering in the affairs of the Lower East Side community when it was really none of his business.

Emmett fell into Gruen's trap by getting angry and asked him what the fuck he was talking about! The reporter shot back that there was all sorts of talk all over the East Village of how Emmett was butting his nose into things that didn't concern him and how he was causing trouble between the different neighborhood groups who got along fine by themselves until he showed up. Emmett caught on, but it was too late. He had already lost his temper. "Man, that sort of jive talk only comes from those East Village marketeering hip-huckster friends of yours and nobody else. Now don't bother me! I'm just a pimp for the kids!" And he slammed down the receiver, angry with John Gruen for baiting him, but more angry with himself for blowing his cool and giving the reporter words to spot quote.

The gang returned to Candy Sand's place full of descriptions of their "Alan Burke Special Performance" which they wouldn't view until it was televised the following weekend. Sure enough, early the next day the newsstands of the city carried the *World Journal Tribune* with Gruen's article discrediting Emmett under the banner headline "Hero Hogan Grogan Stirs Up Lower East Side!" The story named all of the neighborhood groups with whom Emmett had been working and claimed that he was pitting them against each other without citing any reason why he would want to, except that he was a pimp for the kids!

He wondered for a moment where he came up with the certainly Freudian symbol of himself as a pimp, and furthermore why he ever slipped it to the reporter. But he'd been doing too much wondering lately, so he quit it and got angry instead. "Will you look at that! The East Village power punks are trying to impress me with their contacts! That guy turned everything neatly around and made it all come out backwards to make me look like some nitwit troublemaker! He's probably got half the Lower East Side believing it, too! The power of the press! A real slick trick! A real cutie! I wonder where he lives?"

By midafternoon the phone was steadily ringing with people calling to ask Emmett if he saw the "Hero Hogan Grogan" story, and reporters looking for follow-up stories of their own. Even the police captain of the neighborhood precinct, Captain Fink, called, asking whether Emmett would like to come into the station house to talk things over. Fink, like all the other callers, was told that no one at Candy's number knew of any "Emmett Grogan," and when he and the rest were asked where they got the unlisted phone number, there was a momentary silence, then the usual "I don' know. Somebody just gave it to me, I guess . . ." The New York *Times* was particularly pressing since they had been beaten to the story by a rival city newspaper, and Emmett finally agreed to meet with their only black staff reporter, Earl Caldwell. But he had no intention of revealing his true role in the neighborhood or retracting any of the twisted facts of Gruen's piece with statements of his own. No, he was simply going to let the matter die, helping it along a bit by boring it to an early death.

It was easy. A few days before, Emmett had smoked some DMT with the LSD Bear, and some other psychedelic luminaries who gathered for a party at a Tibetan-decorated pad on Mulberry Street. Among the small throng was Leary's sidekick, Richard Alpert, who gave Emmett his phone number and invited him to call whenever he felt the psychic need to do so. And that was now! He phoned Alpert and asked him to meet with him the following morning at the 23rd Street office of *Inner Space*, a psychedelic periodical that wasn't destined to last very long.

He told Earl Caldwell to meet him at the same place, and the following morning he showed up with Alpert only a few minutes behind him. Emmett sat next to Alpert on a funky couch facing Caldwell, who was braced in a straight-backed chair with his pad and pencil all ready. He asked Emmett some sort of lead question about the Gruen article, but instead of answering, Emmett wound Alpert up by asking him to expound on the metaphysics of the psychedelic reality of the Lower East Side, and leaned back into the soft cushion of the sofa, watching as Caldwell began to stop jotting down notes and lifted his head, uncertain about what was going on. He eventually looked back to Emmett and was about to interrupt the good doctor's rambling, but Emmett gestured for him not to and to continue listening, nodding his head with a facial expression that suggested, "Dig Alpert, man! He knows what's happening! He'll tell you what you want to know! Pick up on his vibes, man!"

Earl Caldwell must've sat there for forty minutes trying to figure out why he was there on an assignment, while Richard Alpert went on and on about esoteric philosophies only he knew of, and Emmett sat silently in mock awe of the man whom he had introduced to the reporter as his guru. When Alpert stopped for a moment to ask the publisher of *Inner Space* magazine, who was religiously recording every hollow sound of his voice on a tape recorder, for some water, Caldwell saw his opportunity and took it, splitting from the office with the haste of a man fleeing a fire. Emmett laughed as he watched him run down the stairs like a thief and out of the building.

After Richard Alpert was given his glass of water, he continued his rap into the tape recorder, and Emmett returned to Candy's place where he laid out the scene for the Hun and the others.

Emmett had played it right, and nothing appeared in the *Times*, and the phone suddenly quieted down. By using Richard Alpert and his psychedelic logorrhea, he got himself dismissed as a cracked pothead, and nobody was writing stories about them this late in the game, giving Emmett the pass he wanted and needed to take care of his business.

But it already seemed too late. His name was the only name the straight press knew that was connected with the Diggers, and they were going to keep on using it whenever their stories referred to the "mystery-shrouded group," no matter how much he played the psychedelic buffoon. A flood of articles began to appear in the New York press about the San Francisco Diggers, using the *Ramparts* portrait of Emmett as their "well-known figure" profile and putting imaginary quotes in his mouth without even pretending to have met him.

It was really getting him down, "all this image bullshit!" and he decided it was mainly because he was separated from the reason — the work in San Francisco — which made necessary the Salvation Army cover, and he became anxious to get back, to return to the unshakable reality of Free Food and, at the same time get away from all the image-persona hustle of New York where talk was substituted for action and people were measured by their list of credits.

By now he had given away all of the acid he brought with him from Frisco, and had gone to so many meetings on the Lower East Side where he saw the same faces, that he began to feel that meetings had replaced relationships and organizations had replaced the community. He no longer went to them, but rather casually toured the neighborhood visiting the friends he made in the few weeks he had been there.

It was during one of these late afternoon walks that Emmett was invited by a friend to accompany him to the Theater for Ideas, "for a look at the city's star intellectual radicals, as they sit in a salon, like a forum, and discuss the chosen topic, 'The Enemy Is the Liberal.' " Since he had nothing really better to do, Emmett went to the studio apartment that evening to gawk at the gathering of New York's chic circle of radical superstars. But it backfired on him because he became the star attraction and center of attention and got himself dumped on and hissed at by the glib, pompous audience.

There were about seventy-five persons sitting on rows of wooden, folding chairs facing a dais where a panel of *Ramparts* editors sat behind a cloth-covered table with a pitcher of water and glasses. One of them was old one-eye himself, Warren Hinckle III, and Emmett immediately got his fur up. He should have simply left, but he didn't. Instead he sat there and listened as the panel and the audience had a thoroughly good time patting themselves on the back for their unswerving radicalism, and at the same time condemning the "liberals" as the enemy because of their fearful acquiescence to the establishment political party system. He listened to that kind of self-congratulatory rap for nearly three quarters of an hour before it and the stuffiness of the room and the people who were in it caused him to stand up and accuse the assembled themselves of being the "real enemy," while the liberal was just a patsy and anybody's pawn.

"You're the real enemy because you extend the present system of American society, deluding yourselves with words while paying tribute to the state with taxes, and making believe you're in solidarity with the blacks in Harlem and the peasants in Vietnam from the top-floor windows of your deluxe apartments and East Hampton estates! Who the fuck are you kidding? You're the real enemy! The liberal will always follow whoever's winning, because he usually knows no better or is too frightened! But you people know better, don't you! You know which side you're on in some cocktail conversation like this, sure you do! But when you're in your stockbroker's office, whose side are you on then, huh? Certainly not mine — not for all the crumbs you could ever feed me from your tables! To talk about the liberal as being the enemy is like kicking a dead dog! Talk about yourselves as being the enemy to all those people whose side you claim, you insist, is the same side you're on. Talk about it because you're not on the same side. Talk about it because you're the real enemy, and not the liberal!"

The audience immediately burst out with someone shouting that "the Diggers were merely the Salvation Army in disguise!" and someone else charging that Emmett "was just creating rest camps for teenagers!" Warren Hinckle III jumped in and described Grogan as a "visionary who has the cunning of an Army Supply Sergeant in a B movie." It all added up to "what right does that scraggy hippie social worker have putting us down! Where does he get off, anyway, knocking radicals like us around!"

Then came the clincher that was supposed to prophesy Emmett's co-option by the society he claimed to have dropped out of. Paul Jacobs, who led those Berkeley "Community for New Politics" radicals in that demonstration months before to protest the Haight-Ashbury curfew during the "San Francisco Riot," started screaming from in back of the audience that "like it or not, Grogan, you and the Diggers are going to be exploited because of the fantastic capacity of this country to absorb new ideas and attitudes! Macy's will soon be selling Digger dresses and some company'll put out a candy bar named after you people before long, and they'll put up promotion posters proclaiming, "Eat a Digger!"

The audience laughed and applauded. Paul Goodman, the sixty-year-old author and self-professed "community anarchist," tried to gavel the meeting back to order by declaring, "I'm a Roman senator, not a Digger!" And Emmett got up to leave with Natural Suzanne. There was just no use in wasting energy, and he walked out of the Theater for Ideas, remarking to the crowd that "There are eight million stories in this Naked City, and you people know *every goddamn one of them!*"

Two days or so later, an article about the meeting appeared in the *Village Voice* under the headline, "A View from the Left," and described him as a "tall, lean and scraggy twenty-three-year-old ex-Brooklynite," and went on to say that " 'The Diggers,' according to Grogan, collect free food from merchants or grow it themselves and dispense it free to whoever desires it. They also collect used clothes and give them away,' he said."

It was a good thing Emmett was at the airport when he read the news story, because as soon as he saw that "he said" crap about collecting free food from merchants, he wanted to go and commit some mayhem on the person who wrote the lie. " 'He said!' The guy who wrote this bunk has been reading too much of the *Daily News!*" And he tossed the paper with its "Eat a Digger!" quotes and radical-liberal gibberish into a waste can as his flight was called.

Before he finally left the city, however, he had done one very important thing which he felt he had to do if he really wanted his name to be erased from the files of the mass media. He gave it away. Gave away his name in the same manner he gave his identity to Natural Suzanne for her appearance on the Alan Burke show. He didn't change his name, he just gave it away to whoever wanted to use it, whenever, as had been advertised in *Realist* magazine by Paul Krassner: "The leader of the Diggers doesn't exist, and his name is Emmett Grogan, a hoax unwittingly played upon you by the underground press and the establishment press. Even *Ramparts* was tricked into using the photo of a member of the San Francisco Mime Troupe. Emmett Grogan is the generic term for an existential hero of our time." The name quickly found popular usage among the street kids who started a make-believe game called "Will the Real

Emmett Grogan Please Stand Up!" It got to a point on the West Coast where no one would even believe Emmett *was* Emmett, until he got corroboration from someone he knew personally. He was even able to identify himself to reporters — especially in California — and not be believed. Even the San Francisco *Chronicle* ran a paragraph in one of its stories on the Haight-Ashbury that said, "Whenever a Digger identifies himself as 'Emmett Grogan,' it means nothing since all Diggers call themselves Emmett Grogan on the general principle that anything which confuses the straight world can't be all bad." It was a fantastic success.

However, when it was all over and his name seldom if ever appeared in the media and everything got private once again, Emmett felt a strange uneasiness about the thorough success of his feigned nonexistence, a feeling that maybe he'd been too successful in convincing the media he was only a myth and the name "Emmett Grogan" nothing but a hoax.

He didn't exactly understand why he felt this way. He just did, that was all. But after a while, he decided that it was probably because he was just disappointed in how easy it was to accomplish; bitter at how incredibly easy it had been to dupe the media, and resentful at how quickly they accepted the lie. Emmett finally concluded that he was basically upset about all of it because his ego was insulted. His two cents apparently meant very little to the world.

The Hun returned to San Francisco ten days before, having spent only a few days in New York and leaving right after his appearance on the Alan Burke show. Emmett didn't understand why he came East in the first place, but decided that the Hun had gotten himself a round-trip ticket somewhere and just felt like taking off for a while. The girls, on the other hand, had come to visit their folks. Fyllis' mother had been ailing and Lacey Pines hadn't seen her sisters for what seemed like a long time to a girl just turned eighteen. Natural Suzanne, of course, had wanted to be with Emmett, stopping to see her family on the way to New York. She had been Emmett's old lady now for nearly six months and had grown much older than her eighteen years. She was a tall, beautifully proud-featured girl with a deep-felt shyness which stemmed from a tragic accident that occurred when she was a child.

It happened on her ninth birthday toward the end of a party her family gave her. She was all dressed up in a colorful, chiffon birthday dress and had pinned the tail on a donkey, had dunked for apples, and had popped some balloons, happily enjoying her party, when she brushed by the homemade birthday cake resting on a patio table, and one of the lighted candles fell against her dress, setting it aflame. Her mother turned when she heard Suzanne's screams, and seeing her child about to become immolated by her burning dress, ran for the garden hose, and dowsed the flames with sprays of cold water — the worst thing she could have done because as soon as the cold water came in contact with the child's scorched flesh, it instantly scarred her hips, thighs, and waist.

Because of this scarred portion of her otherwise beautiful body, Natural Suzanne developed a fear of ever being seen without clothing, which made certain activities like swimming and lovemaking impossible for her to enjoy. But when she met Emmett, he was fortunately able to get her to overcome that fear that kept her locked away from the joys of a full life. It was easy.

The first time he returned with her to his Fell Street pad to make love, she said "No," and he asked "Why?" and she replied that she'd been scarred by fire as a child and she was certain he wouldn't want to see the scars because they were ugly. Emmett didn't say anything. He just quietly undressed her in the pale light of a small, broken Tiffany lamp, and when he finished and was standing naked himself, he slowly examined the broad solid lines of Natural Suzanne's South Sea Island girl-like body with its small, round, firm breasts and perfectly shaped brown nipples, and he asked, "What scars?" Then they made sweet love, with him slipping in and out and all over her silky flesh — made satin-smooth by the surplus oils that were transferred to the rest of her body from the patches of slick, dead skin that had no use for nutrients. That night Natural Suzanne began to make up for what she might have missed, and, from then on, she's done whatever she pleased with her body, even gone swimming in a film star's Hollywood pool surrounded by starlets. Whenever anyone asks her how she came to get those scars, Natural Suzanne always answers, "What scars?" and goes on living her life the way people are supposed to.

Emmett arrived in San Francisco on the second Sunday of April with Natural Suzanne, and the two of them moved into a makeshift guest room in the rear of the Webster Street storefront leased by Butcher Brooks and his old lady, Flame. The next day the United States Supreme Court denied a thirty-seven-year-old black Californian's plea for commutation, and Ronald Reagan gave the nigger to his voters as a gift for their electing him governor of the state. Two days later, on April 12, 1967, Aaron C. Mitchell became the

195th man to die in the gas chamber and the 501st man to be executed in the recorded history of California, and, hopefully, the last.

The most important lesson Emmett learned from his trip east was that whatever happens to America doesn't necessarily have to happen first to New York, as that city's inhabitants like to believe. The obvious proof was the San Francisco Haight-Ashbury district's acknowledged position as the birthplace and growth center of the American youth counterculture and the expansion of human consciousness that was going to overwhelm the rest of the country with an astounding energy of awareness in the next few years.

But Emmett could see that Haight-Ashbury was already deep in the throes of a critical dilemma and was quickly approaching disaster with the hordes of arriving runaway youths overburdening the Digger operations which were struggling to meet the needs of these kids and the community.

Brooks, Slim Minnaux, Tumble and, of course, the women, had maintained the daily supply of Free Food for the Panhandle of Golden Gate Park where a growing number of newcomers were gathering to eat at four o'clock every afternoon. The Trip Without a Ticket Free Store was still being managed by the Hun and everything was under control, but the pickings were slim and getting slimmer. There were a whole new string of crash pads which were constantly being closed by the cops, but regularly reopened by young people who called themselves Diggers, whom Emmett had never met.

Emmett returned to his work with Free Food and trucking goods around to be given away at the free store. There hadn't been a party or any kind of free celebration in Haight-Ashbury since he left six weeks before, and he felt like organizing some kind of an event that would put fun back into the streets. So he did. First he got a permit from the Park and Recreation Commissioner because he wanted it to be at night, and he knew that if he planned some sort of happening in the park to take place after dark without legal permission, the cops would vamp on the people who gathered and a lot of heads would be broken because of him. So he got the permit and began putting together the first and only free rock and roll party ever held in a San Francisco public park by the people at night.

The Diggers got together and worked hard, hustling money for the pair of eighteen-foot, flatbed trucks to be used back-to-back as the stage, and for two giant spotlights, like the ones used at movie premieres, to be played on the dew-laden leaves of the park's trees as a light show. The Grateful Dead, Country Joe and the Fish, and Janis Joplin and Big Brother and the Holding Company were invited to play, and they said they would. More different-colored lights were arranged to be strung throughout the area, and someone came forward with a half dozen strobe lights to be played on the people as they danced.

All through the organizing, Bill Graham, who let Emmett use a storefront warehouse below his Fillmore dancehall to stash materials and several boxes of fruit for the event, insisted that the night-time rock and roll party, which was called the "Outlaw Mutation Boogie" among other things, was never going to come off the way it was planned, because he felt the people were incapable of achieving that kind of organization themselves, and he kept telling Emmett that, every time they met during those few days prior to the free dance-concert, adding that he was prepared to pay the Beatles any amount to book them for a free concert which he himself wanted to present in Golden Gate Park. Graham asked Emmett how he felt about the idea of him presenting the Beatles free, and Emmett replied that it would be terrific, but if he really wanted it to be free, totally free, he should leave out the "Bill Graham Presents" part and just let it happen without anyone knowing who was responsible.

Anyway, the Panhandle Park Dance was a phenomenal success, with the giant spotlights lighting up the trees and glistening the tiny dewdrops on the leaves into a sparkling rainbow of a light show, drawing thousands of people towards the strobe-lit area where they danced and hollered and laughed and had a good time. Soon after everything got started and was well under way, working smoothly, Bill Graham showed up with some of his Fillmore auditorium staff and gave out apples to the crowd and helped Emmett and the other Diggers inflate balloons which were being strung around the stage and told them that it was obvious now, and he could see, that he underestimated the people and their power to get it on without professional help and he was glad they were successful. Bill Graham's straight that way.

The park permit read that the gathering had to be dispersed by 11:30 P.M. or be subject to arrest by the police who had been assembling in force two blocks away since nine o'clock that evening, obviously hoping that the permit would be ignored so they could wade in with their nightsticks and incite a riot and fill their empty paddy wagons with bloodied longhairs. Emmett was fully aware of this, as were the rest of the Diggers, and at about twenty minutes after eleven he got up on the stage and stood to one side as the last of the three bands, the Grateful Dead, finished the sixth or seventh number of their set. When they had, he told Jerry Garcia that the next song had to be the last because they only had a few minutes to wind things up before the cops vamped and someone got hurt. Then he told the crowd who were really into partying by this time that the next number would be the last and the music started up before the shouts of disapproval from the audience could be heard.

After the band finished, Emmett stepped up to the microphone once more and told everyone to go home because it was all over now and "Good night!" And they did. The crowd moved quickly and quietly out of the Panhandle Park in all directions, and a police captain, standing next to a squad car that had pulled up to one side of the stage only moments before, stopped the Hun and Coyote and asked them the name of the guy who just spoke over the microphone, and they told him it was just somebody from the crowd, that's all. The captain didn't go for it and asked some more people because whoever the man was, the captain was later overheard telling his sergeant-chauffeur, he was too powerful to remain unknown to them. It doesn't take anyone special to incite a crowd he figured, but it certainly takes someone particular to tell twenty-five or thirty thousand enthusiastically partying people to go home — and be instantly obeyed. The name of the man who could do that they had to know, but no one they asked could tell them, and Emmett left as soon as Coyote and the Hun tipped him off about the inquiries.

It was shortly after that Friday night's Outlaw Mutation Boogie that Emmett began receiving gifts of weapons from his brothers, who felt that his life was now in danger. They sensed that he had exposed himself as a much too popular and powerful figure in the Haight when he stepped up to that microphone and that he was now someone recognized as a dangerous person, not only by the police and other government agencies, but also by the many underground-underworld cabals who didn't want their positions of control in the Haight community jostled or usurped by the likes of him or anyone else.

In fact, Emmett's comrades believed he was dangerous to someone right at that moment, and when you're dangerous enough to someone, they usually try to kill you. So one of his brothers gave him a British Webley revolver and two full boxes of .38 ammunition and a twenty-five-minute-rap which was apparently supposed to fill him with alarm because, "You made yourself a target the other night, Emmett. Put yourself right on the spot for anyone who feels threatened by you or who just doesn't like your looks to draw a bead on you, brother. Yep, you made yourself the number one target around here the other night when you got up on that stage and showed everyone just how much of a heavyweight you really are in the eyes of the people, and you better get used to the idea and get used to it fast, because from now on, you're it!" That was just the kind of comforting encouragement Emmett wanted to hear.

Someone else left a rusted World War II Italian Berretta wrapped in newspaper on the front seat of the Digger pickup, just after Emmett had jumped out of the truck for a moment to buy a can of Ballantine Ale at the Haight Street Liquor Store. When he returned and found the loosely packaged automatic pistol in the cab of the truck, he immediately pulled off the main thoroughfare and quickly parked alongside the curb of an inconspicuous, vacant side street where he read the hastily scribbled note that was stuck into the barrel of the gun:

TO EMET GROGON
Theres been lots a storys going round about how your in danger
Some evil persons dont like what you do for us and they been spread-
ing bad vibes on Haight Street about what is going to happen to you
So we thought you can use this Its all we had and we know it don't
look like much but we thought you can clean it up and its better than
nothing if you dont have nothing else Anyway we want you to have
it because it may help keep you safe and we wanted to show you
that we are behind you 100% on account of we love you
            From all of us who need you and hang out on Haight
            Street and at the Do-nut shop
                                    SIGNED — ANONIMOUS

The sincerity of the note and the trouble the person or persons had gone to in explaining their offering to him convinced Emmett that there was indeed some heavy shit going down on the scene concerning him, and the anonymous chicken-scratched missive and rusty-gun gift did more to put him on edge than anything. It made him feel that there was really something he didn't know about himself or someone or something which was already common knowledge on the street, but which for some fucking reason was unapparent to him!

Or was it just a fucking put-on, a prank someone played on him to make him paranoid? By the time he started up the truck and pulled down to the corner of Fell Street, Emmett didn't care about it anymore and dumped the paper-wrapped rusted automatic, which probably would never have worked anyway, down the sewer and tore the note up into fine, little squares, letting them flutter out his window like a handful of confetti. He geared the truck onto the entrance ramp and along the freeway to North Beach and Tumble's pad without the slightest intention of ever telling anyone about the anonymous package left on the front seat of the pickup or the note that accompanied it, offering a little help from some friends.

It was at Tumble's pad that afternoon that Emmett met Larry Little Bird, a Pueblo Indian who had been raised on the Santo Domingo Reservation near Santa Fe, New Mexico. Little Bird was twenty-five years old and thoroughly maintained his Indianness; a black-pearl-eyed man who was as graceful and strong as a birch tree dancing in the wind. He quietly studied Emmett over a can of malt liquor and within less than thirty minutes of their having been introduced, Larry Little Bird invited Emmett to return with him to New Mexico, because he had the look of a man who could learn what every man needs to learn about himself and what every Indian like Little Bird knows.

Strangely, and to some perhaps selfishly, Emmett didn't have one hesitating thought about leaving with Little Bird that evening for New Mexico, and it would be a month before he'd realize why he went to the wilderness without ever seriously considering his responsibility to his charge — the streets of Haight-Ashbury. The Communication Company issued a handbill the next morning, announcing that "Emmett Grogan has gone for a while," and everyone wondered why, with the promised cataclysmic "Summer of Love" drawing near. So did Emmett Grogan.

It was dawn when they drove up to the comfortable, wood-stove cabin set deep in the woodline on the outskirts of a village called El Rito in the northern part of the state. It was here that Natural Suzanne was to stay with Little Bird's tall, Kentucky-born woman, Cease, while Emmett went into the forests to be taught without words the lessons he had come there to learn.

He had absolutely no money, but Little Bird had a bit and staked Emmett to a short, eighty-pound-pull Bear bow, sleeved in camouflage cloth, and a dozen aluminum-shaft target-and-hunting arrows, as well as a .22 single-shot Magnum, which is treated like a boy's toy by the American Rifle Association, but in reality is a weapon that can bring down the largest game if the person squeezing the trigger is equal to his quarry. They also bought a pair of brown woolen secondhand trousers, a dark green wool shirt, and a pair of low-cut Converse sneakers, which are sturdier and do the same job as moccasins for a man who plans to walk softly in the woods. In fact, all the clothing was bought with the silence of the hunt in mind, and Little Bird painted the sneakers green and brown and spotted the same colors on the pants and shirt to make them blend even more with the background of the springtime forest, as their wool texture would soundlessly harmonize with the quiet of the brush.

Emmett seldom spoke with Little Bird. He simply followed him into the hills every morning after sunrise and coffee, and watched his every quick but careful movement, learning as much as his Indian brother wanted to teach him, until dusk fell and they returned from the woods to the cabin in El Rito where they ate dry bread, deer jerky, and a thick, bean-paste stew and smoked the only tobacco of the long day before undressing in separate rooms and lying down on the matted floor with their women and talking softly with them, while making love for an hour or so until it was beautiful to stop and fall asleep to dream of what the next day might bring.

Emmett followed Little Bird's eyes during their first week together in the New Mexican hills bordering Colorado, and saw the many different creatures who lived there, who sensed their presence but were not alarmed because of their quiet way and the scent Little Bird spread on their camouflaged clothing — a scent that came from tiny sacs of liquid found above the hind hooves of deer. Little Bird had acquired and saved this liquid from the many deer he had slain over the years. It was Little Bird's knowledge of the ways of the wilderness and Emmett's careful attention to his teacher's planned style of movement that allowed them to approach and get within yards of the splendid animals of the land.

Emmett flashed on his past experience in the wilderness of the Italian Alps, but he felt more of a closeness here with the earth and the life which lived from it. He was especially awed by the delicate nearness he was permitted by the animals. The cottontails and jackrabbits, the skunks and raccoons, the feathered tribes of birds perched by their nests at the base of the hills by the cabin in El Rito. And higher up toward the range of mountaintops where the wilderness was truly unspoiled, it was the same. Snowshoe rabbits gave them a glance, porcupines eyed them from the underbrush;

flocks of wild turkeys trooped by them, always being led by a tough old gobbler; a brown bear lumbered along after being assured he was in no danger; a herd of antelope enjoyed the vegetation along the edge of a woodline fencing in an open meadow and curiously gazed for a moment at the frozen-still duo; the proud, antlered bucks stood tall and strong, surrounded by their yearlings and the does whose bellies were just beginning to swell with their unborn fawns. Each one of those magnificent stags was strikingly individual and solely responsible for his small herd — and the sight of them charged Emmett with a deep feeling that one of them was to be the answer to the question that brought him to New Mexico.

At night after eating his food and salad of wild onions picked from the ground and before lying down to talk with Natural Suzanne, Emmett would sometimes stand alone outside under the stars and listen to the howling of the coyotes and the whistling of the elks' mating calls and understand that whatever it was he was about to discover, it would be soon. This made him feel warm and open to the smells carried by the brisk, dark air, but nervous, that there was so much to manhood and being a man.

It was ten days after he arrived at El Rito that the meat was finished and more was needed for the women to make a new stew. Little Bird told Emmett over coffee that morning that today they would go for rabbit, and they went out of the cabin and walked into the hills with the morning sun warming their backs like always, but with a feeling inside them that was different from the other times they left together for the woods. Of course, they had always carried their weapons with them on their walks, but even though they sometimes had been only a few feet away from an animal, Little Bird had never used his bow or Emmett his rifle, because no meat had been needed for their table. However, now there was a need, and the rabbits they had only been watching they now were hunting.

Emmett had practiced a couple of hours every day at twilight with his bow, but it would take a while yet before he would be sure enough with it to make a clean kill. So he left it behind, carrying only his .22 Magnum rifle and some shells when he climbed into the hills with Little Bird, who cradled his Bear bow and ported a pouch of arrows slung across his back.

One thing Emmett quickly understood about the spirit of hunting: you only took what you went in after, and not just anything that you might happen across. Today they were hunting snowshoe rabbits, so Little Bird carried only blunt-tipped arrows to stun and Emmett steel-jacketed bullets to pierce, eliminating the possibility of mangling the meat of the animals with soft, hollow-point shells or thick, razor-edged arrows.

The sun was still low in its dawn, and the air was still chilly and wet with the last moments of night, when Emmett and Little Bird came upon the bunch of snowshoes, nibbling on the underside of a large berry bush right where they knew they would be at that early time of the day. As the rabbits continued eating their morning meal, Little Bird slipped next to a birch tree to break the outline of his figure, and Emmett followed his comrade's example, halving the shape of his image behind the thin, moist trunk of a young sapling, while slowly raising his rifle to his shoulder and bracing his left forearm against the rough bark to fasten his leverage and steady his aim. Little Bird had already eased an arrow from his pouch and stood poised with the shaft resting across his bow and the two fingers of his right hand pinching it in position with the still-relaxed string.

There were three rabbits, and the men were on both sides of them with Emmett closest to a pair and Little Bird not more than ten yards from the pudgiest. Emmett had a bullet already in the chamber, and a five-shot clip. He would hit the brace nearest him while Little Bird stunned the outsized one who was eating alone. Emmett kept both eyes open as he took bead on the tip of the nose of the snowshoe farthest from him, and watched Little Bird pull back his bowstring with one swift, silent motion. Emmett began to squeeze his trigger when he saw the blunt arrowhead nearing the shaft of his Indian brother's bow and returned his attention solely to his target.

The arrow and bullet shot through the air simultaneously with the crack report of the rifle overwhelming the clean sound of the snapped string — and the sweet whistle of the feathered arrow's flight was lost in the resounding echo of the gun blast. Emmett rapidly ejected the casing of the spent shell and bolted a fresh round into his chamber, and Little Bird unsheathed another arrow and quickly placed it flat across his bow, but Emmett's bullet tore into the bone above the third rabbit's twitching nose before Little Bird pulled taut his string. His unsheathed arrow did not go unused, however, because Little Bird's alert black eyes caught sight of another snowshoe leaping from beneath a bush some twenty yards away toward the protective cover of a large patch of underbrush. Emmett also saw the rabbit racing frantically, and he bolted another round into the chamber of his rifle, but waited, calmly leading the running snowshoe with the blackened sight of his barrel.

He could have dropped the rabbit four times while Little Bird was smoothly pulling back on his waxed string and bending his bow to its full arch, but he didn't, because no one had to tell him that the first shot belonged to his Indian friend and brother who spotted the animal begin his frightened dash, before Emmett. This time the sharp twang and the soft swoosh of the arrow's release and its swift flight and its thumping contact with the body of the rabbit was not drowned out by the unnatural sound of exploding gunpowder. Little Bird had stun-killed the animal with a direct blow above his tiny heart just as he was about to escape into a hole over thirty yards away.

Both men stood still for a moment, making sure that there was no more activity in the area before moving towards their catch. Emmett placed the safety on his rifle while Little Bird made sure both his hits were dead by breaking their necks. Emmett's pair, of course, had been killed instantly, and there was only a small inedible portion missing from the front of each of their heads where his bullets had ripped away some bone. If he had hit the rabbits anywhere else, there would have been very little left to eat. But he hadn't, and so now he had his first clean kills as a hunter.

They gathered the four rabbits together, and Little Bird made a slight incision in each of their stomachs to check their livers for spots which would mean they had some springtime or early-summer disease and could not be eaten. But there were no spots on any of them which was not unusual, because they were rather high up in the hills where the temperature seldom rose to the type of sultry heat which supposedly abets such disease in rabbits.

Emmett watched with a certain amount of amazement as Little Bird deftly moved his fingers around the insides of the rabbits, examining their innards and skillfully handling their entrails, searching for some trace of disorder. His amazement was caused by the obvious excitement that Little Bird was experiencing as he dealt with the warm bodies of the freshly killed animals. His eyes were wide and alive with a sort of spiritual enthusiasm, and in fact his whole body seemed involved in a climaxing orgasm that wasn't sexual, but rather religious. Sweat poured out of him and his muscles trembled and his mouth watered and his face jumped and twitched, while his whole body shook with the death experience. No words passed between them, but Emmett began to understand part of what he was there to learn by sensing the enormity of Little Bird's reaction to the kill. The words of an Indian hunting song which Little Bird had translated to him one evening started to beat their message into his brain: "I aim my golden bow; I pull on my golden string; I let fly my golden arrow; and it strikes the heart of the target, and I fall dead. For I am the target. And the target is me."

There were many more snowshoes, cottontails, and jackrabbits, and three wild turkeys taken during the next two weeks, and each time the animals were treated with the same respect that both men would have had for themselves had they been the targets of their own weapons. Also, during that time, Emmett became more and more one with the creatures he hunted and soon Little Bird could see that his pupil — who was only a bit more than two years his younger — was now ready to learn what he brought him there to teach.

One morning, the two men did not leave together for the usual walk in the northern hills. Emmett left alone, to hunt the three-year-old buck he chose to be his first deer when he saw him standing proud against the waters of a rain brook in the light of a falling sunset. He picked the buck from dozens he saw on his walks with Little Bird through the woods, because there was something about the stag that told Emmett it was him.

It was a three-hour walk to the place in the forest where Emmett knew the buck had eaten his dawn meal and bedded himself down on pine needles to sleep away the sunlight in the shade of the tall, thick cover of a thousand trees. When he reached the outside of the young buck's territory, Emmett knelt quietly against a birch and slowly checked every inch of the area with eyes that were now trained to see what they had been blind to a month before. He remained frozen, moving nothing but his eyes and, ever so carefully, his head, for a timeless hour, before relaxing the stiffness of his muscles against the soft, dew-moist earth.

Emmett could sense the presence of his buck nearby, and his eyes showed him at least a dozen places where he might be lying, but gave no definite hint as to which of them was the actual resting place of his deer. Emmett had learned well not to be anxious, and so he waited motionlessly for some sign that would bring the stag to him. He was downwind, and it was a brisk one, rustling the leaves and covering any sound of his humanity or his rough asthmatic breathing.

He would do absolutely nothing to startle the buck to his feet and spook him out of whichever shadow he was lying in. He didn't want it to be that way. He wanted to hit the animal as he calmly rose from his sleep, so that the kill would be the cleanest of kills, and the deer would not even have to suffer a moment's shock of apprehension. Emmett loved this stag he had come to hunt. He had seen him three or four times, and the buck was always alone by the watering hole or pulling buds from the oak brush. That may have been the main reason Emmett chose to hunt him as his first deer: he always saw him alone. This was curious because he was obviously a young, strong buck who should have been followed by at least a brace of does and a yearling or two.

But Little Bird had pointed out that it wasn't that odd, because his mates might have recently been hunted by the handful of Indian men who ventured this far north "out of the white man's hunting season," or else they might have fallen prey to the many predatory cats who roamed this particular area. Either of Little Bird's observations could be true, and Emmett wondered whether animals like his young buck felt loneliness in some way at all. He didn't feel silly in supposing that they did sense something similar to man in their instinct toward life, and he looked up at the clouds and watched them roll and lumber around the blue sky for what seemed like hours until a formation appeared in the mass of white billow and separated itself from the rest of the cumulus puffs to stand alone and apart — a cloud shaped like his antlered stag deer.

Emmett was stunned when he lowered his eyes and saw rising up in front of him, not more than a few yards to his left, the buck he had come to hunt. He blinked his eyes to clear them of the sky and swung his rifle slowly around the trunk of the tree, until the barrel was aimed at that sharp, smooth surface of hide-covered bone alongside the buck's right ear which showed no sign of alarm or fear. He was magnificent, with a strong, handsome face and taut-muscles beautifully framed in a hard body. His legs were long and he casually shook the stiffness of sleep out of them and muffle-pounded his razor-edged hooves on the ground, snorting himself awake.

As Emmett began to squeeze off the round with both his eyes open, the refrain of the Santo Domingo Pueblo hunting song played on the rhythms of his mind and the beat of his heart. The .22

Magnum explosion momentarily blurred the vision of himself falling gracefully, but hard, dead to the ground, the target of the bullet he had just fired. For he was the target, and the target was him.

Emmett fought to keep from trembling at the sight which now lay only a few feet away on the ground, twitching the last nerves of life from his body. He looked at the buck and saw himself, and watched as the animal's spirit left the creature still, and saw how it would be when the time came for him, and he waited silently and allowed the splendid buck to unsufferingly die in peace and in private.

The hollow-point bullet exploded inside the creature's brain and killed him instantly, but that instant was eternal for Emmett. He moved slowly toward the downed buck, after he was satisfied that the magic of his death had ended. Now kneeling beside him, Emmett sensed an overwhelming oneness with the deer.

He slit the animal's belly neatly open and gutted him like a young surgeon performing an abdominal operation on a live body for the first time. Then he tied first the front and then the hind legs of the deer together as he'd been told to do by Little Bird, using some stringy, cordlike sinew he removed from the stomach along with the rest of the entrails. He paused for a moment to look again at the strong beauty of the buck and to let the poetic harmony of the song he learned from his Pueblo Indian brother beat throughout his being.

The past month he spent stalking in the woods and climbing in the mountain forests had strengthened his body to a point where he could feel the difference in himself. By using all of this built-up strength and by exerting all of his pent-up energy, Emmett was able to hoist the slain stag onto his shoulders. He stood calmly for a moment afterwards to adjust the weight on his back and to achieve a snug one-to-one balance with the two-hundred-pound animal he now had to carry all the way back down to the cabin in El Rito. When he was satisfied with the way the deer sat on his shoulders, he picked up his .22 and slid it through both the pairs of corded legs, resting his forearms over the butt and barrel ends of the rifle to apply just enough easy pressure on the coupled legs which were folded over his round, bony shoulders and down against the upper part of his heaving chest. With his arms hanging loosely in this position, Emmett felt he would be able to keep the animal braced easily in place and maintain the even distribution of its weight across his back.

He flexed and rolled his shoulders one final time to see if the deer would shift on him, and when it didn't, he began the way back to El Rito, sure that his burden would stand the test by staying put for the entire walk down through the quiet, wooded foothills of the Carson National Forest and Tierra Amarilla.

Once he found the proper and comfortable rhythm for his stride, Emmett settled into the march and walked with the silent and stern, but graceful, determination of a man in a footrace with darkness and fatigue. He instinctively knew that if he began to take rest stops along the way, his body would tempt him to lengthen each respite until he gave up the agony of his effort. So he didn't stop at all during the next three hours, refusing to acknowledge the ache, while stepping quickly and carefully along the damp ground, cautiously choosing every spot before planting his feet with a firmness that might have been mistaken for anger by someone who was unaware of the enormous energy which Emmett Grogan had discovered within himself that seemingly timeless afternoon. A vital, spiritual energy which surged through his body, filling him with an invisible physical strength from the moment he aimed his rifle at the wilderness within himself and fired on the target of his own animality.

It was dusk when Emmett stepped out of the woodline and made it across a dusty, dry, flat field and the rest of the way to the cabin on the outskirts of El Rito. Little Bird stood in the shadow of the back wall and came forward to greet his friend, student, and brother with a strong, silent, calm look of love, and helped him remove the deer from his back which was now screaming with a pain that was only overcome by the ecstasy of Emmett's triumph over himself.

They laid the magnificent buck softly down on a large piece of canvas tarpaulin which Little Bird had spread on the earth at the rear of the house a good hour before Emmett emerged from the forests. Then Emmett stood straight and watched from above as Little Bird checked the inside of the belly of the slain stag for anything that might have been missed and which, if left in the deer much longer, might have spoiled the obvious quality of the meat. But there was nothing, and Little Bird was privately proud that his white brother had cleaned out the innards so well, and he quickly completed his examination of the rest of the animal, pleased with the single, small round hole on the side of the noble head where the .22 bullet had struck and which he knew had felled the deer instantly and painlessly.

After Little Bird satisfied himself about the cleanness of the kill, he rose and stood alongside Emmett and silently regarded the magnificence of the buck with the man he now knew he had taught well. They remained standing there together for a solid five minutes before Little Bird spoke the word Emmett badly wanted to hear. "Good," was all he said.

Cease and Natural Suzanne appeared out of the rear door of the cabin with a piece of fry bread and a single bowl of stew, which they laid down on the canvas next to the buck's proud, antlered head. He would eat the same food they were going to eat that evening so his spirit would not go hungry on its voyage to the ethereal hunting ground in which the Indians believe. The women also stood with their men for a few moments, silently regarding Emmett's splendid buck in the last minutes of twilight before darkness. They, too, were proud of Emmett for he was now a hunter — which was what his being there was all about.

As soon as they finished their supper and Emmett briefly relieved his body's exhaustion with two soothing hand-rolled cigarettes, he and Little Bird went back outside where they carefully skinned the buck and sectioned up his meat to be cooked later as steaks, or thinned and hung to dry as jerky, or used in stew. It was exacting work and it was nearly midnight before Little Bird salted down and buried the skin in the earth, and Emmett scooped out and jarred what was left of the buck's brains for use in the future tanning of the skin.

When they were finished cleaning down the animal and had sliced most of the meat up for jerky, Natural Suzanne and Cease quick-fried several small but delicately delicious steaks taken from the backbone of the deer, and they ate what Emmett considered the finest meat he had ever tasted. Afterwards, each couple went to their section of the cabin's divided main room where they lay down together. Emmett was too completely exhausted to talk with his woman, but she understood and kissed him with her juice-filled mouth, softly raising his cock hard with her lips and her tongue, easing forth an ejaculation that burst full-loaded wet against the inside of her cheeks, splashing like a hot wave down her slender throat and sedating Emmett into the slumber of a long, deep sleep.

He didn't wake up until the uncommonly late hour of nine o'clock the next morning. He felt a strange urge swelling up inside of him, even before he came fully awake and opened his eyes. Little

Bird's younger brother had driven to El Rito earlier that morning to visit, and the two of them were out on the huge prairie field, picking wild onions, potatoes and other green vegetables to be used in the stew, and Cease and Natural Suzanne were already boiling down the deer's bones for stock over the wood-burning stove in the kitchen.

Emmett pulled on his dungarees and went out back to take a good, healthy shit in the outhouse and get some well water to wash himself awake. As he splashed the water on his face and scrubbed the sleep from his eyes, the sensation got stronger and stronger, pulling him away from the dry New Mexican earth where he was standing and setting him down on the concrete sidewalks of San Francisco. It was a powerful feeling rather than a stubborn thought, which was priming his instincts and telling him to move on, to leave the country for the city, to get back to the place he came from. The towel flapped against his face, as the energies he acquired the day before joined with his old primal instinct to overwhelm him with a force that made his whole body tremor and understand that it was time to go. To go to the place and the people that were flashing in visions behind the lids of his closed eyes. The place and the people he left to come to the mountain by himself. The mountain where Little Bird showed him all there was to see and where Emmett Grogan, for one split second of eternity, became a magnificent, buck deer.

He spent all the time he needed to spend on the mountain and had learned what he needed to learn. Now it was time to return to the valley where the earth was covered with cement and where the people lived their lives hoping for a moment's relief, and show his brothers and sisters what he saw, simply by returning.

The women were still busy in the kitchen, and Natural Suzanne poured Emmett a large tin cup of strong, black coffee sliced with chicory when she saw him coming. But Emmett didn't stop to drink it after he entered the back door. In fact, he wasn't conscious even of having crossed through the kitchen on his way to the section of the cabin's main room where his belongings were neatly stacked. There was nothing in his thoughts but the knowledge that it was time.

He moved like a man possessed but unfrantic, and within a few minutes he had packed his few things into a knapsack, sleeved his bow in its case, bound his arrows together and strapped them onto the side of the pack. He decided to leave the .22 in the corner of the room where it was leaning against the wall next to a couple of boxes of shells, a pair of shotguns and two Colt .45s. He stood up straight and quietly for a second, swinging the backpack over his right shoulder and loosely clutching his bow in the fingers of his left hand. When he was satisfied that he had made no mistakes in picking and choosing what to leave behind and what to take with him, he looked slowly around the room for what he knew would be the last time, and nodded his head at a robin that was winking at him through the only window.

Emmett walked out the front door of the cabin and down the dusty dirt road to El Rito where he would begin his long hitchhike back to the city of Saint Francis. He never said a word to Natural Suzanne or to Cease, nor did he search out Little Bird to say good-bye. He didn't have to.

It took him four days and all of the eighty-five cents he had in his pocket to get back to Frisco with only the heavy deer scent on the Black Bear, Rain-tite jacket Little Bird had given him to protect his senses from the immediate, hard, cold, unnatural assault of the city and its streets. Emmett kept one of the lapels tucked near his nose, using the perfume of the wilderness to defend himself against the industrial smell of progress and modern civilization. At first he felt weird in the midst of the rush-hour city, like he felt those few times he was released from the slow pace of the jails and prisons where he had been forced to sit out too much of his life. It was almost the same way now, returning from the mild, casual environ of the forests to the rapid, nonsensical, heated game of the city.

Instead of hitching rides, he walked through the downtown area and across to the Fillmore district where he knew Coyote would be in the large bottom floor of a house in which he was living with his woman, Sam, and a number of other people. Emmett walked because he wasn't tired and because he wanted to let the feel of the city work him over and massage him back into the shape he would need if he was going to pick up where he left off.

It was the first week of May, and while Emmett was walking toward his brother's pad with a bow in his hand and arrows on his back, Bobby Seale, twenty of his brothers, and six of his sisters, were walking around the Capitol in Sacramento with guns pointed straight up in the air or straight down to the ground, propagandizing to the urban blacks and to all the low-money people who live in the cities of America that the Second Amendment of the Constitution of the United States gives them the right to bear arms for their own self-defense — a right Ronald Reagan and his state legislature were, at that moment, attempting to infringe by passing a bill called the Mulford Act which was aimed at keeping the lower classes disarmed and powerless, while at the same time increasing both the firepower and the repressive investigative powers of the police agencies throughout California.

The Mulford Act meant a lot at the time because, as the Panther Party mandate stated that day in the Capitol at Sacramento, the bill pending before the legislature ". . . brings the hour of doom one step nearer. A people who have suffered so much for so long at the hands of a racist society, must draw the line somewhere . . . to halt the progression of a trend that leads inevitably to their total destruction." It doesn't really matter what eventually happened to that act any longer, whether it's still pending, was shelved or passed. It's just another fucking bill to pay, and that's the way it's always been, until it isn't anymore.

Emmett walked heavy through the city, smelling himself as much as possible to prolong his taste of the mountain. Coyote was glad to see his brother looking so raw-meat wild, and his old lady, Sam, gave Emmett a plate of food, a beer, and made ready a place for him to crash the weariness of the four-day journey out of his system with a good sound sleep, alone.

No one in the house asked him any questions he might not want to answer, and he told them little because his had been a private voyage, and he came back smelling good and that was enough.

Coyote and Communication Company Claude told him all the news he needed to know and within two days he was back with Tumble and Brooks and the women and Slim, delivering food and stealing meat and whatever else wasn't nailed down. Billy Landout even returned from wherever he had been, settling on the outskirts of San Francisco in Daly City with a family he formed along his way and getting back into Free Food again with the others.

Thirty days of solid, hard, relentless work came and went for Emmett like a flash. The food was now rolling once more after it lagged for a while, and there were thousands of kids coming into town from all over with flowers in their eyes and bellies to be filled with hot Digger stew and Super-Spade grass. It was getting very crowded around the Haight and the glint-glimmer of the summer of love fast faded for those who came, wanting what was never there.

Besides the physical labor of trucking around free food for the people and all sorts of free goods for the Trip Without a Ticket free store and checking every once in a while on the rapidly opening and closing Haight-Ashbury crash pads, and taking doctors around on their evening runs and transporting loads of piled-up garbage to the dump and getting busted on charges that were always dismissed, and trying to see and oversee that every one of his brothers and sisters had what they needed for doing what was necessary. Besides being overactively involved in all of that and more, Emmett also began to write about things which he understood and which concerned the people toward whom he felt a responsibility. The Communication Company would print his writings as single papers and distribute them throughout the city, and instead of signing his name at the end of each piece, Emmett drew which is the universal signature of primitive man.

The first paper he wrote was:

THERE IS A GREAT DEAL TO BE SILENT ABOUT

Contemporary history is a money conspiracy — the key to the atom. The facade of present seeming normalcy shows signs of weathering. Each day the cement crumbles a little more and the consequence is an increasing self-division. Portents of chaos everywhere as we grow aware of our own nakedness and impotence. Time is shrinking into itself; only the present seems to hold possibility. We are no longer the heroes of history.

Long-term goals and institutions have lost their relevance. Work is time spent in thrall. *Now* is an accumulation of ends with all goals immediate. Children are tearing away the false front of dignity and status. They are entering existence knowing that today is the first day in the rest of their lives. They want an authentic identity. A new barbarian race flashing on pagan energy, searching for rituals and tribal touch. As they fly from banality and approach the essence of horror.

New determination to pursue experience to its farthest limits. Mad exuberance and hunger for sensation are a constant goad. A demonic circle. A response to existence in last century, at the bottom of personality looking up. Efforts not wasted in games which kill time, deaden awareness and brutalize feeling. Masks thrown off and one enters the inescapable truth and squalor of own being. Beyond the reach of compulsion. *Beyond the possibility of defeat.* Ideology of failure.

Flow with real tides of existence which reach into an underground beyond guise, hate, or love. All contacts immediate and intense. All real things are to be faced in all moments of agony and joy. Everything else is a deception. Politics is an arena where words are juggled in a gigantic hoax. Sharpen senses to continue and improve dialogue with existence. Meaning only found beyond experience. Basic impulse always religious, a cold light on our own incompleteness. Like a debauched child's face.

Another news sheet of Emmett's had to do with another Human Be-In that was proposed by the editors of the San Francisco *Oracle*, the HIP merchants' association, and the Leary-like community shamans dressed all in white. These brilliant wizards wanted to gather 500,000 people on a reservation near Gallup, New Mexico, to celebrate the summer solstice of June 21, 1967. They had already gone to speak with the Hopi Indians who lived there about it, but were given no answers to questions they had just begun to ask, when the reservation's Indian sheriff and his deputies threw them off the land because of their total disrespect and utter arrogance toward the elders of the tribe. For a group of some thirty-year-old hippies who purported to have an enormous regard for the Indians, they did all they consciously could to insult and disturb them.

Fancy, spangled-dressed HIP merchants committed sacrilege after sacrilege by entering the sanctity of hogans and coming back out with the secret, traditional masks of dancers they ripped off the walls and exposed to crowds of uninitiated children who gathered outside the doors of the huts and tepees, startled by what the hippies with their "Santa Claus" beards were doing in the face of thousands of years of spiritual tradition. Longhaired couples flung off their clothes and quick-fucked and gangbanged one another on ground the Indians considered holy, as an expression of the freedom they found by dropping out and as a symbol of their unfailing love for and solidarity with the Indian and his culture. But the Indians didn't see it quite that way. In fact, most of them got plenty god-damn mad at all the hippie men and women running around naked and copulating in the dirt in front of the Indian men, women and children. Some of the stray white women even tried to seduce a few of the young Indian bucks which brought a swift reaction from their wives and wives-to-be.

On top of all of this banality, marijuana and LSD were given to the children. This was the final outrage to the Hopi who had not even invited these "Indian lovers" to be their guests. So they kicked them off their land and told them never to return, no matter how much money the Haight merchants insisted the Indians could rake in behind a Human Be-In. It was shortly after the hippies had driven away in their VW buses that the elders of the tribe discovered that several masks and other spiritual ornaments and accessories were missing — stolen by children born of the same race of people who once before robbed the Indian of everything and left him with nothing.

Emmett's piece about the self-appointed, Haight-Ashbury community leaders' meeting with the Hopi Indians was much different from the account that had been reported to the people of San Francisco by the hippies who were there, and it went on to point out the mercenary absurdity of having a "Be-In" at Gallup, New Mexico, in the first place — because of things like the 120 degree heat, the lack of food or water, the antipathy of the Indians and all residents of the area who would surely, with the cops on their side, violently resist an invasion of hippies.

This tight, two-page report regarding the proposed event was picked up and spread around the underground press and turned out to be enough to cancel all the shopkeepers' plans for a Grand Canyon blast. The marketeers' dream of another West Coast Human Be-In got what it deserved.

The 🔣 series of papers were becoming well-known editorials among the underground, and speculation was high as to who was writing them, with Emmett taking every precaution against his being discovered as their author. He wrote several more of these articles on the attitude New Mexico and its people had towards the longhairs, informing persons who were thinking of migrating to that state about an entrenched animosity the Indians had for almost everyone and the Chicanos had for the Anglos, especially the hippie Anglos.

There has always been a smoldering resentment on the part of the Chicanos against Anglos, because the cities they once dominated in New Mexico, like Albuquerque, were taken from them by Anglo immigrants who had been moving there since 1940 to work for the federal government. It was the atom bomb and these federal payrolls that made Albuquerque a more or less major city, a center for atomic weaponry, increasing its population by almost 800 percent in three decades, from 40,000 to 320,000, and thereby drastically changing the culture of the whole state from Spanish to Anglo.

This tension between the Chicanos and the Anglos skyrocketed with the arrival of the longhairs, who began traveling to the state for its high altitude and desertlike climate, which made it something of a health resort for them. The gap between these money-from-home-counter-all-cultures Anglo immigrants and most of the state's poverty-stricken, unemployed Mexican-Americans was immediate and deep. The longhairs treated the land as a giant playpen, running around drugged and naked in a false spirit of liberation and goofing on the dirt-eating-poor Chicanos whom they considered "unhip." These same impoverished Chicanos — their live-down-the-road neighbors — who tried to scratch a living out of the earth, the earth that mocked their labor in the same way that the frivolous, wasteful behavior of the Anglo hipsters mocked their back-breaking lives, watched what they considered the hippies' debauchery and grew very angry.

This anger continued to smolder within, until it was given a chance for release by the fundamentalist Protestant preacher Reies Tijerina, who came from Texas to lead the first Brown Power uprising of the desperately poor in northern New Mexico during that summer of '67. This seizure of a whole county of land from the Anglos by Tijerina and his Alianza brothers and sisters gave the state's Chicano population a new pride in themselves as a people, and with that pride came a strong desire to strike out at these "young, white, longhaired punks" who taught the Chicano children to disrespect their parents and betray their Mexican-American traditions with talk of rock and roll music and free love.

The many tension-filled spots throughout the state suddenly exploded in a series of violent incidents in which the solitary were murdered and the together were raped and beaten. The situation continued and grew into an open war with the governor of the state publicly saying, "Yes!" to the Chicanos, giving them the Go sign to attack the longhairs for their arrogant life-style which was "bound to make anarchists of their Chicano young anyway." It went on like that until the longhairs armed and began defending themselves, and the war against the "outsiders" reached the stalemate it remains at this day. Only one or two incidents occur each year that ever make the front pages of the big city Albuquerque newspapers, which only thirty years ago were printed in Spanish.

Emmett wrote strongly in these articles about the then-developing situation in New Mexico, and through them tried to temper the arrogance of a group of transient white children who thought flowers were lovely and poverty still an adventure. He never knew if any of the things he wrote had any effect on the migration of longhairs to the Southwest, but he did discover that the Chicanos who lived in the Mission district of San Francisco responded favorably to his reports, and it was eventually through those very same few words he wrote on white pieces of paper that he met and joined some of the emerging young radical street leaders in their fight against the poverty and hard-drug epidemic in that Spanish community of the city.

Every night Emmett would try to piece together some message to himself and anyone who cared to read and understand. He attacked the lackadaisical hedonism of the Haight by shouting over and over that ". . . the point of life is not rest, but action. Death is rest! And everyone will have enough rest for eternity. Now is the time for action, because the world must be seen clearly . . . Western society has destroyed itself. The culture is extinct. Politics are as dead as the culture they supported. Ours is the first skirmish of an enormous struggle, infinite in its implications." And on and on, every chance he got, Emmett tried to smack awake those people who he felt were being duped to death by themselves and others.

Who the fuck are you, anyway! Sitting there in lotus and desperately suffering Anglo Entertainment Syndrome. Hungry for rituals and tribal touch. Lack of elders to initiate you into the magic of yourselves. You are starving! Most of you would be soldiers if not acid. Dig the lack of sensitivity to the Indian thing, obvious on its face; murder all over again. First: the physically meat bodies of Indians gunned down all over the place. Second: the treatment of Indians as property by the Haight Independent Proprietors' attempted wipe-out of the Indian soul simply by camping on it. You're all romantically Indian struck! Witness the horror of HIP *Oracle* newspaper staff sitting on Third Mesa in Hopiland, chanting Anglo, Super-Culture Prostitution of Hari Krishna to uninitiated children. Nervous status maneuvers! The time-worn, white-man arrogance of a million questions with backup answers. The Indian message to mankind is simply, *"Go with silence and closed eyes."* Stop looking into another man's world! Turn onto yourself! Don't consume someone else! Eat yourself and kiss the now with full-blown lips! *Courage is implicit!*

One day Emmett found a hand-lettered poem taped onto the steering wheel of the pickup truck. He had just stepped out for a moment to buy a can of Ballantine Ale:

> IF I AM DOING IT
> AT ALL, IT'S FOR
> LOVE NOT FOR OIL.
> I LOVE CRUSADERS!
> WHOES GOT THE GRAIL?!
> IF IT'S FULL OF OIL

THERE'S A BETTER ONE MADE.
IT'S NEW AND IT'S
THEOREY, BUT MAYBE
WE CAN GIVE IT AWAY
SO THAT THIS TIME
THE SECRET IS A
GIFT FROM
A FRIEND.

It was signed with the same ancient swastika marking with which Emmett had been ending all of his Communication-Company-published material, and he folded it up and put it in his pocket, understanding that he was never going to be able to use that mark as a pseudonym again, because he just wanted to sneak all the way, and that's all there was to it!

June came up fast, and, a few weeks before the country's schools were scheduled to close and release their students to take part in the invasion of the Haight-Ashburys of America in search of a highly prepublicized "Summer of Love," the Diggers were invited by members of the East Coast national leadership of the Students for a Democratic Society to attend one of their annual weekend meetings in a woodsy campground in Michigan. Coyote was back acting with the San Francisco Mime Troupe in their free outdoor commedia dell'arte productions in the parks around the city and wasn't interested in the invitation. But the Hun had resigned his position with the company long ago and thought it would be a good idea to catch a breather from the free store guerrilla theater before the hordes of flower children descended on the Haight. The formal invitation was mailed to the Diggers at the Trip Without a Ticket on Cole Street, and the Hun, therefore, was given first notice of the conference.

Emmett and Billy Landout found out about it a couple of days later when Coyote mentioned that he wouldn't be going. Soon afterwards, the Hun had a meet at his house with Emmett, Billy and Tumble, and the four of them decided they'd go to the conference for the specific purpose of disrupting it — calling the white radicals' bluff which hadn't been done since the days of civil rights when the integration ne plus ultra of all integration promised to the black people had turned out to be their integration into one of the most absurd systems of isms in the modern world of commodities, universally based and dependent on class conflict for its survival.

Anyway, the four men felt that a five- or six-day drive to and from the heartland of America would be a refreshing break from the heavy routine of their daily Digger activities. Also, the "Digger phenomena," as it was called in the media, had begun to sprout up in other areas of North America in all sorts of shades, shapes and sizes. Emmett thought it was about time something was revealed to separate the heavyweight life-style of the San Francisco Digger family from the lightweight dilettantism of the credit-card-carrying-Christian-do-gooders in Los Angeles, the do-nothing, ideologically rhetorical "digger Provos" in Berkeley, the hip-social workers of Toronto — and above all the New York diggers, who were publicly led around by Abbot Hoffman and his publicity-seeking cronies.

Emmett didn't like all of that nonsense very much and neither did the rest of the San Francisco Digger people, who felt put down by all the vaudeville clowning that was being carried on in their name, while they themselves actually were overburdened with real, unfunny slave labor, trying to begin the construction of a world *where you didn't have to laugh anymore*! So that Thursday morning the four of them climbed into the Hertz car rented with a finders-keepers-losers-weepers credit card and began their long drive to Michigan with intent, as well as with jugs of whiskey and wine, cans of beer, and plenty of amphetamines to get them there nonstop the next afternoon.

It was one hell of a run with the four men taking turns behind the wheel to maintain an average speed in excess of ninety miles an hour, and the tires blowing out one, two, three, four, five, six times on the salt-hot, flat stretches of highway from Nevada to Nebraska — where in the town of North Platte the local, fat-bellied sheriff pointed out Buffalo Bill's house as he escorted them out of his limits with a "Be on yer way an' don't you never think 'bout comin' back this town again, specially after the sun go down. You understan' my meanin' or do I have to spell it out more plain for you freaky fellas, huh?" And on into Kalamazoo, Michigan, the next day at about five in the evening where a giant, lime-colored, neon sign was screaming *Insulin! Insulin! Insulin!* in the front window of a country drug-store, flooding the dim dusk of the main street with its loud green message and advising them to pull over 'cause it was time to sponge up the two days' booze with a hot supper before continuing on to Denton and the conference.

They pulled into a space along the empty curb in front of a bar-restaurant-grill that looked small-time hokey-light from the outside, but was huge, bigtime, country-heavy on the inside, which they discovered on entering the place and walking right smack into the jowls of a giant, loose, Friday-evening-crowd of one hundred steel workers, spending the lid off of the wages they had just been paid at the town's mill before bringing the rest home to their old women.

Emmett walked through the front door first, and the laughing, yelling, loud-talking, bulk-muscled, short-sleeved, polo-shirted, white workmen fell into a stone-faced silence the instant they saw him and his long hair hanging below the shoulders of the canvas, Rain-tite jacket he always wore. The silence grew louder and colder as each of his brothers stepped inside behind him and followed him the thirty or so feet past a pair of pocket pool tables toward the long, walnut bar along the back wall, where room was quietly made for them by men who were standing with their feet on the rail.

As he moved forward, Emmett could see that none of the seventy or eighty tables in the place was empty, and his quick glance also told him that the burning sensation he felt flushing at the base of his neck was the glare of the one hundred or so pairs of clean, midwestern eyes seated in the jungle of chairs around those tables, deadpanning their shaggy clothes and two-day auto grime. When he got to the bar the bartender was waiting, and the man seemed a little frightened about what Emmett guessed he figured was going to happen after the silence broke. "He must be the owner, and that's why he's worryin'. He don't care nothin' 'bout us, it's only the damage to his place that he's feelin' anxious 'bout," thought Emmett, as he looked into the man's eyes and ordered what they had been drinking for the past two days on the road. "Four double Four Roses rye whiskies 'n four bottles of Budweiser beer, please."

No one moved except the man behind the bar, as he set up the order and asked with his voice cracking if there'd be anything else. The menu was written in chalk on a blackboard above the bar, and Emmett glanced at his brothers about what they were going to eat, and back up at the board, then down again into the worried owner-bartender's face that was all rosy pink from capillaries broken by booze and said clearly, "Four hot beef stews 'n plenty of bread and butter, please." Emmett calmly tucked the corner of a twenty-dollar bill under his still-full bottle of beer, so the man could see that no matter what might go down, he would get paid.

Whispers began to break through the quiet, and as they grew louder the men closest to the four of them returned to whatever they'd been talking about, minding their own business. The jokes about beatniks and hippies quickly followed, but never loud enough to become a challenge, and the laughter came back into the strong bellies of the crowd of hard-working men who lived what was left of their lives only on weekends.

Everything looked like it was going to be all right, when the Hun, for some singular, absurd, irrational reason of his own, walked brazenly over to the rack of pool cues along the side wall, took one out and returned to the bar with it in his hand. Emmett was just as surprised at the Hun's crazy move as most of the workmen who saw him make it. The food hadn't come yet, and it was going to be another five or ten minutes before it did, and then it would take the four of them about five or ten minutes more to eat it all which made it almost a solid half hour before they'd be leaving the place, and "What the fuck are you going to do, just sit here at the bar with that pool stick between your legs to be ready in case you have to beat away someone or somethin', huh! You goddamn, ignorant prick!" Emmett, Billy and Tumble didn't say any of that out loud to the Hun. They just looked at him that way and tried to let their eyes do the talking for them, but he didn't hear them, or wouldn't, being too busy out-hippin' himself which was his usual pose during tight situations.

Some of the men in the joint thought the Hun's action was funny, and they laughed uproariously. But some of the others didn't think his move was hilarious at all, and in fact seemed to consider it downright insulting to the "live and let live" hospitality they were willing to display. It didn't take long before one of them came over to the little, five-foot-eight-inch, 130-pound Hun to see whether he wanted to play out the move he'd just made.

The guy was about fifty with long, stringy muscles and white hair, and he already had half a bag on. He stood next to the Hun who was sitting on a stool at the end of the bar with the cue stick resting on his left leg, and Emmett standing by his right elbow. The guy had a mixed drink of rye and ginger ale in his hand, and he swayed a little bit as he stood looking at the pool cue, and finally lifted his head clumsily to ask, "Wha' you gonna do with that?"

Emmett felt he couldn't allow the Hun the chance to answer the dude with his usual flip-lip, because his answer would set off whatever was going to happen to all four of them. So Emmett slid between the guy and the Hun's back and politely, but soundly, answered that "he ain't gonna do nothin' with it, 'cause I'm gonna use it for what it was made to do. That's what my friend brought it over here for in the first place — to shoot a game of pool. But after he brought it over, he just realized how tired he really was from all the

388

drivin' he done today, and I decided to play the game he ain't goin'
to. Is that all right, mister?"

The white-haired, wiry guy looked at Emmett for a moment before walking away and back to the other end of the bar where he
came from. A young guy picked up where the older man left off,
however, by approaching Emmett and asking him if he cared to
shoot a game with him. There was no animosity visible in the
younger fellow's face, just a bit of curiosity maybe. So Emmett said,
"Sure, but we'll have to make it a quick game of nine ball, 'cause my
food'll be comin' up soon. That okay with you?" The cat said that it
was, and Emmett racked the nine balls, using only his forearms and
hands to shape them together, and everyone in the bar saw by the
way he packed the balls into the difficult diamond formation without a wooden frame that Emmett knew what to do with a pool
table.

They flipped a coin and Emmett won the toss. He shot the cue
ball hard into the right side of the diamond pack, sinking the number three ball on the break and scattering the rest all over the table.
He sank four more balls into the pockets with his next four consecutive shots before missing an easy bank into the corner, leaving the
other guy to run off the last four neatly positioned balls on the
table, including the nine ball which meant the game. Emmett paid
off the dude with what they agreed to play for, a drink, and also
thanked him for letting him shoot a quick game, shook his hand
with a "much obliged," and then sat down on the stool at the bar
where his hot beef stew had just arrived from the kitchen.

It was dark by the time the four of them left the bar with their
bellies warm and full and their minds toying with the refreshing
idea of a little sleep. Denton wasn't far, and Emmett said he'd drive
the rest of the way to the campground. He had no idea how tired he
was nor how juiced he'd gotten in the bar, and therefore had no
reason to slow down from the ninety-mile-per-hour pace they maintained across more than half the country. There were very few cars
on the road, and after he was at the wheel for about forty minutes
he began to get the feeling they were lost.

The others were all sound asleep, so Emmett picked up the piece
of paper from the dashboard that was the hand-drawn map the
owner of the bar had given them to find their way to the camp in
Denton, Michigan, and held it up in front of him, resting it on the
steering wheel without slowing down, and shifting his eyes from the
road to the paper and back.

He traveled about five miles this way and had just taken another glance at the map, when the asphalt-covered side road he was whipping along suddenly opened onto and across a four lane highway. During the seconds Emmett was glancing at the map, his eyes missed the road sign which would have told him to stop for the intersection, so he didn't know to slow down or even what he was approaching until it happened. The car leaped across the interstate highway between a pair of oncoming trailer trucks whose drivers more than likely shat in their pants, and ended up on the other side of the crossroad that was paved only with gravel-dirt which couldn't handle the high speed of the car's wheels, sending it into a side spin that startled the other three awake just in time for them to see what Emmett's eyes were screaming about. The right side of the car was rapidly sliding toward a concrete road abutment with terrific, slow-motion, instant, fast energy, as if it were being drawn to it by some hidden magnetic force. Everyone jumped to the left side of the car, Billy literally climbing into Emmett's lap, to get away from the roaring, oncoming, concrete block. The split-fraction-of-a-second it went out of view, they all cringed, waiting for the impact that never came, because fate or whatever squeezed the car a hairbreadth past the deadly stone abutment and sent it jumping into the air where it floated still for a moment, before crashing down into the river on the left side of the road and breaking in half.

It all occurred, from start to finish, in about two, three, or four seconds' time, but it seemed longer — much longer. No one was hurt, only a few bumps and the after-shock of waking up into a nightmare and nearly dying. They stood in the thigh-high, quiet water of the small river for a while, each one silently musing to himself about what just happened, and all of them trying to come out of the stupor their brush with sudden death caused their systems. Billy Landout was sitting out of the water on top of the car's trunk; Tumble had his leg hanging over one of the front fenders; the Hun was standing a few feet from the cracked auto and checking out his eyeglasses to see whether or not they were damaged; and Emmett was leaning against the side of the car with his arms outstretched across the top of the roof, thinking the same thoughts as the others.

A farmer turned onto the road with his wife in the cab and his six or seven children in the rear of a tailgate pickup. He stopped, of course, and looked agape at the sight he knew he never would believe if he hadn't seen it with his own two eyes. The man gestured for his family to remain in the truck as he stepped out and approached the bank where he asked the four brothers, who were still standing in the middle of the river, whether he could oblige them in any way, like by telephoning the local sheriff's office or a garage or something.

There was a pleasant smile on the farmer's face which couldn't help show how amusing the outrageous spectacle seemed to him. Tumble asked the farmer to please use his phone in both the ways he mentioned and told him they would all wait for the police and garageman to show. Tumble closed with a sincere "Thank you," and the farmer headed back toward the cab of his truck, but he didn't climb into it. Instead, he leaned inside for a second and turned back around with what looked like. a Brownie Hawkeye camera, complete with flash attachment, in his worn, hard hands.

He returned to the edge of the bank, holding the camera and shyly asked, " 'Scuse me, fellas. I know it might seem downright impolite, but I jus' hadda ask you or I'd be kickin' myself for weeks if I didn't. You see, ain't nobody gonna believe it when I tell 'em 'bout you 'n the river 'n the car 'n all, 'n I would be much obliged if you let me take a snapshot of you 'n everything before I git on back to my house 'n make those phone calls you asked me to."

Tumble and the Hun whispered something like "Nothing doing!" to themselves under their breath with the latter going on to the others about how the photo could be used later to identify all of them, if anything happened at the conference or someplace else nearby. Emmett stopped him before he got himself and the others caught up in paranoia, cutting him off with logic. If the four of them didn't oblige the farmer with a snapshot that each of them could simultaneously blur with a bit of slight movement and closed eyes, the guy might become insulted enough not to oblige them with the necessary phone calls, and they'd be spending the whole goddamn night wet and cold.

All this discussion was done in quick whispers while paying unflinching attention to the farmer who was standing above them and returning their shit-eating-grins with an enthusiastic, hopeful smile. Billy Landout delighted the guy by yelling up to him, "Sure, it's all right for you to take a picture. But just make it no more than two, okay? 'Cause we're gettin' kinda cold here in this river, 'n we'd like to get on out and into some warm clothes. Just tell us when you're ready, so we can pose real nice for you, okay?"

The farmer got real happy very fast and clicked off the two photos with a polite, "Ready, aim," each time, cuing the four Digger brothers on exactly when to jerk their images slightly and guaranteeing that when the film was developed the farmer would have two pictures of four ghostlike blurs hanging around and on top of two halves of a car in the middle of the neighborhood river. He probably would say something like, "Shucks! They all moved!" But his evidence would be good enough to convince his cronies of the freakiest scene he had ever seen in his life.

The guy was overjoyed about what was obviously going to be a lively topic of conversation for months, and he got his whole family to wave excitedly "Thank you! And goodbye!" at the four subjects of the area's future gossip, before pulling on down the road a few miles to his home where he made the phone calls he promised plus several more to his buddies, a few of whom showed up along with the local sheriff and garage mechanic.

Tumble told the cop he was driving the car when it slipped off the road, because Emmett didn't have a valid license and was still a bit too obviously drunk. As it turned out, the sheriff believed everything Tumble said to him except the part about how fast he was traveling when he inadvertently put the car into a skid by trying to avoid hitting a rabbit. Tumble insisted that he had only been doing forty-five or fifty miles per hour, and the sheriff kept denying that it was possible to do all the things that were done to the car and make the kind of skidmarks that were clearly visible in the churned-up dirt road, without going at least eighty, if not ninety miles per hour. So he told Tumble he was going to have to take him into town before the justice of the peace where the matter would be settled, and he'd pay a fine.

Emmett, in the meantime, was talking with the garage guy about how Hertz would pay the expense of towing it out, and they'd have to pay his price, that is, if Emmett didn't call them first and tell them where it was now located on that back-country road. In return for not calling the Hertz Company until the next morning when it was too late, Emmett asked the not unfriendly young mechanic if he'd be kind enough to drive him and his brothers to the Denton campsite where they were supposed to have been hours before. The fellow said it'd be no trouble at all, and also thanked Emmett for the fifty-to-seventy-five-dollar job he just gave him by promising not to call.

The sheriff was writing something in his book when Emmett walked over to hear the Hun inquire of the cop, "What are the people like around here?" The stout fifty-year-old sheriff raised his head, so his eyes were level with the Hun's, staring into them with complete understanding of what the Hun meant. He wasn't angry or nothing; he simply wanted to let the slick-city Hun know he wasn't so goddamn smart or talking to no goddamn civil-servant fool either, and he waited for a moment before answering with a mild sense of his own country wisdom. "If you can generalize what all the people might be like 'round here by regardin' one individual, you might just as well use me as an example, or Hank, the garageman over there, 'cause I'm one of the people 'round here, mister, same's him 'n same's them other folks that stopped by here before. There ain't no difference 'tween them 'n me, 'cept the jobs we do, that's all. I'm one of 'em 'n have been all my life 'n will be till I die. Now, if that answers your question, you're welcome." Then he walked over to his car and told his office on the radio what happened and that he was taking the car's driver into town to stand before the justice and pay a fine.

Emmett talked it over with Tumble, and they decided that the best thing to do was for Emmett, Billy and the Hun to go to the meeting at the camp outside Denton, where there had to be a lawyer whom they could bring back to the justice of the peace's office to argue Tumble's case, if the fine was too stiff to pay. The other two agreed since there was very little else they could do.

The sheriff called Tumble over, and the two of them drove off with Tumble sitting next to the cop on the front seat. The others went with Hank, the garageman, who knew exactly where the summer camp was, and they were there in less than ten minutes. Hank also knew what was going on there, and after writing his name, garage address, and phone number down on a piece of paper for Emmett to phone in to Hertz, he split in a hurry.

The main cabin where the first of the organizational meetings was already under way, was all lit up inside with white light, and the three Frisco Diggers could see it was packed with the type of young and old people they expected to find at such a dry-crusted-dull shindig. The three of them looked at each other for a moment, smiled, and someone said, "Let's go get that lawyer."

Emmett opened the door and stepped inside first, right in front of a long table covered with mimeographed papers and lined up next to the knotty-pine wall on the right side of the room. It was the dais, and Thomas Hayden, a neatly middle-class-dressed, short-haired, pockmarked, college-graduate radical, political careerist and SDS leader, was in the middle of his welcoming address to his fellow delegates, who were all attentively seated on rows of wooden folding chairs that entirely filled up the rest of the room.

Hayden stopped speaking when Emmett moved to a spot directly between him and his audience and silently stood there for the moment it took the Hun and Billy Landout to enter the large rec room and plant themselves on each side of the open door. Everyone else was also quiet, probably startled by their curiosity as to who the three men were who interrupted their meeting.

Emmett's left side was facing the delegation, and his right side faced Tom Hayden and the other speakers seated at the platform, to whom he nodded a slight greeting before turning his back on them to full-face the audience. As soon as he did this, there was a yelp of recognition from the rear of the room where Abbot Hoffman was sitting against the back wall with his pseudo-Digger buddies Paul Krassner, Jim Fourat and Keith Lampe, all dressed up in their beaded, purple-colored hippie costumes and Mexican cowboy hats. Emmett gave them the same sort of nod with which he greeted Hayden and the dais.

"My name's Emmett, 'n that fella over there's the Hun, 'n the one next to him playing the flute is Bill Landout. We're here representing the San Francisco Diggers which we'll get around to later. First, we have to do somethin' more important. You see, we had an accident 'bout six miles from here, 'n one of us, our brother Tumble, was taken to town by the sheriff to stand before the justice. Now, to make sure he don't end up in the slam 'n to get him back here with us, we need a lawyer 'n someone with a car, unnerstand?"

Emmett waited, looking around the room for some sign of someone willing to volunteer. When he felt he waited long enough, which was about a minute, he took a different tack, and with extreme politeness asked one paunchy, bifocaled man in his mid-thirties whether he was a lawyer. The man said that he was and replied to the next question with, "Yes, I've got a car."

This was Emmett's cue to rip the fat guy from his seat and forcibly lead him outside to his car which they drove away with Billy Landout behind the wheel following the lawyer's directions on how to get to the town of Denton. Emmett soothed the very ruffled attorney by explaining that he should have identified himself as a lawyer immediately and volunteered, because "we've been on the road for two solid days now, 'n we're not in no mood to waste no time. Anyway, you're here to show how you're concerned for the

394

people, ain't you? Well, just think of us as two fellows who're giving you an opportunity to exemplify your radicalism and responsibility to the people. Okay? Okay!"

The Hun remained behind to make sure that the meeting wasn't reconvened in the orderly manner in which it started. He accomplished this by simply stepping over to the speaker's platform behind the dais, pushing Hayden out of his way with a handshake and a "Thank you kindly," and swinging on the audience with an excited ramble-rap, the likes of which they never heard before and most of them probably never have again.

He poured it on them with his sweet 'n sour, white-nigger-hipster tongue, lashing out the Trip Without a Ticket message that "Property's the enemy and has gotta have its inanimate values destroyed by any means necessary. Which means that one has to begin by assaulting oneself — attacking all the conditioned misconceptions in one's own head first, before waging warfare against the various machines of the system. Organize your own goddamn heads! Get yourselves together! And quit all this make-believe bullshit! Bullshit, like organizing the teachers, the workers or this 'n that! Don't organize the motherfucking schools! Burn them down! Or just walk away from 'em and leave 'em alone, and they'll rot! Drop out of the system, 'cause you're only kidding yourselves if you don't, and your own children know that, and that's why they're leaving you alone, why they're running away from the lies that are your lives!"

On and on the Hun blazed about guerrilla theater and about Free! for all, because it's yours, and about how Moscow was more fucked up than Mississippi. All the young persons and all those in the audience who had any minds left were completely turned on and overjoyed. The older lefties, however, who had been wrapped in their make-believe, international Communist workers' game since the thirties, forties and Joe McCarthy fifties didn't want to hear it but had to, and were physically upset by almost every word. They came to that cabin-campground in Denton, Michigan, to continue the Workable Lie that allowed them to play with ideological rhetoric and join in harmless activities which didn't interfere with their private financial welfare, and here was the Hun, yelling at them, demanding that they drop completely out of the capitalist economic system and stop their kidding around. It disturbed them very much, because they didn't come to hear the truth.

As soon as Billy Landout pulled the lawyer's car onto the main street of Denton, Emmett spotted Tumble standing alone outside an empty bar with a brown-paper-bagged can of beer in his hand. He got into the car, and Billy turned it around and headed back toward the camp while Tumble told them the story of his appearance before the justice of the peace and his subsequent release with no fine, but with an open invitation to dinner and to spend the night in an empty bedroom in the wooden frame home which doubled as the courthouse. Tumble insisted it was true and that the judge just liked him, that's all.

They were all still laughing when they walked into the main cabin where the Hun was just ending his scattered speech, and the attorney sheepishly returned to his seat, glad to be back in the safe milieu of his not-so-serious comrades. The lawyer wasn't even brave enough to ask for the return of his own car keys, so Billy left them hanging in the ignition.

Billy Landout walked over to the far end of the dais table and sat down on top of it, crossing his legs in the lotus position and smiling. He continued playing a low-keyed melody on his flute — which was all he had driven more than halfway across the country to say to these persons assembled in Middle America, and it was beautiful.

The Hun finished, and an older man of fifty or sixty commented very loudly that what he said was negated by the simple and obvious fact that he'd never been a member of the proletariat working class, and therefore had never dropped out of anything because he had always been on the outside, whereas, the man went on, he himself spent the past thirty-five years or so as a rank-and-file member of the Auto Workers Union and had been, and still was, working goddamn hard every goddamn moment of that time to change the capitalistic mentality of his fellow workers and the structure of the union which, he concluded, was a goddamn more important revolutionary role for him to play "than to be sittin' on a table like that fella over there playin' with a toy flute!"

There was a boisterous round of applause by the majority of the assembled for the workingman's brief statement. When the hand-clapping and backslapping died down, Emmett held back the Hun from making a hip rebuttal, and Tumble stepped forward to take up the gauntlet.

All eyes were on Tumble, waiting for how he was going to answer the challenge, and watching as he removed two cards from his wallet. When he was ready, he struck a heavy stance and stabbed the old leftist dead with his black, shiny eyes.

"You see these two cards, fella? All of you, d'ya see 'em?! Well, a little less than a year ago these cards were me, and they'd been me for over twelve years before that or for just about one third of my life. I got them both at the same time and from the same man, when I was twenty years old and fresh out of a California penitentiary. This one here is the card that says I was a longshoreman on the San Francisco waterfront every day of those dozen years. And this one says I was a member in good standing of the American Communist party, when I was just that, up until I became twenty-four or five, and it didn't seem to make much sense for me to renew my membership. Now, both of these cards were given to me by the same man, or, I should say, by the associates of the same man — Mr. Harry Bridges, who I'm sure all you members of the working proletariat know to be the head of the San Francisco longshoreman's union, as well as a radical champion of all workers' rights.

"What I'm driving at is that neither of these cards is me anymore. Oh, they still have my name on them all right, but they ain't me no more — no way! The reason they no longer are, is a long, long story which I'll shorten by simply reachin' its conclusion for you. But I want you to all understand that I didn't jump to no quick conclusion then, when I actually canceled both of these cards out of my life forever. It was a goddamn long-drawn decision I made after tryin' to work within their confines for all those years of my youth. I didn't jump to no fuckin' conclusion! I thought about it slowly for a long time — too long!

"Anyway, the reason I gave up my card-carrying membership in both these organizations was I realized they were full of shit, and I didn't want to be a part of that shit. Part of the lie that says all socially relevant change is brought about through the power of the working class. You see, I really want to do something to change this goddamn system we got here, and when I realized that I *really, really* did want to do something relevant to change the miserable way most people live in this fuckin' world, I knew I had to stop kidding myself by going to monthly Party meetings, while at the same time earning over three hundred dollars in take-home pay every week. I mean, *I* had no real beef with anything, really, as long as the two hundred dollars for my thirty-five hours' work was coming in every week. And it was basically those wages that made me see that my involvement with the Communist Party, U.S.A. was nothing more than an elitist hobby that made me feel self-righteously good once a month, that's all, and did nothing for no one. One day, I just looked 'round at all my friends who were all playing the same

397

make-believe union, party, workers-of-the-world-unite! game, and I could see that they were all comfortably fat, and so I decided that I was finished with all of that running-in-place bullshit, and I dropped out of the lie and into the truth of myself.

"Then I was lucky enough to meet my brothers here, and ever since I've been working with them to change things. To change things not by demanding that things be changed by protest marches or by demonstrations that *ask* that the changes be given to the people. No! But by changing things ourselves.

"It's as simple as that. We see a change that has to be made, we don't ask or demand that someone else make it happen. We just fucking well make it happen, and if anyone tries to stop us, then we're prepared to defend our right to make those changes that are relevant to our lives and the way we live them.

"I'm talking now about immediate, localized changes, like stopping poor kids from being hungry by getting food for them to eat, or letting a landlord know that he better fix his slum buildings up with heat and hot water in the winter, or we'll burn his own family's fucking suburban house down for him. And he understands, because we let him know that we know where he lives. You dig? And all sorts of real, actual, relevant things like that, like the Free Stores, where a poor person who can't afford something might find it, and not secondhand either, but brand fucking new, so's she or he can get a taste of what it could be like, if we worked together to change things, instead of just jerking off together, masturbating high-falutin' words all over each other — words that sound real good, but don't do nothin'! Nothin' for nobody, never! Like I done for those twelve years, those boxcar years of my life, when I tricked myself into standing still because I was getting good pay for it — for making believe, mister! For making believe that, because I was a worker and a Communist party member, I had the integrity of a true, revolutionary human being, when in reality I was a stone liar, lying to myself and everyone else and not even capable of gettin' a nigger a gig with my own union or any other union for that matter, except the janitors' union.

"I was just like you, mister! Like most of you people right here, playing trick-the-tricker, but only succeeding in tricking myself. I'd still be throwin' those same boxcars and crappin' out on history if I hadn't accepted the truth that I was doing nothing for nobody but my own goddamn selfish self, and if I hadn't met these men here who're now my brothers. This one's gonna speak to you next now, 'cause that's what he came here to do. So you listen to him, 'cause he just might save some of your lives from never living and from never changing the routine limbo of the Workable Lie that's got you coming up boxcars every time and never changing nothing to do with even yourselves, much less history, for chrissake!"

The persons who clapped and hollered and yelled their approval at Tumble as he backed off from center stage were mostly the young who, within a couple of years, were going to drastically change the direction and focus of SDS, but not the basic motives for their involvement in the activities of the organization. Their personal motivations would remain the same as the Old Left's, even though the activities would switch from do-nothing ideological conferences to do-nothing terrorist tactics. Their motives would be just as selfishly personal and as deliberately unconcerned with the needs of the people. They would give vent to their own private frustrations with pseudo-guerrilla, war-game playing and romantic adventurism, and do about as much — these "weathermen" — for the liberation of the country's low-money people into a classless society as George Metesky, the Mad Bomber of New York, did. Nothing! Except some sensational headlines in the newspapers for the voyeurs to get a giggle over. And it's a shame.

Emmett moved forward between the rows of chairs and climbed up on a table in the back of the room, squatting down on top of it and making everyone turn around to see him. He picked up where Tumble left off, telling the crowd about the importance of anonymity to persons who seriously attempted to effect relevant changes in any social order and tried to achieve at least a token independence from the economic system, with the ultimate goal of course being autonomy. An individual and collective autonomy, a spiritual and material autonomy that would eventually lead to the long, hard struggle which would have to be fought to establish a post-competitive, comparative, classless society where all power would be decentralized and given to the people through a form of democratic socialism.

He then began to explain how the Diggers in San Francisco simply assumed their own freedom to serve the people by trying to get every brother and sister whatever they needed, to do what it was they had to do. It was this assumption of freedom, he continued, that caused the radical movement to falsely believe that the individual Diggers and their organization were anarchistic and led the straight establishment into believing that they were just a bunch of

399

"mod monk, hippie, social workers." Both assumptions were wrong, but did provide them with the cover they needed, at the time, to continue their work.

"However, now it's gotten to the point where everyone's missing the point and that's why we come here — to let you know the truth of what we're doin' in San Francisco, so's you can understand and tell your comrades, and only them, that we ain't what everybody says we are, but just what we've now explained to you. We did this 'cause what we're doin' in Frisco needs to be done everywhere and done right! Not like no Salvation Army or no bunch of romantic Robin Hoods, but like, and by, plain and simple free men and women who do it 'cause they love the people! Love the people, not with the slop-bucket love of liberal do-gooders who've got false commitments to humanity, but love with a muscle 'n gut love that sweats and lives and dies for the people. The people who need to be doing what the Diggers *in San Francisco* are doing and nowhere else. Let that be clear — *nowhere else!* The people need to see other people giving it *all* away, before they can dig the basic absurdity of this goddamn parasitical society! It heightens the human contradictions of existing within this inhuman capitalistic system where the best man wins if he kills his brother or sister or a couple of hundred thousand faceless, yellow people in Asia. It heightens the human contradictions of surviving within or under any system of government that's now maintaining some form of social order in the world today. It heightens the human contradictions to such a degree that a person, if he's really a good man or a good woman, will have to refuse to acquiesce to any society that doesn't fulfill its social responsibility to every human being in it!

"Now, when you go around liberating stuff to give away to the people, you gotta watch your ass 'n stay as invisible as possible! You gotta be and remain anonymous, because the society you're fuckin' with is, sooner or later, gonna start flexing its muscles in anger at the thought of swallowing the bitter, Digger pill of 'It's free, because it's yours!' And their police lackies are gonna slam your ass away! If you ain't anonymous, if you got your name written all over everything you do, you ain't doing nothing! 'Cause if you was, and you had your name on all of it, they'd lock you up forever or blow you away for good!

"In other words, if you're really serious and you're actually doing something serious, ain't nobody supposed to know what you look like except the people you're doin' it with and some, never all, of the people you're doing it for. And, of course, the police — they always know what you look like, but if you're really slick, they won't know who you are or what you're doing. And if you don't get what I mean, that's your blues, 'cause that's all you're gonna get from me except my best wishes that y'all don't get got."

The younger, hipper ones laughed as Emmett stood up straight on top of the table to stretch his legs. There was some loud movement behind and to the left of him, and when Emmett turned, he saw that Abbot Hoffman raised his stumpy body, instead of his hand, to ask a question or say something.

"Emmett, you know, whether you like it or not, you're going to get co-opted, because you're too together, too singlehanded, and they're gonna make an image out of you and steal your anonymity and sell you across the country as the 'new antihero'! Before this year's out or sometime in 1968, they're going to put you on the cover of *Time* magazine or *Life* or *Newsweek* and sell your charisma as the fashionable way to be. Whether you like it or not, within a year you're gonna be on a lot of posters on a lot of walls!"

It was the same riff that Paul Jacobs used, to try to cancel Emmett and the Diggers out months before at the Theater for Ideas in New York. This time, however, Emmett was determined to handle the always-the-same challenge of his probable co-option differently. He could feel the whole load of the past year's slave labor and solitude swelling up inside of him and taking the love right from his eyes, leaving them dead cold. He was going to blow it, but he was going to do it his way, for his own reasons, and not as an emotional response to a punk's lame remark.

As he squatted slowly back down, Emmett ran his eyes into those of Tumble, the Hun and Billy, giving them the sign that it was time to effect the epilogue to their already disruptive performance at the SDS conference. Then he sucked the audience into the eye of the storm that was squalling inside of him by speaking softly.

"Abbot . . ."

"It's Abbie, Emmett!"

"Abbot, you're wrong. I'm not goin' to be on the cover of *Time* magazine, and my picture ain't goin' to be on the covers of any other magazines or in any newspapers — not even in any of those so-called underground papers or movement periodicals. There ain't gonna be no posters of me anywhere, and I ain't goin' to put me on sale this year or next year or the year after that, until I feel it beautiful to stop.

"Now that's probably very difficult for you here to understand, 'cause you're always jumping up and pointing at yourselves on TV and in the press to show everyone that you were there, too! But not me, nor my brothers and sisters, understand? And do you know why I'm so sure of that? Do y'all know how I know that what I'm sayin' right now's the truth? Huh?

"Well, it's simple. You see, I'm not kidding! I'm not kidding you, me or anyone else about what I do to help make the change that has to be made in this country of ours, here!

"Must be real fuckin' hard for you motherfuckers to understand that, huh! Most of you suckers'd give your rectums to get yourselves plastered all over the cover of any one of them magazines as the *Big, Bad Radical!* Huh, wouldn't ya! And now you're all lookin' at me — me who's more beautiful 'n heavier than any motherfuckin' man or woman in this room! And you're wondering why I don't let 'em take my picture 'n become the big, bad radical of the year to all America, ain't ya!

"Why such a beautifully muscled, aquiline-featured, rough 'n ready, romantically hip, heavyweight, handsome cat like me who's got more style in the heel of his motherfuckin' foot than any of you'll have forever — why ain't I coppin' the front pages of all them fuckin' rags that'd just gobble up everything I said 'n make me the national, hip, radical Hero Number One overnight?! *Why? Why? 'Cause I ain't kiddin', you ugly, motherfuckin', lyin' cocksuckin', punk-faced, pussy-whipped assholes!*"

Emmett jumped off and suddenly flipped over the Formica lunch table on top of the seated crowd as his words erupted throughout the room, and Tumble watched Emmett's back so nobody would hit him with something from behind. The Hun sat on a windowsill looking at the mad spectacle of Emmett Grogan knocking down girls, punching cats in the face, slapping the older SDSers left and right and all over the fucking place, screaming that they were all *"Cowardly ugly!"* while Billy Landout giggled into his flute and kept right on calmly playing. It was good theater, with people scurrying all around to get out of Emmett's maniacal way, and him screaming and them screaming, but only passively resisting the one-man, violent assault against the dignity of their Workable Lie.

It lasted a full few minutes and ended with Emmett throwing a black cat out the front door because he was the only black person there. "You goddamn nigger, you shouldn't be *here!* Your people need you! There's a war on, so get your fucking black ass back to your black brothers and sisters where you belong! And the rest of you motherfuckers, get outta here 'n go to bed! Go on, it's past your bedtime! But not you, lawyer man! Not you! You're going to drive with us in your car to get something to eat in the all-night diner in Denton town and, later on, to Kalamazoo where we're going to pick up a brand-new car from the nice Hertz man. Won't that be nice, huh? Get goin'!"

Emmett awoke the midmorning of the next day stretched out on the rear seat of a fresh sedan he vaguely remembered getting from the Rent-a-Car company to replace the one he totaled the night before. He sat up to discover that he was alone and the car parked next to the curb of Wells Street in the Chicago neighborhood known as Old Town. It took him a while to figure out how to open the rear door of the car because of a jackhammer, hangover headache and because there wasn't any rear door. It was a two-door sedan and, when he couldn't find the catch to release the back of the front seat, he slammed against it hard with both feet, and it snapped free, bowing broken toward the dashboard and giving him the access he needed to climb out the front side of another moronically designed Hertz wreck-a-car.

He stood for a moment with both his legs spread wide and planted firm on the sidewalk to get his balance and let his dizzy spell pass. Thoughts of the previous night's SDS meeting and the role he and his brothers played in its disruption competed with the pain and filled his brain. "The Diggers are an avant-garde gang of a new kind of status-free people! Basically young, hip, ageless, street-wise-savvy, ballsy, macho, righteous, with chutzpah, flexible in that we can do almost everything to the degree that we are capable of doing anything, resourceful, beautiful, courageous heroes of history! Romance is the routine of our daily lives — uninhibited, unpredictable lives without fear of spontaneity! Unordinary, mystery individuals collected together in a bonded union of commitment to muscle 'n gut love of the people! Our inevitable deaths will be the products of the lives we've chosen to live with a healthy respect for both history and eternity!"

"Ooooeee!" Emmett emptied whatever other thoughts were coming up next by blowing them out of his mind with a whistling sigh, as he walked toward the two plate-glass windows of the shop in front of him. It was a bookstore, "Barbara's Bookstore" read the sign, and Emmett glanced back at all the things he'd just said to himself for the umpteenth time and muttered a line from one of

Texas black-bluesman Lightning Hopkin's songs, "It's kinda crazy to keep on rubbin' at that same ole goddamn thing!"

Then he entered the bookstore where everyone was frozen still, except his three brothers who'd taken it over for a while. Billy Landout was sitting up cross-legged-lotus on the checkout counter with his back against the cash register, playing a sweet, close-your-eyes tune on that wooden, penny flute of his. The Hun had Miss Barbara, the owner, pinned in a hypnotic trance which he induced with his deluxe-special, super-hip-riffster, rap-elixir that had her narcotized and mesmerized into the magic of his flash-brilliant-spinning web of words. The customers, an employee, and whoever else was in the store, were all in the back-left side of the room where Tumble, unconcerned with their presence, was scratching an on-the-spot-inspired poem with a black crayon on a plasterboard wall that partitioned the stock storage room from the rest of the place. It was a long poem, eventually filling the entire, empty, top-to-bottom space of the wall with Tumble's articulation of his own sense of the reality in which he lived and worked with his Digger brothers and sisters. Emmett watched Tumble on his knees painstakingly writing down what was on his mind and read:

STATE OF THE SOUL PREPARED FOR WAR

A document using the word love-life. Not using the word hate. But by implication incorporating negative energy as incisive scalpel wielded by brains, hands, hearts of loving brothers.

CHOOSE YOUR WEAPONS

Flowers or guns — stand by them; learn their essential energies. Apply them as the use permits. You can have both; only you can't shoot flowers and guns make lousy flower pots.

PREPARE TO SURVIVE

America throttles herself in abstract property wars, consumer vessels floated on the blood of our own. We wear flowers in our hair because they're there and beautiful.

SUICIDE OR MURDER?

(What are *you* thinking about)
(What are *you* thinking about)
Guns are
Machines of death

We prepare our minds with.
To perpetuate life. Protect
Our women and children.
Machines we intend never to use
Except in defense.
And when those of you who would
Strangle our only human possibility
Die by our bullets — they will have been fired
Into your brains thru eyes of our loving you.
Your blood soaking the ground will be our blood —
Your death our death.
But we shall pass gently on from there in this body
To tend further children and other flowers; and
Your body shall rot and nourish the planet's new
Seeds long before ours.

/?/!/?

And the winner shall be man; and man shall survive.
My people shall live because they know — each one —
Unto himself IS THE LEADER — and every invention
Of slave politic trickery will fail and crumble,
IMMEDIATELY, in this source dialectic of one to one
Confrontation with all things.

THE FACE OF THIS INDIVIDUAL'S REVOLUTION:

YOU ARE THE LEADER ....

the san francisco diggers
june — 1967

Later that night, the four of them were in a diner in Drag City,
Kansas, eating the last hot meal of their trip back to Frisco. There
were some hot-rod country boys in the place, hanging on the jukebox and posing for their girl friends. They were big, but there
wasn't going to be no fight or trouble or nothing, because they were
only as big as high-school football players are big and just as young.
The food was good, and the four brothers were glad it took the
youngsters a long time to come over to ask them questions about
Haight-Ashbury, because they wanted nothing to distract their attention from enjoying the savory meal.

The kids were nervous at first, because Tumble answered their
questions, and he was nearly twice their age and hard-fisted tough
with a face to match, the kind of a man who would've been a very
big fish in the little pond of their small town and someone who
would never have even spoken with them, much less politely answered their queries. The boys asked all kinds of things about San

Francisco persons whose names they read or heard somewhere. Then one said, "Y' know me 'n a few others are goin' out there in a couple of weeks t' join up with Emmett Grogan 'n his Diggers. Did any you fellas ever meet him?"

The statement made Billy Landout laugh and the Hun drop a dime into the jukebox to play a Hank Williams record. Tumble looked at Emmett who was sitting next to him and slowly turning around toward the seven or eight kids to ask them something. "Where'd you fellas hear about that guy and what-did-you-call-'em, the Diggers?"

The kids sort of looked at each other with a mild disbelief that four grown-up, longhaired, on-the-road, real-live Haight-Ashbury, San Francisco hippies didn't know everything there was to know about Emmett Grogan and the Diggers. The one who seemed to be doing all the talking started up again saying, "Man, everyone knows 'bout Emmett Grogan 'n the Diggers, even 'round here! Why they run the Haight-Ashbury 'n make sure everyone gets 'nough to eat 'n a place to sleep 'n clothes to wear 'n everything a body needs to do his thing! Why there's a girl livin' less than a mile away from here right now who ran away 'bout six months ago when she turned fifteen, 'n went to Frisco where she lived with the Diggers 'n even made it with Emmett Grogan himself. Swear to God! Right, fellas? And talk is she's carryin' his baby right now, but nobody knows fer sure, so's it could be just talk. But she was there all right, 'n she stayed with them people, 'n they done right by her, too. Otherwise, even she said, she'd never of made it alone through those three months she spent out there 'fore the fuzz picked her up. Man! You fellas just gotta know 'bout Emmett Grogan and the Diggers, if you're from Frisco!"

"Oh, we do! We heard about 'em, but we'd already hit the road, drivin' around the country by the time they really started their operation in the Haight. Good people! What's the check, chief, 'n put it all on one, okay? Well, I guess we'll be seein' you fellas out on the coast soon, huh?! Been nice talkin' with you. Be seein' you."

"Yea, later, man!"

An unexpected and strange phenomenon began to take place among the four men inside the car as soon as they were on their way. The brief encounter in the diner with the young teenyboppers, and the way they spoke about "Emmett Grogan" and *"his* Diggers" and "*their* leader" set Emmet apart from his three brothers, not as a matter of his choice, but rather theirs.

Billy Landout thought that Emmett's underground-superstardom as an invisible American cultural hero was mildly hilarious. "They've already got you in the Hipsters Hall of Folklore Fame, and they don't even know what the fuck you look like! You're just hearsay, Emmett. Just a whole lotta hearsay." Then, Tumble suddenly became sullen toward Emmett and showed signs of remaining glum for the entire last lap of the journey. The Hun was predictably bitter at so outrageous an assault on his ego. After all, he was one, too, wasn't he? He even began to make insinuations that Emmett had been using "him" and "his" Free Store all along and was further conspiring to employ "him" and "his" thing as the main rung in the ladder that he was planning to climb to success and fame!

Emmett remained jocular about the whole absurd affair, assuming that his brothers knew it was all a ridiculous matter and he had nothing consciously to do with a media image which he himself had done the most to liquidate. "I mean, look! They were just a bunch of kids who are still a year behind in history and haven't heard yet that I don't really exist. That's all!" But when the Hun went on to insist that "No!" that wasn't all, with his wild-eyed, paranoid, conspiracy-against-him fantasy, Emmett felt like an asshole apologizing for something he could only control by dying.

So he blew it, and started over the front seat for the Hun, to maybe slap some sense into him or at least crack him in his mouth, but Tumble grabbed him, pulling him back down into the rear just as Billy almost lost control of the ninety-mile-per-hour speeding car, driving it along the metal guard rail for a few yards before being able to swing it back into the lane and down on the highway. All of them knew at once that very little was ever going to be the same between them again, and Emmett, especially, felt it was the beginning of the end for their always more or less tenuous solidarity as brothers, and for the name "Diggers" — just a word meaning "Free" — which had somehow already gotten out of hand and onto the charts.

The proof of this pudding came in its eating early the next morning, when the four men pulled into a service station alongside the Route 80 Freeway that bypasses Sacramento. This was to be their last stop, because they were in the home stretch with only eighty-five more miles to go to San Francisco which they left back-to-back together, but to which each of them was now returning somehow alone in the same car.

While the attendant checked out the radiator water and put four or five dollars' worth of gas in the car, the four men used the facilities in the separate ladies' and gents' bathrooms to wash away the sleep none of them had during the night, especially Billy. He had driven the past dozen hours, only stopping here and there for gas and never saying a word, just softly playing a tune on a ten-cent harmonica that appeared from his same old floppy jacket somewhere along the way. He didn't trust any of the other three with his life anymore, since the deal between all of them had gone down in the diner, and he wasn't going to put himself in any of their hands by riding in a car that one of them drove. So he hadn't, and even though the Hun complained that he wanted to share some of the driving to relax his nerves, Billy Landout silently refused with Tumble fully backing him up because his eyes could see that it was the only sensible thing to do with a strange, unknown road blanketed in the darkness of a night filled with tension. Emmett didn't say anything, for as long as Billy Landout was behind the wheel, he knew he was safe.

The four of them were standing by the coffee-dispensing machine, sipping the boiling hot, tan-colored water, when the Hun went into a sarcastic riff, asking Billy if he could please drive the rest of the way home, now that it was daylight and the freeway was jammed with traffic, making it impossible for him to endanger any of their precious lives by speeding. Billy said he didn't mind a bit, if the others didn't, because he was going to lie down on the back seat and sleep the last leg of the journey into the city. Then he walked toward the car and began unlacing his shoes for his nap.

Tumble walked over to the attendant, paid him the money, and chatted about what the traffic was probably going to be like at that time of the day. Emmett took a minute or two getting change of a quarter, so he could buy a couple of packs of Dentine gum to get the taste of the watered-down coffee out of his mouth and also make believe his teeth were clean. The Hun was already behind the wheel, gunning the engine to announce that he was ready to depart, and Emmett ran over and climbed into the front seat with Tumble after they tossed a coin for who was going to ride shotgun.

The three of them had more than enough room in the front seat. Emmett, in the middle, fiddled with the dials of the radio, trying to locate a San Francisco station, and Tumble leaned his head out the window to catch the breeze that would hopefully resurrect his face from the exhausted numbness of his head. The Hun pulled into the middle land of the freeway and was driving unusually smoothly, only using the express lane now and then to pass a Sunday driver, being careful not to draw the attention of a state highway cop.

They had been driving nearly two hours and had just bypassed Berkeley, swinging off the freeway and onto the entrance ramp of the bridge to take them across the bay to San Francisco, when Emmett turned around to wake up Billy Landout in the back seat, only to discover he wasn't there. "Billy! Billy's gone! He's not there!" Tumble jumped around surprised, then up on his knees, bending over the back of the front seat to check out the rear floor of the car. "Where the fuck is he?! Billy!"

As soon as they crossed the Bay Bridge they turned off an exit and pulled the car onto a city side street, double-parking it for a moment to finally make certain that Billy wasn't there. His shoes were there, underneath the woven cotton blanket where he was supposed to be, but wasn't. The three of them looked at each other, and at the same time each realized that they had left Billy Landout back at the Sacramento service station without his shoes and with no money. They left him there, and whether they did it consciously or unconsciously it didn't matter. It was all the same. They left him there, and it didn't make any difference who was driving or who wasn't. They *all* left him there.

They left Billy Landout back there in a service station nearly one hundred miles away without his shoes, because they really didn't care about each other anymore, and now everything was finally different. Everything Emmett imagined the night before had just proved itself to be brutally true, and he was more sad than angry because he instinctively knew that his brother Billy Landout would never forgive him for having left him behind like that without even his shoes, and he wouldn't be his brother any longer and would never speak to him again. And he never has, not even to listen to Emmett simply tell him, "Sorry, Billy. Sorry."

After that real and symbolic purge of one of the brothers, only the Digger women remained a united front while the men took care of what they had to in their separate ways. Emmett did practically nothing besides work with Free Food, picking it up or stealing the meat and delivering it to the women who cooked it for the now outrageous "Summer of Love" hordes who crowded into the Panhandle every day at four in the afternoon. He did the Free Food work mostly by himself, but whenever he did have a partner to help him with the operation, it was usually a woman. Women who weren't on the make to become "Emmett Grogan's old lady" or looking for a chance to play a role in a romantic, Robin Hood-adventure trip — rather, women who were strong, sincere, loyal and brave in their determination to serve the people and help liberate them from the oppression of their poverty.

These women were only girls to most men because the majority of them were still in their middle or late teens or had just turned twenty. To Emmett, however, they were always women and will always be women — every one of them more beautiful than the rest. It wasn't long before he came to trust them more, much more, than he did most men who claimed to be his brothers.

The Hun was involved only in the theater of the Trip Without A Ticket free store and spent the rest of his time developing the guerrilla theater possibilities of the streets. Tumble managed as many trucks as he could get hold of and used them to deliver goods to the free store, transport garbage from the crash pads to the dump, bus people around the city, and every other conceivable usage he could think of. Coyote kept himself busy performing with the San Francisco Mime Troupe for what he promised would be the rest of the summer. Billy Landout split from the city and never came back there to live or work again, just to stop on his way to someplace else.

Emmett seldom regularly saw anyone but the women, and he would only get together with the rest on special occasions, as when they'd all work with each other to stage a celebration for something like the summer solstice or the Fourth of July. His job, which he usually did with Tumble during the production of each of these free-for-all extravaganzas, was always the same: to arrange with the leaders of the rock groups, like Janis Joplin or Jerry Garcia, for them to play; to get enough eighteen-foot, flatbed trucks to use, coupled back to back, as stages for the bands — of which seldom less than two were ever set up in one of the expansive meadows of Golden Gate Park; to supply the meat or poultry and to make a deal with a special group of elderly black men from the Fillmore district to prepare a huge vat of barbecue sauce with which they'd baste the meat they cooked over an open charcoal pit all morning and afternoon of the day's event, giving each piece away to the hungry crowd as soon as it was browned and the unhurried black men felt it was ready to be eaten.

They were always monstrous affairs with thirty to fifty thousand people attending, even though they were always purposely held on a weekday to keep the crowds down. There were at least twenty-five or thirty such "parties," as they were called, which were all paid for by money hustled for whatever was needed, like the flatbed trucks, and arranged, produced and given away by Emmett, Tumble, the Hun, Coyote, the women — by all the Diggers! Everyone else simply took care of incidentals or offered their services, like the rock groups. Only a handful of intimate outsiders knew at that time that the Diggers were entirely responsible for practically every free party ever held in the Golden Gate Park of San Francisco during those years of '67, '68 and early '69. Almost everyone else assumed that the rock bands, like the Grateful Dead, the Airplane or Country Joe and his Fish, put on the affairs to show people how much they appreciated and loved them for buying their albums, and also concluded that the various record companies paid the expenses for everything like the free barbecued chickens or ribs, as well as the salaries of the half dozen or so "old, nigger cooks."

The reason no one knew who was responsible was that the Diggers wanted it that way, since "free" means not copping credit. What began to make Emmett and the others bitter and crazy was that, after each of these events, some of the musicians in the bands, as well as several well-known HIP figures who considered themselves spokesmen for the Haight, made statements to the establishment and underground media which more than just suggested that they were responsible for the entire organization and cost of the celebration, because they wanted to express the love they felt for their brothers and sisters in the community, and "Blah, blah, blah!"

It was a burn all right, but neither Emmett nor anyone of the people he worked with said anything or did anything to set the record straight. Eventually, however, after all the bands made it to the big time, the one group whose manager claimed most of the responsibility for most of the free parties most of the time, found themselves in New York — facing an angry East Village community who were duped by their own stupidity and plenty of publicity about "the hip people's band" into believing that the only live music this particular rock group played was always heard for free. It got to a point where the leader of the band had to make a speech explaining the reason they were actually charging an admission price for entrance to their New York concerts. He was forced into all sorts of strenuous positions, trying to defend his group's right to earn money from the hippie community, until he obviously was stretched to a point by all the interviews poking the same old "But we thought you always played for free . . ." line at him, that he finally screamed something like, "There's no free lunch! No free lunch! No such thing, okay?! We play music for money, and a long time ago, when we felt like it, in the park with our friends, okay?! I mean, we're professionals and this is a business, man!" And that was that, but it sure took a long time for it to go down, and it still didn't come out like it really was.

It was right after one of these free parties celebrating the Fourth of July, '67, that the Diggers finally gave the last thing they collectively had of themselves away — their name, the Diggers. No one knew it had been given away until the moment it happened. Heavyweight scribe and poet Kirby Doyle, author of *Happiness Bastard,* the first free novel published by the Communication Company, broadcast the news to the people in this street paper:

The Birth of Digger Batman

O sky glorious, O sky divine — People — dominions — nations — Heavens — door — O walking deliverance — O Passage — People — O People — Machines — Animals — Trees — Towers & Bridges — O Seed — O colors — Faces — All Moving Things — Life, hello . . . I want to tell you of the birth of Digger.

Morning, about 9:30, July 5th, 1967 — clear and sunny upon the city, the sky echoing with happiness, the streets still and clean and just to walk on them is to be silent in the bright rising from the night after a big 4th of July electric music and free feed celebration out in the park where Emmett and the cooks from the Fillmore had made barbecue for about 4,000 people.

I am up early and out into the street from Coyote's on Pine Street where the Communication Company lived — out and standing in the good day with the smiles all over me, just letting the warmth and the light honey about on me, my clothes glowing and the fine feeling seeping to the skin and a touch tasting to my innards, and O the head is just wanting to face with smiles in all directions. I had driven Susan Parker to the airport a couple days before and still had her car so I swings over a few blocks to Geary thinking to have coffee and a morning smoke with the Jahrmarkts, Billy and Joan and the kids.

Up two flights, rap rap on the door and Bill answers to my hello half-dressed and happy. "The baby's coming," is what I remember of him having said. And there is Joan sitting in the sun of those bright windows looking out over downtown and the bay, sitting on the bed, the mattress inevitably close to the floor, and the three kids — Jade, Hassan and Caledonia — kind of hushed and happy because they know the baby is coming and have been waiting too.

So Joany's been in labor since the night before and now sits very calm with a $3 tin watch in her hand timing the contractions — about every 7 minutes and getting closer together. So me and Billy just standing there kind of stunned and sunny, not thinking too much about what to do. "You got any arrangements made?" I says, and "no" is his reply.

It kind of goes like that, having a cigarette and a cup of coffee in the warmth of the morning in the corner room with just one fact we're standing in — the baby's coming and we are smiling and blinking lumenant with speech in soft sounds. Nobody is thinking too much about hospitals though we figure lightly first about getting Joan into one of those places, but not too serious.

I sound on Joan if she thinks she got time for me to go phone around and see what I can do, get help I guess is what I meant, and she says there's plenty of time, so I cut out and drive over to Margo St. James's place on Nob Hill and start phoning.

I get ahold of Kaiser Hospital and after about seven switchings back and forth, I get ahold of some voice that says No, there is no chance of getting into their facilities without two hundred and fifty dollars in front even if the baby is on the way right now, and that the only thing that They, this voice can suggest is to take The Expectant to County Hospital, which said set of instructions vis-à-vis that exhausted brick pile of agony so offends my ear I come near to throwing the phone across the room.

So, I phone Tumble to let somebody else know what's happening (who tells Emmett who sends an ambulance which nobody quite knows what to do with except send it away). So I clean out Margo's refrigerator of all its food and drive back over to the Communication Company where is lovely Sam and Cassandra and Claude and Helene who I break it down to.

Right away Claude is on the horn talking here and there. I get Cassandra and head back to Billy's, drop off Cassandra and split down to the store to get some smokes and am just rounding the corner on Geary when Claude pulls up to tell me he is on his way to Bolinas to get John Doss, a friend and head of pediatrics at Kaiser.

Upstairs is Cassandra cleaning the kitchen, making coffee and a bit to eat for the kids. It is late morning now and we relax — everything seems to be going along unmolested by even the quiet logic of time— Cassandra softly busy in the kitchen, Billy sitting with Joan in the sunny corner room, the kids hushed and talking among themselves in their room, and I with the stillness of no thinking in my head gazing out the window under the Bat flag at the greenish dome of city hall.

Rap rap on the door and I go to open it to Richard Brautigan who comes in under a soft tan hat, checks out the action, spots Cassandra in the kitchen, decides everything is cool, walks once again through the rooms, tall, slightly stooping like a gentle spider standing up (we are all spiders, or ants, or something, I remember wondering, watching Richard putting his hands in his pockets and taking them out), decides to split. "Be back in a while — need anything?" "No, nothing." Out the door he goes.

It's early afternoon now. Quite suddenly Joan gets up, walks into the kitchen and squats down flat-footed on the floor with her back leaning to the wall, contractions coming quicker, Billy kneeling with her, Cassandra calm, me getting nervous — smoking cigarettes.

Knock on the door and in comes Claude and Helene with John Doss, way over 6 foot, a tower of a man with those huge gentle hands that by mere holding can take the panic from a hurt child. All of a sudden it seems we got the best. Right away he's with Joan, coat off, talking real easy, squat'd down, laughing with the simplicity of things. Claude asks me if I want to smoke some gold and lays a joint on me — I take it and put it on Billy.

People begin arriving — Tumble and Lenore, Tumble much calmer than the day before in the park loaded on acid and telling Richie Marley real anxious, "There's a warp in the continuum!" Emmett arrives. Diggers start coming.

By now the kitchen is a place of prayer — Joan in labor on the big patch quilt now in the middle of the kitchen floor and around her kneeling and sitting silent people — silent and back within listening to what silence says at self to birth.

John Doss moves in from the crowded front room every now and then and kneels his huge person down to speak quietly to Joan as he feels with those giant hands across her belly for the baby within. Billy squats Arab-silent flat-footed beside Joan, his hair long about his shoulders, staring into the thick air that holds the deep flux of his unspeaking Arab Prayer.

Now the city has darkened for night, and Geary Street outside the window crawls alive with the homeward bound. Across the street the huge sign of an auto-agency — BOAZ, in Hebrew "the lion-hearted" — in black and white and red letters sends ancient benedictions into the rooms, and the green dome of city hall is alit as if it were a mosque removed one world and glowing not with bulbs nor candle but rather ringed with another light.

Now from out the night John and Sara and Coyote and Sam and Gandolf and Natural Suzanne and more Diggers arrive like a troupe or miming chorus bearing brown paper sacks filled with sandwiches — huge Poor Boys from some ecstasy delicatessen — the picture: Joan about to give birth on the kitchen floor, one dim shaded desk lamp by her feet, and a dozen people encircling her eating sandwiches and smoking weed, faces all in shadow of the only lamp.

The contractions have begun to quicken and Joany is saying over and over again softly, "Come on little Baby . . . come on" — a little song over and over again directed inside as if by this time the intelligence of the as yet enwombed Baby was beginning to be focused on its birthing passage by the soft speech of Joany's song — "Come on Baby . . . come on little Baby . . . come on."

The labor was becoming long, more than 24 hours now and the concentration of Joan's song had drawn the muscle lines tensed above her eyes pointing to a spot between them, slightly above them, and directly within.

John Doss had a slightly worried look as his hands felt over her belly. He seemed to be trying to gauge the position. Reaching within he felt for the baby's head which seemed to be turned in a wrong direction. The contractions were now great visible waves that moved down across Joan's belly and with each one her tightened face appeared to have the full focused power of everything behind it pouring down through her body toward the slow and heavy workings and waves of force that carried the baby in its passage.

"I need an instrument," he said mentioning some sort of birthing clamp. "I have to turn the baby's head." He turned to someone there and told them to go across the street to the hospital and get an instrument and an intern.

Meanwhile John begins instructing Billy in how he, Billy, is going to receive his baby. Beneath the belly skin you can see the baby making its movements. Around Joan about a dozen Diggers and Digger ladies looking like all the accumulated faces of the Universe, the Divines of Ever pouring from each eye.

Like no time there is a bang on the door and two white coated hospital guys come in stiff and important with shiny metal in their hands, take one look at the scene and decide it won't do for them to have anything to do with it. John Doss goes to meet them and they start backing off real quick. John grabs one of the guys by the lapels and starts to jerk the doctor's jacket off and gets it down to around the guy's elbows.

"Take off that coat and get to work in here, for Christ's sake. Be a doctor for once in your life!" he says to the guy.

"Take it easy, John, take it easy," the other guy tries to soothe. "This can't be done here . . . it's not sterile. She must be moved to the hospital."

About this time I start to ride up. "She isn't going anywhere," I says leaning across Joan at the guy. "Cool it," Bill says from the floor. They split threatening an ambulance, and for all we know, the Heat, so everybody settles down again with "Come on baby" going very strong.

So John is back down with Billy showing him how to receive the baby, when it starts to come out and so quick and easy it seems a miracle but Billy has the baby's head in his hands and it looks like throughout the whole scene of deliverance the baby had turned its own head and decided to come on out and with a thick liquid *whoosh* is right in Billy's hands. I am on my knees by Joany's head and I lean down with little more than a whisper, "It's a boy."

With some cotton string John Doss ties off the umbilical cord and cuts it with a pocketknife and the baby is born, out, free, alive and beautiful crying in his father's hands so fast that it was not a process of birth at last but life occurring.

John Doss begins cleaning up Joany and places the afterbirth in a basin.

"Eat!" he says to the circle of joyously lighted faces holding out the basin. "Everybody eat!" and starts carrying the basin around from one to one and each dips a hand to the stuff of birth and blood and tastes and never, from no dope I have ever taken, have I got so instantly high. Somebody marks the time, 10:41, and asks Billy the baby's name.

"Digger!" Billy answers back with a voice loud with single word as its own rising song.

The bloodied ends of the umbilical tying string Billy takes and wraps up in a poem I had made that afternoon to lay on the kitchen floor:

Velvet kneeling meat —
Crazyblood in his prayers.

is all I remember.

At the instant Billy Batman called his child by their name, the Diggers knew it was given away and they never used it to refer to themselves again. Of course, it was a slow process to hip the San Francisco community to the fact that they were no longer to be known as the Diggers, but rather as the Free City Collective or Commune or whatever. Within a few months, however, no one in the Haight-Ashbury, except the press, used the word that is now simply the name of a burly, blond-haired boy who's already demonstrated that he's got the strength and the vision to go with his birth tag.

Emmett only left the city one more time that so-called Summer of Love to go to New York again to take care of some business and also on to London for a few days to take part in a conference billed as

"The Dialectics of Liberation." As usual, it turned out to be a mistake and a waste of time for him, especially since he was now alone and traveled that way. It was quite uncomfortable at times, when all around him were apparently surrounded by their "brothers and sisters." He hadn't as yet resigned himself to the fact that he was, once again, the loner he had been for most of his prior life, and it was still hard and confusing for him to be working with and for men who didn't particularly care about him or each other as brothers anymore. The hard, nitty-gritty reality of this wouldn't directly strike him with its naked cold-bloodedness for another six or seven months. And so he went on about his business, as if everything was the same between him and his people and without letting on to even himself, much less anyone else, that the San Francisco family of which he was a member was coming apart at its seams.

The business that Emmett went to take care of in New York had to do with money. He fortunately didn't have to spend much time getting what was needed together and sending it back home, using a dozen different money orders to make sure that the few thousand dollars was spread evenly among the people he wired it to — the Free City Collective.

This money he posted back to the people with whom he worked was not raised at any benefit function or charity ball. Even though times were often harder than it was possible to endure and the pickings were nowhere to be found, much less slim, the Free City people never broke their word to themselves by holding a rock concert benefit that would probably have raised enough money to bankroll all their operations for an entire year or more. They never did it, because it was too easy, and more important, they didn't want the common, low-money people or even their children to end up paying for their trip.

The money they always needed was always gotten in the same various ways that Emmett was able to get it during those few July days in New York. That is to say, it was sometimes stolen or sometimes hustled from persons or corporations that didn't miss it anyway. Some of the dollar energy they needed to operate was simply given to them, however, through a tax-deductible middleman by friends who'd made it in a legitimate business enterprise or in one sort of larcenous activity or another, in which case the necessity of using the tax-deductible middleman was eliminated. This money, given to them without any stipulation as to its use, was only taken from friends, never from strangers, because these individuals were sincere and had no other way of participating in what Emmett and the rest were doing.

It was only after he sent the money back to the West Coast and was getting ready to return there himself that Emmett was invited to the conference in England by its London organizers. From the moment he found out the details of "The Dialectics of Liberation," Emmett felt he had a responsibility to attend because the forum was packed solid with hard-core-radical-political careerists, headlined by Stokely Carmichael, and including John Gerassi, Paul Goodman and Herbert Marcuse whom Emmett regarded with a respect he holds for few men. Also in attendance and representing their various fields of endeavor were the brilliant, vanguard psychiatrist, R.D. Laing; ecologist and student of mammals, Gregory Bateson; poet, scribe and the kind of good person that *is* hard to find, Allen Ginsberg.

He was the only one invited, however, to lay out what was going down among the young people for whom he apparently was selected as representative. So Emmett decided he had to go, but he didn't have any money or means to get there since he'd already mailed nearly all of what he had back to San Francisco. He was standing in Greenwich Village's Sheridan Square at the time, right in front of the *Village Voice* newspaper offices, and that was just about the only reason he had for entering and asking the receptionist if he could please speak with the publisher.

"Is he expecting you?"

"No, but it's an important personal matter, you understand. Just ring him up 'n tell him Grogan, Emmett Grogan, from San Francisco's here to see him, and I'm sure everything'll work out."

The secretary did just that, and, when she put down the phone, she told him that Mr. Edwin Fancher, the publisher, would see him in a few moments, as soon as he was finished with whatever had him occupied. Then she asked Emmett with a phony, rich-man's-daughter shyness, "Is it true?"

"Is what true, pretty lady?"

"That part in the *Ramparts* story — did you really get away with the meat after the butcher hit you over the head?"

"No."

"No?"

"No. Sorry. Next time I'll try harder. Just for you."

A jovial man whose looks Emmett immediately forgot came forward from the rear, introduced himself as the publisher, and after shaking hands invited him into his office which was stuffed-cluttered with political rhetoric printed in every shape and form. It was in that cramped, stocked-with-papers office that Emmett made his less-than-five-minute pitch about how he had to go to England, and Mr. Edwin Fancher listened as the touch was put to him in the form of an exclusive writing proposition which both men knew would never be fulfilled. But he came through, anyway, like an old gambler staking a young fighter to his first main bout or playing a long-shot hunch.

Emmett left the *Village Voice* with a five hundred dollar personal check and was escorted across the street to a bank where he exchanged it for cash. Afterwards, he stood alone in Sheridan Square, counting the money and hoping that the publisher man didn't feel he'd been messed over with a smile and a grin or had come out on the short end of a dirty deal. For that wasn't the case. Emmett didn't hustle him; he simply asked and was given. But just the same, as he walked away, Emmett peeled an eye over his shoulder back at the newspaper office, thinking to himself that if he got any bolder, life was going to end with him being treated a hell of a lot colder. Amen!

At the Fifth Avenue office of the British Overseas Airlines later in the day, Emmett bumped into Danny the Riff, the twenty-four-year-old co-manager of the Grateful Dead rock group. He, too, was buying a ticket to London, and they on-the-spot decided to travel there together on the same flight that night. Both of them had some loose ends to tie up around the city before they left, so Danny suggested they meet around early evening in the Park Avenue apartment of a friend of his. He gave Emmett the address with a "See you there later, brother!" before bouncing away, looking real good, dressed in tattered-patched jeans and carrying an attaché case in one hand, a real, made-in-Africa, cast-iron-tipped spear in the other, and an enormous, kinky, Afro-like hairdo flopping all over his head, covering up most of his gentle Moroccan-Jewish face. Emmett watched him trip down the avenue past Saint Patrick's Cathedral, freaking everybody out, stopping them in their tracks and forcing them to turn their heads to get a better look at this costumed monster who was one of their children. He was a peaceful, gentle guy who never intentionally hurt anyone. Maybe that's why Emmett liked him and they were friends. Danny the Riff was a sweet cat.

Emmett shot into Brooklyn on the subway to see his family, and they were glad he did. His parents couldn't for the life of them understand the length of his hair or his name change or the things they heard or read about him and what he was doing. But they were happy to see he was healthy, except his mother commented that he looked a little thin, and his father was a bit disconcerted by the gold earring pierced through his son's left ear. "What does it mean, anyhow?" he finally asked.

Usually, when he was asked this sort of question, Emmett would reply, "It means that you don't know what it means, and I ain't never gonna tell you, ever!" But this man was, after all, his father, and he wasn't being in the least bit arrogant, just curious as to why any young man, especially his own son, would have a thing like that done to him. So Emmett told him, simple and clear, that his brother named Tumble put it there, and all it really meant was that there was going to be a hole in his ear forever which would never let him forget who put it there and what they had both been to each other. The gold earring that was fitted into the hole was given to him by another of his brothers, Coyote, for more or less the same reason. The only difference being that the earring could be removed or changed or lost, like in a fight, or even stolen, but the hole was going to be there for as long as he lived.

His father understood. It all sounded like a story he once read about a group of Rumanian gypsies, but he understood and thanked his son for explaining the matter to him. Then they drank some beer together and reminisced about Grandpa for a while before Emmett felt comfortably certain that he wouldn't offend his father by asking him about his own job and how it was treating him. His father was a proud, sensitive and extremely gentle man, and, even though he was his only son, Emmett wasn't exactly on familiar terms with him, having been away from home for most of his life, ever since he reached puberty.

There was still a bond between them, however, the same kind of bond that's always between two men who are father and son, regardless of whatever else they might be. And so Emmett heard that things weren't going as well as they should be and that his father was quitting the firm he'd been with for over twenty years to accept an offer from a long-time Greek friend of his who was about to open his own stock brokerage house. Leaving Delafield and Delafield, the place he worked at for half of his life, was a difficult decision for his father to make, but it was made easier by his friend who showed him that his seniority and devoted service in that firm's business meant little in actual terms of pension or retirement benefits. In fact, it meant absolutely nothing at all, except maybe a thousand dollar kiss-off when he reached the age where he'd be too old to work.

Therefore, the next week was going to be his last at that house, and he'd be getting a lot more pay, future benefits and an executive-level managerial position where he wouldn't have to take all the orders, but give some of them, when he made the move to the new brokerage business owned by his Greek friend who he was sure would do right by him. "Good!" Emmett said to his father, and he was very glad that he might just be catching a break for once in his life.

He left shortly after that with a kiss for his sister, who said she'd be out to the West Coast soon, which for some reason didn't make Emmett happy at all, but he didn't have time then to discuss it with her. His parents walked him to the elevator and asked that he return soon and maybe stay awhile. They waved to him and shouted "Goodbye!" through the small window of the door as it closed and the car began its descent to the ground floor. It didn't matter to his mother and father that the window wasn't the porthole of a ship carrying him out to sea or the rear windshield of a taxi driving him to some air or bus terminal. It was still the window of a vehicle that was again taking their son away from them, and they couldn't care less that it was just an elevator bringing him downstairs. It was still taking him away, so they waved and said goodbye, and his mother began crying as she walked the few yards back to the apartment with the man who still made love to her in the same beautifully gentle way he had when he sired their son who, once again, was gone.

It was nearing five o'clock when Emmett entered the Park Avenue building, and the doorman showed him the way to the velvet-lined private elevator that would take him where he wanted to go. The difference between the funky, graffiti-scratched, slow-running elevator that his parents had to use every day, all the time, and the fine, delicately exquisite, smooth flowing quickness of the elevator in which he was now ascending, was maybe what it was all about: the difference between the way the inherited or chosen few live and the way most of the rest are made to live their lives. It was definitely one of the differences that Emmett wanted to eliminate somehow not only from his life, but from life itself.

The double steel outside doors rolled silently open, and Emmett gently slid apart the two glass-windowed, wooden doors of the car's interior. Before stepping out of the elevator into the red-carpeted, satin-lined foyer, however, he looked down at the polished brass edge of the car's floor and saw that the name of the company that designed and manufactured both the elevator in his parents' building and la crême de la crême of lifts in which he now stood was the same, Otis. He silently congratulated Mr. Otis on his ability to touch all the bases and, smiling to himself, left and sealed up the car.

The door chimes were answered by a blond woman who obviously refused to accept the fact that she was approaching her middle thirties and was rich enough to purchase things which enabled her to fake her twenties. The moment she shook his hand at the door, Emmett knew how old she was, even though he was fooled at first. He could feel the years in the skin covering the fingers and knuckles of her hand which still clasped his, coaxing him toward the large salon that was the rear of the apartment, with a skylight for a ceiling and an immense, articulate, psychedelic painting drawn on one of its otherwise orange-red walls. She introduced herself to Emmett and, upon hearing her surname, he immediately assumed that she was the daughter of a famous film director who hadn't made a good movie in years. But she wasn't.

Danny the Riff was late and had phoned, saying that he'd be by within the next hour which would have left Emmett quite alone with the lovely, good lady, if it hadn't been for the seven or eight men seated around the comfortably furnished salon. Emmett forgot each of their names as soon as they were introduced to him, except for one who was apparently the woman's brother because he had the same surname, wore no wedding ring and looked a lot like her.

Emmett couldn't get over how difficult it was for him to handle people's names, especially when they had two more besides their first. "No big deal," he concluded as he sat down in a billowy armchair to wait for Danny the Riff in a room full of strangers who had already given him a large snifter half-filled with good brandy, because it was what he wanted, and were now trying to get him into their cocktail conversation. But that he didn't want and made it clear by playing spaced and not answering or saying anything. They finally left him alone and returned to what they were talking about among themselves which was business, the stocks and bonds business.

Emmett listened attentively, but unnoticeably, to everything that was said, trying to make something out of the abbreviations and figures being tossed around. He'd been there about thirty-five or forty minutes and had only really spoken a few words to the good lady hostess, when something added up and he began to realize what it was: within the web of numbers and abstract letters of the alphabet that was most of the men's conversation, there was a message signaled to him, and he suddenly found himself decoding it.

The realization started slowly to build itself up inside of him and quickly became more visible and full. It had to do with the younger brother of the good lady. It had to do with who he was and what he did in the stock market and how he was connected to a pair of names that were mentioned during the course of the conversation. The names were Delafield and Delafield, and, as soon as Emmett heard them, he listened to everything real good, until he was able to figure out that the brother, the man in his very early thirties who was sitting across the room from him, was an allied-member partner of Delafield and Delafield, and was Emmett's father's boss and had been Emmett's father's superior, ever since he graduated from whatever college he attended.

It was immediately after that discovery that Emmett sat back in his chair, astounded at what he was beginning to understand about this brother and sister and about what they really had to do with him. You see, not only was "younger brother" over there Emmett's father's employer, but the guy belonged to the family who owned the Pennsylvania coal mines in which Emmett's grandfather had gone to work when he was eight years old, ninety or so years before. This sister whose penthouse he was sitting in and her younger brother were the children of the family for whom Emmett's father and grandfather had worked their entire fucking lives! They were the children of the men and women who owned It! Who still own It! Who bought and paid for the last two heads *of his family!*

He couldn't believe it, even though he knew it! He was fired with an immediate impulse to leap across the room and scar someone for the rest of their life with his glass. It was all so goddamn, overwhelmingly, unbelievably real that it was, at once, surreal and absurd. He began to calm himself with the thought that he'd never end up working for them, the children. The children who inherited his father's employment would never salary his son — or would they? Their family owns so much that one could end up working for them without even knowing it. The only way to be sure, certain, Emmett thought, was never to work — never to take wages from anybody as long as he lived, which was preposterous, but probably true just the same.

Emmett was still in the exploding throes of this startling revelation that their family owned his family, and he was really working himself up toward something, when Danny the Riff showed, and they had to go right away or miss their plane to London. Danny seemed to be very tight friends with the sister and brother pair, or at least he was acting that way, so Emmett decided not to blow it, but simply cool the message that was boiling inside his brain.

He began shaking everyone's hand goodbye with a "Be seein' you!" and making damn sure that he didn't come up on younger brother too fast, rather saving him for last. When he did reach him standing at the end of the half-circle of men, Emmett listened to him say something like, "If there's ever anything I can do for you when you're in New York, don't hesitate to call. My sister always knows where I can be reached, okay? Good! Nice meeting you and have yourself a good trip. Bye now." Then he released Emmett's hand from his clasp, but Emmett grabbed his right back and held it tight, looking straight-eyed and softly telling him, so that no one else could really hear, although they knew that something was going down.

"There *is* one small thing you could do for me, if you have the time and would?"

"Sure, what is it? If I can do it, I certainly will."

"Well, there's this friend o' mine, see, who works at your place there, Delafield 'n Delafield. And I was just wonderin' if you'd say hello to him for me?"

"Of course, what's his name and what does he do at Delafield?"

"I really don't know what you call what he does. But he's been doin' it for over twenty years in one of them margin clerk's cages, you know what I mean?"

"Yes . . . uh, what was his name . . .?"

"His name's Grogan. Mister Grogan. He's my father!"

As soon as he said it, Emmett instantly knew that he did the righteous thing and that whatever it was he meant before, he meant it more than ever now.

In the elevator on their way down, Danny asked him what his whispered tête à tête with the brother had been about, commenting that it looked serious. Emmett told him that it wasn't nothing, really. "Just wanted to let the man know that the both of us inherited the wrong side of the tracks."

"Who? Me and you?"

"No, me and him."

They landed in London before noon the next morning, and after taking a coach from the Heathrow Airport to the Piccadilly Circus passenger terminal, they hopped in separate cabs with Danny confirming where they were to meet that evening, before driving off to take care of the business end of music with a promoter in whose house he would also be staying for the next few days. Emmett read the address which had been given to him by friend and poet Allen Ginsberg, who told him that was where he'd be, and where Emmett could stay if he came over for the "Dialectics of Liberation."

When Emmett told the driver where he wanted to go, the man turned to have a look at this longhaired bloke sitting in the rear of his MacNab and asked him if he was certain he had the address right. Emmett looked again at the piece of paper to make sure and repeated it to the cabbie, assuring him that was where he wanted to go. There was a long pause during which Emmett was given a more careful once-over, and, only after the driver was satisfied that his scrutiny hadn't detected whatever it was he thought might be wrong, did he put the roomy sandy in gear and pull away in the direction of Regent's Park with his passenger enjoying memories of the view from the window, while dropping a questioning line or two about the July cricket matches at Lord's Ground to let the cabbie know that he knew London and didn't want to be driven around to fatten the meter.

Emmett had never heard, or at least couldn't remember ever having heard, of the street that was the address he repeated to the driver. He understood the reason behind this unfamiliarity when they finally got through the thick traffic and arrived in front of one of only four brilliantly white, Grecian-columned houses, standing side by side with a dignified magnificence that was designed to accentuate the exclusiveness of what was not a street, but a "terrace" bordering the rolling green splendor of the very private northwest side of Regent's Park. It was then that the driver again asked Emmett whether he was still sure that this was where he wanted to be let out, because, he explained, he knew for a fact that at least three of the four imperial houses were presently occupied by members of the Queen's royal family and, " 'Scuse me, mate, but you jus' don't look the type t' be visitin' them class of people, 'less you're goin' inside to fix the plumbin' or something. Ya know wha' I mean?"

The fact of the matter was that Emmett *did* know what he meant and wasn't really certain any longer, and, after showing the driver the slip of paper with the address on it which they both agreed he could have written down wrong, he told him to wait a minute, until he found out if he was in the right place by ringing the doorbell to see whether the residents were expecting him.

The door was opened by Marietta, the young, stoically tall woman of pale silence who taught Allen Ginsberg this and that about Indian music, prayers and mantra chants, whose mere appearance in the doorway all dressed in a cotton sari, wrapped warm with a bulky wool sweater told Emmett that this was where he was supposed to be, and he kissed her.

After paying his fare and reassuring the MacNab driver that he was home, Emmett took his small bag filled mostly with notes, papers and an extra pair of socks and walked back up the marble stairs, under an archway, and through the front door. He felt as if he were entering a palace, and he was. A small palace, but a palace just the same, lightly decorated with antiques and furnished with sparse but deliciously mellow Louis XIV furniture to avoid cluttering up the elegant space of walnut-paneled floors and ever-so-grand rooms.

Everyone was there and Allen introduced him first to two of the men who'd affected his life and whom he'd always wanted to meet, William Burroughs and Alexander Trocchi, both writers, poets, prophets and seers. The woman whose place it was came forward with the grace and beauty of years of wealthy refinement and with a delicate whisper greeted Emmett and sincerely expressed hope that his journey across the sea had been a pleasant one. Her name, strangely enough, meant "bread" in certain dialects of Italian and that was exactly what she had to offer and had been offering to poets for years in her role as the chief benefactress of dozens of artists throughout the world. She was a good, gracious woman of whom very few unkind words have ever been spoken. She showed Emmett to his room.

The giant main event of the week-long "Dialectics of Liberation" conference was to occur that night, beginning at 8:00 P.M., and a few short hours before that, Emmett made a mistake. He went with some of the men, whom he considered his elders because of their "beat experience," across town to a communal house where many of the old-timers and founding fathers of white hipsterism lived together as expatriates from their various countries or simply as British artists who felt outcast in their own land. It was a spectacular place full of singular originals — the men and women artists and their work. There was also plenty of dope, but unfortunately only two varieties of it, Lebanese hashish and pure London, drugstore heroin which was, of course, legal there for any registered addict.

The group sat in a quick cluster on the thick, Persian-rugged floor of what appeared to be the living room, — all the rooms looked so much alike it was hard to tell any difference between them with the exception of the kitchen and W.C. There was a tray on the floor, and Emmett helped himself to the papers, cigarette tobacco and hash, using about six or seven papers and mixing the loose tobacco with lots of hash to roll a "splif" which is a joint about as fat as a cigar and just as long. It took him nearly half an hour to smoke it with no help from anyone, because they all had their own or were not interested in anything else but the high-grade pharmacy scag. So was Emmett, and by the time he was loaded on smoke, he started getting a real yen to get off behind some of that fine A-1 stuff, and he did, doing himself up as if he had his last fix the day before, instead of a decade ago.

The moment the rush hit and the dope ran through his veins, every cell in Emmett's body snapped with remembrance of the sensation they had never really forgotten during the ten, long, clean, past years. He nodded out right after what was only a cellular memory became again a real feeling enveloping his body in its own erotic warmth. He didn't even have time for any regrets — if he had any — just enough time to nod his head plop! down on his chest which wasn't heaving with its asthmatic wheeze any longer.

Emmett's nod became a deep sleep with him propped up in the corner of the room, leaning against the interesting walls undisturbed by anything or body. One of the poet elders in the house woke him up after three or four hours, because night was rapidly falling, and Emmett had to get to the "Dialectics of Liberation" conference being held in a gigantic, fantastic, huge dome of a building appropriately called the Roundhouse. It had once been the warehouse, storage depot and garage for the numerous vehicles of London's Metropolitan Transport system.

When Emmett arrived there a little before eight o'clock that Saturday night, he liked the industrial, working-class smell and leftover accoutrements of the brilliantly designed, hollow-mammoth Roundhouse, but he didn't particularly like the look of the weekend crowd of four or five thousand sitting in row after row of collapsible wooden chairs and drinking beer from large gallon cans which was the only way to juice that Saturday night, because all the pubs would be shut down by the time this main session of the conference ended.

Emmett was still loaded with the sleepiness of heroin and very much on the nod, his eyes pinned and glassy and all the love taken from them by a heavy look of coldness. He kept himself together, though, knowing that he had to, because in a few minutes he'd be sitting on the stage with all the left-wing superstars and would make a ten-minute speech. A speech he planned and even researched, but now was too fucked up to deliver properly. He had even forgotten his notes back at the house, but it was no big thing, really, because he'd have another chance the following day when the only speaker billed for the afternoon was him, and he had been assured that the response to hear him rap was well worth his having traveled there. So, tonight he figured he would relax and tomorrow do what he came to do.

They were all standing backstage, and Allen Ginsberg fulfilled his usual sincere diplomatic role by introducing him to everybody, one at a time. Suddenly she was standing in front of him, an elegant, gracefully tall black woman with a coiffeured Afro and dressed in a West African robe. She said her name was Angela Davis and that she had been hearing about Emmett and the Diggers in San Diego where she was a student and teacher in the philosophy department at the University of California. She invited him to look her up whenever he was in that part of the state and then let him go as Allen pulled him away towards the cluster of black people surrounding the man in whose entourage Angela Davis was traveling at the time — Stokely Carmichael.

Allen excused and pardon me'd his way through the group, holding onto Emmett and dragging him toward the center and the man who was all decked out in a bright orange shirt. When they reached him, Allen treated the introduction with the decorum he thought appropriate for a historic meeting. The two men were standing face to face only a few feet apart, and the backstage crowd quieted down to maybe hear what was going to be said as Stokely Carmichael stuck out his hand, his face broadening into a smile, intending to say something like "Glad to meet you, brother." But he didn't, because Emmett didn't raise his hand in greeting or change the cold, hard expression on his face or even give any sign that he intended to. He just stood there, deadpanning Carmichael and his outstretched hand and the smile on Carmichael's face quickly dropped into a frown as he began to realize that this longhaired Digger dude, Emmett Grogan, was making him look like a goddamn fool in front of everybody.

Stokely Carmichael was obviously outraged by this stone affront to his dignity as one of the proclaimed leaders of American radicalism, and he did an abrupt about-face, stomping away and huffin' 'n puffin' thunder and smoke about "Who's that longhaired, motherfuckin' hippie punk think he is . . . !" He walked away fast and furious with his bodyguards and fellow Black Power advocates following him and glaring back at Emmett, mumbling to one another that they should've guarded their leader better and not have permitted that "white motherfucker!" to insult him.

The rest of the backstage groupies were whispering hard and heavy about what they just witnessed, and reporters were asking around about Emmett, like who he *really* was and why he didn't shake Carmichael's hand. A few even concluded that he was a racist and didn't want to touch black skin.

Someone finally asked Emmett himself, and he told them he didn't like Stokely Carmichael and hadn't wanted to meet him, but somebody unwittingly brought them together, and he felt he would've been lying the way all politicians, be they radical or conservative, lie, and so he simply refused to smile back at and shake the hand of a man he disliked extremely. "But it was nothing personal, you understand. In fact, very few things I'll do here or ever do anywhere are personal — they're political."

Shortly afterwards, Emmett was led onto the stage where he sat on the same kind of a wooden folding chair in which the five thousand or so persons in the audience were also seated, facing him with their ten thousand eyes, and he was suddenly very glad that he'd worn his wire-rimmed sunglasses to shade the pinning of his eyes.

The speeches were routine and predictable and were all sponsored by token honorariums from the London Institute of Phenomenological Studies, except Emmett's which was free. Psychiatrist R. D. Laing said everyone was crazy, including himself; John Gerassi had recently returned from Cuba and spoke about the necessity for a violent revolution; Gregory Bateson talked about the scientific apocalyptic aspect of the anxiety syndrome from which everyone was suffering; Allen Ginsberg insisted that the best tactic of psychopolitical action was to "make public all the private hallucinations and fantasies of our priest-hero-politician-military-police leaders, like those of John Edgar Hoover, for instance"; the keynote speaker, Stokely Carmichael, still very upset with Emmett, lashed out at the longhaired hippies who, he claimed, were advocating peace in time of revolutionary warfare and were traitors to the radical movement, because their upper-middle-class affluence afforded them the choice of nonviolence and the means with which to drop out of the fight for liberation which he quoted as "only coming through the barrel of a gun!"; Paul Goodman suggested that governments might begin applying immediate social welfare ideals and principles by paying, for example, people on New York's welfare rolls to live in the country, instead of in the city. "Give them the same money, and say, 'You don't have to live *in* New York, you can live *out* of New York!' "; Herbert Marcuse didn't say anything because he wasn't there, having hopefully found something more important to do with the time; Emmett spoke last.

He had been sitting on the stage for over an hour, wavering in and out of the focus of his consciousness behind his tinted, penny-bun glasses and every once in a while listening to what someone had to say. The only one he was hardly able to hear was Stokely Carmichael who yelled so goddamn loud that the tone finally became the point of his speech rather than the words. The crowd had given him an enthusiastic round of applause which they directed at the singer and not his song. Then, all of a sudden, Emmett found himself standing stage-center in front of the microphone and removing his shades for want of something to do and because none of the other speakers who were wearing them had taken them off to address the audience. It took him a moment to adjust his eyes to the startling lights, and, when he cleared them of the brilliance he focused on one individual out of that whole crowd of five thousand — William Burroughs, seated in the fourth or fifth row way over to the left of everyone with his tortoiseshell glasses, and his thinning hair combed flat to one side of his head, and his black, porkpie hat of ten years resting on his lap with his bony hands holding on to it so it wouldn't be snatched by one of his old-time pals and sold or exchanged for a nicer cap. He looked like an aging Hitler youth, sitting there erect and waiting with his thin lips pressed together and all dressed in black, waiting to be impressed, his narrow, Missouri face turned upwards, looking dead at Emmett with the wry knowledge of its own evil presence.

They locked eyes together for the longest moment as Emmett

remembered that this was the writer-poet-genius man who got his wife to place an apple or avocado on her head at a stoned-tequila-drunken party in Mexico, because his marksmanship was challenged by one of his pals or somebody. Then he carefully aimed the .45 pistol or whatever it was, firing a slug point-blank into the center of his wife's forehead which made her cerebrum hemorrhage and the police gasp. But they quickly called it an "accidental homicide," and everybody else said, "Wow!" except Bill Burroughs, who just sat there, like he was sitting there now, knowing full well that no one was ever going to know the secret that lies hidden in his brain.

Bill Burroughs and the rest of the audience were going to have to wait until the following evening to be impressed by Emmett, because he was too tiredly stoned to say what he wanted. What he did do, therefore, was to open his speech with "Today is the first day of the rest of your life!" which was a line he either made up or picked up somewhere during the last year. Shortly after he said it that night, it began appearing on posters and postcards and everywhere, not as a quote attributed to anyone, but just as a simple, declarative sentence to be sold by persons who never had an original thought in their dollar-billed lives.

He kept his speech short and to the point, which was to say, he refuted all of Carmichael's screamed remarks, not by giving away any secrets about himself or the people with whom he worked, but by simply explaining that the work they did together wasn't any Salvation Army trip, and concluding that neither he nor any of his people were so-called flower children, because they'd known ever since they were little boys and girls that ". . . flowers die too easy, even when they have thorns!"

Then he left. He walked off the stage and down into the audience where he sat and spoke with Michael X, a London black man whom he'd known when he was in London the first time around. Michael X was also the West Indian black leader who was going to end up paying for Stokely Carmichael's bottomless rabble-rousing against "whitey." Michael X was going to pay by being arrested for Carmichael's inciting the residents to riot in the streets of London's black ghetto of Brixton after the conference, creating hysteria and then immediately splitting the country with the promise that he'd be right back, knowing that he'd never return and thereby leaving Michael X to hold the bag which he was to do, for over a year in prison.

Emmett talked solely and briefly with Michael X about money

and how and whether he was getting enough to sustain the political-education operation that he and his brothers and sisters had organized and were attempting to maintain for the black people of Brixton. When he heard that money was very scarce and particularly hard for them to come by, Emmett gave Michael X an angle which eventually financially supported the work he and his comrades were doing for at least the following twelve or thirteen months. It had nothing to do with stealing or hurting anyone, and still has nothing to do with you, no matter who you are.

Early the next evening, Emmett found himself standing in front of the same microphone before about one thousand of the younger, heavier members of the same audience. This time, however, he was alone with no one else on the stage. He also felt a lot younger than the previous night, when his chippy shot of drugstore scag made him feel as old as the hills and as numb-dumb-cold-dry as a dead dog. He still couldn't figure out why he hit himself in the vein with the poison of his youth. Had it just been for old time's sake or had he been trying to impress his Beat elders with his own down hipster style? He gave up attempting to answer himself with a vow that he'd never chip again.

The rows of radicals who came to hear what he had to say were anxious but attentive, and Emmett was ready for them. He had memorized his speech the day before and had thoroughly gone over it that afternoon, blocking out its dramatic pauses and polishing up his delivery. When the moderator of the day's symposium of "Liberation," or whatever it was supposed to be, finished introducing Emmett as a "Digger, a hippie, an acidhead and a living mythical legend in his own time," he stepped forward to the applause and waited for it to subside, feeling ". . . righteously righteous and stone justly just," as his good friend and family doctor once said in a song.

The handclapping died down, and Emmett spoke strong and clearly into the microphone like an actor delivering a soliloquy, and the finger-popping revolutionaries listened to what they wanted to hear:

"Our revolution will do more to effect a real, inner transformation than all of modern history's revolts taken together! . . . In no stage of our advance, in no stage of our fighting must we let chaos rule! . . . Nobody can doubt the fact that during the last year, a revolution of the most momentous character has been swelling like a storm among the youth of the West. Look at the strength of awareness of the young people today! Look at our inner unity of will, our unity of spirit and our growing community of thought! Who could compare us with the youth of yesterday? We are unanimously convinced that strength finds its expression not in an army, in tanks and heavy guns, but rather ultimately expresses itself in the common working of a people's will! The will that is uniting our groups with the conviction that men and women must be taught the feeling of community to safeguard against the spirit of class warfare, of class hatred and of class division! . . . We are approaching a life in common, a common life of revolution! A common life to work for the revolutionary advancement of peace, spiritual prosperity and socialism! Toward a victorious renewal of life itself! . . . Our job is to wake everyone up and do away with illusions! So that when the people are finally awakened, never again will they plunge into sleep!

"The revolution will never end! It must be allowed to develop into streams of revolutions and be guided into the channel of evolution . . . History will judge the movement not according to the number of swine we have removed or imprisoned, but according to whether the revolution has succeeded in returning the power to the people and in the bridling of that power to enforce the will of the people everywhere! . . . Power to the people!"

The entire speech lasted for over ten minutes, and Emmett was satisfied with his convincing delivery that now had the whole audience up on its feet giving him an enthusiastic, standing ovation. He stood motionless by the microphone, where seconds before he was gesticulating like mad, dramatizing every word. He stood still, not bowing, or waving, or moving his lips to say, "Thank you! Thank you!" He just stood there and waited for the crowd to settle back down, so he could finally tell them what he *really* came there to say.

It was a couple of minutes before it was quiet enough for him to again place his mouth near the microphone and say, "I can sincerely appreciate your enthusiasm and honestly understand your excited applause, but, to be perfectly truthful, I can accept neither. You see, I neither wrote nor was I the first person to have ever given this speech. I really don't know who wrote it. I have an idea, but I really don't know. However, I do know who was the first man to make this speech. His name was Adolf Hitler, and he made his delivery of these same words at the Reichstag in, I believe, 1937. Thank you, 'n be seein' you."

There wasn't a sound in the huge main hall of the Roundhouse for a full thirty seconds or more. Nobody even moved. Then, all at once, it exploded with the fury of one thousand persons who thought they'd been had, been messed over, come out on the short end of a dirty deal! They directed their rage at Emmett who got his ass out of there real quick, and then they completely flipped, breaking things up, setting stuff on fire, and spilling their anger outside onto the street where they began fighting with those few who thought that Emmett Grogan had showed them just how jive rhetoric really was by putting them all on, beautifully.

Emmett was still laughing the next day when he returned to the Roundhouse for a discussion workshop that was arranged by those few hundred radicals who dug what he taught them about themselves and revolution. They wanted to learn anything else he could teach them before he left later that afternoon on his week-long return trip to the United States through more than a dozen cities in six or seven countries.

So he opened up his bag of experience, showing them everything he knew that wasn't supposed to be kept secret, and closed the bag by advising them that some of Adolf Hitler's early speeches weren't bad or wrong at all. It was just another case of people ". . . picking up on the singer and not the song, which, of course, usually blows the singer's mind, like it did Schicklgruber's who began to take seriously the lunacy of his own fantasies and proceeded to actualize them, using the people as his pawns. I mean, the cat knew they were digging him and the way he said things, rather than what he had to say. *He* was all he had to say, as far as they were concerned! You can see that in any old newsreel film clip of him standin' up at some podium in the middle of a few hundred thousand screamers and all he's sayin' is numbers! EINS! ZWEI! DREI! You know what I mean?"

What Emmett did best was advise communes or collectives of black or white or yellow or brown or pink radical street people on how to get whatever they needed, how to get themselves economically together to continue their work. After the conference, he spent a rush-hour week, flying around to all the different countries of Europe on the same tourist class ticket for his return flight to New York. He visited every city where he knew something heavy was happening to meet the people responsible, like the Provos in Amsterdam; Joe the Fever in Prague; Communes #1 and #2 and the Free University in Berlin; the Mistral Bookshop and Post Office and a whole lot of young heavies in Paris; everyone from the Exploding Galaxy to Peggy Duff to the Co-op Printing Society to Bromley by Bow's Kingsley Hall in London; and ten more cities on the continent in which there were groups of sincere, serious people at work, trying to lay the foundation for an intercommunal planet where there would be no boundaries dividing up the world, just different tribes of people free to live their lives the way they want, instead of have to — which is the only way to keep it all from dying.

Emmett got back to New York completely wiped out and totally exhausted from his fierce, whirlwind tour through Europe. His repeated discussions with the many different communal groups had him drained, demolished and half crazy behind "rubbin' at that same old goddamn thing!" He had rejoined Danny the Riff somewhere along the way, and they returned to New York together where most members of the Grateful Dead rock family met them at the Chelsea Hotel. It was in a room at the Chelsea that Emmett finally collapsed with exhaustion and slept for thirty straight hours.

It was almost the second week of July when he eventually woke up and a Wednesday he'll never likely forget. The sun was already waning as he had a shower and shave, putting on the same clothes, except for a change of socks, and bopped out to 23rd Street and down Seventh Avenue toward Greenwich Village. He had about fifty dollars in his pocket, and his stomach was craving with the hunger of a man who went to bed hungry and overslept. He wanted to eat a steak, a big, juicy piece of rare meat with some boiled potatoes, maybe, and a green salad on the side. He got exactly what he wanted and more in a Sixth Avenue Italian restaurant and gamblers' bar named Emilio's. The place was across from the corner of West Third Street, meaning Emmett walked a full twenty blocks or a stone mile without even realizing it until he sat down to eat and felt a bit dizzy. He lifted up his feet to look at the soles and heels of his Tony Lama, black Western boots that the free city women bought for him with a hot credit card and muttered something to himself about how they were made for walking on dirt and grass, not concrete and grime.

The food and half bottle of red Bolla wine was just what he needed and the pizziaola sauce covering the thick porterhouse was an added delight. He paid the waiter, but had a little difficulty getting himself up from behind the table and out of the booth, because the food added a good five pounds to his stomach and momentarily made him sluggish and awkward. He finally squeezed himself loose, however, and walked over to the end of the long bar where he ordered a Liquore Grappa to light the burners of his digestive system and lessen the load in his stomach.

He had two more quick shots of the Italian white lightning before leaving Emilio's and slowly walking over to Tenth Street, past the Women's House of Detention where all the boy friends and pimps stood on the sidewalk yelling up to the faces of the inmates in the wire-meshed, pigeonhole windows "Everything's all right, baby! You gonna be back out on the street soon! Don't worry, okay?! Trust me!" Sure.

Emmett walked into Casey's bar where he'd been once before with Candy Sand at that literary party during the early part of spring. He remembered that they made a very good Irish coffee in Casey's, and he wanted one and possibly two or three. He stood in the front corner of the room where the bar curved in toward the wall. The tables were crowded with eight o'clock diners and the bartenders busy, tending aperitifs or sour, before-supper drinks. There was a very solid, strong-looking black man dressed in a gray suit and charcoal tie with his polished Florsheim shoe up on the bar rail next to Emmett's funky boot. He was in his late forties and, glancing at his reflection in the behind-the-bar mirror, Emmett saw that the cat was very happy about something.

The two of them began talking about nothing in particular, and they felt relaxed with each other as only men who have very little to fear or lose can relax with other men. They'd been rapping for about a quarter of an hour and had bought each other a round, when Mercer McKay, as he introduced himself, invited Emmett to follow him outside to the car he had parked down the street. Emmett did so without hesitation and pleased by the invite, because he instinctively knew he was going to find out what this black man, Mercer McKay, was smiling so much about.

The car was a practically brand new Cadillac Coupe de Ville limousine, all black shiny outside and luxurious leather upholstery inside, with one-way tinted windows, so no one could see into the spacious interior. Emmett slid into the passenger's side of the front seat and immediately noticed the gray hat next to him. Mercer was the chauffeur for whoever car this was.

"Lock your door back up, 'n take a blow o' this!" Mercer was handing Emmett a clear plastic vial of pharmaceutical cocaine and an eighteen-carat gold spoon to ever so delicately scoop out the snow and snort it into his nostrils. It was very good coke, and Emmett no longer had to wonder why his man was smiling.

They'd been sitting inside the air-conditioned boat of a car, rapping and listening to music, when it suddenly came over the radio that there was "a riot erupting in Newark," an incredibly corrupt, deadbeat city where everyone is shortchanged, particularly blacks. Both men looked at each other, and Mercer turned the radio up louder to catch the news they were reporting. Then he started the engine and pulled the car away, swinging it toward the West Side Highway. When Emmett asked him where they were heading, Mercer McKay told him straight. "We're goin' t' Newark! I got my woman's there, 'n she ain't good for much, but what she's good for's plenty 'nough for me, 'n I don' want t' lose her in no goddamn police riot! This here car'll get me through, all right. You don' wanna come, you just say so, 'n I'll drop you off at your hotel. Well, what's it gonna be?"

They were in Newark a little more than half an hour later. The city was an explosion of flashing lights, flickering flames and fast moving silhouettes. The sound of running, laughing, screaming, glass-breaking, bottle- and brick-throwing young black bloods was a constant uproar. The gunfire, crisp commands and crackling radios of the police were scattered, but pervasive. The noise was overwhelming and the scene visually surreal.

Mercer drove into an alley where everything else seemed very far away, and he honked the horn twice. The bottom-floor door of a two-story wooden frame house opened cautiously, and out ran a fantastically beautiful black woman in a gold lamé mini-dress. Her name was Lucille, and she was around twenty years old and Mercer McKay's old lady. She hugged him and kissed at his face through the open window of the car, until he stopped her and said that things were getting too hot for them to waste time. "So go back inside 'n get the others, 'n let's get outta here!"

The others were Lucille's four equally beautiful sisters and her mother who wasn't bad looking herself. Emmett was literally dragged into the back seat by the four sisters, leaving the front seat to Mercer, Lucille and mama. The jug of coke also found its way into the rear of the car, and the fun really began, with the girls giggling and howling and grabbing at Emmett's body and him running his hands all over their legs, until he found the one who wasn't wearing any panties. Then he put his fingers to work, and Mercer pushed a button to roll up the window that divided the front from the back part of the car, so Mama wouldn't hear the sound of laughter turn to the sweet soft sighing of sex.

The Cadillac took them right through Newark that first night of the riot and passed the roadblocks the state police had set up, to cordon off the "trouble area." Some of the cops even saluted the limousine as it went by, probably figuring it was carrying a high political official or somebody equally important to their careers. The rest of the night was spent partying in Mercer's downtown pad with Emmett finally returning to the Chelsea Hotel around dawn, the sister who didn't like to wear panties hanging on his arm, happy for a moment away from home.

The Newark riot lasted five more days with Abbot Hoffman getting into the act by calling for "Food for Newark Spades" to be donated at a specified time in Greenwich Village's Washington Square Park. Abbot and his cronies collected about seven or eight cardboard cartons of canned food and brought it over to Tom Hayden who was in Newark, heading the Newark Community Urban Project, facing at that time the terribly difficult decision of whether or not to join the federal government's War on Poverty program. The war on poverty is now, of course, over. Poverty won.

Anyway, Hoffman later exploited to his benefit these few cartons of canned goods which nobody ate, but used as missiles when they ran out of bricks. He claimed in several press conferences that he and his comrades were "Diggers" and that "Diggers are niggers," and, therefore, they smuggled in ". . . seven truckloads in all" to their ". . . underground soul brothers SNCC and NCUP." By using the name "Diggers" which the press had long associated with "Free Food," Hoffman changed a few boxes of Campbell's soup cans and several truckloads of tripsters sightseeing the "riot" into "seven truckloads" of loaves and fishes which they ". . . had a ball passing out!"

The last night Emmett stayed at the Chelsea Hotel in New York, he was talking with Danny the Riff and some of the Grateful Dead people about a "Trip Without a Ticket to Europe" to be completely "free" and unexploited by the media. It would not be for sale! There happened to be a reporter for the *Village Voice* in the room at the time, the late Don McNeill, and he wrote an article entitled "Trip Without a Ticket to Invade Europe" with no one's permission and blew the whole thing out the window. The avarice of film companies like Warner Brothers made it impossible for the trip to happen for "free" by blocking most of the financial possibilities. Years later they would cop the idea and make an obnoxious film with a fat disc jockey and a bunch of no-account, lame panhandlers, entitled *Medicine Ball Caravan* which, as one reviewer put it, "added up to no experience."

Emmett returned to San Francisco sick and tired of having been so long away from the city where he belonged. But very few things were happening to increase his gladness at being back among familiar faces doing his work with the Free Food. One thing did happen, however, that was enough to make him think that things weren't all that bad and even gave him a bit of optimism. Coyote had finally gotten down off the fence, resigning from the Mime Troupe to actively join the Free City Collective as a full-time brother, instead of simply remaining a part-time, lend-a-hand man. What made him decide to choose to play for keeps, only he knows. But when he'd made his decision, he didn't just come around. He came full around, and Emmett was back in time to embrace him.

Coyote had found a middle-aged woman who'd inherited an old hotel that she didn't know what to do with. It was a fifty-year-old, 482-room, huge place that used to cater mostly to prizefighters, like Jack Dempsey, but now was a waterfront flophouse for itinerants called the Reno Hotel. Coyote knew exactly what to do with it, as did his partner at the time, Golden Gloves Davey, a college-graduate boxer and stout worker: they were going to make a free hotel out of it. They intended to renovate the rundown building and redecorate it all in a modern, funky style including in it a free theater, movie house, restaurant and hospital. The woman who owned the hotel was thrilled with the idea and set her lawyers to draw up a nonprofit corporation to cover the turnover of the Reno to the Free City Collective. Unfortunately, their enthusiasm about the possibility of a well-run, free dwelling was not at all shared by the city hall bureaucrats and various police agencies who denounced the planned project as a "bed of evil" and pressured the fine woman into boarding up the hotel and terminating her role in the "free" venture.

It was a heavy disappointment for everyone connected with the Free City Collective, but especially for Coyote and Golden Davey, who thought they'd succeeded in solving at least a portion of the overcrowding dilemma of the Haight-hipster community. They both worked extremely hard to get the undertaking going and gathered large crews of carpenters, electricians and all sorts of skilled persons to reconstruct the Reno when the police forces and city hall powers said no. Of course, they based their veto on the absurd argument that the existence of a free hotel would draw "hippie undesirables" to the city of Saint Francis. Naturally they neglected to mention that San Francisco was already overflowing with more than one hundred thousand "hippie undesirables" who had no permanent or temporary place to reside, except the downtown jail.

The members of the Free City Collective were disgusted, but rather than vent their animosity for the fat cat establishment by blowing up a bank or two, or by protesting with demonstrations and press conferences, they returned to their work. They all knew what no one had to tell them: reactionary terrorism or a few childish tantrum marches would only temporarily relieve their own private frustrations with the so-called government, rather than help the people.

It was at about this time that Emmett began his "Free Food Home Delivery Service" and left the daily, Panhandle, 4:00 P.M., free feeding of the street folks for the women to cook and men like Tumble, Butcher Brooks and Slim Minnaux to deliver. Emmett's idea was exactly as he announced it in the *Free City News*, a service that took over the daily newspaper role of the Communication Company, incorporating the same machinery and people. Free City News was an enlightened, efficient and graphically superior news agency operated solely by members of the Free City Collective, which meant practically anyone who wanted to work and wasn't kidding.

It was a truly informative and beautiful newspaper. So beautiful, in fact, that the research department of the Gestetner Corporation, from whom the mimeograph machines had been stolen, couldn't believe that their equipment could produce such technically fine and attractive color combination graphics; which was probably why they didn't call the cops. Instead they politely asked the publisher of the *Free City News* to let them subscribe to the paper, or, at least, mail them a copy of everything that was printed and drawn with their machines. They were astonished that Billy Batman, who put together several of the most beautiful issues, and Golden Gloves Davey and House-Be-Nimble, who kept the news service from simply becoming a brilliant one-shot review, were using their Gestefax stencil maker to *paint*. It blew their minds!

The announcement that Emmett published in the *Free City*

News was only a beginning, but it really started things off right and in a hurry. It read:

FREE FOOD

LION MEAT   SOUL VEGETABLES   BLUE CHIP DAIRY GOODS
Everymorning Delivered to your Commune.
FRESH FISH   RIPE FRUIT   SOLID GREENS
Everyevening Feed the Brothers and Sisters in your House.
IT'S FREE BECAUSE IT'S YOURS
Give Your Address and the Number of People in the Commune to the Behind the Counter Cousin at the Psychedelic Shop.

. . . MUST BE DONE NOW . . .

At first Emmett found himself delivering only to communal houses filled with young people who came to town looking for what they couldn't see back home. But that was only for the first few days. After some of those matriarchal black women and welfare mothers who hung around the Trip Without a Ticket free store heard about it, as well as some of the young Chicano women who were into the activities of the Mexican-American Mission Rebels — the predecessor group to what is now known as La Raza — after those women heard about his Free Food Home Delivery Service, Emmett was given a whole bunch of names and addresses with the number of children and adults in each household marked clearly on a whole lotta slips of paper.

If he had any intention of sliding along, gradually and calmly developing his operation, these women didn't want to hear about it. They wanted it to happen all at once, now! And if he didn't come through, like he was making out he would, Emmett was going to be called to answer by these women who didn't want to hear nothing about how much time anything takes, but wanted what he himself had said was theirs, and they wanted it today!

"You say that 'it's free because it's yours,' don't you?! Well, I want mine! 'N we all wants ours! Just give us what belongs to us, 'n listen to your own poetry! We wants the food!"

Within ten days of his announcement, Emmett found himself all alone with a list of over a hundred names, addresses, and sizes of families living in slum tenements — from the black Fillmore ghetto all the way across town to the Chicano Mission district ghetto. He looked at that list, and he knew he either had to throw it down the sewer right away or come across for those mothers who used their children to call his hand. He decided to play out his hand, simply because he dealt the cards to himself.

As soon as he committed himself to backing up his own words, the enormity of the task became more than obvious. After a six-day week of stealing and delivering meat on Monday and Wednesday, vegetables on Tuesday and Friday, and dairy products on Thursday and Saturday to Viola on Webster Street with eight kids, Bertha on Lily between Buchanan and Laguna with ten, to the Jasons on Seymour Street with nine, to Baby Jesus on Washington with nine, to Paita Bye on Waller with fifteen, to Carmen on Mission and 22nd Street with eleven, to Ligette and Ward on Ellis Street with nine and six, to Terrell on Hayes Street with seven, to Carlos Cavaze on Treat Street with eight, to the Aurora Glory Alice commune on Cole with nine, and on and on, with ninety more names of families with people to feed — after that week, Emmett understood it was going to be sixteen hours a day, six days a week for as long as he could do what he said he would.

The Free Food Home Delivery Service became not only the most difficult thing Emmett had ever done in his life, but also the loneliest. Seldom would anyone ever accompany him on the daily, except for Sunday, day-long runs. He did most of it all by himself. Whenever someone did help him out, it was usually one of the women, but only a few, and even they would rarely stick it through with him from dawn till dusk.

Even though it was, without a doubt, the most essential aspect of their survival as a communal group, there was just something about the operation that made it unattractive to most everyone within the Free City Collective. It wasn't the tremendous burden of the work, or the length of the hours, or the likelihood of arrest and jail that made the Free Food operation undesirable. It was the thanklessness, the unromantic, unrewarding exhaustion of the cheerless, dismal anonymity which was the basic premise of "free" and the very essence of "Free Food." Anonymity is what made the food "free" and kept the "Free Food" coming right to those families' doors. Kept it coming for not just a week or a month, but every working day for a straight nine months. Kept it coming to people who didn't even know where it came from. They just had an idea, and most of them simply thought Emmett was a delivery driver, salaried by some rich man who wanted to ease his conscience by giving away a little food.

It was the nearest Emmett has ever come to making himself insane, remaining lonely in a way that few men ever have a chance to be lonely.

He not only had to ride with the fact that most of the people to whom he delivered the food thought of him as just a hired driver; he also had to contend with the incredible phenomenon of having his own Free City brothers put him down, bad-mouthing him, and begrudging him even the slightest bit of credit for having accomplished anything, much less acknowledging that he put the food on their table over which they discussed his shortcomings! It had him crazy! Crazy, because he knew he was doing it to himself. He didn't have to continue the Free Food. He didn't have to do any of those things! But he did, and that made it a matter of choice. Though he *really* didn't need the food himself, he somehow, deep inside himself, needed to free the food for those people who needed it. And in that sense, he probably needed it more than they did. He definitely needed it more than he ever needed anything else.

And so, Emmett remained an anonym to most people and allowed those close to him to drive him nearly out of his mind with their maddening insults to his sense of brotherhood. Some members of the Free City Collective resented his rigid insistence that everything be carried out anonymously, while anyone who wanted to could and was taking credit for "free" things they'd never done and words they'd never spoken or written or thought.

The Summer of Love was mainly the result of such a lie. The Haight Independent Proprietors' Human Be-In lie and its result bore witness to what would be in store for a nation that allowed its children to be lied to by comical, fake-radical politicos whose masquerade they nurtured by giving them profitable access to the mass media. The adventure of poverty by young white people in love ghettos throughout the country, like the Haight-Ashbury and the Lower East Side, was pleasant fakery for most of them. But in the same way that real poverty has always given birth to real revolution, this feigned poverty of the adventurous would breed a false-bottomed, jerry-built revolution in which the adventurers would continue their make-believe and be followed by the rock-concert lumpen, tired of their own voyeurism.

Of course, the "Summer" really ended before it ever started, but the sound of the tolling bell only began being heard in that last week of August when one of the most beloved men on Haight

443

Street, 35-year-old Hells Angel, Chocolate George, died in a collision with a car right in the middle of the block and in front of the very people who really liked him for his Cossack general's appearance, his Russian fur hat, and his overall fearless, friendly attitude toward everyone, except would-be tough guys or bullies whom he crushed. His funeral-parlor wake was attended by truckloads of street people, and he was buried with an impressive honor guard of two hundred of his Angel brothers from all over the state on their bikes, and with two quarts of chocolate milk in his coffin, so he wouldn't get thirsty wherever he went. Afterwards, the people had a party in Golden Gate Park where ten thousand gathered to wail Chocolate George goodbye, and a memorial band composed of members of all the rock groups played "Didn't He Ramble!" Emmett arrived with the Free Food pickup truck full of a half ton of shaved snow ice covering a thousand cans of beer. The beer was drunk and the ice used for a snowball fight in August. Then it was over, and he was gone, and it wasn't ever gonna be the same again.

Soon after that, another important Haight Street figure and friend of Emmett's was reported missing until his body was found in a sleeping bag beneath a cliff by the Point Reyes lighthouse where it was thrown by the person or persons who murdered him with a 9-mm., P-38, automatic pistol for the money in his pocket. Super Spade was known to carry a lot of bread around, and that night he supposedly was holding onto $50,000 to pay for a load of grass. But the simple armed-robbery-murder theory wasn't the way most people who knew him thought Super Spade died. They preferred to think he'd been snuffed by Eastern Mafia hit men who were sent out by the syndicate to get rid of anybody who could be an obstacle to their eventual takeover of the Haight-Ashbury territory. The only thing wrong with that bit of speculation was that the Mafia doesn't sell marijuana, and that's all Super Spade ever did. His murder, however, and the subsequent rumors of imminent mob control of the Haight caused a whole, new emigration of older hipsters to the countryside in search of some utopian dream that wasn't there.

There followed a whole string of senseless murders which usually involved some form of torture or bodily mutilation. The first of these was naturally headlined in the press as the "Psychedelic Murder," and the killer was caught driving a car with the cleanly severed, trimly stitched arm of the victim lying in the luggage area behind the back seat. Another was described by the papers as a "Sadistic Orgy Killing," and it was. A nineteen-year-old girl was dragged from her Haight-Ashbury apartment by seven men and three women who stripped and stomped her, scrawling obscene graffiti-slogans all over her nude body with lipstick, before they kicked her head in.

Then the news of the "First Longhaired Hippie Bank Robber" was headlined on the front pages and had everyone laughing, but also bitching that ". . . if the guy had to be the first, why the hell didn't he really impress the motherfuckers, instead of only getting away with twelve hundred and ninety-five dollars? Shit!" Beneath smaller headlines on the back pages there were stories about how the Haight was changing from a place of smiles and the "comfortably poor," to a normal, tension-filled, terror-stricken ghetto in which the peaceful "flower children" were no longer safe in the wake of increasing violence and simmering hostility.

The Summer of Love ended on the thumbs of thousands hitch-hiking someplace else, like Charles Manson, or on the welfare rolls for those who wanted to stay in Frisco and stretch their adventures in poverty as far as they could take it. The David Smith Medical Clinic closed again for lack of funds and want of publicity, and the truth of the Haight-Ashbury seemed to be making itself known now that the "flower children" had gone back to school. It just wasn't what it used to be, "the old Hashbury," one columnist noted, and the cops knew it. More than anyone, they created the overall harder reality of what was left of the "Psychedelic Community" with their harassing "haul-ins" and "sweep-ups," and they were going to get exactly what they deserved. The police commissioner screamed that it had become "a cesspool," right before the first bomb exploded near the park police station and the "law and order" candidate, Alioto, was elected mayor of the city.

The Hun, picking up on an opportunity to produce some good guerrilla theater, organized an appropriate street event for the strangling Haight, entitled the Death of Hippie. There was an orderly funeral procession of pallbearers carrying a coffin filled with hippie paraphernalia such as beads, flowers, hair, and so on, and followed by a large crowd of veiled mourners. The wooden coffin draped in black crepe paper was placed on top of a pyre and set aflame while a bugler played taps and ushers handed out black-bordered remembrance cards to the assembled which read:

Once upon a time, a man put on
beads and became a hippie — Today

445

> *the hippie takes off his beads and*
> *becomes a man — a freeman!*
> *Leaving behind the final remains*
> *of "Hippie — the devoted son of*
> *Mass media and*
> *the boundaries are down.*
> *San Francisco is free! Now free!*
> *The truth is OUT, OUT, OUT!*

A full description of the Death of Hippie production was carried on the front pages of most newspapers nationwide, and even the underground press couldn't resist calling "Freeman," a "Freebie." But the Hun's event did accomplish something of no small import. It influenced the two brothers and co-owners of the Psychedelic Shop to close it up forever, leaving a sign in their front window advising whoever that "Nebraska needs you more."

Soon after the "hippie" street population thinned out a bit, gangs of young, diddy-boppin', black bloods from all over the city began vamping through Haight-Ashbury seeking out "flower children" as prey. But most of them had already gone, making the women of the community the only easy marks for the black youths' blind reactionary acts of rape and robbery against anyone white. Their targets were always the weak, helpless and harmless girls who still thought of flowers as lovely and were attacked simply because they were accessible in the low-income neighborhood. This made the men of the community plenty fucking angry, and there was a series of fights, stabbings and shootings, until it looked like the whole goddamn thing was going to erupt into a race war with the "longhaired, shaggie honkies" led by the Frisco Hells Angels on one side against the "back-stabbin', women-killin' niggers" led by some cats from the Fillmore who identified themselves as "Black Panthers." The cops intended to stand on the sidelines and wait for everyone to beat everyone else to death or at least into exhaustion, before they moved themselves in for the overkill of both sides.

Emmett could see the righteousness of a massive assault on the bloods who were prowling the neighborhood, but he was confused as to who the Fillmore "Panthers" really were. So he called the party's Oakland headquarters and talked about what was going down with Bobby Seale and David Hilliard who put everything in perspective by revealing that those Fillmore dudes weren't Panthers at all, but just some paper cats running around, trying to mau-mau some loose change from the bearded, white, liberal, beaded merchants and rip off whatever else they could from the hip community. They promised to make everything clear to their black brothers and sisters in the next publication of their well-read newspaper, and also issue a warning to those young blacks who were causing all the trouble. The Panther party did this because they wanted to avoid a racist confrontation between their people and the longhairs, not because they were protecting the "hippies" who were perfectly capable of defending themselves by now.

The Black Panther party's statement was printed the following week and picked up and republished on the front pages of the city's newspapers. It was the only reason that open warfare between the two peoples didn't occur. The phony Panthers who were strutting around the Haight stopped after they read this: "Warning to so-called Paper Panthers — stop vamping on the hippies. They are not your enemy, black brothers. Leave them alone or the Black Panther Party will deal with you!"

It was around the same time that the inevitable happened to the man who'd originated and maintained the Black Panthers and who became a dynamic heroic figure to the young people of his community as soon as he began standing up to the intimidation of the Oakland police department. To those black youngsters, Huey P. wasn't just another "bad" brother off the block — he was a "bad" brother who not only was unafraid of the cops, but openly defiant of them. Every time the kids saw him, they asked him one question over and over, again and again: "When you gonna off a pig, Huey P.?!" "Yea, Huey P., when you goin' blow one o' them oinks away?! When you goin' to snuff one o' them motherfuckers, huh, Huey P.? When? When? When, Huey P.? When?"

The kids were a chorus, chanting the same refrain whenever he appeared anywhere. A refrain from a song that was burning with rage inside of him, ever since he realized that men who brutalized other men weren't men, they were animals. They were pigs! And one night, two members of that species appeared behind the car he was riding in and began to harass him, using the power of their uniforms as a badge, a license to insult the humanity of a human being, just because they felt like it and just because he was the uppityist black nigger they or the country had seen since Malcolm X.

When they pulled the car over and told him to get out, he did. They had guns in their hands. Huey P. had a book in his, a bound copy of the Constitution of the United States and the Bill of Rights. One of them shot Huey P. in the stomach, and then Huey P. somehow killed one of them and wounded the other. At least that's what they said happened and what most people believed, because of the way Huey P. had sung his song and the way the young black people's chorus had chanted that one phrase, "Kill the pig! Kill the pig!" until there was practically no one who wanted to believe that he hadn't actually done what they said he'd done in the manner they insisted he had. Almost no one; and possibly even including Huey P. Newton himself.

By then, everyone who was into anything in the streets of the Haight-Ashbury was packing some sort of heavy caliber weapon; either a blade like a machete, or a sawed-off rifle, or simply a pistol. Everyone! Emmett drove around with a piece beneath the dashboard of the Free Food pickup truck. He'd fixed up a tight little rack under the glove compartment to hold his .38, and it fit perfectly and was always there, firmly braced, but forever ready to be put to use in the defense of his life, liberty or pursuit of happiness.

One day a strange thing happened which afforded Emmett a golden opportunity to scare the living shit out of a man who might have been and still may be elected President of the United States. It was late in the afternoon, and he had just finished delivering most of the Free Food with only a few more stops to make before he completed his rounds, when he turned south of Buena Vista Park and drove down to Broderick Street, where there was a giant crowd gathered in front of Huckleberry House, the referral center for runaways. The street being blocked by the throng, he pulled over to have a look at what was taking place.

As soon as he stepped from the pickup, he heard someone calling to him from atop the front stairs of Huckleberry House, insisting, "Emmett! Emmett Grogan! Come on up here! Come on!" It was one of the ministers and leading officials of Glide Church which administered the referral center, and Emmett did what he was told and went up the stairs and inside where he was introduced, with the usual reference to his being a "legendary myth," to none other than the then Governor of Michigan, George Romney, and his pert, little wife Lenore, both of whom were touring the country to test the water for his upcoming campaign as a candidate in the Republican primary elections for President of the whole goddamn country!

Emmett was impressed when George Romney told him that he'd been hearing about his fine charitable work among the poor and misguided youth who found themselves alone and hungry and away from home on the streets of Haight-Ashbury, and he had the utmost

448

respect for the alms-giving services that Emmett and his fellow "What do you call them? Oh, yes, Diggers!" were doing for the young people of the nation who strayed to San Francisco.

A coincidence popped into Emmett's mind, and he couldn't pass up the chance to see if he could pull off a fabulous score — the kidnapping of the governor and his wife. In the most sincere and charming tone of voice he could muster, Emmett informed George and Lenore Romney that coincidentally, at that very moment, there were more than one hundred Indians from his home state of Michigan eating in the park with the "hippies," and it would be wonderful and extremely thoughtful of the governor and first lady to stop by and visit with the people from home. He didn't have to say anything about what good publicity it would be for the folks back in the Midwest. The good governor had already weighed its value, and Emmett watched as it registered with a click of his eyes and a cluck of his tongue.

What happened next, Emmett didn't exactly expect, but immediately picked up on it. The governor threw his arms around him and said with a smile, "Emmett, suppose *you* take me and my wife over there to meet with your people and the Indians from our state. What about it?"

"My truck's right out front, Governor, and I'd be more than happy to oblige. In fact, sir, it'd be an honor."

The three of them moved quickly outside, and George Romney helped his wife, Lenore, into the cab of Emmett's Free Food pickup, just like a midwestern farmer would've helped his wife into a pickup truck, all dressed up for Sunday and on their way to church. Maybe that's when Emmett decided not to do what he didn't, and then again, maybe not.

Besides the three of them, everybody else was confused; the state troopers, the city cops, the FBI, the reporters, the Methodist ministers, everyone, and the only thing they all could think of doing was to go along with the three, in the flatbed open back of the pickup truck. They all started climbing onto the rear of the truck at once. There were over a hundred of them, all fighting for a place to stand, with the reporters pushing and shoving each other but remaining very careful to avoid nudging any of the FBI men, who were already standing up straight in each of the four corners of the truck's rear. They had everything covered.

The half-ton pickup was just about to collapse under the weight of the maddening crowd, when Emmett yelled to the governor to "please tell all them suckers to get off o' the truck, Governor, sir, 'cause it's the only one still running good 'nough to deliver the Free Food, 'n they're gonna break it down for keeps!" George Romney didn't hesitate for a moment. He stood right out up there on the running board and told all them guys to "get down out of this man's truck, immediately! Can't you see what you're doing to it? He needs this pickup more than any of you need a ride, so get off, 'n get off now! You hear me?" Then he waited until every last one of them got out of the vehicle, including the heat, before he sat back down in the front seat, slammed the door closed, and put his arm 'round his wife, Lenore. And maybe that was when Emmett decided not to do it.

A man in a blue suit and sunglasses popped his face into the window on the driver's side and asked where they were going. Emmett looked at the governor, and the governor looked back at him, asking, "Where *are* we going?" Emmett answered, 'Golden Gate Park. We'll meet them there!"

Emmett must have been at least two or three blocks away when the security man realized that Golden Gate Park was a very, very big place and turned back to ask "Where in Golden Gate Park?" only to find that they had already gone with no one following them or anyone knowing where they went except him, and all he knew was that they were going to Golden Gate Park which is thousands and thousands of acres square and extremely easy to get lost in, and practically impossible to find someone in if you have no idea in what direction they're headed. The guy got sick, and hysterically hurried the Greyhound coach carrying the governor's entourage of reporters to Golden Gate Park where he dispersed the cops on motorcycles and in squadrols throughout the huge area, ordering them to search every goddamn inch, "But find the governor!"

Emmett had purposely not specified where in Golden Gate Park, because they didn't drive to Golden Gate Park. At least, not what was considered by most to be the Park proper, but was known as its Panhandle. It was to that long strip of green ground that extends about a dozen blocks from the park's entrance between the two main avenues in and out of town, that Emmett brought George Romney and his wife to meet not a hundred Indians from Michigan, but one Indian, who was or claimed to be a hundred years old, and about five hundred stone-street-freaks and crazies who didn't like the governor very much.

It was only a short, ten-block drive from Huckleberry House to that place in the Panhandle where the Free Food had been eaten every day at 4:00 P.M. for over a year by then. But Emmett didn't go directly there. Instead, he swung around in the opposite direction to make sure none of the cops or the Greyhound would find or catch up to his '56 green Chevy pickup truck, because he wanted to be alone with Governor George Romney and his petite wife for a while or maybe even longer than that, but definitely for as long as it took him to display what he knew about power.

It only took Emmett a couple of sentences to stop the governor's enthusiastic attempt to appear sincerely concerned about the plague he considered Haight-Ashbury to be and to halt the stream of hollow questions that were sure to follow.

"Governor, do you always take these kinds of risks?"

"What do you mean?"

"I mean, you don't know me. Nobody knows me. And yet here you are with your wife, being driven in a pickup truck by me without even knowin' where you're goin' and with no one following us to make sure we ever get there. You see what I mean?"

The governor abruptly turned his head around to look through the cab's rear window back along Oak Street to see if what he just heard was true. And it was. There was no Greyhound bus and no cops anywhere behind them or even within sight.

"Technically speaking, Governor 'n Mrs. Romney, I've just kidnapped both of you. Don't worry about it, though. I ain't gonna do nothin' but talk to you for a minute 'n try to explain something that I think I ought to. Then we'll go eat some corn on the cob with your home folks, okay? Good. Now listen careful, 'cause we only got a minute or two, 'n don't interrupt me until I finish, because I want to say it to you."

Emmett shot a look at the two of them and saw that they were no longer smiling, and the way both of their faces were set told him that they knew whatever happened next was entirely up to him — which was the thing Emmett wanted to show the governor about power.

He talked plain and clear for two solid minutes and one red light about how there will sooner or later no longer be any need for politicians like Governor Romney, because the people, meaning those people who didn't already know and needed to know more than anyone, were going to realize, understand, be educated to the truth, the fact that politics wasn't supposed to be the business of just a few who claimed to be representing the many. It wasn't supposed

451

to be a business! "Politics is life! All our lives, 'n not no profession like you guys make it out to be, 'n want to keep it, so you won't lose your jobs!" And he went on to explain how and why the professional politicians' days were numbered and the games they played in every country in the world, except maybe one, were going to be phased into extinction.

"You see, what you got sitting next to you here ain't just a man, a plain old homo sapiens; he's a political animal. And a political animal is anyone who knows whatever the score is and still refuses to submit to someone else's rule. Anyone who wants to live his own life, and be the only one to control the way he wants to live without messin' over anyone else's right to live the way they damn well want, and vice versa. Now in order to become a political animal, you gotta understand that politics isn't just everyone's business, it's every one of our lives, and *it's never been anyone's vote!*

"After learnin' that, then you have to figure out how you can get hold of enough power to live your life the way you want. And you can't get that kind of power by making a whole lotta money, or by stealing a whole lotta money, or by joining a club that allows you to transcend your blues once a week, or by getting yourself into public office where you can exercise control over the way others live their lives. No, that's all make-believe. It does satisfy quite a few people, but it's never gonna be able to satisfy a whole lotta young people who are just now growing up, and a whole bunch more whose fathers and mothers haven't even met yet. And that goes for all the races, all over the world.

"We're gonna get the power to live our lives the way we want through revolution. And not the same kind of revolution like it's always been, where the few rich people are killed and their property taken away and redistributed among the ones who get there first. Ours is going to be a revolt against power and against leaders and against property. We want it to be free, autonomous, and classlessly equal! All of it! And how we achieve that will be entirely up to you and those like you, because we only believe in defending ourselves when attacked, and we don't want anything from you, except to be left alone! *We* meaning those people sitting on the grass out your window, over there."

Emmett pulled the truck into a space alongside the Panhandle and told Governor George Romney and his wife, Lenore, that they were now where they should be, and he had nothing more to say, except "Let's go 'n eat some corn!" The man and his wife stepped out onto the grass and began walking towards the seated crowd, but before Emmett himself got out of the truck, he tugged his revolver from its brackets and called for the governor to return to the pickup for a second. When he did, Emmett pointed to the .38 lying on the seat inside the cab and asked Governor Romney if he'd forgotten something.

"No . . ."

"Well someone did, and it sure looks like they're not fooling," Emmett said, as he led the governor back to his wife and toward the hundred-year-old Indian from Michigan and the five hundred or so people who were going to keep the governor and his wife in the state of near panic that Emmett had induced. He decided, however, not to exaggerate their panic by holding them, say, for the exchange of unquestionably political prisoners like John Sinclair, a Detroit poet sentenced to ten years for one marijuana cigarette and his radical, political leadership, and many, many others, too numerous to list. Emmett didn't feel like it.

As soon as Emmett moved the governor and his wife into the center of the still-seated circle of a thousand faces, he introduced them, got someone to get each of them a cob of hot, buttered corn, and left them standing there, all alone, to be terrified by the intense sincerity of the contempt that each of those young, surrounding faces had for him, Governor George Romney, and for her, his wife Lenore. The two of them were forced to stand there for twenty minutes heavy with abuse and accusations regarding "his" and "her" roles in the continuing Vietnam genocidal war, and in the police riot in Detroit, and in the Algiers Motel executions, and everything else that the political animality of those young people told them the governor and his first lady were responsible for, or had participated in.

A squad car noticed the scene and radioed to the others that they'd found Governor Romney. The Michigan state police with their siren blaring led the Greyhound bus down Oak Street to the spot in the Panhandle where the shouting and waving of clenched fists had reached the point where it looked like there was going to be a hanging with somebody having already gone to get the rope. The governor's aides arrived none too soon and whisked him away without so much as a goodbye, but with about a dozen joints that kids shoved in his coat pockets, hoping for god-knows-what to happen.

Emmett hadn't seen any of that go down, but heard about it later from Slim Minnaux whose photo was in all the papers during that week, standing tall above the seated crowd pointing his long out-stretched arm and a stern finger at Governor George Romney, his face all on fire and his mouth shouting, *"J'accuse! J'accuse!"*

Emmett hadn't seen any of that because he drove away after lead-ing the good governor and his first lady into the eye of the storm. He left them there alone because he felt he did all he could by deliver-ing them to the Panhandle and, more important, because he had to complete the rest of his rounds to the customers of the Free Food Home Delivery Service.

The pressure that Emmett placed himself under as the Free Food delivery man remained constant, the agony growing more painful whenever his loneliness became almost unbearable and he had to face the fact that all of the psychological and physical punishment he suffered was self-inflicted. He knew it was going to be a hand of solitaire as soon as he picked up the cards and began dealing them to himself. But he never figured on the deck being stacked against him like it was.

There were moments of relief, but they were brief and few and far between. Natural Suzanne came back from El Rito, New Mexico, and set up a place for the both of them in the rear of a vacant storefront in the Mission district. It was good for Emmett to have someone to return to after a full day, driving through the streets of the entire city usually alone. Before Natural Suzanne had made it back to San Francisco, Emmett had been sleeping wherever he ended up on any given night. Those nights were sometimes almost as tiring as the days he spent on the road. So when she arrived, Emmett was very glad to see her and welcomed the chance to pick up where they left off.

The one other significant respite that occurred happened a few months later. Emmett was asked to come East by some people who were connected with San Francisco's Glide Church and some New York foundations who wanted to steer money into the Lower East Side and East Village communities. They wanted Emmett and the Free City Collective's advice on how such a project should be set up and what directions it should take.

Emmett leaped at the chance to get away from picking up, steal-ing, and delivering Free Food for a while. The women and one or two of the men, like Slim Minnaux, Butcher Brooks and Golden Gloves Davey came through and said that they would keep things going while he was gone. Nobody particularly cared to go East with him, though, because of the same, old, prevailing attitude among his brothers that Emmett was on a "star trip," and he would cop all the glory for himself once they got to New York. This conclusion of his brothers was legitimate in terms of Emmett's powerful monster ego, but it had no validity at all in point of fact. He had completely honored his vow of anonymity. That wasn't what bothered them, however. What had them always on edge about Emmett was that he had the power to make himself a public hero any time he wanted to, and they just didn't want to believe that he wouldn't.

Apparently, Tumble thought seriously about those same things which were torturing Emmett's mind to insanity, and he decided to go to New York with him. The deal was that they would both watch each other's back and share the burden of doing what had to be done there. The only mistake they made was in bringing along a gun. They should've brought two.

Jerome Rubin, the Cleveland sportswriter turned Berkeley radical, had already joined up with Abbot Hoffman in New York to form the fabulous duo that was going to get them both top billing on the radical vaudeville circuit. About the same time Rubin arrived in the East, Hoffman received a phone call from Emmett telling him to stop using the name "Diggers" as the title of his act and advising him to find another one, which he did with Rubin, Krassner and their wives, and with the help of a camp, memory lane, Eddie Cantor-Busby Berkeley film called *Making Whoopee!*

The decision to telephone wasn't Emmett's alone, but was reached by most of the people in the Free City Collective. It was based on an outrageously selfish, thirty-page pamphlet that Hoffman had written while he was employed as one of Mayor Lindsay's aides. The pamphlet was entitled *Fuck the System,* and Abbot was enormously proud of himself for having tricked the city into printing it.

The contents listed the various places where and how adventurers in poverty could have gotten anything from free vegetables and meat to free buffaloes, if the pamphlet hadn't been written. You see, instead of actually doing any of these things to get something for nothing, which he heard about like anyone else who lives in a poor district, Hoffman wrote them down on paper for his own self-aggrandizement as a "Oh, look how hip he is!" hipster. He wrote down the addresses of all the places that poor people in New York City had been hitting for food and other stuff, ever since they existed, and he made it all into a joke. He made a joke out of the way people who didn't choose to be poor got what they needed once in a while to

455

make their lives a little easier. He made a joke out of what Emmett and his brothers and sisters took seriously and actually did sixteen hours a day, every day for two years, working to serve the people, of whom they were a part. He made a joke, and those who didn't need any of the things he listed thought it was all very funny, and they laughed and gave Abbot the applause he was searching for. But if he had written a pamphlet like that about where and how people in San Francisco got what they needed for free, the joke would have been on Abbot Hoffman, and he would have been killed just like any other snitch.

Since they were given some money to cover their expenses by those people who wanted their advice, Tumble and Emmett decided to get a large double room at the Chelsea Hotel instead of flopping at someone's pad. They no sooner checked in and entered their room, when the phone rang. The voice on the other end told them that there was a meeting scheduled for later that afternoon in a loft on the Lower East Side, and that everyone whose names the two of them had previously suggested to the man would be there, as well as a few others. After they hung up, Emmett and Tumble went to sleep. It was only eight o'clock in the morning, and they had been up all night on the plane, discussing what would be the best solution for the problem of directing financial energy into the East Village.

At 3 P.M. they arrived at the Second Avenue loft and were greeted by a Methodist minister from San Francisco's Glide Church who showed them upstairs and into a very big room filled with many men and a few women, most of whom didn't like the idea of the two of them coming from the West Coast to tell them how to take care of their business at all. Others remembered Emmett from his last visit East and didn't like him very much. And he didn't like them a whole lot either.

Emmett spoke first and flatly stated that whatever money eventually came into the hip community should be used for "popular," rather than "public," events. "The money should be thought of as energy, and used to create popular alternatives, such as changing the slum environment by getting it cleaned up and painting visuals on the vacant sides of buildings. Now, the point of a popular alternative is that, if there are enough of them around, they will turn the people of the neighborhood on to their own power, and they'll begin to fight for the right to live, instead of quietly dying!"

Tumble said that the money, however it's put to use by the hip community, should only be used within the area of the Lower East Side and never outside the neighborhood, "to, say, protest the war or anything else for that matter. Let someone else put up the money for those kinds of events. Let them that own all of it pay for the marches to go exorcise the Pentagon. You keep whatever money you get from these foundations at home, here on the East Side, and use it to produce changes. Changes, not in newsreel footage, but in the way people have been made to live around here! Changes for the better! It's already for the worse!"

Then Emmett took the proposal that he and Tumble had drawn up on the plane, and laid it out for everyone in the room, including those whom they excluded from what they called the "Ten to Fifteen Group." It was a list of fifteen names of men and women who Tumble and Emmett knew were considered, by their East Village peers, capable of handling the kind of energy that sums of money would bring to the area. Emmett read off all fifteen names and explained how the money would flow through the tax-deductible front of the New York City Mission Society before it came around to them and was placed inside whatever type of free money structure they chose to develop among themselves.

When he finished and was satisfied that he had covered everything, Emmett tacked up the paper outlining all that he just said and walked out of the meet with Tumble. As far as the two of them were concerned, all was said and done. The realization of the proposal was entirely up to those people who were sitting in that Second Avenue loft and considered themselves leading members of the community. Apparently, those community "leaders" didn't feel much like doing any leading, because they never took any individual or collective action on the proposed free money structure. Even though there were half a dozen men with signed checks in the inside pockets of their vested suits standing against one of the side walls representing the foundations that wanted to hand the bread over with no strings attached.

Maybe these "leaders" are still sitting around on their asses up in that loft, bullshitting about how "unhip" it is to take money from establishment funds. They could afford to do that. Of course, they never thought of tipping off those who don't have any qualms about taking money from strangers so that someone could have used it.

That night Emmett and Tumble had a heavy falling-out because Emmett borrowed Tumble's gun when he went for a walk alone. At least that was what ticked off the almost violent argument between

457

the two men who came on like brothers to everyone else but themselves. What it finally came down to, though, was the old "star trip" number. Both their strong, powerful egos clashed because a team of groupies who hung around the Chelsea slighted Tumble to get next to Emmett. The two of them played "dozens" for a good fucking thirty minutes. It was incredible, but real, and Tumble was right and he split to the airport, catching the next flight back to Frisco, and Emmett, once again, was alone. He got loaded, and around dawn there was a knock on the door to his room. He opened it, half hoping to see Tumble, but it was the pair of groupies who recognized him from the couple of months they spent on the West Coast, they said, before he punched both of them in their faces, just hard enough to keep them from ever saying hello to him again.

The next evening Emmett was still upset about Tumble's leaving. They had both acted like mugs. He turned on the television set to listen to the six o'clock newscast, while he washed and shaved. He was drying himself off when he heard it. The 4:30 movie of that gray New York afternoon was still on the TV screen, and he heard a corny line of dialogue he was going to remember. "The only reason friends pat you on the back is to find a place to break it."

Emmett left the tube on to play to an empty room and rode the Chelsea Hotel's slow-poking elevator to the lobby, where he bumped into a woman he knew, and they went into the adjacent El Quixote bar for a drink. They had two, and before he finished his second Southern Comfort, the woman had him red-hot mad with the news of a book that Abbot Hoffman was compiling for publication. According to her, it was all about how Abbot and his Costello friends were everything and did everything that Emmett and his once Digger, now Free City Collective, brothers and sisters were and did and were still doing.

Emmett was stewing with steam over his drink like an out-of-town mark who'd just been taken for all he had. Then he got a flash. He remembered that giant stack of papers he gave to Abbot almost a year before. The pile of papers that Emmett, Coyote, Tumble and, most important, the Hun had written — that were published by the Communication Company in San Francisco and given away free throughout that city.

It was that pile of papers which supplied Abbot Hoffman with all the superficial information and hipster phrases that enabled him to act like he was one of the died-in-the-wool originals. The Hun's pieces were particularly valuable to Hoffman because they gave him the key to explaining how everything he did was theater — brilliant, guerrilla theater in the streets.

Emmett hopped into a cab and was knocking on the door of Hoffman's ground-floor apartment at St. Mark's Place within ten minutes. His wife, Anita, answered and was glad to see Emmett, but told him Abbot was in Boston giving a lecture and trying his best to get himself arrested for some misdemeanor or another. Emmett decided to play it cool and try to find the papers that had to be somewhere in the railroad flat. He rapped for a moment with Anita whom he didn't dislike in the least, when the phone rang. It was her husband.

When she finished talking, Emmett took the receiver and asked Abbot how everything was going and listened to the childish enthusiasm of a lightweight who could hardly wait to get himself arrested for jumping over the turnstile in the subway or something.

Emmett was seething, but didn't let on to Abbot. "Oh, by the way, man. You remember those papers I gave you early last spring? Well, I want to give them to Carol what's-her-name, so she can reprint them for the Angry Arts folks. You still got them. Where are they?"

The reply he heard he half expected. Abbot told him that he didn't have them anymore. Somebody took them home to read one night and never brought them back, and he couldn't remember who it was. He went on to say that Emmett could look around the pad if he wanted, but they really weren't there any longer.

Then Emmett blew it and laid it on the line. "Listen, Hoffman, I've been hearin' that you're writing some sort of a book, and I wanna tell you, if you print or paraphrase any of those pieces, especially the Hun's stuff on theater, without saying that you didn't write those words, we're gonna make you answer for it plenty, unnerstand. And we're not going to consider it a misdemeanor either!"

Hoffman came back with words to the effect that it was all "free", wasn't it? So how could he or anyone else steal "free"? Emmett explained as calmly as he could that guys like Abbot could steal "free" and had been doing that ever since he was given those papers, because he made believe that he was what they represented, and what the people who wrote them worked at all the time — "Free!" Abbot answered by saying that he *was* "free" and that everything he had *was* "free" and nobody could steal anything *from him*, because it was all free!

Emmett knew by now that the papers were safely tucked away someplace else and that he wasn't going to get them away from

Hoffman. So he decided to demonstrate to Abbot how something that's "free" can be stolen and how it feels to have something that's "free" taken.

He asked Abbot whether he was sure that he was "free" and whether everything he had was really "free." Then Emmett mentioned some things around the apartment, like the typewriter that was in front of him and the record player, and Abbot replied that it was *all* "free," further remarking that Emmett could take anything he wanted. "It's free, because it's yours!" he said.

Emmett hung up and walked to the front room where Abbot Hoffman's wife, Anita, was sitting on a large, cloth-covered mattress that doubled as couch and guest bed. She was watching a movie on television and hadn't heard the telephone dialogue between Emmett and her husband which was good, because she would've thought it was ugly, and it would've upset her. That's the way she was at the time.

Emmett got himself a can of something from the refrigerator and watched the movie and talked with Anita for a while, before he took what he had to take, to show Abbot Hoffman how something "free" could be stolen and how it felt to have it taken.

The next morning Emmett made a reservation on an evening flight back to San Francisco and took his last walk around the Lower East Side for what he knew would probably be a while. He loved the city of New York and all its different neighborhoods, particularly the section of the Lower East Side south of the Houston Street dividing line, because it still contained the Old World flavor, hundreds of tongues flapping in a hundred different languages. He didn't like the northern section of the neighborhood since it was renamed the East Village.

He was walking along what used to be called the Yiddish Broadway, but was now only Second Avenue, looking at the refreshing arbor in the tiny park fronting St. Mark's-on-the-Bowery Church, when he bumped into one of them. There were five of them, and Emmett could see by the way they were all decked out in funky denims with the lame colors of their club stitched on their cut-away jackets that they were sidewalk bikers: guys who stomp around like they belong to an outlaw motorcycle gang, but don't have any bikes and more than likely never had. They just make believe.

The one he bumped into stepped back and stared at Emmett for a moment, saying, "Hey, man, I know you!" The guy also looked familiar to Emmett, who decided something that made him reply, "Yea, I seem t' know you, too. But I ain't gonna brag about it!"

"Hey, fellas, you know who this cat is? He's Emmett Grogan! The big, bad motherfucker himself! *The* Emmett Grogan — the fastest gun in San Francisco 'n probably in the whole wild West! Ain't that right? You supposed to be the baddest, ain't ya?!"

Emmett knew that it was Billy the Kid showdown time and that he was gonna get got anyway, so he grabbed the punk who was doing all the jawing and ran him backwards, bashed his skull open against the cast-iron fence and threw a punch at the one coming up on his left side. It never landed. The piece of lead pipe landed, though, on the top right side of his forehead, and Emmett went down, but not completely out, leaving him with enough sense to cover up his head and face with his arms to block the engineer boots that were kicking at his skull, fast and hard from every which way. One of the round steel toes rammed clean into his balls, taking all the mickey out of him and also any chance his body might have had to scramble up and get him away from the trouble he was *now* hopelessly in.

He was just about to go under when the pounding of the kicks stopped, and he heard a lot of shuffling noise. He didn't look up until his hearing told him they had all run away. The dude whose head he cracked was still slumped against the fence, but a pair of black shoes suddenly blocked his view, and the blue pants bent down at the knee and a voice he didn't look at asked him how bad he was hurt and what were they after.

"I'm okay, just a little sore, officer. They were after my money, I guess."

"All right, the ambulance'll be here in a moment to take you to the hospital where they'll fix you up. You wait here, understand? I'm going after my partner who's chasin' 'em down Ninth Street."

The cop handcuffed the guy who started it all to the cast-iron fence and ran back to his squad car, burning rubber up Ninth Street after everybody else. Emmett heard other sirens coming from a long way off, and he figured he'd better get the fuck up and out of there before they got to him and he ended up staying in New York City for a very long time. The way the dude was slumped against the fence over there told him that it might be more than just a hassle he was in for if he stayed. So he pulled himself up to his feet and hailed a cab going crosstown to the West Side.

461

The driver dropped Emmett off in the vicinity of the Chelsea. If the prick lying against the fence was really serious, the cabbie could only tell the cops the address of an Eighth Avenue IND subway station which was what his trip sheet read.

He made sure the cab continued uptown before walking the block to the midmorning-empty bar connected to the Chelsea, slipping through it to the hotel's staircase unnoticed, and on up to the room. He turned off the television and phoned a doctor friend who came by within twenty minutes. The double lacerations on the top right side of his head took quite a few stitches to close, and his face was turning all black and blue and was already swollen, but it wasn't all that bad. After all, he hadn't been stabbed, and he considered himself lucky.

It was his friend's off day, so Emmett picked up the phone and asked Pernnell, the Chelsea's bellman, if he'd get them a bag of ice cubes, a bottle of Comfort and a couple of glasses. They drank away the afternoon with reminiscences, and Emmett's friend drove him to the airport where he caught his flight back to San Francisco, sleeping all the way home.

Tumble's return alone had opened a permanent chasm that was going to keep Emmett firmly divided from his once-were brothers, probably forever. Natural Suzanne was waiting, though, and she told him all the nitpicking gossip that went down after Tumble came back by himself. After a while Emmett didn't want to hear any more of it and stopped her with a "Fuck it! Fuck all of it!"

He picked up where he left off with the Free Food the next day, and it was the first time he didn't *really* want to do it anymore. He was sick and tired and wasted by the rift between him and the other men, as well as some of their old ladies in the Free City Collective. Sure, a lot of it was his own damn fault! Emmett knew he had a monster ego, but he always kept his vanity personal, never letting it get beyond the private bounds of the Collective. What the fuck did they want from him? Couldn't he be crazy? Wasn't he allowed? He never blew the covers off any secrets by making himself *public* like they did. He was just *popular,* and that's what probably got them all twisted about him. Everything he did was popular! He had the most popular act going in the invisible circus of the Free City Collective, and they were scared he was going to make his popularity public and cop all the chips! So they begrudged him even the pleasure of their company and left him alone, like only other men can leave another man alone.

Then one day the devil came to see Emmett in the form of a recently returned Chicano soldier from Vietnam who brought a gift with him. The present was just a small part of what he said he brought back to the States and had already sold for a whole lot of money that he sort of felt guilty about and wanted to remedy somehow. The only way he could think of doing that was "Here!" and he gave Emmett almost half an ounce of 90 percent pure heroin. The last thing he said before he split forever was, "It's free!"

Emmett stood in the thin hallway that led to the side doorway of his storefront crib, looking at the tiny, aluminum-foiled package in his hands. When he raised his eyes, there was no one standing in the doorway, and the vacuum that remained made it seem almost as if no one had been there at all. He closed the door and went into the kitchen where he opened up the aluminum package, and as soon as he laid his eyes on the flat mound of dull white powder, he knew he was going to use every grain of it all by his lonesome. Alone, just like he'd been doing practically everything else for what, all of a sudden, was much too long.

For the first few weeks, everything went along all right. He got out of bed at dawn, took his wake-up fix in the bathroom and coasted through the day, making his Free Food deliveries and returning back to his Mission district storefront pad at dusk where he headed directly for the john to get high again. Natural Suzanne noticed that something was wrong with Emmett immediately. He stopped drinking the usual two or three nightly quarts of Ballantine Ale to get the sweat back in him; he hardly ever ate; he was always unusually tired, often nodding right out and sleeping till morning; he lost his sense of humor, and never smiled; and he no longer made love with her as he used to each night before they fell asleep and each morning when they woke up.

"Emmett, Emmett, what's the matter?"

"What's the matter? I got syphilis! That's what the matter. Leave me alone!"

It went on like that for a while longer, until the morning finally arrived when Emmett couldn't get out of bed to make his rounds. Natural Suzanne was already up in the kitchen making the coffee he seldom drank anymore, and he called to her. She came and knelt down on the floor-mattress bed and listened to her man talk about how tired he was and how she was the only one. He gave her the keys to the truck and the list of names and addresses with the number of people in each of the families written in a circle alongside every name.

"It's Tuesday, so today's vegetables. You've done it with me, 'n you know how it's all supposed to go. Get a couple of sisters to help you, 'n maybe even one of our brothers who's not too busy doin' his own goddamn thing! You don't have to do everyone on the list, just those with the asterisks next to their addresses. They need it the most, and our Collective. Okay?! Hurry up, 'cause if you don't get to the Produce and Farmers market quick, Synanon 'n them nuns'll beat you 'n cop everything. Thanks, sweetheart. Thank you."

For the rest of the week and from then on until the city and state governments put a stop to it, most of the women like Natural Suzanne, Lacey Pines, Fyllis, Nana Nina, Vicki Sparks, House Jane, Almond Judith, to name a few, and some of the Free City men, Slim Minnaux, Little Robert, Clearwater, Coyote, Butcher Brooks, House-Be-Nimble, G. G. Davey, Tumble, Strong Vinnie, to name a few, took over the Free Food Home Delivery Service and kept it happening for as many as they could. After a while, however, it became impossible for them to complete the entire route for a whole lot of obvious reasons, such as their lack of familiarity with it, and they condensed it to those families who were part of the Free City Collective or close to the work they were doing. At least some of the people were still eating. But even that ended in the spring, when most of the Free City Collective, in an attempt to stretch the long, dull winter out of their systems and to demand that the city and state do what *they* had been doing, began to perform a daily guerrilla theater production of poetry readings, agit-prop skits and song singing at lunch hour on the front steps of City Hall.

It went on every day for weeks and was called "City Hall Noon Forever!" — thoroughly entertaining the civil servants who came out to spend their lunch hours in the sunshine of the adjacent park. It ended abruptly however when the Hun and several others demanded to read a not unreasonable proposal to Mayor Alioto or his assistant, Michael McCone. The cops moved in, clubs swinging, and arrested forty of the male and female participants in the joyous Free City Collective event on the insistence of Municipal Judge Albert Axelrod who accused one of the Thelin brothers, owners of the then-closed Psychedelic Shop, of violating California Penal Code 650-A,

464

which means committing the offense of appearing in public with one's face partially covered with a bandana. The nineteenth-century law had been enacted against those who had intent to conceal their identity, like members of the Ku Klux Klan. Thelin was only anticipating the cops' use of tear gas.

The arrest was banner-headlined, "The Poetry Bust!" and the newspapers printed the Free City Collective's sensible proposal in its entirety:

PROPOSAL

San Franciscans, in the interest of eternity, and out of respect for their Mayor, will recommend the following course of action to that office this afternoon.

1. That city-owned buildings remaining empty be restored to the people for reconstruction, embellishment and refurbishment, so that those people might live there freely.
2. That all foodstuffs and material in surplus not accounted for in current welfare distribution be returned to the people for redistribution "free" through ten autonomous neighborhood "free stores" whose rent shall be paid by the city.
3. That presses and trucks be made available for the dissemination of "Free News" throughout the city, so that the people will come to know one another and make channels of access available to each other.
4. That the city provide resources for autonomous neighborhood celebrations of the city, the planet and their own free beings.
5. That parks and other public spaces be returned to the people of San Francisco. The Mayor's office is invited to share in that vision. City-wide celebration of Summer Solstice will mark the entrance of FREE SAN FRANCISCO into eternity.
   "Welcome Home!"

Emmett was totally against the City Hall Noon Forever event, arguing with the Hun that the only productive result would be the reprinting of the proposal in the newspapers, and that wasn't worth the violation of the Free City Collective's never-ask-or-protest-for-anything rule. Furthermore, Emmett argued, the establishment powers were bound to retaliate for making such "popular" ideas "public."

No one was listening to Emmett after he stopped delivering the Free Food to the people and folded in his hand before playing out all the cards he dealt to himself. So, even though they knew he was probably right, the members of the Free City Collective opted for the guerrilla theater event, if for no other reason than it was more fun than actually assuming the freedom to do the real thing. The authorities did retaliate by ordering the Produce and Farmers' markets to stop supplying the collective with fruit and vegetables and also legislating all sorts of new regulations on the distribution of Free Food which were impossible to comply with. The only free food they could scrounge up after the city hall deal went down forever was just enough to feed themselves and seldom anyone else. And that was that.

The amount of scag Emmett used each day increased along with his tolerance for the drug, and it wasn't long before someone pinned him nodding in public and the word rapidly spread throughout the city, and eventually from coast to coast, about what everyone began to call "Emmett's problem." He was a junkie, and everybody he knew wrote him off like a bad check. It was as if he betrayed them all, and in a way he had, but no more than he betrayed himself.

The stuff from Nam was gone before he knew it, and Emmett found himself with a motherfucker of a jones! After using up that pure horse, nothing he could cop on the street could get him straight. It just took his sick off, and it was costing him eighty to a hundred dollars a day simply to do that. He got the money in the same way all down junkies get the bread they need: any way he could. Soon he was being blamed for every rip-off that occurred in the Haight Community, and all at once, all the people he had known and who loved and admired him, but never told him, didn't like him anymore. In fact, most hated him, and some were so angry at what he was doing to them and to himself that they tried to physically hurt him. A few of them actually did. The only person who showed pity to him was Shig at the City Lights Bookstore in North Beach who lent him money once in a while, until it got to be too much even for him, and all Emmett could ever say was, "Thanks, Shig. Be seein' you."

Finally it got to be too much for Emmett, and he checked himself into Mendocino Hospital where they said they would detoxify him with methadone. It would have worked, except that they only gave him a small amount of the synthetic opiate for four days — a very short way to come down, very fast, especially for a man with a monster, gorilla habit like the one Emmett had on his back. It didn't work, and on the morning of the fifth day, Emmett's nervous system was rattling itself to death in a vicious Saint Vitus's Dance all its own. He called Natural Suzanne who had been for months cheated out of all the love Emmett could have been giving her, because of some white powder and the pinning of his eyes. But she was one of the few still willing to stand by him, so she came when he phoned and drove him back into the city where he scored a fix at the Ellis Hotel in the Fillmore district, paying for two twenty-dollar balloons with a batch of James Brown stamps that Natural Suzanne had been saving.

Emmett knew he would never be able to satisfy the hunger of his addiction with more and more dope, and the quantity of methadone he needed to detoxify himself wasn't available on the streets of California at the time. There seemed to be no way out, when Emmett got a flash. He went to the pharmacology section of the main public library and copied exactly what he wanted out of a book. Then he drove to Berkeley and the house of a doctor of chemistry who made LSD and methedrine in a laboratory in his basement. They were casual friends, and Emmett talked to him for a while, testing his water, before telling him what he came there to ask him to do, and giving him the piece of paper with this written on it: *Dolophine*, a synthetic opiate invented by German scientists at the insistence of morphine addict Herman Goering and named after Adolf Hitler and usually known as methadone.

Methadone (dl-4,4-diphenyl-6-dimethylamine-3-heptanone)

The doctor of chemistry said it would take awhile, but he could make it, and would, and as much as he could, for "free." The cat even had a machine that would turn the product out in pill form — the same tab-making machine he regularly used to stamp his acid out. After a while, Emmett returned to Berkeley and picked up thousands of methadone pills. He kept enough himself and stashed the rest for distribution later among the junk population of San Francisco.

Then he went out to a ranch near Point Reyes, California, where

Coyote had taken over a fifty-dollar per month house with his blond-haired Louisiana woman, Sam, and a whole lot of other people. Emmett drove there alone because Natural Suzanne had finally become sick and tired of their loveless relationship and was making up for what her old man had been unable to give her. The last thing he said to her when she was forced to split to save the youth and vitality of her less than nineteen years was, "Have a nice life, Natural Suzanne. Have a nice life." And he meant it with all the sincerity he could ever mean about anything.

Coyote's ranch was a stone heavy spread where only heavyweight men and women came from the city to do nothing that wasn't them. Some rode in on choppers, others in cars and trucks. A few walked the mile from the front gate to the house. Nobody ever tiptoed, and no one was a stranger. Everything was always going on, and it was a free-for-all. A man silhouetted against the falling sun, churning up the earth on the side of a hill with the rat-tat-tat 45-caliber bursts from his Thompson submachine gun. A woman giving birth in the green, high grass reflected in a hundred watching eyes and in the sound of a child's first liberated cry. Musicians who made millions playing for ears that paid to hear, and musicians who never made anything at all, jammed their hard, mellow souls together and filled the place with the sound of whatever points they were trying to get across in the music that never stopped.

The ranch was a bayou of heartaches and good times, where people overworked each other in a devil dance that made their bones beg for another chance before they gave in. It was a sunup-to-sundown refusal to guard the truth and a shifting center where no one's imagination would leave them alone. A place where anyone who knew the address could come to live or die, get married, find each other or themselves, or, like Emmett, kick a habit and return to finish what he started out to do. It was called Olema, and it's not there anymore, and Richard Brautigan didn't have to mention it in the poem he wrote about how Emmett Grogan left his habit there.

DEATH IS A BEAUTIFUL CAR PARKED ONLY
for Emmett

Death is a beautiful car parked only
to be stolen on a street lined with trees
whose branches are like the intestines
of an emerald.

468

You hotwire death, get in, and drive away
like a flag made from a thousand burning
   funeral parlors.

You have stolen death because you're bored.
There's nothing good playing at the movies
   in San Francisco.

You joyride around for a while listening
to the radio, and then abandon death, walk
away, and leave death for the police
   to find.

Still weak and in a sag of wondering which way his body was going to go next, Emmett decided it was time to document what they had all tried to accomplish together as the Free City Collective. They held what turned out to be their last formal meeting as a family and planned the one-shot review magazine for which a young, stand-up Los Angeles man handed Emmett forty-hundred-dollar-bills-cash energy to help get it compiled. The collective chose a slick detective-magazine format to say what they had to say, but since the cost of such a glossy, highly stylized review was beyond their limits, they had to settle for simple newsprint and go along with seeing it distributed and sold for thirty-five cents in exchange for forty thousand "Free" copies which were theirs to give away.

The cover of the document was titled "The Digger Papers," and none of the contents therein were copyrighted, so that anyone might reprint anything without permission. On the outside back cover was what many people who knew him thought was the Hun's most brilliant and poignant statement in art. It was a black-and-white reproduction of a six-by-three-foot, blue-and-white poster of two Tong assassins, calmly biding their time, leaning against the corner of a brick building. Above them hung a sign with the Chinese character from the I Ching that spelled revolution, and written below their feet in black letters was the slogan *1% FREE*. The Hun designed the original poster with a friend called Red-Cock Don and with several others posted them on walls throughout Chinatown and all over the city, to the consternation of the Chinese and the wonderment of everyone.

Most of the information and news that was broadcast between the front and back covers of the Digger Papers was written in poetry, except for what became the most important piece of the collection for those who really wanted to know how to organize and maintain a Free City. That was written in straight prose by Emmett.

THE POST-COMPETITIVE, COMPARATIVE GAME OF A FREE CITY

Our state of awareness demands that we uplift our efforts from competitive game playing in the underground to the comparative roles of free families in free cities.

We must pool our resources and interact our energies to provide the freedom for our individual activities.

In each city of the world there is a loose competitive underground composed of groups whose aims overlap, conflict, and generally enervate the desired goal of autonomy. By now we all have guns, know how to use them, know our enemy, and are ready to defend. We know that we ain't gonna take no more shit. So it's about time we carried ourselves a little heavier and got down to the business of creating free cities within the urban environments of the western world.

Free Cities are composed of Free Families (e.g., in San Francisco: Diggers, Black Panthers, Red Guards, Mission Rebels and various revolutionist gangs and communes) who establish and maintain services that provide a base of freedom for autonomous groups to carry out their programs without having to hassle for food, printing facilities, transportation, mechanics, money, housing, working space, clothes, machinery, trucks, etc.

At this point in our revolution it is demanded that the families, communes, black organizations and gangs of every city in America coordinate and develop Free Cities where everything that is necessary can be obtained for free by those involved in the various activities of the individual clans.

Every brother and sister should have what they need to do whatever needs to be done.

Free City:
An outline . . . a beginning
Each service should be performed by a tight gang of brothers and sisters whose commitment should enable them to handle an overload of work with ability and enthusiasm. "Tripsters" soon get bored, hopefully before they cause an economic strain.

Free City Switchboard/Information Center
should coordinate all services, activities, and aid and direct assistance where it is most needed. Also provide a reference point for legal aid, housing, machinery, etc.; act as a mailing address for dislocated groups or individuals and guide random energies where they are most needed. (The work load usually prevents or should prevent the handling of

470

messages from parents to their runaway children . . . that should be left up to the churches of the community.)

Free Food Storage and Distribution Center

should hit every available source of free food — produce markets, farmers' markets, meat-packing plants, farms, dairies, sheep and cattle ranches, agricultural colleges, and giant institutions (for the uneaten vats of food) — and fill up their trucks with the surplus by begging, borrowing, stealing, forming liaisons and communications with delivery drivers for the leftovers from their routes . . . best method is to work in two shifts: morning group picks up the foodstuffs and the afternoon shift delivers it to the list of Free Families and the poor peoples of the ghettos everyday. hard work.

This gang should help people pool their welfare food stamps and get their old ladies or a group to open a free restaurant for people on the move and those who live on the streets. Giant scores should be stored in a garage-type warehouse equipped with freezers and its whereabouts known only to the Free Food Gang. This group should also set up and provide help for canning, preserving, bread baking, and feasts and anything and everything else that has to do with food.

Free City Garage and Mechanics

to repair and maintain all vehicles used in the various services, the responsibility for the necessary tools and parts needed in their work is entirely theirs and usually available by maintaining friendly relations with junkyards, giant automotive schools, and generally scrounging around those areas where auto equipment is easily obtained. The garage should be large enough and free of tripsters who only create more work for the earnest mechanics.

Free City Bank and Treasury

this group should be responsible for raising money, making free money, paying rents, for gasoline, and any other necessary expenses of the Free City Families. They should also organize and create small rackets (cookie sales, etc.) for the poor kids of the ghettos and aid in the repair and maintenance of the machinery required in the performance of the various services.

Free City Legal Assistance

high-style, hard-nosed, top-class lawyers who are willing to defend the rights of the Free City and its services . . . no honky, liberal, bleeding-heart, guilt-ridden advocates of justice, but first-class case-winners . . . turn on the best lawyers who can set up airtight receivership for free money and property, and beat down the police harassment and brutality of your areas.

471

Free City Housing and Work Space
rent or work deals with the urban gov't to take over spaces that have been abandoned for use as carpentry shops, garages, theaters, etc., rent whole houses, but don't let them turn into crash pads. Set up hotels for new arrivals or transients by working out deals with small hotel owners for free rooms in exchange for light housework, porter duties, etc. Big warehouses can be worked on by environmental artists and turned into giant free dance-fiesta-feast palaces.

A strong trio of serious business-oriented cats should develop this liberation of space within the cities and be able to work with the lawyers to make deals and outmaneuver urban bureaucracies and slum landlords . . . one of the main targets for space are the churches who are the holders of most real estate and they should be approached with a no-bullshit hard line.

Free City Stores and Workshops
nothing in these stores should be throwaway items . . . space should be available for chicks to sew dresses, make pants to order, recut garments to fit, etc. The management should all be life-actors capable of turning bullshitters into mud. Important that these places are first class environments with no trace of salvation army/st. vinnie de paul charity rot. Everything groovy. Everything with style . . . must be first class. *It's all free because it's yours!*

Free Medical Thing
should be established in all poverty areas and run by private physicians and free from any bureaucratic support. The Free City Bank should try to cover the expenses, and pharmaceutical houses should be hit for medical supplies, etc. Important that the doctors are brothers and do not ask to be salaried or are not out to make careers for themselves (witness Dr. David Smith of the Hippie Free Clinic in San Francisco who is far from a brother . . . very far).

Free City Hospital
should be a house converted into bed space and preferably with a garden and used for convalescence and people whose minds have been blown or who have just been released from a state institution and who need the comfort and solace of their own people rather than the cold alienated walls of an urban institution.

Free City Environmental and Design Gang
gangs of artists from universities and art institutes should be turned on and helped in attacking the dank squalor of the slums and most of the Free City Family dwellings . . . paint landscapes on the sides of tenements . . . fiberglass stairwells . . . make crazy. Tight groups of good painters, sculptors, designers who comfortably construct environments

for the community. Materials and equipment can be hustled from university projects and manufacturers, etc.

Free City Schools
schools designed and run by different groups according to the consciousness of their Free Families (e.g., Black Man's Free School, Anarchist's Creative Arts School, etc.). The schools should utilize the space liberated for them by the Free City Space Gang.

Free City News and Communication Company
providers of a daily newspaper, monthly magazine, free Gestetner and printing notices for other groups and any special bulletins and propaganda for the various families of the Free City. The machinery should be kept in top condition and supplied by any of the various services. Paper can be scavenged at large mills and cut down to proper working size.

Free City Events . . . Festival Planning Committees
usually involves several Families interacting to sponsor tours for the kids . . . Balls, Happenings, Theatre, Dance, and spontaneous experiments in joy . . . Park Events usually are best set up by hiring a 20-foot flatbed truck for the rock band to use as a stage and to transport their equipment; people should be advised by leaflets to bring food to exchange with their neighbors; banners, props, balloons, kites etc., should be handled by a committee; an electrician should be around to run the generator and make sure that the PA systems work; hard work made easy by giving responsible people the tough jobs.

Cooperative Farms and Campsites
the farms should be run by experienced hands and the Free Land settled on by cottage industrial people who will send their wares into the Free City. The farms must produce vital food for the families . . . some free land that is no good for farming should be used as campsites and/or cabin areas for Free citizens who are in need of country leisure, as well as kids who could use a summer in the woods.

Scavenger Corps and Transport Gang
is responsible for garbage collection and the picking up and delivery of items to the various services, as well as liberating anything they think useful for one project or another. They are to be responsible for the truck fleet and especially aware of the economic strain if trucks are misused by tripsters.

Free City Tinkers and Gunsmiths, Etc.
will repair and keep things going in the houses . . . experienced repairmen of all sorts, electricians, and carpenters. They should maintain a warehouse or working space for their outfit.

demand Free time on radio and TV stations; demand a Free City frequency to set up your own stations; rent computers to call the punches for the revolution or use them in any constructive way possible.

On April 6, 1968, two days after Martin Luther King was assassinated standing on a Memphis motel balcony, Lil' Bobby Hutton, the first rank-and-file member to join the Black Panther party, was shot down dead with his hands on top his head, essentially because he refused to strip himself naked like Eldridge Cleaver and his other Panther brothers did before they walked out of that basement and into the mercilessness of the Oakland Police. The insurrections that swept through the ghettos of America that spring weekend were in response to the cowardly way in which both men were killed while unarmed, symbolizing for the nation how most men who are both poor and black usually die in a "gun battle" with the police. Later on, some of the students at Columbia University were to take over that institution for five days in a revolt that promised to change the manner in which things were run around there, and demanded employment for minority workers on all construction jobs that took place on school-owned property.

Only superficial changes occurred in the ghettos and at Columbia on account of the so-called "riots," except that all of the construction crews at the university are now made up of minority workers who are very busy tearing down housing that the people of the Morningside Heights and Harlem communities desperately need and replacing it with university buildings. Emmett knew that nothing but a few good news stories was going to come out of all the "rioting," but he wished all those involved "luck" just the same, especially a Columbia student named Mark Rudd who looked like he needed something real bad, because he sure didn't have no brains.

Around the same time Emmett went over to Oakland to speak with Black Panther Party Chairman Bobby Seale, and Chief of Staff David Hilliard, giving them a couple thousand copies of the Digger Papers which had a "Free Huey!" advertisement collage by Natural Suzanne on the inside back cover. The Papers were later distributed among Panther party members and throughout the black community. The conversation among the three men was crisp and to the point. Emmett outlined what he did and asked the two party leaders what they needed, besides money, that he could possibly get for them. They began discussing a plan they had to start a Free Breakfast for Children program that would put some nourishment into the normally empty bellies of black kids before they went to school. It was a good idea, and Emmett was glad to hear that the Panthers were seriously intending to serve the people in other ways besides providing political education — the only thing Eldridge Cleaver ever considered important.

Without letting on to the Panthers, Emmett accumulated within a few days enough powdered milk, cereal, eggs, etc., from those same sources he tapped when he operated the Free Food Home Delivery Service. Just after dawn he arrived at the Black Panther party headquarters in Oakland and unloaded the breakfast food, stacking it along the wall in the driveway next to the Panthers' storefront premises. He left without anyone seeing him, except the police surveillance squad in the building across the street. Dave Hilliard arrived a bit later that morning, to do the type of organizational work that few men are capable of doing well, he found the stuff and the Breakfast for Children Program that was never going to end was begun shortly afterwards by the Black Panther party.

Emmett spent the next few weeks carefully distributing the 10 mg. methadone pills he had stashed throughout a good deal of the addict population in San Francisco, by using a complicated system of dead-letter drops to protect himself from arrest and prosecution. Each packet contained fifty pills, and all of them were stashed in different "drop" locations, and only one packet was allotted to each addict he contacted. It was a one-to-a-customer policy, except none of it was for sale, it was all, like the man said, "for free!"

The junkies are probably the only minority group in the United States that doesn't have its own "Liberation Front" to fight for their human and constitutional rights to be treated by the medical profession as diseased patients, instead of by police agencies as fiendish criminals. Emmett wasn't particularly concerned with *how* the free methadone was used by the addicts who connected for it. He knew some of them would sell it for heroin or simply use it to reduce their level of tolerance for scag, enabling them to get high again for a while, or use it when there was no dope available on the streets, or to supplement their habits. But he also knew that others would use the medication to kick — and that, plus the knowledge that, for a brief moment at least, the absurd, unnecessary desperation of addiction would be gone for a handful of strung-out men and women, was well worth the insane effort and dangerously difficult skullduggery he put himself through to make it happen for what was really only a second.

It was immediately after Emmett completed that Free chore that William Bendix was replaced in the leading role of America's favorite pastime of "Kill the Umpire" by Sirhan Sirhan, who fired a bullet into the brain of Robert Kennedy with almost exactly the same demeanor and in much the same way as Saigon's police chief fired a round from his revolver into the temple of a Viet Cong suspect and commented afterwards on television that "Buddha will understand." Sirhan Sirhan had Allah on *his* side.

The chicken also came home to roost in the cold hype and media scam of the Haight-Ashbury, when it became the only truly racially integrated neighborhood in America to riot in July, '68. It all began with the cops, of course, who tried to arrest two brothers on suspicion of selling LSD, and it ended three nights later after what the newspapers headlined as a "Fiery Riot." The truth of the matter was that there were about two thousand people in the streets, most of whom were either just watching the five or six guys who were doing all the rock-, bottle-, and fire-bomb throwing, or trying to stop them with such sophistical statements as, "Violence is the last resort of the incompetent!" But three nights of that large a crowd, and that small a group of violent activists, was enough to smash every shopwindow on Haight Street and burn out the Bank of America building, before the squad of tactical cops got wise and launched a sweep in two directions, quelling all the action and emerging from the contest victorious.

After that, most of the Haight Independent Proprietors threw in the towel and boarded up their stores for good. As it turned out, many of the Head shops and hippie boutiques that closed had been owned by a corporation with a Nob Hill dentist for chairman, which only used the bearded longhairs as managers for their storefront.

Another result of the "Fiery Riot" was that the media began to include explosives as a part of the terms of hipsterism, while also looking back longingly to when the district was the home of the flower generation. The epilogue to the Haight "riot" came from a group calling itself the Haight-Ashbury Neighborhood Development Corporation, which proposed a hundred million dollar plan to resuscitate the district with an ambitious face-lift to make it the most attractive business area in the city, hoping to hide all the ugliness with the paint of success.

Bonnie and Clyde was big at the movies, and Hoffman and Rubin were making Yippie! on radio and TV, trying to get the young and foolish to go to Chicago that August to play "Crowd" in a piece entitled *Law and Order.* Those two geriatric longhairs were raising the underground to the height of its alternative shuck with a make-up title for a make-believe number that was to be the Yippie Festival of Life Convention in Chicago. Even though Emmett was in New York while the YIP propaganda was manipulating lame middle-class kids into its pseudo–street culture, he simply refused to believe that anyone real was going to fall for their obvious scam, and he went up to Woodstock to visit with the man who invited him there.

Bob Dylan was exactly unlike what Emmett Grogan expected him to be.

Emmett was in Europe during those first years that Bob talked the music and played the news to his starving generation, and broke the hearts of every American poet with his singing of the song. Of course, he heard the records overseas, but it wasn't like listening to those same albums in the country where they were cut. By the time, Emmett finally came home and settled into things, it was already "Blonde on Blonde," and he just temporarily didn't know. He found out later without having to tramp through the green, hard-sell, crystal swamp of positively Fourth Street, image-persona, media hustle.

Now Emmett was sitting on the second step of a warped wooden flight of four front stairs that led up and into the funky, screened porch of a pine-walled cabin where a film editor, who used the name Al Gable whenever he seldom took a credit, lived with his wife, six hound dogs and two dozen cats. Bob was sitting on the same step, and in him Emmett saw a man who somehow made it through that swamp and settled down alive on the other side. A man who had a wife and five kids and simply played music for a living. A plain and easy-dressed man, complicated only by the hearsay. A physically small man who was strong for his size and not fat at all, but wiry with coached stringy muscle and shoulders that stuck out wider than you'd think. A man with a lot of friends, but afraid of those who weren't, just the same. A man who kept a matchstick in his mouth to keep from smoking and who was sliding with the knowledge of growing older and leaving the brassy, punk snide of his younger-than-that now behind him. Dylan was clean.

They talked soft and casual for as long as it took them both to find where the other was at. Then Bob told Emmett about a place he'd been to, not too long before, and about what he saw there and how it looked. What impressed him most was the gravestones planted all around on top of this old-time, boot-hill cemetery. It wasn't the shape or age of the headstones or the way they were carved. It was the words that were chipped into their rough, flat surfaces that impressed him; not on account of their particular wisdom or peculiar wit, but because they were there at all. Bob wondered whether they were the last words of the persons buried beneath them.

Probably not, but it got them both talking about last lines they'd heard of some people saying — just before the little dirt road exploded into dust, and roaring up it and pulling onto and across the crabgrass toward the two of them was a pink Lincoln Continental convertible with the top down, two passengers, and Gregory Corso driving. The pink-lemonade topless limo skidded to a stop along the slick, dew grass, and America's number one "Gasoline" poet leaped out of the driver's seat and over the front door with a nearly empty pint of Swiss Colony wine splashing in his left hand and sticking forth his right to shake hello, saying, "How ya doin', *Robére*? Heard you were here, Emmett, 'n came down from the farm t' see you! This is my woman, Bel, 'n you both know Julius Orlovsky, right? What's happenin'?"

Bob was silent. Emmett mentioned that they'd been comparing famous last lines, when Gregory halted him. "Last lines, heh! Well I don' know about what anybody else has to say but me, see. An' I'm gonna tell you somethin'. I already got my last line stashed for when the time comes to use it! How's that for being prepared, huh?! An' I went to jail instead o' the Boy Scouts! You wanna know the way I want it to be? I'll tell you!

"I wanna be layin' in a bed, see, with all my friends around me. An' when I got just a little more time left, hardly none at all, I want one of my friends to lean over 'n ask me, 'Gregory, you *lived* your whole life, 'n now that it's almost over, Gregory, tell us. Tell us what it was like, Gregory.'

"That's when I props myself up on my elbows 'n look at all o' them waitin' to hear what I got to say, 'n that's when I tell 'em what it was like, boy. I tell 'em! I tell 'em! *It was nowhere!*"

Emmett enjoyed the country pleasures of Woodstock until the leaves began to turn and the air became crisp with autumn. He spent the kind of time with Bob that they both needed to get to know each other better. They went to listen to music together and did some walking and talking. There was a screening of the very funny, personal film Bob made about one of the last times he took to the road, touring England as *Dylan*, the on-the-make kid in a mysterious, Hitchcockian train where nothing happened and no one was allowed more than a taste of anything. It was entitled *Eat the Document*, and Emmett laughed at what he felt had to be one of the most honestly hilarious movies any man ever had that special sense of humor to make, about whatever he once had been.

Then there was the Band, and listening to them play together and their "Big Pink" debut album, which was going to let everyone in on the well-kept secret that they were the best. Their music taught Emmett that if anything was ever going to be really good, it was going to be a long time coming; and that San Francisco was, by far, not the only place where something was happening.

Afterwards Al Grossman said, "Anytime," and he doesn't talk that way to many people. So Emmett answered, "Thanks," before he said, "Be seein' you," and ran to catch the plane that would take him to Chicago and another man from whom he would learn a few more things he had to know.

Fred Hampton was waiting for him at the Illinois Chapter head-quarters of the Black Panther party on West Madison Street. The Panthers had just come above ground in Chicago, opening their office only a few days before, and Emmett was the first man who wasn't black or a Panther to walk up the steep, narrow staircase and into the long, barren room which the dozen sober faces who watched him move were willing to defend with their lives.

After Linda Fitzpatrick and Groovy were murdered in New York, a "hippie" detective squad had been assigned to circulate through the Lower East Side area in hippie clothes in an effort to protect the "East Village flower people" from the niggers and spics. This knowledge was just as common among Chicago's low-money people as it was among those in New York. That, plus his middle-of-the-back-length hair and the stone-corny, fraudulent activity of the Yippies who had just made fools and suckers out of most of Chicago's hipsters, were more than enough reasons for the black men and women in that office to be cold-eyed wary of Emmett Grogan, no matter what sort of references the Party's Central Committee phoned in about him from Oakland.

So Emmett stood in the middle of the empty room alone, conscious of the glare of the surrounding eyes, but understanding why they felt that way toward him. He was waiting to meet the man he came there for, who was now busy taking care of some other business in a small cubicle of a side room.

Emmett had money in his pocket. Money that film editor Al Gable arranged, during his negotiations with an Illinois movie company about making a film to show why the hard-poor and heavy people of America stayed away from all the protests of the '68 Democratic National Convention. Emmett insisted the money was necessary to insure the cooperation of the southwest black neighborhood that was the Panthers' turf in the making of the film. The money wasn't really necessary for that purpose, but it was badly needed by the Panthers to function, now that they were above ground and out in the open, and Emmett thought they would be able to put it to good use. The film that was eventually going to come from this initial meeting would be *American Revolution II*, and Fred Hampton would use the making of it as a medium for forming the Rainbow Coalition, a political alliance among the Black Panthers, the Puerto Rican Young Lords, the group of Appalachian whites known as the Young Patriots, and the unaffiliated, young, white street radicals who considered the singular newspaper, *RISING UP ANGRY*, their speaking organ. Fred's ability to overcome each of these groups' prejudices towards the others and his successful formation of the enormously strong Rainbow Coalition would prove how very powerful and, finally, dangerous a man he really was to the Illinois status quo. And they would kill him.

A muscular young blood who introduced himself as Odignga, chief of security, escorted Emmett into the tiny side office and left him, closing the door from the outside. Emmett then found himself being offered a chair by the solid, two-hundred-pound, bulk-muscled black man sitting on the opposite side of an old, battered, flat-top desk piled high with papers. He sat down and immediately felt at ease in the presence of this totally joyful and obviously fearless man.

Fred Hampton had the large, big-boned face of a plain, young, hard worker who only used one simple tool to do what it was he needed to do. The clarity in his bright eyes and the sharp definition of the muscular dimples in his thick-skinned cheeks told you right away that the tool he used was his brain. Emmett liked Fred because he had none of that East-Coast-West-Coast, mau-mau, noble savage, nickle-dime, nigger-flip jive about him. He was straight goods all the way, and he had just turned twenty years old around the time Emmett met him, and he already seemed to know that he was going to be dead when he was twenty-one.

Emmett handed the money over to Fred and told him what kind of a deal was going down with the film group. Then they got to talking about how you could really smell the way the money is made in Chicago, from the pungent odor from the back-of-the-yards district where the animals are slaughtered for their meat. The scent is always hovering over the entire city, keeping the people in line and walking the straight and narrow for the wages they earn, but are made to believe they're being given.

Suddenly there was some hollering and a noise that made both men look up just in time to see the door fling open and a giant, big-bosomed, black woman come crashing inside the tiny office. She stopped in front of the desk and without even giving Emmett a glance asked, "Is you Fred Hampton?"

"Yes, ma'am . . ."

"Is you chairman o' these here Black Panthers?"

"Yes, I . . ."

"Is you for the people, all the black people?"

"Yes'm!"

"Is you ready t' serve the people?"

"Yes'm!"

"Well, we ain't got no goddamn heat! It's gonna be ten below after it's dark, 'n we ain't got no heat 'n no hot water! Now, what I wanna know is, you sittin' there tellin' me you fo' the people, tellin' me you ready t' serve the people! Well, *I'* one o' the people 'n ain't none o' us gots no steam heat, never mind water in *our* buildin'! Now, if you all those things you say you is, 'n we the people, what you gonna do 'bout gettin' us some heat, brother? What?"

"What's the address of the building, ma'am?"

"What you gonna do, call the health department 'n ask 'em t' send an inspector 'round or sumptin'?!"

"No, ma'am, me 'n my brothers are goin' to get you the heat you need t' live through these cold, wintry nights. An' never you mind how, but t'morrow mornin' you gonna hear the steam whistlin' inside your pipes, 'n your radiators is all gonna be sizzlin'. When the people in the buildin' start askin' who done got the heat turned on, you be sure t' tell 'em all, mama, that it was the Illinois Chapter of the Black Panther party that done did it! 'Cause we here t' serve the people 'n not just talk 'bout how nice it'd be if we did."

481

That night around twelve or one o'clock, Chairman Fred was in the basement of the thirty-unit slum tenement building where the superintendent was doing his job, saving the landlord a little extra money by letting about three hundred people nearly freeze to death in the dead-of-winter cold of their apartments. One of his Panther brothers knocked on the door of the cellar flat, and when it opened they could see the red-hot, potbellied stove warming the super's place like a piece of toast. The man who opened the door was just standing still, his eyes frozen on the gaping barrel of the enforcer Chairman Fred was holding against his nose. The superintendent was just waiting to obey the orders that Chairman Fred gave him. "Stoke up the boilers, nigger! It's cold outside."

As soon as the people in that building heard and felt the heat steaming up, there was no way for that super or any other superintendent to shut it off for the rest of that winter of '68–'69, and no way those tenants were ever going to quietly acquiesce to the cold during any other winter thereafter. That's how Fred Hampton served the people, and that's why Fred Hampton died for the people. He was a teacher but he only made speeches on weekends.

John Huggins and Bunchy Carter had been shot dead in the lunchroom of U.C.L.A., and the spring was trying to break apart the solid wall of winter when Emmett returned to San Francisco, only to find out too late that he made a mistake in ever leaving Chicago. Everybody in Frisco still had a heavy attitude towards him, and nobody would believe he wasn't still using horse. So he resigned himself to the fact that it was all going to stay that way and even tried pushing it further beyond his reach by hanging as loose and as bad as he could without becoming corny.

He hustled a man he didn't need to hustle out of more than a thousand dollars cash, and a wise man named Pete, who was going to teach Emmett almost more than anyone had about himself, helped him buy a Harley-Davidson '74 and chop it down into a low-slung, extended-front-wheel, quality scooter.

Emmett rode that scooter up and down California's coastline and back and forth to San Francisco no matter what the weather. He came to love that bike of his, like a man could only love his horse. Most times he rode that red fandango along the open road alone with the air burning against his face and pushing him to jack the throttle and weave the bike in and out, between the square, eight-cylindered machines bought on time spent in thrall. Sometimes he would ride with a buddy or two, and they would get ripped with wine the chicks were always made to pay for, and roll in the laughing blood they caused themselves or anyone else to lose. A few times — too few — he was invited on runs with the club, which made him understand that he really hadn't seen all there was to see in being "*1% FREE*," once more.

Emmett went to Los Angeles for the umpteenth time, but he didn't go alone. He was with a slender, soft, milk-skinned blond of an always-by-your-side-when-you-want-me, good woman named Blanche who wore a mink coat and hardly anything else at all. The moment he decided to stay in that town awhile, he already stayed too long. Two years to the hour of the day that George Jackson was going to go down in the San Quentin prison yard with a bullet in his back, Emmett was arrested driving a car. The cops charged him with having kidnapped and robbed a man at gunpoint, someplace else. It didn't matter to them that there was no gun or money in the car or that the guy who actually pulled the caper only a few minutes before was described as being short with black hair. Nothing seemed to matter to them, except getting Emmett booked and locked up in the Hollywood police station where a few of them used him for exercise.

Early the next morning, he was cuffed to a chain around his waist, shackled, and brought downtown for arraignment on the nonbailable kidnapping and other charges. Then he was transferred with many other prisoners to the Los Angeles County jail where he was separated from them and taken upstairs to a tier of six-by-ten-foot cells, each occupied by a single inmate. Although the rest of the jail was comprised of larger cells which usually held four or five prisoners and more on weekends, this section only had cells built for one person. Emmett recognized it immediately as the high power module of the L.A. County jail. There were no low riders in this section, just alleged capital offenders, four-time losers, and those considered violently dangerous. As a guard escorted him to his cell, shaving mirrors began popping out from between the bars of each cell so the inmates could see who was coming down the freeway.

Emmett lay on his bunk and thought about the word "module," remembering he had heard it repeated often a month before, when Neil Armstrong stepped out of the lunar module and onto the moon, but failed to claim it as territory, thus voiding the concept behind every national boundary in the world, and theoretically making imperialism obsolete. "Module?" Emmett thought. "Mod-

LISA LAW

ule?" over and over, before he picked up a five-day-old newspaper lying on the floor and looked it over to pass a bit of time, reading the headlined story about the peace and harmony of the Woodstock Festival and how there'd been over four hundred thousand people there who still believed in the flower children's philosophy and practiced what they preached, making it into a beautiful event for everyone.

"Flower children, my motherfuckin' ass! If it hadn't been rainin' so goddamn hard all of those three days, somethin' more than mud pies would of been made there! Who the fuck they think they're kiddin'?"

Emmett didn't know that the cops had found the address of the house in Los Angeles where he was staying. They got it off the back of an envelope where he wrote it along with his new telephone number. He also had no idea that the coppers invaded the place, arresting Blanche, her three young daughters, and a friend of hers who just happened by to visit, charging them all with possession of marijuana. He discovered all this a couple of days later when Brownie, a good, stand-up, Colorado woman who moved to L.A. from San Francisco with her old man to get into the film industry, told him about Blanche and her kids. It was thanks to Brownie and her husband that Blanche finally got cut loose on bail along with her friend and got her children released into the legal custody of her parents. Both of them also did all they could for Emmett, even though they, as most San Franciscans he knew way back when, didn't particularly like him very much anymore.

Emmett took the news about Blanche and the kids getting popped really bad, and it made him sick because no matter how you looked at it, he brought it down on all of them, and now the children were taken away from their mother which was disgustingly wrong and made him sick. A short time after, there was more news — this time it was good, but not good enough to offset the bad that had already taken place.

The United States Supreme Court decreed that the merely technical kidnapping law for which Caryl Chessman had been smothered in the gas chamber nearly a decade before was unconstitutional. Therefore, that charge against Emmett was dropped and bail subsequently set. The bail money was raised by Natural Suzanne, Lacey Pines, and Fyllis, who came to southern California to help Blanche get Emmett out. The money came from people whose names were in Emmett's little phone book. Since no bondsman would ac-

487

cept even a one-hundred-thousand-dollar house as collateral because their insurance companies were told that Emmett was a bad risk, the total bail had to be posted in cash, and it was by people scattered throughout the country and for reasons of their own for which Emmett was grateful.

It was definitely the wrong time to be in Los Angeles with the heat running all around, looking for the Sharon Tate-La Bianca killers. Yet it wasn't that kind of heat that had Emmett sweating out his stay. After he was released on bail, Emmett was arrested at his house and on the street on several different occasions on suspicion of practically anything. Several police agencies were now beginning to combine their efforts to piece together the jigsaw puzzle which Emmett Grogan had purposely created of himself. They knew they were onto *something*, but whatever it was they really didn't know. They just had a hunch. So they kept picking him up for questioning in an attempt to uncover the picture hidden within the folds of paper they gathered from all over the world which they knew was bound to become clear sooner or later. Fortunately for Emmett, it came later.

The preliminary hearing in the case of *State* v. *Grogan* occurred during the same week the Chicago Conspiracy Trial began in Chicago. Emmett's brilliant young defense counsel, Mr. Barry Nakell, considered that fact, and they both decided to keep all the proceedings of his case quiet and private, not even notifying the L.A. *Free Press*. They thought it best to approach and attack the entire matter as a straight beef, leaving all the political implications untouched, unless the prosecution brought them up, in which event Attorney Nakell assured his client, "We'll bury them!"

At the preliminary hearing, Attorney Nakell thoroughly impeached each of the so-called witnesses who identified Emmett only after he was pointed out to them in the courtroom. The final capper came when Emmett's good friend Max, who taught black adults in Watts how to read and write and had never been arrested for anything, testified on the stand that one of the so-called witnesses had, earlier in the day, talked amicably with the defendant about courtrooms in general, asked him where he came by his leather Cardin jacket, and accepted several cigarettes, obviously not recognizing Emmett as anyone he ever saw before, until he returned from having lunch with the prosecutor and arresting officers with whom he discussed a forgery case he had pending against him.

The judge still bound Emmett over for trial, but it didn't matter.

Nakell surprised the prosecution by waiving a jury trial and simply giving the youngest black judge sitting on a California bench the manuscript of the preliminary hearing along with a brilliantly comprehensive brief he wrote about the lack of any evidence and the thorough weakness of the case which he insinuated the state had fabricated against his client. The district attorney's office was caught with their pants down, and they demanded more time and all kinds of continuances to counter the slick, tactical defense. The judge replied that they had had enough time and adjourned for the day.

A week later, the newspapers were full of stories about Charles Manson and his family's arrest and the Weathermen's so-called "days of rage" in Chicago where they trashed a few windows of downtown stores, and lots of windows of poor, elderly pensioners living out their last years in boardinghouses that just happened to be scattered throughout the wealthy Gold Coast neighborhood.

At ten o'clock one morning of that same week, Emmett went into an empty courtroom to refuse a motion of dismissal of his case from the district attorney, before accepting the judgment of his honor who found him "not guilty" of anything.

A few hours later, after sincerely saying "Thanks, be seein' you," to twenty-nine-year old Barry Nakell, Emmett was riding his bike along the California coast highway back to San Francisco alone and into Altamont for which he had laid the groundwork with the Rolling Stones, their road management and the Grateful Dead, while he was awaiting the conclusion of his case.

Emmett rode to Altamont on his chopped red Harley fandango '74. He went there knowing what might happen to the rock concert lumpen, simply because the weather was good. He also went there knowing which side he would be on. He jumped his scooter up and over a dry, brown hill and into the giant crowd that had gathered for the last of the best "Free for Alls!"

Fred Hampton had been murdered in his bed while he slept two days before, and something he once said was rolling around inside Emmett's brain ever since he heard the news. It was the kind of phrase that wasn't easy to shake, and Emmett kept hearing it to himself all that day — "I'm too proletarianly intoxicated to be astronomically intimidated!" And the weather was too good for things not to turn bad, especially since they were for "free."

A long while later, Emmett was going to explain to the New York *Post* columnist, Alfred G. Aronowitz, just why and how and what he was responsible for, at that last California festival ever to be "free":

"In 1890, fifteen years after Custer's mistake, the Ghost Dance was introduced to the Sioux by the Paiute seer Wovaka. It was a religion which promised the return of the buffalo and the disappearance of the white man. The Sioux were enthusiastic advocates. With equal vigor, however, their dream was destroyed by the massacre at Wounded Knee where thousands of Indian men, women and children fell at the hands of the United States artillery. Since that disaster, the Sioux have never recovered. And the straight goods is that the Altamont Festival of December 6, 1969, remains the only workable criterion for uprooting the Ghost Dance. Nobody wants to save what's best left dead." This is a quote from a heavy article that has been appearing in the American and European underground press during the last ten months. No one knows much about the guy who put the piece together and he likes it that way. His name is Emmett Grogan and last night I sat and talked with him and this is what he had to say:

"It was my fault. It was my fault because in October '69 I poorly represented the people of the Bay Area Community when I invited the Stones to a party which we were planning to throw in Golden Gate Park. My right to represent anyone had been negated by the lying, cheating, scheming, rip-off-artist reputation that I was tagged with in certain circles of professional musical swells, as well as a few other places.

"It was my fault that during the pre-concert discussions, I was ego-blind to the fact that Jagger and Company had no intention of fulfilling our agreement that the people of the community construct and control the free festival while the Stones simply show up on one of the planned multiple stages whenever they felt like it and play just like any of the other 'name' bands that were going to be there.

"It was my fault that they not only didn't take me seriously but that they also didn't take the people seriously or even think that we were capable of getting it together by ourselves like we had done thirty times before.

"It was my fault because I returned to San Francisco from Los Angeles and pumped everyone up about the wailing, 'free because it's yours!' party we were gonna have. A party which I said was gonna knock the despair and depression of the winter of '69 right on its ass.

"It was my fault that I didn't contact Allen Klein and advise him to tell his nephew and his friends to back off, when I realized that Ronnie Schneider was doing a 'trick the tricker' on us by saying that Golden Gate Park was too small (meaning that it was too big for a star-stoned-Mick-showcase) and the issuance of the permit for the use of the park was blocked.

"It was my fault that I didn't tear the lower lip off the punk who was leaking information to a San Francisco reporter who galloped around on a white horse and wrote inciting columns prior to the event which, more or less, demanded a disastrous chaos to salve his Wild West bruise and which inadvertently predicted Jann Wenner's *Rolling Stone* rag's yellow-journalistic smear of the people instead of the business.

"It was my fault because I didn't try to stop in any way that I could, the four hundred thousand people who were specifically convened to appear as extras in someone's idea of a home movie, promising that a percentage of the take from the film's profits would go toward a permissive-loony-bin-of-a-playground for the adventurers-in-poverty freaks, instead of toward reality which is Haight Street and Hunters Point in San Francisco and Uptown in Chicago and the Lower East Side in New York.

"It was my fault that the California Hells Angels who came to drink beer, have a good time and party with the community like they've been doing for years, ended up hassling to protect a trembling stage for a pussy who loves to provoke audiences into childhood hysteria and who thought that he was appearing before a flock of teenyboppers and flower children, rather than before a crowd of four hundred thousand men and women who discovered a long time ago that flowers die too easy. Even if they have thorns.

"It was my fault that several groups in the Bay Area came to distrust me because my silence duped them into thinking that the Altamont affair was sanctioned, when actually I should have blown the covers off of the fiasco weeks before it was allowed to take place and make suckers of us all.

"It was my fault because I permitted hip San Francisco chauvinism to dictate my silence into a belief that a good time would be had by all, even after the adequate Sears Point site had been vetoed when the professional sharks of the Filmways Corporation demonstrated that the business acumen of Schneider was that of a minnow and forced him to play out his dead hand of solitaire at a barren racetrack in the town of Livermore which no one even knew was in California.

"It was my fault that the Workable Lie which was the Rolling Stone Concert at Altamont wasn't seen clearly until, as Sweet William says, 'Everything it ever was, is all being sold.'

"And to the people to whom I was totally irresponsible, all I can say is *mea culpa*.

"And to all those false-bottomed-hipsters and the short-change-artists who like to deal dead hands and who like to think that they run things around here, *un bacio d'morte*.

"And Meredith Hunter dying like a sniveling maniac instead of like a determined man — that was his fault."

It was the first month of the 70s, and just about thirty days after Altamont went down forever, replacing Woodstock in the hip lexicon of expresssions, when Emmett Grogan began to feel he had done all he ever would in California with its people, at least for "Free!" anyway. He had been running free up and down and back and forth across the entire tapestry of the state and it all remained just as unknown to him as when he started back in '66. Now, every instinct he depended on told him it was time to split and leave it all behind, before it did just that to him.

He was anxious, but not fearful, of the future, and he wanted to get hold of the soundest, most truthful information, so he could devise himself a plan for that next unavoidable step he knew he was going to have to take into the unknown. There was no way for him to stay where it had become familiar, because all those old ways had proven themselves to be deadly. The West had become his home, and he pushed it as far as it could take him without dying. He understood that there was a time to die, but also that his time hadn't come as yet. He decided to head back to where it all began, when he was supposed to have been a boy. He decided to return to New York and Brooklyn, and he was going to walk all the way because he wanted to listen carefully to whatever sounds America was making. Everything he ever heard anybody say about America was true. This time around, he wanted to hear what America had to say, and the only real way for him to do that was by walking through it alone.

He left not a moment too soon. The various police agencies finally fitted the pieces of the jigsaw puzzle together, and they came up with a picture of a man named "Emmett Grogan." It wasn't all that clear, so they badly wanted to find and talk with him. FBI agents questioned some of his friends, and those who put up some of his bail money in Los Angeles. Plainclothesmen in San Francisco picked up his sister who had been in that city for almost a year, interrogating her with their hands about the whereabouts of her brother. In Chicago, they asked around, but kept coming up with the empty-handed "nonexistence" line. In New York City, agents steadily harassed his parents, dropping hints about how Scotland Yard wanted some answers from their son, but always assuring them that it was just routine, until his exasperated mother asked "Which routine? Which routine?" One FBI man even left a note for his father which read, "Sorry I missed you. Please call my office tomorrow. Best time 8:30 A.M. to 10:00 A.M., or 4:30 to 5:00 P.M. AGENT JOSEPH WALSH, FBI."

Emmett didn't know any of this when he walked away from San Francisco, leaving it all behind. He just had a feeling, a feeling that it would be better for him to be hanging sheetrock in Davenport,

Iowa, and thinning out trees in the thick, overgrown forests that skirt the Canadian border, than to be nailed to the chauvinism of San Francisco with someone constantly explaining that "the best is always yet to come, so just do your thing, and you'll be king!"

The moment he took that first step out of what no longer was his home, Emmett knew he'd made a righteous move and that he was on his way to making it real once more, compared to not.

His legs carried him through the absurd wave of do-nothing terrorism that began and ended with the explosion of the bomb factory in the wealthy Greenwich Village townhouse. They took him past Eldridge Cleaver's threat of "race war," if white radicals failed to rally to the defense of Bobby Seale, and on by the subsequent May Day weekend held to protest the chairman's "railroad" trial in a town where some Broadway shows close before they get to open in the Big Apple. He didn't even stop to take a look at those shot at Kent and Jackson State or the ones missing in the jungles of Cambodia. He did, however, pause for a moment in bewilderment at Huey P.'s release, just to figure what it might mean, now that Fred Hampton was long dead. Finally his legs brought him back to "Go" and a humid, hot summer that was lightened up a bit by a blond mouthful of a woman who was simply another day in another week.

Then Pearl died, and Emmett watched Nixon squash the prosperity that spawned the country's counterculture, causing the hardhat, blue-collar guys to beat on marching students, in hope that the President would grant some grace to labor in the economic wage-price freeze. He didn't, though, and neither did they have to stomp down the college kids who already reconsidered and subdued themselves to the yoke now that jobs were scarce.

And so, Emmett saw it all come down to money once again. On the street he heard that it had cost twenty-five thousand to bust out Leary from the San Luis Obispo minimum security farm, and that Cleaver put him under house arrest in Algiers because he didn't come through with the ten grand he promised him. Later, after three of the twenty-one Panther defendants had jumped bail from their trial in New York, two of them allegedly returned to liberate money by taking the wages from some of their black brothers and sisters, humiliating them by forcing them to strip naked in a Harlem after-hours social club where they were trying to forget their jobs as chauffeurs and domestics.

After the split became forever in the Black Panther Party, Cleaver really showed himself to be nothing more than crazy by threatening to kill all and anyone, no matter who, and finally offing one of his own brothers in Algeria who, he boasted, ". . . was only the first to be buried in the Panther graveyard, leavin' plenty room for more!" Just another low-riding mug who, like all mugs, started knifing his brothers in the back when he got himself in a jam by leaving the country he couldn't handle — in the same way he couldn't handle women.

Cleaver finally parodied himself by holding an absurd press conference in Algiers to announce his imminent return to America where, he said, he was going to organize "urban guerrilla units" patterned after those in Latin America, Quebec and Northern Ireland. Their deeds would include political kidnappings "of such a nature that they will receive nationwide and worldwide coverage, as well as other exploits that we will openly and proudly admit throughout the Pigs' news media!"

Later that same day, H. Rap Brown was shot, apparently, in a gun duel with some New York cops after he and three St. Louis black men allegedly stuck up the Red Carpet Lounge, robbing all the nonwhite patrons and some kids who were having a penny-ante dice game outside the bar. Some people would say that sticking up saloons was a revolutionary act. It wasn't, and probably no one knew that better than H. Rap Brown. Apparently, Cleaver doesn't know it, even though the conviction of *his* Black Panthers, Richard Moore and Eddie Josephs, who pleaded guilty to the robbery of the after hours club, gave proof to the lie of his announced "threat" of organized urban guerrilla warfare in America.

Emmett listened to the black, brown and white people on the streets of New York that day, as they reacted to Cleaver's statements with angry contempt for his false-bottomed threat against the "Pigs!" In the end, they all seemed to know that whenever the deal finally went down for Eldridge Cleaver, he would prey on his "own people" and, just like the other two brothers of *his* Panther faction, would call it a "political act" instead of simply another street crime committed against the poor. The low-money people didn't like it very much, and neither, Emmett suspected, did such legitimate, stand-up, serious organizations as the FLQ, the IRA and the Tumpamaros.

Huey P., Bobby Seale and David Hilliard, however, stood in front of the men and women who chose their side, and that major faction of the Panther party finally began to get down to what it was all about by serving the people through fulfilling their needs, rather than filling their ears with words. Emmett watched the change and was glad that it happened the way it did, heightening the contradictions to the point of no return.

The money theme kept beating its rhythm into Emmett's mind, forming a pattern that became a medley of riotous melodies from the ghetto insurrections to the student uprisings to the prison rebellions which for him became the most important — the Attica massacre spelling it out for those who, until then, just didn't understand.

He thought about the word Attica, which was the name for that part of Greece which encircled the ancient city of Athens. He saw the analogy between the city and state of New York. Most inmates in that Attica state penitentiary were city slickers being guarded by hokey, upstate appleknockers in the same way the law-abiding citizens of the city of New York are legislated against by country-boy "representatives" who have no *real* idea about the problems of running an urban environment.

Emmett decided to concern himself with what was once known as urban blight, now as urban abandonment. He knew that in New York City thirty thousand to forty thousand dwellings were abandoned each year, in Philadelphia twenty thousand, and much the same, in St. Louis, Chicago, Detroit, Oakland and San Francisco. There was a section of Brooklyn called Brownsville which he chose as a plausible spot to maybe do it. To send out a general alarm to all those wandering, heavy hipsters who learned the trade of how to live their lives, and invite them all to converge on Brownsville, occupy it, reconstruct it as a community and try to do what most of them had sought to do in other places without making all the same mistakes. This time as a really postcompetitive, comparative collective community.

Emmett knew who they were by now, and he thought of them as eagles: "Individuals, families, communes, gangs, who are bound together by the blues life. The ones that throw it all away. They're everything anyone wants to be. They're the cream of the streets and their frame of reference is a style of life and death that has been censored from history and condemned to hearsay since man learned to read and write. They are the ones to survive the plagues, the ones in this country who are not in an illusory bag and the ones who get more than the oakey-doke without askin'.

"The best music — the best of everything that is expressive of all this country's got to give is by and about them.

495

"The blues are finally a people who are going to take care of business."

Emmett knew it would work and that something like that had to work if the cities were to be saved. To be saved in an ideological age where ideas lived a greater life than man and words were juggled in a gigantic hoax and where he needed more than the skeleton to make the vision walk. He needed to lift off something that was neither beauty nor truth, but only a plaster false face, if he was to be one of the only ones to discover the grin of the skeleton.

The only ones were those that had reached their own rock bottom and got up. They always got up. They searched for brothers and sisters, not friends. They did not play the role of crowd in remakes of the *Law & Order vs. Riot* movie. They didn't sell their vision — to sell their vision would have been to pretend it was theirs. They didn't put themselves on, fall guy. They were wise to the educated fools who look to confront fake situations where pretensions can be made to self-defense. They killed who had to be killed. They were sick and tired of being sick and tired. They dug that the goin' up better be worth the comin' down. They deceived deception with truth. They were spreading the cheeks and kissing the little brown asshole of democracy. They dealt with all real things in all moments of agony and joy. They didn't waste their efforts in games which kill time, deaden awareness and brutalize feeling. They did not let themselves be suicided by a Judas-goat society. They were no longer lonesome for their heroes. They took care of business. They did not nickle-dime bomb make-believe numbers. They did what was necessary (not unnecessary) to end the desperation of illness, hunger, nakedness, addiction, poverty, eviction, jail, oppression and the money conspiracy which decimated the streets and backwoods. They were all innocent. They were felons. They were good at it. They did not intend to spend any more time in penitentiaries. They did not use the courts for redress. They were silent about almost everything. They remembered Michael Collins and what his comrades had done to him. They did not own it. They loved. They were the offspring of mid-twentieth-century broken consciousness. They were beyond the possibility of defeat. "They, that unnamed, 'they.' Well, nothing moves a mountain but itself. And they — I've long ago named them me."

Then Emmett Grogan sat down to write a book for all the heartbroke lovers he left behind awaiting release. And for Kenny Wisdom and his suntan.

498

ACKNOWLEDGMENTS

To Mrs. Gladys Hansen, Senior Librarian, Special Collections Department, San Francisco Public Library

To Peter Dinella, Head Librarian, and Blaze Curci, New York *Post* Library

To Peter Draz, Head Librarian, and the men and women of the Time, Inc., Reference Library

To the men and women of the New York *Daily News* Information Bureau and Main Library

To the men and women of the New York Public Library's Telephone Reference Service

To *Allen Baker*
    Janet Lee Bart
    Paula Carrigan
    Liz Clarkson
    Doris Dynamite
    Bennett H. Glotzer
    B. Rose Gross
    Albert B. and *Sally Grossman*
    Michael S. Hamilburg
    Elaine Kaufman
    Louise Latraverse

To Susan Lee
    Felix Leneman
    Norman Mailer
    Max Mendes
    Pearl
    Bill Phillips
    Sylva Romano
    Andrew Seubert
    Ann Sternberg
    Rip and Geraldine Torn
    and to THE PEOPLE

[signature: Thank you, Emmett Grogan.]

TITLES IN SERIES

*For a complete list of titles, visit www.nyrb.com or write to:
Catalog Requests, NYRB, 435 Hudson Street, New York, NY 10014*